A HISTORY OF THE BLACK WATCH
[ROYAL HIGHLANDERS] IN THE
GREAT WAR, 1914–1918

VOLUME THREE

VOLUME ONE: REGULAR ARMY
1st, 2nd and 3rd (Special Reserve) Battalions

VOLUME TWO: TERRITORIAL FORCE
4th, 5th, 4/5th, 6th, 7th and the Reserve Battalions
and Allied Regiments
The Royal Highlanders of Canada
and The Sydney Scottish Rifles

VOLUME THREE: NEW ARMY
8th, 9th, 10th, 11th, 12th, 13th and 14th Battalions

"K.I. 1914." A BLACK WATCH SOLDIER OF "THE FIRST HUNDRED THOUSAND"
After the drawing by "Snaffles"

A HISTORY OF THE BLACK WATCH
[ROYAL HIGHLANDERS]
IN THE GREAT WAR, 1914–1918

EDITED BY
MAJOR-GENERAL A. G. WAUCHOPE, C.B.
Author of
"The Black Watch, 1725–1907"

AM FREICEADAN DUBH

LONDON
THE MEDICI SOCIETY LIMITED
MCMXXVI

Printed and bound by Antony Rowe Ltd, Eastbourne

TO
THE MEMORY OF
THE EIGHT THOUSAND MEN
OF THE
REGULAR, TERRITORIAL AND SERVICE BATTALIONS
OF
THE BLACK WATCH
WHO GAVE THEIR LIVES IN THE GREAT WAR
THIS HISTORY IS DEDICATED

"*Without labour there is no coming to rest, nor without fighting can the victory be obtained.*"

PREFACE

THIS record of The Black Watch during the Great War shows how some thirty thousand men served in the Regiment in France, Belgium and Salonika, in Palestine and Mesopotamia, of whom eight thousand were killed and over twenty thousand were wounded.

The long days in the trenches encouraged a very close understanding between officers and men, and many hours were spent talking over what might best be done for the good of the Regiment after the war. Serving in the earlier part of the war as a company officer, I gathered from these discussions that there were three schemes which great numbers of our men hoped might, one day, be realized.

The first of these schemes entailed the reorganization of the Regimental Association, in order that help might be given to the large number of men, who, it was feared, would find themselves in difficulties or in distress after the war. This first object has been achieved through the labours of many officers of The Black Watch, among whom I must mention the names of the Earl of Mansfield, Colonel S. A. Innes and Major L. Gibson.

The second scheme often spoken of was that of a War Memorial, which should not only be a visible monument to those who fell, but, at the same time, be of help to those who had suffered through the war, and to all widows and children.

This object has also been achieved by the establishment of the Dunalistair Home, the successful foundation of which was so largely due to the labours of the late Brigadier-General W. McL. Campbell and of Colonel H. H. Sutherland.

The third object which I found so many of our men were anxious to see fulfilled was that a history of The Black Watch during the war should be written and published at such a price as would render its purchase possible by all ranks and their relatives. It was hoped that this history would form a true record of the main achievements of our Regular, Territorial and Service Battalions, that is to say, a record of the gallantry of all those men who bore the Red Hackle and crossed the seas in the service of the Regiment; and further, that this account, written by those who shared equally in the hardships and in the fighting, might also furnish a picture of the life led by our men in various lands and campaigns throughout these years of trial and danger.

It has been, therefore, in the endeavour to realize this last object that this history has been written. In these volumes the work of each separate battalion is described mainly by officers who took part in the actual actions and scenes here set out; and the thanks of the Regiment are due to those who have given so much time and labour to this end. But as these accounts have

PREFACE

been revised, and in many parts re-written by me, I accept full responsibility for the whole.

Our Territorial Battalions, direct descendants of The Black Watch Volunteer Battalions, had long held a fine reputation in Scotland for discipline and soldierly bearing. The conduct of their contingents which served as reinforcements to the Second Battalion during the South African War, served but to enhance this reputation and to knit all units of the Regiment yet more firmly together. It was no surprise therefore that our four Territorial Battalions were among the earliest ready to take the field, and among those who earned the highest praise for gallant deeds and unstinted good work.

Unlike the Territorial Battalions, the Service Battalions had no organization and no history, yet from the first day that they went into battle till the end of the war they nobly upheld the traditions of The Black Watch. This was partly due to their well-trained officers, to the splendid quality of the recruits who came so very largely from our 42nd Regimental District, and, above all, to the fine spirit—of which the Red Hackle is the symbol—that enheartened every man and, though unseen, was felt by every man to be the link that binds together each platoon, company and battalion of The Black Watch.

The task of editorship has at times seemed almost beyond my powers. As editor I am conscious of many defects, both of omission and commission. None the less I believe that this history, which describes the many gallant deeds and cites the names of those who fell in action, gives a faithful record of all those Battalions whose spirit and achievement have brought yet more honour and glory to The Black Watch. I believe also that this history shows that the same spirit of trust and good fellowship which has united all ranks of the Regiment since its earliest days still flourishes: that this spirit which inspired The Black Watch in the great victories of the Peninsula, Waterloo and Seringapatam, and sustained the heroes of Fontenoy and Ticonderoga, is the same spirit which filled the hearts and strengthened the resolve of those who in this last war gave their lives in the service of their King, their Country and their Regiment.

It is impossible for me to thank all those officers, non-commissioned officers and men who have given their help in the writing of this history, but I well know that they gave their help willingly and for the good of the Regiment. I must, however, take this opportunity to thank Colonel John Stewart and Captain G. S. M. Burton for their assistance in revising proofs and arranging the appendices of these volumes.

It is therefore with the hope that the great deeds described

PREFACE

in these pages will serve as an example and an encouragement to all those who in future years join The Black Watch and wear the Red Hackle that I am emboldened to publish this history.

I am greatly indebted to Sir William Orpen, to Mr. Charles Payne ("Snaffles"), and also to Sir Bruce Seton (the owner), and Mr. J. Beadle, the painter of the "Pipes of War," who have been good enough to grant me permission to reproduce certain pictures as illustrations to this history.

I ask all readers who detect errors in the text, or who are in possession of additional material or facts dealing with the history of the Regiment in the Great War, to send any information or corrections to the Officer Commanding, The Black Watch Depot, Perth.

A. G. WAUCHOPE,
Major-General.

BERLIN,
November, 1925.

Note. The two months delay in the publication of Volumes II and III has been due to Strikes and other unforeseen causes, and although unavoidable is very greatly regretted.

CONTENTS OF VOLUME THREE

	PAGE
EDITOR'S PREFACE.	vii
BATTLE HONOURS OF THE BLACK WATCH.	xviii
FOREWORD BY GENERAL THE RIGHT HON. SIR JOHN G. MAXWELL, G.C.B., K.C.M.G., C.V.O., D.S.O.	xix

THE EIGHTH BATTALION

CHAPTER I—August, 1914, to August, 1915.
    Early Days in England and France.   3

CHAPTER II—September, 1915.
    The Battle of Loos.   9

CHAPTER III—September, 1915, to May, 1916.
    Trench Warfare.   16

CHAPTER IV—June to October, 1916.
    The Battles of the Somme and Vimy Ridge.   22

CHAPTER V—November, 1916, to April, 1917.
    The First Battle of Arras.   31

CHAPTER VI—February to June, 1917.
    The Battles of Arras.   35

CHAPTER VII—July, 1917, to March, 1918.
    Havrincourt.   42
    Battle of Passchendaele.   45

CHAPTER VIII—March to May, 1918.
    The German Offensive.   50

CHAPTER IX—May to September, 1918.
    Hondeghem Area.   58
    Attack at Meteren.   60

CHAPTER X—September to November, 1918.
    The Advance to Victory.   64

CHAPTER XI—November, 1918, to November, 1919.
    On the Rhine.   70
    Demobilization.   71

CONTENTS

LIST OF APPENDICES—

		PAGE
I.	Record of Officers' Service.	75
II.	Summary of Casualties.	84
III.	Casualties—Officers.	85
IV.	Nominal Roll of Warrant Officers, Non-Commissioned Officers and Men Killed in Action or Died of Wounds or Disease in the Great War, 1914-18.	87
V.	Honours and Awards.	99
VI.	List of Actions and Operations.	103

THE NINTH BATTALION

CHAPTER I—SEPTEMBER, 1914, TO JULY, 1915.
    Formation of Battalion and Training in England.   107

CHAPTER II—JULY TO OCTOBER, 1915.
    Early Days in France.   116
    The Battle of Loos.   124

CHAPTER III—OCTOBER, 1915, TO JULY, 1916.
    Trench Warfare.   132

CHAPTER IV—JULY, 1916, TO MARCH, 1917.
    The Somme.   138

CHAPTER V—MARCH TO JUNE, 1917.
    Arras.   145

CHAPTER VI—JUNE TO SEPTEMBER, 1917.
    Ypres.   155

CHAPTER VII—SEPTEMBER, 1917, TO MAY, 1918.
    The Battle of Arras.   168
    Amalgamation with 4/5th Battalion.   173

CHAPTER VIII—MAY, 1918, TO JULY, 1919.
    Formation and Movements of 2/9th Battalion.   174

LIST OF APPENDICES—

		PAGE
I.	Record of Officers' Service.	177
II.	Summary of Casualties.	186
III.	Casualties—Officers.	187

CONTENTS

LIST OF APPENDICES (*continued*)— PAGE

   IV. Nominal Roll of Warrant Officers, Non-Commissioned Officers and Men Killed in Action or Died of Wounds or Disease in the Great War, 1914–18.   189

   V. Honours and Awards.   198

   VI. List of Actions and Operations.   201

THE TENTH BATTALION

CHAPTER I—SEPTEMBER, 1914, TO NOVEMBER, 1915.
    Formation of Battalion   205

CHAPTER II—NOVEMBER, 1915, TO JULY, 1916.
    Salonika.   213

CHAPTER III—JULY, 1916, TO MARCH, 1917.
    Salonika (*continued*).   223

CHAPTER IV—MARCH TO AUGUST, 1917.
    Salonika (*continued*).   233

CHAPTER V—SEPTEMBER, 1917, TO JULY, 1918.
    Salonika (*continued*).   243

CHAPTER VI—JULY TO OCTOBER, 1918.
    France.   251

LIST OF APPENDICES—

   I. Record of Officers' Service.   257

   II. Summary of Casualties.   261

   III. Casualties—Officers.   262

   IV. Nominal Roll of Warrant Officers, Non-Commissioned Officers and Men Killed in Action or Died of Wounds or Disease in the Great War, 1914–18.   263

   V. Honours and Awards.   265

   VI. List of Actions and Operations.   266

THE ELEVENTH BATTALION

OCTOBER, 1914—Its Formation and Service.   269

APPENDIX—

   Nominal Roll of Non-Commissioned Officers and Men who Died of Disease in the Great War, 1914–18.   281

CONTENTS

THE TWELFTH BATTALION

PAGE

May, 1916—Its Formation and Service.   285

LIST OF APPENDICES—

    I. Record of Officers' Service.   289
    II. Nominal Roll of Non-Commissioned Officers and Men who Died of Wounds or Disease in the Great War, 1914–18.   290

THE THIRTEENTH BATTALION

August, 1914—Its Formation and Service.   293

LIST OF APPENDICES—

    I. Record of Officers' Service.   301
    II. Summary of Casualties.   306
    III. Casualties—Officers.   307
    IV. Nominal Roll of Warrant Officers, Non-Commissioned Officers and Men Killed in Action or Died of Wounds or Disease in the Great War, 1914–18.   308
    V. Honours and Awards.   310
    VI. List of Actions and Operations.   312

THE FOURTEENTH BATTALION

PREFACE.   315

CHAPTER I—January, 1917, to April, 1918.
    Palestine.   317

CHAPTER II—April, 1918, to May, 1919.
    France.   323

LIST OF APPENDICES—

    I. Record of Officers' Service.   331
    II. Summary of Casualties.   335
    III. Casualties—Officers.   336
    IV. Nominal Roll of Warrant Officers, Non-Commissioned Officers and Men Killed in Action or Died of Wounds or Disease in the Great War, 1914–18.   337
    V. Honours and Awards.   340
    VI. List of Actions and Operations.   342

INDEX.   343

ILLUSTRATIONS TO VOLUME THREE

"K. 1., 1914." *A BLACK WATCH SOLDIER OF "THE FIRST HUNDRED THOUSAND."* AFTER THE DRAWING BY "SNAFFLES."   *Frontispiece*

THE EIGHTH BATTALION.   *Facing page*

PIPE BAND PLAYING AFTER THE CAPTURE OF LONGUEVAL, JULY, 1916.   24

EIGHTH BATTALION DRAWING THE RUM RATION AFTER THE CAPTURE OF LONGUEVAL, JULY, 1916.   26

"A SUBALTERN OF THE BLACK WATCH, 1917." AFTER THE DRAWING BY "SNAFFLES."   104

THE NINTH BATTALION.

OFFICERS BEFORE EMBARKATION FOR FRANCE, 1914.   112

"A SOLDIER OF THE NINTH BATTALION." FROM A SKETCH DRAWN IN FRANCE, 1917   138

THE TENTH BATTALION.

ON THE MARCH TO AMBARKOI, SALONIKA, 1916.   218

WOUNDED MEN BEING TAKEN TO HOSPITAL ON SALONIKA FRONT, 1918.   218

THE ELEVENTH BATTALION.

THE PIPE BAND.   272

LIST OF MAPS TO VOLUME THREE

THE EIGHTH BATTALION. *Facing page*
    THE BATTLE OF LOOS, 25th SEPTEMBER, 1915.   10
    THE BATTLE OF THE SOMME, JULY, 1916.   28

THE NINTH BATTALION.
    THE BATTLE OF LOOS, 25th SEPTEMBER, 1915.   128
    CAPTURE OF GUÉMAPPE, 23rd APRIL, 1917.   150
    BATTLE OF THE 25/27th APRIL, 1917, FOLLOWING THE CAPTURE OF GUEMAPPE.   150
    ATTACK ON THE LANGEMARCK-GHELUVELT LINE.   156
    OPERATIONS EAST OF ARRAS, MARCH, 1918   168

THE TENTH BATTALION.
    MACEDONIA, VARDAR-DOIRAN FRONT.   240
    THE SALONIKA FRONT.   248

THE FOURTEENTH BATTALION.
    GENERAL MAP OF PALESTINE.   317
    GENERAL MAP OF FRANCE.   342

BATTLE HONOURS OF THE BLACK WATCH

The Royal Cypher within the Garter. The badge and motto of the Order of the Thistle. In each of the four corners the Royal Cypher ensigned with the Imperial Crown. The Sphinx, superscribed " Egypt."

" GUADALOUPE, 1759," " MARTINIQUE, 1762," " HAVANNAH," " NORTH AMERICA, 1763-64," " MANGALORE," " MYSORE," " SERINGAPATAM," " CORUNNA," " BUSACO," " FUENTES D'ONOR," " PYRENEES," " NIVELLE," " NIVE," " ORTHES," " TOULOUSE," " PENINSULA," " WATERLOO," " SOUTH AFRICA, 1846-7, 1851-2-3," " ALMA," " SEVASTOPOL," " LUCKNOW," " ASHANTEE, 1873-4," " TEL-EL-KEBIR," " EGYPT, 1882-4," " KIRBEKAN," " NILE, 1884-5," " PAARDEBERG," " SOUTH AFRICA, 1899-1902."

The Great War—25 Battalions.—" Retreat from Mons," " MARNE, 1914, '18," " Aisne, 1914," " La Bassée, 1914," " YPRES, 1914, '17, '18," " Langemarck, 1914," " Gheluvelt," " Nonne Bosschen," " Givenchy, 1914," " Neuve Chapelle," " Aubers," " Festubert, 1915," " LOOS," " SOMME, 1916, '18," " Albert, 1916," " Bazentin," " Delville Wood," " Pozières," " Flers-Courcelette," " Morval," " Thiepval," " Le Transloy," " Ancre Heights," " Ancre, 1916," " ARRAS, 1917, '18," " Vimy, 1917," " Scarpe, 1917, '18," " Arleux," " Pilkem," " Menin Road," " Polygon Wood," " Poelcappelle," " Passchendaele," " Cambrai, 1917, '18," " St. Quentin," " Bapaume, 1918," " Rosières," " LYS," " Estaires," " Messines, 1918," " Hazebrouck," " Kemmel," " Béthune," " Scherpenberg," " Soissonnais-Ourcq," " Tardenois," " Drocourt-Quéant," " HINDENBURG LINE," " Épéhy," " St. Quentin Canal," " Beaurevoir," " Courtrai," " Selle," " Sambre," " France and Flanders, 1914-18." " DOIRAN, 1917," " Macedonia, 1915-18." " Egypt, 1916." " Gaza," " Jerusalem," " Tell 'Asur," " MEGIDDO," " Sharon," " Damascus," " Palestine, 1917-18," " Tigris, 1916," " KUT AL AMARA, 1917," " Baghdad," " Mesopotamia, 1915-17."

The list of Honours given above shows that The Black Watch had won 28 Battle Honours before 1914, and gained 69 Battle Honours during the Great War. As it was impossible to emblazon all these Honours on the King's or Regimental Colours, the Army Council decided that only ten Great War Honours selected by the Regiment should be emblazoned on the King's Colour. A committee therefore was appointed, under the Chairmanship of Sir John Maxwell, Colonel of the Regiment, which selected the following ten Honours to be borne on the King's Colour :—

(1) MARNE, 1914, '18
(2) YPRES, 1914, '17, '18
(3) LOOS
(4) SOMME, 1916, '18
(5) ARRAS, 1917, '18
(6) LYS
(7) HINDENBURG LINE
(8) DOIRAN, 1917
(9) MEGIDDO
(10) KUT AL AMARA, 1917

These 10 Honours were chosen as being the most representative of the various Campaigns in which the twelve Battalions of the Regiment who fought overseas took part.

The Regimental Colour still bears the 28 Honours won before the Great War, and the 10 Honours chosen by the committee are emblazoned on the King's Colour.

FOREWORD

BY

GENERAL THE RIGHT HON. SIR JOHN G. MAXWELL,

G.C.B., K.C.M.G., C.V.O., D.S.O., COLONEL, THE BLACK WATCH

THIS year, 1925, is the 200th Anniversary of the formation of the Independent Companies from which, in 1725, The Black Watch originated. The commissions of the six Captains of these Independent Companies are dated 1725, therefore it seems very appropriate to publish this year *The History of The Black Watch in the Great War*.

I, as its Colonel, have been asked to write this "Foreword," a task rendered no easier by the admirable Preface of Major-General A. G. Wauchope, the editor of this history.

In no part of the Empire was there a more hearty response to the call for men than in Scotland. We, of The Black Watch, are not given to boasting unduly of our deeds: we prefer to rest assured that every man who had the honour of wearing the Red Hackle acted up to and, collectively, enhanced the glorious traditions of our Regiment. No less than twenty-five Battalions served in the Great War, and eight thousand men of The Black Watch laid down their lives for their King and Country.

The official record of the battles and engagements in which these Battalions served shows that in whatever theatre of war the Regiment was represented, the traditions of The Black Watch were most worthily upheld. It is therefore right and proper that, as far as possible, a complete and true story of the exploits of each Battalion, in the various theatres of war, is recorded and incorporated in this history.

I desire to emphasize what General Wauchope has said, that no matter its shortcomings, if there be any, this history is written by the Regiment for the Regiment and for the countless friends of The Black Watch all the world over. No outside aid has been evoked. Every endeavour has been made, consistent with the design of the work, to keep within certain limits, so that the history can be published at such a price to bring it within the reach of all. One would like to know that a copy is in the hands of all past and present Black Watch men, as well as the relatives of those whose loss we mourn.

We are proud of our Regiment, and of the fact that His Majesty the King is our Colonel-in-Chief. We are justly proud of our records, both of the past and of the Great War. We hope that this history will be kept as a treasured heirloom and handed down to future generations of Black Watch men in order that they may emulate the valour and devotion of their predecessors.

FOREWORD

Our thanks are indeed due—and I offer them in the name of the Regiment—to Major-General Wauchope, and all who have assisted him in the compilation of this history. It has been an onerous task, though one of love and pride, and we congratulate them on having accomplished so successfully that which they set out to do.

J.G. Maxwell

COLONEL, THE BLACK WATCH.

THE EIGHTH
BATTALION

CHAPTER I

AUGUST, 1914, TO AUGUST, 1915

Early Days in England and France

THE 8th (Service) Battalion of The Black Watch was raised in August, 1914, by Lord Sempill of Fintray, Aberdeenshire. A member of a famous fighting family, he had served with The Black Watch and Cameron Highlanders in the Soudan in 1886, and with Lovat's Scouts in the South African war. The Battalion he was now to raise held a place of honour. It was a unit of the leading Brigade, the 26th Infantry Brigade, later called the 26th (Highland) Brigade of the 9th (Scottish) Division, the first division of Lord Kitchener's " New Army," and, as the senior battalion in that Brigade, it can claim to have been the vanguard of the " First Hundred Thousand."

The Battalion was formed at Albuera Barracks, Aldershot, in August, and about the middle of September it moved to Maida Barracks, which were shared with the 5th Cameron Highlanders. Hard training was carried out daily. The Battalion had a backbone of regular and ex-regular officers, most of whom had served formerly in The Black Watch. These included the Colonel; the Second-in-Command, Major J. G. Collins, an ex-adjutant of the 1st Battalion; the Adjutant, Captain J. L. S. Ewing; Major N. G. B. Henderson, A company; Captain G. H. M. Burnett, B company; Major O. H. D'A. Steward, C company; and Captain Sir George Abercromby, formerly of the Scots Guards (who left after a few months to become A.D.C. to Lieutenant-General Sir Charles Fergusson in France, but rejoined the Battalion as Second-in-Command in January, 1916), D company. A number of the subalterns had served in University Officers' Training Corps, and all were full of enthusiasm for their work. The ranks of warrant officers and senior non-commissioned officers were filled with serving soldiers or ex-soldiers. The rank and file came mainly from city offices, from the plough, and from the Fife collieries. Some at first had little idea of military discipline, but a genuine patriotism had inspired them to enlist; they were keen to become efficient, to join the fighting line, and therefore rapidly grew into a disciplined and organized body. Training weeded out the physically unfit, and as the strength of the Battalion was often far above the normal establishment, the 8th when it went abroad represented the pick of a large number of men.

The issue of uniforms and rifles was slow. Supplies were long in coming, and quartermasters of battalions made desperate efforts, moral and immoral, to be the first to secure articles of clothing and equipment for their own units. A battalion with glengarries thought themselves better soldiers than one without, and as equipment of all kinds arrived piecemeal, the battalions presented a curious spectacle on parade. Just after the formation of the 8th, on August 26th, it was inspected on Laffan's Plain by the King, the men being then in mufti, but by January, 1915, equipment was nearly complete except for machine guns and transport. The ordinary day's training began at 6 a.m., with an hour of marching, running and physical training before breakfast. After breakfast the Battalion usually marched several miles to a training area, and only returned to barracks in time for tea. After tea general instruction and short lectures were given.

Before leaving Aldershot the Battalion fired its first musketry course on the ranges. On January 16th, 1915, the 26th Infantry Brigade (8th Black Watch, 7th Seaforths, 8th Gordon Highlanders, and 5th Camerons), commanded by Brigadier-General E. G. Grogan, moved from Aldershot to Hampshire; where the 8th were billeted in Alton, with the machine gun section about a mile away at Holybourne. Here training was continued, and on January 22nd the Battalion was inspected, with the rest of the 9th Division, on Laffan's Plain by Lord Kitchener and M. Millerand, then French Minister of War. This inspection took place in a downpour of rain, in which the troops waited for hours.

On March 21st the Battalion marched to Oxney Farm Camp, near Bordon, where a very cold week was spent under canvas, after which it moved into St. Lucia Barracks, Bordon. Here a final musketry course was fired on Longmoor Ranges, and also a machine gun course, in which the 8th Battalion section came out first on points in the Brigade. During March and April the 8th received the remainder of its equipment, including the Battalion transport, the days being fully occupied in training.

In the beginning of May the long hoped for order arrived for the Brigade to proceed overseas. The following is a list of the officers, warrant officers and senior non-commissioned officers who accompanied the Battalion to France :—

Lieut.-Colonel Lord Sempill (Commanding Officer).
Major J. G. Collins (Second-in-Command).
Captain J. L. S. Ewing (Adjutant).
Major N. G. B. Henderson (O.C. A company).
Captain H. M. Burnett (O.C. B company).
Major O. H. D'A. Steward (O.C. C company).

DEPARTURE FOR FRANCE, MAY 10TH, 1915

Captain E. M. Murray (O.C. D company).
," W. E. Houston-Boswell (Second-in-Command), A company.
," The Hon. F. Bowes-Lyon (Second-in-Command), B company.
," F. H. C. McTavish (Second-in-Command), C company.
," J. S. S. Mowbray (Second-in-Command), D company.

Lieutenants and 2nd Lieutenants

R. N. Duke (Battalion Machine Gun Officer).
G. B. McClure.   M. E. Pelham-Burn.
H. Butter.   H. S. Sanderson.
D. S. Anderson.   P. H. Shaw.
H. St. J. Strange.   W. R. J. Forbes.
G. B. Gilroy.   L. McKenzie.
P. A. Cox.   R. N. M. Murray.
E. H. MacIntosh.   W. H. Scott.
H. M. Drummond.   P. H. Forrester.
Capt. Rev. O. B. Milligan, C.F. (Chaplain).
Lieut. and Q.M. P. Goudy (Quartermaster).
Lieut. A. L. McLean, R.A.M.C. (Medical Officer).

Battalion Headquarters

R.S.M. W. H. Black.   Colour-Sgt. A. Wilson, O.R.S.
R.Q.M.S. T. Tinley.   Sgt. G. Simpson.

A company

C.S.M. Bissett.   C.Q.M.S. E. Hamilton.

B company

C.S.M. F. Fraser.   C.Q.M.S. G. Shirran.

C company

C.S.M. A. G. Hill.   C.Q.M.S. W. Henderson.

D company

C.S.M. D. Mitchell.   C.Q.M.S. W. Barlow.

On the 9th of May, 1915, the machine gun section and Battalion transport, including three officers and 109 other ranks, left Bordon for France via Southampton and Havre. The remainder of the Battalion, 26 officers and 898 other ranks, started the next day and travelled via Folkestone to Boulogne; there they were joined by the transport party under Major O. H. D'A. Steward, and the whole Battalion went on by train to Arques, near St. Omer.

THE EIGHTH BATTALION THE BLACK WATCH

Arques was reached in the early hours of the morning of May 11th, and the 8th was billeted there for the next few days, Battalion Headquarters occupying the Château. Here the distant rumble of the guns at Ypres was heard for the first time.

On the 16th of May the Battalion marched out of Arques to billets in farms north-east of the village of Staple, and on the following day moved into Bailleul. Four days later the Commanding Officer and ten others rode to Armentières and were attached to the 18th Infantry Brigade, spending twenty-four hours in the trenches at Le Touquet with the 2nd Battalion Durham Light Infantry. At 5 a.m. on May 24th the whole Battalion marched to Armentières, and spent the next night attached to various units of the 16th Infantry Brigade. There were no casualties, and the following night the Battalion came out of the trenches and returned to Bailleul.

On the 27th the Battalion marched to Pont de Nieppe and was quartered partly in billets but mainly in bivouacs near a brickfield. Here A and D companies worked entrenching near Le Touquet, and the first casualty occurred, Second Lieutenant Mackenzie of A company being wounded in the arm by a bullet.

On the 3rd of June the 8th moved into billets at Steenje, and from there marched twenty-one miles to Burbure, near Lillers. The march was carried out by night, starting at 6.30 p.m. on the 5th. Not a single man fell out. The troops were in full marching order, much of the way lay over stretches of cobbles, and the night was hot and dusty. It was a fine performance, and testified to the fitness of all ranks.

While the 8th was at Burbure, the 9th Division was in G.H.Q. reserve, and on the 24th the Battalion moved to billets at Fouquereuil, near Béthune, and on the 25th to Busnettes. The Brigade Commander was now Brigadier-General Ritchie, the Divisional Commander being Major-General Landon.

On June 28th a move was made to Essars, and next day the 8th marched to billets just south of Le Touret, in Brigade reserve, while the Seaforths and Camerons went into trenches east of Festubert in relief of the 21st Brigade (7th Division). As battalions at this time had only two Vickers machine guns each, those of the 8th went into the line with the 7th Seaforths.

After dark on the 4th of July, D company relieved the reserve company of the 5th Camerons, and next day the remaining companies relieved the other Cameron companies in the front line, due east of Festubert. The trenches in this area were much knocked about by shell fire, and had been captured only about three weeks previously by a battalion of the Bedfordshire Regiment. The sector included a dangerous salient known as "The Orchard," but on this tour, its first of trench warfare,

TRENCH WARFARE, JULY TO AUGUST, 1915

the 8th suffered lightly, losing only three men killed and seven wounded. War, however, was found to have a humorous as well as a serious side, and all ranks chuckled when Sergeant McHardy, machine gun section, had to go kiltless because the kilt which he had hung up to dry was blown away by a shell.

The 10th Highland Light Infantry took over the line on July 7th, and the Battalion returned to billets near Locon in the small hours of the morning. On the same day Lord Kitchener inspected the Battalion, drawn up in line on a road south of Locon.

On the 14th the 8th relieved the 11th Royal Scots in the line east of Le Plantin in heavy rain. The night was pitch dark, and the trenches were full of mud and wet clay. The following day three small mines were exploded in the crater opposite the right front, just north of Givenchy village, and on the 17th the enemy blew another mine at the south-east side of this crater. One or two night alarms drew rapid fire from both sides and made the night exciting; and two or three small bursts of shelling by the enemy damaged the trenches and caused a few casualties.

On July 15th the 8th Gordon Highlanders relieved the Battalion which then went back to reserve. The losses for the tour were four killed and two wounded. While occupying the reserve line a few more casualties occurred, including Captain E. M. Murray. D company was then taken over by Captain J. S. S. Mowbray. On July 29th B and C companies under Major Collins moved into the reserve trench of the sector immediately on the left, in support of the 7th Seaforths, and on August 1st the whole Battalion returned to billets north-west of Locon.

Between August 6th and 16th the Battalion occupied the front line about midway between Le Plantin and Festubert, relieving the 12th Royal Scots. This sector contained a part of the front line known as "The Glory Hole," which was always heavily shelled by the enemy, and over seventy 10·5 cm. shells fell on this part of the trenches on the 11th. By the 16th, when relieved by the 6th Royal Scots Fusiliers, the Battalion had lost nine killed and 12 wounded, including Sergeant Malcolm of B company and Company Sergeant-Major Fraser of C company.

On the 17th a move was made to billets at Robecq, where a pleasant time was spent at rest in country surroundings, during which the 9th Division was inspected by Field-Marshal Lord Kitchener on August 19th near Busnes. On September 2nd the Battalion, after spending the previous night in Béthune, relieved a battalion of the Loyal North Lancashire Regiment between Annequin and Vermelles.

THE EIGHTH BATTALION THE BLACK WATCH

It now became clear that preparations were being made for a great offensive action ; large numbers of new trenches were dug, and saps were pushed forward from the front line ; recesses were prepared in the bays of the fire trenches for the reception of gas cylinders, and large stocks of ammunition and other material were brought into the line.

In September the following moves took place :—

On September 7th the Battalion moved to Béthune, being relieved in the front line by 6th Royal Scots Fusiliers. On September 11th to billets in Sailly Labourse. On the 15th to the front line Y 4 sector. On the 18th to Béthune. On the 20th in the front line Y 4 sector, and on the 21st, a four days' continuous bombardment, the prelude to the battle of Loos, began.

CHAPTER II

SEPTEMBER, 1915

The Battle of Loos

IN the Battle of Loos, the front allotted to the 9th (Scottish) Division east of Annequin and Vermelles was opposite the famous Hohenzollern Redoubt, a strong salient projecting from the enemy line. Behind this redoubt lay a coal pit, " Fosse No. 8," a large slag heap, and a little mining village, the east part of which was known as the Corons de Maroc and the Corons de Pekin. In the distance lay the towns of Haisnes and Douvrin. Hohenzollern Redoubt was on a small spur, and, though invisible from the nearest point of the British line owing to its situation on a gentle reverse slope, it had a wide command over No Man's Land both north and south. On the right of the 9th Division, now commanded by Major-General Thesiger, was the 7th Division, and on the left the 2nd Division.

The 9th Division was ordered to attack with the 26th Brigade on the right, the 28th Brigade on the left, and the 27th in reserve. The 26th Brigade attack was to be delivered by the 7th Seaforths on the right and 5th Camerons on the left; the 8th Gordon Highlanders were in close support to the Seaforths, and the 8th Black Watch to the Camerons. The front of the Camerons and The Black Watch, together with the line held after the attack, is shown on the accompanying map (p. 11).

During the four days' bombardment, which started on September 21st, the Battalion held the firing line on this front, and it was a period of strain and tension. The enemy batteries retaliated, and the ceaseless thunder of the British artillery and rattle of machine gun fire, which sprayed the enemy's lines to impede his communications and prevent repairs to his wire, kept even tired men from getting much sleep. In addition to this much labour was needed to complete the final preparations for the attack, particularly the carrying up of gas cylinders to the front line. Great secrecy had been maintained about the use of gas, which was referred to in Divisional orders as " the accessory," this being the first occasion on which gas was used by the British Army. On the eve of the attack the 5th Camerons took over the front line from the 8th, who spent the night before the battle closely packed in reserve trenches.

At Zero, 5.50 a.m. on September 25th, the gas was released from the cylinders and a light westerly wind carried it slowly towards the German trenches. As there was insufficient gas for a continuous discharge up to the hour fixed for the assault, 6.30 a.m., it was let off in bursts, smoke candles being thrown out between the intervals of gas discharges so as to keep up the

THE EIGHTH BATTALION THE BLACK WATCH

appearance of a gas cloud. The spectacular effect of this drifting cloud of intermingled whites, greys, yellows and browns was singularly impressive.

Shortly after 5.30 a.m. the Battalion began to move up to the front by various communication trenches, arrangements having been carefully prepared for this movement by Lord Sempill.

The attack was ordered to be carried out with three companies, A, B and C, in line, each company moving forward in four waves of one platoon each, D company remaining in support. A moved up Central Boyau, its leading platoon reaching the front line between Sap L 2 and Sap M (see map) in time to advance immediately behind the Camerons, with the other three platoons ready to follow on in the old Fire and Support Trenches. B company moved via Left Boyau, its front platoon moving to the front line between Sap M 2 and Sap M. C company moved by way of Quarry Boyau, its leading platoon assembling in the front line with its right at Sap M 3. D company had been intended to hold the front line between L 2 and M 4, but as things fell out it followed the advance of the leading companies. Before moving forward, packs had been dumped by companies in depots off one of the communication trenches, where they were left behind in accordance with orders from Headquarters, an unfortunate plan, as it was found impossible to recover them after the battle.

After a final burst of intense artillery and machine gun fire the assault was delivered at 6.30 a.m. By 7 a.m. Hohenzollern Redoubt and Little Willie Trench—running northwards from the Redoubt—had been taken, and the Battalion and Camerons combined, pressed on and took Dump Trench, the main German trench in front of Fosse No. 8.

The losses, however, had been very severe. The 28th Brigade on the left had attacked most gallantly, but found the enemy wire on their front uncut, and had been completely held up at the start, with very heavy losses. This exposed the left flank of the 26th Brigade advance, and the Camerons and The Black Watch, advancing along the north slope of the slight Hohenzollern spur, came under close enfilade machine gun fire from Madagascar and Madagascar Point on their left, mingled with some shrapnel fire from the east and north-east; consequently both battalions suffered great losses.

Enemy artillery fire was comparatively light, but probably at no other time during the whole war did the 8th ever come under machine gun fire so intense and deadly as that at Loos. Officers and men were mown down. Colonel Lord Sempill was badly wounded near Fosse No. 8, and lay, his legs paralysed, until

BATTLE OF LOOS, SEPTEMBER 25TH, 1915

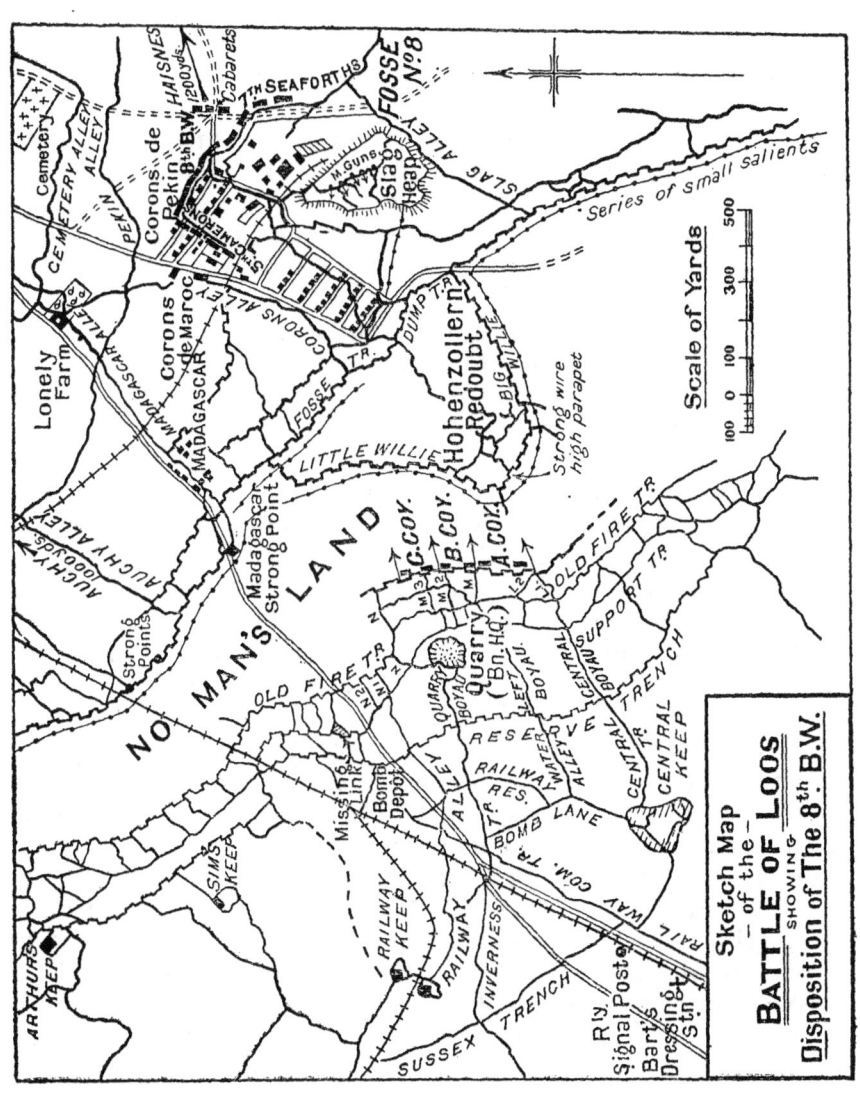

bearers were able to carry him back. His orderly, Corporal W. Smith, lay all day in the open with him, and assisted in carrying him in at dusk. An unlucky shell, which pitched into D company when in the front line trench, killed Captain Mowbray and Lieutenant Sanderson. Two of the other three company commanders, Major Henderson, A company, and Major Steward, C company, were wounded; Lieutenants E. H. MacIntosh and Shaw were killed; and all but four or five of the other officers were wounded.

From Dump Trench the advance was continued, and by 9.30 a.m. the whole of the Corons de Pekin and Fosse No. 8 was held by a mixed force of The Black Watch and Camerons. A large number of prisoners, many wearing gas respirators, were taken in the Corons. What effect the gas achieved is doubtful; the Battalion Medical Officer reported that three of the enemy were killed by it; it certainly induced the Germans to wear respirators, and probably had considerable moral effect.

Meantime, on the right, the Seaforths and Gordon Highlanders, with a few men of the 8th, somewhat sheltered from the Madagascar machine gun fire because the line of their advance lay along the south side of the Hohenzollern spur, had pushed on further and reached the outskirts of Haisnes. It was near Haisnes that Lieutenant McClure was wounded. The exposed left flank, however, made the retention of this position impossible, and they were obliged to fall back.

The command of the Battalion now devolved on Major J. G. Collins, who organized the remaining men on a line extending from the south-east corner of the Corons de Pekin along the eastern face, then turning sharply back short of the fourth house from the north-east end to the pit manager's house. Before retiring the enemy flooded one of their communication trenches by means of a sluice, and in one place two German dead were seen floating in the water. The Camerons were on the left, and on the right the Battalion was in touch with the Seaforths. In spite of the water in the trench, increased by heavy rain during the day, it was a good position, as most of the heavy bursts of enemy shelling crashed into the brick houses in rear, and the spirits of the men remained serene in spite of a thorough soaking by the rain. The position was consolidated so far as material and time permitted, and a brick wall near the right flank was loop-holed for rifle fire.

About 6 p.m. a Royal Engineer officer reported that the Brigade on the right had retired, and as the left flank was already fully exposed, both flanks were now unprotected and telephone communication with the rear completely failed. The 26th Brigade, however, held on in this position, under

HOHENZOLLERN REDOUBT, SEPTEMBER 26TH, 1915

considerable shell fire, every effort being made to prepare for a possible counter-attack. A Lewis gun had been issued to each company before the attack, and three of these were still in action, though there were only a few drums of ammunition remaining. Two of the four Vickers machine guns were also in position. One had been left out of action at Railway Well, and the other—under Sergeant Anderson, who was killed—had been lost near Haisnes, together with the entire team, after doing good work and engaging a German battery at short range.

About midnight a relief consisting of the 73rd Infantry Brigade, 24th Division, was sent up. This Division had just arrived in France, and it was thrown into the line in the midst of the battle after a long and trying march. Before the relief had been completed an enemy counter-attack developed upon the right flank near three buildings known as the Three Cabarets. The night was pitch dark, and it was difficult to grasp the situation, but enemy bullets kept raining upon the brick houses behind the trench, while salvos of shells crashed into the Corons. Rapid fire was instantly opened by all rifles and machine guns, and the attack was beaten off. When the situation had again become quiet the relief was completed and the 8th withdrew to the old front line, where it took up position at 2.30 a.m. on the 26th in reserve to the advanced Brigade. Lieutenant Goudy, the quartermaster, was waiting at the old Battalion Headquarters at the quarry with rations and rum, which the wet and exhausted troops badly needed. It is interesting to note that during the day the transport had been kept loaded ready to follow the Battalion on a long advance ; the general scheme of the battle had contemplated a sweep eastwards by the British at Loos, and a drive northwards by the French in Champagne, so that the two armies should meet at Valenciennes and thus " pinch out " a large enemy salient ; but three years of war had still to pass before so ambitious a plan became possible.

On the 26th the Battalion held its old line all day and during the following night. Several officers who had been left out of action on the first day—Lieutenants Gilroy, Forrester and C. O. C. MacIntosh—came up from the transport lines to join the few who had survived the battle.

At dawn next morning it became clear that the 73rd Brigade in front were in difficulties, and men were observed falling back. Very shortly German bombs were seen bursting in Hohenzollern Redoubt and close to Little Willie Trench, and it was obvious that Fosse No. 8 had been lost and that the enemy was rapidly regaining hold upon the Redoubt itself. Lieutenant-Colonel Cameron of Lochiel then ordered a force of 70 men of The Black Watch and 30 Cameron Highlanders under Captain

Bowes-Lyon, commanding B company, 8th Black Watch, to advance to the redoubt and to rally any men seen retiring. This advance was carried out, and the enemy were prevented from advancing further; but about 10.30 a.m. Captain Bowes-Lyon and Lieutenant C. O. C. MacIntosh were both killed by enemy bombs. The situation later on again became threatening, and General Thesiger and some of his staff went forward to the redoubt where, most unfortunately, the divisional commander was killed. To help the 73rd Brigade urgent requests came back for Black Watch and Cameron bombers, and there was no lack of volunteers amongst the tired survivors of these regiments. Several men of the 8th also went forward repeatedly and gallantly across the open to the redoubt carrying supplies of bombs and ammunition.

About 3 p.m. orders were received for the whole of the 26th Brigade to advance and occupy Dump Trench, east of the redoubt, as the 73rd Brigade had fallen back. There was no time to make any arrangements or issue any instructions. Word was passed from man to man along the trench, and they immediately clambered over the parapet and moved forward to the Hohenzollern. The redoubt was reached without many losses, in spite of considerable shelling, but any further advance proved to be impossible owing to the extremely heavy German machine gun and rifle fire, and a further attempt to advance met with heavy loss. Major Collins then decided to hold the redoubt, and a fierce bomb fight ensued in " Little Willie," a short distance from the junction of that trench with the Hohenzollern. The heavy "Béthune" and " cricket ball " bombs, though most effective on explosion, were no match in point of range for the lighter German " stick " grenades, but the 8th bombers fought on and held their own against this handicap, though at heavy cost. Lieutenant Forrester was mortally wounded while engaged in leading the bombers, and many casualties occurred among the rank and file. Owing to these losses the Battalion was soon without any trained bombers, but classes were at once organized in the rear trenches. Men were quickly shown how to light and throw grenades, and then went forward to keep up the fight, while others were employed detonating and passing forward supplies of grenades as they arrived from the rear.

During the afternoon Major Collins and Regimental Sergeant-Major Black were both killed. The Battalion was then commanded by Captain Ewing, the Adjutant.

In spite of persistent bombing by the enemy in " Little Willie " the Germans were prevented from making any advance, and the redoubt was successfully held under heavy shrapnel fire

TO RESERVE, SEPTEMBER 28TH, 1915

until 9.30 p.m., when the 85th Infantry Brigade came up and relieved the 26th, who were withdrawn to their old lines in Y 4 sector.

At 5 a.m. on September 28th the Battalion was withdrawn to the reserve line, and at 9.30 a.m. moved back to billets in Béthune, the whole of the 9th Division having been relieved by the 28th.

In this battle the 8th lost 19 officers and 492 other ranks in the three days' fighting. Of the officers nine were killed, and of the 20 combatant officers who went into action on the first day of the battle only three remained when the Battalion left the line. In losing Lord Sempill the Battalion lost a gallant Commanding Officer who had worked unsparingly for the success of his men; and by the death of Major Collins, whose experience and high sense of duty made him a worthy successor in command, the 8th suffered a further blow and one from which it could not quickly recover.

CHAPTER III

TRENCH WARFARE. SEPTEMBER, 1915, TO MAY, 1916

THE 29th of September was spent resting and cleaning up in Béthune, but early the following morning the Battalion entrained and proceeded by St. Omer to Abeele in Belgium, marching from there to billets in Poperinghe, which was reached about 12.30 p.m. on October 1st.

The period after Loos was a difficult one for the Battalion; the only original officers now with it being Captain J. L. S. Ewing in command, Captain R. N. Duke, Lieutenants D. N. Anderson, G. B. Gilroy and P. A. Cox, the Quartermaster, Lieutenant P. Goudy and the Medical Officer, Lieutenant A. L. McLean. It was thus very weak in numbers, nearly all the old non-commissioned officers were gone, and much equipment was deficient. New officers and drafts of men soon arrived, but it was clear that much training and re-organization would be necessary before the Battalion could regain its former efficiency as a fighting unit.

On October 2nd the Brigade commander, Brigadier-General Ritchie, addressed the Battalion and complimented all ranks on their part in the fighting at Loos. At 6 p.m. next day a move was made to huts near Dickebusch, and on the evening of the 4th, after an inspection of the Brigade by General Plumer, G.O.C. Second Army, the 8th went into the front line between the Ypres–Courtrai railway and the Ypres–Courtrai canal, taking over trenches " 34 " and " 35 " from a battalion of the Border Regiment, and trench " 33 " from the South Staffordshire Regiment. This tour passed uneventfully until the 9th, when Lieutenant Cox was wounded. The same night the 5th Camerons took over the line and the Battalion went back to Brigade reserve Headquarters, D company occupying a ruined château known as " Bedford House," while the other three companies remained further forward.

On the 13th the 8th returned to the front line slightly further north, relieving the 7th Seaforth Highlanders in trenches " 36 " and " 37," with its left flank resting on the Ypres–Courtrai railway, which, at this point, ran through a deep cutting. Just across the railway, and in enemy hands, lay the famous " Hill 60," a low mound which mines and shells had converted into a heap of muddy brown earth. Battalion Headquarters were a little way back along the railway, behind a curious pile of soil known as " The Dump."

Two days later several mines were exploded by the enemy on the right of the Battalion, the unit on that flank suffering many casualties. Enemy snipers were at this time very active, and Brigade sharpshooters were formed to deal with them. The

IN THE TRENCHES NEAR YPRES, OCTOBER, 1915

trenches were close together, and wet weather soon brought parapets tumbling down, thus adding to the danger. Losses from sniping were probably heavier during this time at Ypres than at any other throughout the war. On October 18th the G.O.C. V Corps, Lieutenant-General E. H. H. Allenby, went round the Battalion trenches.

The 21st was an unfortunate day for the 8th as trench "37" was shelled by heavy minenwerfer. Immediate steps were taken to clear the trench, but while the men were filing to a flank a heavy bomb pitched amongst them, killing 13, wounding five, and completely destroying the trench for thirty yards. The tour ended with a relief by units of the 27th Brigade on October 23rd, when the 8th marched back to rest in huts, "Scottish Lines," at Ouderdom. On the 24th Major H. R. Brown, 5th Camerons, took over command temporarily from Captain Ewing, and on the 30th, when the Battalion was still at rest, Major G. B. Duff, D.S.O., Cameron Highlanders, joined and took over command from Major Brown. The total losses during this month, which included two tours in the front line of five days and ten days respectively, were one officer wounded, 15 other ranks killed, and 10 other ranks wounded.

After some time in reserve, which was spent in training and route marching, the Battalion took over trenches "35" and "36" from the 6th Royal Scots Fusiliers on November 4th. Headquarters and two and a half companies were in the line; D company and half C company were in Bedford House furnishing guards. The trenches were very wet, Johnson's Trench—the main communication trench back from Headquarters at the Dump—being nearly full of water and impassable. The front trenches were little better, and in many places men had to stand knee-deep in liquid mud. Fortunately a supply of gum boots made these conditions tolerable, and leather jerkins and goatskin coats helped to keep out the cold. Much work was done on the trenches in spite of the bad weather conditions.

On the 6th enemy trench mortars caused nine casualties, and the British 60-pounder mortars failed to give an effective reply, as a high percentage of rounds fired were "blind." Afterwards, however, a carefully arranged system by which immediate retaliation was obtained by a direct call from the Battalion to an 8-inch howitzer battery proved successful in stopping further trouble from the German heavy minenwerfer.

Next day the trenches were much improved, and at night B company, holding trench "35," was relieved by the 12th Royal Fusiliers, 24th Division. After the relief B company occupied two strong points, R 7 and R 8, about six hundred yards behind the front line, and just in rear of the ruined village of Verbranden Molen and Blauweport Farm, a little further back. On the 8th A company in trench " 36 " was relieved by the 8th Gordon Highlanders, after which A and B companies moved back to dug-outs a mile or two in rear, C going to Blauweport Farm, and D with Battalion Headquarters to Bedford House.

On November 10th the Battalion relieved the 8th Gordon Highlanders as follows: A company, trench " 36," B and C companies, trench " 37," D company, trench " 38," Battalion Headquarters, the Dump. Rain had again reduced the trenches to a bad state and, in spite of energetic repair work, further heavy rain on the 12th and 13th made things worse. On the 14th, on relief by the 8th Gordon Highlanders, the Battalion went into rest at Canada Huts, but as two companies were under canvas and the ground was a sea of mud they were little better off than in the line. The official records contain an entry that on November 16th the Battalion went to baths at Dickebusch—possibly a minor incident of regimental history, but one which conditions of life in " The Salient " in November, 1915, made notable.

Between November 18th and 22nd the 8th was again in the line, holding the same trenches as before. On both occasions the trenches were drier, and after much work were left in better condition.

After three days in Brigade reserve the Battalion was again in the line from the 26th to the 30th. It was then relieved by the 8th Gordon Highlanders, and proceeded to Canada Huts. A touch of hard frost gave variety to the weather during this tour, which was uneventful, except for a bombardment of trench mortars on the 28th. During the month the losses of the Battalion amounted to 44 all ranks, killed and wounded.

December 1st to 4th was spent in Divisional reserve at Canada Huts. From the 5th to the 8th the Battalion was in the line; 9th to 12th, in Brigade reserve at Bedford House and Blauweport Farm; 13th to 16th, in the line; and on the night of the 16th, on relief by the 8th Gordon Highlanders, it moved to Canada Huts. On the following day the Battalion marched to Vlamertinghe and entrained for Steenwercke, whence it marched to billets in farms about a mile south of Bailleul.

The 9th Division was now in Corps reserve. The billets occupied were low lying, floods covered the roads at some places, and made it necessary to use pontoons as ferry-boats. Here the 8th spent its first Christmas in France, and the close of the year found it still at rest, occupied in steady training, chiefly drill, route marching, training of specialists, and bombing. The losses for the month of December, before the Battalion left Ypres, were one man killed and 15 wounded.

IN CORPS RESERVE, JANUARY, 1916

All ranks were glad to be back in France, for, apart from the Flanders mud and cold wet weather, life in the Ypres salient was not inspiriting. Clinging to a low ridge, with nothing but a monotonous and dreary plain behind, over most of which the enemy held observation, was trying. In addition, occupation of " The Salient " made long marches back to rest quarters necessary; and it was disheartening for tired troops when relieved from the trenches to find themselves, after a march of three or four miles, as much exposed to enemy artillery fire as they had been when near the front line. In the line shells often arrived from most unexpected directions, and looking back from Headquarters at the Dump, the enemy Very lights seemed to go up directly in rear—a continual and disquieting reminder that the Battalion was holding part of a deep and narrow salient. The tents or draughty Nissen huts, which formed the " rest " billets, and the bleak and desolate country, helped to make Ypres, between October and December, 1915, a place from which everyone was thankful to escape.

The greater part of January, 1916, was spent by the 8th in billets just south of Bailleul, a pleasant change from the Ypres salient. A great deal of training and re-organization was done here; special attention was paid to the use of hand grenades, all ranks going through a course of bombing and passing a test organized by Divisional Headquarters at the end of the course. There was considerable rivalry among the battalions for the honour of having the most expert bombers, and the 8th obtained second place in the Division—the credit being greatly due to the bombing officer, Lieutenant T. D. S. McLaren.

In the New Year Honours List the Battalion was awarded three decorations: the Commanding Officer, Lieutenant-Colonel G. Duff, received the D.S.O., and Captains J. L. S. Ewing and G. Gilroy the M.C.

During January three small drafts arrived amounting to 146 other ranks, and Captain Sir G. Abercromby rejoined from II Corps Staff. About this time the first consignment of steel helmets reached the Battalion, but they were regarded rather as a joke than as being of any practical use.

On the 24th the 9th Division began to take over the Ploegsteert line from the 25th Division, and the following day the 8th left its billets at 7 a.m. and marched to the " Piggeries," one of the support positions in Ploegsteert Wood.

The line taken over consisted of two sectors; the left the frontage of Ploegsteert Wood, with one battalion extending south of the wood. The right sector continued the line to the Lys river, and was held by the 28th Brigade, the 26th and 27th holding the left sector. Each sector was held with one Brigade in the front system and the third in support. Each battalion always occupied the same trench sector and changed over into support with its linked battalion in the other Brigade; by this means each battalion got to know its line thoroughly, and continuity of work was obtained. The 8th was linked with the 11th Royal Scots and occupied the southern sector of Ploegsteert Wood with Headquarters at Rifle House; the Reserve position was at the further end of the wood, with one company in Touquet Berthe Farm and Battalion Headquarters in the Keeper's Cottage. The tour of duty was six days in the front line and six days in support.

The front line consisted entirely of breastworks, and there were few communication trenches. The parapets were not shell-proof, and in many places were not even bullet-proof. Both battalions, however, worked hard, and during the next few months effected a great change in the situation.

On going into the line the strength of the Battalion was 28 officers and 883 other ranks, the companies being commanded as follows —

A coy. Capt. G. Gilroy, M.C.   B coy. Capt. J. D. Carswell.
C coy.   ,,   H. Butter.   D coy.   ,,   D. Anderson.

Needless to say this was only "paper strength"; actually the 8th was hard pressed to find a sufficient number of rifles to hold the line.

During the next four months the Battalion continued to hold this sector in conjunction with the 11th Royal Scots, and nothing of great importance occurred. In January and February the weather was very bad, but towards the end of April there was a great change for the better, and life in the wood became more pleasant; gardens were started at all reserve billets, and the necessary paths and duckwalks were put in good order.

Although the sector suffered little from shell fire, there was a great deal of machine gun fire at night, and casualties were frequent owing to the lack of communication trenches. The losses amounted to one officer killed and one wounded, 20 other ranks killed and 60 wounded.

On the morning of March 30th, Second Lieutenant W. Johnston was unfortunately killed by a chance bomb when returning from a patrol in No Man's Land, and the same afternoon Second Lieutenant J. L. Burton was wounded by shrapnel when attending Johnston's funeral.

The only notable action by the enemy occurred on the evening of May 13th, when the 11th Royal Scots were holding the line. After a heavy bombardment, during which long stretches of the breastworks were entirely demolished, two German raiding

TRENCH WARFARE, FEBRUARY TO MAY, 1916

parties crossed No Man's Land and entered the Royal Scots lines. They were ejected after a fierce struggle, leaving eleven dead behind. The Royal Scots suffered very heavily during the bombardment, and when the 8th relieved them the following morning the breastworks were found to have been obliterated in many places and had to be entirely rebuilt.

During this period there were several changes in the command of the Battalion. On March 4th Lieutenant-Colonel G. B. Duff, D.S.O., took over command of the 5th Camerons, and Captain Sir George Abercromby succeeded him in temporary command of the 8th. On April 9th, Lieutenant-Colonel C. W. E. Gordon, a Black Watch regular officer, took command of the Battalion from Captain Sir G. Abercromby, who then became Second-in-Command. During the latter part of May Captain and Adjutant J. L. S. Ewing was sent sick to England, Captain R. N. Duke taking his place. In March, Captains J. H. Stewart-Richardson and B. C. A. Steuart and Second Lieutenant A. Duncan Wallace joined the Battalion, and in the same month Regimental Sergeant-Major Mitchell, D.C.M., was sent sick to England and Company Sergeant-Major Barlow became Regimental Sergeant-Major.

At the end of May news came that the 9th Division was under orders for the Somme and would be relieved by the 41st Division. On May 30th the Battalion was relieved in the trenches by the 15th Hampshire Regiment, and went into reserve billets at Creslow, moving back to Steenje the following day, the 9th Division being then in Corps reserve.

CHAPTER IV

JUNE TO OCTOBER, 1916

The Battles of the Somme and Vimy Ridge

ON the 1st of June the Battalion started on its march to the Somme battlefield, and was continually on the move until it arrived at Corbie on the 25th. Occasionally a few days were spent in the same billets, when training and organization work were carried out; several drafts of officers and men arrived, and it was during this period that the number of Lewis guns was increased to sixteen, or one to each platoon.

The Battalion left Steenje on the 1st and marched to Bleu, moving to Morbecque Camp two days later, where it was inspected on the march by the Second Army Commander, General Sir Herbert Plumer. On the 4th the march was continued to Estrée Blanche, where a halt was made till the 13th. Here much training was carried out, but owing to the ground being covered with growing crops, and to continuous bad weather, the work was done only under great difficulties. While at Estrée Blanche, Second Lieutenants W. P. Dunbar, W. Austin and R. B. Bennett and 68 other ranks joined the Battalion. On the 10th the 26th Brigade held a Brigade Horse Show, in which the 8th gained many prizes. On June 13th the Battalion marched to Berguette, and at 10.30 p.m. entrained for the south, arriving at Longueau the following morning. From there the Battalion retraced its steps through Amiens to Argoeuvres, where it arrived about midday, both officers and men being very tired. The next nine days were spent training at Argoeuvres. On the 16th all company commanders and the Second-in-Command proceeded by motor-bus to Bray to reconnoitre the ground previous to the attack. While at Argoeuvres the following Second Lieutenants joined the Battalion: J. E. Hastings, W. F. Hutton, C. M. Alport, J. A. McRae, A. Graham, B. Webster, D. Tindal, W. McA. Cameron, A. Socket and J. K. Cousins.

On the 23rd of June the 8th marched to Longpré, moving two days later by train to Corbie, where all heavy baggage was left, and on the 27th at 11 p.m. started on its last stages towards the battlefield. The 28th and 29th were spent in Welcome Wood, and on the night of the 30th the Battalion moved to Celestine Wood, and the following night to Grovetown, where it was in reserve at instant call. Moving forward to Dillon Copse on July 4th, the Battalion took over the line at Montauban on the 8th from the 11th Royal Scots. During this move heavy shelling by the enemy took place, but the Battalion was lucky in escaping with few casualties.

ASSAULT ON LONGUEVAL, JULY 14TH, 1916

C company, under Captain Butter, took over the trenches on the north and east of Montauban. D company, under Captain L. G. Miles, took over the trenches on north of Bernafay Wood, while A and B companies, under Captains Gilroy and Carswell, remained in support behind Montauban in Train Alley with Headquarters. Transport and the reserve officers, non-commissioned officers, and Lewis gunners remained at Grovetown. On July 11th at 7 p.m. the Battalion was relieved by the 7th Seaforths and went into bivouac at Carnoy.

From the 8th to the 11th Montauban and Bernafay were under continuous shell fire, which was heaviest on the evening of the 11th. Companies in the front line would have suffered severe casualties from this fire had it not been possible to make use of many deep German dug-outs; but by keeping most of the men in these dug-outs, with a few sentries in the line, the losses were comparatively light. Captain Carswell and Second Lieutenants Fergusson and Socket were wounded and nine other ranks killed and 61 wounded. July 12th was spent at Carnoy, and at 7 p.m. on the 13th the 8th moved forward to Breslau Alley Trench in preparation for an attack the following morning.

The objective of the 9th Division on the 14th was the capture of Longueval and Delville Wood, the 26th Brigade being detailed for the attack on Longueval and Waterlot Farm with orders to push on through Delville Wood after the first objectives had been taken. The advance of the 26th Brigade was led by the 8th Black Watch on the right and the 10th Argyll and Sutherland Highlanders on the left; the 7th Seaforths were held in support and the 5th Camerons in reserve.

At 11 p.m. on the 13th the Battalion filed out from Breslau Trench, and by 3 o'clock the next morning was in position on the slopes of Longueval 400 yards south of the village, with the Argylls on the left and the remainder of the Brigade in rear. A covering party under Captain L. G. Miles was in front, and during the night did good work in keeping off hostile patrols. The Battalion was disposed in eight lines of platoons; the first four being D on the right and C on the left, and the second four lines, B on the right and A on the left. The ground on which the 8th lay was heavily shelled during the night, and it was found necessary to move the whole Battalion forward some distance to avoid casualties.

The assault of Longueval commenced at 3.25 a.m. on the 14th, and after severe fighting all objectives were captured by 10 a.m., with the exception of a strong point on the south-east of the village, which did not fall until 5 p.m. After Longueval was captured patrols were sent forward into Delville Wood. At first these met with little resistance, but by the afternoon the enemy was reinforced, and the patrols met with no success. Longueval was heavily shelled all day, and the Battalion was forced to evacuate several advanced posts owing to its exposed position. The losses were very heavy; all four company commanders were either killed or wounded, and the casualties among the rank and file were serious. By nightfall the enemy had filtered back into some of the northern outskirts of the village, but beyond occasional sniping did but little damage.

July 15th opened quietly, but at 11 a.m., after a heavy artillery preparation, an enemy attack was launched from the north-west, but was easily beaten off, and although the village was heavily bombarded for the rest of the day, no further fighting took place. The situation remained unchanged during the next two days. Longueval was under constant shell fire with the result that the 8th suffered heavily, and by the evening of the 17th it was so weak that eight reserve officers and all available non-commissioned officers and men were sent up from the transport lines to reinforce the Battalion. On the night of the 17th the Battalion transport and ration parties were caught in a barrage of high explosive and gas shells just short of Longueval, and suffered many casualties among both personnel and animals.

The 18th was another day of hard fighting. At 4 a.m. the 2nd Gordons, assisted by A and D companies of the 8th Black Watch, recaptured the northern outskirts of Longueval. At 9 a.m. the enemy opened a bombardment of great violence on both the village and Delville Wood, which continued until 7 p.m. Under cover of this they launched a strong attack at 3 p.m., and regained Delville Wood and the greater part of Longueval. A and D companies were driven back from the northern outskirts of the village to the railway line, but here the whole Battalion rallied and checked the enemy's advance. Colonel Gordon then organized a counter-attack and recaptured the line near Clarges Street. From this position another counter-attack not only drove the enemy out of the village, but succeeded in entering Delville Wood. Here, however, the line was outflanked, and the Battalion was forced to retire to Clarges Street having suffered very heavy losses.

Between 7 and 8 p.m. 120 men from the South African trench mortar company arrived as reinforcements and gave great assistance in holding the line. Early on the 19th, the 19th Durham Light Infantry took over Clarges Street, and later in the day the 10th Argylls occupied the railway line, the 8th Black Watch being then withdrawn to Carnoy. The strength of the Battalion was now reduced to six officers and 165 other ranks,

EIGHTH BATTALION PIPE BAND PLAYING AFTER THE CAPTURE OF LONGUEVAL, JULY, 1916

AFTER THE BATTLE, JULY, 1916

On July 20th the Battalion marched to the Sandpit near Méaulte, where it was joined by the transport and a draft of one officer, Captain Taylor, and 165 other ranks.

From July 8th to 19th casualties were as follows :—

Officers

Killed nine, wounded 14, died of wounds two, missing three. Total 28.

Other Ranks

Killed 86, wounded 370, died of wounds 13, missing 71. Total 540.

Officers killed

Capt. H. Butter.	2nd Lieut. W. McA. Cameron.
,, J. D. Carswell.	,, J. A. McRae.
Lieut. J. H. Robertson.	,, J. E. Hastings.
2nd Lieut. W. F. Hutton.	,, J. F. Crichton.
,, J. G. Fergusson.	

Officers died of wounds

Capt. G. B. Gilroy, M.C.   2nd Lieut. E. D. Murray.

Officers missing

2nd Lieut. D. Tindal.   2nd Lieut. E. Milroy.
,, G. H. Sprake.

Officers wounded

Capt. B. C. A. Steuart.	2nd Lieut. C. M. Alport.
,, L. G. Miles.	,, W. H. Scott.
2nd Lieut. L. McKenzie.	,, W. D. Montgomerie.
,, H. B. Dickson.	,, B. Webster.
,, J. C. R. Buchanan.	,, R. B. Bennett.
,, H. A. Clement.	,, W. P. Dunbar.
,, K. R. Cook.	,, A. M. Duncan Wallace

The Battalion remained at Sandpit, Méaulte, till July 23rd, reorganizing and re-equipping, and by that time its strength, including drafts, was 12 officers and about 350 other ranks.

The following officers commanded companies :—

A company. Lieut. Ritchie.   B company. Capt. Taylor.
C company.   ,,   Gauldie.   D company. Lieut. W. G. Hay.

Battalion Headquarters consisted of Lieutenant-Colonel W. E. Gordon, Major Sir G. Abercromby and Captain and Adjutant R. N. Duke. Company Sergeant-Major Henderson

THE EIGHTH BATTALION THE BLACK WATCH

became regimental sergeant-major vice Regimental Sergeant-Major Barlow, wounded.

On July 23rd the Battalion proceeded to Villers Sous Ailly by train and road, and on the 25th to Bruay, where it received a draft of 75 other ranks from the base and nine officers from the Reserve Battalion Argyll and Sutherland Highlanders. During the march to Bruay the 8th passed through the billets of the 9th Battalion The Black Watch, commanded by Lieutenant-Colonel S. A. Innes, and a halt was made for an hour to enable the two battalions to meet.

On July 28th the Battalion left Bruay for Gouy-Servins, a village four miles behind the Vimy Ridge, where the 9th Division held the line. The next fourteen days were spent there, training and reorganizing; the weather was good and much useful work was done, with the result that the Battalion rapidly regained its efficiency after the hard experiences of Longueval and Delville Wood. Unfortunately there was a serious bombing accident on August 8th, which resulted in the death of Lieutenant W. G. Hay, commanding D company, and in the wounding of Second Lieutenant F. R. Fortune.

Some changes now occurred among the company commanders: Lieutenant T. D. S. McLaren took over A company from Lieutenant Ritchie, evacuated sick; Captain H. Forsyth took command of C company from Lieutenant Gauldie; and Lieutenant Austin succeeded Lieutenant W. G. Hay in command of D company.

On August 12th the Battalion took over the Berthonval No. 1 sector from the 4th Battalion Middlesex Regiment. This sector was on the extreme right of the 9th Division line, joining up with the 47th Division. The trenches were dry and deep, but no attempt had been made at revetting, and it was obvious that many would collapse in wet weather; dug-out accommodation was also scarce, but the line was very quiet, there being little activity except occasional trench mortar bombing.

On the 15th, Second Lieutenants A. S. Harper and A. D. Hutchison joined the Battalion. The 8th was relieved by the 4th South African Regiment on the 23rd, and proceeded in buses to La Comte, the IV Corps rest area, where it remained a week, during which the following officers joined from the 11th (Reserve) Battalion:—

Second Lieutenants R. E. Odell, R. C. Ashfield, A. J. Mann, J. A. Anderson, J. M. Whitecross, J. A. Whitwright, J. McK. Taylor, J. L. Young, A. T. Lowen, R. N. Murray, A. Campsie and A. Craven.

From August 23rd to September 1st the 8th remained at

EIGHTH BATTALION DRAWING THE RUM RATION AFTER CAPTURE OF LONGUEVAL, JULY, 1916

TRENCH WARFARE, AUGUST TO SEPTEMBER, 1916

La Comte practising for an attack to be made shortly by the 26th Brigade, but the day before leaving La Comte the attack was cancelled owing to the scarcity of shells. The Battalion returned to Gouy Servins on September 1st, and the following day relieved the 2nd South African Regiment in the Berthonval sector. A great change was now evident in this sector, the German trench mortars being far more active. The British line was full of Stokes guns and 60-pound trench mortars, which fired night and day in retaliation.

This activity culminated on the 14th in a combined raid of 60 men of the Battalion and 60 of the 5th Camerons with the object of securing prisoners and identifications. There was no artillery support to the raid, but a barrage was put down by twenty-four Stokes mortars, which are said to have fired 4500 rounds during the fifteen minutes the raid lasted. The Black Watch raiding party was commanded by Lieutenant A. Hamilton with Second Lieutenants Harper, Lowen and Odell. The raid was successful; only one prisoner of the 101st Saxon Regiment was captured, but the trenches were found to be full of dead; according to the prisoner this was due to the fact that a large party was working in the German trench when the barrage fell. For services on this occasion Lieutenant Hamilton afterwards received the M.C. The total loss during the raid was five men wounded.

On the 16th the weather changed, and rain fell in torrents, with the result that many parapets collapsed and the trenches were filled with liquid mud. On the 19th the Battalion was relieved by the 6th King's Own Scottish Borderers and marched to billets in Gouy Servins, whence, on the 22nd, it proceeded to Mingoval. Lieutenant-Colonel C. W. E. Gordon was now promoted Brigade Commander in the 41st Division, and Major Sir George Abercromby succeeded to the command of the Battalion.

The 9th Division was now warned for a second tour in the Somme battle, and ordered to proceed to the Third Army training area and prepare for a coming attack. On the 23rd the 8th marched to billets in Denier, a miserable little village with poor accommodation. Here constant training was carried out, and several drafts soon brought the Battalion up to strength. On October 3rd the Battalion was inspected by the G.O.C. XVII Corps, and two days later orders were received for the move towards the Somme area.

The 8th was now organized as follows:—

A coy. Lieut. T. D. S. McLaren.   B coy. Capt. N. R. Taylor.
C coy.   „   J. Inglis.   D coy.   „   R. N. Murray.

THE EIGHTH BATTALION THE BLACK WATCH

Battalion Headquarters

Lieutenant-Colonel Sir G. Abercromby, Battalion Commander.
Captain R. N. Duke, Adjutant.
Second Lieutenant P. Ray, Machine Gun Officer.
    "   A. Glen, Signalling Officer.

Starting on the 5th, the Battalion moved by Mézerolles and Franvillers, and reached Albert on the 7th, where it remained two days; on the evening of the 9th the 26th Brigade took over the trenches at Eaucourt L'Abbaye just opposite the Butte de Warlencourt. The 7th Seaforths held the front line with the 10th Argyll and Sutherland Highlanders in support in the Flers line, the 5th Camerons and 8th Black Watch being in reserve near High Wood. The 8th was bivouacked in the old German trenches on the north-east side of the wood, a most unpleasant position, just in front of several batteries which fired day and night, and which were constantly searched for by German heavy guns.

The coming operation in which the Battalion was to take part was an attack by the 9th Division on the Butte de Warlencourt and the trench system surrounding it. The 26th Brigade attack was to be carried out by the Seaforths and two companies of the Argyll and Sutherland Highlanders. Early on the morning of the 12th the Division attacked the Butte in conjunction with other Divisions operating on its right and left. Unfortunately the attack failed, and little ground was gained by the assaulting troops who suffered heavy losses. That night the Seaforths and Argyll and Sutherland Highlanders were withdrawn into reserve, the 5th Camerons taking over the line at Eaucourt L'Abbaye, with the 8th Black Watch in support in the Flers line. The Battalion remained in this position for the next four days, chiefly occupied in clearing the battlefield, during which operation many bodies of men belonging to The Black Watch Territorials were found and buried. On the 17th orders were received that the 5th Camerons would attack Snag Trench early the following day, together with one company of The Black Watch.

A company was detailed for this duty, and Second Lieutenants A. Balkwill and A. Hutchison were sent forward to reconnoitre the ground. Unfortunately, Balkwill was killed and Hutchison seriously wounded by artillery fire on their way up. This left A company short of officers, and the Commanding Officer detailed B company, under Captain Taylor, in its place. On the evening of the 17th the Camerons and B company concentrated in the front line, the remaining three companies occupying the Flers

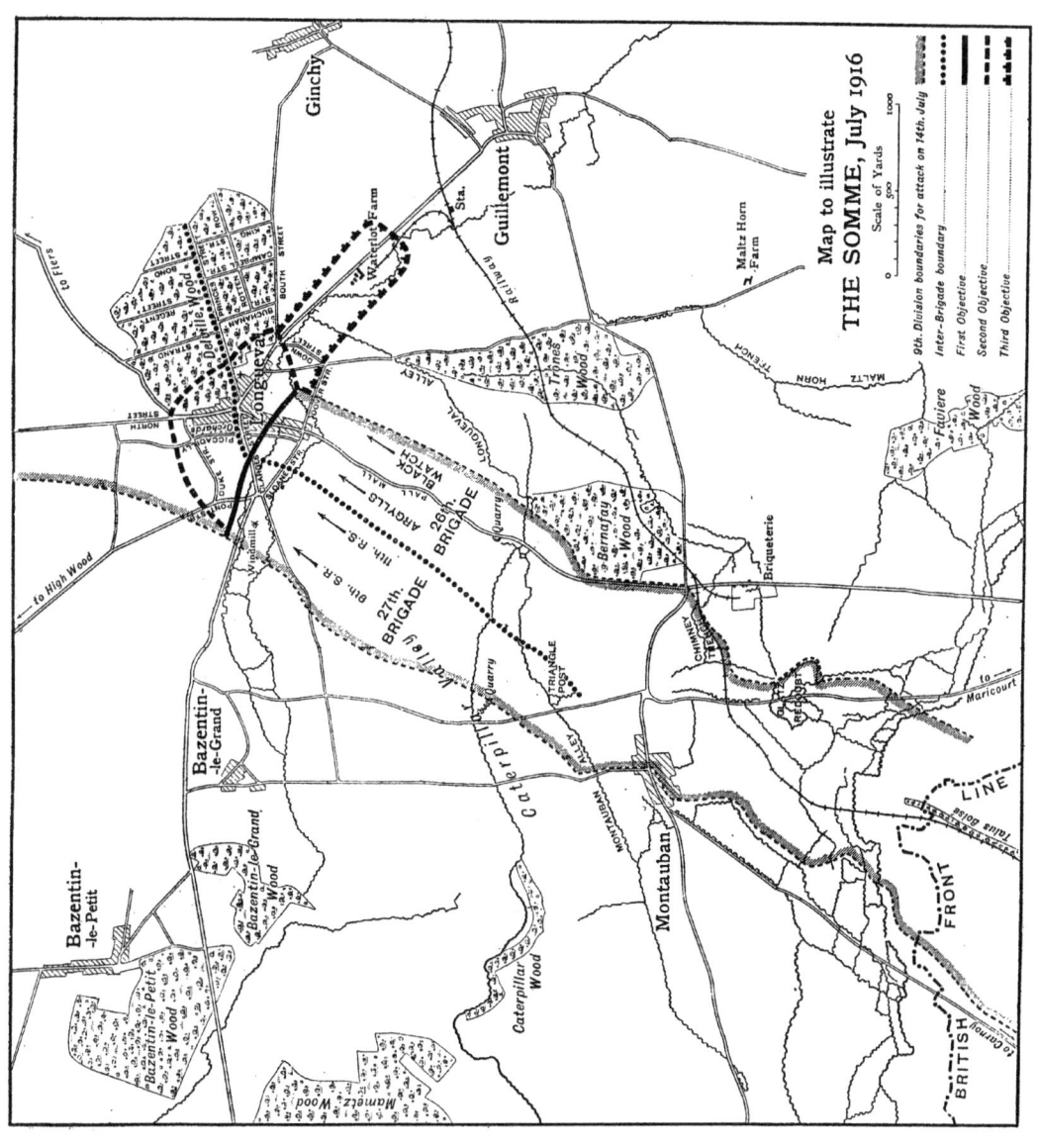

BUTTE DE WARLENCOURT, OCTOBER 18TH, 1916

line, now vacated by the reserve companies of the Camerons. At 3.40 a.m. on the 18th the Camerons attacked and captured Snag Trench. B company did not actually take part in the attack, but remained in the Cameron's old front line in support. During the day the Camerons consolidated their ground, and at 8.30 p.m. the 8th relieved them in the newly captured position, the line being held by D company on the right, A in the centre and C on the left, with B in support in the original front line. The 21st Brigade, 30th Division, was on the right and the South African Brigade on the left.

At 5.30 a.m. on the 19th the Germans started a counter-attack by bombing; on the right D company easily held its own, an attack with a flamenwerfer being stopped by Private Tait with a well-aimed Mills bomb. On the left things went badly, the South Africans were bombed out of their trench and crowded into C company's line, completely blocking the trench. The German bombers were close after them, and, hurling their bombs into the overcrowded trench, inflicted heavy casualties on C company. Second Lieutenant Anderson was killed while trying to organize a counter-attack, and the Company Commander and Company Sergeant-Major were both wounded. During the confusion which followed the Germans succeeded in capturing C company's line and pressed down on to A, but a counter-attack, headed by Second Lieutenants Campsie and Craven, drove them back; Craven was unfortunately killed and Campsie wounded.

At 7.30 a.m. Captain Taylor brought up B company, which had been in support, and by vigorous bombing attacks succeeded in recapturing C company's line, with the result that by noon the 8th had retaken the whole of its line, though touch with the South Africans was not regained until 5 p.m., when the whole position was reoccupied.

Throughout the day rain fell in torrents, and the trenches were in an appalling state, movement along them being practically impossible; in fact, the conditions under which this fighting took place could not have been worse, and its success in recapturing the position speaks highly for the determination and fighting spirit of the Battalion. In the *History of the 9th Division* the author, Major J. Ewing, M.C., concludes the account of the fighting with the following words: " The whole of the defences " were then reorganized, but the enemy did not venture again " to tackle The Black Watch."

Owing to the terrible conditions under which this action was fought, the 8th required time for reorganization, and early on the 20th it was relieved by the 12th Royal Scots, and moved back to its previous bivouac at High Wood, and the following

THE EIGHTH BATTALION THE BLACK WATCH

day to Mametz Wood, from which, on the 25th, it moved to Albert. Some idea of the state of the ground may be gathered from the fact that many platoons took eight hours to cover the four miles between the trenches and High Wood.

The following casualties occurred between the 10th and 20th of October: Officers, killed three, wounded seven; other ranks, killed 21, wounded 152, missing 24. During the fighting the Battalion lost Second Lieutenants A. Balkwill, A. Craven, and A. Anderson killed; Lieutenant J. Inglis, Second Lieutenants A. Campsie, A. T. Lowen, R. Ashfield, J. McK. Taylor, A. D. Hutchison, and A. B. Ruthven wounded; 21 other ranks killed, 152 wounded and 24 missing, a total of 207 all ranks.

On October 14th the Battalion suffered a severe loss when the Quartermaster, Lieutenant P. Goudy, was sent to England sick. He had been with the Battalion since August, 1914, and his long experience, ability and readiness to help had ever been a great asset. His loss was much felt, but in Second Lieutenant D. Soutar a capable successor was found.

CHAPTER V

NOVEMBER, 1916, TO APRIL, 1917

The First Battle of Arras

THE Battalion spent October 25th and 26th in Albert, where several drafts arrived, and three officers, Captain I. W. Shepherd and Second Lieutenants P. J. A. Alexander and G. C. Logan, joined. The quartermaster's department had a busy time replacing clothing and equipment lost or destroyed at High Wood, but on the 27th the Battalion was ready to move to Franvillers, where Captain A. Drummond joined, and on the 28th to Mulliens-au-Bois, and thence by bus to billets in Arras on the 30th. The 9th Division was now billeted in rear of Arras for rest and training. Rumour had it that in the spring of 1917 operations on a large scale, in which the 9th Division would take part, would start from Arras, and the winter, therefore, was to be spent in preparation for this attack.

The 26th Brigade was billeted immediately behind Arras, with one battalion in the town attached to the Brigades holding the line to provide working parties. The 8th was the first battalion detailed for this duty, and was billeted in the Cavalry Barracks with Headquarters and company messes in adjoining houses.

At this time Arras was unusually quiet and peaceful. Scarcely a shell was heard all day, billets were good, and after dark many shops opened, and luxuries, which the Battalion had not seen for months, could be purchased. Movement in the streets by day was forbidden owing to the frequent visits by enemy aeroplanes. This precaution was very necessary as, although it appeared deserted, a large number of troops occupied the city—in fact, after dark the streets were nearly impassable owing to the crowd—and if the enemy had shelled Arras, casualties must have been very heavy.

The 8th remained thus employed till November 20th, during which many small drafts reached the Battalion, and the following officers joined: Second Lieutenants H. B. Dickson, C. W. Bellamy, W. Hunter and H. L. Bryson. In addition 10 officers of the 3rd Gordon Highlanders, and one from the Fife and Forfar Yeomanry, were attached for duty.

On the 20th the Battalion marched from Arras to Izel-les-Hameaux to undergo a period of training for ten days. On the 28th, Second Lieutenants A. Proudfoot and G. H. Watt joined, and four days later the 9th Division received orders to take over the line in front of Arras from the 35th Division, the 26th Brigade being detailed to hold the right or No. 1 Sector.

THE EIGHTH BATTALION THE BLACK WATCH

The line was held by two battalions, with two in support in Arras. The Black Watch and Seaforths were detailed for the first tour in the line, the former on the right and the latter on the left. As soon as these orders arrived, commanding officers and company commanders were sent to Arras in order to inspect the line and make arrangements for the relief. The 8th relieved the 17th Lancashire Fusiliers in the sub-section " I ". An inspection of the trenches showed that while they were fairly well built and dry, there was little cover, and dug-outs were scanty. The Fusiliers reported the line very quiet except for two spots—one, on the right, where a heavy German trench mortar was in position, and the other where the line crossed the Arras–Cambrai road, and was constantly the object of German light trench mortar activity.

On December 3rd the 8th marched to Wanquetin, and took over the front line the following evening. The tour, which lasted six days, passed without incident, and on the 10th the Battalion was relieved by the 10th Argyll and Sutherland Highlanders and moved back to billets in Arras, after which, on the 16th, it relieved the Argylls in the same sector.

A change was now made in the Battalion dispositions in the line, which was found to be too long to hold in the usual manner. A series of strong points were constructed and held by three companies, the fourth being in support in the outskirts of Arras. B company under Captain Taylor, C under Captain Drummond and D under Captain Murray held the line, with A under Captain Shepherd in support.

The line was now becoming far from peaceful. As the Somme battle was now at an end, a great many batteries had been sent north to Arras in preparation for the coming offensive, and their constant activity naturally drew retaliation from the enemy. On the 19th Lieutenant R. Odell was seriously wounded by a trench mortar bomb and died the following day. On the 23rd the Battalion was relieved by the Argyll and Sutherland Highlanders and marched to the reserve billets in Arras.

The 8th now lost the valuable services of Captain R. N. Duke, the Adjutant, who became Staff-Captain to the 27th Brigade. About the same time Brigadier-General A. Ritchie, G.O.C. 26th Brigade, was promoted to command a division and was succeeded by Lieutenant-Colonel J. Kennedy, D.S.O., from the 10th Argyll and Sutherland Highlanders.

The Battalion passed a quiet Christmas in Arras, but on the night of the 28th the billets were heavily shelled with gas shells. The men were sleeping when the bombardment began, and many shells fell in the billets, a number of men being gassed before they were properly awake. The shelling lasted about

RAIDING THE GERMAN FRONT LINE

three hours, during which some 3000 shells fell in the Battalion area. A and B companies were the two most affected, and fog rendered the work of getting men out of their billets and into cellars most difficult; at times the fog was so thick that it was impossible to see through gas masks, and they had to be taken off and the gas chanced. Two sergeants died from gas poisoning, and 65 other ranks were sent to hospital suffering from the effects of gas.

The Battalion returned to the trenches in I Sector on the 30th, and again took over from the Argyll and Sutherland Highlanders. On January 1st, 1917, a heavy German trench mortar bomb fell on a dug-out in C company's line, causing it to collapse, and killing five men in it. The following day Second Lieutenant A. M. Ogilvie was wounded while inspecting the German wire. On the 4th the Battalion was relieved by the Argylls and moved to the Arras billets.

The 9th Division now received orders to obtain prisoners and identifications. The 26th Brigade was given this task, and Brigadier-General Kennedy issued orders to the 8th Black Watch and Argyll and Sutherland Highlanders each to provide a party of a hundred men to carry out a raid on the 6th in daylight, with artillery support. The line to be raided was carefully selected by the two battalion commanders, each being allotted about 150 yards of the German front. Three lines of enemy trenches were to be overrun, the garrison killed or captured, and identification obtained.

The scheme for the raid was as follows: At Zero the leading platoons were to leave the British trenches and occupy the enemy front line, forming blocks on their outer flanks. The second platoons were to follow and go through the leading platoon as far as the German second line, while the third platoons were to "leap-frog" the two others and occupy the third line. The fourth platoon, with the company commander, was to halt in the enemy front line, from which it could be used as support if necessity arose. Fifteen minutes after Zero the retirement was to commence, starting from the German third line—the last platoon to retire to be the supporting platoon with the company commander. C company, Captain Drummond, was selected for the raid, the platoon commanders being Second Lieutenants Whitecross, Whitwright, Proudfoot and Hunter.

On the morning of the 6th the British artillery opened a heavy fire on the enemy line, increasing in intensity at 2.30 p.m.; at 3.8 p.m. the raid took place, and met with complete success. All three lines were occupied, but only four Germans were seen, one of whom was captured and the rest killed. The

THE EIGHTH BATTALION THE BLACK WATCH

remainder of the garrison had taken refuge from the bombardment in deep dug-outs and could not be induced to come up; Stokes' bombs were thrown down the stairways with the result that some dug-outs collapsed and others took fire. The Battalion losses amounted to one man killed and 10 wounded. The Argyll party saw no Germans in their part of the line. The 8th occupied I Sector for the last time on the 10th, and was relieved by the 6th Queen's (12th Division) on the 14th, and moved to billets in Etrun, in the XVII Corps area, where it was joined by Lieutenants M. E. Pelham-Burn and P. H. C. Colquhoun.

After a week's training and rest the 8th, on January 22nd, relieved the 5th Camerons in L.I. Sector at Roclincourt on the extreme south of the Vimy Ridge. This was a bad line, but had the advantage of being quiet, only one casualty occurring during the tour in the trenches.

On the 27th the Battalion was relieved by the Seaforths and went into billets at Maroeuil, when Lieutenant-Colonel Sir G. Abercromby proceeded to England on a month's leave, his place being temporarily filled by Major R. Anstruther, M.C., a Regular Black Watch officer who joined on the 22nd.

From now till February 23rd the Battalion was occupied in providing large working parties for the coming attack, and the Battalion was much scattered in consequence. On the 23rd the 8th assembled at " Y " Huts, close to Etrun, and marched to the XVII Corps training area at Monchy Breton, where it went into billets; here it remained until the 2nd of March, during which time constant training was carried on and several drafts arrived from the base.

CHAPTER VI

FEBRUARY TO JUNE, 1917

The Battles of Arras

TOWARDS the end of February orders were received that the Division would soon return to the line, and on March 2nd the 8th left Monchy Breton for "Y" Huts, an encampment about four miles behind Arras. Here Lieutenant-Colonel Sir G. Abercromby rejoined and took over command from Major Anstruther Captain and Quartermaster P. Goudy also arrived and took over his old duties from Second Lieutenant Soutar.

On March 3rd the Battalion moved into billets in Arras, companies being quartered in the Convent and Battalion Headquarters in the Hotel de Universe. From the 4th to the 7th, the 8th was employed in finding working parties for R.A. and R.E. in St. Catherine on the outskirts of Arras. This area was crowded with batteries of every description, which were constantly bombarded by the enemy, as indeed was the whole city. By this time the Germans had become aware that something was brewing, and the consequent increased activity of their guns caused many casualties. Fortunately the Battalion was lucky in escaping lightly, only one officer, Second Lieutenant Young, being wounded.

On March 8th the Battalion moved into the support trenches of J Sector in relief of 5th Camerons, and on the 9th took over the front line from the 7th Seaforths, Second Lieutenant Chambers being wounded by an aeroplane bomb during the relief.

The Battalion was now holding the line which would eventually be the starting-point of 26th Brigade in the Arras battle. The line was over a thousand yards long, with its right resting on the River Scarpe. As a trench line, it left much to be desired, especially on the right, where hostile heavy trench mortars had completely flattened the parapets of the front line trenches. The Battalion remained in the line until the 14th, and had a quiet tour, the only incident being an attempted enemy raid on the 10th, which did not materialise owing to timely notice of its coming having been given by the Battalion patrols. On the 14th the 8th was relieved by the 9th Scottish Rifles and moved back to "Y" Huts, and on the 21st it returned to J Sector in relief of the 12th Royal Scots.

South of Arras the enemy had suddenly retreated, and touch had been temporarily lost. The Army Commander feared that the same might happen north of Arras and thus bring to nothing all preparations for attack. Orders, therefore, were issued that all work was to be hurried forward,

THE EIGHTH BATTALION THE BLACK WATCH

and that the great attack would take place as soon as possible. The Battalion spent four busy days hastening on their preparations; assembly trenches were dug, gaps cut in the wire, and dumps containing all manner of material were formed. By the 25th everything was ready, and on the 26th the Battalion was relieved by the Seaforths and marched back for a period of rest before the battle. On arrival at " Y " Huts, orders were received for a further move the following day, and on the 27th the Battalion moved a few miles further back to poor billets at Hautes Avesne, where it was joined by Second Lieutenants D. Harrison and J. Monday.

The weather now broke completely, rain and snow fell constantly, and the date of the operation was postponed from day to day in the hope of better weather. Finally, the attack was fixed for April 9th, and on the 6th, in torrents of rain, the Battalion began its move back to the line. To effect this movement the 8th was divided into two parties, and on the evening of the 8th B and C companies with Battalion Headquarters marched back to J Sector, where B took over the exact frontage from which the Battalion was to attack on the 9th; C company went into billets in Arras, and Battalion Headquarters occupied the 26th Brigade Battle Headquarters in Forrestier Redoubt. The day before, A and D companies, under Major Anstruther, had moved to billets in Arras, and on the night of the 8th to assembly trenches in J Sector, where they joined the rest of the Battalion.

The Divisional attack was made on a three-brigade front, each brigade assaulting with two battalions in the front line and two in support, brigades being allotted a frontage of 600 yards, 300 yards to each battalion. The 26th Brigade was the right brigade of the 9th Division line with its right flank on the River Scarpe, the South African Brigade being on the left. The Seaforths on the right and the 8th Black Watch on the left led the advance; the Argylls and Camerons were held in support and reserve respectively.

The 26th Brigade had three definite objectives. The first was the German 3rd Trench System line, about 100 yards from the British front line. This Black Line was to be captured by the two leading companies of attacking battalions. The second objective was the Arras-Douai railway, Blue Line, about a thousand yards beyond the Black Line, and its capture was the task of the rear companies of the leading battalions; the third and final objective was the village of Athies, a thousand yards still further in advance, and this was to be captured by the supporting battalions, the Camerons and the Argyll and Sutherland Highlanders.

BATTLE OF ARRAS, APRIL 9TH, 1917

The 8th was organized for the attack as follows: Front line, C company under Second Lieutenant A. Proudfoot on the right, and B company under Second Lieutenant P. Alexander on the left; the Second line was made up of A company under Captain I. Shepherd on the right, and D company under Lieutenant W. Austin on the left; Battalion Headquarters were midway between the two lines. The transport and personnel not employed in the battle remained at St. Catherine.

At 10.30 p.m. on the 8th the Battalion began moving into the assembly trenches, and by 3 o'clock the following morning was in position. There had been considerable shelling during the night, but casualties were few.

Zero hour was fixed for 5.30 a.m. on the 9th, and ten minutes before that time the bombardment—which had already lasted for three days—increased to its greatest intensity. Punctually at 5.30 a.m. the leading companies left their trenches. They originally started in four waves, fifteen yards apart, but such was the confusion of shell holes and battered trenches that the four lines soon joined together and the companies swept forward in a single line. Little resistance was met with at first, and the Black Line was easily taken, as the garrison appeared to be cowed by the long bombardment and anxious to surrender. Four officers, including a Battalion Commander, and 150 men were captured by the leading companies, and many more were taken from deep dug-outs by two platoons of the Argylls, who were "mopping up." By 6.10 a.m. the Black Line had been captured, and the Battalion was in touch with the troops on its right and left who had been equally successful. The losses of B and C were light, amounting to two officers and about 60 other ranks; Lieutenant Pelham-Burn was killed and Second Lieutenant Grey wounded.

A and D companies, who had already suffered considerably from shell fire, now formed up behind the Black Line, and at 7.35 a.m. began their advance on the Blue Line, coming under heavy shell fire almost at once. German machine guns from south of the Scarpe also caused many casualties. Here Second Lieutenant Mann was killed and Second Lieutenants Bryson and McLaren were wounded, but the two companies, ably led by Captain Shepherd and Lieutenant Austin, pressed on and, although edging off northwards, eventually gained an entrance to the railway cutting at its northern end. During this advance Second Lieutenants Gawne, Tyser and Ross were killed. There was a stiff bomb fight in the railway cutting, but finally the whole line was taken and touch gained with the Seaforths on the right. Six officers, one a regimental commander, and 100 men were captured in the Railway line. Directly they had taken their objective, A and D companies started to consolidate their position, while the Camerons and Argylls passed through them to be ready for the attack on Athies.

By this time A and D companies were very weak, having lost six officers and about 140 other ranks, and a platoon each from B and C was sent up to reinforce the Black Line. The total losses in this fighting amounted to five officers and 50 other ranks killed; six officers and 147 other ranks wounded; and three men missing.

The attack on Athies by the Camerons and Argylls was successful, and they were in turn passed through by the 4th Division which advanced to attack Fampoux.

The Battalion remained in the captured positions on the Railway and Black Line for the remainder of the day, and on the following day A and D companies withdrew from the Railway line to the original British front line, B and C companies with Battalion Headquarters remaining in the Black Line. On the 12th the 9th Division was ordered to pass through the 4th Division and attack Greenland Hill, north-east of Roeux, the 27th and South African Brigades being detailed for the attack; the 26th Brigade remained in support behind Athies with orders that if the attack were successful a further advance would be made against Roeux; but as the attack by 27th Brigade and South Africans was driven off with heavy loss, the 26th was not called on to move.

On the evening of April 12th the 8th took over the line in front of Fampoux from three weak battalions of the 4th Division, and held this line until the 15th, when it was relieved by the 7th Black Watch. Unfortunately there was a great deal of shelling during this relief, the 7th suffering heavily; Lieutenant A. Glen, Adjutant 8th Battalion, being wounded while acting as a guide to the 7th. After the relief, the 8th assembled in Arras in the early hours of April 16th, and that afternoon marched back to "Y" Huts, where it was joined by the Battalion transport.

The next four days were spent in reorganizing and re-equipping, the 9th Division having been warned it would soon be required for a fresh attack. On the 19th, Captain R. Hadow joined the Battalion, and on the 21st it moved, by train and road, to billets in Foufflin-Ricametz, close to St. Pol. This was the best billeting area the Battalion had occupied for some time, and all ranks were thoroughly comfortable.

On the 23rd a draft of 97 men arrived, composed mainly of men from the Army Service Corps who had recently been in hospital. The men knew little of infantry work, and some were hardly able to load their rifles. The Commanding Officer protested, but without result, and the Battalion had to absorb the

TRENCH WARFARE, ARRAS, MAY, 1917

draft, and try to train the new-comers in two days. On April 25th a start was made back to Arras, and that evening the 8th was once more in " Y " Huts. Two days later, on the 27th, the whole Division moved to the Black Line in Corps reserve in readiness for a further attack on Greenland Hill which had so far resisted all efforts to capture it. The Division now practically consisted of two weak Brigades, the 26th and 27th. The South African Brigade, which had lost heavily on the 12th and had received no drafts, was now organized as one weak composite battalion and formed the 9th Division reserve.

The 8th moved up to the Black Line on the 27th, and concentrated in Obermeyer Trench, its total battle strength being 16 officers and about 470 other ranks. Company commanders were as follows: A company, Lieutenant Mackenzie; B, Captain Taylor; C, Lieutenant Proudfoot; and D, Lieutenant Monday; Battalion Headquarters consisting of Lieutenant-Colonel Sir G. Abercromby, Captain and Adjutant R. Murray and Lieutenant D. Soutar, signalling officer.

On the 28th the Battalion moved up to the Railway line, relieving the 5th Camerons. The line was constantly shelled, and on the 29th Second Lieutenant T. D. Speed was mortally wounded in the cutting. The same day the following five officers arrived at the Transport lines: Captain A. Duncan Wallace, Lieutenants W. Forbes, H. D. McMillan and Second Lieutenants J. Robertson, F. H. Bradley and H. A. Clement.

The 8th remained in the Railway line till May 1st, when it moved forward to the front line, taking over from the Seaforths. This line was about 250 yards in front of Greenland Hill, and consisted of two lines of trenches, the front line being known as Cuba Trench and the support as Clasp Trench, with only one communication trench, Chili Trench, connecting the two lines with the rear. On the 2nd orders were received that the Division would assault Greenland Hill at dawn the following day. In this attack the 26th Brigade had the 4th Division on its right and the 27th Brigade on its left, the attacking battalions being the Camerons and two companies of the Argylls on the right and 8th Black Watch on the left, Headquarters of both battalions being in Chili Trench, whilst the Seaforths and remaining two companies of Argylls were in support.

On the night of May 2nd the Battalion moved into its assembly position as follows: A and B companies in the front line, with C and D in support. The Battalion was in position by 1 a.m. on May 3rd, and although there was continual shelling during the movement, casualties were not heavy, but, unfortunately, Lieutenant Mackenzie and Second Lieutenant Harley were wounded. Previous to this Second Lieutenants Soutar and Whitecross had been evacuated sick.

Zero hour had been fixed for 4 a.m. on the 3rd, when there would have been enough light to get the right direction; but a few hours earlier the hour was changed to 3.45 a.m., which necessitated attacking in the dark; in consequence, there was no time to take bearings, and the exact direction could not be accurately taken.

The moon went down at 3 a.m., and the attack started in pitch darkness at 3.45 a.m. From the first the attacking troops were in trouble. Owing to darkness, and the impossibility of keeping a straight line on the broken ground, all direction was lost, and a gap was left between the Black Watch and Camerons. On the left of the Battalion the 27th Brigade had to incline to the right, and this movement was carried to excess, with the result that the Battalion of the 27th Brigade came across into the 8th's area, thus adding to the confusion. The Germans, who apparently expected this attack, at once opened heavy shell and machine gun fire on the advancing troops, which caused very heavy casualties and brought the attack to a standstill. Owing to the fact that all officers and non-commissioned officers of the leading companies were either killed or wounded, it is impossible to give a complete story of the fight, but it seems probable that few, if any, of A and B companies reached the enemy's trenches, and the survivors of the Battalion retired to the original front line; here the only two unwounded officers, Second Lieutenants McNeal and Wilson, aided by Company Sergeant-Major M. McArthur, organized a line of defence. Second Lieutenant H. Clement was sent up from Battalion Headquarters to assist, but was killed directly he arrived.

The losses had been very heavy, nearly half the Battalion being either killed or wounded in about fifteen minutes. Four officers were killed, six wounded and two missing, and 21 other ranks killed, 148 wounded and 43 missing. Officers killed: Lieutenant J. Monday, Second Lieutenants H. Clement, T. D. Speed and H. Bell. Officers wounded: Lieutenant J. MacKenzie, Second Lieutenants D. Harrison, J. R. Fairley, W. C. Harley, H. J. Walker and A. Proudfoot. Missing: Captain N. R. Taylor and Second Lieutenant P. G. Fraser.

During the remainder of the day the 8th, now consisting of four officers and about 250 men, held Cuba Trench, and that night was relieved by the 7th Seaforths and went into support in the Fampoux line. On May 5th a further move back was made to a position behind the Railway line, and on the 10th the Battalion moved back to " Y " Huts to reorganize, and on the 12th the whole Division proceeded to St. Pol training area, the 8th

TRENCH WARFARE, JUNE, 1917

being billeted at Averdoingt. Here drafts amounting to 205 other ranks arrived, and the following officers joined: Captain E. Harnett and Second Lieutenants Walcott and Robson. On May 21st Lieutenant-Colonel Sir G. Abercromby was invalided to England, Major R. Anstruther taking over command, Captain R. Hadow becoming Second-in-Command. From the 12th to 29th the Battalion was engaged in training, and during this period was nearly brought up to strength by frequent drafts. On the 30th the Division received orders for its return to the line, and the 8th then moved by bus to St. Catherine on the outskirts of Arras, relieving the 7th Argyll and Sutherland Highlanders (51st Division) in the line at Roeux the following day.

Battalion Headquarters were located in Roeux Wood, and according to custom a certain number of officers and men were left behind and billeted in Arras. The shelling was heavy throughout this tour; Major Anstruther was seriously wounded on June 2nd, and command of the Battalion then devolved on Major R. W. Hadow. The 5th Cameron Highlanders relieved the 8th on the night of 4/5th June, to support an attack to be carried out by the 27th Brigade, and the Battalion then returned to the Railway Embankment in Brigade support, leaving A company in the Sunken Road (Crump Trench) under orders of the Officer Commanding 5th Camerons. The casualties during this tour were one man killed and 19 wounded, in addition to Major Anstruther, who was sent to England.

The 10th Argyll and Sutherland Highlanders relieved the three companies of the Battalion in Brigade support on June 6th, and the 8th then proceeded to Stirling Camp, in the Blue Line, in Brigade reserve, A company rejoining the following day, having been delayed by heavy enemy shelling, from which three men were wounded.

For the next five days the Battalion provided large working parties of about five hundred men to consolidate the new front line on the 27th (Lowland) Brigade front. All ranks set about this task with a fine spirit, working under extreme difficulties. A number of new officers joined the Battalion from the Base during the few days it was in reserve, and on June 12th the 8th proceeded to St. Nicholas, the Battalion having been relieved by one from the 11th Brigade. That evening the Battalion went by bus to rest billets at Moncy Breton, where it remained until the end of the month. Further reinforcements joined, and the time was spent in reorganization and in company and battalion training; special attention was given to musketry, as it was now realized that although the bayonet and bomb are useful weapons, it is the rifle and Lewis gun on which the infantry soldier has chiefly to rely.

CHAPTER VII

JULY, 1917, TO MARCH, 1918

Havrincourt—Battle of Passchendaele

ON June 30th the Battalion marched to Dainville Wood, where training, including night operations, was continued in the Wailly area. Here the 26th Brigade Games were held with great success on July 11th, and it was not until the 24th that orders were received to move the following day into the IV Corps area.

For this move the transport was divided, part moving by road and the remainder by train. The former, under Lieutenant B. Webster, reached its destination, Ruyaulcourt, in IV Corps area, two days later. The Battalion marched from Dainville at 4.30 a.m. on the 25th and entrained at Beaumetz Station at 6.30 a.m. for Bapaume, whence it marched to camp at Ruyaulcourt, moving into the line in relief of the 2/10th London Regiment (58th London Division) the same night. The transport lines then moved to Ypres.

The sector now held by the Division extended on the left as far as the Canal Du Nord, which at this point was much damaged by shell fire. The outpost and front line trenches were in bad repair and very wet, and the first few days were spent in draining, deepening and improving them. The work was somewhat impeded by bad weather, but the enemy remained quiet so long as they were left undisturbed, which suited the Division and allowed it to make the trenches habitable and secure.

The main German line ran along the hill in front of Havrincourt village, giving a commanding view of the trenches held by the Division on the edge of the wood. Patrolling by the Germans was active, and it was some time before the Division obtained full command of No Man's Land. Considerable improvements, however, had been made before the Battalion was relieved by the 7th Seaforths, on the night of the 3rd of August. Two officers and two men were wounded during the tour. After relief the Battalion moved into Brigade reserve at the west of Havrincourt Wood, where it remained until August 7th, when it again returned to the right sector and took over the line from the Seaforths, who had continued the improvements made on the trenches; this work went on steadily during the second tour until the night of August 13th, when the Battalion moved into Divisional reserve in Ruyaulcourt.

There were few losses during this period, but the weather and conditions of the trenches made long tours in the front line system impossible, and the 8th again took over the same sector on the night of August 19th, remaining in until the 24th, when

MOVE TO YPRES, SEPTEMBER, 1917

it returned to Brigade reserve west of Havrincourt Wood. The Havrincourt sector had been one of the quietest the 8th had so far occupied, and although the trenches were bad when taken over a month before, they were now in a satisfactory state, but the weather throughout the past month had necessitated continuous draining by means of trench pumps. On the 30th the 9th Royal Irish Fusiliers, 36th Division, relieved the Battalion in Brigade reserve. The 8th then moved by Bertincourt to Velu, where it entrained for Achiet-le-Grand, reaching Bradford Camp near Gomiécourt that night.

From the 1st to the 12th September the Battalion remained in this camp. The training included battle assault practice, trench to trench assault, attack in the open, and field firing. It soon became evident that another attack would take place shortly, and, on September 8th, an advance party was ordered to proceed to the Ypres area. On the 13th the Battalion moved by train from Bapaume and the following day marched to Hill Camp in the Watou area, the Division now becoming part of the V Corps under Lieutenant-General Sir E. A. Fanshaw. The next day it marched to B Camp in the Brandhoek area, and two days later to Toronto Camp, relieving the 5th Battalion Manchester Regiment (27th Brigade) in Divisional reserve, the 27th Brigade and the South Africans taking over the front line.

After dusk on September 19th the 8th moved by lorries and train to bivouacs in the Ypres south area. Shortly before midnight a move was made by road to the forward areas of assembly and thence by " F " track. Battalion Headquarters was in a German pill box in Wilde Wood, the move being completed without loss by 2.30 a.m. on the 20th.

At 5.40 that morning an attack was launched on the Divisional front by the 27th Brigade and South Africans, the objective being Hanebeek Wood and Zonnebeke Redoubt. The attack was successful and all objectives were taken. The 8th, being in reserve, remained in assembly positions until the 22nd, when it returned to Toronto Camp, platoons moving at quarter hour intervals. The following day the Battalion moved to Highgate Camp in the Winnezeele area, where it remained until the 26th, when it returned to Toronto Camp, and the same evening moved forward again to the old German front line in Corps reserve to assist, if necessary, operations to be carried out by the 3rd Division. Here it remained for three days, and though not in the battle, suffered from heavy shelling. Six men were killed by a direct hit on a pill box, and several others were sent to hospital suffering from the effects of gas, among them Captain J. M. Scott, commanding C company.

THE EIGHTH BATTALION THE BLACK WATCH

Early on the 30th the Battalion moved by train to Esquelbecq, and thence by road to billets in Eringhem, Nieuwland-Holland, where training was carried out for over a week, when several Brigade night operations were practised. These proved most useful to the 8th in the next action. Captain W. French, who had been Adjutant of the 10th Argyll and Sutherland Highlanders, now joined the Battalion as Second-in-Command.

The Battalion entrained at Esquelbecq for Brielen on October 8th, and on arrival marched to Siege Camp, where preparations were made to take over the line. This camp, like most of those in the forward areas near Ypres, was not pleasant; persistent bombing was carried out by the enemy, and each tent was surrounded by a wall of earth a foot thick and about three feet high. At 8.45 a.m. on the 10th the 8th left Siege Camp and proceeded by road to Reigersburg Camp where it remained until dusk, parties being sent forward that evening to reconnoitre the forward positions of assembly and to tape out assembly positions for the following night. At 7.15 the same evening the Battalion proceeded by platoons at fifty yards interval to the following forward positions: A and B companies to Canopus Trench, C and D to California Drive, and Battalion Headquarters to Cheddar Villa.

The 8th remained throughout the day in Canopus Trench and California Drive, and each company left by different routes at 7 p.m. to take up positions for attack the following morning. From 2 to 4 a.m. the Battalion was subjected to a heavy gas shell bombardment which necessitated the wearing of box respirators. A and B companies, on reaching the arranged place, on the right of the Assembly positions of the 7th Seaforths, were not met by guides, and found no tapes or platoon discs laid out for their assembly. However, with the help of the tapes marking the front of the right companies of the Seaforths, the assembly of A and B companies was completed about 4 a.m. It was afterwards found that the taping party had suffered severe losses from shell fire, and had been unable to complete its work.

Shelling continued throughout the assembly, but fortunately the shells fell some hundred yards in rear. Touch was established with the 3rd New Zealand Rifle Brigade on the right, but could not be gained with C and D companies on the left; C and D, however, had gained touch on their left flank with the 5th Cameron Highlanders, and the 10th Argyll and Sutherland Highlanders, and also with the companies of the Seaforths who were holding the line during the assembly.

At Zero all four companies moved forward to their respective lines and advanced close in rear of the barrage as it began to creep forward. A gap was formed between the right and left

PASSCHENDAELE, OCTOBER 12TH, 1917

companies owing to their having failed to get in touch with each other on assembly. This gap was immediately filled by the left support company of the 7th Seaforth Highlanders. At the start, A company, under Captain Ian W. W. Shepherd, met with serious opposition from enemy rifle fire, which checked its advance. This fire increased near Adler Farm, but was overcome by Lewis gun and rifle fire, and a few prisoners were taken. The enemy fought chiefly in the open, lined up behind the remains of a hedge, and did not occupy the ruins of the farm or any strong points. The shelling was heavy, and the company as it advanced came under heavy machine gun fire from both flanks at close range. Good progress was made, however, and the company reached its objective. A halt was then made and a line of shell holes consolidated so far as the state of the ground would permit.

During the advance several enemy machine guns were put out of action, but the company suffered heavily from shell and machine gun fire during and after consolidation. B company, under command of Lieutenant P. J. Alexander, passed through A, and pushed on towards the final objective. They were, however, unable to reach this, being held up by fire from a pill box which, after severe fighting, was captured, Lieutenant P. J. Alexander being killed.

On the right, the New Zealand troops and Royal Scots (9th Division) were held up by a belt of wire about thirty yards in front of them, and an endeavour was made by B company—now commanded by Second Lieutenant A. L. Milroy—to dig in, but it was found that the position was subjected to machine gun fire from both flanks, and from snipers behind the wire, from which the company lost heavily. About half an hour later the New Zealanders and Royal Scots were ordered to retire, and when they had done so Lieutenant Milroy had no alternative but to withdraw and conform to the troops on his flank. This he did, and took up a position between the cemetery and the road, where a line was organized in conjunction with some Seaforths under Captain Reid, some 12th Royal Scots under their signalling officer and about 25 men of A and B companies who had been collected by Second Lieutenant H. F. C. Govan of A company. About 3 p.m. a small, and apparently unorganized, counter-attack by the Germans was driven off without difficulty. Later in the afternoon the new front line was heavily shelled, and German machine guns and snipers were very active.

On the Battalion left the attack had not gone so well. C company leading, advanced at Zero, keeping close up to the barrage, and, unfortunately, suffered a number of casualties. After advancing about a hundred yards the company turned quarter right, in order to avoid the danger of a gap occurring between companies.

No serious opposition was encountered during the early part of the attack, but the company was held up on reaching the enemy support line by snipers and machine gun fire, and among those killed was Lieutenant H. B. Dickson, the company commander. A further advance of a hundred yards was accomplished by section rushes under cover of rifle and Lewis gun fire, and C company then consolidated, as far as practicable, on a line of shell holes level with what remained of A and B companies, it being realized that further advance was impossible.

D company, who advanced in rear of C, moved off " half left " at the commencement of the attack. This loss of direction was caused by the company having assembled facing that way owing to the lack of guiding tapes, and also because touch had not been established with B on the right before Zero. Shortly after the attack opened D company came under severe enfilade machine gun and rifle fire from the direction of Oxford Houses. The company advanced on the left of C, and had been drawn into the fight before it was intended. Lieutenant A. S. Harper, who was in command, went forward with one section and Company Headquarters with the object of capturing a pill box, from which the company was being enfiladed. Of this party all became casualties except the company sergeant-major. Unfortunately Lieutenant Harper was killed in his gallant attempt. The enemy, who offered a most determined resistance here, were about a hundred strong, the assumption being that they had sheltered in the pill box during the barrage. The survivors of D company, under Lieutenant J. Robson and Second Lieutenant Yule, were now held up in front of a small copse by machine gun and rifle fire, thereby losing the barrage.

On the capture of Oxford Houses by the Battalion on the left, D company consolidated on a line in touch with that battalion, with their left flank on Oxford Houses, and also in touch with C company on the right. The situation remained the same until nightfall, when the 8th was relieved by the South Africans, and, sadly depleted in numbers, returned to Siege Camp. Casualties amongst runners had been exceptionally heavy, whereby it was found impossible to get messages to and from Battalion Headquarters. Great difficulty had been experienced throughout, and it was impossible to recognize objectives, nearly all landmarks having been obliterated by shell fire. The ground over which the attack took place was literally a sea of mud, and in consequence movement was extremely difficult, most of the shell holes being more than half full of water.

Mention must be made of the Medical Officer and his

TRENCH WARFARE, NIEUPORT, NOVEMBER, 1917

personnel, who worked under extreme difficulties and with great gallantry. Captain G. R. B. Grant, R.A.M.C., personally attended to the wounded in the open under heavy fire; the supply of stretcher bearers was unequal to the demand, and the " carry " for them was far too great in view of the state of the ground. Throughout the attack the shelling was constant, heavy and well placed, and the enemy put up a most determined resistance. On relief being completed on the 14th, a few days were spent at Siege Camp resting and reorganizing, after which, on the 22nd, a move was made to School Camp, and another the following day to billets in the Wormhoudt area, where a draft of 189 men joined the Battalion.

Next day the Battalion moved to billets for one night in the Teteghem area, south-east of Dunkerque. The final destination was reached on the evening of the 25th, when it was billeted in the Casino at Malo-les-Bains in the Coast Defence sector. Three days later orders were received to relieve the 10th Royal West Surrey Regiment, 124th Brigade, in the right sub-sector of the Nieuport-Bains sector, and this relief took place on the night of October 28th.

Starting at 11.45 a.m. on the 28th, the 8th moved by bus to Coxyde Bains, where it bivouacked on the sand dunes till 9 p.m., and then proceeded into the line by platoons at four hundred yards interval. Guides met each platoon at Oostdunkerke, and the relief was completed without loss by 1.30 a.m. D company took over the right sector, with C on the left and A and B in support. The front line was well revetted, and fortunately the trenches were dry owing to the sandy ground.

After the fighting round Ypres this sector was looked upon as a haven of rest. As the support line was overcrowded, A company was withdrawn to Yorkshire Camp. The Battalion was relieved by the 7th Seaforths on the evening of November 3rd, and moved to Yorkshire Camp, where it remained for six days, furnishing working parties for the removal of Lieven gas projectors from the front line, and carrying ammunition for the artillery. On the 7th a reconnoitring party proceeded to take over from the 1st South African Battalion in the right sector of the Coast Defences, the 8th relieving the South Africans two days later with three companies—A being detached for duty under the 289th Company Royal Engineers at Zeepanne.

During the period in the Coast sector there was desultory enemy shelling with both high explosive and gas shells, but on the whole the sector was quiet. On November 16th the Officer Commanding a French battalion arrived, and details of a relief were arranged for the following day by the 1st Battalion 3rd (French) Infantry Regiment.

THE EIGHTH BATTALION THE BLACK WATCH

When this relief had been completed, the 8th marched to Uxem in the Teteghem area, the following day to Esquelbecq in the Wormhoudt area, and on the 19th to Rietveld. These long marches told on some of the men who had recently joined, and the medical officer had to treat a large number of men for sore feet before the Battalion reached Herly on the 22nd. From November 23rd to the 30th the Battalion remained in billets in the villages of Herly, Avesnes and Bellevue-Fruges. Inspections of equipment and the usual company and platoon training were carried out daily, and on the 28th the Brigade Commander inspected the recently arrived drafts.

On December 1st the 8th was again on the line of march, billeting the first night at Blangy, and two days later at Peronne, having moved there by train from Wavrans overnight. On the 4th the Battalion marched to Heudecourt and relieved the 2nd Coldstream Guards in support at Gouzeaucourt on the 5th. After three days in the support line the Battalion relieved the 7th Seaforths in the right sub-sector in front of Gouzeaucourt on the night of December 8th, and remained there until again relieved by the Seaforths four days later. The enemy made more than one determined attempt to improve his position, but the weather did not permit of more serious fighting, as the ground was frost-bound and heavy falls of snow were frequent.

During December the Battalion occupied the front, support and reserve lines successively. Christmas Day was spent in the front line. The 8th was relieved the following day and returned to the front line on the 30th. A few days later the Battalion occupied huts on the Fins road. Here several drafts of non-commissioned officers and men joined the Battalion, mostly men of category B who had been reclassified and passed as fit for service in the field. Some training was carried out, but the chief work consisted in protecting the huts from aerial attack by building walls of sandbags round them.

At this time rumours of an impending German attack were frequent, and intelligence reports showed signs of great preparations behind their lines. On January 22nd the Battalion was relieved by the 7th Seaforths, and moved the following evening to huts at Sorel-le-Grand, and thence by Decauville railway to another camp in the Bois de l'Epinette. A company was left at Nurlu, but the remainder moved to billets at Chipilly on the 29th, where A company rejoined. Here the first two weeks of February were spent in training, and on the 13th the Battalion was inspected by the General Officer Commanding at Bray-sur-Somme.

On the 16th the 8th moved to Hem to work for ten days

TRENCH WARFARE, DECEMBER, 1917, TO MARCH, 1918

on light railways under the Royal Engineers, and on the 28th it moved to York Camp at Moislains. During the latter part of February the weather was stormy and extremely cold, and the Battalion did not enjoy the comfort of a standing camp for long, as, on March 4th, it moved to bivouacs at Sorel-le-Grand. While at Sorel large working parties were furnished for work in the forward zone of the 39th Divisional area. On March 11th the Battalion moved forward to the Yellow System trenches at Gouzeaucourt in relief of the 6th Cheshire Regiment, Headquarters being situated at Dead Man's Corner, the details moving forward from Moislains to Sorel-le-Grand.

Work on the Yellow System and on strong points nearby was continued for, although the situation was quiet, an enemy offensive was expected any day, and work was pushed forward with all possible speed, wiring and strengthening trenches and posts being continued by all units in the area. During the next week the enemy shelling gradually increased, his aeroplanes became more active, and gas shelling of the rear areas became general.

CHAPTER VIII

MARCH TO MAY, 1918

The German Offensive

ON the night of March 19/20 the Battalion relieved the 5th Camerons in the left sector of the Brigade front. Patrols were sent out from various points, but nothing of an unusual nature was reported. The enemy was known to be in strength, and an attack was expected the following morning but, while battle positions were maintained, work was continued on the front line positions. The following morning the attack was again expected, but it was not until about 4.30 on the morning of March 21st that the enemy launched his long looked-for effort.

When the German bombardment opened the 8th was disposed as follows:—

Right front company:
  B company, plus 1 platoon D company (Capt. Inglis).
Left front company:
  A company, plus 1 platoon C company (Lieut. McLaren).
Gouzeaucourt Defences:
  D company, less 1 platoon (Capt. Austin).
Red Line Defences:
  C company, less 1 platoon, and Pioneer platoon (Capt. Duncan Wallace).
Battalion Headquarters:
  In sunken road forward from Dead Man's Corner.

The heavy gas shell bombardment which fell on the front system, the valleys behind Gouzeaucourt and on the Yellow System was not unexpected, and box respirators afforded the troops complete protection, even after they had been worn for nearly five hours. There was a thick ground mist, which hung about the valleys most of the day.

Before the attack the posts in the front line had been withdrawn—except S.O.S. posts—to the support line in front of the railway, but as far as possible observation was kept on any attempted move on the part of the enemy by posts pushed out from the support line, and by patrols as far as the front line. Thanks to the efforts of Second Lieutenant A. W. Miller and his signallers communication was maintained throughout the day, in spite of the heavy shelling.

No general attack was made by the enemy on the Battalion sector that day, and all arrangements had been made for the

THE GERMAN OFFENSIVE, MARCH 21ST, 1918

front line posts to be manned as usual at dusk, when orders were received that the 8th would withdraw from the forward zone, including Gouzeaucourt village and the Red Line to the Brown Line in front of Desart Wood, the withdrawal to be completed by 5 a.m. on the 22nd. Orders to this effect were issued to companies immediately, and the operation was carried out without incident, the companies being distributed in the following order:—

1. Right and left front line companies under cover of battle posts. 2. One company in Gouzeaucourt Defences. 3. Pioneer platoon with Battalion Headquarters. 4. One company in the Red Line. On completion of the withdrawal, A, D, and C companies, from right to left, took up positions in the sector allotted to the Battalion in the Brown Line from just north of Desart Farm to the junction with a company of the 7th Battalion; C company occupying a line of posts in Gouzeaucourt Wood astride Queen's Cross–Metz road.

As the advance of the enemy by Revelon Farm and Chapel Hill had turned the Yellow and Brown Line systems on the right, orders were received shortly after noon on March 22nd to withdraw to the Green Line system. This was repeated to companies, and the withdrawal by small parties was completed by dusk, when the Battalion occupied the Green Line system in front of Equancourt from the railway line southwards for about 1600 yards to the junction with the 12th Royal Scots. On the right the 26th Brigade details under Major A. Hunter, 5th Camerons, prolonged the line northwards from the railway to a point about fifty yards north of the Equancourt–Fins road, where touch was eventually established with troops on the left. The dispositions of companies in the Green Line from right to left were as follows: D, B, A, C companies each with one platoon in the observation line, and two platoons and Company Headquarters in the support line; Battalion Headquarters and the pioneer platoon occupied Equancourt village.

The enemy followed hard on the withdrawal of the Camerons and Seaforths from the Yellow Line system and arrived in increasing numbers in front of the Green Line from 9 p.m. onwards. Throughout the night of March 22nd, enemy machine gun fire was constant and his patrols active. One party was dispersed by a patrol from the 26th Brigade details near the Equancourt-Fins road, and the body of a German soldier was secured for identification. Otherwise the night passed without incident.

The enemy began his attack on the Green Line soon after daylight on March 23rd, supported by fairly heavy artillery and trench mortar fire, combined with intense machine gun fire,

THE EIGHTH BATTALION THE BLACK WATCH

under cover of which his wire cutting parties were particularly bold in their endeavours to cut the wire defences. All attacks were, however, repulsed by Lewis gun and rifle fire on the Battalion front, with heavy loss to the enemy and, as far as could be seen, the line was still intact at 10 a.m. Orders, however, were then received to withdraw and fight a rearguard action to the ridge beyond Etricourt and Manancourt. The 8th were then to take up a defensive position from the Sugar-beet Factory on the left to Hennois Wood on the right.

Just as these orders were issued, it was seen that the line some distance on the right had been forced, and the Germans were pressing their vantage with vigour. In spite of this, the withdrawal was carried out in good order and with considerable skill under cover of the supporting companies of the 5th Camerons and 7th Seaforths, assisted later by the 8th Battalion Pioneer platoon, and some details under Second Lieutenant W. M. McCash, who took up a line about six hundred yards in front of the canal, and pluckily held up the enemy until the rearguard had cleared the canal. After this they withdrew in good order, Second Lieutenant H. F. C. Govan and Company Quartermaster-Sergeant Stewart swimming the canal in full equipment.

During the fighting on the Green Line, and the subsequent withdrawal to the new position behind the canal, Captains Austin, Inglis and Wallace, and Lieutenant McLaren handled their companies with judgment and determination, inflicted considerable losses on the enemy, and thereby materially helped the withdrawal. Lieutenant McLaren, who was reported wounded and missing, was later on found to have been made a prisoner during this fighting.

On reaching the new positions, the line was organized and touch gained on both flanks of the Battalion. During the afternoon there was a slight lull in the fighting, and advantage was taken to push forward posts which were maintained till dusk, and also to replenish ammunition under the supervision of Regimental Sergeant-Major Mitchell, M.C., D.C.M., who was subsequently wounded. After dusk the enemy attacked the right of the 47th Division—on the left of the Battalion—causing the left company to yield some ground, and to expose its left flank. Lieutenants Robertson and Farmer showed quick appreciation of the situation by immediately organizing flank defences, and not only maintained the line, but also inflicted severe losses on the enemy, who attempted no further operations in that quarter during the night.

About 11.30 p.m. orders were received that the Brigade would withdraw, whether relieved or not, by 4 a.m., and take up a line on the eastern edge of St. Pierre Vaast Wood, and north-

THE GERMAN OFFENSIVE, MARCH 24TH, 1918

wards east of Saillisel. Details of this withdrawal and those for a reconnaissance of the new positions were at once arranged with company commanders. The movement was begun about 3 a.m. on the 24th, through Le Mesnil-en-Arrouaise and Saillisel, and was completed by 5 a.m.

On arrival at Saillisel, it was found that the enemy was already in possession of the northern part of the new position, the remainder being held by one company of the 5th Camerons with units of the 27th Brigade and the 9th Seaforths. After consultation among the Battalion Commanders, it was decided to take up a position on the Sailly–Saillisel Ridge north-west of St. Pierre Vaast Wood, covering the Bapaume–Péronne road, the 8th being in the centre of the Brigade front, with the Seaforths on the right and Camerons on the left. On taking up this position, about four hundred yards in front of the main road, strong fighting patrols were immediately pushed forward to secure the ridge in front. This ridge was, however, found to be occupied by the enemy, who drove back one of the Battalion patrols with considerable loss. D company, under Captain Austin, was therefore ordered to withdraw to a support position west of the main road to cover a retirement should this become necessary.

About 8 a.m. it was observed that the troops on the right were withdrawing, closely followed by the enemy in considerable strength, and this sudden and unexpected development rendered a general and immediate retirement by the 8th necessary. This was accordingly arranged, and was carried out by companies from the right, under cover of strong rearguards.

The advance of the enemy on the right was very rapid, and although groups of riflemen and Lewis gun sections, taking up position in odd trenches and sunken roads, inflicted some loss and hampered the enemy's advance, it was not possible to hold a defensive line until the Morval ridge was reached. Here, under cover of artillery, a position was taken on a line running southwards towards Combles, to cover the withdrawal of troops still in front, the line being prolonged to the north-east in front of Morval by detachments of C and D companies. On finding his advance delayed by this line, the enemy again tried to turn the right flank by Combles, at the same time making a holding attack on the left flank of the 8th, but neither attempt was successful.

About 11.30 a.m. instructions were received to continue the withdrawal by Guillemont to Maricourt. The Battalion therefore assembled on a line west of Bouleaux Wood, towards Guillemont, and was divided into a Right or southern force, and a Left or northern force. The Right force withdrew about

2.30 p.m. to a line about three hundred yards east of Guinchy. This line had been already established by a battalion of the Royal Welch Fusiliers, in order to cover the cross roads at Guinchy, so as to assist the withdrawal of a large amount of transport. As there were less than a hundred men with this Right force, it was impossible to prolong the right flank to Guillemont. This line was held for upwards of three hours, until all the transport was cleared, and considerable losses were inflicted on the enemy; after which, between 5 and 6 p.m., the force was withdrawn to a line around the eastern edge of Delville Wood and Waterlot Farm.

Meanwhile the Left force, taking up a line south-east of Morval, maintained its position till about 2 p.m., and considerably delayed the enemy's advance. It then withdrew to the ridge along Cordoroy road and the railway from Morval to Guinchy, where it took up another position in support to some Vickers guns which had been pushed forward to the ridge. About 5 p.m., however, the enemy had turned both flanks of this line and the Left force then withdrew to Flers, where detachments of various units, amounting to about three hundred men, were collected.

About 6 p.m. the Right force, on the edge of Delville Wood, received orders from Brigade to withdraw and reorganize at Maricourt. Accordingly detachments of the 8th assembled in Longueval, and under Lieutenants Barr and Hyslop moved off to Maricourt by Bernafay Wood road. Just as this party started, an enemy high velocity shell burst at the head of the column, killing the two officers, and killing and wounding about 10 other ranks. After attending to the wounded and burying the dead, the party reformed and moved off to Maricourt, where it heard that the Brigade was assembling at Montauban, and thither the detachment moved in the course of the night of March 24th.

Soon after daybreak on the 25th the Brigade took up a position west of Montauban, along the Montauban–Mametz road, supporting the left flank of the dismounted cavalry then holding this sector. Here it remained until 6 p.m., when orders were received to withdraw in small parties by Carnoy and Le Plateau to Bronfay Farm, and thence to Etineham, which was reached between 9 and 10 that night. Shortly after midnight the order was given to "stand to" and be ready to move at 1.30 a.m. The 8th, now organized as a company with four platoons of an average strength of 28 other ranks, accordingly moved with the remainder of the Brigade via Morlancourt and Ville-sur-Ancre to Dernancourt, arriving about 7 a.m. Here the Brigade rested till about noon, when news was received of the enemy's advance through Méaulte, and orders were issued for trench positions east and south of Dernancourt to be manned, covering the

MOVE TO PONT NOYELLES, MARCH 28TH, 1918

bridges and crossings of the Ancre, the line following the river and railway. In the course of the afternoon several attacks on positions north-east of Dernancourt were driven off and the line held. After dusk ammunition was brought up, platoons reorganized, and the night of March 26th passed without incident.

Soon after daylight on the 27th the enemy developed an attack in strength against the 35th Division on the right, and the right flank of the 26th Brigade was forced to withdraw, but the centre and left, held by the 8th, maintained their positions. A support line, formed from stragglers, was now taken up along the ridge behind the village and parallel to the railway, about a thousand yards in rear.

Throughout the day the enemy shelled Dernancourt and all positions round it heavily, but without causing much loss, and at noon the appearance of supporting troops enheartened all ranks after the four days of severe fighting and almost constant movement by night. The Battalion was relieved about 8 p.m. by part of the 47th Battalion Australian Infantry; it then withdrew to Hennecourt Wood and rested there till morning. At 10 a.m. on the 28th it moved to Pont Noyelles, where the details of the Left force rejoined. The following day the 8th moved to Cardonnette, where for the first time since the attack commenced a hot meal was provided; late in the afternoon the Battalion moved to billets in Flesselles, spending one day there and moving on the 31st to Montrelet.

The casualties during the week had been heavy: one officer killed, seven wounded and four missing; 30 men killed, 136 wounded and 271 missing—a total of 12 officers and 437 other ranks. Fortunately many of the missing, including Lieutenants H. F. C. Govan and T. D. S. McLaren, were eventually found to be prisoners of war.

Leaving Montrelet on April 1st, the 8th entrained at Candas that evening and arrived at Butterfly Farm the following morning. General Sir Herbert Plumer, Commanding the Second Army, inspected a detachment of the 9th Division near La Clytte, before they moved by train from Kilmarnock Siding to Spoil Bank to relieve the 12th New Zealand Regiment in support. On April 6th, the Battalion relieved the 5th Camerons in the left sector of the front line.

The line was quiet, but conditions were bad, and much work was carried out on the defences before the 12th Royal Scots relieved the Battalion on the night of April 9th, after which it moved by light railway to Parret Camp, where it was joined by the details. By this time drafts had arrived and the 8th was fairly strong, but many of the new-comers were boys who had seen no active service. Reorganization took place at once, as enemy operations were reported to have taken place in the Lys and Kemmel sectors.

On the morning of the 10th, the enemy attacked the right flank of the 19th Division, and by three o'clock in the afternoon Wytschaete was reported to be in the enemy's hands. As a result of this, orders were issued for the Battalion to move forward and reconnoitre the area in front of Grand Bois, between Hollebeke and Wytschaete, to clear up the situation on the right flank of the 27th Brigade at Spoil Bank and the White Château, the 26th Brigade ordering the right flank of the 27th to be secured at all costs.

The Battalion eventually took over a line from Goudezuune Farm to the corner of Ravine Wood. Although the situation was somewhat obscure, a line Oustaverne Wood–Goudezuune was organized and by 4 p.m. Wytschaete and Messines were reported to have been regained. Early in the evening A company was detailed to proceed to the cutting south of Wytschaete, in support to the troops of the 58th Brigade who were defending Wytschaete itself. Fighting continued during the night, and early the following morning patrols were pushed forward under a barrage to try and establish forward posts throughout the Corps system.

On April 12th the 8th took over the front line from Dome House to Somer Farm, and the following night was relieved by the 1st East Yorks Regiment and 15th Durham Light Infantry, to enable it to take up a line in support of the 5th Camerons in the lines Oaten Wood–Triangular Farm–Louwaege Farm. Here D company occupied a strong point at Piccadilly Farm, C was in positions in St. Eloi, A in support in Oaten Wood and B on the northern edge of Triangular Wood. Heavy artillery fire continued throughout the day, Triangular Wood and Piccadilly Farm being shelled with 5·9 and 8 inch shells. During the night of the 13th, B and D companies withdrew to huts in rear of Battalion Headquarters; A and C remaining in support to the 5th Camerons, A on the right and C on the left.

Heavy artillery fire continued for the next few days, Oaten Wood being severely shelled at intervals. Three enemy balloons were up over the lines most of the time, and enemy machine gun fire was active. On the 15th, as there were indications of further activity on the part of the enemy, B and D companies were again moved forward to the support trenches. Intermittent shelling continued throughout the next day, and about 8 a.m. on April 17th, the enemy put down a slight barrage on the line held by the Battalion. Two Lewis guns were pushed forward north-east from Dome House in order to deny the sunken road

GERMAN ATTACK ON KEMMEL HILL

of the Daamstrasse to the enemy should he attempt to advance by that way. At this time the Germans held the wood behind the Daamstrasse and Pheasant Wood, and were reported to be in force further back.

During the next few days heavy shelling continued in the forward area, and the 8th was held in readiness for immediate action. On April 20th the following redistribution of companies took place:—

5 platoons in front line posts of organized shell holes.
7 platoons in the main line St. Eloi–Dome House.
1 company in Stong Points, St. Eloi–Piccadilly Farm.

The next night the Battalion was relieved by the 7th Seaforths, and took up the following positions for the night: A and C companies in the Corps line, round Vierstraat; B and D with Battalion Headquarters at Hallebast Corner. On April 22nd the 8th relieved the 6th West Yorkshire Regiment and South African Brigade in the front sector of the Vierstraat line, A and B companies taking over the sector held by the South Africans, the relief being completed by 2 a.m. The following day the enemy attacked the French on the right and reached their support line, but a quickly organized counter-attack restored the situation. Apart from heavy shelling, particularly in the rear areas, the situation remained normal for the remainder of the tour.

On the night of the 24th the 9th Scottish Rifles relieved the Battalion in the Vierstraat system, the relief not being completed until about 4 a.m., when the 8th came under the orders of the 28th Brigade. The Battalion had scarcely settled down in bivouacs when the enemy launched an attack on the Kemmel Hill sector held by the French, and broke their line north of the hill. Orders were at once issued to the 8th to try and reach the Cheapside line and hold it at all costs. This was achieved, and the Battalion gained a position in advance of the Cheapside system near the Vierstraat line, and held it throughout the day, at a cost of about forty casualties, B company taking 61 prisoners. That night the 8th was relieved by a West Riding battalion, and withdrew to support in the Cheapside line. Here it remained until relieved by the 9th Scottish Rifles on the evening of the 26th, when it proceeded to Camps 19 and 20 in the Brandhoek area, moving the following day to a camp between Abeele and Poperinghe, and on the afternoon of the 28th to camp in the Watou area. Here a few days were spent reorganizing and cleaning, and a large number of reinforcements joined the Battalion, which had been considerably reduced in strength during the recent operations.

CHAPTER IX

MAY TO SEPTEMBER, 1918

Hondeghem Area—Attack at Meteren

ON the 3rd of May the Battalion marched to Eringhem, where a further draft joined on the 4th. It remained here until the 6th, and then marched the next day by road to La Pierre Camp, near Racquinghem. Here the 8th remained until May 23rd, each company in turn spending a few days at the Second Army Musketry School at Lambres. All ranks thoroughly enjoyed the change after their strenuous days in the Kemmel sector.

On May 18th the Battalion was inspected by the Army Commander, who presented medal ribbons to several non-commissioned officers and men, and three days later a party under Major Ian W. W. Shepherd moved forward to reconnoitre the position held by the 92nd Infantry Brigade in the Meteren sector. All details were arranged, and on the 23rd the 8th moved by bus from Racquinghem to Caestre and thence by road to reserve huts in relief of the 11th East Yorks Regiment, the relief being completed by 2 a.m. on the 24th. At 9.30 that evening the Battalion relieved the 13th York and Lancaster Regiment in the left sector of front line taken over by the 26th Brigade, the 7th Seaforths being on the right and the 160th (French) Regiment on the left.

Throughout the tour the enemy shelled the line intermittently, causing some loss. There were no dug-outs and few shelters in this sector; the Battalion Headquarters were in the cellar of a house, and the Medical Aid Post in a room with little protection. On May 28th the details were moved into the Thieushouk Defences, and on the night of May 30th the Battalion was relieved by the 11th Royal Scots, 27th Brigade, and moved back to camp in XV Corps reserve in the Hondeghem area, where it supplied working parties for the Corps signal company.

Late on the evening of June 5th, the Battalion left Hondeghem area and moved to the right sector of the Divisional front, where it relieved the 9th Scottish Rifles in support. Here the Battalion remained until June 11th, supplying working parties for the Royal Engineers, and on the night of the 11th, it was relieved by the 2nd Battalion Royal Scots Fusiliers, and took over the left front sector from the 6th King's Own Scottish Borderers of the 27th Brigade, companies being disposed as follows: Right front, D; Left front, A; Support, C; and Reserve, B.

Few casualties were sustained until the night of June 14th,

TRENCH WARFARE, MAY TO JULY, 1918

when the Battalion carried out a raid with the object of securing identifications. The raiding party consisted of Second Lieutenant R. Potter in command, Second Lieutenant M. S. Stuart and 60 men with two Lewis guns. The raiders, divided into two parties of one officer and 30 men each, moved forward in line of sections at 1.5 a.m. under a good artillery barrage. On arriving within ten yards of a hedge in front of the German lines they were met by heavy rifle fire, to which they immediately replied, and continued the advance. The wire had been cut in places, and parties were able to push through. Along the hedge the enemy had dug a line of narrow holes, each capable of holding one or two men, and each having overhead cover. Once through the hedge no serious opposition was encountered, and one or two farms in the vicinity were immediately surrounded and searched. No enemy, however, were found and no identifications were obtained. Rain began to fall an hour before Zero and continued until the raid was over. The night was so dark that it was impossible to discover any of the enemy dead; and patrols which were sent out the next night found none. During the raid enemy shelling was comparatively light, one officer and one man were killed, four men wounded, and three missing. After this raid the Battalion continued to hold the line until relieved by the 6th King's Own Scottish Borderers, 27th Brigade, on the night of the 17th, when it moved back to reserve billets in Hondeghem area, where a few days were spent and where parties were supplied for work under XV Corps signals. During the last tour influenza was very prevalent, and nine officers and 74 other ranks were sent to hospital.

One or two small drafts joined at Hondeghem. On the 23rd a party proceeded to the line to reconnoitre the front of the left battalion, right sector, Meteren front, and the 8th took this sector over on the night of the 24th from the 2nd Battalion Royal Scots Fusiliers. This sector was comparatively quiet, and the Battalion was relieved by the 7th Seaforths on the evening of the 26th, when it took over the support trenches, and supplied working parties at night to improve the new reserve trenches. On this front the field of fire was bad owing to crops growing in No Man's Land; but these were gradually cut down at night for a considerable distance from the front. On the 2nd of July personnel of the 78th (American) Division were attached to the Battalion for instruction. During these few days the sector was comparatively quiet, with the exception of a heavy bombardment of Meteren village with 8" shells. Patrolling was actively carried out, and much work was done to improve the trenches.

On the night of July 6th the 8th was relieved in the front

line by the 12th Royal Scots, and moved back once more to the Hondeghem area, where it remained for five days. During this period several attacks on the aerodrome were practised and the Battalion was reorganized. The 8th left Hondeghem during the evening of the 12th, to relieve the 12th Royal Scots in the front line of the left sector. During this move the enemy dropped many bombs from aeroplanes. This tour was uneventful, but heavy rain flooded the trenches, which entailed much work in draining them. On the 16th the sector was taken over by the 7th Seaforths, and the Battalion moved back to bivouacs in reserve trenches at Thieushouk.

An attack to secure Meteren was ordered for July 19th. Accordingly, on the afternoon of the 18th, the 8th, commanded at this time by Major W. French, moved from Thieushouk to battle positions in the left battalion sector, where it was established by 3 a.m. the following day.

Zero was fixed for 7.55 a.m. At 7.45 a.m. the artillery barrage opened and was effective and regular; the attacking companies came into position and followed close to it, with the support company in rear. At 9.10 a.m. a message was received that the left company and one platoon of the supporting company were held up near the hedges in front of the enemy's line, and were unable to move further forward owing to heavy machine gun fire from posts behind the hedge, and from emplacements in the fields further back. At 11.30 a.m. a message was received from Second Lieutenant McDonald of the right attacking company stating that he had reached his platoon objective on the left of the Camerons, also that he was holding a line in touch with that battalion on the right, and had established a post on the south side of the Meteren–Bailleul road, but was unable to gain touch with the remainder of his company on the left. A reconnaissance was therefore made by an officer from Battalion Headquarters between 10 a.m. and 12 noon, who found that the 8th, with the exception of McDonald's force, had been held up by the hedges referred to, the wire in front of the hedges being almost intact. Attacking and supporting companies had suffered severe losses in attempting to force this line, and it was eventually found necessary to withdraw the remnants of these companies to the jumping-off posts.

By this time, movement above ground had become almost impossible owing to enemy machine gun and rifle fire from the posts in the hedges; enemy snipers were also active, and it was not until late in the afternoon that it was definitely ascertained that no effective portion of the right company had reached any position between the jumping-off posts and the line reached by the right platoon, thus a gap of about five hundred yards was

ATTACK ON METEREN, JULY 19TH, 1918

left in the line. This was filled between 5 and 6 p.m. by a platoon of the reserve company establishing a post on the left of the Meteren–Foe cross roads, and by two platoons of the 7th Seaforths establishing a post between the cross roads and the Meteren–Bailleul road. That night the enemy kept up constant rifle and machine gun fire, and continued to hold the line of hedges in front of the Battalion.

During the night of July 20th the front line was readjusted, the 7th Seaforths taking over the Battalion line south of the Meteren-Foe cross roads, while D company took over the posts in front, and A, B and C companies were withdrawn to the old front line, each company being reorganized as a strong platoon. Heavy enemy shelling took place that night, but when patrols were pushed forward about 9 a.m. on the 21st, it was discovered that the enemy had withdrawn from the hedges, and forward posts were at once established by the Battalion.

The non-success of this attack was mainly due to the Stokes mortar barrage having failed to destroy the wire in front of the line of hedges. The artillery barrage had been good and was thickened with smoke shells to prevent enemy observation; the smoke, however, was rather thin by the time the attack was within thirty yards of the hedges. The advance was also delayed owing to entanglements placed among the growing crops, some by the enemy and some by our own troops. Patrols had reported gaps in the wire and in the hedges, but these were later found to be very small and of little use to the attackers.

The losses during this attack were heavy: Killed, 87; wounded, 111; missing, 28. Total, 226.

The following were the officer casualties:—

Killed in action

Lieut. (A/Capt.) H. D. McMillan.
„ J. L. Young.
2nd Lieut. J. Burt.
„ R. L. Brown.

2nd Lieut. P. Peebles.
„ J. A. Tillie.
„ J. W. Musgrove.
„ T. D. Don.

Wounded

Lieut. (A/Capt.) H. L. Bryson.
„ G. H. Watt.

2nd Lieut. G. G. Herd.
„ A. J. McKenzie.
„ A. Brownlie.

The Battalion was relieved on July 24th, and moved to camp in the Hondeghem area, where it remained until the end of the month, the few days being spent in reorganizing and refitting; an inspection of the Brigade by the Divisional Commander also took place. On the last day of the month a move was made to

THE EIGHTH BATTALION THE BLACK WATCH

Thieushouk in relief of the 9th Scottish Rifles, and on August 1st the 8th took over the support positions, disposed as follows:—

B company, two platoons in Fontainhouck south and two platoons in the Reserve lines; D company in the switch line astride the Fontainhouck–Meteren road; A and C companies in Roukloshille switch line.

The Battalion remained in these positions until the night of the 3rd, and supplied working parties for the Royal Engineers; on that night it relieved the 7th Seaforths in the left front sector, A and D companies taking over the front line trenches with C in support, and B in reserve. Heavy shelling took place during the relief, and enemy aircraft dropped several bombs on the back areas and approaches. The bombardment was not unexpected, as an enemy wireless message had been picked up during the day to the effect that their artillery would shoot on this area; 25 casualties were caused by this bombardment. During the tour much drainage work was carried out, as the trenches were very wet.

On the 8th, news was received of enemy withdrawals at various points, but fighting patrols sent out to verify this reported the enemy were still holding the posts in considerable strength. During the night of the 8th a bombardment by gas projectors was carried out by the Division on the left. This was directed towards Mural Farm, and although the enemy alarm whistles were heard, the result of the bombardment was not known. The following night the 8th was relieved in the front line by the South African Composite Battalion, and on completion of the relief about midnight it moved to camp, where some days were spent in cleaning up, inspections of kit, bathing and training.

On August 16th the Brigade Commander inspected the Battalion, and the following day it moved to reserve positions, with Headquarters in Flêtre Château, in reserve to the 27th Brigade. This Brigade attacked on the 18th, and all objectives were taken. That night the 8th relieved the South African Battalion in the left front sub-sector, the relief being carried out without casualties. By this time the enemy artillery was much less active; his guns were apparently very far back, indicating a possible withdrawal.

The 36th Division carried out a minor operation on the night of August 21st and captured Mural Farm. At 1.30 a.m. under a separate barrage a platoon of D company, 8th Black Watch, advanced from the outpost line without encountering any of the enemy—a further indication of a withdrawal on this front. During the night of the 22nd the 7th Seaforths relieved the Battalion, which moved back to support positions in

MOVE TO RACQUINGHEM, AUGUST, 1918

Roukloshille switch, and was relieved the following night by the 12th Battalion Norfolk Regiment (94th Infantry Brigade). When this relief was completed, the 8th moved to Hondeghem Camp, and entrained the next day for the Racquinghem area, detraining at Renescure and marching to billets in Orchard Camp. Here several days were spent in training and reorganization.

CHAPTER X

SEPTEMBER TO NOVEMBER, 1918

The Advance to Victory

THE period in the Racquinghem area came to an end on the 11th of September, when the Battalion marched to Wormhoudt "C" area, billeting for the night in farmhouses in and around Buysscheure, and marching the following day to Wormhoudt, where a halt was made for one day. On the 14th it entrained, and moved by light railway from Ledringhem to Orillia Camp, in reserve to the 14th Division, and held the left sector of the II Corps front until the 18th. That night the Battalion relieved the 13th York and Lancaster Regiment (41st Infantry Brigade), C company on the right and A on the left, taking over the front line with Company Headquarters in Potijze Château and Dragon Farm respectively; B company in support and D in reserve. The relief was completed without incident, but Salvation Corner and Dead End were slightly shelled during the day.

About 5 a.m. on September 20th a man of an enemy patrol, a Bavarian, came into the right company's line and gave himself up. The forward areas in this sector were quiet, but the troops in rear were at times heavily shelled. Enemy working parties could be seen on the Frezenberg Ridge, near the well-known pill boxes, Kit and Kat. On the evening of the 21st the 7th Seaforths took over the front line, and the 8th moved to billets in Siege Camp, where it remained until the 26th, carrying out practices in assembling for attack and making all necessary preparations for the coming operations, which were to prove the beginning of the final stages of the war.

On the night of September 27th the Battalion moved into the left sector of the Brigade front, ready for an attack on Passchendaele Ridge to be carried out the following day by the Second Army in conjunction with the Belgian Army on the left. C was on the right and A on the left in the front line, with D in support to C, and B in support to A. Battalion Headquarters were in Potijze Château, where, by 4 a.m. on the 28th, all companies reported themselves in position. Liaison was established on both flanks, and one platoon from the 8th, under Lieutenant B. M. Laing, was detailed to attack along the international boundary on the Battalion left flank to maintain touch with the Belgians. Lieutenant H. F. Calder remained with the Belgian Battalion Headquarters with four runners from his own battalion, so that reports could be sent from time to time during the attack.

Zero hour was at 5.30 a.m. on September 28th. At 6.15 a.m.

CAPTURE OF BROODSENDE RIDGE

the attack was reported to be going well; a quarter of an hour later, Battalion Headquarters moved forward and established themselves at Railway Post pill box. The first objectives were reported captured by 8 a.m. and all companies prepared to follow in support of the 5th Camerons, who were to continue the attack, liaison being kept up with the 7th Seaforths on the right and the Belgians on the left.

At 9.20 a.m. the 5th Camerons moved forward behind the barrage with the object of capturing the Broodsende Ridge. The attack progressed favourably and the ridge was captured by 11.30 a.m., when the Camerons took up a line in front of the Ridge with the 8th Black Watch and 7th Seaforths in close support. A company now moved across in support of the 7th Seaforths, who prolonged the front line on the right, and joined up with the 27th Brigade. Casualties were light, as the enemy positions had not been held in strength and their guns had been moved far back. The night of the 28th was quiet, there being little or no shelling.

About 9 a.m. on the 29th the advance was continued due east, the 8th being in Brigade support. The Belgians, however, met with opposition from the village of Moorslede, and the Battalion, with the remainder of the Brigade, was ordered to bear slightly north of the original line of advance in order to assist them. This extra force had the desired effect, and the advance continued throughout the day, the 8th being still in support, while the 5th Camerons came into line between the Belgians and the 28th Brigade.

Between 5 and 6 p.m. enemy resistance stiffened considerably, and B company, under Lieutenant Paul, advanced into a gap in the line between the Belgians and the 5th Camerons, D company, under Captain Austin, eventually extended the line and joined up with the Belgians on the left. Shortly after 6 p.m. orders were received from Brigade that a halt would be made for the night on the line held. Battalion Headquarters were established in a pill box north of Slypskappelle; B and D companies remaining in the line, with A and C companies in close support. The night of September 29th passed quietly, and during the course of the day Scip Wood was penetrated and an advance on both flanks was attempted. Owing to determined resistance, however, the wood had to be evacuated and the Battalion withdrew to the original line.

About 8 a.m. on September 30th orders were received that the advance would be continued at 6.15 a.m. the following day, the advance to be east, through the villages of Rolleghemcappelle, Winkel, St. Eloi, Capelle, St. Catherine's cross roads and Harlebeke, halts for reorganization to be made on a line north and south through the villages, and each advance to be continued on orders from Brigade Headquarters. The Battalion was ordered to advance on the left, with the 7th Seaforths on the right, and the 5th Camerons in support; the Belgians were not to begin their advance till 11 a.m.

All companies had reached their assembly positions by 5.45 a.m. on October 1st, and half an hour later the attack was launched. This met with immediate success, and about 7 a.m. a halt was made and A and B companies reorganized as arranged, while C and D acted as flank guard. Orders were received that the advance would continue at 8.45 a.m., but five minutes before this hour the enemy launched a heavy counter-attack through a gap on the left. After considerable difficulty, this flank was secured, and two companies of the 5th Camerons were employed to prolong the line from the railway south-west, so as to join up with the Belgians. This left C and D companies in a very advanced position, and they had suffered severely before they could be withdrawn. Captain Ritchie, commanding C company, and Lieutenant Paul, B company, were killed. On the right the Seaforths were forced back on the railway, but the line was secured for the time being, and the night of October 1st passed quietly.

On the next day considerable movement was observed in the enemy's lines, and about 5 p.m. the Germans put down a fairly heavy artillery barrage and made a feeble attack, which was easily repulsed on the front held by the Battalion. On the right and left, however, the enemy attacked in some force, but were driven back; a few succeeded in establishing themselves on the right, but were soon ejected.

Shelling increased during the night of the 2nd, but the day was quiet except for occasional bursts of machine gun fire, and the activity of snipers. On the night of the 3rd the Battalion was relieved by the 12th Royal Scots, 27th Brigade, and moved back to billets east of Strooiboomhoek village, along the road to Dadizeele. The relief was completed about midnight, and after a good rest the day was spent in refitting and reorganizing. About 5 p.m. on the 5th the 8th moved, at short notice, to shelters around Celtic Wood and the night passed without incident. On the next day drafts to the number of 140 men arrived. During the night of the 6th enemy bombing operations were carried out around Celtic Wood, but not in the immediate vicinity of the Battalion shelters.

On the 7th the Battalion moved by light railway to X Camp, and the transport to Macpherson Camp, both north of Poperinghe; this move occupied the whole day. Here the 8th was joined by a draft of 124 men. Three days were spent

CAPTURE OF ST. ELOI, OCTOBER 14TH, 1918

in X Camp, where the Battalion was inspected by the II Corps Commander, Lieutenant-General Sir Claud Jacob. On the 9th of October orders were received to move into the line again on the night of the 10th in relief of the 2nd Royal Scots Fusiliers. Advance parties were despatched early on the 10th, and at 4 p.m. the 8th moved by light railway from Byng Junction to Moorslede Sidings, and thence by road to the line. The Battalion took over the left sector, and the trenches were held by A company on the right and D on the left, with C and B in support and reserve. The day passed quietly, and after dusk patrols were pushed out by the front line companies. Cook Copse was reconnoitred and occupied by patrols of the 8th, one man of A company being killed in this operation. The enemy remained fairly quiet during the next day or two, but patrols, which were out continuously after dark, reported no signs of any retirement. Some heavy gas shelling took place on the 13th, but caused no casualties.

The advance was continued the following day and at 5.27 a.m. on October 14th an artillery barrage fell on the enemy lines, and two minutes later the Germans bombarded the St. Pieter–Menin road. At 5.30 a.m. the Battalion advanced, D company leading, with the 28th Brigade on the right, and the 9th Belgian Regiment on the left. B, C and A companies were in support and organized in depth. D company was held up at Mogg Farm about 6 a.m., and B and C were then ordered to assist it by working round the flanks, and the farm was soon cleared of the enemy. Smoke was then drifted across the front from the south-west; this completely obliterated everything, and hampered operations for some time. By 7.30 a.m., however, the Battalion had reached a line 600 yards east of the light railway and continued its forward progress. Battalion Headquarters then moved forward and by 11 o'clock was established at Jerry Farm. As the smoke cleared the Battalion continued to advance through Winkel—St. Eloi, halting on the eastern outskirts of the village. The advance was continued at noon, but was eventually held up by machine guns on the high ground east of woods near the village; by 4 p.m. it became evident that further progress was impossible and it was decided to consolidate for the night on the line gained. Strong patrols were sent forward to protect the left flank, as the Belgians were in advance of the Battalion; but, later, in face of strong machine gun opposition, the Belgians withdrew from their advanced position. All companies of the Battalion were then in the front line. During these operations Lieutenant Potter, A company, and Second Lieutenant W. G. Sim, D, were killed, and Lieutenants W. Elder, C, and B. Webster, B, and Second Lieutenants

THE EIGHTH BATTALION THE BLACK WATCH

D. K. Johnston, W. G. Yeoman and H. W. Leitham, D company, were wounded.

At 9 a.m. on October 15th a battalion of the 27th Brigade passed through the 8th and continued the advance, the Battalion remaining in reserve at Winkel—St. Eloi, where it stayed until the 18th, on which day it took over the line from the 88th Brigade and from the 9th Belgian Regiment. The Battalion was held in support to the 5th Camerons and 7th Seaforths.

The attack on the River Lys position began at 11 a.m. on the 19th, the Camerons and Seaforths crossing first, followed by the 8th Black Watch in close support. The river was successfully crossed by boats which were pulled across, and by two pontoon bridges hurriedly built by the Royal Engineers, and Harlebeke was occupied and held. At 6 p.m. the advance was continued, and Deerlyck on the left was taken, but on the right the advance was considerably delayed in crossing the Gaverbeek. Here the whole attack was held up by machine gun fire on the crest of the hill at St. Louis, and a line was established about two hundred yards south-east of the St. Louis–Vichte road. A company held the front line, with D company in close support, B and C companies being in reserve in farms behind the ridge.

Throughout the 21st there was heavy enemy artillery and gas shelling, and at night the 8th took over the whole of the 26th Brigade front. At 9 a.m. on October 22nd units of the 27th Brigade passed through the 26th and continued the advance, which, however, was seriously impeded by the activity of the enemy artillery and by a dense fog. At 5 p.m. orders to fill a gap on the right between the 27th Brigade and 29th Division were received. A company was sent forward to find the left flank of the 29th Division, and B to find the right flank of the 27th Brigade. This task was extremely difficult in the mist and darkness, but was eventually carried out with complete success, and the gap, which extended to more than 2000 yards, was filled by all four companies. The 8th then came under orders of the General Officer Commanding 27th Brigade, the line held being through Laaten, facing south-east. This line was held until the 24th, when the 5th Camerons and 7th Seaforths relieved the Battalion, which withdrew to billets in farms east of the St. Louis–Vichte road, and rejoined its own Brigade.

At 9 a.m. on the 25th a further advance was made under cover of an artillery barrage, the Battalion being in support to the 5th Camerons on the right and 7th Seaforths on the left. The leading battalions were held up about one o'clock by machine gun fire from the ridge south-west of Ooteghem, and C company was sent up in close support to the Camerons and pushed

THE ARMISTICE, NOVEMBER 11TH, 1918

forward 200 yards over the crest of the ridge, the other three companies remaining in reserve. The following day the Battalion was relieved by the 11th East Yorkshire Regiment, 31st Division, and returned to billets near Deerlyck, moving again the next day to Harlebeke area, where a large number of officers joined.

Here reorganization and refitting were carried out until the 29th, when the Battalion marched to Lendelede, where it was billeted in the village. A further draft joined here and parades were held and musketry practice was carried out. The total losses during the operations from October 10th to 26th were: Officers killed, two; wounded, five; other ranks killed, 23; wounded, 125; missing, 23. Total, 178 all ranks.

These operations were the last the 8th took part in, and after a few days' training at Lendelede the Battalion moved by road on November 3rd to the Steenen–Stampkot area, where, two days later, the Division was inspected by the King of the Belgians. The inspection took place in the Hulste Aerodrome and His Majesty, who was accompanied by the Queen, rode down the front of the Division. The troops marched past in column and then advanced in line in review order. After a few days' training the Battalion, on November 10th, marched back to billets in Harlebeke, where news of the acceptance of the Armistice terms was received about 7 p.m. Troops and civilians thronged the streets of the village, and the bands of the Brigade played until nearly midnight.

On November 11th information was received that the Armistice was to take effect from 11 a.m., and the day was observed as a holiday. On the 13th Lieutenant Farmer and the Battalion Chaplain went to Meteren and put crosses on the graves of men who were killed in the taking of that village on July 19th.

CHAPTER XI

NOVEMBER, 1918, TO NOVEMBER, 1919

On the Rhine—Demobilization

AFTER the Armistice, plans were made for the advance to the Rhine, and on November 14th the Battalion moved on the first stage of this journey to the Renaix area. The march was resumed the following day at 8.20 a.m. to north of Louise-Marie, where the Battalion remained until the 18th, when it advanced to Lierde—St. Martin. After a day's rest the Battalion moved forward to billets in Nieuwenhove, and on the 21st to Lennick-St.-Quentin. As the Battalion marched through this town the local bands formed up in the Square and played the British National Anthem. The band of the Battalion was sent to Brussels to take part in the state entry of the King of the Belgians into the capital, and the following day many men were allowed to go to Brussels to witness the ceremony.

On November 23rd a further move was made to Malaise, where one day was spent cleaning up and resting before marching to Longueville. The next move was on the 27th, to billets in Jauche, and on the following day to Vieux-Waleffe; the 30th was spent at Plemalle-Haute in the valley of the Meuse, and a number of men were given leave to visit Liège. On December 1st the 8th marched to Nessonnaux; on the 4th it moved to Limbourg, and the following day crossed the Belgian frontier into Germany at Stockem, where it was billeted in the village of Raeren. The advance continued on December 6th from Raeren to Gressenich; on the 7th to Duren; on the 8th to Bottenbroich, and on the following day to Nieppes, a suburb of Cologne, where a halt was made for a few days.

The Rhine was crossed on December 13th, just a month after the Armistice, and the 8th Black Watch led the Division, preceded by an advanced guard composed of one composite company of the Battalion under Captain D. A. Soutar, one section Royal Engineers and one section Divisional Machine Gun Corps. The Brigade bands were massed and marched at the head of the main body to the Mulheim Bridge, where they halted and played the "March Past." The Governor of Cologne and the II Corps Commander were present at the bridge. The route followed on this march was Mulheim—Weisdorf to Opladen, where the Battalion billeted for the night.

On the 14th C and D companies under Major Ian W. W. Shepherd moved by road from Opladen to Solingen to relieve the 15th Hussars, 9th Cavalry Brigade. The posts were taken over by 8 a.m. the following day, and the remainder of the

DEMOBILIZATION

Battalion marched to Solingen and billeted in schools and halls in the town. On the 23rd A company relieved B as outpost company, and took up quarters in the forward zone. Battalion Officers' and Sergeants' Messes were formed, and Christmas Day was observed as a holiday. Demobilization began on the 27th, and the first draft, sixteen miners from various companies, proceeded to England. Educational classes were formed and the usual drill parades were held daily. New Year's Day was also observed as a holiday, and on January 4th the Corps Commander, Lieutenant-General Sir Claud Jacob, K.C.B., presented French decorations to the officers and men of the Division. During the month a number of inter-company football matches and boxing classes were organized.

Demobilization continued, and by the end of the month three officers and 117 non-commissioned officers and men had returned to civil life. The demobilization of such an army was no light task and required continuous work and careful organization; coal miners had priority at first, and 71 miners were despatched. Agriculturists were next called for, and 15 ploughmen were demobilized. It was obviously desirable to give preference to those men who had served longest in the field, but it soon became evident that many cases of hardship must occur, since men had to be demobilized as they could most usefully be employed in their various trades at home. One man, No. 202,203 Private V. Donaldson, B company, who had served three years and ten months overseas, was not demobilized until January.

In February many of the older hands were released. On March 1st the Battalion left the 9th Division to join the 187th Infantry Brigade, 62nd Division, as the 9th Division was under orders to be disbanded owing to the rapidity of demobilization. When the 8th moved by train from Solingen to Mechernich the band of the 5th Camerons played the Battalion to the station, the massed pipes and drums of the 7th Seaforths and 5th Camerons played a "farewell," and the long connection of the 8th Black Watch with the 9th Division was severed. The following day the Battalion marched to billets in Burvenich, and came under orders of the 187th Infantry Brigade. On the 7th a move was made to Zulpich, where the Battalion entrained for Duren, marching from the latter town to Merzenich. Several drafts increased the strength of the Battalion, which moved to billets in Vettweiss before the end of the month. The final for the Army Cup was played on March 28th between the Battalion team and that of the 1st Camerons, at Blucher Park, Cologne, the 8th being beaten by two goals to one.

THE EIGHTH BATTALION THE BLACK WATCH

The Battalion remained at Vettweiss with D company at Malmedy until April 7th, when it marched to Buir under the command of Lieutenant-Colonel V. M. Fortune, D.S.O., who had formerly commanded the 1st Battalion The Black Watch.

The total number demobilized during April was 10 officers and 183 other ranks. The Battalion remained at Buir until May 9th, when it moved to Maubach, near Duren, remaining there until well on in June, D company joining from Malmedy on May 24th. Demobilization was continued as quickly as possible, and 60 non-commissioned officers and men were released during the month.

On the 17th of June the Battalion left Maubach for Benrath, where it took over posts held by the 9th Scottish Rifles, which were inspected on the 24th by the Commander-in-Chief.

On June 28th news was received that the Peace Treaty had been signed by the Germans. On the last day of June the Battalion was relieved by troops of the Lowland Division, and advance parties were despatched to Birksdorf and Unt-Maubach. Educational classes were continued during June, and about 13 men were demobilized.

In July the Battalion moved to Unt-Maubach, where it remained for the rest of its stay in Germany. The 9th of June was observed as Peace Day by the Army of the Rhine, and company sports were held. On the 11th the Commander-in-Chief visited the Battalion and inspected camps and training. Major R. E. Anstruther, M.C., rejoined at Maubach on the 22nd as Second-in-Command, and on July 29th Lieutenant-Colonel V. M. Fortune, D.S.O., took over command of the Rhine Army School of Musketry, and was succeeded in the Battalion by Major Anstruther.

Only 13 men were demobilized in July, as the Battalion was soon to return to England. Preparations for this move were begun on August 7th, and No. 3 Rest Camp, near Calais, was reached on the morning of the 13th. The Battalion disembarked at Folkestone and marched to Shorncliffe, where it entrained for Milford and Brocton. During August, 143 men were demobilized.

September was spent at Brocton, and during the month 295 men were demobilized, but the Battalion was strengthened later by absorbing the 6th Battalion The Black Watch. In October the Battalion left Brocton for Mansfield, and by November 15th the 8th was reduced to Cadre strength. After the dispersal of the remaining officers and other ranks, Lieutenant-Colonel R. E. Anstruther and Captain Milroy proceeded with the Quartermaster to the Depot at Perth. By the middle of December all matters were settled, Lieutenant-Colonel

DISBANDMENT

Anstruther went on leave, and the remaining officers were demobilized.

Thus, after an existence of over five years, during which it had added many laurels to those won by the other Battalions of the Regiment, the 8th (Service) Battalion ceased to exist, except in the hearts of those who had served in its ranks, and in the memories of all who love The Black Watch and will never forget the gallant deeds and great achievement of the 8th.

APPENDIX I

Record of Officers' Services

THE EIGHTH BATTALION

Abbreviations:—"K."—Killed. "D. of W."—Died of Wounds. "W."—Wounded. "M."—Missing. "P. of W."—Prisoner of War.

Abercromby, Sir G., Bart., Capt. Rejoined from Staff 18th Jan., 1916. Assumed temporary command of Battn. 7th March, 1916, to 9th April, 1916. Promoted Major. Assumed command of Battn. 22nd Sept., 1916. Promoted Lieut.-Col. To hospital 21st May, 1917. Awarded D.S.O. 23rd May, 1917. Rejoined 9th Sept., 1917. To hospital 16th Sept., 1917.
Alexander, P. J. A. 2nd Lieut. Joined 22nd Oct., 1916. To hospital 29th Oct., 1916. Awarded M.C. 23rd May, 1917. Promoted Capt. *k.* 12th Oct., 1917.
Alport, C. M. 2nd Lieut. Joined 20th June, 1916. *w.* 15th July, 1916. Rejoined 12th July, 1917. To hospital 16th Sept., 1917.
Anderson, D. L. 2nd Lieut. Joined 5th July, 1917. *w.* 1st Oct., 1918. Promoted Lieut. Rejoined 25th Nov., 1918.
Anderson, D. S. Capt. Joined 2nd Feb., 1915. To hospital 20th March, 1917. Rejoined 29th April, 1918.
Anderson, J. A. 2nd Lieut. Joined 25th Aug., 1916. *k.* 19th Oct., 1916.
Anstruther, R. E. Capt. Joined 22nd Jan., 1917. Assumed command of Battn. 21st May, 1917. Awarded M.C. 23rd May, 1917. Promoted Major.
Ashfield, R. C. 2nd Lieut. Joined 25th Aug., 1916. *w.* 18th Oct., 1916.
Austin, W. 2nd Lieut. Joined 6th June, 1916. Awarded M.C. 23rd May, 1917. Promoted Capt. To hospital June, 1918.

Balkwill, A. T. J. 2nd Lieut. Joined 4th Sept., 1916. *k.* 18th Oct., 1916.
Barbour, K. 2nd Lieut. Joined from Argyll and Sutherland Highlanders 27th Oct., 1918.
Barnett, G. A. 2nd Lieut. Joined 11th June, 1917.
Barr, J. W. 2nd Lieut. Joined 19th Oct., 1917. *k.* 24th March, 1918.
Bates, J. V. Lieut. R.A.M.C. Awarded M.C. 29th Aug., 1916.
Bell, H. 2nd Lieut. Joined 16th Feb., 1917. *m.* 3rd May, 1917.
Bellamy, C. W. 2nd Lieut. Joined 14th Nov., 1916. Left Dec., 1916.
Bennett, R. B. 2nd Lieut. Joined 6th June, 1916. *w.* 18th July, 1916.
Bowes-Lyon, Hon. F. Capt. *k.* 25th Sept., 1915.
Bradley, F. H. 2nd Lieut. Joined 29th April, 1917. *w.* and *m.* 27th March, 1918.
Brand, E. J. 2nd Lieut. Joined from 3rd Battn. 27th Oct., 1918.
Brown, H. R. Major. Joined 24th Oct., 1915. (In temporary command for short period. Left in Nov., 1915, to take temporary command 71st Seaforth Highlanders.)
Brown, R. L. 2nd Lieut. Joined 20th Feb., 1918. To hospital sick 4th June, 1918. Rejoined 13th June, 1918. *k.* 19th July, 1918.
Brown, W. Capt. R.A.M.C. Joined 27th Oct., 1915. Transferred to Rouen 28th April, 1916.
Brownlie, A. H. 2nd Lieut. Joined 22nd April, 1918. *w.* 20th July, 1918.

THE EIGHTH BATTALION THE BLACK WATCH

Bryson, H. L. 2nd Lieut. Joined 17th Nov., 1916. *w.* 9th April, 1917. Rejoined 26th April, 1917. To U.K. 31st Jan., 1918. Rejoined 22nd May, 1918. *w.* 20th July, 1918.
Buchanan, J. C. R. 2nd Lieut. *w.* 14th July, 1916.
Burness, C. 2nd Lieut. Joined 13th July, 1916. Left Battn. to take up duty as Permanent Base Commandant XIX Corps 31st March, 1917.
Burnett, G. H. M. Capt. *w.* 27th July, 1915.
Burns, D. C. 2nd Lieut. *k.* 30th Sept., 1918.
Burt, J. 2nd Lieut. Joined 23rd June, 1917. *k.* 19th July, 1918.
Burton, J. L. 2nd Lieut. *w.* 30th March, 1916.
Butler, H. Lieut. *w.* 25th Sept., 1915.
Butter, H. Capt. *k.* 14th July, 1916.

Cameron, S. 2nd Lieut. Joined 17th Feb., 1918.
Cameron, W. McA. 2nd Lieut. Joined 20th June, 1916. *k.* 14th July, 1916.
Campsie, A. 2nd Lieut. Joined 25th Aug., 1916. *w.* 19th Oct., 1916. Awarded M.C. 8th Dec., 1916.
Carswell, J. D. Capt. *k.* 14th July, 1916.
Chambers, T. E. 2nd Lieut. Joined 16th Feb., 1917. *w.* 9th March, 1917.
Clement, H. A. 2nd Lieut. Joined 21st April, 1916. *w.* 14th July, 1916. Rejoined 29th April, 1917. Mentioned in Despatches 4th Jan., 1917. *k.* 3rd May, 1917.
Collins, J. G. Major. *k.* 25th Sept., 1915. Mentioned in Despatches 1st Jan., 1916.
Colquhoun, P. H. L. C. Lieut. Joined 14th Jan., 1917. Transferred to 1st Battn. 19th Feb., 1917.
Cook, K. R. 2nd Lieut. *w.* 14th July, 1916.
Cousins, J. K. 2nd Lieut. Joined 20th June, 1916.
Cox, P. A. Lieut. *w.* 9th Oct., 1915.
Craig, A. 2nd Lieut. Joined 7th Nov., 1916.
Craven, A. 2nd Lieut. Joined 25th Aug., 1916. *k.* 19th Oct., 1916.
Crawford, S. Major. Joined 1st Oct., 1915. To 26th M.G. Coy. 29th Jan., 1916.
Crichton, J. F. 2nd Lieut. *k.* 18th July, 1916.

Davidson, A. F. 2nd Lieut. Joined 17th July, 1917. Accidentally *w.* 1st Aug., 1917. Rejoined 20th Feb., 1918. *w.* 24th March, 1918.
Dempsey, M. V. 2nd Lieut. Joined 25th Aug., 1918. *w.* 1st Oct., 1918.
Diamond, J. 2nd Lieut. Joined from 5th Argyll and Sutherland Highlanders 27th Oct., 1918.
Dickson, H. B. 2nd Lieut. Joined 21st April, 1916. *w.* 14th July, 1916. Rejoined 14th Nov., 1916. Promoted Lieut. *k.* 12th Oct., 1917.
Dingwall, J. 2nd Lieut. Joined from 8/10th Gordon Highlanders 4th Nov., 1918.
Don, T. D. 2nd Lieut. Joined 19th April, 1918. *k.* 21st July, 1918.
Drummond, D. 2nd Lieut. Joined from 6th Argyll and Sutherland Highlanders 28th Oct., 1918.
Drummond, H. M. Lieut. *d. of w.* 26th Sept., 1915.

APPENDIX I

Duff, G. B. Lieut.-Col. Joined and assumed command of Battn. 24th Oct., 1918. Left Battn. to command 5th Cameron Highlanders 4th March, 1916. Awarded D.S.O.

Duffus, P. B. Lieut. Joined 8th Oct., 1915. To 26th M.G. Coy. 11th Jan., 1916.

Duke, R. N. Capt. and Adj. Promoted Capt. 10th May, 1915. Appointed Adj. April, 1916. Awarded M.C. 1st Jan., 1917. Mentioned in Despatches 1st Jan., 1917. Awarded D.S.O. 3rd June, 1918. Mentioned in Despatches 3rd June, 1918.

Dunbar, W. P. 2nd Lieut. Joined 6th June, 1916. w. 18th July, 1916.

Duncan, A. 2nd Lieut. Joined 23rd July, 1918.

Elder, W. R. W. Lieut. Joined 23rd July, 1918. w. 14th Oct., 1918. (F. and F. Yeomanry.)

Elliott, A. E., Hon. Lieut. and Q.M. Joined 2nd June, 1918. Evacuated to U.K. 25th July, 1918.

Ewing, E. L. O. 2nd Lieut. Joined 7th Aug., 1918. w. 1st Oct., 1918. Awarded M.C. 15th Feb., 1919.

Ewing, J. L. S. Major. Joined from 9th Scottish Rifles 3rd Aug., 1917. Awarded M.C. Mentioned in Despatches. To hospital 11th Sept., 1917. Rejoined 10th Nov., 1917.

Fairley, J. R. 2nd Lieut. Joined July, 1916. w. 3rd May, 1917.

Farmer, G. A. 2nd Lieut. Joined 5th July, 1917. Awarded M.C. March, 1918.

Farquhar, J. 2nd Lieut. Joined 11th June, 1917. To hospital 11th Sept., 1917.

Fergusson, J. G. 2nd Lieut. To hospital 7th March, 1916. Rejoined 9th April, 1916. k. 14th July, 1916.

Fleming, C. P. Lieut. Joined 9th Oct., 1915. To hospital 7th Feb., 1916.

Forbes, W. R. J. Lieut. w. 25th Sept., 1915. Rejoined 29th April, 1917. To U.K. 10th Feb., 1918.

Forrester, P. H. 2nd Lieut. w. 25th Sept., 1915. Mentioned in Despatches 1st Jan., 1916. d. of w.

Fortune, F. R. 2nd Lieut. Accidentally w. by grenade 7th Aug., 1916.

Fraser, A. 2nd Lieut. Joined 3rd Jan., 1918. w. 26th March, 1918.

Fraser, P. G. 2nd Lieut. Joined 7th Nov., 1916. w. and m. 3rd May, 1917.

French, W. Major. Joined as Second-in-Command 1st Oct., 1917. Awarded M.C. 10th Jan., 1918. To 10th Argyll and Sutherland Highlanders in temporary command 3rd Jan., 1918. Rejoined 3rd Feb., 1918. Assumed command of Battn. 19th Aug., 1918. Bar to M.C. 30th April, 1918. Awarded D.S.O. 15th Feb., 1919.

Gawne, W. Z. 2nd Lieut. Joined 7th Nov., 1916. k. 9th April, 1917.

Gilruth, D. 2nd Lieut. Joined 1st Nov., 1916. Transferred to 5th Cameron Highlanders 27th Dec., 1916.

Gilroy, G. B. Capt. Awarded M.C. 3rd June, 1916. d. of w. 15th July, 1916.

THE EIGHTH BATTALION THE BLACK WATCH

Glen, A. 2nd Lieut. To hospital 21st March, 1917. Rejoined 27th March, 1917. Promoted Lieut. 17th Feb., 1918. Promoted Capt. To hospital 24th April, 1918. Rejoined 30th May, 1918. Awarded M.C. 1st Oct., 1918.

Goalen, J. M. Lieut. Joined Battn. 17th Feb., 1918. *w.* 25th April, 1918.

Gordon, C. W. E. Lieut.-Col. Assumed command of Battn. 9th April, 1916 (from 8th Gordon Highlanders). To Fourth Army Staff 22nd Sept., 1916. Mentioned in Despatches 4th Jan., 1917. Awarded Order of Danilo (3rd Class) 9th March, 1917. Mentioned in Despatches 15th May, 1917; 11th Dec., 1917.

Goudy, P. Hon. Lieut. and Q.M. To hospital 14th Oct., 1916. Awarded M.C. 1st Jan., 1918. Promoted Capt. To U.K. 1st June, 1918.

Govan, H. F. C. 2nd Lieut. Joined 11th June, 1917. *w.* and *m.* 23rd March, 1918. Mentioned in Despatches 7th May, 1918.

Gowie, J. M. 2nd Lieut. Joined 1st Nov., 1916.

Graham, A. 2nd Lieut. Joined 20th June, 1916.

Grant, G. R. B. Capt. M.C. R.A.M.C. Evacuated sick 6th May, 1918.

Greig, J. C. W. 2nd Lieut. Joined 1st Nov., 1916. *w.* 9th April, 1917.

Hadow, R. W. Capt. 2nd in command of Battn. 21st May, 1917. Promoted Lieut.-Col. Awarded D.S.O. To U.K. 17th Aug., 1918.

Hamilton, A. L. G. Lieut. Awarded M.C. 14th Nov., 1916.

Hammond, J. W. Lieut. Joined 25th July, 1918.

Hardie, J. A. 2nd Lieut. Joined from 4th (Reserve) Battn. 11th Nov., 1918.

Harley, W. C. 2nd Lieut. Joined from 5th Cameron Highlanders 27th Dec., 1916. *w.* 3rd May, 1917.

Harnett, E. St. C. Capt. Joined 16th May, 1917.

Harper, A. S. 2nd Lieut. Joined 15th Aug., 1916. *k.* 12th Oct., 1917.

Harrison, D. R. 2nd Lieut. Joined 27th March, 1917. *w.* 3rd May, 1917.

Hastings, J. E. 2nd Lieut. Joined 17th June, 1916. *k.* 18th July, 1916.

Hay, W. G. 2nd Lieut. To hospital 16th March, 1916. Accidentally *w.* by grenade 7th Aug., 1916. *d. of w.* 8th Aug., 1916.

Henderson, G. R. B. 2nd Lieut. Joined 11th June, 1917. *k.* 24th March, 1918.

Henderson, N. G. B. Major. *w.* 25th Sept., 1915. Awarded D.S.O. 1st Jan., 1919.

Herd, G. G. 2nd Lieut. Joined 4th May, 1918. *w.* 19th July, 1918.

Houston-Boswell, W. E. Capt. *w.* 25th Sept., 1915.

Howieson, W. V. 2nd Lieut. Joined 4th Sept., 1916. Promoted Lieut. July, 1917. Division Gas Adviser 78th American Division Nov., 1917.

Hunter, W. A. D. 2nd Lieut. Joined 15th Nov., 1916. *w.* 12th Jan., 1917. Rejoined 19th Oct., 1917. To French 160th Regt. as liaison officer 23rd May, 1918. Awarded M.C. *k.* 1st Oct., 1918.

Hutchison, A. D. 2nd Lieut. Joined 15th Aug., 1916. *w.* 19th Oct., 1916.

Hutchison, R. H. Lieut. Attached 1st Black Watch. *k.* 13th Nov., 1915.

Hutton, W. F. 2nd Lieut. Joined 17th June, 1916. *k.* 14th July, 1916.

Hyslop, W. D. 2nd Lieut. Joined 6th Nov., 1917. *k.* 24th March, 1918.

APPENDIX I

Inglis, J. Lieut. Joined July, 1916. w. 19th Oct., 1916. Rejoined 31st Oct., 1916. To hospital 14th Sept., 1917. w. 23rd March, 1918.
Irons, W. 2nd Lieut. Joined 6th Nov., 1917. Left Battn. 20th March, 1918.

Jackson, D. 2nd Lieut. Joined 6th Nov., 1917. k. 16th Dec., 1917.
Jeffrey, J. 2nd Lieut. Joined 26th Aug., 1918. w. 28th Sept., 1918.
Johnston, D. K. 2nd Lieut. Joined 21st July, 1918. w. 14th Oct., 1918.
Johnston, W. 2nd Lieut. k. 30th March, 1916.

Kincaid, A. D. 2nd Lieut. Joined 5th July, 1917. To hospital 11th Sept., 1917. d. of w. 23rd March, 1918.

Laing, B. M. 2nd Lieut. Joined 5th July, 1917. w. 12th Oct., 1917. To hospital 19th April, 1918. Rejoined 30th May, 1918. To hospital 16th June, 1918.
Lawrence, W. R. Lieut. Joined 4th Oct., 1915. Accidentally w. 5th Nov., 1915.
Leitham, H. W. 2nd Lieut. Joined 15th May, 1918. w. 14th Oct., 1918.
Lightbody, W. P. 2nd Lieut. Joined 28th Aug., 1918.
Lindsay, R. 2nd Lieut. Joined from 3rd Battn. 27th Oct., 1918.
Logan, G. C. 2nd Lieut. Joined 29th Oct., 1916. To hospital 11th Nov., 1916
Louden, W. R. W. 2nd Lieut. Joined 8th July, 1917. To hospital 15th June, 1918. Promoted Lieut. To U.K. 23rd July, 1918.
Lowen, A. T. 2nd Lieut. Joined 25th Aug., 1916. w. 19th Oct., 1916.
Luke, H. A. 2nd Lieut. Joined 22nd April, 1918. w. 25th April, 1918.

MacIntosh, C. O. C. 2nd Lieut. k. 25th Sept., 1915.
MacIntosh, E. H. Lieut. k. 25th Sept., 1915.
MacKenzie, L. w. 3rd May, 1918.
MacLachlan, D. G. 2nd Lieut. Joined 23rd July, 1918.
MacLaren, D. R. Lieut. Joined from 10th Battn. 4th Oct., 1918. To hospital 18th Oct., 1918.
McCash, W. M. 2nd Lieut. Joined 11th June, 1917. To U.K. 28th April, 1918. Awarded M.C.
McClure, G. B. Capt. Mentioned in Despatches 1st Jan., 1916. k. 2nd Oct., 1915.
McDonald, J. M. 2nd Lieut. Joined 4th May, 1918. To hospital 15th June, 1918. Awarded M.C. 15th Oct., 1918.
McDowall, C. G. Lieut. Joined 24th July, 1918. w. 28th Sept., 1918.
McKenzie, A. J. 2nd Lieut. Joined 26th April, 1918. w. 19th July, 1918.
McKenzie, V. A. 2nd Lieut. Joined 21st July, 1918. Awarded M.C. Oct., 1918.
McKenzie, L. 2nd Lieut. w. 27th May, 1915. w. 14th July, 1916. Rejoined 13th Sept., 1916. w. 3rd May, 1917.
McLaren, D. R. Lieut. Joined 30th Oct., 1915. Sick 4th May, 1916. Rejoined 4th Oct., 1918. Sick 17th Oct., 1918. Rejoined 6th Jan., 1919.
McLaren, T. D. S. Lieut. w. 9th April, 1917. Rejoined 7th Oct., 1917. p. of w. 23rd March, 1918.

THE EIGHTH BATTALION THE BLACK WATCH

McLean, A. H. 2nd Lieut. Joined 6th Nov., 1917.
McLean, A. L. Capt. R.A.M.C. (attached). Awarded M.C. 15th Feb., 1919.
McLeod, J. F. 2nd Lieut. Joined 11th Sept., 1916. To U.K. 15th Feb., 1917.
McMillan, H. D. Lieut. Joined 29th April, 1917. Appointed Instructor Fifth Army School 3rd Jan., 1918. *k.* 19th July, 1918.
McNeal, T. D. F. 2nd Lieut. Joined 1st Nov., 1916. Transferred to 1st Gordon Highlanders. Rejoined from 1st Gordon Highlanders 27th Oct., 1918.
McNeil, J. T. Lieut. Joined 28th April, 1917.
McRae, J. A. 2nd Lieut. Joined 20th June, 1916. *k.* 18th July, 1916.
McTavish, F. H. C. Capt. *w.* 25th Sept., 1915.
Mann, A. J. 2nd Lieut. Joined 25th Aug., 1916. *w.* 9th April, 1917. *d. of w.* 10th April, 1917.
Mathews, P. L. S. 2nd Lieut. Joined 5th July, 1917. To U.K. 2nd Feb., 1918.
Miles, L. G. Capt. *w.* 14th July, 1916. Awarded D.S.O. 29th Aug., 1916.
Miller, A. W. R. 2nd Lieut. Joined 11th June, 1917. To hospital 17th June, 1918. Awarded M.C. 27th July, 1918.
Milligan, O. B. Capt. C.F. (attached). Awarded M.C. 17th Dec., 1917.
Milroy, A. L. 2nd Lieut. Joined 11th June, 1917. Awarded M.C. 12th Dec., 1917.
Milroy, E. 2nd Lieut. *k.* 18th July, 1916.
Monday, J. C. 2nd Lieut. Joined 27th March, 1917. *k.* 3rd May, 1917.
Montgomerie, W. D. 2nd Lieut. To hospital 16th March, 1916. *w.* 15th July, 1916.
Morbey, H. J. 2nd Lieut. Joined 9th Nov., 1916.
Mowbray, J. S. S. Capt. *k.* 25th Sept., 1915.
Munro, D. L. 2nd Lieut. Joined 7th Nov., 1916. *w.* 12th Oct., 1917. *d. of w.* 13th Oct., 1917.
Murray, E. D. 2nd Lieut. *w.* 18th July, 1916. *d. of w.* 21st July, 1916.
Murray, E. M. Capt. *w.* 27th July, 1915.
Murray, R. N. M. 2nd Lieut. *w.* 25th Sept., 1915. Rejoined 25th Aug., 1916. Promoted Capt. and Adjt. To U.K. 21st Dec., 1917. Rejoined 12th May, 1918. Appointed A.D.C. to G.O.C. 9th Division 29th May, 1918. Awarded M.C. 15th Feb., 1919.
Musgrave, T. A. 2nd Lieut. Joined 22nd April, 1918.

Niven, A. 2nd Lieut. Joined from 4th Battn. 27th Oct., 1918.

Odell, R. E. 2nd Lieut. Joined 25th Aug., 1916. *w.* 18th Dec., 1916. *d. of w.* 19th Dec., 1916.
Ogilvie, A. M. L. 2nd Lieut. Joined 7th Nov., 1916. *w.* 2nd Jan., 1917.

Paul, J. R. Lieut. *k.* 1st Oct., 1918.
Peebles, P. 2nd Lieut. Joined 4th May, 1918. *k.* 19th July, 1918.
Pelham-Burn, M. E. Lieut. Joined 14th Jan., 1917. *k.* 9th April, 1917.

APPENDIX I

Phillips, E. G. M. Capt. Joined from 10th Battn. 27th Oct., 1918.
Pitcairn, E. G. Lieut. Joined from 10th Battn. 4th Oct., 1918. To hospital 5th Oct., 1918. d. of pneumonia 6th Oct., 1918.
Pollock, J. B. 2nd Lieut. Joined 23rd January, 1918. w. and m. 26th March, 1918.
Poore, S. W. 2nd Lieut. Joined 23rd July, 1918.
Potter, R. 2nd Lieut. Joined from 1st Battn. 13th June, 1917. To hospital 7th Sept., 1917. To U.K. 8th Feb., 1918. Rejoined 22nd May, 1918. Promoted Lieut. Promoted Capt. k. 14th Oct., 1918. Awarded M.C. 15th Feb., 1919.
Prosser, J. Lieut. Joined 7th Aug., 1918. k. 28th Sept., 1918.
Proudfoot, A. 2nd Lieut. Joined 28th Nov., 1916. w. 3rd May, 1917. Rejoined 16th May, 1917. Awarded M.C. 23rd May, 1917.

Ramage, A. G. Lieut. Joined 7th Oct., 1915. To 26th M.G. Coy. 11th Jan., 1916.
Ray, P. O. 2nd Lieut. Joined 8th Aug., 1916.
Reeves, F. L. Lieut. Joined from 1st Life Guards and appointed Adj. 8th Feb., 1918. Awarded M.C. 30th April, 1918.
Rice, P. H. 2nd Lieut. Joined from Indian Army 27th Oct., 1918.
Ritchie, A. S. 2nd Lieut. To hospital 7th March, 1916. Rejoined 9th April, 1916. Awarded M.C. 29th Aug., 1916. Promoted Capt. Rejoined 25th Aug., 1918. w. (at duty) 28th Aug., 1918. k. 1st Oct., 1918.
Roberts, H. J. 2nd Lieut. Joined 16th Feb., 1917. w. 9th April, 1917. Promoted Lieut. Rejoined 12th July, 1917. To Base 17th Feb., 1918.
Robertson, J. H. Lieut. k. 18th July, 1916.
Robertson, J. K. A. 2nd Lieut. Joined 29th April, 1917. Awarded M.C. 17th December, 1917. To U.K. sick 24th April, 1918.
Robson, J. 2nd Lieut. Joined 16th May, 1917. Promoted Lieut. w. 25th Dec., 1917.
Ross, G. D. 2nd Lieut. Joined 7th Nov., 1916. k. 9th April, 1917.
Rowan, N. 2nd Lieut. Joined 28th April, 1917. Rejoined from 10th Battn. 4th Oct., 1918.
Ruthven, A. B. 2nd Lieut. w. 19th Oct., 1916.

Sandeman, L. G. Lieut. Joined 20th Feb., 1918. w. 23rd April, 1918. (Attached 7th Seaforth Highlanders.) Awarded M.C. April, 1918.
Sanderson, H. S. Lieut. k. 25th Sept., 1915.
Scobie, A. 2nd Lieut. Joined 19th July, 1917.
Scott, J. M. Capt. Gassed 28th Sept., 1917.
Scott, W. H. 2nd Lieut. w. 15th July, 1916.
Sempill, Lord. Colonel. w. 25th Sept., 1915. Mentioned in Despatches 1st Jan., 1916.
Shaw, P. H. 2nd Lieut. k. 25th Sept., 1915.
Shepherd, I. W. W. Capt. Joined 11th Oct., 1916. Awarded M.C. 23rd May, 1917.
Shiach, W. L. 2nd Lieut. Joined 6th Nov., 1917. Awarded M.C. 15th Oct., 1918.
Sim, W. G. 2nd Lieut. Joined 14th May, 1918. k. 14th Oct., 1918.

THE EIGHTH BATTALION THE BLACK WATCH

Simpson, W. F. 2nd Lieut. Joined 11th June, 1917. Accidentally w. 1st Aug., 1917. Rejoined 29th Aug., 1917. w. 24th March, 1918. Rejoined 5th Sept., 1918.
Slade, F. E. 2nd Lieut. Joined 6th Nov., 1917. To M.G. Coy 27th April, 1918.
Smith, J. P. 2nd Lieut. Joined 11th June, 1917. w. 12th Oct., 1917.
Socket, A. 2nd Lieut. Joined 20th June, 1916. w. 8/9th July, 1916.
Soutar, D. A. 2nd Lieut. Joined 11th Sept., 1916. Awarded M.C. 3rd May, 1917. Promoted Lieut. 19th April, 1917; Capt. 24th Aug., 1918. Awarded Bar to M.C. Oct., 1918.
Speed, T. D. Lieut. w. 29th April, 1917. d. of w. 2nd May, 1917.
Sprake, G. H. 2nd Lieut. k. 18th July, 1916.
Steuart, B. C. A. Capt. Joined from 11th Battn. 16th March, 1916. Gassed 14th July, 1916.
Steward, O. H. D'A. Major. w. 25th Sept., 1915.
Stewart-Richardson, J. H. Capt. Joined from 11th Battn. 4th March, 1916. To U.K. for training 27th June, 1916.
Storrs, G. B. 2nd Lieut. Joined from 8th Argyll and Sutherland Highlanders 27th Oct., 1918.
Strange, H. St. J. Lieut. w. 25th Sept., 1915.
Stuart, A. H. Lieut. Joined 7th Oct., 1915. Ordered to Egypt 2nd June, 1916.
Stuart, M. S. 2nd Lieut. k. 14th June, 1918.
Sutherland, E. J. 2nd Lieut. Joined from 3rd Battn. 11th Nov., 1918.
Sutherland, D. H. 2nd Lieut. Joined 8th Sept., 1918. Awarded M.C. 15th Feb., 1919.

Taylor, J. McK. 2nd Lieut. Joined 25th Aug., 1916. w. 18th Oct., 1916. Rejoined 30th Dec., 1916 Transferred to R.F.A. 22nd April, 1917.
Taylor, N. R. 2nd Lieut. Awarded M.C. 8th Dec., 1916. k. 3rd May, 1917.
Tillie, J. A. 2nd Lieut. k. 19th July, 1918.
Tindal, D. 2nd Lieut. Joined 20th June, 1916. w. 18th July, 1916.
Tyser, H. E. 2nd Lieut. Joined 21st April, 1916. k. 9th April, 1917.

Walcott, E. P. M. 2nd Lieut. Joined 16th May, 1917. w. 11th June, 1917.
Walker, H. J. 2nd Lieut. Joined 7th Nov., 1916. w. 3rd May, 1917.
Wallace, A. M. D. 2nd Lieut. Joined 26th March, 1916. w. 18th July, 1916. Promoted Capt. Rejoined 29th April, 1917. w. 24th March, 1918.
Watson, D. Lieut. Joined 11th Nov., 1918.
Watt, G. H. 2nd Lieut. Joined 28th Nov., 1916. w. 9th April, 1917. Promoted Lieut. Rejoined 20th July, 1918. w. 22nd July, 1918.
Watterston, J. 2nd Lieut. Joined 6th Nov., 1917. Transferred to 26th Brigade Trench Mortar Battery (no date).
Webster, B. 2nd Lieut. Joined 20th June, 1916. w. 15th July, 1916. Rejoined 16th Feb., 1917. Promoted Lieut. Rejoined 8th Sept., 1918. w. 14th Oct., 1918.
Whamond, J. 2nd Lieut. Joined 5th Aug., 1918. w. 20th Aug., 1918.
Whitecross, J. M. 2nd Lieut. Joined 25th Aug., 1916.

APPENDIX I

Whitwright, J. A. 2nd Lieut. Joined 25th Aug., 1916.
Wilson, D. 2nd Lieut. To hospital 24th April, 1918.
Wilson, J. B. 2nd Lieut. Joined from 7th Argyll and Sutherland Highlanders 28th Oct., 1918.
Wilson, R. O. S. Lieut. Joined from 9th Battn. 27th Oct., 1918.
Wimbs, J. 2nd Lieut. Joined 6th Nov., 1917. To U.K. 19th April, 1918. Rejoined 22nd Oct., 1918.

Yeoman, W. G. 2nd Lieut. Joined 21st July, 1918. *w*. 14th Oct., 1918.
Young, J. L. 2nd Lieut. Joined 25th Aug., 1916. *w*. 3rd March, 1917. Rejoined 9th Nov., 1917. Promoted Lieut. Awarded M.C. *k*. 19th July, 1918.
Yule, G. L. 2nd Lieut. Joined 11th June, 1917. Awarded M.C. 30th April, 1918. Mentioned in Despatches 3rd June, 1918.

The names of officers who joined the 8th Battalion after the Armistice have not been included in this Appendix. The names of the following officers were omitted from the first proofs in error :—

Black, J. Captain. Joined May, 1918.
Drummond, A. M. Captain. Joined Feb., 1917.
Fraser, J. Lieut. Joined Dec., 1917. Transferred to Seaforth Highlanders May 1918.
Gauldie, K. Lieut. Joined July, 1916. *k*. when serving with Royal Engineers 1917.
Sandeman, S. A. Lieut. Joined June, 1918.
Wilson, A. T. Lieut., M.C. Joined from Argyll and Sutherland Highlanders Sept., 1916.

APPENDIX II

Summary of Casualties. The Eighth Battalion

The discrepancy between these figures and those given by the war diaries is accounted for by the fact that, save in the case of regular battalions, the diaries seldom give a record of casualties other than those suffered in main actions.

OFFICERS, 1914–18

Year.	Killed. D. of wounds. D. on service.	Wounded.	Missing.	Total.	Year.
1914	—	—	—	—	1914
1915	10	15	—	25	1915
1916	27	24	2	53	1916
1917	13	27	1	41	1917
1918	18	27	5	50	1918
Totals:	68	93	8	169	

OTHER RANKS, 1914–18

Year.	Killed D. of wounds. D. on service.	Wounded.	Missing.	Total.	Year.
1914	—	—	—	—	1914
1915	201	(a) —	(a) —	492	1915
1916	259	587	95	941	1916
1917	288	523*	83	894	1917
1918	375	563	332	1270	1918
Totals:	1123	1673	510	3597	

TOTAL:

Officers, 169.   Other Ranks, 3597.

(a) No numbers given.   * Including 219 on May 2nd, unclassified.

APPENDIX III

Casualties—Officers

THE EIGHTH BATTALION

* Killed in action.   † Died of wounds.   § Died.

Name.	Rank.	Date.
Alexander, P. J. A.	Capt.	*12.10.17. M.C.
Anderson, J. A.	2nd Lieut.	*19.10.16.
Balkwill, A. T. J.	2nd Lieut.	*18.10.16.
Barr, J. W.	2nd Lieut.	*24.3.18.
Bell, H.	2nd Lieut.	*3.5.17.
Bowes-Lyon, F. Hon.	Capt.	*25.9.15–2.10.15.
Bradley, F. H.	2nd Lieut.	*27.3.18.
Brown, R. L.	2nd Lieut.	*19.7.18.
Burt, J.	2nd Lieut.	*19.7.18.
Butter, H.	Capt.	*14.7.16.
Burns, D. C.	2nd Lieut.	*30.9.18.
Cameron, W. McA.	2nd Lieut.	*14.7.16.
Carswell, J. D.	Capt.	*14.7.16.
Clement, H. A.	2nd Lieut.	*3.5.17.
Collins, J. G.	Major.	*25.9.15–2.10.15.
Craven, A.	2nd Lieut.	*19.10.16.
Crichton, J. F.	2nd Lieut.	*18.7.16.
Dickson, H. B.	Lieut.	*12.10.17.
Dingwall, J.	2nd Lieut.	
Don, T. D.	2nd Lieut.	*21.7.18.
Drummond, H. M.	Lieut.	*25.9.15.
Fergusson, J. G.	2nd Lieut.	*14.7.16.
Forrester, P. H.	Lieut.	*25.9.15.
Fraser, P. G.	2nd Lieut.	*3.5.17.
Gawne, W. Z.	2nd Lieut.	*9.4.17.
Gilroy, G. B.	Capt.	†15.7.16.
Harper, A. S.	Lieut.	*12.10.17.
Hastings, J. E.	2nd Lieut.	*18.7.16.
Hay, W. G.	2nd Lieut.	†8.8.16.
Henderson, G. R. B.	2nd Lieut.	*24.3.18.
Hovan, H. F. C.	2nd Lieut.	*23.3.18.
Hunter, W. A. D.	Lieut.	*1.10.18.
Hutchison, R. H.	Lieut.	*13.11.15.
Hutton, W. F.	2nd Lieut.	*14.7.16.
Hyslop, W. D.	2nd Lieut.	*24.3.18.
Jackson, D.	2nd Lieut.	*16.12.17.
Johnston, W.	2nd Lieut.	*30.3.16.
Kincaid, A. D.	2nd Lieut.	*23.3.18.
MacIntosh, C. O. C.	2nd Lieut.	*25.9.15–2.10.15.
MacIntosh, E. H.	Lieut.	*25.9.15–2.10.15.
Mann, A. J.	2nd Lieut.	*9.4.17.

THE EIGHTH BATTALION THE BLACK WATCH

Name.	Rank.	Date.
McClure, G. B.	Capt.	*25.9.15–2.10.15
McMillan, H. D.	Capt.	*19.7.18.
McRae, J. A.	2nd Lieut.	*18.7.16.
Milroy, E.	2nd Lieut.	*18.7.16.
Monday, J. C.	2nd Lieut.	*3.5.17.
Mowbray, J. S. S.	Capt.	*25.9.15.
Munro, D. L.	2nd Lieut.	*12.10.17.
Murray, E. D.	2nd Lieut.	†21.7.16.
Odell, R. E.	Lieut.	†19.12.16.
Paul, J. R.	Lieut.	*1.10.18.
Peebles, P.	2nd Lieut.	*19.7.18.
Pelham-Burn, M. E.	Lieut.	*9.4.17.
Pitcairn, E. G.	Lieut.	§6.10.18.
Pollock, J. B.	2nd Lieut.	*26.3.18.
Potter, R.	Capt.	*14.10.18.
Prosser, J.	Lieut.	*28.9.18.
Ritchie, A. S.	Capt.	*1.10.18. M.C.
Robertson, J. H.	Lieut.	*18.7.16.
Ross, G. D.	2nd Lieut.	*9.4.17.
Sanderson, H. S.	Lieut.	*25.9.15–2.10.15.
Shaw, P. H.	2nd Lieut.	*25.9.15–2.10.15.
Sim, W. G.	2nd Lieut.	*14.10.18.
Speed, T. D.	Lieut.	†2.5.17.
Sprake, G. H.	2nd Lieut.	*18.7.16.
Stuart, M. S.	2nd Lieut.	*14.6.18.
Taylor, N. R.	Capt.	*3.5.17.
Tillie, J. A.	2nd Lieut.	*19.7.18.
Tyser, H. E.	2nd Lieut.	*9.4.17.
Young, J. L.	Lieut.	*19.7.18. M.C.

APPENDIX IV

Nominal Roll of Warrant Officers, Non-Commissioned Officers and Men Killed in Action or Died of Wounds or Disease in the Great War, 1914–18

THE EIGHTH BATTALION

* Killed in action. † Died of wounds. ‡ Died at home. § Died.

Abbot, D., L/Cpl., S/10407	*14.7.16	Baird, R. T., Pte., S/7726	*21.11.15
Abbot, J. F., Pte., S/40765	* 9.3.17	Baird, W., L/Cpl., S/3835	*18.7.16
Adams, A., Pte., 291670	†25.4.18	Balsillie, T., Pte., S/40536	†20.10.16
Adamson, C. V., Pte., S/11325	†18.7.16	Barclay, D., Cpl., S/3599	*17.7.16
Adamson, H., Pte., S/2913	§16.10.16	Barclay, J., Pte., S/11581	*12 4.16
Adamson, W., Pte., S/40726	*16.4.18	Barclay, W., L/Cpl., S/3600	‡23.9.16
Aitken, A., Pte., 202206	†11.4.18	Barclay, W., Pte., S/3619	*25.9.15
Alexander, J., Pte., 266689	*16.12.17	Barclay, W., Cpl., 40535	*19.7.18
Alexander, R., Pte., S/23060	*22.3.18	Barn, J. D., Pte., S/21378	*23.3.18
Allan, D. McD. F., Pte., S/41675	* 1.10.18	Barnett, C., Pte., S/12745	†18.2.17
Allan, D. McG., Cpl., 292581	† 6.10.18	Barnett, E. C., Pte., S/40453	* 9.4.17
Allan, J. K., Pte., S/40930	*24.3.18	Barter, A., Pte., 268727	† 4.6.17
Allan, T., L/Cpl., 350304	*24.6.18	Barton, J., Sgt., S/8646 (M.M.)	*12.10.17
Allan, T., Pte., S/40450	*16.12.17	Barton, W., L/Cpl., S/3077	*17.5.16
Allan, W., Pte., S/8898	*25.4.16	Bastain, E., Pte., S/21352	*12.10.17
Allen, A. C., Pte., S/13095	*19.10.16	Battison, J., Pte., 292828	*24.6.18
Allison, J., Pte., S/13945	†21.10.18	Baxter, A., Pte., S/2957	* 3.5.17
Amos, F., Pte., S/10071	* 8.10.15	Beattie, A., Pte., 3/2972	*10.4.18
Anderson, A., Pte., S/40528	*20.10.16	Bedwell, J., Pte., S/19900	*19.7.18
Anderson, C., Sgt., S/3042	*27.9.15	Belcher, F., Pte., S/20932	*12.10.17
Anderson, G., Pte., S/2978	*25.9.15	Bell, A., Pte., S/16773	† 9.4.17
Anderson, J., Pte., S/41552	†26.4.18	Bell, A. S., L/Cpl., 10268	*12.10.17
Anderson, R., Pte., S/43225	*28.9.17	Bell, G., Pte., S/25831	‡ 3.8.19
Anderson, T., Pte., S/3602	*27.9.15	Bell, H. J., L/Cpl., S/7912	* 9.4.17
Andrew, J., Pte., S/3761	*18.7.16	Bell, J., Pte., S/17546	*23.3.18
Andrews, G., Pte., S/7411	†16.2.16	Bell, P., Pte., S/8660	*21.10.15
Angus, A. M., Pte., 3/3150	‡25.6.16	Bell, R. G., Pte., S/40452	†14.10.17
Angus, J., L/Cpl., 3/2883 (M.M.)	†24.7.16	Bell, T., Pte., S/11331	*14.7.16
Angus, J. W., Pte., 201983	* 1.10.18	Bellingham, J., Pte., S/11542	*19.10.16
Angus, R., Cpl., S/3217	*12.10.15	Benson, W. J., Pte., S/17560	* 1.1.17
Annan, C. M., Pte., S/18111	*19.7.18	Bent, W. J., Pte., S/3884	* 9.4.17
Appleby, D., A/Cpl., S/3663	*19.10.16	Beveridge, R., Pte., S/40533	* 9.4.17
Archer, A., Pte., S/8966	† 4.5.16	Birch, T., Pte., S/13757	‡24.10.17
Archibald, R., Pte., S/6292	†18.4.17	Birrell, R., Pte., S/13755	*28.9.18
Archibald, W. J., Pte., S/41553	†17.4.18	Bissett, D., Pte., 2430	*10.10.16
Armit, D. B., L/Cpl., S/40525	* 1.10.18	Black, A., Pte., S/7532	*14.7.16
Armstrong, J., Pte., S/3384	*25.9.15	Black, J., Pte., S/6453	*25.9.15
Atkinson, R., Pte., S/3738	*25.9.15	Black, N., Pte., S/3200	*25.9.15
		Black, R., Pte., S/8220	*18.7.16
Baillie, P., Pte., S/23969	*19.7.18	Black, W., R.S.M., 6580	*27.9.15
Bain, C. J., Pte., S/19954	*12.10.17	Blagrove, C. F., Pte., S/40691	* 9.4.17
Bain, J., Pte., S/9186	* 9.7.16	Blaikie, R., Pte., S/7362	* 9.4.17
Bain, J., Pte., 350265	*19.7.18	Blaikley, W., Pte., 3713	*25.9.15
		Blair, C., Pte., S/11255	*18.7.16
		Blair, J., Pte., 235059	*27.5.18

THE EIGHTH BATTALION THE BLACK WATCH

Blair, W. N., L/Cpl., S/11719	*14.7.16
Blake, G Pte., S/40697	*12.10.17
Blyth, J., Pte., S/10718	*30.6.16
Blyth, J., Pte., 10191	*18.7.16
Boland, C., Sgt., S/6525	†28.12.16
Boles, W., Pte., 3/3495	*25.9.15
Bonnar, D. E., Pte., S/40722	*19.7.18
Borthwick, C., Pte., S/43540	*19.7.18
Borthwick, G., Pte., S/40786	* 9.4.17
Borthwick, G., Pte., S/8890	* 7.5.16
Bowman, A., A/Sgt., S/7698	* 3.5.17
Bowman, W., Pte., S/6386	*25.9.15
Bowman, W., Pte., 266638	*15.12.17
Boyd, G. O., Pte., 3694	*18.7.15
Boyd, W., Pte., S/12594	*30.7.16
Boyle, H., Pte., S/16479	*19.7.18
Boyter, A., Pte., S/43129	*19.10.16
Bradford, J., Pte., S/11218	*13.4.18
Bradie, P., Pte., S/9927	*18.7.16
Bradwell, J., Pte., S/3413	*16.4.18
Brash, J., Pte., 268709	* 3.5.17
Brewster, J., Pte., S/8948	†18.7.16
Bridgeman, G. A., Pte., S/19901	*12.10.17
Briggs, A., Pte., S/16344	* 9.4.17
Briggs, W. C., Cpl., 9743	*17.7.16
Brotherston, G. A., Pte., S/12271	*14.10.16
Brough, J. G., Pte., S/40456	*19.10.16
Brough, T., L/Cpl., S/14982	†25.3.18
Brown, A., L/Cpl., S/3522	††11.7.16
Brown, F. B., Pte., S/16938	†21.7.18
Brown, J. F., Pte., S/18277	§ 2.4.18
Brown, T., L/Cpl., 10487	† 2.10.18
Brown, T., Pte., S/22132	*30.12.17
Brown, T. B., Pte., S/3586	*25.4.16
Brown, W., Pte., S/13343	*17.10.16
Bruce, A., Pte., S/22015	†30.3.18
Bruce, D., Pte., S/43009	* 3.5.17
Bruce, J. W., Pte., S/8714	† 2.7.16
Bruce, J. M., Pte., S/11343	*15.7.16
Bruce, W., Pte., S/43194	* 3.5.17
Brunton, R., Pte., S/11221	†15.7.16
Brunton, T. L., Pte., S/40540	†11.4.17
Bryce, R., Pte., S/8632	†15.10.17
Buchanan, A. C., Pte., S/8569	‡12.11.16
Buchanan, J., Sgt., S/3860	*18.7.16
Buchanan, J., L/Cpl., S/9246	*18.7.16
Burchall, J., Pte., 202411	*30.9.18
Burns, J., Pte., S/3808	‡28.7.18
Burns, R., Pte., S/3757	†11.11.15
Burns, W. A., Pte., S/41458	*21.4.18
Butchart, M., Pte., 291159	*12.10.17
Cadger, J., Pte., S/18778	*21.3.18
Callan, J., Pte., S/43318	*19.10.16
Callum, A., Pte., S/3554	*16.7.16
Calvert, W. E., Pte., S/12333	*12.10.17
Cameron, A., Pte., S/9023	*21.10.15
Cameron, A., L/Cpl., 268730	*12.10.17
Cameron, J., Pte., S/22837	*28.9.18
Cameron, R., Cpl., S/3849	*25.9.15
Cameron, W. J., Pte., 266402	†13.10.17
Campbell, A., Pte., S/16336	* 2.10.17
Campbell, A., Pte., S/40785	* 4.3.18
Campbell, D., Pte., S/22109	§15.9.18
Campbell, H., Pte., S/10382	*25.9.15
Campbell, J., Pte., S/9448	*14.7.16
Campbell, J., Sgt., S/10414	* 9.4.17
Campbell, J., Pte., S/24111	*21.3.18
Campbell, M., Pte., S/20115	*12.10.17
Campbell, N. S., Pte., S/19955	‡ 2.6.17
Campbell, R., Pte., S/24055	*16.4.18
Campbell, T., Pte., S/12964	†30.10.17
Cant, J., Pte., S/8952	*31.3.16
Cargill, D., Pte., S/6479	*25.9.15
Carlin, J., Pte., S/9192	*21.10.15
Carmichael, J., Pte., S/2800	*14.10.15
Carnegie, D., Pte., 292943	*19.7.18
Carr, J., Pte., S/19956	*12.10.17
Carrie, D., L/Sgt., S/16463	*20.10.18
Carrie, P., Pte., S/2778	*29.9.15
Carswell, D., Pte., S/40462	*19.10.16
Carter, G., Pte., S/17059	*19.7.18
Cartledge, W., Pte., S/21356	*24.6.18
Casey, P., Pte., 266502	†28.9.17
Catto, G., Cpl., S/6204	† 6.5.17
Chalmers, J., Pte., S/10495	*21.10.15
Cheesman, H. B., Pte., S/10950	†26.4.18
Chisholm, A., L/Cpl., S/6226	*19.7.15
Christie, G. N., Pte., 291849	*12.10.17
Christie, J., L/Sgt., S/3193	*14.7.16
Christie, T., Pte., S/41461	†20.4.18
Chrystal, A. A., Pte., 268732	*12.10.17
Clark, A., Pte., S/6985	‡18.5.16
Clark, D., Sgt., 3/3219	*18.7.16
Clark, G., L/Cpl., S/43027	†21.10.16
Clark, J., L/Cpl., S/4599	* 9.4.17
Clark, J., Pte., S/43003	*19.10.16
Clark, J., L/Cpl., S/9127	*21.10.15
Clark, W., Pte., S/40465	*19.10.16
Clyde, L., Pte., S/4207	*12.10.17
Cockburn, F., Pte., S/9528	†21/4/17
Cogan, J. P., Pte., S/9155	*12.10.17
Colgan, J., Pte., S/3190	*14.8.15
Collins, G., Sgt., 678 (M.M.)	* 3.5.17
Collister, J. E., Pte., S/9923	* 9.7.16

APPENDIX IV

Colville, G., Pte., 268998	*11.4.18	Davidson, W., Pte., S/43593	‡ 8.11.18
Conacher, J., Sgt., S/6909	*14.7.16	Davis, F., Pte., 292181	†22.7.18
Condie, W., Pte., S/24291	* 2.10.18	Davis, A. W., Pte., S/12230	*19.7.18
Connelly, P., Pte., S/3257	*27.9.15	Day, F. C., Pte., S/18180	* 1.10.18
Constable, A., Pte., S/12987	* 3.5.17	Dean, R., Pte., S/14520	*12.10.17
Cook, A., Pte., 291889	†19.7.18	Dear, C., Pte., 240217	† 1.4.18
Cook, A., Pte., S/3185	*17.7.16	Dechan, P., Pte., S/6209	* 9.4.17
Cook, S., Pte., 3/2955	* 7.7.15	Dewar, J., Sgt., S/3118	*14.7.16
Cook, H.M., Pte., 8762	* 3.5.17	Dewar, J. R., Pte., S/9875	
Coomber, F., Pte., S/9006	*13.7.16	(M.M.)	*12.10.17
Coombes, A. G., Pte., 11677	†19.10.16	Dewar, P., Pte., 292897	† 6.9.17
Cooper, J. C., Pte., S/22970	† 2.10.18	Dewar, R., Pte., S/11897	*15.7.16
Cooper, J., A/Cpl., S/40552	†17.10.17	Diamond, P., Pte., S/18025	* 3.5.17
Corstorphine, G., Pte., 7569	‡10.8.17	Dickson, D. D., Pte., S/7657	*12.10.17
Cosh, A., A/Sgt., S/6678	*19.7.18	Dickson, H., Pte., S/43218	* 3.5.17
Cosh, C. J., L/Cpl., S/9320	*14.7.16	Doe, A., Pte., S/10211	†28.10.15
Coulter, J., Pte., 203224	§24.3.18	Doig, T., Pte., S/3741	*25.9.15
Coutts, H., Pte., S/41688	* 1.10.18	Doig, W., Pte., 268710	*19.7.18
Coutts, J., Pte., 267978	*19.7.18	Donaghey, C., Pte., S/43007	*24.3.18
Cowie, J. M., Pte., S/16991	*28.9.17	Donald, A. S., Pte., S/18842	*24.3.18
Cowper, A., Pte., S/16520	*12.10.17	Donald, R. S., Pte., S/22844	*24.3.18
Cox, W., Pte., 3/2980	* 6.12.16	Donaldson, J., Pte., S/14364	*12.10.17
Craig, W. McF., Pte., S/24113		Douglas, A., Pte., S/40468	† 9.2.17
	*19.7.18	Douglas, J., Pte., S/9870	*21.10.15
Craik, G. P., C.Q.M.S., 5804	*14.10.18	Douglas, W., Pte., S/3153	*25.9.15
Crawford, G. B., Pte., S/3683	*25.9.15	Douglas, W., Pte., 268347	*21.3.18
Crawford, J., Pte., S/2866	*25.9.15	Dow, D., Pte., S/18820	†28.3.18
Crawford, T., Pte., S/3687	* 6.10.15	Dowie, R., Pte., S/13696	* 3.5.17
Crawford, W., L/Cpl., S/8770		Dowie, W., Pte., S/12648	*30.6.16
	*19.10.16	Downie, D., Pte., S/22107	*23.3.18
Creer, T. E., Pte., S/12420	*19.7.18	Drew, J., Pte., S/43590	* 1.10.18
Crerar, J., Pte., 202046	*16.12.17	Dryburgh, C., Pte., S/3461	* 9.4.17
Crichton, W. F., Pte., S/3701	† 7.10.15	Duncan, D., Cpl., S/9900	*19.10.16
Crighton, W. R., Pte., S/18877	*28.9.17	Duncan, C., L/Cpl., S/6294	*25.9.15
Croll, A., Pte., 351121	†21.7.18	Duncan, C., Pte., 202830	*12.10.17
Crombie, A., Pte., S/8870	*21.10.15	Duncan, F. W., Pte., S/18974	†10.1.18
Crombie, J., Pte., 350119	*12.10.17	Duncan, J., L/Cpl., S/8598	*16.7.16
Crow, J. L., Pte., 3/3397	*25.9.15	Dunn, W., Pte., S/2923	†26.4.18
Crowe, A., Pte., 267650	*23.3.18	Durie, H., Pte., S/20111	†16.10.17
Cruickshanks, A., L/Cpl., S/17592		Duthie, W., Pte., 291568	* 1.10.18
	*12.10.17	Eadie, W., Pte., S/12695	*30.6.16
Cullen, J., Pte., S/3601	*18.7.16	Easton, J., Pte., S/3872	*25.9.15
Cullen, J. C., Pte., S/22849	* 1.10.18	Easton, W., Pte., S/12665	*30.7.16
Cumming, A., Pte., S/4996	*12.10.17	Edgar, A., Pte., S/10384	*25.9.15
Cunningham, A., L/Cpl., 3/2542		Edmonson, H., Pte., S/7704	*25.9.15
	*19.10.16	Edward, D., Pte., S/12430	*19.7.18
Currie, R., Pte., S/9360	*15.7.16	Emslie, J. W., Pte., 290779	‡15.5.18
Currie, T., Pte., S/40037	† 8.12.17	England, A., Pte., 267593	*19.7.18
		English, J. B., Sgt., S/8602	*14.10.18
Dalrymple, J., Pte., S/16202	* 3.5.17		
Darby, E., Pte., 10267	*13.7.16	Fabian, G., Pte., S/24194	*20.10.18
Darrock, H., Pte., S/24368	* 1.10.18	Fairgrieve, P., Pte., S/3612	§17.7.18
Davidson, R., Pte., S/40743	* 3.5.17	Farroll, J., Pte., S/6287	*21.11.15
Davidson, T., A/L/Sgt., S/8835		Farmer, C., Pte., S/11606	*19.3.16
	*12.10.17		

89

THE EIGHTH BATTALION THE BLACK WATCH

Farquhar, J., Pte., S/3202	*25.9.15	Gilchrist, T., Pte., 202846	*12.10.17
Farquhar, W. A., Pte., 10215	*12.2.16	Gildea, H., Pte., S/8801	* 9.4.17
Fearery, G. H., Pte., 19920	*12.10.17	Gilhooly, D., Pte., 3/2562	*14.7.16
Fearn, D., Pte., S/7326	* 9.8.15	Gillies, J., Pte., S/40559	* 3.5.17
Fearn, H., Pte., S/41694	* 1.10.18	Gillings, C W., Pte., S/6258	*18.7.16
Felgate, W., Pte., S/16899	* 3.5.17	Gilmour, D., Pte., S/17594	* 6.1.17
Ferguson, D., Sgt., S/4216	*14.7.16	Gilmour, D., Pte., S/43324 (M.M.)	*19.7.18
Ferguson, H., Pte., 292177	†27.3.18		
Ferguson, J., L/Cpl., S/10399	* 3.5.17	Gilonis, J. A., Pte., 11594	*19.7.18
Ferguson, J., Pte., S/8759	*16.10.15	Girvan, T., Pte., 42069	*19.7.18
Ferguson, J., Pte., S/40471	*19.7.18	Glen, A., Pte., S/16884	* 3.5.17
Ferguson, W., Pte., S/10976	*19.7.18	Glen, J., Pte., S/9022	* 9.4.17
Ferry, L., Pte., 25310	*22.10.18	Glen, J., Pte., S/22800	*16.12.17
Findlay, S., Pte., S/22427	*24.10.18	Gloag, D. G., Pte., S/9545	† 7.11.15
Finlayson, H., Pte., 310040	* 1.10.18	Goldsmith, M., Sgt., 3/4214	*24.3.18
Finney, G., Pte., 351139	*19.7.18	Gordon, D., Pte., S/3482	*25.9.15
Fisher, C., Pte., S/11910	* 3.5.17	Gordon, P., Pte., 240039	*19.7.18
Fisher, J., Pte., S/40557	*19.10.16	Gordon, W., Pte., 201042	*16.12.17
Fisher, T., Pte., 1786	*19.10.16	Gordon, W., Pte., S/9207	‡14.3.16
Fitchett, W., Pte., S/23251	*1.10.18	Gordon, J. O., Pte., S/3068	*25.9.15
Fitzsimmons, H., Pte., S/21816	*28.9.18	Gorrie, T., L/Cpl., S/5327	†14.10.18
		Gourdie, J., Pte., S/3493	*25.9.15
Flannagan, T., Pte., S/3570	†16.9.15	Gourlay, A., Pte., S/40716	* 9.4.17
Fleming, T. M., Pte., 41510	*19.7.18	Gourlay, A., Pte., S/16651	*12.10.17
Flood, T., Pte., S/3259	*11.8.15	Gourlay, G., L/Cpl., S/18149	*30.9.18
Forbes, J., Pte., 268884	*19.7.18	Gow, D., Pte., S/10342	*25.9.15
Forbes, J., Pte., S/10341	*27.9.15	Gow., J., Pte., S/41518	*30.9.18
Forbes, J., Pte., S/40469	†18.11.16	Goodwillie, A., Pte., S/6577	*27.9.15
Forbes, T., Pte., S/40866	*19.7.18	Graham, J., Cpl., S/7940	*11.7.16
Forbett, J., Pte., S/40137	*12.10.17	Graham, D. C., Pte., S/25903	*24.10.18
Ford, J., Pte., S/8738	*13.7.16	Grainger, A., Pte., S/40475	†20.10.16
Ford, D. McD., Pte., S/11579	*15.7.16	Grainger, W. S., Cpl., S/24118	*23.3.18
Fordyce, W. A., Pte., S/41535	†22.4.18	Gray, C., Pte., S/9295	*13.7.16
Forrest, J., Pte., S/10376	* 9.7.16	Gray, D., Pte., S/43238	*12.10.17
Fraser, F., C.S.M., 9660	*14.8.15	Gray, J., Pte., S/6308	† 7.10.15
Fraser, J., Pte., 235055	*19.7.18	Gray, J., Pte., S/23081	†17.5.18
Fraser, R., Pte., S/19724	*24.3.18	Green, F., L/Cpl., S/10483	*18.7.16
Fraser, M. M., Pte., S/9745	*14.7.16	Green, J., Sgt., S/3923	*25.4.18
Frazer, G., Pte., S/10024	*19.10.16	Green, T. W., Pte., S/12804	†11.7.18
Frazer, W. J., Pte., S/12784	*14.7.16	Gregory, G. L., Pte., 266319	*12.10.17
		Greig, P., Pte., S/2990	*12.10.17
Gabriel, A., Pte., S/16756	†29.10.18	Grierson, D., L/Cpl., S/2967 (M.M.)	*14.7.16
Galloway, J., C.S.M., 5766	*19.7.18		
Galloway, J., Pte., S/2946	†14.4.17	Grewer, A., Pte., S/8243	*26.9.15
Gardiner, J., Pte., S/3689	*14.7.16	Grieve, J., Pte., S/13338	* 9.4.17
Gardner, A. G. M., L/Cpl., S/9187	*18.7.16	Gunn, J., L/Cpl., S/6466	*25.9.15
		Gunn, J., L/Cpl., S/10494	*14.7.16
Garvie, J., Pte., S/8998	‡ 2.11.16	Gunn, J., Pte., S/24060	‡10.4.18
Geary, D. K., Pte., S/23131	*24.3.18	Gunning, D., Pte., S/24120	*23.3.18
George, F. C., L/Cpl., S/9367	*14.7.16	Gunning, J., Pte., S/9221	* 3.5.17
		Guthrie, A., Pte., S/9565	‡ 4.10.16
Georgeson, G., Pte., S/8698	† 9.7.16	Guthrie, A., Pte., S/8697	* 3.5.17
Gibson, A., Pte., S/9892	§ 3.4.18	Guthrie, W., Sgt., 530	†28.12.16
Gibson, J. D., Pte., S/40440	*19.10.16	Guthrie, W. J., Pte., 26139	*24.10.18

APPENDIX IV

Haggarty, C., Pte., S/17651 *21.3.18
Haig, W., Pte., S/13003 † 9.4.17
Haldane, T., Pte., 203182 § 1.3.18
Halliday, J., Pte., S/3790 †15.7.16
Hamilton, A., L/Sgt., S/9286 * 3.5.17
Hamilton, A., Pte., 3/3170 * 7.7.15
Hamilton, E., C.S.M., 7113 *27.9.15
Hamilton, T., Pte., S/3868 *25.9.15
Hannah, J., Pte., S/4283 * 3.5.17
Hannah, T., Pte., S/9941 § 8.5.16
Hargreaves, A., Pte., S/2948 *18.7.16
Harrower, D. J., Pte., S/40791
    *19.7.18
Harris, D., Pte., S/13270 * 9.4.17
Harrison, C., Pte., 3692 *25.9.15
Harrison, A. C., Pte., 10111 †20.10.17
Hart, W., Pte., S/40793 *14.10.18
Hastie, A., Pte., S/4435 * 3.5.17
Hastie, W., L/Cpl., S/10302 *25.9.15
Hay, A., Pte., S/40818 *19.7.18
Hay, J., Pte., S/18252 †12.4.18
Hay, W., Sgt., 290531 *12.10.17
Hazlett, D., Pte., S/5216 *28.9.18
Heaney, J., Pte., S/5594 *18.7.16
Heathcote, J., Pte., S/40771 *12.10.17
Heeley, W. H., Pte., S/11392 †22.7.16
Henderson, A., L/Cpl., S/17595
    *19.7.18
Henderson, A. G., Pte., S/22986
    *19.7.18
Henderson, J., Pte., 3/3381 *18.7.16
Henderson, J., L/Cpl., S/43314
    †17.6.18
Henderson, J., Pte., S/16182 †26.5.17
Henderson, S., Sgt., 3/3309 *10.7.16
Henretty, J., Pte., 292093 *12.10.17
Henry, J. A., Pte., S/40444 *26.3.18
Hepburn, L., Pte., S/16981 * 2.6.17
Hepburn, R., Pte., S/41707 †27.8.18
Heron, J., L/Cpl., S/40477 *13.8.17
Heslin, J., Pte., S/40282 *17.12.17
Hewitt, W., Pte., 3/4276 *28.9.17
Hebenton, G., Pte., 3/6332 *15.7.16
Hickson, H., Pte., S/4278 * 9.4.17
Higgins, F., Pte., S/3485 *14.8.15
Hignett, G. E., L/Cpl., S/10734
    †11.4.17
Hill, J., Pte., S/9133 †23.11.15
Hislop, J., Pte., S/7638 *18.7.16
Hodge, J., Pte., S/19917 * 3.5.17
Hodges, G. W., Pte., S/10208 *25.9.15
Hogg, J., Pte., S/12989 *19.10.16
Hogg, W., L/Cpl., S/3607 *25.9.15
Holland, H., Pte., S/12362 * 1.1.17
Honess, A., Pte., S/11805 †22.10.17
Hood, R., Pte., S/8811 *18.7.16
Horner, J., Pte., S/43044 *22.3.18
Horsburgh, A., Pte., S/9227 †13.11.15
Horsburgh, W., Pte., 3/3147 *15.7.16
Hort, W., Pte., S/7733 *19.7.18
Houghton, W., Pte., S/12192 *15.7.16
Houston, W., Pte., S/9357
    (M.M.) *12.10.17
Howat, E., Pte., S/6549 *11.8.15
Howie, F., Pte., S/18091 †11.3.17
Hughes, J., Pte., S/9919 *14.7.16
Hughes, J., Pte., 285104 † 3.10.18
Hughes, W., Pte., S/3276 *25.9.15
Hunter, A., Pte., 6 *29.1.16
Hunter, W., Pte., S/6395 †27.9.15
Hurst, T. V., Pte., S/17066 * 9.4.17
Husband, W., Pte., 350824 *23.3.18
Husselbee, C. S., Pte., S/3681 *25.9.15
Hutton, P., Sgt., 9828 *19.7.18
Hynd, J. K. A., Pte., S/25832 †24.10.18
Hynd, F., Pte., S/8501 *16.7.16

Imrie, R., Pte., S/6472 † 3.10.15
Inglis, A., Pte., S/12543 *19.7.18
Ireland, D., Pte., S/7212 *25.9.15
Irvine, W., Pte., S/22073 †26.7.18
Izatt, P., Pte., S/43327 †20.10.16

Jackson, J., Pte., S/41583 *14.10.18
Jamieson, D., Pte., S/8939 *17.4.16
Jamieson, G., Pte., S/6280 *11.7.16
Jamieson, W. D., Pte., S/8645 *12.2.16
Japp, D., Pte., S/2915 ‡12.7.16
Jarvis, D., Pte., S/11047 †15.4.17
Jenkins, E., Pte., S/26862 *14.10.18
Johnston, A., Pte., S/16761 †12.6.17
Johnston, C., Pte., 240492 *1.10.18
Johnston, D., Pte., S/9026 †11.7.16
Johnston, G., Pte., S/40734 †13.4.17
Johnston, J., Pte., S/40721 * 3.5.17
Johnston, J., Pte., S/12793 †17.10.16
Johnston, R. J., Pte., S/40752 * 9.4.17
Johnston, T. T., Pte., S/24038
    *24.3.18
Johnston, W., L/Cpl., S/40514
    † 5.2.17
Johnstone, A., Pte., S/2952 *25.9.15
Johnstone, G., Pte., S/24124 †27.4.18
Johnstone, W. N., Pte., S/20758
    *19.7.18
Jones, J., Pte., S/3396 *28.11.15

Kay, J., Cpl., S/8955 * 9.4.17
Keir, W. J., Pte., S/41477 *25.4.18
Keir, W., Pte., S/40479 *19.10.16

THE EIGHTH BATTALION THE BLACK WATCH

Kellas, T T., Pte., S/24125	*21.3.18	Livingston, T., A/L/Sgt., 1971	*19.7.18
Kellock, R. H., Pte., S/12572	*30.6.16	Lockhart, D., L/Cpl., S/3244	*18.7.16
Kelly, J., Pte., S/8512	†19 9.16	Logan, W., Pte., S/7308 (M.M.)	*12.10.17
Kennedy, A., Pte., S/10756	*19.10.16	Logie, J., Pte., S/41530	†25.4.18
Kennedy, J. R., Pte., S/42071	*19.7.18	Longham, P., Pte., S/6457	*14.7.16
Kerr, C., Pte., 267228	*19.7.18	Longmuir, P. W., Pte., S/3898	†19.7.16
Kerr, G. M., Pte., S/17005	*12.10.17	Longmuir, G. W., Pte., S/43024	* 3.5.17
Kerr, R., Pte., S/40562	*12.10.17	Longmuir, W., L/Cpl., 240624	*24.3.18
Kerr, W., Pte., S/22901	* 1.10.18	Lorimer, A., Pte., S/9190	†17.4.17
Kerrigan, J., Pte., S/40744	*24.3.18	Louden, G., A/Cpl., S/11358	† 3.5.17
Kidd, J., Pte., S/43317	* 3.11.17	Louden, J., Cpl., S/3240	*25.9.15
Kidd, J., Pte., 202597	*19.7.18	Louden, R., Pte., S/40703	*12.10.17
Kiddie, A. M., Pte., 267920	*19.7.18	Low, D. M., L/Cpl., 265427	*23.3.18
Kimm, R., Pte., S/6682	*18.7.16	Low, P., Pte., S/17564	*10.4.18
King, A., Pte., S/6469	*14.7.16	Low, R., Pte., S/12759	*17.9.17
King, T. A., Pte., S/15963	*19.7.18	Low, S., Pte., S/40432	*22.3.18
Kinleyside, H. S., Pte., S/9202	*22.3.18	Low, W. H., Pte., S/41520	*19.7.18
Kinnear, W., Pte., S/11893	* 3.5.17	Low, W., Pte., S/10373	*25.9.15
Kinnear, W. H., Cpl., S/5141	*27.9.15	Lunan, T., Pte., S/8799	*18.7.16
Kirby, W., L/Cpl., S/8095	12.10.17	Lunn, G., Pte., S/19925	* 3.5.17
Kirk, A., Pte., S/6481	*27.1.17	Lynch, G., Pte., 2697	*27.9.15
Kirk, G., Pte., S/16400	* 9.4.17	Lynch, J., Pte., S/3657	†20.9.15
Kyle, A., Pte., S/10779	* 7.4.17	Lyon, J., Pte., S/20874	*20.7.18
		Lyon, R., Pte., S/11212	*19.10.16
Laing, G., Pte., S/3336	† 7.11.15		
Laird, A., L/Cpl., S/7772	*25.9.15	Macaulay, J. M., Pte., S/8983 (M.M.)	*12.10.17
Laird, A. S., Pte., S/3412	*14.7.16	MacDonald, A., Pte., S/21752	†29.3.18
Lamb, S., Sgt., 1487	*25.9.15	MacDonald, R., Pte., S/41543	*19.7.18
Lambert, D., L/Cpl., S/3735	*14.10.15	MacDougall, I., Pte., 350357	* 1.10.18
Lamont, P. J., Pte., S/24126	§ 7.5.18	MacFarlane, J., Pte., S/9800	* 9.4.17
Lane, F., Pte., 12450	* 3.5.17	MacKay, W. W., Pte., S/41495	*25.4.18
Langlands, A., Pte., S/40516	* 3.5.17	MacKenzie, D. C., Pte., S/42077	*30.9.18
Lauchbery, R., Cpl., S/7328	†15.7.16	Magie, L. B. K., Pte., S/40736	* 9.4.17
Laughlin, D., Pte., S/6342	*14.7.16	Maguire, J., Pte., S/4182	*12.5.16
Laurence, W., Pte., S/13461	*23.3.18	Mair, A., Pte., S/7365	† 6.8.16
Law, J., L/Sgt., S/3322	*25.9.15	Malcolm, J., Sgt., S/2905	†13.8.15
Lawson, J., Pte., S/9840	†19.7.16	Malpas, H. J., Pte., S/40567	* 3.5.17
Lawson, P. D., Pte., 268713	* 3.5.17	Malpas, S. E., L/Cpl., S/40508	†19.10.16
Ledger, E., Pte., S/4604	*13.7.16		
Ledingham, G. M., Pte., S/16690	*19.7.18	Marlow, J. M., Pte., S/41499	*25.4.18
Lees, G., Pte., S/12513	*18.7.16	Marshall, P., Sgt., S/40436 (M.M.)	*19.7.18
Leitch, J., Pte., S/6470	*25.9.15	Marshall, A. W., L/Cpl., S/10491	*21.10.15
Leith, A. M., Pte., S/24039	*24.3.18		
Leitham, A., Pte., S/40749	* 3.5.17		
Leslie, A., Cpl., S/8004	*14.7.16		
Leslie, H., Pte., S/12022	*12.10.17		
Lester, A. W., Pte., S/8757	†16.7.16		
Lewis, H., L/Cpl., S/10275	*14.7.16		
Lindsay, A., Pte., S/9001	*12.10.17		
Linkston, W., Pte., S/12811	*22.10.16	Martin, A. T., Pte., S/22808	† 1.4.18
Little, R., Pte., S/8617	* 7.11.15	Martin, J. H., L/Cpl., S/8610	*14.7.16
Littlejohn, D., Sgt., S/3445 (M.M.)	* 3.5.17		

APPENDIX IV

Mason, A., Cpl., S/2961 *25.9.15
Masterton, G., Pte., S/8476 *12.10.17
Masterton, J., Pte., S/18387 *15.6.18
Mathieson, L., Pte., S/40043
 (M.M.) *23.3.18
Matthew, J., Sgt., S/3618 * 9.4.17
Matthew, R., Pte., 202037 †16.10.17
Maxwell, A., Pte., S/11700 *19.7.18
Maxwell, D., Pte., S/3696 *28.7.15
McAlise, T., Cpl., 3/2958 *16.7.16
McAllister, A., Pte., S/6555 *27.9.15
McAndrew, J., L/Cpl., S/3045
 *19/10/16
McAndrew, J., Pte., 291127 †25.6.18
McAngus, A., Pte., S/7586 *14.7.16
McAra, J. S., Pte., S/40913 *27.6.18
McAvoy, J., Pte., S/9873 *21.10.15
McCafferty, F., Pte., S/10441 *19.7.16
McCann, P., Pte., 201807 *12.10.17
McClymont, D., Pte., S/8425
 *19.10.16
McColm, A., L/Cpl., S/6551 * 9.7.16
McCondoch, R., Sgt., 2305 * 9.4.17
McConnell, J. A., Pte., S/40727
 *25.5.18
McCormack, W. H., Pte., S/6539
 *27.9.15
McCready, W., L/Cpl., S/3759
 *25.9.15
McCue, J., Pte., S/41567 *28.5.18
McDonald, A., A/Sgt., S/17540
 (M.M.) *19.7.18
McDonald, A., Pte., S/10343 *21.10.15
McDonald, D., Pte., S/3409 *27.9.15
McDonald, G., Pte., S/9042 *21.11.15
McDonald, G., L/Cpl., S/7765
 *25.9.15
McDonald, J., Pte., S/41725 † 2.10.18
McDonald, J. E., L/Cpl., 268723
 *12.10.17
McDonald, O., Pte., 10085 *16.4.17
McDonald, R., Pte., S/6219 †30.9.15
McDonald, R., Pte., S/16612 * 3.5.17
McDonald, W., Pte., S/4746 †21.8.16
McDonough, J. O., Pte., S/12374
 *13.7.16
McDougall, D., Pte., S/8015 *14.7.16
McDougall, T., Pte., S/4237 *18.7.16
McDowall, A., Pte., S/8722 †19.7.16
McFarlane, A., Pte., S/10427 *14.7.16
McFarlane, G., Pte., S/16920 *12.10.17
McFarlane, J., A/Sgt., 7314 *12.10.17
McFarlane, J., C.S.M., S/3323 *24.3.18
McFarlane, T. B., Pte., S/22923
 *24.3.18

McFarlane, W., Pte., S/16683 * 9.4.17
McFarlane, W. P., Pte., S/43601
 †14.10.18
McGibbon, A., L/Cpl., 10388 *14.9.16
McGilvray, J. A., Pte., S/12569
 †26.7.16
McGinty, J., Pte., S/9889 *14.7.16
McGregor, D., L/Cpl., S/10294
 *23.3.18
McGregor, G., Pte., 2296 *12.10.17
McGregor, J., L/Cpl., S/11338
 (M.M.) * 3.5.17
McGregor, J., Pte., 266302 †16.12.17
McGregor, R., Pte., 266521 *19.7.18
McGregor, W., Pte., S/11188 *19.7.18
McGregor, W. R., Pte., 200423
 † 3.10.18
McGuiffick, P., Pte., S/41532 *25.4.18
McGuire, H., Pte., S/3709 *25.9.15
McIndeor, P., Pte., 285033 *19.7.18
McIntosh, A., Pte., S/3097 †10.4.17
McIntosh, J., Pte., 203629 *14.10.18
McIntosh, J., Pte., S/3917 †12.7.16
McIntosh, W. B., Pte., S/12598
 *30.7.16
McIntyre, A., L/Cpl., S/8650 *28.9.18
McIntyre, J., Pte., S/3145 *25.9.15
McIntyre, J., Pte., S/42076 *19.7.18
McIntyre, J., Pte., 3/731 †12.10.17
McKaig, J., Pte., S/10309 †21.10.15
McKail, J., Pte., 292778 †28.12.17
McKay, D., Pte., S/3327 *25.9.15
McKay, N., Pte., S/3722 *18.9.15
McKay, W., Pte., S/24041 †30.9.18
McKenna, T. C., Pte., S/41746
 * 2.10.18
McKenzie, H., Pte., S/24244 *30.9.18
McKenzie, J., Cpl., S/3066 *17.7.16
McKenzie, W., Pte., 266708 *12.10.17
McKenzie, W., Sgt., S/3167 *25.9.15
McKie, M., Pte., S/3720 *16.7.16
McKinlay, J., L/Cpl., S/3816 *27.9.15
McKinnon, J., Pte., 17605 * 9.4.17
McLaggan, W., L/Cpl., S/22000
 †26.11.18
McLaren, J., Pte., S/3877 *25.9.15
McLaren, W., Pte., 3/2752 *19.10.16
McLaren, W. M., Pte., S/26123
 *24.10.18
McLaughlin, E., Pte., S/8997 *21.10.15
McLaughlin, R. F., Sgt., S/8482
 (M.M.) †29.9.18
McLean, A., L/Cpl., S/7964 *25.9.15
McLean, A., Pte., S/40575 *20.10.16
McLean, J., Pte., S/7208 *25.9.15

THE EIGHTH BATTALION THE BLACK WATCH

McLean, M., Pte., 202224 *19.7.18
McLean, T., A/Sgt., S/40506 * 9.4.17
McLeary, J., Pte., S/11618 *14.7.16
McLennan, J., Cpl., S/8669 *14.7.16
McLennan, J. D., Pte., S/41570
         *27.5.18
McLeod, J., Pte., S/9826 *24.3.18
McLeod, J., Sgt., 7401 †11.4.17
McLeod, J., Pte., 475 † 3.5.17
McLeod, R., Pte., S/3352 *27.9.15
McLorie, D., Pte., 7812 *14.7.16
MacMurchie, J. S., Sgt., 2301
 (D.C.M., M.M. and Bar) * 3.5.17
McMath, J., Pte., S/3630 *25.9.15
McNaughton, A., Pte., S/6377
         † 5.10.15
McNaughton, W., Pte., S/22884
         *19.7.18
McMillan, J., L/Sgt., 2616 *23.3.18
McMillan, J., Pte., S/12853 †18.10.16
McNeil, J., L/Cpl., S/40517 *19.10.16
McNeill, E., Pte., S/5344 †15.7.16
McPheat, J., Pte., S/3517 *25.9.15
McPhee, J., Pte., S/6047 *13.7.16
McPherson, D., Pte., 202298 * 1.10.18
McSween, T., Pte., 8522 *22.3.18
McTavish, D., Pte., 266988 *12.10.17
McWhirr, T., Pte., S/6511 † 9.4.17
Mears, C. H., Pte., S/19803 *13.10.17
Meek, G., Pte., 200995 *14.10.18
Meldrum, H., Pte., S/5333 †19.7.16
Meldrum, J., Pte., S/40519 † 4.5.17
Meldrum, J. G., Pte., S/17061 * 9.4.17
Meldrum, W. R., L/Cpl., S/8806
 (M.M.) *18.7.16
Mellon, J., Pte., S/3004 *27.9.15
Menzies, A., Pte., S/17947 *16.12.17
Menzies, R. G., L/Cpl., 265912
         *16.7.18
Metcalfe, A., L/Cpl., S/17031 * 1.10.18
Millar, J., Pte., S/7684 *25.9.15
Millar, J., 3/3059 *27.9.15
Millar, J., Pte., S/10002 *27.2.16
Miller, R., Pte., S/9050 * 3.5.17
Miller, W., Pte., S/10260 ‡ 3.8.16
Miller, W. B., L/Cpl., S/43417
         *28.9.18
Miller, W. T., Cpl., S/40438 * 9.4.17
Milne, J., Pte., S/17539 * 1.1.17
Milne, J., Pte., S/9029 *24.3.18
Milne, T., Pte., S/3234 * 9.4.17
Milne, T. A. D., Pte., S/3205 *13.7.16
Mitchell, D., Pte., 16427 *12.10.17
Mitchell, D. McL., Pte., S/9224
         *16.10.15

Mitchell, J., Pte., S/3611 *18.7.16
Mitchell, J., Sgt., S/3774 *25.9.15
Mitchell, R., Pte., S/12993 * 1.1.17
Mochan, D., Pte., S/5592 *22.3.18
Moir, J., Pte., S/3826 *16.7.16
Monro, A., Pte., S/10378 *25.9.15
Morgan, A., Sgt., S/6679 ‡ 8.10.17
Morgan, R., Pte., S/6358 *27.9.15
Morrison, A., Pte., S/2995 *27.9.15
Morrison, A., Pte., S/7294 ‡25.4.17
Morrison, D., Pte., S/13164 ‡25.1.18
Morrison, J., Pte., S/40488 *19.10.16
Morrison, J., Pte., 2434 *25.9.15
Morrison, W., Pte., S/10542 †20.7.18
Moses, J. P., Pte., S/2937 ‡ 1.5.15
Moulter, E., Pte., S/19930 * 3.5.17
Mount, J., A/Cpl., 3/2499 *19.7.18
Moyes, A., Pte., 202104 *19.7.18
Muir, H., Pte., S/6195 *16.4.17
Muirhead, R., Pte., S/7671 *25.9.15
Mullins, J., Pte., S/6159 *12.10.17
Mumford, W., A/L/Cpl., S/16582
         * 19.7.18
Munley, W., L/Cpl., S/3500 *16.7.16
Munn, J., L/Cpl., S/10422 *15.7 16
Munro, J., Pte., S/8664 *12.10.17
Murdoch, R., Pte., 351095 *21.3.18
Murphy, T., Pte., 8073 *25.9.15
Murray, A. G., Pte., S/10421
 (M.M.) *15.6.18
Murray, C., Pte., 996 †15.10.18
Murray, D., Pte., S/41723 * 2.8.18
Murray, F., Pte., 3/2344 *19.7.18
Murray, G. A., Pte., S/19968
         *28.9.17
Murray, J., Pte., S/24713 *14.10.18
Murray, R., C.S.M., 1606 *19.7.18
Murray, W., Pte., S/8808 †10.4.17
Murrie, A., A/Sgt., 268719 *12.10.17

Napier, J., Pte., S/3846 † 1.10.15
Napier, W., Pte., S/3092 *25.9.15
Nelson, J., Pte., S/9532
 (M.M.) *12.10.17
Nelson, S., Sgt., 846 *19.7.18
Ness, G. S., Pte., S/14567 *12.10.17
Ness, J., Pte., S/8147 *12.10.17
Neville, J., Pte., S/41748 †21.10.18
Nicol, D., Pte., S/16614 †10.4.17
Nicol. W., Pte., 3/2498 †17.7.16
Nicholson, R., Pte., S/18880 *31.10.18
Nicholson, R., Pte., S/2982 † 4.10.15
Nisbitt, H., Pte., S/5068 *19.7.18
Noble, T. H., Pte., 291805 *21.3.18
Norrie, A., Pte., S/42008 † 6.9.17

APPENDIX IV

Oag, W., Pte., S/7185 — *25.9.15
Ogilvie, G., Pte., S/9795 — *24.3.18
O'Kell, J. E., Pte., S/12133 — * 9.10.16
Ord, A., Pte., S/3249 — * 9.8.15
Orr, D., Pte., S/17722 — *23.3.18
Osborne, A., Cpl., S/6290 — † 1.8.16
Osler, C., L/Cpl., 17610 — †12.4.17
Oswald, W., Pte., S/13360 — *12.10.17

Page, H., Pte., S/10444 — †18.7.16
Page, R., Pte., S/40581 — *19.10.16
Park, G., Pte., S/40583 — * 9.4.18
Parker, R., Pte., S/8841 — †19.10.16
Parker, T., Pte., S/18412 — *12.10.17
Parker, W., Pte., S/2801 — *25.9.15
Paterson, R., Pte., S/3660 — *25.9.15
Paterson, R., Cpl., S/3141 — *27.9.15
Paton, A., Pte., 235057 — †23.4.18
Paton, D., Pte., S/7316 — *19.10.16
Payne, F., Pte., 291717 — †25.4.18
Peddie, J., Pte., S/20927 — *12.10.17
Peden, A., Pte., S/8861 — *21.11.15
Peden, W., Pte., S/10820 — †13.12.17
Peggie, A., Pte., 203157 — *24.3.18
Penman, A., Pte., S/9032 — §22.7.18
Penman, A., Pte., S/7324 — *25.9.15
Peterson, P. J., Sgt., S/13096 — *28.9.18
Petrie, J. L., Pte., S/7972 — *27.9.15
Petrie, P., L/Sgt., S/3645 — *27.9.15
Philip, G., Pte., S/41469 — *14.10.18
Phillip, G., Pte., S/9369 — *19.7.18
Phillips, G., Pte., S/3353 — *25.9.15
Phillips, W., Pte., 240374 — *19.7.18
Philp, H., Pte., S/40767 — * 9.4.17
Philp, J., Pte., 267766 — †12.4.18
Plumley, G., Pte., S/19934 — * 3.5.17
Pollock, J., Pte., S/3552 — *25.9.15
Porter, J., Pte., S/41481 — *19.7.18
Potter, G. A., Pte., S/41750 — *28.9.18
Potter, J., L/Cpl., S/6553 — †26.9.15
Pratt, A., Pte., S/2959 — *25.9.15
Pratt, G., Pte., S/6260 — *24.9.15
Pratt, J., Pte., S/40088 — † 4.6.17
Preston, W. J. H., Pte., S/9319 — †16.7.16
Pringle, W. F., Pte., S/3589 — *27.9.15
Proudfoot, A., Pte., 266077 — †26.7.18
Proudfoot, J., Pte., 2684 — †15.7.16
Pryde, A., Pte., S/12821 — † 8.2.17
Puller, J., Pte., S/9394 — *19.7.18
Purves, D. A., Cpl., S/3804 — *25.9.15

Quinn, H., Pte., S/3414 — *18.7.16
Quinn, R., Pte., S/41474 — *19.7.18

Rae, A., Pte., S/41460 — *19.7.18
Rae, W., Pte., S/41448 — †19.4.18
Raeburn, R., Pte., 17534 — * 3.5.17
Rafferty, P., Pte., S/3400 — * 7.7.15
Ramage, A., L/Cpl., S/3360 — ‡25.7.18
Ramage, H., Sgt., S/2962 — *12.10.17
Ramsay, A., Pte., S/3557 — *16.7.15
Ramsay, J., Pte., S/43737 — †15.10.18
Ramsay, W., Pte., S/15524 — †19.10.17
Rankin, J., Pte., S/6270 — † 9.7.16
Rankin, W. A., Pte., S/13087 — * 3.5.17
Rattray, C., Pte., S/3095 — *12.10.17
Rattray, D. L., Pte., S/41464 — † 3.10.18
Reekie, A., Pte., 266928 — † 7.10.18
Reid, J., Pte., S/42082 — *15.6.18
Reid, W., Pte., S/40586 — * 3.5.17
Reid, W. C., Pte., S/3477 — * 3.5.17
Reilly, W., Pte., S/3375 — *25.9.15
Rennie, J. R., Pte., S/42016 — *24.10.18
Rennie, W., Cpl., S/9244 (M.M.) — * 3.5.17
Renton, D., Pte., S/7719 — †18.7.16
Reoch, J., Pte., S/18785 — †29.11.17
Riley, R., Pte., S/43019 — *21.3.18
Rintoul, R., Pte., S/16598 — * 9.4.17
Ritchie, E. G., Pte., S/23113 — * 1.10.18
Ritchie, F. S., Pte., S/42019 — *19.7.18
Roberts, A., Pte., S/43400 — *12.10.17
Roberts, W., Cpl., S/9668 — †12.4.17
Robertson, D. D., Pte., S/13349 — *24.3.18
Robertson, D. E., L/Cpl., S/9365 — * 3.5.17
Robertson, E., Pte., S/25833 — *14.10.18
Robertson, J., Pte., S/3556 — *17.7.16
Robertson, J., Pte., S/16317 — * 3.5.17
Robertson, J., L/Cpl., 293121 — *23.3.18
Robertson, J. S., Pte., S/24292 — *20.10.18
Robertson, P., Pte., S/10379 — * 9.4.17
Robertson, R., Pte., S/9315 (M.M.) — * 3.5.17
Robertson, R., Pte., 268869 — *16.4.18
Robson, D., Pte., S/10367 — *24.3.18
Robson, G., Pte., 8560 — *14.7.16
Rochford, J., L/Cpl., S/3510 — *19.7.18
Rodger, J., Pte., S/15914 — *19.10.18
Rodger, J., Pte., S/3531 — † 8.10.15
Rodger, J. D., Pte., S/43012 — *19.7.18
Rodger, J., Pte., S/11525 — † 7.5.16
Rodgers, J. T., Pte., S/19936 — * 3.5.17
Rose, G., Pte., 41573 — *27.5.18
Ross, A., Pte., S/40588 — * 3.5.17
Ross, C., Pte., S/42025 — *19.7.18
Ross, J. P., L/Cpl., S/18226 — *14.10.18

Ross, J., Pte., S/9188	*18.7.16	Sloan, J. R., Pte., S/18839	*12.10.17
Ross, J., Pte., S/6430	*13.12.15	Smart, A., Pte., S/41512	† 6.8.18
Ross, T. M., Pte., 203316	*12.7.18	Smart, A., Cpl., S/43010	* 3.5.17
Rousell, G., Pte., S/6462	* 9.4.17	Smedley, J., Pte., S/10264	*14.7.16
Rowell, J. G., L/Cpl., S/10457	* 1.4.16	Smith, A., L/Cpl., S/2992	† 1.8.16
		Smith, A., Pte., S/8672	* 7.11.15
Roy, G. F., Pte., S/41781	* 1.10.18	Smith, A., Pte., S/16385	†20.7.18
Rugg, S., Pte., S/22967	*23.7.18	Smith, A. H., Cpl., S/3608	*18.7.16
Russell, J., Cpl., S/6475	*14.7.16	Smith, A. P., Pte., S/18563	*12.10.17
Russell, J., Pte., S/16839	†19.2.17	Smith, C., Pte., S/8924	†30.11.15
Rutherford, J., Sgt., S/5144	*20.10.16	Smith, D., Pte., S/11053	*14.7.16
Rutledge, R. J. J., Pte., 202873	†13.10.17	Smith, G., A/Sgt., S/3024	* 2.10.18
		Smith, G., Pte., S/6531	*14.8.15
		Smith, J., A/Cpl., S/2809	* 2.6.17
Sandeman, F., Pte., S/23141	* 1.10.18	Smith, J., Pte., S/10370	*25.9.15
Sanderson, W., Pte., 3715	*25.9.15	Smith, J., L/Cpl., S/11054	* 9.6.16
Saunders, H., Pte., S/13269	*12.10.17	Smith, J., Pte., S/19974	* 3.5.17
Saunders, J., Pte., S/40738	*12.10.17	Smith, J., L/Cpl., S/2836	*27.9.15
Scott, A., Pte., S/22906	*19.7.18	Smith, O., Pte., S/6425	†25.3.18
Scott, A., Pte., 10077	†24.2.16	Smith, P., Sgt., 203515	*23.3.18
Scott, C., Pte., S/17021	‡29.1.19	Smith, S. P., Pte., S/19941	* 3.5.17
Scott, G., Pte., S/9033	*18.7.16	Smith, T., Pte., S/17613	* 9.4.17
Scott, G., Pte., S/41486	†20.7.18	Smith, V. W., Pte., S/42035	*19.7.18
Scott, J. L., Pte., 315215	*19.7.18	Smith, W., L/Cpl., S/9019	*19.10.16
Scott, J., Pte., S/25719	*14.10.18	Sneddon, J., Pte., S/9045	†10.11.15
Scott, T., Pte., S/3418	*27.9.15	Somerville, J., Pte., S/16430	§18.5.18
Scott, W., Pte., S/12184	*18.7.16	Spark, J. G. H., Pte., S/11846	*12.9.16
Scott, W., Pte., S/22129	† 3.1.18	Speed, A., Pte., S/43130	*19.10.16
Scott, W., Pte., S/40592	* 9.4.17	Spence, A., Pte., 350252	*19.7.18
Scoular, H. R., Pte., S/12917	* 9.4.17	Spence, W. P., Cpl., S/41533	*14.10.18
Scullion, G., Pte., S/6359	*25.9.15	Spencer, A., Pte., S/12457	*19.7.16
Seaton, T., L/Cpl., S/40698	*19.7.18	Sproll, T. S., Pte., S/10196	*15.7.16
Shanks, J. R., Pte., S/15043	* 9.4.17	Stairmand, W., Pte., 292019	†20.9.18
Shannon, J., Pte., S/42030	*19.7.18	Stark, W., Pte., 268225	*19.7.18
Sharp, D., Pte., S/40596	*12.10.17	Starr, A., Pte., 10243	* 3.5.17
Sharp, P., L/Cpl., 310149	* 2.10.18	Stevenson, A., Pte., S/3666	*27.9.15
Sharpe, J., Pte., S/6351	†14.12.15	Stevenson, A., Pte., S/41575	*16.4.18
Shaw, W., Pte., S/3289	*27.9.15	Stevenson, D., Pte., S/8497	*18.7.16
Shepherd, A. B., Pte., S/41482	*19.7.18	Stevenson, J. McP., Pte., S/22851	*19.4.18
Shepherd, G., Pte., S/43072	*24.3.18	Stewart, A. J., Pte., 268216	*19.7.18
Shepherd, J. L., Sgt., 9970	*25.4.18	Stewart, C., Pte., S/7327	*25.9.15
Shepherd, W., Pte., S/6309	*27.9.15	Stewart, C. H., Pte., S/6266	*25.9.15
Shields, A. N., Pte., S/9243	*18.7.16	Stewart, D. R., Pte., S/11757	† 6.8.16
Short, J., Pte., S/7319	*27.9.15	Stewart, F., Cpl., S/8810	*10.7.16
Sim, J., L/Cpl., 292003	*19.7.18	Stewart, G., Pte., S/17776	*12.10.17
Sim, T., Pte., S/8523	*18.7.15	Stewart, G., Pte., 267554	*22.3.18
Simpson, D., Pte., S/3019	*24.3.18	Stewart, G., Pte., S/22103	*16.4.18
Simpson, G., Sgt., 3/3168	*27.9.15	Stewart, H., Pte., S/12608	*28.9.17
Simpson, T., Pte., S/3007	*18.7.16	Stewart, J., L/Cpl., S/3266	*13.7.16
Sinclair, J., Pte., S/41761	*14.10.18	Stewart, W., Pte., S/3751	*27.9.15
Sinclair, W. J., Pte., S/3549	†31.12.17	Stirling, A., Pte., S/22848	*19.7.18
Skae, J. B., Pte., S/8671	*19.5.16	Stocks, A., Pte., S/10350	†17.10.15
Sloan, D., Pte., S/9311	* 1.1.17	Strachan, J. M., Sgt., S/8717	†19.7.18
Sloan, J., Sgt., S/3851 (M.M.)	† 1.2.17	Strain, D., Pte., S/7270	*27.9.15

APPENDIX IV

Stronach, T., Pte., S/22276 *14.6.18
Sturgeon, E., Pte., S/6989 *14.7.16
Sturrock, D., Pte., S/12903 *25.5.18
Sturrock, G., L/Cpl., S/43013 *19.10.16
Sutherland, A., Pte., S/41455 *19.7.18
Sutherland, J. N., Pte., S/16339
    * 9.4.17
Sutherland, T., L/Cpl., 7513 *25.9.15
Swandle, J., Pte., S/7193 *25.9.18
Swanson, M., Sgt., S/4176 *12.10.17
Sweeney, E., Pte., S/41756 *14.10.18
Sweeney, W., Pte., S/41472 †27.9.18
Swinley, G., Pte., S/2945 †14.10.17
Swinley, R., Pte., S/4584 §23.7.15
Syme, J., Pte., 12470 †14.4.17
Symon, D., Cpl., 266429 *19.7.18

Taggart, J., Pte., S/10081 *14.7.16
Taylor, D. W., Pte., S/40255 *19.7.18
Taylor, D., Pte., S/2828 ‡29.1.18
Taylor, E., A/Sgt., 19944 *22.10.18
Taylor, G., Pte., S/6390 *25.9.15
Taylor, J., Pte., S/2829 *25.9.15
Taylor, J., Pte., 266466 *12.10.17
Taylor, T. L., L/Cpl., S/3540 †18.9.15
Taylor, W. R., Pte., S/25562 †26.10.18
Taylor, W. R., Pte., S/6501 *19.7.15
Tennant, J., L/Cpl., S/16309 *12.10.17
Thain, H., Pte., 265736 §11.9.18
Thom, A., Pte., S/41456 †11.4.18
Thompson, G. G. B., Pte., S/42047
    *16.4.18
Thompson, T., Pte., S/8934 *28.3.16
Thompson, V. L., A/Cpl., S/40434
    *19.10.18
Thomson, A., Pte., 8419
    (M.M.) *19.7.18
Thomson, A. J., Pte., S/41414 *19.7.18
Thomson, C. R., Pte., S/42046
    *19.7.18
Thomson, D., Pte., S/3806 *25.9.15
Thomson, J., Pte., 3/3064 *13.7.16
Thomson, J., Pte., 2737 * 1.11.17
Thomson, J., Cpl., S/3876 *25.9.15
Thomson, L., Pte., S/12809 *19.10.16
Thomson, P., Pte., S/6447 *15.7.16
Thomson, R., L/Cpl., S/42066
    † 7.10.18
Thomson, W., Pte., S/2932 *25.9.15
Threlfell, A., Pte., S/9897 * 3.5.17
Todd, A., L/Cpl., S/4417 *27.3.18
Todd, H., Pte., S/42050 *19.7.18
Todd, M., Pte., S/3130 *25.9.15
Tomkins, P., Pte., S/17615 * 3.5.17
Tonner, C., Pte., S/3475 †25.9.15

Townley, W., Pte., S/24048 *24.7.18
Trench, J., Pte., S/11442 * 9.4.17
Tucker, R., Pte., S/40275 † 5.10.18
Tulloch, W. G. J., Pte., S/41576
    *19.7.18
Tully, B., Pte., S/42083 *19.7.18
Tully, H., Pte., S/7215 *19.7.16
Tully, W., Pte., S/7216 *25.9.15
Tunstall, A., Pte., S/3410 *19.10.16
Turnbull, G., Pte., S/42051 † 3.8.18
Turnbull, S. H., Pte., 290443 *19.7.18
Turner, E., Pte., S/8629 *17.7.16
Turner, R. W., Pte., 241251 *12.10.17

Vass, T. K., Pte., S/40757
    (M.M.) * 3.5.17
Vaughan, D., Pte., S/22558 *22.3.18
Vowell, R., Pte., S/40605 *23.3.18

Wade, W., Pte., S/41768 *29.9.18
Wagstaff, T., Pte., S/3275 *25.9.15
Walkden, A., Pte., 3699 * 6.10.15
Walker, A., Pte., S/16605 * 3.5.17
Walker, H., Pte., S/40928 *24.3.18
Walker, J., Pte., S/7676 *27.9.15
Walters, I., Pte., 3/2143 * 3.5.17
Wann, A., Pte., 293001 †16.10.17
Wann, J., Pte., S/8766 †30.3.16
Ward, J., Pte., S/11340 *15.7.16
Ward, J., Pte., 293199 *16.4.18
Watson, A., Pte., S/17581 * 3.5.17
Watson, D., Sgt., S/2931 ‡27.12.16
Watson, T., Pte., S/6543 *27.9.15
Watt, D., Pte., S/4012 †18.7.16
Watt, P., Pte., S/3180 *27.9.15
Watt, W., Pte., 3/3925 * 9.4.16
Webster, D., Pte., S/42056 *19.7.18
Webster, J., Pte., 292953 †20.12.17
Welsby, W., Pte., S/12357 *18.7.16
Welsh, T. R., Pte., S/6494 *25.9.15
Welsh, W., Pte., S/9943 *14.10.18
Wemyss, W., Pte., S/9914 *17.7.16
Whitewell, V., Pte., S/26055 *14.10.18
Whitson, J., Pte., 291642 †27.4.18
Whyte, A., Pte., S/3121 *14.7.16
Whyte, A., Pte., S/40612 *19.10.16
Whyte, J., Pte., S/8784 *14.7.16
Wibberley, C. H., Pte., S/10140
    * 3.5.17
Wilkie, C. J. P., Pte., S/17767 † 2.4.18
Wilkie, G., Pte., S/40608 †28.3.18
Wilkinson, J. C., Pte., S/12561
    † 6.1.17
Williamson, A., Pte., S/41471 †26.7.18
Williamson, J., Pte., S/24346 *15.6.18

THE EIGHTH BATTALION THE BLACK WATCH

Wilson, C. S., Pte., S/40615   * 9.4.17
Wilson, D., L/Cpl., 3/3014   *27.9.15
Wilson, D. G., Pte., S/6548   *25.9.15
Wilson, F., Pte., S/9356   †15.5.16
Wilson, H. C., Cpl., 3/3428   ‡28.7.16
Wilson, J., Cpl., S/6278   *13.7.16
Wilson, J., Pte., S/43267   *12.10.17
Wilson, R., Pte., 350803   *22.3.18
Wilson, T., Pte., S/43319   * 3.5.17
Wilson, T. S., Pte., S/7266   †16.7.16
Wingate, R., L/Cpl., S/8173   *14.9.16
Winn, A., Pte., S/9808   †25.3.18
Wonnacott, W. H. S., Pte., S/18822   *12.10.17
Wood, C., Pte., S/12649   *30.7.16
Wood, J., Pte., S/15501   † 5.5.17
Woods, T., Pte., S/9040   †20.10.15
Woods, T., Pte., S/6533   *27.9.15
Woolnough, F. J., L/Cpl., 17536   * 3.5.17
Wright, D., Pte., S/23279   *19.7.18
Wright, J. H., Pte., 292712   †13.11.17

Yeadon, N., Pte., S/11109   * 3.5.17
Yellowlees, J., Cpl., S/7677   *16.3.16
Young, A., Pte., S/43242   *25.12.17
Young, A. M., Pte., S/40619   *23.3.18
Young, H., Pte., S/3677   *25.9.15
Young, J., L/Cpl., S/2861   *27.9.15
Young, J. F., Cpl., S/3637   †19.5.16
Young, P., Pte., S/16459   †18.4.17
Young, W., Pte., S/7693   †27.7.16
Young, W., Pte., 201807   *23.12.17
Younger, G., Pte., 291084   *11.10.18

APPENDIX V
HONOURS AND AWARDS
The Eighth Battalion
D.S.O.

Lieut.-Colonel Sir G. W. Abercromby, Bart.
Major R. N. Duke.
Lieut.-Colonel G. B. Duff.
Major W. French.
Major R. W. Hadow.
Major N. G. B. Henderson.
Capt. L. G. Miles.

Bar to M.C.

Major W. French.
Lieut. D. A. Soutar.

M.C.

2nd Lieut. P. J. Alexander.
Lieut. W. Austin.
Major R. E. Anstruther.
Lieut. J. V. Bates.
2nd Lieut. A. Campsie.
Capt. R. N. Duke.
Capt. E. L. O. Ewing.
Capt. J. L. S. Ewing.
Major W. French.
Capt. G. B. Gilroy.
Lieut. A. Glen.
Capt. P. Goudy.
Lieut. A. L. G. Hamilton.
Lieut. A. W. R. Miller.
Capt. The Rev. O. B. Milligan.
Lieut. A. L. Milroy.
R.S.M. J. Mitchell.
Capt. R. N. M. Murray.
2nd Lieut. J. M. McDonald.
Lieut. A. L. McLean, R.A.M.C.
2nd Lieut. R. Potter.
2nd Lieut. A. Proudfoot.
Capt. F. L. Reeves.
2nd Lieut. A. S. Ritchie.
Lieut. J. K. A. Robertson.
Capt. I. W. W. Shepherd.
2nd Lieut. W. L. Shiach.
2nd Lieut. D. A. Soutar.
2nd Lieut. D. H. Sutherland.
Capt. N. R. Taylor.
2nd Lieut. G. L. Yule.

Bar to D.C.M.

Pte. T. May.
C.S.M. P. McArthur.

D.C.M.

Sgt. J. Anderson.
A/Sgt. R. Barclay.
Sgt. G. Birrell, M.M.
C.S.M. A. Bissett.
C.Q.M.S. W. Clark.
Sgt. M. Corbett.
Sgt. P. Craig.
Sgt. G. Cowie.
Corpl. G. S. Doig.
Sgt. C. Eggie.
A/Corpl. T. Ferguson.
Sgt. A. C. Gammie.
Corpl. A. Gray.
A/Corpl. J. Halkett.
Pte. T. May.
L/Corpl. J. M. Macdonald.
C.S.M. D. Mitchell.
R.S.M. J. Mitchell.
C.S.M. A. Moir, M.M.
Sgt. A. Murray.
C.S.M. P. McArthur.
Sgt. W. McDougall.
A/Sgt. J. McFarlane.
C.S.M. J. McHardy.
Pte. A. McIntosh.
Pte. W. Paterson.
Sgt. McN. N. Peacock.
C.S.M. H. Redpath, M.M.
Pte. D. Richardson.
Sgt. P. Robertson.
C/Sgt. D. Ross.
R.S.M. D. Sinclair.
Sgt. J. Smellie.
Sgt. D. Smith.
Pte. H. S. South.
Corpl. D. Stewart.
C.S.M. J. Walls.

THE EIGHTH BATTALION THE BLACK WATCH

M.S.M.

Sgt. J. Dewar.
Sgt. J. K. Downie.
L/Corpl. J. G. Fotheringham.
A/Sgt. A. Holmes.
R.Q.M.S. A. Ramage.
Corpl. W. Stevenson.

Bar to M.M.

Corpl. J. W. Arundel.
Pte. T. M. Fast.
Sgt. D. Forsyth.
Pte. J. Hogg.
Corpl. R. MacFarlane.
Pte. T. Morton.
Pte. R. F. McLaughlin.

M.M.

Sgt. J. Abbie.
Sgt. A. Agnew.
Corpl. A. Anderson.
L/Sgt. J. Alexander.
Pte. J. Anderson.
Pte. J. Anderson.
L/Corpl. J. Angus.
Pte. W. Annan.
Corpl. J. W. Arundel.
Sgt. J. Barton.
L/Corpl. J. Beattie.
L/Corpl. H. Beveridge.
L/Corpl. J. Birkinshaw.
Sgt. G. Birrell, D.C.M.
Pte. D. Blyth.
A/Corpl. J. Brown.
L/Corpl. R. Brunton.
Pte. R. Bryson.
Pte. W. Carter.
Sgt. G. Collins.
Pte. R. Cormack.
Pte. J. Coutts.
Pte. A. Craik.
Pte. W. Dall.
Pte. J. R. Dewar.
Pte. F. Duncanson.
L/Corpl. D. Ewing.
L/Corpl. A. Fairhurst.
Pte. T. M. Fast.
Pte. M. Fletcher.
Corpl. J. Ford.
Sgt. D. Forsyth.
L/Corpl. A. Fraser.
Pte. A. Gibson.
Pte. D. Gilmour.
Pte. R. Glen.
Corpl. J. Gordon.
Sgt. J. Gourlay.
Pte. J. Gourlay.
L/Corpl. D. Grierson.
Pte. G. Grieve.
Sgt. M. Henderson.
L/Corpl. R. Henderson.
Pte. R. Henderson.
Pte. H. H. Hodgson.
Pte. J. Hogg.
Pte. J. Houston.
Pte. W. Houston.
Pte. J. Hume.
Pte. E. Hunter.
Pte. J. Hutchison.
Pte. J. L. Innes.
Pte. R. Ironside.
Pte. T. Irwin.
Pte. S. Jenkins.
Pte. G. Kirk.
Sgt. W. Laird.
Sgt. J. Lee.
Sgt. J. Lees.
Pte. R. Leggate.
Sgt. D. Littlejohn.
Corpl. W. Lowden.
Pte. P. Luke.
Pte. J. M. Macaulay.
A/Corpl. A. MacDonald.
Corpl. R. Macfarlane.
Pte. W. Mackrell.
Sgt. J. Marr.
A/L/Sgt. P. Marshall.
Pte. L. Mathieson.
Pte. B. Mathews.
Pte. T. Mayes.
L/Corpl. W. R. Meldrum.
Pte. A. Moir.
L/Corpl. P. Morrison.
Pte. T. Morton.

APPENDIX V

M.M. (contd.)

Pte. J. Moyes.
Sgt. D. J. Munro.
Pte. A. Murray.
Pte. J. Murray.
L/Corpl. N. McBrayne.
L/Sgt. E. MacCaffrey.
Pte. F. McDonald.
L/Sgt. G. R. McDonald.
Pte. A. McFadyen.
Pte. W. McFadyen.
L/Corpl. A. McFarlane.
L/Corpl. J. McGregor.
Pte. J. McIntyre.
Pte. J. M. McKenzie.
Corpl. J. McLaren.
Pte. R. F. McLaughlin.
Pte. J. Nelson.
Corpl. A. Newlands.
Pte. J. Orchison.
A/C.S.M. H. Redpath, D.C.M.
Pte. W. Reid.
Pte. W. Rennie.
Pte. W. J. Ritchie.
Corpl. J. Robertson.
Sgt. P. Robertson.
Pte. R. Robertson.
Pte. P. Scullion.
A/Corpl. P. Shevlin.
Sgt. J. Sloan.
Sgt. D. Speed.
Pte. W. P. Spence.
Pte. D. T. Stewart.
Corpl. H. Stewart.
L/Corpl. N. Stewart.
L/Corpl. J. M. Strachan.
Pte. W. M. Sutherland.
Pte. J. S. Tait.
L/Corpl. A. Thorpe.
L/Corpl. D. Turner.
Pte. T. K. Vass.
L/Corpl. A. Walton.
Pte. W. Welsh.
Pte. C. Whyte.
Pte. T. A. Wilkin.
Corpl. J. Wilson.
Sgt. W. Wiltshire.
L/Corpl. J. Young.

Mentioned in Despatches

2nd Lieut. H. A. Clement.
Major J. G. Collins.
Capt. R. N. Duke.
Capt. J. L. S. Ewing.
2nd Lieut. P. H. Forrester.
Lieut.-Colonel C. W. E. Gordon (3).
Lieut. H. F. C. Govan.
Capt. G. B. McClure.
Col. Lord Sempill.
2nd Lieut. G. L. Yule.

Sgt. J. Abbie.
Pte. G. Boak.
Sgt. H. Bowman.
L/Corpl. J. Devine.
Sgt. J. Dewar.
Sgt. J. Downie.
Pte. A. Fairhurst.
Pte. J. Hardy.
Sgt. J. Henderson.
A/R.S.M. W. L. Henderson.
L/Corpl. A. May.
Pte. W. J. Murray.
Pte. P. J. Peterson.
Sgt. D. Simpson.
Corpl. H. Sutton.
Sgt. T. Taylor.
Pte. J. Tod.

THE EIGHTH BATTALION THE BLACK WATCH

FOREIGN DECORATIONS

ORDER OF DANILO, 3rd Class (MONTENEGRO)
Lieut.-Colonel C. W. E. Gordon.

CROIX DE GUERRE (FRENCH)
A/C.S.M. G. Birrell.
A/Corpl. G. G. Blair.
L/Corpl. J. Burton.
Corpl. T. Ferguson.
C.S.M. W. L. Henderson.
L/Corpl. J. Shankland.
Sgt. W. Wiltshire, M.M.

CROIX DE GUERRE (BELGIAN)
C.Q.M.S. W. Clark, D.C.M.
Pte. T. Cunningham.
Sgt. J. Henderson.
A/C.S.M. P. McArthur.
R.S.M. D. Sinclair.

MÉDAILLE D'HONNEUR AVEC GLAIVES (EN BRONZE)
Pte. A. Donald.

BRONZE MEDAL (ITALIAN)
Sgt. J. Abbie.

APPENDIX VI

List of Actions and Operations

The Eighth Battalion

1915. Landed in France. 10th May.
  Trench warfare. Armentières, Festubert, Le Plantin, Givenchy, Hohenzollern Sector.
  BATTLE OF LOOS. (Hohenzollern Redoubt.) 25th September.
  Trench warfare. Ypres Salient. September–December.

1916. Trench warfare. Ypres Salient, Montauban.
  BATTLE OF BAZENTIN RIDGE. (Capture of Longueval.) 14th–18th July.
  Trench warfare. Berthonval, High Wood, Arras. July–December.

1917. Trench warfare. Arras, Roclincourt. January–April.
  FIRST BATTLE OF THE SCARPE. (North of River Scarpe.) 9th April.
  Trench warfare. Fampoux Area. April–May.
  THIRD BATTLE OF THE SCARPE. 2nd May.
  Trench warfare. Greenland Hill, Havrincourt, Ypres Area. May–October.
  FIRST BATTLE OF PASSCHENDAELE. October 12th.
  Trench warfare. Nieuport, Gouzeaucourt. October–December.

1918. Trench warfare. Bois d'Epinette, Gouzeaucourt. January–March.
  FIRST BATTLE OF BAPAUME. (Dèsart Wood, Equancourt, Etricourt, Denancourt.) 21st–25th March.
  BATTLE OF MESSINES. (Kemmel, Goudezoune Farm.) 10th–11th April.
  FIRST BATTLE OF KEMMEL RIDGE. 17th–19th April.
  SECOND BATTLE OF KEMMEL RIDGE. 25th–26th April.
  Trench warfare. Caestre Area, Meteren Sector. April–July.
  CAPTURE OF METEREN. 19th July.
  Trench warfare. Meteren Sector, Ypres Area. July–September.
  BATTLE OF YPRES (1918.) (Passchendaele Ridge.) 28th September–2nd October.
  BATTLE OF COURTRAI. (Winkel, St. Eloi.) 14th October.
  ADVANCE TO VICTORY. September–11th November.

"A SUBALTERN OF THE BLACK WATCH, 1917"
After the drawing by "Snaffles"

THE NINTH
BATTALION

CHAPTER I

SEPTEMBER, 1914—JULY, 1915

Formation of Battalion and Training in England

WHEN the Regular and Special Reserve had been mobilised, Lord Kitchener's historic telegram which brought the New Armies into being reached Perth. The original Army Order, dated August 21st, 1914, dealt with the First New Army, namely the 9th to 14th Divisions, the ranks of which were soon filled to overflowing. In September instructions were received authorizing the formation of three more Armies, to the second of which the 15th Division belonged and of which the 9th Black Watch formed part.

The first " Service Battalion "—as the new formations were termed—was the 8th, and its ranks were filled by September 3rd. On the 6th a further draft of two hundred men left Perth for Aldershot, where the newly formed 8th Battalion was stationed, and this date may be taken as being the first birthday of the 9th Battalion. Three days later sanction was obtained to form the drafts which had reached the 8th Battalion between the 6th and 9th into a separate unit, the command being given to Major T. O. Lloyd (Reserve of Officers), who had served for many years in the Regiment, and had retired from the 1st Battalion in 1909.

In a very few days the new Battalion was, numerically, up to strength, but, with the exception of a few retired non-commissioned officers, too old to be called up with the Reserve, there were no non-commissioned officers and, with the exception of the Commanding Officer, and Quartermaster, the few officers were second lieutenants, and few at that. It was, of course, necessary to appoint an Adjutant without delay, and the Commanding Officer, 8th Battalion—Lord Sempill—came to the rescue by consenting to the transfer of Lieutenant A. K. McLeod, one of the three regular officers given him by the War Office, for that purpose. A few days after the Battalion came into being Captain J. Stewart, who had retired from the 1st Battalion a few months earlier, joined and took over command of A company, being promoted Major and Second-in-Command shortly afterwards.

The 9th was fortunate in its Quartermaster, Lieutenant W. Clark. Coming from the Royal Scots, Clark served the 9th Black Watch loyally and affectionately from its birth till, in May, 1918, it lost its identity when merged with the 4th/5th Battalion. In the early days it was by no means easy to clothe and feed the Battalion, but apart from his very thorough knowledge of the Regulations (and ways round them) Clark's priceless gift of ever seeing the bright and humorous side of any situation was of the greatest value.

Another important appointment made by Colonel Lloyd was that of G. D. Bedson to be Regimental Sergeant-Major. He had left the Regiment in 1902, discharged to pension after twenty-nine years' service, during which he had received the medal for the Egyptian campaigns, 1882–85, with five clasps, and the Khedive's Star. He had been, for some years, exempt from liability to recall, but, like many others, Bedson was one of the first to answer Lord Kitchener's call for men. It very soon became apparent that, in his quiet and unostentatious way, he was busy inculcating into the newly appointed non-commissioned officers and men the pride in the traditions of the Regiment in which he himself had served so long.

In addition to Regimental Sergeant-Major Bedson, the Battalion was fortunate in securing the services of two former colour-sergeants of the Regiment, J. Hampton and J. Lindsay. The former was at once appointed Regimental Quartermaster-Sergeant, and did splendid service for two years with the 9th Battalion, when he received a commission and was appointed Quartermaster of another battalion. Lindsay was made Orderly Room Quartermaster-Sergeant, which appointment he held throughout the war with great credit to himself and to the Battalion.

Nearly all the company officers were first gazetted as second lieutenants. Few had any military experience at all and it was a difficult matter to select company commanders and their second-in-command, but Colonel Lloyd accomplished this difficult task with rare discrimination and, after the first few weeks, hardly a change was found necessary.

The choice of suitable men for the non-commissioned officer ranks was a still more difficult task. The few old—and some were very ancient—non-commissioned officers were, of course, at once given acting rank, the remaining vacancies being filled on the recommendation of company commanders. It is astonishing how few mistakes were made. It is worth recording that the 9th Black Watch was the first battalion in the 15th Division to report that it had filled its appointments of company sergeant-majors and quartermaster-sergeants, this having been accomplished within a week after Colonel Lloyd assumed command.

As regards the men. No words can express what they went through in those early days and the enthusiasm and entire absence of grumbling with which they went to work and put up with the manifold discomforts then existing. At first "K 2" was "nobody's child." The First Army had to be dealt with before much attention could be paid to the wants of the

ALDERSHOT, SEPTEMBER TO NOVEMBER, 1914

Second, and therefore they had to endure many discomforts and hardships unknown to their elder brothers.

Work and instruction were constant. At first ten hours a day, including Sundays, was the rule. Fortunately the weather was good, and, except that towards the end of their stay at Aldershot, when the men's clothing became so ragged that many could not be allowed out of barracks, nobody minded how hard they worked as long as they were making themselves fit. With enthusiasm such as this it is not surprising that the task of instruction was easy, and it was not long before the 9th became what it was throughout the war—a smart and well-disciplined Battalion.

The 44th, 45th and 46th Brigades formed the infantry of the 15th (Scottish) Division, which was first commanded by Major-General A. Wallace, C.B., the 44th, or Highland Brigade, consisting of the 9th Black Watch, 8th Seaforths, 9th and 10th Gordon Highlanders. Four months after it had been formed the 9th Gordons left to become Pioneer Battalion to the Division, its place in the Brigade being taken by the 7th Camerons. Brigadier-General M. Grant Wilkinson, M.V.O., was the first Brigadier of the Highland Brigade, serving with it until April, 1916, and it is safe to say that no other Brigadier was ever more popular among all ranks or more proud of his command.

September to November 10th was spent at Aldershot, where for the first few weeks the Battalion shared Albuhera Barracks with the 8th Black Watch till September 22nd, and then with the 8th Seaforths. The first occasion on which the Battalion fell in as a unit was on September 26th, when Their Majesties the King and Queen and Lord Kitchener inspected the 15th Division. On this occasion, with the exception of a few officers, the whole Division wore civilian clothes. The men, however, stood in the ranks like veterans, and it was obvious that His Majesty was greatly impressed.

The first uniforms issued arrived about the end of September. These consisted of "Brodrick" caps, red serge tunics of the pattern worn some ten years earlier by line battalions, and blue trousers with red stripes. These articles did not all arrive at the same time but by degrees sufficient supplies made it possible to discard the rags (literally) in which the Battalion had worked for weeks, and by the middle of October the men were all dressed alike, but civilian greatcoats were retained for some long time afterwards.

On September 30th, Colonel the Hon. H. E. Maxwell, D.S.O., was gazetted to command the 9th Black Watch. He was in every sense a "Black Watch" officer; he had been Adjutant of the 2nd Battalion, and had commanded it for four years after the war in South Africa. Unfortunately he was unable to pass the medical authorities as fit for active service, and, in consequence, the command was given to Major T. O. Lloyd, with the temporary rank of Lieutenant-Colonel.

Early in October, thanks to the help of generous friends, the Battalion was able to purchase pipes and drums, which helped many a footsore man on the long and uninteresting route marches.

While at Aldershot, Major-General Wallace left the Division on appointment to a command in Egypt, his place being taken by Major-General Colin J. Mackenzie, C.B., from command of a brigade in France.

About November 10th orders were received to the effect that the Battalion would shortly move into billets at Liss, about fourteen miles from Aldershot. The move was accomplished on November 23rd without difficulty, and, although the inhabitants were at first somewhat dubious as to the manners of soldiers in general, and the Highlander in particular, the Battalion soon settled down and all ranks became the fast friends of their various hosts and hostesses. Never during its existence did the 9th Black Watch receive as much kindness and hospitality as it did from the warm-hearted inhabitants of Liss. So much so, that when the news of the battle of Loos became public many letters of both condolence and admiration were received in the Battalion from their friends at and round Liss. It is interesting to record that, in 1922, when the 2nd Battalion was quartered at Bordon, four miles from Liss, they were received as old friends, on account of the pleasant recollections of the 9th Battalion retained by the inhabitants.

The following is a list of the officers who accompanied the Battalion from Aldershot on this its first move:—

Headquarters

Lieut.-Colonel T. O. Lloyd (in Command).
Major J. Stewart (Second-in-Command).
Captain A. K. McLeod (Adjutant).
Lieut. and Quartermaster W. Clark.
Lieut. F. A. Bearn, R.A.M.C. (attd. as M.O.).

A company	*B company*
Captain D. H. N. Graham.	Major M. W. Henderson.
Lieut. S. Norie-Miller.	Captain S. D. Stevenson.
„ J. C. Henderson-Hamilton.	Lieut. R. E. Harvey.
	„ G. A. Rusk.
„ J. Crighton.	2nd Lieut. A. O. Dennistoun.
2nd Lieut. D. J. Glenny.	„ J. Campbell.
„ G. Scott-Pearse.	„ R. Stirling.
„ R. H. Robertson.	„ R. W. Reid.
With 285 other ranks.	With 277 other ranks.

TRAINING AT LISS

C company	D company
Captain J. Gilchrist.	Captain J. M. Bell.
„ A. D. Carmichael.	„ J. H. S. Richardson.
Lieut. J. H. Cameron.	Lieut. C. S. Tuke.
2nd Lieut. R. Andrew.	2nd Lieut. J. D. G. Miller.
„ E. R. Wilson.	„ W. Story-Wilson.
„ R. H. C. Ewart.	„ E. N. L. Raymond.
With 281 other ranks.	With 298 other ranks.

Total, 32 officers and 1141 other ranks.

The time at Liss passed quickly, being mostly taken up by musketry on a miniature range and company training, although the area for this was somewhat restricted.

At New Year all ranks received seven days' well-earned leave, half the Battalion being away at a time. This concession was much appreciated, although to those coming from the Western Isles and the far north of Scotland it meant only a few hours with their relations.

Many comforts, in the shape of warm garments, etc., were from now onwards received from friends and well wishers, and among them came hundreds of pairs of khaki hose-tops in anticipation of the issue of kilts which was expected in the near future. At this time the warrant officers and non-commissioned officers entertained the children of Liss at tea and a Christmas tree, the officers organizing a concert for the elders, to the success of which Brigadier-General Wilkinson and his daughter largely contributed.

A great event occurred on January 20th/21st, namely, the issue of kilts of The Black Watch tartan. These were worn on the following day, when, with the rest of the Division, the Battalion was inspected at Frensham Common by M. Millerand, the French War Minister, and Lord Kitchener.

Few who were present on that occasion are likely to forget it. Snow commenced to fall shortly after the Battalion left Liss and continued until Frensham was reached, by which time everyone was wet through. After forming up, the Division waited in a biting wind for two hours before Lord Kitchener's party arrived. The inspection consisted of a hurried walk along a road on each side of which the Division was drawn up. The whole ceremony lasted barely ten minutes, after which the half-frozen troops marched back to billets. The distance the 9th Battalion covered that day was 28 miles, the return journey through mud and slush being exceptionally trying, but only three men fell out.

In an Order dated 23/1/15, General Sir A. Hunter, commanding Aldershot Training Centre, congratulated the troops and said:—

"They will understand that paramount consideration necessitated this demand on their personal exertions regardless of the weather conditions, which have been without parallel, even in this wet winter," adding: "The Secretary of State for War has desired that every officer and man on parade should be told of the satisfaction with which he noted the splendid bearing and appearance of all ranks and the pleasure with which he inspected so fine a body of troops."

Khaki tunics and military greatcoats were issued on the 26th when the Battalion was properly clad in the uniform of The Black Watch for the first time, nearly five months after its formation.

Transport animals were drawn on February 2nd, Lieutenant W. Story-Wilson being appointed transport officer. No selection could have been better, for both in England, where he supervised the training of his staff, and later in France, this officer did excellent work, his animals and vehicles being always in first-class condition and order.

About this time it became known that the Battalion would shortly move to Chisledon, near Swindon, where facilities for training were better and where it would be accommodated in huts. The move took place by train on the 23rd, when the 9th took over the hutments from the 8th Battalion Cheshire Regiment in Draycott Camp, the 8th Seaforths taking over the adjacent lines, while Headquarters and the remainder of the 44th Brigade were in billets at Cirencester, the Division now coming under the command of Major-General Sir Pitcairn Campbell, G.O.C. Southern Command.

Musketry commenced on March 1st. Twenty-five service rifles only were available, but with these the whole Battalion was put through Tables A and B by Major Stewart with satisfactory results. When this was completed Battalion training recommenced and, together with bayonet fighting, continued until well into April, during which time much hard and interesting work was accomplished.

On March 22nd command of the 15th Division changed for the third time, Major-General Colin Mackenzie vacating on appointment to the War Office, and Major-General F. W. N. McCracken, C.B., D.S.O., from a brigade in France, taking over command.

On the 23rd the Battalion moved into new hutments in Chisledon Camp, where greater comfort was enjoyed, although the environments of the huts left much to be desired, as the contractors, when building the camp, had evidently overlooked the necessity for roads, with the result that in wet weather the ground

OFFICERS OF THE NINTH BATTALION, SALISBURY PLAIN, 1915

Back Row: 2nd Lt. O. A. Bearn, 2nd Lt. L. G. Morrison, 2nd Lt. R. Andrew, 2nd Lt. W. J. Leslie, Lt. E. R. Wilson, 2nd Lt. J. Campbell, Lt. S. Norie Miller, 2nd Lt. A. Sharp, 2nd Lt. W. S. McIntyre

Centre Row: 2nd Lt. J. Millar, 2nd Lt. D. J. Glenny, 2nd Lt. L. Murray-Stewart, Lt. J. C. Henderson-Hamilton, 2nd Lt. R. H. Robertson, 2nd Lt. R. Stirling, 2nd Lt. J. D. G. Miller, Lt. G. A. Rusk, 2nd Lt. A. O. Dennistoun, Lt. J. Crighton, Lt. W. Story-Wilson

Front Row: Capt. J. M. Bell, Lt. and Q.M. W. Clark, Capt. J. H. Stewart-Richardson, Capt. A. K. McLeod, Major J. Stewart, Lt.-Col. T. O. Lloyd, Lieut. and Adjt. R. E. Harvey, Capt. J. Gilchrist, Capt. S. D. Stevenson, Capt. F. A. Bearn, R.A.M.C., Capt. D. M. Graham 2nd Lt. R. W. Reid

Vol. III

TIDWORTH, MAY AND JUNE, 1915

round the huts and the parade ground was a sea of mud. An extract from a company diary dated March 24th states :—

"The state of the camp, owing to the mud, is such that it almost excludes the possibility of getting the men out of the huts now that they are in them."

Things rapidly settled down, however, and by the 27th the Battalion was comfortably housed, the whole of the 44th Brigade being by this time concentrated in Chiseldon and Draycott Camps. Here, for the first time, the massed pipes and drums of the Brigade, about fifty pipers in all, sounded Retreat.

Training continued without intermission. That of specialists, such as signallers and machine gunners, was carried out under great difficulties due to the lack of material, but it was accomplished "somehow," as indeed was most of the training; but was done was thoroughly done, as was proved later in the Field.

On May 12th the 44th Brigade moved by road from Chiseldon to Parkhouse Camp, near Tidworth, a distance of 26 miles. At the time, Parkhouse Camp was still in course of construction and the Battalion was accommodated under canvas. This proved a blessing in disguise when, shortly afterwards, sleeping in the open in France, the men were singularly free from sickness.

For the next four weeks Brigade training took up all the time and good progress was made. On May 19th the Brigade was inspected and marched past Lord Kitchener, then Secretary for War, who expressed himself as highly pleased with its soldierly bearing.

In June the Brigade held Highland games, the chief prize being a silver cup presented by the Brigadier for the battalion that gained most points in certain events. This was won by the 6th Camerons, but the 9th Black Watch managed to win its share of the prizes.

On June 21st, His Majesty the King inspected the Division at Sidbury Hill. Fully equipped and ready to take the field, it was a very different formation to that which His Majesty had last seen in September, 1914, and anyone not closely associated with it would have had difficulty in believing that such a change could have been effected in so short a time. The spirit and patriotism which had manifested themselves in the early days never dwindled, and it was this that made all ranks fit to take their places in the line by June 21st, 1915. Shortly after this inspection general leave was granted, and everyone felt that it would not be long before they left for the front.

Embarkation orders came somewhat suddenly. On Sunday,

THE NINTH BATTALION THE BLACK WATCH

July 4th, the following message from the Division reached General Wilkinson:—

"44th Brigade will embark for France on Thursday 8th AAA.
"Transports under Seconds in Command on Wednesday 7th."

The next four days were busy ones indeed. Fully one-fifth of the Battalion were on leave, mostly in Scotland, when the message was received: these were recalled at once, and there was not a man absent when the Battalion marched out of Parkhouse Camp on the 8th.

The transport, machine gun section and signallers, under Major Stewart, left at 3.45 a.m. on the 7th, reaching Southampton four hours later, where, together with a similar detachment from the 8th Seaforths, the Headquarters unit of the Division, and a detachment of Divisional Artillery, they embarked on the s.s. *Mount Temple* and sailed the same night under destroyer escort, reaching Havre the following morning. Here they proceeded to a well-found rest camp some three miles from the town, where they remained till the evening, when they entrained and left about midnight on the 8th for an unknown destination. On this occasion the transport section gave proof of the efficient manner in which it had been trained by Lieutenant Story-Wilson. Although the men had had no opportunity of practising entrainments there was not a hitch of any kind throughout the journey, and, with the exception of one suffering from the sea voyage and exchanged at Havre, every animal arrived at its destination in first-class condition.

The Battalion left on Thursday the 8th, crossing from Folkestone in the s.s. *Invicta* with the Brigadier, his staff, and the Headquarters and two companies of the 8th Seaforths, reaching Boulogne at 9.50 that night.

The day before leaving the following message from His Majesty the King was communicated to all ranks:—

"Officers, non-commissioned officers and men of the 15th
"Division.
"You are about to join your comrades at the front, in bring-
"ing to a successful end this relentless War of eleven months'
"duration.
"Your prompt patriotic answer to the Nation's call will never
"be forgotten. The keen exertion of all ranks during the period
"of training has brought you to a state of efficiency not un-
"worthy of my Regular Army. I am confident that in the Field
"you will nobly uphold the traditions of the fine Regiments
"whose name you bear.

THE MOVE TO FRANCE, JULY 8TH, 1915

"Ever since your enrolment I have closely watched the growth and steady progress of all Units.

"I shall continue to follow with interest the fortunes of your Division.

"In bidding you farewell, I pray that God may bless you in all your undertakings."

To this gracious message, General McCracken replied as follows:—

"On behalf of myself and the officers, non-commissioned officers and men of the 15th Scottish Division, I beg to express our humble thanks for His Majesty's gracious message.

"All ranks hope to uphold the glorious traditions of the Regular Army and, if possible, to add to them."

CHAPTER II

JULY TO OCTOBER, 1915

Early days in France—The Battle of Loos

ON reaching Boulogne the Battalion disembarked and proceeded to Ostremond Camp, about three miles from the quay, arriving there about midnight, the first battalion of the 15th Division to set foot on French soil. Here, on the site of Napoleon's camp when he contemplated an invasion of England, the 44th Brigade concentrated during the night of 8th/9th July.

At 4.20 p.m. the following day the 9th Black Watch marched to Pont de Briques station, where, at 6.30 p.m. the train conveying the Second-in-Command and transport, etc., arrived from Havre and the Battalion entrained. A three hours' journey brought them to Watten, where they were met by Captain O'Connor, Staff-Captain 44th Brigade, with orders to proceed by road to Moulle, where billets would be provided by the Maire. On Colonel Lloyd enquiring where Moulle was, the Staff-Captain pointed somewhat vaguely, in the dark, to the west, and when further asked for a map he replied that he had only one and that no others were available! However, after annexing the one and only map, and with the guidance of Sergeant André Bonsargent, the interpreter who had joined the Battalion at Boulogne from the French "Corps de Liaison," the 9th reached its destination soon after midnight. Companies moved off to their areas and, after some trouble, finally reached their billets about dawn.

Nothing could exceed the kindness of the inhabitants. No British troops had been billeted in the area prior to the arrival of the 15th Division, and the villagers gave of their best to the troops. The Commanding Officer, Second-in-Command and Adjutant were lodged in the château of M. Dupont, a very courteous French gentleman who, with his wife, did everything to make them comfortable. When thanked on the eve of departure, he replied that it was nothing, adding, " C'est pour nous sauver que vous êtes venu."

On the 13th of July the Commander-in-Chief, General Sir John French, paid the Battalion an informal visit while on his way round the 15th Division area.

The following day orders reached battalions to the effect that the Division would move on the 15th *en route* to join the IV Corps, General Sir H. Rawlinson, then holding the line between Grenay and La Bassée Canal. The march to IV Corps area occupied three days, the first stage—twenty-two miles for the 9th Battalion—to Hazebrouck being accomplished as a Division. The day was hot and the roads paved with cobble-stones were trying to

TRENCH WARFARE, MAROC, JULY, 1915

young soldiers, but only six failed to march in when the Battalion reached its billeting area at Grand Hasard, near Hazebrouck.

The next day a comparatively short march of twelve miles, in which brigades moved independently, brought the Battalion to Bas Rieux, near Gonnhem.

The final march to its area was a wet one and was carried out on the night of the 17th. Again brigades moved independently, the 44th assembling at Chocques and reaching billets in and round Houchin about 2 a.m. on the 18th. Here the billeting area was restricted and bad. The Commanding Officer therefore obtained permission to bivouac A and B companies in a wood near by, where they made themselves far more comfortable than C and D, who were in billets. Here the Battalion remained till the 2nd of August, when it went into the line. The first ten days were occupied in company marches and physical training.

On July 20th detachments of parties were sent from battalions, etc., in the Division, to similar formations then in the line for instruction, those from the 9th going to the following battalions on the dates mentioned:—

24th/26th July. Second-in-Command, machine gun officer, two company sergeant-majors, two company quartermaster-sergeants, and one machine gun non-commissioned officer, to 21st London Regiment (T.).

27th/28th July. Same party to 2nd Battalion Sussex Regiment.

28th/30th July. Commanding Officer, Adjutant, two company sergeant-majors, two company quartermaster-sergeants, and one machine gun non-commissioned officer, to 22nd Battalion King's Royal Rifles.

31st July/1st August. Same party to 22nd Battalion London Regiment.

28th/30th July. A company (by platoons) to 22nd London Regiment. B company (by platoons) to 23rd and 24th Battalions London Regiment.

30th July/1st August. C company (by platoons) to 22nd London Regiment. D company (by platoons) to 23rd and 24th Battalions London Regiment.

During these periods much useful knowledge of trench warfare was gained from the exceedingly efficient battalions to which the men were attached.

The 9th Black Watch first took over a portion of the front line on Monday, August 2nd, when the 44th Brigade relieved the 23rd and 24th Battalions London Regiment (6th London Infantry Brigade, 47th Division) in what was known as W 3 Section, 2 Sector, east of Maroc and opposite the famous "Double Crassier." Here the 15th Division held the right sector of the IV Corps

THE NINTH BATTALION THE BLACK WATCH

front from the Grenay—St. Jeanne D'Arc road to Le Rutoire–Loos road, a frontage of about 4200 yards. The sector was divided into two sections and was held by the 44th Brigade (right) and 45th (left), the 46th being in Divisional reserve.

At this time the Grenay—St. Jeanne road was the extreme right of the British front, and on this occasion the 9th Black Watch held the right of the line, next to a battalion of the French 58th Division, XXI Corps. Here the opposing lines ran roughly north and south, between the ruins of Maroc and Cité St. Jeanne D'Arc, thence due north, and west of Hulluch and on to La Bassée Canal.

The front line was held by C right sub-section, D left sub-section, B in the support line and A in reserve at Maroc, where Battalion Headquarters were established in some ruined cottages.

The sector was a particularly quiet one, the enemy contenting themselves with occasionally shelling Maroc and the back areas. There was, however, an enormous amount of work to be accomplished; the wire defences were in bad order, dug-outs were conspicuous by their absence, and " keeps " or strong points required construction. To the uninitiated, the work appeared colossal, but all ranks tackled the job with energy, and, at the conclusion of the tour, General Wilkinson published a Special Order congratulating his battalions on the work accomplished.

The Battalion was relieved on the night of the 9th of August by the 10th Scottish Rifles, 46th Brigade, and moved to Noeux-les-Mines in Divisional reserve with the remainder of the 44th Brigade. It did not suffer a single casualty on this its first tour, which fact drew favourable comment from Major-General McCracken.

On Sunday, the 15th of August, an episode occurred which is of interest to all who have ever had the honour of wearing the Red Hackle.

" When the 9th Black Watch landed in France the only head-
" dress was the Glengarry, but, on July 22nd, the Khaki Balmoral
" bonnet was issued. Colonel Lloyd immediately wrote to the
" Commanding Officers of the 1st and 2nd Battalions saying that
" he presumed that neither of the Regular Battalions would
" object to a Service battalion wearing the much envied ' Red
" Hackle.' They both agreed that a Service battalion had every
" right to do so, and the Hackles were at once ordered from
" England.

" When the Battalion arrived at Noeux-les-Mines some few
" dozen ' Hackles ' had arrived and been issued to officers and
" non-commissioned officers who, of course, at once wore them.
" On August 14th General McCracken visited the 9th Black
" Watch billets at Noeux-les-Mines, and on his departure, the

TRENCH WARFARE, PHILOSOPHE, AUGUST, 1915

"Brigade Commander informed Colonel Lloyd that, while the Divisional Commander had no objection to the 'emblem' being worn behind the line, he considered it too conspicuous and had decreed that it must not be worn when the Battalion was in the trenches.

"Here was a serious situation. Never had a battalion of the Regiment ever gone into action without it since its award in 1795. Fortunately Colonel Lloyd dined with the Divisional Commander on the 15th and took the opportunity of explaining what the 'Red Hackle' meant to every Black Watch man, and on hearing this General McCracken immediately withdrew his veto. By September 12th every man in the 9th Battalion was issued with a Hackle which was always worn until the adoption of the steel helmet precluded its continuance while in the trenches."

On the 17th of August the 44th Brigade moved into the line east of Philosophe, the 9th Black Watch being in support at Mazingarbe. Here large working parties, averaging about 12 officers and 450 other ranks, were employed by day and night in digging new trenches, gun emplacements and in constructing a Bombing School at Noeux. The Battalion took over Section X 1, east of Philosophe, from the 8th Seaforths on August 26th. This time three companies held the front and support lines—A on the right, C in the centre, and D on the left. One platoon of B company holding two "keeps" while the remaining three were in reserve, with Battalion Headquarters at Quality Street.

On the day it went into the line the first casualty occurred, Private McKenzie, of C company, being wounded. Three days later, on the 29th, Captain J. Gilchrist, Second-in-Command of D, went out into No Man's Land just after dawn to remove a paper placed there by the enemy during the night. As he was returning he was fired on and mortally wounded. Sergeant Nisbet, Sergeant McCann and Lance-Sergeant Hunter, all of D company, went to his assistance and with some difficulty got him through the wire and into the trench. He was at once taken to Quality Street and from thence to Chocques, where he died the same day. For their gallantry on this occasion the three non-commissioned officers were publicly commended by Colonel Lloyd by order of the Divisional Commander. Captain Gilchrist was one of the first officers appointed to the Battalion, having received his commission from Company Sergeant-Major 8th Battalion Gordon Highlanders in September, 1914.

The following day the Battalion was suddenly withdrawn to Mazingarbe, where it became Divisional reserve, being relieved by a battalion of the Royal Scots Fusiliers.

THE NINTH BATTALION THE BLACK WATCH

For some time previous to this, rumours of a British offensive had been rife, but it was not till August 30th that definite information was given to commanding officers. Notwithstanding this secrecy, however, the great activity displayed in construction of new works, coupled with the ever-increasing flow of heavy artillery now arriving, encouraged everyone to guess what might occur. These outward signs, and the fact that the Battalion, together with the 8th Seaforths, was suddenly withdrawn from the line after a tour of four days, led the 9th Black Watch to assume that it was meant to play some part in the coming offensive.

The Battalion remained billeted in Mazingarbe from August 30th to September 24th, during which time it supplied large working parties for the construction of dug-outs, capable of accommodating a whole battalion, and on other works under Royal Engineers, and although many parties were employed in the front and support lines, it was very fortunate in having only one man killed and four wounded in that time.

It was not long before the many rumours were substantiated and it became known that an attack on a large scale would take place in the near future. One of the first signs was an order from General McCracken directing the Second-in-Command, Major Stewart, to make the necessary arrangements for the distribution of gas cylinders along the whole of the 15th Division front line. This order reached the Battalion on September 6th, and the work was finished by dawn on the 11th, by which time 1500 cylinders were in position in the front trenches. It was no easy task. Each cylinder weighed 140 lbs. and required two men to carry it. However, with the assistance of 25 officers picked from all battalions of the Division, a large working party, numbering over 1000 men, carried out the task without a hitch of any kind. On the last night, the men of the 9th Black Watch performed two journeys in order to complete the work, and on completion the workers received the thanks of the Divisional Commander. The secret was really well kept, for, until the morning of attack, the enemy had not the slightest idea that their own weapon would be turned against them.

From the 6th onwards the time was taken up in perfecting all details for the forthcoming battle. There were frequent, almost daily conferences—divisional, brigade or battalion—and by the 18th all was ready.

Russia, who had suffered severely earlier in the year, had recovered and was once more such a cause of anxiety to Germany that the latter was obliged to move a number of divisions from her western front eastwards. She felt she could do this safely, as she did not believe it possible that England

PREPARATIONS FOR BATTLE OF LOOS

could, by this time, have trained sufficient men to make any serious attack in either France or Flanders. She scoffed at what little she had heard of the " New Armies," and never dreamt that the Allies contemplated an attack at one of their weakest points—namely, at the junction of the French and British forces.

Sir John French's intentions were—

(1) To break through the German line at a selected place.
(2) To prevent the enemy from re-establishing his line.
(3) To defeat decisively the then divided forces.

To carry out the above intentions, the British First Army, under Sir Douglas Haig, then holding the line Grenay–Festubert, was detailed to lead the attack assisted by the French (Tenth) Army operating north and south of Arras, while demonstrations were to be made at other points to prevent the enemy from reinforcing the main point of attack. This main attack was to be made on Loos and the ground immediately north of Lens, which large and awkward town was to be left alone in the hope that it would fall automatically as a result of successful attacks of the French from Souchez on the south and British on the north.

The main attack of the First Army was assigned to the I and IV Corps, from Grenay to La Bassée Canal, the dividing line between them being the Vermelles–Hulluch road. South of this road the IV Corps attack was to be carried out as follows:—On the right the 47th (London) Division was to capture the " Double Crassier," east of Maroc, and having done so, was then to form a defensive flank facing south-east. On its left, the centre of the Corps attack, the 15th (Scottish) Division was ordered to attack the high ground north of Loison-sous-Lens, while on the left the 1st Division was to take Hulluch and cross the Haute Deule Canal.

By this time the British artillery in France had been considerably augmented, the IV Corps having in its area 253 guns of all calibres, including 36 howitzers of 8 in. and over, with which to support the attack. Ammunition for these guns had been provided on what was then considered a generous scale, and it was hoped that the hail of shells that would fall on the enemy trenches at Zero hour would materially assist in keeping down the fire of any enemy surviving the gas attack.

The Divisional front was some 1500 yards in length, running due north from the Quality Street–Lens road, and on this General McCracken decided to attack with the 44th Brigade on the right and 46th on the left, keeping the 45th in reserve.

The leading brigades were directed to attack in two columns each consisting of one battalion, a section of R.E. and one platoon

THE NINTH BATTALION THE BLACK WATCH

9th Gordons (Pioneers), those of the 44th Brigade being composed as under:—

Right Column. No. 1. Lieutenant-Colonel Lloyd, 9th Black Watch, No. 2 Section 73rd Field Company R.E., and one platoon G company 9th Gordons (P.).

Left Column. No. 2. Lieutenant-Colonel Thomson, 8th Seaforths, No. 3 Section 73rd Field Company R.E., and one platoon G company 9th Gordons (P.). The 19th Battalion London Regiment, 47th Division, was on the right of the 9th Black Watch. In support of the 44th Brigade attack were the 7th Camerons, Lieutenant-Colonel J. Sandilands, with the 10th Gordons, Lieutenant-Colonel Wallace, the 73rd Field Company R.E. (less two sections) and G company 9th Gordons (P.) less two platoons.

On August 30th the preliminary battle orders issued gave five objectives, namely: the German front and second lines, Loos village, Puits 15 (east of Loos) and the Redoubt on Hill 70. To these were added, on September 21st, (*a*) the Cité St. Auguste and (*b*) the high ground north of Loison-sous-Lens, two miles further east.

A few words are necessary to explain the country over which the attack was to take place. On the whole it was undulating and open, the chief features being (*a*) a spur running north-east from Grenay to Hulluch, (*b*) the high ground south and east of Loos and (*c*) the valley between the two. In September, 1915, the opposing trenches crossed the spur, following a north and south line, at its highest point on the Lens–Quality Street road, and nothing could be seen beyond the German front line from the British trenches. On the other hand, the enemy were able to keep the whole of the country to the north, south and west under direct observation from the high ground east and south of Loos, the spur only concealing a small portion of the British line. Thus the advantage as regards ground clearly lay with the enemy and, so long as he held Loos under observation, neither guns or reserves could be safely brought up to assist a further advance. It was therefore imperative that the " Double Crassier," Loos, Hill 70, east of it, and " The Dump " further north, should be taken quickly.

For some days prior to the attack all guns had been engaged in cutting the German wire by low-bursting shrapnel fire. On the 15th Division front this had been fairly well done, but further north, on the 1st Division front, it was not successful, which fact had a great bearing on the whole operation.

One point of vital importance was impressed on all concerned. It was " Keep going: a constant flow of reinforcements will be following you." How far this promise was kept will be seen later.

BATTLE OF LOOS, SEPTEMBER 25TH, 1915

The attack, originally planned for the 18th, was, for various reasons, postponed till the 25th, by which time everything was ready, and for three days prior to that date the German positions had been subjected to a continuous bombardment.

On Friday the 24th, at 4.30 p.m., the 9th having stacked their packs and kits in a farm in Mazingarbe,[1] commenced moving down the long communication trench leading to its battle position. It was a trying march of about three miles, but by midnight all companies had reached their respective positions, which ran from " C.T.6 " inclusive to " C.T.7 B " exclusive, in which area they were distributed as follows:—

A company (Captain Graham) in the fire trench.
B ,, (Major Henderson) in support trench.
C ,, (Captain McLeod) in Trench 27.
D ,, (Captain Bell) in C.T.21, Battalion Headquarters occupying a small dug-out in C.T.6.

In the above order the attack was to be launched, each company advancing in two lines of two platoons each. Neither the four company Second-in-Command, Captain Carmichael and Lieutenants Norie-Miller, Rusk and J. D. G. Miller, or the four company quartermaster sergeants were, to their great disgust, permitted to accompany the Battalion, being left behind to form a reserve in case of undue losses, a most fortunate provision as it proved.

For some days prior to the attack doubts had been expressed as to the advisability of using gas. The weather at the time was by no means favourable, there being little or no wind; so calm was it, indeed, on the 24th that all troops were ordered to " stand fast." This order was, however, cancelled late in the afternoon as the wind from the west seemed to gain strength; but when dawn broke on the 25th what wind there was was very slight and from the south-south-west veering to south-west and by no means ideal for the operation.

Until an hour before " Zero " the actual moment for discharge of the gas was not known, but at 4.50 a.m. the following message was received from Brigade Headquarters:—

" ' Zero ' hour is 5.50 a.m. AAA You will inform officers of " 187 Coy. R.E. in your Sector of this hour."

[*Note.*—These were the Officers i/c Gas Cylinders.]

Punctually at 5.50 a.m. the gas was released, and at the same time the rate of artillery and machine gun fire doubled. The

---

[1] Known afterwards as " Black Watch Farm." It was owned by a M. Hennequet, whose daughter, Mlle Henriette was, and is to this day, a firm friend to all who wear the Red Hackle.

lack of sufficient wind, and its uncertain direction, minimized the results expected from the gas; in fact, a good deal blew back, causing some casualties, especially to battalions further north, but as far as the 9th Battalion was concerned no ill effects were felt.

At 6.30 a.m. the infantry advance began.

No one present will ever forget that attack. As one man, the leading two platoons of A company leapt on the parapet and, making their way through the British wire, steadily advanced towards the German front line, followed by the remainder of the Battalion at regular intervals. It seemed impossible to realize that these lines of disciplined soldiers had been, twelve short months before, almost all civilians. Perfect steadiness prevailed, regardless of the heavy fire which, coming more especially from the "Lens Road Redoubt," swept the ground over which they had to cross. There was no shouting or hurry; the men moved in quick time, picking up their "dressing" as if on a ceremonial parade. The distance to be crossed varied from 80 to 200 yards, and, despite the fierce fire, not a line wavered or stopped. The day after the Battalion came out of action Lieutenant-Colonel, now Major-General Sir John Burnett-Stuart, G.S.O.1, 15th Division, told Colonel Lloyd that the finest sight he had ever seen was that of the 9th Black Watch advancing on the German first line.

The most formidable point in the enemy front line was the Lens Road Redoubt, or "Jew's Nose," as it was called. This strong point was in the Battalion area, and as the dividing line between the 9th Black Watch and the left battalion of the 47th Division was the Philosophe–Lens road, it was necessary for the right of the Battalion line to advance half-right towards it and gain touch with the 47th Division after its capture.

Within five minutes both the German front and support lines had been taken, but at what a cost. Three of the company commanders, Major Henderson and Captains Graham and Bell, together with Lieutenants Henderson-Hamilton, Crighton, Cameron and Millar, had been killed, together with all four company sergeant-majors and over 200 other ranks; while Captain McLeod, nearly all the remaining officers and a large number of other ranks had been wounded.

As he lay on the ground, Major Henderson's last words to his company were "Keep going." His example, and that of all the others, was not lost, for, regardless of the heavy casualties, which might well have affected the spirit of more seasoned troops, the lines swept on irresistibly.

After the capture of the "Jew's Nose" and the remainder of the German front system the attack went on over the third line and down the slope, where communication trenches filled with German dead bore silent but eloquent testimony to the fury

CAPTURE OF HILL 70, SEPTEMBER 25TH, 1915

of the assault. Loos village was quickly reached, and through it the Seaforths and The Black Watch, now reinforced by the Camerons, fought their way. Just before arriving at the village a treacherous act on the part of the enemy increased the fury of The Black Watch. A German officer approached Second Lieutenant A. Sharpe and threw up his hands, whereupon Sharpe ordered his men not to fire on him. At that moment another enemy officer, standing behind the other, shot Sharpe dead with his revolver.

Desperate hand-to-hand fighting took place in the village itself, where a large number of prisoners were taken in the cellars and buildings, mostly after the leading lines had passed on to Hill 70, some, in fact, not being " rounded up " until the following day.

At 8.20 a.m. Colonel Lloyd, who by this time established his headquarters near some haystacks west of Loos, received a message that the 9th had got through the village and were advancing up the slopes of Hill 70 together with the Seaforths, Camerons and Gordons, who had been sent up from reserve as Loos was reached, and on receiving this message Battalion Headquarters moved forward through the village. By this time all four battalions of the Brigade had become intermingled owing to the fighting in Loos, but with the same dash and determination they swept on up the Hill and over the crest towards Cité St. Auguste.

On the left of the Brigade, the 46th had done equally well and were abreast of the 44th; but on the right the 19th London Regiment had been held up by machine gun fire from Loos Cemetery and were delayed until the afternoon. This had a considerable bearing on the situation, as far as The Black Watch was concerned.

When the Hill was reached it was found that the 15th Division was in an unenviable position. Both flanks were exposed, for the 1st Division, on the left of the 46th Brigade, had been held up at the outset by uncut wire, and there was no sign of the 19th London Regiment on the right. About 9 a.m. Battalion Headquarters was established at a house on the extreme eastern outskirts of Loos, and about fifty yards from the base of the Loos Crassier, which effectively hid all that was going on further south. Shortly afterwards a report reached Colonel Lloyd that the enemy were bringing machine guns forward at the eastern end of the Crassier and that, in consequence, the small party of his battalion there (about twenty men under Corporal J. Connely) had been obliged to refuse its right flank, and were thus holding the enemy at bay.

The situation on this flank was therefore precarious. Colonel Lloyd had only a handful of men, consisting of the Battalion staff, signallers and a few runners, at his disposal to meet the

THE NINTH BATTALION THE BLACK WATCH

menace, but these, and the party under Connely, effectively prevented the enemy from turning the right flank of the Division. Confirmation of this situation is found in an account of the battle written by a German officer who took part in it. He says that the Highlanders were almost taken in flank on the German left. It was this party of The Black Watch who successfully stopped the attack on this flank.

While this was going on, on the right, the leading men of all four battalions had crossed the Hill and some had actually reached the houses of The Dynamitière, but of these none returned, all being either killed or captured. The remainder endeavoured to dig in about 400 yards down the eastern slope of Hill 70, but exposed to heavy fire from the Cité St. Auguste, they were compelled to fall back and dig themselves in just below the western slope. A half-completed redoubt crowned the hill, and six or seven times the rapidly diminishing numbers of the 44th and 46th Brigades stormed and took the work only to be driven out each time by heavy machine gun and rifle fire.

Matters remained thus till late in the afternoon. Many and urgent calls were made for the promised reinforcements, but none arrived until 3 p.m., when the situation was somewhat relieved by the arrival of six motor machine guns, under Major Hall, sent up by Division to report to Colonel Lloyd. Of these, two went to reinforce Corporal Connely's party on the Hill, while the others were sent to Colonel Sandilands, 7th Camerons, on the crest, where they did very good work. The work done by these machine gunners deserves more than passing reference. They showed great determination in making their way up, and lost severely in doing so. Abandoning their motor-cycles before reaching Loos, the men carried both guns and ammunition up to the front line in the face of heavy and continuous fire, rendering magnificent service to the hard-pressed Highlanders.

Throughout the day no communication with Brigade Headquarters had been possible except by runners, many of whom had been killed before delivering their messages. No communication could be established with the 47th Division, and it was not till 4 p.m. that some men of the 19th London Battalion were seen creeping across the Loos Crassier, thus, for the first time in the day, establishing communication with the 9th Black Watch. On the left, too, matters had improved, for during the afternoon the 1st Division was able to get forward and in line with the 46th Brigade in the neighbourhood of Puits 14.bis.

At 4.30 p.m. Colonel Lloyd received the following message from General Wilkinson:—

" The 62nd Brigade is marching on Loos. AAA If Hill 70

BATTLE OF LOOS, SEPTEMBER 25TH, 1915

"is held by us they will support and, if necessary, relieve the 44th Brigade. AAA and, if situation admits, will assist in further advance on Cité St. Auguste. AAA 45th Brigade are being ordered to hold on to Loos."

On receipt of this message, Colonel Lloyd sent the following to the Seaforths, Gordons and Camerons:—

"In view of Brigade message reference 62nd Brigade. AAA What are your views, do you consider relief desirable?"

Colonel Sandilands replied that he considered the relief urgent, as he had only about 100 men left; while Colonel Wallace reported that he could not estimate his casualties, as his battalion was so split up, adding that he agreed with Colonel Sandilands. No reply was received from the Seaforths. As to the 9th Black Watch, the reply was obvious, there being barely 90 men remaining, including Headquarters and the party at the end of the Crassier. Taken as a whole the Brigade had lost about 75 per cent of its total strength in the battle. True, it had captured four lines of German trenches together with Loos village and the crest of Hill 70, but the survivors in no condition to hold its gains without help, which seemed as far away as ever. A message was therefore sent stating the situation, and at midnight orders were received from General Wilkinson to the effect that the Brigade would be withdrawn on relief by the 21st Division. This took place during the early hours of September 26th, when the 9th Black Watch was relieved and marched back to Philosophe, arriving there at 3.30 a.m. Out of a total of 940 who went into action, only 98 all told returned to Philosophe that morning. The Battalion had lost 360 other ranks killed or missing and 320 wounded, together with the following officers:—

Killed	*Wounded*
Major M. W. Henderson.	Captain A. K. McLeod.
Captain J. M. Bell.	Lieut. R. Andrew.
,, D. H. N. Graham.	,, A. O. Dennistoun.
Lieut. J. C. Henderson-	,, D. J. Glenny.
Hamilton.	,, E. R. Wilson.
,, J. Crighton.	2nd Lieut. J. Campbell.
,, J. H. Cameron.	,, R. Stirling.
2nd Lieut. J. Millar.	,, G. Scott-Pearse.
,, A. Sharpe.	,, W. J. Leslie.
Captain C. S. Tuke (Bde.	,, E. R. Wilson.
M.G. Officer).	Captain F. A. Bearn, R.A.M.C. (attd.).

Died of Wounds
Captain and Adjutant R. E. Harvey. A total of 701 all ranks.

THE NINTH BATTALION THE BLACK WATCH

At Philosophe the Battalion went into billets. Here it was joined by those officers and non-commissioned officers who had been left behind on the 24th. Their arrival, early in the morning of the 26th, materially assisted in the task of reorganization.

About 9 a.m. the Commanding Officer received a message directing him to move the Battalion at once into what was known as the Grenay–Vermelles line (a trench system about a mile behind the original British front line) and to be in readiness to repel any attack thereon. This move had hardly been completed when another message, much delayed in delivery, arrived, to the effect that the 44th Brigade was to occupy the original British front trenches south of the Philosophe–Lens road and to be in readiness to cover an attack on Hill 70 which would be made by the 45th and 62nd Brigades in the afternoon.

This move was made at once, and the Battalion went forward to the original German front line and set to work reversing the parapet and putting the line into a state of defence.

Unfortunately the attack on Hill 70 that afternoon failed for no reasons in any way connected with the 15th Division, and when night fell the general situation was about the same as it had been on the evening of the 25th, the 45th Brigade still holding on tenaciously to the western slopes of Hill 70.

At 1.20 a.m. on the 27th the Brigade was ordered to withdraw and concentrate at Mazingarbe, billeting in the north-west corner of the village. Five hours later the 9th Battalion reached its area, where the whole Battalion was accommodated in " Black Watch Farm," which prior to the battle had been scarcely large enough to take in A company alone.

Thus ends the story of the 9th at Loos. No words can ever do justice to its deeds on that occasion. Leading, as it did, the right of the Highland Brigade attack, it had perhaps the hardest task in dealing with the enemy front system, in the taking of which most of its casualties occurred. Writing some time after the battle, Brigadier-General H. F. Thuillier, destined later to command the Division, says :—

"A day or two after the first attack I had occasion to pass
" over the ground where the 15th Division had assaulted the
" German trenches. In front of the remains of that work known
" as the ' Lens Road Redoubt ' (Jew's Nose), the dead High-
" landers, in Black Watch tartan, lay very thick. In one place,
" about 40 yards square, on the very crest of the ridge, and just
" in front of the enemy's wire, they were so close that it was
" difficult to step between them. Nevertheless the survivors had
" swept on and through the German lines.

BATTLE OF LOOS
SEPTEMBER 25TH, 1915
Advance of the 15th Division.

Objectives shown ----
Barrages " ▼▼▼

Scale of Yards
0 500 1000

The 7th Objective was "the high ground N. of Loisons-sous-Lens."

THE BATTLE OF LOOS

"As I looked on the smashed and riven ground, ... I was amazed when I thought of the unconquerable, irresistible spirit which those newly raised units of the 'New Armies' must possess to enable them to continue their advance after sustaining such losses."

It was neither the fault of the Highlanders, nor of the 15th Division, that the operation so successfully begun should have ended as it did. General McCracken's instructions to push forward to the utmost were obeyed to the letter, as he himself acknowledges in his report. Unaided, mortal men could have done no more than did his Division at Loos, and in the performance of those orders the 9th Black Watch well upheld the credit of its parent regiment. Although the incident did not occur until some days later, it is worth recording that one morning, as the Commanding Officer and Second-in-Command were walking through Mazingarbe, the 42nd passed them, on their way to the front line. The Commanding Officer, Lieutenant-Colonel C. E. Stewart, stopped and, on behalf of the 1st Battalion, congratulated Colonel Lloyd on what the 9th Battalion had achieved at Loos—a very much treasured compliment. This was made known to all ranks in the following Order :—

Special Order. 9th Black Watch

"The Commanding Officer of the 1st Battalion has just been over to express to the Commanding Officer the great pride which all ranks in the 42nd feel at the splendid work of the 9th Black Watch on September 25th."

On September 28th the Battalion, with the rest of the 44th Brigade, moved back to Houchin.

15TH DIVISION SPECIAL ORDER

"The following message has been received from Sir Henry Rawlinson :—

"'The Corps Commander is anxious that you should communicate to all ranks of the 15th Division his high appreciation of the admirable fighting spirit which they displayed in the attack and capture of Loos village and Hill 70.

"'Sir Douglas Haig has also desired the Corps Commander to convey his congratulations to the Division.

"'The Major-General wishes to say that he is very proud of his Command.

"'(Sgd.) J. T. BURNETT-STUART, Lieut.-Col.,
"'Gen. Staff, 15th Division.'"

THE NINTH BATTALION THE BLACK WATCH

SPEECH BY MAJOR-GENERAL MCCRACKEN, COMMANDING 15TH DIVISION, ON OCTOBER 2ND, 1915, AT HOUCHIN

"Colonel Lloyd, officers, non-commissioned officers and "men of the 9th Battalion The Black Watch.

"I have come here to say just two or three words only.

"You have heard already, and everyone knows, that your "behaviour during the recent operations has been much appre-"ciated.

. . . . .

"I have already heard that your people know which Division "took the great part in the operations—you will have told them "yourselves. If they do not know they will in the course of the "next few days.

"I want to add one word more. I want to impress upon you "the quality which made you perform the deeds of that day.

"The quality you possess is discipline. Without discipline an "Army is only a mob, but with discipline it is an instrument "with which a Commander can do almost anything. You have "discipline. Officers, non-commissioned officers and men should "work to this end all the time.

. . . . .

"I grieve for your losses. Remember lives that have been "given up, have been given up ... in the best cause of all— "fighting for their country.

"Your country is proud of you."

Immediately after the battle the French Government, as was their custom, conferred a certain number of awards on British soldiers. Three of these were allotted to the Division, and one, the Croix de Guerre, was awarded to Lance-Sergeant J. McKellar.

During the 27th and 28th of September a certain number of men who had become detached during the fighting, and had fought with other battalions, reported themselves, with the result that on the 28th the Battalion stood on parade eight officers and 320 strong. The remainder of the Battalion had been either killed or wounded in the heavy fighting.

The Battalion remained at Houchin five days, during which the work of reorganization commenced. The feeling of dismay at the task before them of those who had helped to train it in 1914 may be well imagined. There was no time, however, for lamentation and all turned to and started work with a will.

On the 1st of October, Lieutenant S. Norie-Miller was appointed Adjutant vice Captain Harvey, died of wounds.

During these few days the task of collecting and burying those

IN CORPS RESERVE, OCTOBER, 1915

who had fallen was accomplished. Large parties from all battalions in the Brigade were sent up daily and gradually got together as many of their fallen comrades as was possible. A few of the 9th had been buried by parties from other brigades and divisions, but the majority were collected by men of their own battalion, under Captain Carmichael, often exposed to enemy fire from the new positions east of Loos. The bodies of Major Henderson, Captains Graham and Bell, Lieutenants Crighton, Henderson-Hamilton and J. Millar, were buried together just north of the Philosophe–Lens road, about ten yards east of the original British front line. Here they rest undisturbed to this day, their graves kept in order and fresh flowers placed on them by the villagers of Mazingarbe. Close to them are the graves of over 150 men who fell before reaching the German trenches.

CHAPTER III

OCTOBER, 1915 TO JULY, 1916

Trench Warfare

THE Division was now in IV Corps reserve, and on October 3rd it marched westwards to Lillers and the neighbourhood to rest, train and re-equip. At Lillers, where the 44th Brigade were billeted, the work went on smoothly and rapidly. A large amount of material was obtained to replace that lost. Specialists, such as machine gunners (who had almost all been killed or wounded), signallers, runners and above all, non-commissioned officers were selected and their training commenced. Between the 1st and 12th of October eighteen second lieutenants from the 11th Battalion in Scotland reported for duty, amongst them being J. H. Robertson, R. W. Reid, R. H. C. Ewart and L. G. Morrison, all of whom had served with the 9th in England. The other officers were: Lieutenants E. G. Pitcairn, H. E. Reynell, O. L. Bearn (brother of the medical officer), L. Stewart-Murray; Second Lieutenants A. McGregor, J. Dewar, J. Small, J. B. Robertson, R. Carswell, A. Howard, J. Waldie, A. McPhee, T. Tweedie and A. McKenzie.

During this time drafts amounting to 505 other ranks joined, bringing the Battalion again up to strength but by no means up to the standard of efficiency at which it had been a month earlier. Such could not be expected, but the new comers worked hard, and soon the effects of that spirit of discipline which even Loos could not eradicate became apparent throughout the Battalion.

All this time the battle, which had commenced on the 25th of September, still raged round Loos, and, as further operations were contemplated, the 15th Division was ordered to return to the front line on October 12th, on which day the Battalion moved by train to Noeux-les-Mines, where it went into billets. Here it remained carrying out training of all kinds till the 22nd, when it moved to Noyelles. The reason for this move was that, as the battalions of the 46th Brigade, then in support to the 45th in the line, were weak, General McCracken placed the 9th Black Watch at the disposal of the G.O.C. 46th Brigade. Reports had been received that the enemy were massing for an attack in the neighbourhood of the Quarries. Nothing happened, however, and the Battalion spent an uneventful but rather unpleasant three days in Noyelles.

On the 25th the 9th went into the line, this time in Brigade reserve, the Gordons and Camerons holding the front line with the Seaforths in support, relieving the 45th Brigade.

The sector in which the Battalion now found itself was a bad one. It was overlooked from both the Hohenzollern Redoubt and

TRENCH WARFARE, NOVEMBER, 1915

Puits 14.bis. The trenches were in an appalling condition, especially those which had been made since the September fighting. It is not surprising, therefore, to read in the Battalion Diary that when it relieved the Gordons in the front line on the 29th, the relief took six hours to complete, " all the trenches being water-"logged and full of mud, while heavy shelling and close " proximity to the enemy made it impossible to move up over " the open ground."

From this date till November 19th the weather was extremely bad, with gales of wind. On one occasion, when the Battalion moved up through Vermelles, the wind was such that it blew the walls of ruined houses down as though they were being shelled. Fortunately, tours in the front line were now restricted to three days at a time, but even this short period was as much as the men could stand.

The worst sector of all was that opposite Hulluch. Here most of the trenches were waterlogged, some literally impassable and many almost obliterated by shell fire. That portion known as "The Hairpin" was the worst, for, besides shallow and crumbling trenches, enemy snipers and bombers were especially active. The front line was close to that of the enemy; in fact, at one place Germans occupied the same trench. Each had blocked their flank, leaving a narrow No Man's Land of about four yards in width. Under such unfavourable conditions rationing the Battalion was a difficult matter, but the transport officer and quartermaster never once failed and, although they might be late on some occasions, the men always had their rations.

On the whole, the enemy was unenterprising, except with bombs, and when orders were issued that for every bomb sent over by the enemy six were to be sent back, things quietened down considerably. Casualties were few. The Diary only mentions that on November 8th, Second Lieutenant A. McKenzie and two other ranks were killed and four wounded; later that Lieutenant J. D. G. Miller was killed in " The Hairpin."

The Battalion suffered a great loss on November 19th. On that day Lieutenant-Colonel T. Lloyd was ordered, on the recommendation of the medical officer, to be evacuated sick. For some time previously he had been suffering from sciatica, aggravated by the bad conditions then prevailing, and was now compelled to leave the Battalion. He left with the greatest grief, hoping to return and resume command; but although he remained, on paper, in command for some time, he was never passed medically fit, and thus his active association with the 9th Black Watch ended.

Concluding his own period with the Battalion, Colonel Lloyd wrote:—

THE NINTH BATTALION THE BLACK WATCH

"Never can I adequately express my admiration for this great Battalion, nor can I find words to thank all ranks for the loyal support extended to me during the many and varied experiences between 6th September, 1914, and 19th November, 1915. . . . Ever conspicuous shone that indomitable spirit of cheerful sacrifice. . . . My proudest recollection is that, although only for a short period, I had the great honour to command it."

Major, now Lieutenant-Colonel, N. W. MacGregor, 9th Gordon Highlanders, assumed command of the Battalion on the departure of Colonel Lloyd, after which it returned to the "Hairpin" sector on the 19th, remaining there till the 23rd, when it moved into Divisional reserve, billeted at Vaudricourt, where it received a draft of two officers, Lieutenant W. Binnie and Second Lieutenant E. N. Raymond, and 22 other ranks.

On December 1st the Battalion moved back to Noyelles, and the following day the Brigadier presented the French Croix de Guerre to Lance-Sergeant McKellar for his gallant services during the battle of Loos.

Three days later the 9th relieved the 10th Gordons in the "Hairpin" sector, remaining there for two days, when it was relieved and moved to Philosophe, going up again to the front line on the 11th. This proved its last tour of trench duty in 1915, for on the 14th it was relieved by the 18th London Regiment, 47th Division, and proceeded by train to Lillers and thence to Lozinghem, the 15th Division then becoming IV Corps reserve.

Apart from the vile weather, the last tour had been a quiet one with a few casualties: two other ranks killed and six wounded.

A draft of 48 other ranks joined on the 29th, bringing the strength of the Battalion on December 31st up to 22 officers and 944 other ranks.

While at Lozinghem, much-needed training, including a Divisional exercise and various route marches and reorganization, were carried out. In January, Major J. Stewart rejoined from hospital, taking over command from Lieutenant-Colonel MacGregor, and on the 14th the Battalion, with the rest of the Division, moved up to the front line.

At this time the Division line ran from the Loos—St. Laurent road to Devon Lane, just north of the Vermelles–Hulluch road. This was held by two brigades, the dividing line being Vendin Alley, the Battalion taking over the left sub-section of the right sector (from Posen Alley to Vendin Alley inclusive). The trenches were by no means in good order, and work on them continued unceasingly. The enemy gave little trouble and the tour was comparatively a quiet one. On the 26th the Battalion

TRENCH WARFARE, JANUARY TO MARCH, 1916

was relieved by the 10th Scottish Rifles and went into billets at Noeux-les-Mines; but the four machine guns, under Lieutenant Waldie, remained in the line, as the Commanding Officer had a premonition that the enemy contemplated an attack that night. This proved correct, and The Black Watch guns played such a prominent part in repelling the attack that messages of congratulation were received from both the Division and Brigade Commanders, together with one from the G.O.C. 46th Brigade, under whose orders the guns had remained. Later, Sergeant Bayne and Lance-Corporal Thomson received the D.C.M. for their good work on this occasion.

After a few days rest the Battalion moved to Philosophe and, three days later, took over the line from Vendin Alley to Devon Lane, relieving the 8th Seaforths. This tour proved unfortunate. The enemy were more aggressive, especially with artillery fire, and consequently casualties were somewhat heavy, two officers being killed, one wounded, seven other ranks killed and 29 wounded.

On the 13th, on relief by the 10th Scottish Rifles, the Battalion moved back to Mazingarbe, where it was joined by Second Lieutenants R. J. L. Scott and J. S. Stirling, and, on the 20th, took over the line opposite Puits 14.bis, where it only remained for two days, moving back to the old German trenches northwest of Loos, in Brigade support, on relief by the 10th Gordons.

From here the Battalion moved to Noeux-les-Mines on March 2nd, where it remained for a week, during which the whole Battalion went through a course of instruction in the use of gas helmets; every man passing through a chamber filled with gas eight times as strong as that then employed by the enemy. A great deal of care was taken in the instruction of the men in the use of these helmets, which, as will be seen, proved invaluable not long afterwards.

The next tour, this time in the Hulluch sector, lasted from the 9th to 17th March, when the Battalion moved back to Philosophe, where Lieutenant R. B. A. MacDonald and Second Lieutenant H. M. Drummond reported for duty. Like the last, the period was uneventful except for the last day, when the enemy shelled the Battalion line heavily; two officers, Second Lieutenants Howard and Clow, and two other ranks were killed and 16 other ranks wounded.[1]

On March 25th the Division went into Corps reserve with Headquarters at Lillers, the 44th Brigade occupying the villages of Burbure and Allouagne, the 9th Black Watch being allotted

---

[1] It may be of interest to mention that Howard was an officer in the U.S. Army. Directly England declared war he threw up his commission, crossed to England and enlisted, being granted a commission shortly afterwards. He did *not* inform the U.S.A. authorities of his intention.

THE NINTH BATTALION THE BLACK WATCH

Burbure. Here a month was spent "resting," which relaxation took the form of hard and necessary training culminating in a Divisional exercise which lasted for two days.

On the 17th, Brigadier-General Wilkinson handed over command of the 44th Brigade to Brigadier-General F. J. Marshall. Before leaving he visited the Battalion and said good-bye, thanking them for what they had accomplished under his command and congratulating them on the high standard of discipline they had attained.

Towards the end of April news came that the next move would be back to Loos, and on the 25th the 9th moved up to Noeux-les-Mines by train and road, taking over the right section of the "Quarry" sector from the 11th Middlesex (12th Division).

Two days afterwards the enemy sent over a cloud of gas which did little or no harm, but on the 29th to cover an attack on another Division further south it was repeated. Unfortunately this caused many casualties, due to the fact that the wind changed just after the cloud had passed over, and many men of the Right company took off their masks, thinking that it had blown over. One officer (Lieutenant J. Small) was killed, and three (Captain G. A. Rusk and Second Lieutenants J. McIntyre and J. M. Dewar) were gassed, and Second Lieutenant H. M. Drummond wounded, in addition to nearly a hundred other ranks, some of whom died from the effects of gas.

The next rest period, from the 11th to 19th May, was interrupted by a determined enemy attack from Hohenzollern Redoubt. On this occasion the enemy succeeded in taking "The Kink," and the 9th Black Watch was hurried up to support in an attempt to re-take it; this was, however, finally abandoned and the Battalion returned to Sailly for the remainder of its period in reserve. On the 17th, Lieutenant R. W. Reid died from wounds received on April 27th. Although small in stature, and little more than a boy in years, this young officer was a real man and was held in high esteem by all ranks. He received his wounds while successfully repelling an enemy bombing attack which had reached his trench.

From this time till the end of July little of interest occurred. The time was spent either in Hulluch or Hohenzollern sectors with short periods of rest at Sailly or Béthune, where between the 14th and 18th of July Highland games were held.

On June 16th, Lieutenant-Colonel Stewart, one of the few remaining original officers of the Battalion, was evacuated sick, and Lieutenant-Colonel S. A. Innes assumed command. During the period the following officers reported for duty:—

2nd June: Second Lieutenants A. F. Watson, H. S. Muir, S. Allan and N. Bartmann.

MOVE TO THE SOMME, JULY 22ND, 1916

28th June: Captain R. F. Bruce and Second Lieutenant F. Proudfoot, with 10 other ranks.

23rd July: Second Lieutenants T. E. Reid and D. W. Cuthbert.

At this time the battle on the Somme was raging fiercely and rumours of a move in that direction had been rife. These were substantiated by orders received on July 20th to the effect that, on relief by the 2nd Battalion Lincolnshire Regiment on the 22nd, the Battalion would move to Houchin, preparatory to marching south with the Division, and on that day the 9th Black Watch said farewell to the Loos area in which it had fought so long.

From January to 23rd of July the casualties were as follows:—

	Officers		Other Ranks		
	Killed or Died of Wounds.	Wounded.	Killed or Died of Wounds.	Wounded.	Missing.
January	Nil	Nil	5	16	1
February	3	1	9	32	2
April	1	5	40	117	4
May	3	1	14	56	2
June	Nil	Nil	8	45	Nil
July	Nil	4	7	40	Nil

CHAPTER IV

JULY, 1916, TO MARCH, 1917

The Somme

THE move to the new area commenced on July 23rd with a march of fourteen miles westward to La Thieuloye, where a halt was made for two days. From there the Battalion proceeded south, halting successively at Magnicourt-sur-Canche, Occoches, Longuevillette (one day's halt), Naours (three days' halt), Mirvaux, La Houssoye and Bazieux, at which place it met the 1st Battalion bivouacked there, and finally, on August 8th, the 9th Black Watch reached Albert, where it was joined by a draft of 40 other ranks under Second Lieutenant Dow. During the whole march the weather was hot, and this, combined with want of practice in marching, made the first stages of the move rather trying; few men, however, fell out. The change was welcome, and all ranks benefited greatly.

The fighting in this area had commenced in July, and therefore when the 9th Black Watch joined the III Army Corps, (General Pulteney), it went almost straight into the battle. Unfortunately no accounts from officers of the Battalion who participated in the operations are available, and the following very bald account is taken from the War Diary and other official documents.

The first operation against the enemy positions immediately south of Martinpuich, found the 9th with the 44th Brigade, in Divisional reserve, the initial attack being made by the 46th and 45th Brigades. Here The Black Watch found the conditions under which they had to exist very different to those prevailing in the Loos salient. Instead of living in a maze of trenches, everyone moved freely in the open, undeterred by even more shelling than that with which they were familiar round Loos.

The Battalion moved first to reserve in front of Albert, where it was accommodated in tents. The sensation of shell fire, with nothing between the splinters and the occupants but a thin canvas tent, was, understandably, somewhat novel to those accustomed to the deep dug-outs in and round Loos. Further up, however, things were very different, and here, in the areas just taken from the enemy, vast and well-equipped dug-outs were found. It was extraordinary to note the comfort in which the enemy had lived for the past two years right up in their front line. In one instance, the German commander at Fricourt had a dug-out consisting of several rooms, all completely furnished with beds, kitchen, etc., in which he had not only his wife and daughter, but the latter's governess to stay with him. What

A SOLDIER OF THE NINTH BATTALION
From a sketch drawn in France, 1917

ATTACK ON "THE ELBOW," AUGUST 14TH, 1916

trenches existed were merely lines of connected shell-holes giving little cover from either fire or view. These were, of course, improved later, but the task of doing so was herculean, and it was a long time before they were in anything like order.

The initial attack by the 46th and 45th Brigades did not prove entirely satisfactory, being hung up on the right owing to another Division encountering too strong a resistance, with the result that the 44th Brigade was ordered up to continue the operation on the 14th, on which date the 9th Black Watch found themselves in the line near Contalmaison, ready to support the attack of the 7th Camerons on the "Switch Line" and "The Elbow." A heartening sight met the 9th as it marched through Contalmaison on this occasion in the shape of two German guns labelled "Captured by the 1st Bn. The Black Watch."

This attack was, at first, successful and about two hundred yards of trench was captured, but the enemy, making a counter-attack down "The Elbow," recaptured the ground and about fifty yards beyond it, where he was checked and held up by a Stokes gun and rifle grenades. By this time all the officers of the Camerons had become casualties, so Captain Binnie, with two companies of the 9th Black Watch, was sent forward and preparations were at once made to consolidate and to organize a fresh attack to recapture "The Elbow."

This was launched in conjunction with the Camerons and two platoons of the Seaforths and was completely successful; but that night all consolidation work was suspended owing to heavy enemy artillery fire. On this occasion The Black Watch captured one machine gun and seven men of the 179th Regiment. Unfortunately the losses were severe, Second Lieutenant R. B. A. MacDonald being killed, whilst Lieutenant D. C. Eglington and Second Lieutenants J. F. MacRae, A. F. Watson, R. J. McMurray and J. S. Strang were wounded, besides 25 other ranks killed, 113 wounded and 12 missing, a total of 157. In addition, and to the great regret of every man in the Battalion, Captain F. A. Bearn, the Battalion medical officer who had been with it from the early days of 1914, was severely wounded and thus left The Black Watch which he had served so devotedly throughout. Captain Bearn received the Military Cross for his services at Loos, and later was awarded the D.S.O. for his subsequent and continuous efforts. A good story of "The Apothecary" may be told here: While holding the rat-infested trenches near Loos, Bearn was in the habit of practising on the rodents with his revolver—generally with some success. On one evening, seeing in the dark what he took to be a sitting rat, the medical officer drew his revolver, took careful aim and fired. As the animal remained stationary he took another shot to make sure, and as it still remained immovable he then proceeded to investigate, to find that he had been firing at a *live Mills grenade!*

On the 19th, when relieved by the Seaforths, the Battalion moved to Scots Redoubt, and on the 24th to Contalmaison, relieving the Camerons. Here it occupied a line of small strong points some 150 yards in front of the front line. This tour and the next in the same place were more unpleasant than usual, owing to heavy enemy shelling by which Second Lieutenants D. O. Tweedie and H. B. Johnstone were wounded.

There came now a lull in active warfare, during which plans for the next offensive were being prepared, and in the interval the 9th Black Watch, on relief by the 27th Northumberland Fusiliers, moved back into Divisional reserve one mile east of Albert, where the 44th Brigade took the place of the 103rd, and where it was joined by a draft of 51 other ranks under Second Lieutenant Gordon.

In the recent fighting the Battalion had lost heavily, the total casualties being nine officers and 240 other ranks.

September 6th found the Battalion once more in the front line, between High Wood and Bazentin le Petit, with a battalion of the 1st Division on the right and the 7th Camerons on the left. This position, owing to its being overlooked by the enemy in High Wood, was difficult to reach and could only be approached through the left battalion. In its new position much preparatory work, in the way of " jumping off " trenches, fire-steps and saps, was accomplished under continuous shell and machine gun fire, Captain J. B. Robertson and three other ranks were killed on one occasion by shell fire.

On September 7th the Battalion was ordered to attack an enemy trench just outside the north-west corner of High Wood, the attack to take place on the following day.

Colonel Innes detailed B and D companies to carry out the operation under Captains Stirling and Binnie. The attack was launched at 6.30 p.m. and, in face of heavy machine gun fire, the trench was taken and 30 prisoners captured. Consolidation commenced at once, and a strong enemy counter-attack made an hour later was driven off with considerable loss. Shortly afterwards, however, a battalion on the right, which had been co-operating, found it impossible to maintain its position and sent word that it was going back. This led to enemy pressure from that flank and also from the front, besides a certain amount from the left, and at 8 p.m. this became so strong that the two companies were forced to fall back to the original front line, which was reached with slight loss. The losses were Lieutenant Ireland wounded and missing, Captains Stirling and Binnie and Second Lieutenants Humble and Drummond wounded; 24 other ranks

MARTINPUICH SECTOR, SEPTEMBER, 1916

killed, 14 missing and 59 wounded. In addition to those taken prisoner it was estimated that 70 Germans were killed. During this action a prisoner was taken who belonged to the Bavarian division that had been opposite the Battalion at Hohenzollern Redoubt. He had on him a German trench map showing the Battalion positions in that area.

The following day was spent repairing damaged trenches and in reorganization generally, and that night the Battalion, on relief moved to billets in Albert, where the next few days were spent in rest and re-equipping. Here Lieutenant E. W. Wilson and a draft of 30 other ranks joined the Battalion.

The Battalion next moved, on September 11th, to Shelter Wood, in Brigade support, going up to the front line in the Martinpuich left sector on the 17th. This was an exceptionally unpleasant tour. Not only did the enemy deluge the area with heavy artillery fire, but torrents of rain converted the half-finished trenches into quagmires, making work on them wellnigh impossible. Fortunately they only remained here for two days, but during that time they lost seven other ranks killed, 37 wounded and one missing.

On the 19th the Battalion was relieved and, with the rest of the 44th Brigade, marched to Laviéville, the 15th Division having been replaced in the line by the 23rd. Here Captain W. Story-Wilson rejoined, and Lieutenant G. Forsyth and Second Lieutenants R. McRoberts and D. G. Hodge joined from the 11th Battalion.

This last period had been a long and trying one. The Division was forty-four days in the line, during which it had taken part in heavy and continuous fighting all the time. All formations had done well and in recognition had received the gracious thanks of His Majesty the King, and congratulations of the Commander-in-Chief, the Army Commander (twice) and the Divisional General (three times). Casualties had been heavy, those of the 9th Battalion from the 12th August to 19th September being:—

	Killed.	Missing.	Wounded.
Officers	1	1	15
Other ranks	62	29	294

In addition to which six officers and 71 other ranks were evacuated sick.

While the Division was in Corps reserve the 9th spent the time at Franvillers, from September 20th to October 6th, during which time the usual training was carried out. Here Second Lieutenants R. A. Hastings and C. G. MacDowall joined from the 11th Battalion, while Major A. D. Carmichael went home to attend a Senior Officer's Course of Instruction.

THE NINTH BATTALION THE BLACK WATCH

The next move took place on October 6th, when the Battalion marched to Bécourt, relieving the 13th Duke of Cornwall's Light Infantry in Le Sars area on the 8th. This short tour—it only lasted two days—cost the Battalion one officer, Second Lieutenant Turnbull, killed and four other ranks killed, 11 missing and 36 wounded; and from there it moved to rest at Bresle Camp, where, on the 20th, the 44th Brigade was visited by the Corps Commander, Lieutenant-General W. P. Pulteney, who addressed them as follows:—

"Officers, non-commissioned officers and men of the 44th
"Infantry Brigade. I have come here to-day to thank you for
"the magnificent service you have rendered while under my
"command. You have had to face and overcome many diffi-
"culties. The advance over the Pozières–High Wood Ridge, the
"capture of Martinpuich and the defence of Le Sars, testify to
"your good work. I want you to keep fit and in training during
"the coming winter as there are more difficulties before you.
"If a rifle gets rusty it is not of as much use as it was before.
"So it is with you men. Therefore keep fit both morally and
"physically. I am pleased to see you looking so well after all
"you have come through.
"In conclusion let me congratulate the 15th Division on
"having had a longer turn in the trenches than any Division in
"the Army."

While at Bresle the following officers joined the Battalion: Major H. F. F. Murray; Second Lieutenants D. C. Fraser, A. D. McDiarmid, W. Ferguson and R. O. Wilson. It was here also that news reached the Battalion that their Quartermaster, Lieutenant Clark, had been awarded the Military Cross. Never was an honour more deserved. From the birth of the Battalion in 1914, Clark was untiring in his efforts to forward and conserve its interests. At Loos and on the Somme no amount of shelling was heavy enough to prevent him coming up with the rations, and no trouble was too great and no "wangle" too large, if by so doing the 9th Black Watch would benefit.

The rest of their time in the Somme area was peaceful as far as actual fighting was concerned. Of course, there was continuous heavy shelling by day and night which took toll from The Black Watch. Worse than any shelling, however, was the condition of the areas in which the men lived and the prevailing weather conditions. Until the Division themselves constructed them there were very few dug-outs, the only shelters being narrow slits in the ground, exposed to the vile weather which now prevailed. Most of the so-called "trenches" were merely

TRENCH WARFARE

chains of waterlogged shell holes in which all ranks had to live as best they could, and finally rations had, in many instances, to be carried up four miles by men of the reserve company, and in some cases men had to be dug out of the mud into which they had fallen and from which they could not extricate themselves unaided.

Things were so bad that General McCracken decided that battalions would only spend two days in the front line at one time. Although this was a good measure, it entailed many miles of walking over churned-up and waterlogged country which somewhat discounted the good effect of longer " rest " periods. It was, in truth, a very trying period, and it is not surprising that a good deal of sickness occurred. Even when battalions were in Divisional reserve at Shelter Wood and Scots Redoubt, under canvas, they found fully eight inches of mud and no tent boards.

Under such conditions the 9th Black Watch spent the remainder of 1916 in the front, support and reserve lines. Losses were few, even from shell fire, but when moving out of the line on December 27th three companies were caught in a gas-shell bombardment and were fortunate in escaping with only three casualties, Second Lieutenant Hastings and two men.

On December 1st the strength of the Battalion had dwindled to 22 officers and 411 other ranks; but on the 11th a draft of 199 arrived, followed by another of 112 on the 1st of January,

The New Year found the Battalion in Brigade reserve in Pioneer Camp, from which it moved the following day to Seven Elms in support, going again to the front line on January 3rd, in the Flers Switch.

The New Year Honours list contained the following names:

D.S.O. Lieutenant-Colonel S. A. Innes and Captain F. A. Bearn, R.A.M.C. (attd.).

M.C. Regimental Sergeant-Major G. D. Bedson, the following being "mentioned": Lieutenant-Colonel Innes; Major A. D. Carmichael; Captain S. Norie-Miller; Second Lieutenants J. F. N. MacRae and G. B. Mackie, and Lieutenant and Quartermaster W. Clark.

Twice more in January did the Battalion occupy the front line, the first time in 26th Avenue and the second in the right sector, Flers Switch, during which one officer was killed and three wounded, and nine other ranks killed and 36 wounded. When the 15th Division was relieved by the 2nd Australian, The Black Watch moved with the remainder of the 44th Brigade to Bécourt Camp on February 1st, marching to Bresle on the 4th, where it remained until the 11th, and where, on the 8th, the New Year dinner was held, a little late perhaps, but none the less enjoyable.

In January and February three drafts joined the Battalion: the second included Second Lieutenants T. Byers and T. Edwards with 80 other ranks, and the third, Second Lieutenant J. L. Burton and 42 other ranks. The Battalion spent eleven days at Bresle. The weather was intensely cold, but training and sports of all kinds took place and did much good after the recent trying time.

The 15th Division was now destined for the Arras front, and before it left received a farewell message from General Sir H. Rawlinson, Commanding Fourth Army, in which he said:—

" The capture of Martinpuich with more than 1000 prisoners, " accomplished as it was after six weeks of hard and continuous " fighting in the line, was a feat of arms deserving the highest " praise and illustrates the endurance and fine fighting spirit for " which the Division has always been renowned.

" The work which they have done at and about Le Sars has " been of the same high standard as that which they accom-" plished at Loos, and I know no Division in which a higher " standard of discipline and moral exists, nor one to which I " would entrust a difficult undertaking with greater confidence."

On February 14th the Division joined the VI Corps (Lieutenant-General Haldane) in the Third Army (General Allenby), and that day commenced its march to Arras. The time spent in the muddy trenches of the Somme and in bad rest camps had lowered the vitality of the men, and this, added to the biting cold wind which prevailed throughout the whole four days, rendered the march no easy task. The 9th, moving with the 44th Brigade, billeted at the following places: February 14th, Beauval; 15th, Outrebois; 16th, Ligny; 17th, Croisette; and 18th, Buneville, where Second Lieutenants W. Anderson and M. Duggan reported for duty and where it spent five days, moving on to Ambrines on the 23rd, where training recommenced and reorganization was carried out in accordance with instructions received from General Headquarters. Here, on March 8th, the Battalion was inspected by the Commander-in-Chief, and on the same day a draft of 50 men, under Second Lieutenant E. Dale, joined.

CHAPTER V

MARCH TO JUNE, 1917

Arras

THE Battalion went into the new front area on the 11th of March, relieving the 13th Royal Scots. It had moved up to Arras the night before, and all ranks were somewhat surprised at the ease with which they reached the front trenches. Here the line ran north and south, about a quarter of a mile east of Arras, from which city covered communication trenches made it possible for reliefs to be carried out in daylight. In the city itself large cellars and caves, the latter many hundreds of years old, were utilized to provide billets for support and reserve troops. In this area the enemy was quiet and, except for somewhat severe shelling on several occasions, did not interfere with the many preparations which were now in progress for forthcoming operations. In Blangy suburb, where the opposing lines were only about fifteen yards apart, everything was quiet, both sides being so wary of each other that no casualties occurred. Whilst holding this sector the 9th Battalion held the left of the 15th Division line, and the 8th the right of the 51st Division, thus enabling them to exchange greetings daily.

The aggressive spirit of the troops was, however, kept up by constant raids on the enemy trenches, one of which, carried out by two platoons of B company under Second Lieutenants R. K. McRoberts and J. L. Burton, on the 8th of April, was particularly successful, many dug-outs being bombed and one prisoner taken at a cost of five other ranks wounded and two missing.

With the exception of the above-mentioned raid there is little of importance to chronicle before the Arras fighting commenced. On March 19th Captain W. Story-Wilson was awarded the Italian Silver Medal for Military Valour. A draft of 41 other ranks arrived on the 22nd, and, on the 30th, the Battalion was inspected by the VI Corps Commander.

The object of the forthcoming attack was the capture of Vimy Ridge, Monchy le Preux and the high ground to the south of it, in order to drive the Germans back on to the lower ground to the east. To the 15th Division was allotted the first stages of the attack on Monchy. By this time it was realized that no troops, however good, could force their way through the enemy system more than a given distance, and the objectives on this occasion were therefore strictly limited.

The task of the 15th Division was to capture and consolidate a position known as the Brown Line, the second line of the German resistance just east of Feuchy village. When this had been taken, the 37th Division were to go through the 15th and capture Monchy le Preux. Between the front line and the Brown Line were two other objectives, namely, the Black and Blue Lines, the former being the German front-line system and the latter some rising ground known as " Observation Ridge."

General McCracken detailed the 44th Brigade (right) and the 45th (left) to carry out the attack on the Blue Line, reserving the 46th Brigade for the capture of his final objective, the Brown Line, and in accordance with these instructions Brigadier-General Marshall entrusted the attack on his front to the 8/10th Gordons (right) and 9th Black Watch (left), the battalion on the left of the 9th being the 7th Royal Scots Fusiliers, 45th Brigade.

By April 4th everything was ready for the forthcoming battle and the preliminary bombardment of the German trenches commenced. The 9th, who had taken over the left sector of the Brigade line on the 3rd, was accommodated in cellars, dug-outs and a large cave, which latter held over 200 men, the front line being lightly held by one platoon and two Lewis guns, and disposed thus they remained during the five days' bombardment.

Starting at midnight on April 8th, the Battalion took up its position for the attack. In the front line were C (right) and D (left) companies, each in four waves. B company found the support line, in two waves; whilst A followed in reserve, also in two waves, each wave consisting of two lines. By 3.40 a.m. all were in position, and at Zero hour (5.30 a.m.) the attack commenced.

The enemy front trenches were reached by 5.45 a.m., where consolidation at once commenced and preparations made to continue the attack. So far there had been few casualties, not more than fifty in all, mostly caused by the German barrage which fell promptly one minute after the attack was launched. In this stage Second Lieutenant J. O. Fraser was killed, and Second Lieutenants T. W. Hunter, D. W. H. Cuthbert, R. K. McRoberts and A. Marshall wounded.

At 7.10 a.m. the advance on the Blue Line began, and soon a stiff enemy resistance was encountered by the Gordons on the right, the Royal Scots Fusiliers and The Black Watch on the left. By this the Battalion was held up along a line running north and south through the centre of the " Railway Triangle," from the embankments of which machine gun and rifle fire enfiladed the ground over which the 44th Brigade had to advance. Snipers, too, were active, and during this pause in the advance the Battalion lost heavily, especially in officers, Captain Story-Wilson and Second Lieutenants S. M. Reid, T. E. Reid, J. Callan, F. Proudfoot and J. W. Barr being all hit.

IN RESERVE AT FEUCHY, APRIL, 1917

The delay lasted for three hours, when, with the assistance of a tank and the support battalion, 7th Camerons, the line moved forward to the Blue Line, where it consolidated uninterrupted by the enemy. At 2.20 p.m. the 46th Brigade went through the line, and a few hours later the 9th Battalion was relieved by the 7th Camerons and went back to Hermes Trench in reserve.

The operation had been entirely successful and had been accomplished without undue loss. In addition to those officers already named, Captain H. J. Collins, Roman Catholic Chaplain to the Brigade, attached Black Watch, was killed, and Second Lieutenant D. W. H. Cuthbert died of wounds the same day. Captain and Adjutant S. Norie-Miller, Second Lieutenants H. Muir and R. M. Dinwiddie, the transport officer, were wounded.

Captain Collins' death was felt by all ranks. He joined the Battalion before it left England, and no officer was more proud of being attached to the Battalion than was Captain Collins. He accompanied it on every tour in the trenches and was ever to be found in the front line with a haversack full of cigarettes, his own gift to the men. On many occasions did he carry out the funeral service on men killed in the front line, sometimes under rifle and machine gun fire, and always, but most of all when conditions were bad, did his cheery presence enhearten all ranks. Captain Collins was recommended for the Military Cross some months before his death. On the 8th of June, 1917, his name appeared in the list of officers " Mentioned in Despatches."

The captures by the Battalion included over 200 prisoners, four machine guns, one trench mortar, and some mining instruments.

A word must be said regarding the weather. Up to the date of attack it had been fine, but scarcely had operations commenced than rain fell and continued throughout the day, turning to snow as the final objective was reached. The work of consolidation was carried out at night in blinding snow and a gale of wind. It was a most arduous task, but the knowledge of all they had accomplished that day raised the spirits of all ranks, and by dawn the captured line was in defensive order.

April 10th was spent in burying the dead, clearing the captured ground and furnishing a large working party. On the following day the 9th was ordered forward to Feuchy, where it remained all day in reserve for the attack on Monchy by the Division, returning the same night to Arras on relief by the 17th Division. Here it was billeted in cellars in the Grand Place, from thence moving to Schram Barracks, where it received the congratulations of the Commander-in-Chief, Army, Corps and Divisional Commanders, and where it remained till the 19th, when it moved up to Wancourt, relieving the 1st King's Own

THE NINTH BATTALION THE BLACK WATCH

Scottish Borderers (29th Division), in readiness for the second phase of the battle.

This time the task of the Division was the capture of Guémappe and the ground east of it as far as St. Robart Factory and the Bois du Vert, which constituted the Red Line, whilst the Green Line, or final objective, was 2000 yards further east. This attack was to be made by the 44th Brigade (right) and 45th (left), the 46th being in Divisional reserve. The task of the leading brigades was the capture and consolidation of the Red Line, from the Cojeul River on the right, due north, east of Cavalry Farm (both of which were in the 44th Brigade area), to a copse 700 yards north of the farm. The 50th Division was on the right of the 44th Brigade, the Cojeul River being the dividing line.

The 8th Seaforths (right) and 7th Camerons (left) led the 44th Brigade attack, the 9th Black Watch and 8/10th Gordons being in support and reserve respectively; but the capture of Guémappe itself was entrusted to the Seaforths alone. It was an awkward position, overlooked from the high ground south of the Cojeul, and it appeared very unlikely that, even if the village was captured, it could be held until the high ground round Wancourt Tower had been taken by the 50th Division. This proved correct.

At 2.30 on the morning of April 23rd the Battalion moved up to its position for attack, just west of Spear Lane, with Headquarters at Marlière, relieving a battalion of the 87th Division. At 4.45 a.m. the attack was launched under a barrage from the combined guns of the 3rd and 15th Divisions, and it was soon apparent that the attack was held up. The enemy had, during the past fortnight, heavily reinforced his front line both with men[1] and machine guns, and the fire from the latter in Guémappe entirely stopped the Seaforths until, about 11 a.m., the guns were silenced a further advance was made and the Seaforths gained the village. Unfortunately, however, they were compelled by machine gun fire to evacuate it shortly afterwards, but a party of about 70 men of the 9th Battalion, under Captain L. G. Morrison, had managed to reach Hammer Trench and Dragoon Lane, just north of Guémappe, and here they remained fighting stubbornly for four hours until directed to withdraw in order to straighten the line. This movement was necessary as the 50th Division had been driven back, which left Guémappe exposed to heavy enfilade fire from the high ground south of the Cojeul. While in this position, with their right flank exposed to the enemy still in Guémappe, this party suffered heavily from the fire

---

[1] The position was strongly held by the *3rd Bavarian Division*, most of the prisoners taken by the 9th belonging to the 18*th Regiment*.

SECOND ATTACK ON GUÉMAPPE, APRIL 25TH, 1917

of their own artillery, whose officers were unaware that they were still holding out, and it was but few who could obey the order to withdraw with Captain Morrison. At 6 p.m. that very gallant officer organized another attack, this time with a mixed force of Black Watch, Seaforths and Camerons. Morrison himself was killed leading the assault before he had gone many yards, but his attack was entirely successful, all the lost ground being regained and some beyond it. The initial advance of Captain Morrison's party was greatly assisted by the gallant conduct of No. 240046 Sergeant J. Gibb, 9th Black Watch, who "single handed, "worked his way round the end of the trench and destroyed "an enemy machine gun and its crew who were holding up the "advance."

Thus ended the first attempt to take Guémappe. By this time night had fallen, and no further attempt was made that day. At 2.30 a.m. on the 24th the 9th was withdrawn to shell-hole bivouacs just west of the old German second line, where that day and the next they spent re-equipping, as far as possible, from salvage found on the battlefield.

The fighting throughout had been fierce. In addition to those already mentioned, Lieutenant O. L. Bearn (an original officer of the Battalion) and Second Lieutenants A. F. Watson and J. Wilson were killed, and Second Lieutenant W. Anderson died of wounds. Second Lieutenants C. K. Young, J. N. Humble, J. B. Third, G. Leslie, R. A. M. Hastings and J. L. Burton were wounded; whilst five other ranks were killed, 12 missing and 155 wounded, the company officers being now reduced from 16 to six. The very gallant conduct of Captain Morrison and his devoted party that day added another leaf to the laurels of The Black Watch.

During the two days that elapsed before the 9th Battalion was again engaged, the 46th Brigade had been able to push forward and take Guémappe and had reached a line running almost due north and south from the Cojeul, west of Cavalry Farm, along Knife Trench and thence to the Copse. From this new line (known in orders as the Brown Line) General McCracken made arrangements to launch another attack on the Blue Line with the 44th Brigade on the right and 45th on the left at 10.30 p.m. on the 26th, the 9th Black Watch on the right and 7th Camerons (left) being detailed by Brigadier-General Marshall to carry out the task of the 44th Brigade.

At 11 p.m. on the 25th the 9th Battalion took over the right sector of the Brown Line. It consisted of a few half-finished trenches dug by the 46th Brigade. They were not linked up and communication was difficult. No opportunity for reconnoitring the ground in front was possible on account of heavy rifle and machine gun fire; in fact, the whole operation presented considerable difficulties.

At Zero hour the attack began under a close and very accurate artillery barrage. On the right, next the river, it was held up after only fifty yards had been covered. The left of the Battalion attack succeeded in reaching the Blue Line, and along the front of this line they were eventually able to establish a line of posts, in continuation of others made by the Camerons, who had also reached the objective. Later that night, first the 45th Brigade, and then the Camerons, were compelled to withdraw from their positions by strong enemy counter-attacks, with the result that by dawn on the 27th, The Black Watch posts were completely cut off. Early that morning the enemy succeeded in rushing the two nearest to the Cojeul, but the others were able to hold on throughout the day until relieved that night by the 8/10th Gordons. The garrisons of these posts put up a magnificent fight. Most of the officers were either killed or wounded, but still the men fought on without food or water until nightfall.

At midnight what was left of the Battalion moved to Dragoon Trench and Spear Lane, west of Guémappe (strength, two company officers and 130 other ranks), and on the 28th it moved back to Arras, when the Division was relieved by the 56th.

On the 29th the Battalion marched to Simencourt, where, with the remainder of the 44th Brigade, it went into billets to rest and refit. The fighting round Guémappe had cost the Battalion dear. Second Lieutenant J. L. Burton was reported missing, and Second Lieutenants A. D. McDiarmid and T. B. Allison (attached to the Brigade Trench Mortar Battery) were wounded; 13 other ranks were killed, 27 missing and 175 were wounded, bringing the total casualties for the battle to:—

	Officers	Other Ranks
Killed	9	66
Missing	1	39
Wounded	19	361
Totals	29	466

The above casualties resulted from fighting spread over fifteen days, during which the Battalion was engaged in two distinct and separate operations. It is of interest to compare these losses with those sustained in the Somme battle and with those at Loos on 25th September, 1915. The spirit and fighting will of the Battalion was unquestionably the same on all three occasions. Why should it, therefore, have lost over 600 men in September, 1915, 488 a year later on the Somme in forty-four days, and about the same number

BATTLE OF GUÉMAPPE, 25TH–27TH APRIL, 1917

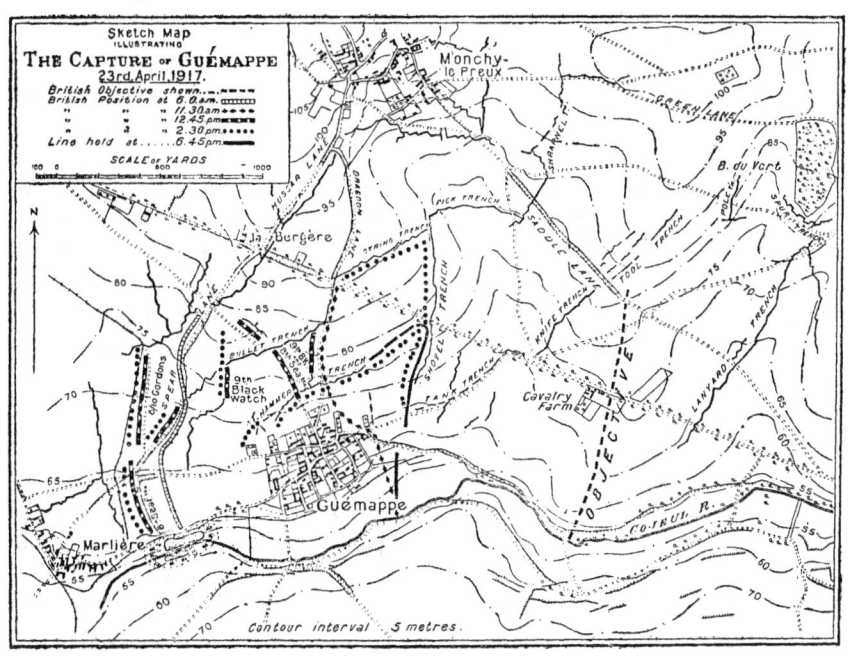

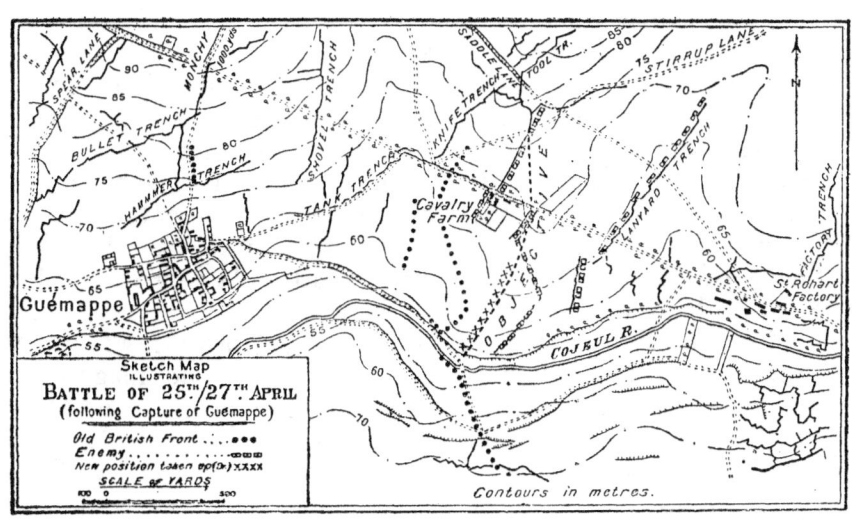

THE NINTH BATTALION THE BLACK WATCH

at Arras in April, 1917? The answer is that in 1915 there was no limit given as regards objectives. It was, in fact, an order at Loos that the Division was to "push on to the full extent of its power." That battle, gravely as it affected the personnel of the 9th Black Watch and other equally gallant battalions, served the purpose of demonstrating that, however gallant the company officers and other ranks, they could not be expected to achieve the impossible. On the Somme, and in fact on every other occasion after Loos, a battalion was set a definite task, and when that was accomplished another went through to the next objective. Again, at Loos, the artillery barrage was unknown, and though at Arras it had not reached that pitch of perfection which it did later, even then it had the effect of reducing losses in the attacking force.

While at Simencourt the following messages were received and communicated to all concerned:—

15TH DIVISION, No. G.762

"The Corps Commander has written to the Divisional Commander asking him to convey to Commanders, Staffs, and to all ranks of the Division 'his appreciation and thanks for the splendid work they have done' both in preparation for and in execution of the attack. The Corps Commander is 'particularly gratified by the energy displayed by all ranks after the third objective was captured.

"'The great reputation of the 15th (Scottish) Division has been more than maintained.'

"The Divisional Commander feels sure that this generous acknowledgment of the work of the Division will be highly valued by all. He wishes to add his own thanks. He is proud to have under his command a Division in which officers, non-commissioned officers and men are inspired with so fixed a determination to do their duty. The task given the 15th Division in the battle of Arras was a heavy one entailing hard work in preparation and great gallantry in attack. The difficulty of the operation only inspired all ranks to greater effort and brilliant success has been achieved.

"The crushing defeat of the enemy on April 9th was due to the discipline, hard work, untiring energy and magnificent gallantry of all ranks. Another page of honour has been added to the glorious records of the Division.

"The Divisional Commander wishes to thank every officer, non-commissioned officer and man, and he feels that it is indeed an honour to command the victorious 15th (Scottish) Division.

"(Sgd.) H. H. S. KNOX, Lieutenant-Colonel.
"General Staff, 15th Division."

IN CORPS RESERVE, MAY, 1917

Eight days were spent at Simencourt, resting and reorganizing, during which the following officers and two drafts of 286 other ranks joined: Second Lieutenants J. E. Drummond, G. R. Kerr, R. J. McMurray, C. B. Ritchie, A. Graham, G. E. Young, E. M. Drummond, J. H. Fraser and A. D. Tatham.

On May 7th Lieutenant-Colonel Innes was admitted to hospital, Major H. F. F. Murray assuming temporary command. The next day the Battalion moved to Grand Bullecourt, on the Division becoming part of the XVIII Corps, and here it remained a fortnight, during which the usual recreation and training in all branches was resumed. Here a further draft of 38 other ranks and the following officers joined: Captain J. Donaldsons; Lieutenant J. S. Strang; and Second Lieutenants J. Taylor, J. G. Scoular, C. F. Neish, W. R. Tovani, R. Stevenson, W. K. McGregor, N. G. Johnstone, J. C. Deasy, A. W. McLeod and R. B. Anderson.

Whilst at Bullecourt the first British list of "Immediate Awards" came out on May 10th. It was invariably the practice of the French Government to bestow such honours, but till now the British had not followed their example. It was certainly a further incentive to distinction, and these awards were far more appreciated than those given months after the recipients had distinguished themselves. In this list appeared the names of Second Lieutenant F. Proudfoot and No. S/16677 Private A. Black, who received the Military Cross and Distinguished Conduct Medal respectively for conspicuous service during the first phase of the Arras fighting.

On the 15th a Divisional Horse Show and football match took place at Le Cauroy at which the Commander-in-Chief was present. The 9th Battalion won the Football Cup, defeating the 8/10th Gordons in the final round by 4 goals to nil. It also won the first prize for pack ponies, and the third for the best turned-out limber and wagon mules. A main feature of the Show was witnessed at the close, when the massed pipes and drums of the Division played together, 232 men in all. It was probably unique and made a great impression on those who saw it.

From Bullecourt the 9th Battalion moved to Vieil Hesdin on the 22nd, when the Division joined the XIX Corps, where a draft of 15 other ranks joined, and here it remained until June 21st, when the Division marched north to Ypres. This month of rest and quiet was perhaps the most enjoyable the Battalion spent throughout the war. The weather was good; all ranks knew that they had played no small part in the Arras fighting, and their *moral* was as high as it had ever been. On the 31st

THE NINTH BATTALION THE BLACK WATCH

the list of awards for Arras was issued. It contained the following :—

Bar to D.S.O.
Lieut.-Colonel S. A. Innes.

Military Cross
2nd Lieut. T. Byers. C.S.M. J. McKercher.
  ,, T. B. Allison.   ,,   T. Price.

Distinguished Conduct Medal
L.-Corpl. J. Sandilands.

In addition to the above honours and the " Immediate Awards," the following also received recognition for their gallant conduct at Arras :—

Military Cross
2nd Lieut. H. S. Muir.

Military Medal
Sgt. J. Gibb.   Pte. S. Isles.
 ,, A. Crisp.   ,, W. Mechan.
Corpl. W. Wilson.   ,, W. Dick.
L/Corpl. W. Lindsay.

Medaille Militaire
Corpl. T. Park.

During its stay at Hesdin the Battalion lost the services of Regimental Quartermaster-Sergeant Munro, who received a commission as Lieutenant and Quartermaster and was posted to the 8/10th Gordons. He had served with distinction in the 9th since its birth, and it was to the very great regret of all ranks that he left it. The day after he departed his name appeared in *The Gazette* as having been awarded the D.C.M. for devoted service whilst Regimental Quartermaster-Sergeant and also for gallant conduct in the Loos salient.

Two drafts joined during May and June. The first consisted of 15 other ranks, and the second of 101 other ranks; on the 8th of June Lieutenant-Colonel Innes resumed command from sick leave.

CHAPTER VI

JUNE TO SEPTEMBER, 1917

Ypres

ON the 18th of June, three days before the Division commenced moving north, Major-General Sir F. W. N. McCracken, K.C.B., C.M.G., D.S.O., relinquished command to Major-General H. F. Thuillier, C.B., C.M.G., on appointment to command the XIII Corps. He had commanded the Division since January, 1915, and every man knew his intense pride in it and its achievements. On leaving General McCracken issued the following Special Order:—

" In bidding farewell to the 15th Division I wish to express
" my heartfelt thanks to all ranks for their continued assistance
" to me during the period of over two years since I assumed
" command.
" The standard of discipline and training which has enabled
" the results already obtained will, I am convinced, lead in the
" future to still greater success. The maintenance of this stan-
" dard, added to the high sense of duty of all ranks in the Division,
" will inevitably enable the same to obtain the final victory before
" returning to the land of their birth, which is already so justly
" proud of their fine achievements.
" I shall at all times watch their movements with the deepest
" interest, and I wish them every possible success in the future."

The march to Ypres, where the Division was to fight next, commenced on the 21st of June, the Battalion billeting as follows: 21st June at Henricourt; 22nd, Pernes; 23rd, St. Hilaire; 25th, Steenbeek; 26th, Caestre; finally reaching its destination, Toronto Camp, on the 27th, on which day it was inspected on the march by Major-General Thuillier.

Many true and vivid descriptions of " The Salient " have already been written, and it is not necessary here to dwell on the conditions prevailing in that area, except to say that it fully came up to what all ranks had heard concerning it; even the camps behind the line were in a shocking condition.

The Division now took over the right sector of the XIX Corps from the 55th. This line ran from the Ypres–Roulers railway to Warwick Farm, a distance of about 1300 yards, which was held by one brigade at a time, the 46th being the first Brigade to hold it, taking over from the 166th on June 20th. On the 30th the 44th Brigade began to move up in relief of the 46th, the 9th Black Watch relieving the 10/11th Highland Light Infantry (support battalion) on the Menin road, $3\frac{1}{4}$ miles south-east of Ypres, and he following day the Battalion took over the left sub-section of the front line from the 12th H.L.I. Here, the Diary says, "heavy shelling of reserve line and back areas was "continuous, far heavier than any previously met with by the "Battalion."

After a tour of seven days, three of which were spent in the support line, the 9th was relieved by the 13th Royal Scots on July 9th and returned to Toronto Camp, marching the following day to Poperinghe, where they entrained to Arneke and marched from there to Rubrouck. This first tour seems to have been singularly free from casualties, mention only being made of Second Lieutenants W. K. McGregor and T. Edwards as wounded on July 6th.

It was not long after their arrival at Rubrouck that the reason for the move became known. Some time previously General Thuillier had received instructions regarding a projected offensive in which his Division would take part, and on receipt of these instructions he decided to make a temporary change in the composition of two of his brigades, namely the 44th and 46th, the first of which was to lead the attack. This reconstituted, or "mixed" Brigade, as it was called, consisted of the 9th Black Watch, 8/10th Gordons, 7/8th K.O.S.B.'s and 10/11th H.L.I., with half the 44th Brigade M.G. Company and Trench Mortar Battery, the remaining formations of both brigades making up the "mixed" 46th Brigade which was to support the 44th in the coming operation.

By the 20th these alterations had been completed, and, on the 21st, the 44th "mixed" Brigade moved to Winnezeele and Watou, where it practised the attack over ground flagged out representing the enemy trench system, moving to Watou on the 22nd and to Toronto Camp the following day. To obtain ground suitable for practice and for drill, the Battalion was employed in harvesting the Belgian crops. This work was carried out with both zeal and efficiency, but it is doubtful if its labours were always appreciated by the owners of the crops.

Whilst at Watou, Privates J. Keating and A. Black were presented with the Military Medal for gallantry performed near Potijze on July 2nd. (See Appendix V.)

From Toronto Camp the Brigade moved up nearer Ypres, where, as the date of the attack had been postponed, it remained in bivouac one mile west of Ypres from July 25th to 30th. During these five days representatives from all formations down to companies made frequent visits to the front line, thus familiarizing themselves with the route they would have to follow on going up to the line. This was a wise precaution, and when the move took place every one of the attacking and supporting battalions moved up to their positions without a hitch, although the tracks

THE LANGEMARCK-GHELUVELT LINE

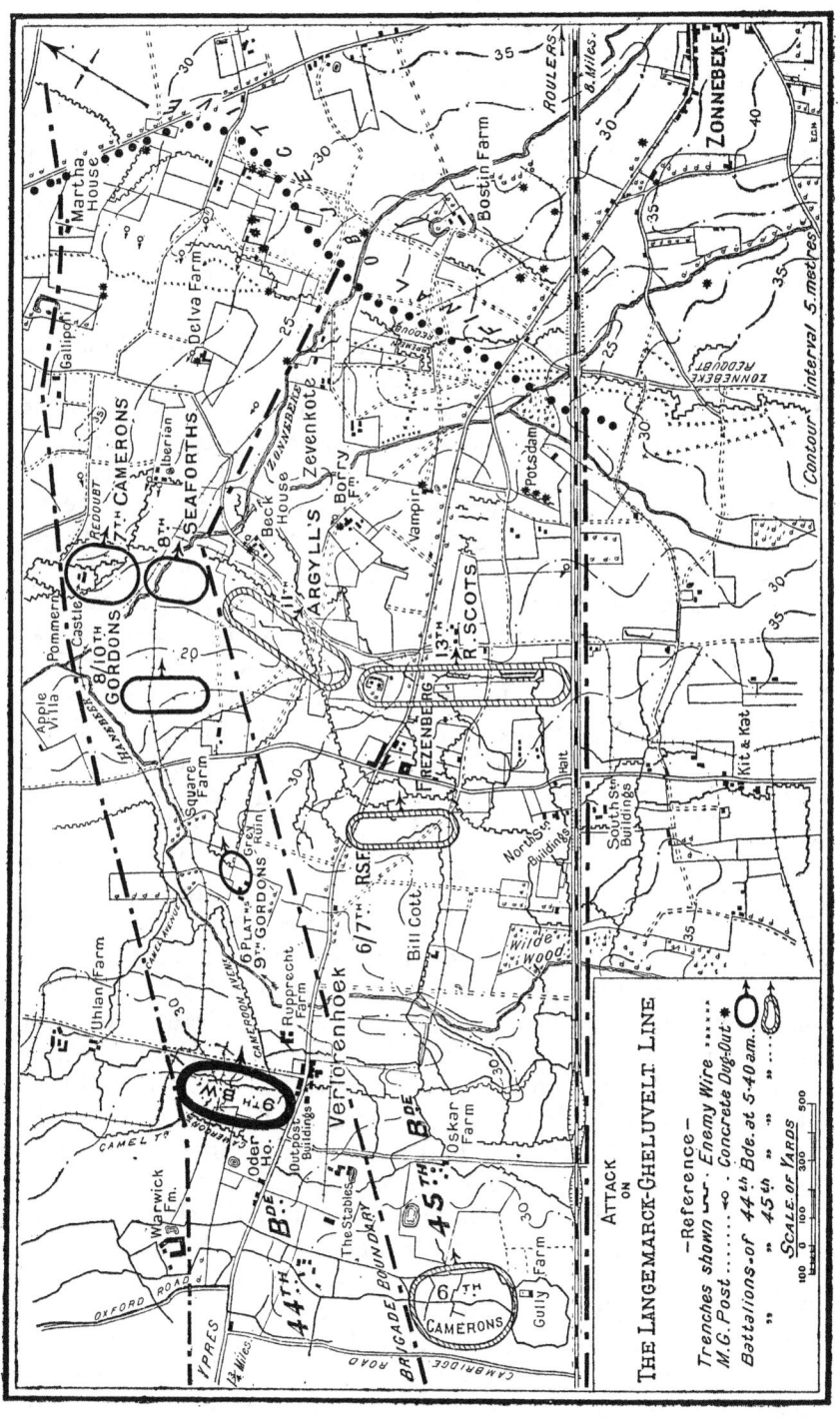

THE NINTH BATTALION THE BLACK WATCH

were not easy to find and the whole area was subject to heavy and intermittent artillery fire.

The attack about to take place was part of that which ushered in the Third Battle of Ypres, designed to drive the enemy from the high ground north-east and east of Ypres, the Division front being that with which it was familiar, namely, the ground between the Ypres–Roulers railway and Warwick Farm.

The objectives of the Division were three. First, the Blue Line, or German front trenches; second, the Black Line, some 500 yards further back; and, thirdly, the Green Line, which consisted of a line of trenches and strong points 1500 yards further back. In Orders, a note was added to the effect that should the Green Line be reached, a further advance would be made to the Gravenstafel–Broodseinde road, a fairly optimistic view of things, considering the enemy positions and strength.

General Thuillier's attack was to be carried out by the 44th (right) and 46th (left) Brigades, having on the right and left of the Division the 8th and 61st Divisions respectively. He gave the capture of the Black and Green Lines to these two brigades, keeping the 45th in reserve for a further advance on the Gravenstafel road line. The right of the 44th Brigade line ran along the railway, while the left commenced at Oskar Farm, thence north of Frezenberg and south of Frost House. General Marshall's attack was to be carried out by the 8/10th Gordons (right) and 9th Black Watch (left), the other two battalions of the "mixed" Brigade being in support and reserve.

At midnight on the night of July 30/31st the Battalion was formed up in the "jumping-off" trenches—A, B and D companies being in the front line, with C in close support.

The attack was launched at 3.50 a.m. on the 31st, little opposition being encountered until the enemy reserve line was reached, where a couple of machine guns caused slight delay and some casualties, amongst whom were Captain Grant and Second Lieutenants W. Marchbank and T. McGregor. From this point onwards stiff opposition was met with, mainly from hidden machine guns and snipers, but, regardless of losses, the Battalion advanced and by 4.45 a.m. had reached the Blue Line, or first objective, in the neighbourhood of Hill Cottage.

Here the leading companies reorganized in shell-holes and, at 5.15 a.m., continued their advance towards the second objective, the Black Line, a road some 300 yards east of Frezenberg village. This road was hidden by the Frezenberg Ridge, just in front of which ran a trench strongly held by the enemy. On reaching this trench, the Battalion found that the wire had been very well dealt with by the artillery, and, advancing by section rushes, the platoons were able to capture the trench and Frezen-

THIRD BATTLE OF YPRES, JULY 31ST, 1917.

berg Redoubt just behind it. While this had been taking place the "moppers up" had, with the assistance of a tank, cleared the ground behind, taking 80 prisoners. An hour later the advance was continued to the final objective, about 400 yards east of Frezenberg. This was reached at half-past six, and the Battalion started consolidating its position by linking up a line of shell-holes and a few concrete dug-outs; while thus engaged it suffered severely from snipers on the Zonnebeke road. For the next two hours the situation remained unchanged, but between 8.30 and 10 a.m. the enemy attempted two counter-attacks, both of which were driven back with severe loss, especially the second, when the Germans came under rifle fire at 200 yards.

At 10.10 a.m. the advance of the 45th Brigade on the Green Line commenced. The barrage for this was opportune, as it caught the second counter-attack, the enemy turning tail and being practically annihilated.

The position the Battalion now held was anything but ideal. It was on the eastern slope of the Frezenberg Ridge and under direct observation from the ridges further east and north, some 2000 yards away. In addition, by this time the enemy had brought up more guns, and these, directed by aircraft, brought an exceedingly accurate and heavy fire to bear on the new line; so heavy was it that the Diary states:—

"The shelling was very heavy, worse than any of us remember "having received on the Somme, and this continued all day."

The remainder of the day was passed in this exposed position, it being impossible to reorganize or work under such conditions. During the afternoon Battalion Headquarters moved forward as far as Ibex Drive, but were constantly compelled to change their position owing to artillery and enfilade rifle fire, from which both the Commanding Officer and Adjutant were slightly wounded.

About five o'clock the 45th Brigade was obliged to withdraw as far as the Black Watch line owing to the retirement of the 8th Division on the right; but nothing further occurred until, at 11 p.m., the Battalion was relieved by the 8th Seaforths, and at 3 a.m. on August 1st was withdrawn to Brigade reserve in the old German front line, in which for the next two days it was employed in carrying up ammunition, rations and water to the troops in the front line, always under heavy and constant artillery fire.

On the 3rd the Battalion, together with the rest of the 44th Brigade, was relieved by the 47th and proceeded to bivouac two miles west of Ypres, moving by bus transport to Winnezelle area the following day, when the 15th Division was relieved by the 16th (Irish).

THE NINTH BATTALION THE BLACK WATCH

During this fighting the Battalion lost fairly heavily, 20 other ranks killed, 180 wounded and 45 reported missing, while Second Lieutenant J. Taylor had been killed and the following officers wounded: Captain N. A. Grant; Second Lieutenants E. M. Drummond, J. H. Fraser, C. F. I. Neish, W. R. Tovani, W. Marchbank, T. McGregor, J. E. Drummond, R. B. Anderson and J. C. Woodburn. In addition, Lieutenant-Colonel S. A. Innes and Captain S. Norie-Miller were wounded but remained at duty.

This first phase of the battle had gone well on the whole. The Battalion had assisted in advancing the Division line some 2000 yards, and, although the final objective had not been reached, the important Frezenberg Ridge had been taken and held. The weather throughout had been as bad as it could be, but, notwithstanding this and heavy artillery fire which swept the back areas, ammunition, rations, water and R.E. material were brought up to the new front line after the fighting by large parties from the 9th Black Watch after it had been withdrawn to Brigade support.

While at Winnezeele the Divisional Commander visited the Battalion and, on behalf of the Army and Corps Commanders, thanked them for the work they had done on this occasion.

A fortnight was spent near Winnezeele resting and reorganizing. It was by no means a pleasant time owing to heavy rain which turned the ground into a sea of mud, and to exceedingly bad tent accommodation; so bad, indeed, was the weather that further operations were postponed, thus giving the enemy opportunity to re-establish his line, a fact which had a great bearing on the second phase of the battle.

During this period drafts amounting to 214 other ranks joined the Battalion, but when it again took part in the battle, on August 21st, its strength in the line was only 14 officers and 442 other ranks.

The weather having improved, operations were resumed on August 15th, and on the 17th the 15th Division commenced moving up to the front line, the 9th Battalion marching to Poperinghe, and from there to Toronto Camp, the rest of the 44th Brigade being bivouacked near Ypres, in readiness for the second phase of the battle, which, as far as the Division was concerned, was to commence on August 22nd. On this occasion the 44th Brigade was on the left of the Division, with the 45th on its right and the 184th (61st Division) on its left.

The area over which the attack was to be carried out was that which had been allotted to the Division in the first phase, with the exception that the left boundary of the Division had been extended to include Hill 35 and Gallipoli Farm, both important

ATTACK ON GALLIPOLI FARM

points on the left front. For the initial attack, General Marshall employed the 8th Seaforths on the right and 7th Camerons on the left, keeping the 8/10th Gordons and 9th Black Watch in support and reserve respectively, and, in addition, he had with him six platoons of the 9th Gordons Pioneers at Grey Ruin as a supplementary reserve.

During the night of August 21st the 9th Black Watch moved up to its reserve position in the old German trenches between Rupert Farm and Oder House. Hardly had it reached this when the enemy subjected the area to a heavy gas-shell bombardment which caused some 30 casualties, 10 being killed, and Second Lieutenant G. R. M. Kerr gassed.

The attack commenced at 4.45 a.m. on the 22nd, and at once the leading battalion came under exceedingly heavy machine gun fire from concrete emplacements which the enemy had evidently been able to erect during the unforeseen lull in the fighting.

All accounts as to what took place in this assault are vague. Few men from attacking formations were able to tell what occurred, as nearly all were either killed or wounded before getting far, but from what is known the Seaforths and Camerons, assisted by the six platoons (9th Gordons), fought their way forward as far as a line well east of Beck House to just west of Iberian Farm and from there to Pommern Redoubt. No further progress was possible in face of intense machine gun fire, and the situation remained stationary throughout the whole of the 22nd and the following day. Battalions in the front line were so mixed up that on the night of the 22nd, Brigadier-General Marshall sent the 9th Black Watch up to relieve the 7th Camerons (left), while the 10th Scottish Rifles, lent from the 46th Brigade, did the same with the Seaforths on the right. This move was completed by 10 p.m., when orders were received that two companies of The Black Watch were to attack Gallipoli Farm at 1.30 a.m. on the 23rd.

There was little or no time for reconnaissance; the attack was made under most adverse conditions, and it is not surprising that the Battalion failed to gain its objective. All touch with flank battalions was lost, and barely 100 yards of ground was gained before the attack was brought to a standstill by intense fire from Hill 35. The ground gained was, however, at once consolidated and linked up with the original front line before dawn. In this somewhat hastily devised attack the Battalion lost Captain J. Donaldson killed and about 50 other ranks killed or wounded, a large total for such a small gain.

At 11 a.m. nothing less than a tragedy to the Battalion occurred. The Commanding Officer, Major H. F. F. Murray, temporarily in command owing to Lieutenant-Colonel Innes having been ordered not to take part in the attack, on account of the necessity for keeping at least one senior officer to replace a possible casualty, had made his headquarters in a captured German concrete dug-out. Unfortunately the entrance faced the enemy, and a shell entered it, killing 12 of the Battalion Headquarters staff and wounding nine others, among the former being Major Murray and the signalling officer, Second Lieutenant R. Stevenson, and among the latter the Acting Adjutant, Second Lieutenant G. E. R. Young.

No further fighting took place on the Battalion front till late on the 25th, but the front line was always under heavy shell fire, some of it being from British guns firing on Gallipoli and Hill 35.

On the death of Major Murray, Captain W. B. Binnie took command, and shortly afterwards instructions reached him that the Battalion was to make another attempt to capture Gallipoli Farm at 11 o'clock the following night. From this time till the moment of this next attack nothing of importance took place. The front line was, of course, under constant shell fire which interfered greatly with the transport of rations, water and small-arm ammunition, but no counter-attacks were made by the enemy, and there was time in which to prepare for the coming attack.

At 11 p.m. the attempt was made by about 170 men of the 9th under Captain G. F. Young. The right of the attack managed to reach the summit of Hill 35, where it was held up by machine gun fire from a point west of Gallipoli Copse. On the left, the attackers reached the outskirts of Gallipoli, which was strongly held, but were eventually compelled to withdraw level with the right attack. The ground thus gained, about 200 yards, was consolidated during the night and linked up with the original front line. Two prisoners were taken, and Captain Young and Second Lieutenants S. Graham and C. B. Ritchie were wounded.

The 26th passed quietly except for enemy shelling. During the afternoon the Battalion was relieved by the 10/11th Highland Light Infantry and, in pouring rain, marched to Toronto Camp, strength seven officers and 245 other ranks.

The last phase of the fighting was, if anything, more trying and cost the Battalion more than that which preceded it. Major H. F. F. Murray, Second-in-Command; Captain J. Donaldson, Second Lieutenant Stevenson and 35 other ranks had been killed; whilst Captains G. F. Young and J. S. Strang, and Second Lieutenants G. R. M. Kerr, G. E. R. Young, S. Graham, C. B. Ritchie and another, together with 143 other ranks, were wounded and 12 missing—total 200.

Thus ended the fighting in the Ypres area as far as the 9th Black Watch was concerned. The remainder of the 15th Division

TO CORPS RESERVE, AUGUST 29TH, 1917

left the line during the night of the 29th of August, and, on the 31st, the 44th Brigade marched to Watou area, where it remained for a week resting and reorganizing. While at Watou drafts amounting to 393 other ranks, together with the following officers, joined: Lieutenants J. I. Buchan, D.S.O., L. McKenzie and Viscount Drumlanrig, and Second Lieutenants C. K. Young, G. H. Gordon, J. M. Brown and P. E. Kerr.

On the 30th the Battalion was inspected by General Sir H. Gough, Commanding Fifth Army, who congratulated it on the work accomplished. At the same time General Gough sent Lieutenant-Colonel Innes a copy of the following letter from the Commander-in-Chief:—

"General Sir HUBERT GOUGH, K.C.B., K.C.V.O.,
"Commanding Fifth Army.

"I desire to inform you, and the men under your command,
"that although adverse weather conditions have impeded pro-
"gress, and imposed great hardships on the troops, their efforts
"have nevertheless already produced very important results.

"Despite all difficulties, positions of great importance cover-
"ing a wide area have been won in the face of determined
"resistance on the part of the enemy. Even more important than
"this is the degree to which the enemy's powers of resistance are
"being used up and the rapidity with which his reserves are
"being exhausted. Judged by this test, far more has been accom-
"plished than is apparent, even to the extent of territory gained.

"In addition to the fact that the enemy has found it neces-
"sary already to employ a large proportion of the whole of his
"forces on the Western Front in his efforts to stop your advance,
"it is becoming evident that the drain on his man-power is out-
"stripping his resources.

"For him everything is at stake in this battle. Failure to stop
"our progress will shake the confidence of his Army, the trust in
"it of the civil population of Germany, and the faith of his Allies.
"With this knowledge he has concentrated his best troops to
"oppose us, and is throwing them into the battle at a rate which
"he has not the means to continue for long.

"In conveying to you personally, to your Staff, to the Com-
"manders and Staffs serving under you and to your troops my
"congratulations on all they have already accomplished, please
"assure them that the prospect for the future is good, and that
"their steady courage and determination in spite of bad weather
"and great hardship has done much towards bringing us nearer
"to final victory.

"(Signed) D. HAIG,
"Field Marshal."

THE NINTH BATTALION THE BLACK WATCH

By this time it became known that the Division would move back to Arras in the near future, but before it left a list of "Immediate Awards" was published. It included the following:

Bar to Military Cross
Lieut. F. Proudfoot.

Military Cross
2nd Lieut. J. E. Drummond.   C.S.M. J. McCall.
  „   W. R. Tovani.

Distinguished Conduct Medal
Corpl. A. Johnstone.

Bar to Military Medal
Pte. A. Jack.

Military Medal

Sgt. C. Ogilvie.	Pte. J. Moffat.
„ C. Cody.	„ A. Stone.
Corpl. J. H. Davidson.	„ J. Grant.
„ W. Sharples.	„ A. Gowk.
„ G. Wright.	„ W. Brown.
L.-Corpl. R. Ross.	„ J. Johnson.
„ H. Brown.	

An account of the deeds for which these honours were awarded will be found in the Appendix.

CHAPTER VII

SEPTEMBER, 1917, TO MAY, 1918

The Battle of Arras—Amalgamation with 4/5th Battalion

ON September 2nd the Battalion marched to Caestre, entrained for the Arras sector with the rest of the 44th Brigade, and on reaching its destination went into billets in the Agnes–lez–Duisans area. Two days were spent here resting, during which the following farewell message from General Sir H. Gough was promulgated:—

" The Commander of the Fifth Army bids good-bye to the
" 15th Division with great regret. Its reputation has been earned
" on many battlefields and has never stood higher than now. He
" wishes it all good fortune and many further successes in the
" future. ' Will ye no come back again? ' "

The Division was now part of the XVII Corps, and, on the 22nd, the 9th Black Watch took over the left sub-sector of the Divisional front, immediately north of the Scarpe, the river being the dividing line between it and the 8th Seaforths on the right.

The line was quiet and nothing of importance occurred for some time. After their experiences round Ypres the peaceful atmosphere of Arras was gladly welcomed. The weather was fine to begin with, but broke in October, doing great damage to trenches and entailing much hard work in keeping them in order. In this the Battalion was engaged more or less continuously even during the so-called " rest " periods, large working parties being employed under the Royal Engineers in revetting miles of damaged trenches.

On October 10th, Major-General H. L. Reed, V.C., took over command of the Division from Major-General Thuillier, who had been appointed to the Ministry of Munitions, and the same day Lieutenant Colonel Innes proceeded to the Commanding Officers' course at the Third Army School, Major W. B. Binnie taking over temporary command.

When the Battalion arrived at Arras for the second time it was greatly under strength in both officers and other ranks, but during September and October drafts arrived, and by November 1st it was up to strength once more. Many new officers reported for duty together with others who had been wounded, amongst them being Captain W. Story-Wilson, Captain Norie-Miller, and the Quartermaster, Lieutenant Clark, who were now the only three officers remaining who had landed with the Battalion in July 1915.

On October 8th, whilst in reserve at Rifle Camp, a further

list of awards for good service was received, of which the following relate to the 9th Battalion :—

Bar to Military Cross
Major W. B. Binnie.   Lieut. S. Graham.
Captain J. S. Strang.   ,,   N. G. Johnstone.

Military Cross
2nd Lieut. J. Addison.   2nd Lieut. T. Calvert.

Bar to Military Medal
Sgt. J. Mullen.   L.-Corpl. R. Ross.

Military Medal
Sgt. W. Murphy.   Pte. W. W. Kennedy.
Corpl. W. Rankin.   ,, G. W. MacIsaac.
L.-Corpl. J. Smith.   ,, R. Duffy.
Pte. T. Ross.   ,, J. Beveridge.
,, J. Somerville.

Under the heading October 9th, whilst the Battalion was at Wilderness Camp, the following entry occurs in the Diary :—

"Lieutenant-Colonel S. A. Innes, D.S.O., gazetted to "Command, vice Lieutenant-Colonel T. O. Lloyd, C.M.G., "d/4/9/17."

Another link with the original Battalion was lost when, on November 1st, the Adjutant, Captain S. Norie-Miller, went to England on six months tour of duty. He succeeded Captain Harvey, killed at Loos, and from the first day he joined at Aldershot served the Battalion faithfully and well.

Although, on the whole, this period was quiet, the Division was continually occupied in raiding the enemy lines and keeping up that aggressive spirit for which it was famed. On one occasion, after a raid, a German prisoner escaped, but returned voluntarily to the 9th Black Watch line, stating that he considered life as a prisoner decidedly more comfortable than that in his countrymen's trenches.

On November 27th, while holding the line near Monchy, a small party, consisting of Second Lieutenant E. W. D. Wilson and 12 other ranks, were successful in taking two prisoners from a crater near Harness Lane. The capture must have been of some importance, as both the Brigadier and Division Commander told Colonel Innes that information of great importance had been thus obtained.

By the end of 1917 the 15th Division had been in the fighting line for over six months, two of which had been spent in the

TRENCH WARFARE NEAR ARRAS, WINTER, 1917

Ypres salient. All battalions were in need of a rest, and it was with delight that they heard they would be relieved by the Guards Division early in January. The move took place on the 2nd, when the 9th Black Watch was relieved by the 1st Battalion Scots Guards and proceeded to Baudimont Barracks, in Corps reserve. While here, on January 15th, the Battalion was inspected by Major-General Reed, the parade state showing 29 officers and 757 other ranks as present. On the following day the New Year dinner was held in the Expeditionary Force canteen, 811 being present.

The rest period lasted until the first week in February, the latter part of the time being occupied in Brigade and Divisional training, during which the 44th Brigade held various competitions, the Brigadier's cup for the best Lewis gun team being won by the Battalion.

As the Battalion was on the point of going into the line once more at Arras a change was made which affected it greatly. Instructions had been issued reducing divisions from thirteen battalions to ten, which involved the reorganization of existing brigades. To their great sorrow, though for reasons highly complimentary to themselves, the 9th Black Watch left the 44th (Highland) Brigade and, on February 7th, became part of the 46th (Brigadier-General A. F. Lumsden) with the 7/8th K.O.S. Borderers and 10th Scottish Rifles.

Throughout the latter months of 1917 and the commencement of 1918 it became increasingly evident that Higher Command expected the enemy to make a prodigious effort to end the war, and one which would tax the resources of the Allies to counter. Every available man was employed in strengthening existing defences, in constructing others behind the line, and in making preparations for evacuating the front line if forced to do so. This entailed an enormous amount of work, much hampered by bad weather which made the use of communication trenches impossible, and tracks overland were used increasingly.

January and February, 1918, passed without incident, the Battalion taking its usual turns of trench duty. There are few entries recording casualties—in fact, this period might be well termed a calm before a storm. From March 3rd to 10th the Battalion occupied billets in Arras, taking over the left subsector of the Division line on that day from the 7/8th K.O.S. Borderers, with the 6th Camerons on the right and 1st Coldstream Guards (Guards Division) on the left.

An enemy attack was expected to be made on the 13th, but this did not materialize, and, on the 17th, the Battalion was relieved by the 10th Scottish Rifles, moving to Happy Valley in Brigade support.

THE NINTH BATTALION THE BLACK WATCH

The long-expected German attack began on March 21st, when the enemy assaulted the Allied line further south, at the junction of the French and British Armies, and almost at once broke through the line. For the first two days nothing except intense artillery fire occurred on the 15th Divisional front, but by the evening of the 22nd it became apparent that the Division would be compelled to withdraw to conform with the movements of those further south, if Arras was to be saved. As has already been stated, a contingency such as this had been prepared for, and a new position, known as the Army Line, had been constructed some 4000 yards further back which General Reed had made all arrangements to occupy at short notice; therefore when, on the 22nd, it was known that the withdrawal was necessary a few men from each battalion in the Division were left to cover the movement whilst the remainder took up new positions, mainly in Halifax and California trenches between the original front and the Army Line.

The 9th Battalion came into the line on the 22nd, and that evening found it disposed as follows: D company holding a line of shell-holes from Jamaica Trench to Chinstrap Lane, 200 yards north-west of Johnson Avenue, with A in support, while C, on the right, held from Jamaica to Jerusalem Trench, with B in reserve in Halifax Trench with Battalion Headquarters.

About 10 a.m. on the 23rd the enemy began to occupy the original front line, abandoned, according to orders, by the Division rear-guard. Advancing slowly and in groups, they offered ideal targets for both artillery and machine gun fire and suffered severe losses. From the somewhat aimless way in which they advanced it seemed that the Germans could not realize that all troops had withdrawn, and it was not until noon that they reached Les Fosses Farm, where they stopped and dug in. Nothing further occurred on that day or on the following one, when the Battalion was relieved by the 7/8th K.O.S. Borderers and moved to the Army Line, with Headquarters at Wilderness Camp.

Unfortunately, on the 23rd, the Commanding Officer, Lieutenant-Colonel Innes, was evacuated to hospital, his place being taken by Major W. B. Binnie. His departure, after having commanded the Battalion ever since it left the Loos salient, was greatly felt by all ranks.

Content with their successes, the enemy made no further attack on the Division front until the 28th. This interval was usefully employed in strengthening and elaborating the new positions now occupied by the Division, which work, especially on the right, proved of great value later, when the troops further south were driven back and that flank became exposed.

OPERATIONS EAST OF ARRAS

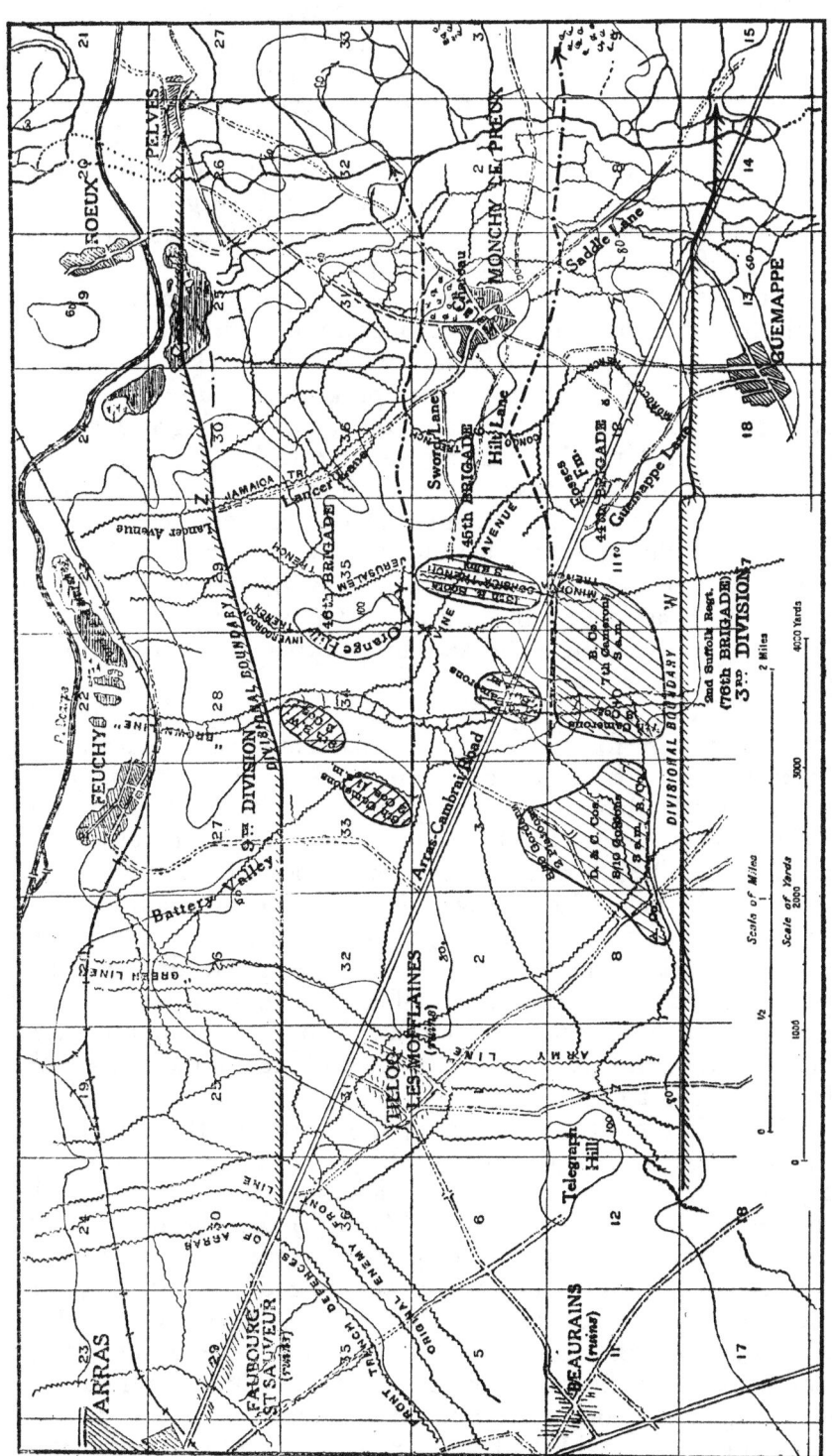

THE OPERATIONS EAST OF ARRAS, MARCH, 1918
(*By permission from* The History of the 15th Division)

THE NINTH BATTALION THE BLACK WATCH

On the 25th a message reached Battalion commanders that the enemy might be expected to attack the following day. This proved incorrect. No attack was made until the early morning of the 29th, when the Battalion, having relieved the 10th Scottish Rifles in the line two days before, was distributed as follows: A and B companies in Jerusalem Trench, D in support in Cromarty Trench, C (less two platoons) in Invergordon Trench (reserve) and two platoons as escort to the Vickers guns, two hundred yards west of Feuchy-Chapel road.

At three o'clock on the morning of the 28th a platoon from both the front companies was withdrawn to Invergordon Trench, whilst those of C in that trench withdrew to Halifax Trench. While this readjustment was in progress an intense artillery barrage developed over the whole front, culminating at 7.30 a.m., when the fire " lifted " and the enemy attacked.

On the right, as far as the Battalion was concerned, the attack struck the centre of B company. Here the Germans succeeded in breaking through and, having done so, bombed north along the front line until stopped and held up by a block. Unfortunately this was shelled and, on its destruction, the enemy made further progress until checked by another block still further north.

While this was going on, the left company (A), with the remainder of B, formed a defensive flank along a trench running north-east from Invergordon Trench, and held on to this trench until severely shelled and compelled to withdraw about nine o'clock, when they retired to Pelves Lane, where, together with the 7/8th K.O.S. Borderers, they formed another defensive flank from which they inflicted severe losses on the advancing enemy. In the meantime D company, in Invergordon Trench, found its right flank in the air owing to B having withdrawn north. All the officers had been either killed or wounded, but the men hung on for over half an hour until the few remaining were driven out about 8.15 a.m. by a combined attack from the front and right flank.

Meantime matters had been going badly further south and, by 8 a.m., both the 45th and 44th Brigades had been driven back, owing to the withdrawal of the Division on the right, and a considerable portion of the 45th (centre) Brigade had reached Halifax Trench, which formed part of what was known as the Brown Line. Here they were reorganized, and at 8.15 a.m. the remnants of D company 9th Black Watch fell back to that line, and the mixed force came under the orders of the Commanding Officer 9th Black Watch, Halifax Trench then becoming the front line, and new support and reserve lines being hurriedly established further east and west of Feuchy road.

GERMAN OFFENSIVE, ARRAS, MARCH, 1918

For the next hour enemy artillery fire on the new front line ceased almost entirely, although heavy machine gun fire continued without a pause. About 9.30 a.m. the enemy, whose attacks had continued further south, succeeded in breaking through the Brown Line and, although the 9th Battalion, occupying the support line west of Feuchy road, held on until 12.45 p.m., they were once more compelled to withdraw, this time to the Army Line further back. Here the Battalion was reorganized by Captain Story-Wilson, who had assumed temporary command when Major Binnie was wounded earlier that day.

By this time the force of the German attack had spent itself, and in the course of the afternoon the situation became "normal." The two companies of the 9th who had formed a defensive flank along Pelves Lane were withdrawn to the Army Line, when the 4th Division on their left withdrew. No further attack was made, and the enemy contented themselves with establishing their line in the valley immediately west of Orange Hill. The night passed quietly, and the Battalion was able to establish an outpost line east of the Army Line without molestation.

Thus ended the last German attempt to take Arras. In the part played by the 15th Division in its defence the 9th Black Watch had had a great share. It is true the Battalion had been compelled to withdraw, but at the most it had only yielded from one-half to three-quarters of a mile and in doing so had taken heavy toll from the enemy. One company sacrificed itself during the resistance, nearly every man in it being killed or wounded.

The Corps Commander's message ran:—

" I knew you could be relied upon to stick it out to the end.
" Well done. There are fresh troops in support of you now, but
" I want the honour of holding Arras to be yours alone."

In the recent fighting the Battalion had, like all others in the Division, lost heavily. Captain J. S. Strang, originally reported as wounded and missing, and Second Lieutenants J. McVeigh and L. McKenzie had been killed; and Major W. B. Binnie, Second Lieutenants G. E. Gowan and A. S. Loxton were wounded. Three officers were reported as missing, namely, Second Lieutenants W. A. Forrest, E. P. Walcott and Lieutenant J. W. Morris. The latter officer belonged to the United States Medical Service and was acting as medical officer to the Battalion; a very gallant comrade, his loss was keenly felt by all. In addition to the above, Captain Story-Wilson was also wounded, but remained at duty and in command of the Battalion until relieved by Lieutenant-Colonel Dudgeon, D.S.O., M.C., Cameron Highlanders, on April 1st. Nineteen other ranks were killed, 122 wounded and 76 were reported as missing, a total of 227 all ranks.

Although it might have been expected that after so long a period in the front line, culminating with three days' fierce fighting, the troops should have been given some rest, it was impossible, owing to the gravity of the situation and to the lack of reserves, to take the Division out of the line. Fortunately the enemy had shot his bolt and was in no condition to make any further effort. It is of interest to note that information obtained from prisoners pointed to the fact that by this time the discipline in the German Army was on the point of breaking, the main topic amongst the men being a coming combined attack by the French, British and American Armies.

From April 1st to 23rd the Battalion was engaged in holding the line and in working on new trenches round Blangy, spending the usual few days in Brigade reserve in Imperial Caves. While in the line no enemy action took place, but the usual patrol activity was displayed and on several occasions the Black Watch patrols pushed out over four hundred yards in front of their line without discovering any trace of the enemy.

The Battalion left the line on April 23rd, moving back to Etrun, where Lieutenant-Colonel R. A. Bulloch, a well known Black Watch Regular officer, took over command from Lieutenant-Colonel Dudgeon, and on the following day the 9th moved by omnibus transport to Burbure, the 15th Division having now been transferred from the XVII to the XIII Corps, then in Army reserve.

On this occasion Lieutenant-General Sir C. Fergusson wrote the following letter to Major-General Reed :—

"I wish to express to you and to all ranks of the 15th Division
"my great regret at your departure from the XVII Corps. We
"have now been associated for many months, and I had hoped
"that we might have seen this battle through together. That,
"however, is not to be, and I can only hope that the fortune of
"war may some day bring us together again. The 15th Division
"has a great reputation and may well be proud of it. I know
"that the honour of Scotland is safe in its keeping and that those
"who are now serving in its ranks will prove themselves worthy
"of those gallant men who have won glory for the Division in
"the past. I wish you all good luck and success from the bottom
"of my heart."

Only a few days were spent at Burbure, and even these were

AMALGAMATION WITH FOURTH-FIFTH BATTALION

broken by orders issued the day after arrival to the effect that the Division was to return to Arras at once. These orders were afterwards cancelled, but the Battalion had actually entrained before the move was countermanded.

At Burbure the following awards for services on March 28th were promulgated:—

Military Cross

Lieut. A. K. Hamilton. Lieut. A. Marshall.
  ,, E. W. D. Wilson.

Military Medal

L/Corpl. T. Callaghan. Pte. A. R. Robertson.
  ,, J. Clink.   ,, A. Rowley.

On May 2nd orders were received to the effect that the Division would rejoin the XVII Corps at once, and on the following day the Battalion entrained at Pernes for Maroeuil, marching thence to its former quarters in Baudimont Barracks, Arras. The same evening it went into the line once more as Battalion in Brigade support, when the 46th took over from the 10th Canadian Brigade in the Fampoux sector, north of the Scarpe River.

From the entries in the War Diary it is clear that this tour, which proved to be the last for the original 9th Black Watch, was very quiet, the only reference to enemy activity and the last occasion on which casualties are mentioned being: May 9th, "Intermittent shelling two O.R.'s died of wounds." Thus, with this tiny flicker, died out that glorious light of the 9th Black Watch which had shone so brightly for over three and a half years.

On the 11th the Battalion left the line and proceeded to Wakefield Camp, where, on the 16th, it ceased to be a separate unit and was merged with the 4/5th Territorial Battalion. The amalgamation was completed by the 19th, on which date the Training Staff of the 9th, consisting of 10 officers and 51 other ranks, left to join the 39th Division, then employed as a training centre for the American Forces which were now arriving in France in large numbers.

Of the original members of the 9th Black Watch, one officer and 83 other ranks were still serving with it in May, 1918. Several had been wounded more than once and were indeed veterans.

The command of the newly constituted, or rather amalgamated, 4/5th and 9th was given to Lieutenant-Colonel Bulloch, a well-deserved compliment to the 9th. The rest of the story is told in the chronicle of the 4/5th Battalion, and it is now the duty of the historian to turn to an entirely new 9th Battalion.

CHAPTER VIII

MAY, 1918 TO JULY, 1919

Formation and Movements of 2/9th Battalion

THE foundation of the 2/9th Battalion consisted of the training Cadre already mentioned, which, after a short period with the American troops, proceeded to Aldershot in May, 1918, where it was engaged for the next two months in raising and training the newly formed unit.

Nearly all the officers had seen service with one or other of the Black Watch battalions,[1] but the men were mostly youngsters, partly trained in depots and formed into a Battalion to help to fill the gap caused by the casualties resulting from the enemy's March offensive. Every available man was required in France and very little time for training was possible, so, at the end of July, the Battalion found itself under orders for France as part of the 47th Brigade (Brigadier-General B. C. Dent), 16th Division (Major-General A. B. Ritchie), the other battalions being the 14th Leicestershire Regiment and the 18th Welch Regiment.

Leaving Bourlay Camp, Aldershot, on July 30th, and travelling by Folkestone and Boulogne, the Battalion reached Hodecq the following day, where it went into billets. The first eighteen days were spent in training, during which, on the 14th, General Sir H. S. Horne, the First Army Commander, paid the Battalion a visit, the Division having joined the I Corps.

Its first move to a battle area took place on August 19th, when the Battalion moved by omnibus to Noeux-les-Mines, marching from there to billets at Barlin, where it relieved the 1st Battalion, who sent their band to play the 9th in, a graceful compliment much appreciated by every man in this the youngest battalion of the Regiment.

On the 21st the Battalion proceeded by rail to Sailly-Labourse, taking over the Annequin defence system in support of the 14th Leicesters and 18th Welch, then holding the front line, Hohenzollern sector.

At this time it was known that the enemy contemplated a general retirement, and, in consequence, front-line troops carried out constant and vigorous patrolling. In this the 9th took part, and on September 2nd made a raid on the German trenches, in which it lost 31 men.

The time passed quietly until October 14th, on which date the following entry occurs in the War Diary:—

[1] The War Diary does not contain any list of the officers who accompanied the Battalion abroad. It was commanded by Lieutenant-Colonel J. Cruickshank, with Captain D. N. Grant as Adjutant.—Ed.

2/9TH BATTALION RETURNS TO SCOTLAND

" This day it was ascertained that the enemy had withdrawn
" from his position on the Haute Deule Canal bank, and the
" Welch crossed without opposition. .... During the early part
" of the night The Black Watch moved forward, through the
" Welch, and took up an outpost line running N. and S. between
" Bauvin and Provin with three companies, B, C and D, with A
" in support."

From this date until the Armistice the Battalion moved forward with the 16th Division until, on October 20th, it arrived on the banks of the Scheldt, in the neighbourhood of St. Maur. Here it was obvious that the enemy resistance was stiffening and the advance was held up. The Battalion took no further part in active operations after this time, being employed on road repairing round Rumes and Escoeuilles, where it was when the Armistice was declared on November 11th. The occasion was somewhat marred—as the Diary states—by the " fact that there was a complete absence of whisky in the Battalion."

The rest of the 9th Battalion story is soon told. Moving from place to place on the dates given below, it was employed on training and in carrying out the numerous instructional schemes designed to occupy the time during the difficult period of demobilization.

November 12th at Le Préau.
      „   15th at Corbrieux.
      „   16th at Avelin.
      „   27th at Fretin.

The Battalion remained at Fretin for the rest of the winter and during the spring of 1919 until it was reduced to Cadre strength, and then moved to Pont-à-Marcq. The 9th returned to Scotland in July and was then finally disbanded.

APPENDIX I

Record of Officers' Services

Abbreviations :—" K."—Killed. " D. of W."—Died of Wounds. " W."—Wounded. " M."—Missing.

THE NINTH BATTALION

Addison, J. 2nd Lieut. Joined 27th March, 1917. Awarded M.C. 4th Oct., 1917.
Allan, J. 2nd Lieut. Rejoined 30th June, 1916. To U.K. sick 23rd Jan., 1917.
Allan, S. 2nd Lieut. Joined 12th June, 1916.
Allison, T. B. 2nd Lieut. Transferred to 44th L.M. Battery. *w.* 26th April, 1917. Awarded M.C. for gallantry Battle of Arras, 1917.
Andrew, R. Lieut. Went to France with Battalion 7th July, 1915. *w.* 25th Sept., 1915.
Anderson, R. B. 2nd Lieut. Joined 11th May, 1917. *w.* 31st July, 1917. To U.K. 4th Aug., 1917.
Anderson, W. 2nd Lieut. *d. of w.* 23rd April, 1917.

Baille, A. 2nd Lieut. Joined 7th April, 1916.
Barr, J. W. 2nd Lieut. Joined 9th Jan., 1917. *w.* 9th April, 1917.
Bartmann, N. 2nd Lieut. Joined 12th June, 1916. *w.* 10th July, 1916.
Bearn, F. A. Capt. M.O., R.A.M.C. *w.* 25th Sept., 1915, at duty. *w.* 18th Aug., 1916. Awarded M.C. Jan., 1916. Awarded D.S.O. 5th Jan., 1917.
Bearn, O. L. 2nd Lieut. Joined 5th Oct., 1915. To hospital 28th Nov., 1915. Rejoined Battalion. *k.* 23rd April, 1917.
Belford, C. R. 2nd Lieut. *k.* 2nd Sept., 1918.
Bell, J. M. Capt. Went to France with Battn. 7th July, 1915. *k.* 25th Sept., 1915.
Bell, T. H. 2nd Lieut. Joined 11th Dec., 1915. *k.* 9th Feb., 1916.
Bellamy, C. W. 2nd Lieut. Joined Sept., 1917. Promoted Lieut. 19th Nov., 1917. Left Battn. Aug., 1918.
Binnie, W. B. Lieut. Joined 25th Nov., 1915. Promoted Capt. Awarded M.C. 17th Aug., 1916. *w.* 8th Sept., 1916. Rejoined 9th Jan., 1917. Rejoined 3rd July, 1917, from Senior Officers' Course. Bar to M.C. 4th Oct., 1917. Promoted Major 24th Aug., 1917. *w.* 28th March, 1918.
Birrell, H. L. 2nd Lieut. Joined June, 1918. To U.K. 31st Oct., 1918.
Brand, W. R. Capt. C.F. To Base 17th Feb., 1918.
Brown, D. D. 2nd Lieut. Joined 5th April, 1916.
Brown, J. M. 2nd Lieut. Joined 25th Aug., 1916. *w.* 22nd Dec., 1916. Rejoined 27th Aug., 1917. Promoted Lieut. 19th Nov., 1917. To U.K. sick 20th Jan., 1918. To hospital 10th Oct., 1918. To U.K. 5th Nov., 1918.
Browne, G. B. 2nd Lieut. Joined 5th Dec., 1915. *k.* 7th Feb., 1916.
Bruce, R. F. Capt. Joined 28th June, 1916.
Buchan, J. I. Lieut. D.S.O. Joined August 1917.
Burton, J. L. 2nd Lieut. Joined 11th Feb., 1917. *m.* 27th April, 1917. Body found where he was last seen on 27th April, 1917, and buried by 1/4th Yorkshire Regt.

THE NINTH BATTALION THE BLACK WATCH

Byers, T. 2nd Lieut. Joined 8th Feb., 1917. Awarded M.C. for gallantry Battle of Arras. Promoted Capt. To hospital sick 19th June, 1918. To U.K. 8th Oct., 1918.

Callan, J. 2nd Lieut. Joined 22nd Sept., 1916. *w.* 9th April, 1917.

Calvert, T. 2nd Lieut. M.C. Joined 10th Aug., 1917. Awarded M.C. 4th Oct., 1917. Promoted Capt. Gassed 23rd March, 1918. To U.K. 3rd April, 1918.

Cameron, A. J. 2nd Lieut. Joined 7th Oct., 1918.

Cameron, J. H. Lieut. Went to France with Battalion 7th July, 1915. *k.* 25th Sept., 1915.

Campbell, J. 2nd Lieut. Went to France with Battn. 7th July, 1915. *w.* 25th Sept., 1915.

Campbell, W. P. 2nd Lieut. Joined 8th Oct., 1917. Transferred 1/6th Battn. 30th Oct., 1917.

Carmichael, A. D. Capt. Went to France with Battn. 7th July, 1915. Promoted Major. Mentioned in Despatches 5th Jan., 1917. Left Battn. Sept., 1917.

Carswell, R. 2nd Lieut. Joined 6th Oct., 1915. To hospital 30th Nov., 1915.

Clark, R. T. 2nd Lieut. Joined 22nd Sept., 1916. To U.K. for 6 months tour of duty 15th Feb., 1918. Promoted Lieut. 7th April, 1918.

Clark, W. Q.M. & Lieut. Went to France with Battn. 7th July, 1915. Awarded M.C. 28th Nov., 1916. Mentioned in Despatches 5th Jan., 1917. Struck off Strength 30th June, 1917. Promoted Capt. 9th Sept., 1917.

Clow, G. R. 2nd Lieut. Joined 18th Nov., 1915. *k.* 17th March, 1916.

Cochrane, J. Lieut. Joined 7th Oct., 1918.

Collins, C. K. 2nd Lieut. Joined 25th April, 1918.

Collins, H. J. Capt. C.F. Went to France with Battn. 7th July, 1915. Awarded M.C. 8th June, 1917. *k.* 9th April, 1917.

Cook, G. N. 2nd Lieut. Joined 23rd Sept., 1917. To U.K. sick 1st April, 1918.

Crighton, J. Lieut. Went to France with Battn. 7th July, 1915. *k.* 25th Sept., 1915.

Cronne, F. W. 2nd Lieut. Joined 14th Nov., 1915.

Cruickshank, J. Lieut.-Col. Arrived in France in Command of re-formed Battn. 30th July, 1918. Left Battn. 24th Oct., 1918

Cullen, T. Capt. Joined 12th Oct., 1916. To Town Major Buneville 18th Feb., 1917. Rejoined Battn. 20th May, 1917. Left to Town Major Vieil Hesdin 24th May, 1917. To command 15th Div. reception camp 2nd July, 1918.

Cunningham, D. M. 2nd Lieut. Joined 9th May, 1918. *w.* 10th June, 1918. *d. of w.* 11th June, 1918.

Cuthbert, D. W. H. 2nd Lieut. Joined 23rd July, 1916. *k.* 9th April, 1917.

Dale, E. E. 2nd Lieut. Joined 6th March, 1917. Dismissed the Service 5th Oct., 1917.

Davies, H. S. 2nd Lieut. Joined 12th Oct., 1918.

Deasy, J. C. 2nd Lieut. Joined Battn. May, 1917.

Dennistoun, A. H. O. Major. Joined 13th Dec., 1916. Mentioned in Despatches 18th Dec., 1917. Struck off strength of Battn. 23rd April, 1918.

APPENDIX I

Dennistoun, A. O. 2nd Lieut. Went to France with Battn. 7th July, 1915. w. 25th Sept., 1915.
Dewar, J. M. 2nd Lieut. Joined 6th Oct., 1915. Gassed 29th April, 1916.
Dinwiddie, R. M. 2nd Lieut. w. 9th April, 1917.
Donaldson, J. Capt. Joined 11th May, 1917. k. in a. 23rd Aug., 1917.
Dow, W. 2nd Lieut. Joined 29th July, 1916. w. 24th Jan., 1917.
Drumlanrig, Viscount F. A. K. D. Lieut. Joined 27th Aug., 1917. w. 24th Dec., 1917. To U. K. 9th Jan., 1918.
Drummond, E. M. 2nd Lieut. Joined 1st May, 1917. w. 31st July, 1917. To U.K. 4th Aug., 1917.
Drummond, H. M. 2nd Lieut. Joined 23rd Nov., 1915. Rejoined 18th March, 1916. w. 28th April, 1916.
Drummond, J. E. 2nd Lieut. Joined 25th Aug., 1916. w. 8th Sept., 1916. Joined 1st May, 1917. Awarded M.C. for gallantry 31st July, 1917. w. 2nd Aug., 1917. Rejoined Battn. from hospital 17th Sept., 1917. Promoted Capt. 18th Oct., 1917. To Base sick 1st Jan., 1918.
Dudgeon, R. M. Lieut.-Col. D.S.O., M.C. Assumed command of Battn. 1st April, 1918. Struck off strength of Battn. 23rd April, 1918.
Duffy, W. J. 2nd Lieut. M.C. Joined 2nd Dec., 1917. To U.K. sick 20th Jan., 1918.
Duggan, M. 2nd Lieut. To hospital (shell shock) 13th June, 1917. To U.K. 20th June, 1917. Promoted Lieut. 19th Nov., 1917. Relinquished commission on account of ill health 10th Feb., 1918
Duke, J. M. S. Capt. Joined 9th July, 1916. Left Battn. for Base 11th March, 1917.
Dundas, W. F. 2nd Lieut. Joined 26th Oct., 1917. To U.K. sick 14th Dec., 1917. Rejoined 29th April, 1918. w. 21st May, 1918. Transferred to U.K. 3rd June, 1918.

Edwards, T. 2nd Lieut. Joined 8th Feb., 1917. w. 7th July, 1917. Rejoined 9th May, 1918. To U.K. 5th June, 1918.
Eglington, D. C. Lieut. w. 18th Aug., 1916.
Ewart, R. H. C. 2nd Lieut. Joined 5th Oct., 1915.

Fairley, J. R. Lieut. Joined June, 1918.
Fell, F. J. 2nd Lieut. Joined 31st March, 1916.
Ferguson, W. 2nd Lieut. Joined 25th Nov., 1916. To U.K. sick 30th Jan., 1917.
Forrest, W. A. 2nd Lieut. Joined 8th Oct., 1917. m. 28th March, 1918.
Forsyth, G. 2nd Lieut. Joined 19th Sept., 1916.
Fraser, D. C. 2nd Lieut. Joined 25th Nov., 1916.
Fraser, J. H. 2nd Lieut. Joined 1st May, 1917. w. 31st July, 1917. To U.K. 19th Aug., 1917.
Fraser, J. O. 2nd Lieut. k. 9th April, 1917.

Gilchrist, J. Capt. Went to France with Battn. 7th July, 1915. w. 29th Aug., 1915. d. of w. same date.
Gilchrist, J. S. Capt. R.A.M.C. Joined Battn. 20th April, 1918.
Gillatt, J. M. Major. To command 16th Royal Scots 11th Dec., 1916.
Glenny, D. J. 2nd Lieut. Went to France with Battn. 7th July, 1915. w. 25th Sept., 1915.

Gordon, E. Capt. R.A.M.C. Joined Battn. as M.O. 1st Oct., 1916.
Gordon, G. H. 2nd Lieut. Joined 2nd Sept., 1916. *w.* 5th Jan., 1917. Rejoined 27th Aug., 1917. Promoted Lieut. 19th Nov., 1917.
Govan, G. E. M. 2nd Lieut. Joined Battn. 18th Sept., 1917. *w.* 28th March, 1918.
Graham, A. 2nd Lieut. Joined 1st May, 1917. Promoted Lieut. 19th Nov., 1917. *k.* 30th Dec., 1917.
Graham, D. H. N. Capt. Went to France with Battn. 7th July, 1915. *k.* 25th Sept., 1915.
Graham, S. 2nd Lieut. *w.* 25th Dec., 1916. Promoted Lieut. 24th April, 1917. *w.* 25th Aug., 1917. Awarded M.C. 4th Oct., 1917.
Grant, N. A. Lieut. Joined 9th July, 1916. Promoted Capt. *w.* 31st July, 1917.

Hamilton, A. K. Lieut. Joined 10th Feb., 1918. Promoted Capt. Awarded M.C. To U.K. sick 12th July, 1918.
Hamilton, A. K. Capt. Joined 18th Sept., 1918.
Harley, B. H. 2nd Lieut. Joined 25th April, 1918. To hospital sick 20th June, 1918.
Harvey, R. E. Capt. and Adj. Went to France with Battn. 7th July, 1915. *d. of w.* 25th Sept., 1915.
Hastings, R. A. M. 2nd Lieut. Joined 21st Sept., 1916. *w.* 23rd April, 1917.
Henderson, M. W. H. Major. Went to France with Battn. 7th July, 1915. *k.* 25th Sept., 1915.
Henderson-Hamilton, J. C. Lieut. Went to France with Battn. 7th July, 1915. *k.* 25th Sept., 1915.
Hill, J. W. 2nd Lieut. Joined 31st Oct., 1918.
Hodge, D. G. 2nd Lieut. Joined 19th Sept., 1916. To U.K. April, 1917.
Howard, A. J. 2nd Lieut. Joined 7th Oct., 1915.
Howard, R. T. P. 2nd Lieut. Joined Oct., 1915. *k.* 17th March, 1916.
Hughes, R. 2nd Lieut. Joined 9th May, 1918.
Humble, J. N. 2nd Lieut. Joined 6th June, 1916. *w.* 8th Sept., 1916. Rejoined 5th March, 1917. *w.* 23rd April, 1917. Promoted Lieut. 19th Nov., 1917.
Humphries, C. M. Lieut. Joined 22nd June, 1918. To U.K. 24th Oct., 1918.
Hunter, T. W. 2nd Lieut. Joined 20th March, 1916. *w.* 9th April, 1917. Promoted Capt. 27th March, 1917.

Inch, R. Lieut. Joined 9th May, 1918
Innes, S. A. Major. Joined 16th June, 1916. Promoted Lieut.-Col. Awarded D.S.O. 5th Jan., 1917. Mentioned in Despatches same date. Awarded Bar to D.S.O. for gallantry, Battle of Arras, 1917. To hospital 7th May, 1917. Rejoined and assumed command of Battn. 4th June, 1917. Mentioned in Despatches 18th Dec., 1917. To hospital sick 23rd March, 1918. To U.K. 2nd April, 1918. Mentioned in Despatches 8th June, 1918.
Ireland, J. B. 2nd Lieut. Joined 6th June, 1916. *k.* 8th Sept., 1916.

APPENDIX I

Johnstone, H. B. 2nd Lieut. Joined 16th Aug., 1916. *w.* 25th Aug., 1916.
Johnstone, N. G. 2nd Lieut. Joined 11th May, 1917. Awarded M.C. 4th Oct., 1917. Promoted Capt. 15th Aug., 1917. *k.* 30th Dec., 1917.

Kerr, G. R. M. 2nd Lieut. Joined 1st May, 1917. Rejoined from Base 16th Aug., 1917. Passed unfit for service 22nd Oct., 1917.
Kerr, P. C. 2nd Lieut. Joined 15th July, 1917. To U.K. gassed 8th April, 1918.
Kerr, P. E. 2nd Lieut. Joined 31st August, 1917.
Kilgour, R. L. Capt. Joined July, 1918.
Kinnoch, D. 2nd Lieut. Joined 26th Oct., 1917. To U.K. sick 4th May, 1918.
Kirk, D. K. Capt. Joined 26th Sept., 1918.

Lakeman, A. F. 2nd Lieut. Joined 30th Sept., 1917. To Tank Corps 22nd Dec., 1917.
Lambroughton, M. 2nd Lieut. Gassed 5th Sept., 1918. *d.* of Influenza 16th Nov., 1918.
Lauder, J. H. 2nd Lieut. Gassed 14th Sept., 1918.
Leitch, A. 2nd Lieut. Joined 8th Oct., 1917. To 4/5th Battn. 19th May, 1918.
Leslie, G. C. 2nd Lieut. Joined 22nd Oct., 1916. *d. of w.* 17th Aug., 1917.
Leslie, W. J. 2nd Lieut. Went to France with Battn. 7th July, 1915. *w.* 25th Sept., 1915. Promoted Lieut. 3rd Oct., 1917. To U.K. sick 18th Feb., 1918.
Lloyd, T. O. Lieut.-Col. Went to France with Battn. as commanding officer 7th July, 1915. To hospital sick 18th Nov., 1915. Awarded C.M.G. June, 1916.
Loxton, A. S. G. 2nd Lieut. Joined 8th Oct., 1917. *w.* 28th March, 1918.

MacDonald, A. W. 2nd Lieut. Joined 23rd Sept., 1917. Promoted Lieut. 26th Oct., 1918.
MacDonald, R. B. A. 2nd Lieut. Joined Battn. 18th March, 1916. *k.* 18th Aug., 1916.
MacDowall, C. G. 2nd Lieut. Joined from 11th Battn. Oct., 1916. To U.K. 14th Aug., 1917. Promoted Lieut. 19th Nov., 1917.
MacFie, J. D. A. 2nd Lieut. Transferred to R.F.C. 31st July, 1916. Promoted Lieut. 19th Nov., 1917.
MacGregor, J. 2nd Lieut. Joined 7th April, 1916.
MacGregor, N. W. Major. D.S.O. Gordon Highlanders. Assumed command Battn. 18th Nov., 1915. Left Battn. Jan., 1916.
MacGregor, W. 2nd Lieut. Joined 9th May, 1918.
MacRae, J. F. N. 2nd Lieut. Joined 2nd June, 1916. *w.* 18th Aug., 1916. Mentioned in Despatches 5th Jan., 1917.
MacWilliam, H. Lieut. *k.* 28th May, 1916.
McCluer, B. B. Lieut. M.O.R.C., United States Army, attached. Joined 2nd April, 1918. To hospital, badly *w.* 21st April, 1918.
McCullum, J. R. 2nd Lieut. Rejoined 5th Nov., 1918.
McDiarmid, A. D. 2nd Lieut. Joined 25th Nov., 1916. *w.* 26th April, 1917. Promoted Lieut. 19th Nov., 1917. Rejoined 31st Oct., 1918.

THE NINTH BATTALION THE BLACK WATCH

McGregor, A. W. 2nd Lieut. Joined 6th Oct., 1915. *k.* 27th Feb., 1916.
McGregor, T. 2nd Lieut. *w.* 23rd May, 1916. Rejoined 27th June, 1917. *w.* 31st July, 1917. To U.K. 14th Aug., 1917. Promoted Lieut. 19th Nov., 1917.
McGregor, W. K. 2nd Lieut. Joined 11th May, 1917. *w.* 6th July, 1917. To U.K. 9th July, 1917. *w.* 14th June, 1918. Rejoined. *m.* 28th July, 1918.
McIntyre, J. 2nd Lieut. Joined 31st March, 1916. Gassed 29th April, 1916.
McIntyre, W. S. 2nd Lieut. Went to France with Battn. 7th July, 1915. From hospital 4th March, 1916. To hospital 7th March, 1916.
McKenzie, A. 2nd Lieut. Joined 9th Oct., 1915. *k.* 5th Nov., 1915.
McKenzie, L. Lieut. Joined 30th Aug., 1917. *w.* and *m.* 28th March, 1918. *d. of w.* 2nd April, 1918.
McLean, R. Major. Joined 16th Oct., 1918. To 15th Division 25th Nov., 1918.
McLeod, A. K. Capt. Went to France with Battn. 7th July, 1915. *w.* 25th Sept., 1915.
McLeod, A. W. 2nd Lieut. Joined 11th May, 1917.
McMurray, R. J. 2nd Lieut. *w.* 18th Aug., 1916. Rejoined 1st May, 1917.
McPhee, I. D. A. 2nd Lieut. Joined 9th Oct., 1915.
McRoberts, R. K. 2nd Lieut. Joined Battn. 19th Sept. 1916. To U.K. 21st April, 1917.
McVeigh, J. 2nd Lieut. Joined 26th Oct., 1917. *d. of w.* 28th March, 1918.
Machin, B. W. 2nd Lieut. *w.* 7th Dec., 1917. To U.K. sick 31st Dec., 1917.
Mackie, G. B. 2nd Lieut. Joined 25th Aug., 1916. To U.K. sick 25th Nov., 1916. Mentioned in Despatches 5th Jan., 1917. Promoted Lieut. 19th Nov., 1917.
Malcolm, T. G. 2nd Lieut. Joined 23rd Sept., 1917. To 4/5th Battn. May, 1918.
Malcolm, W. 2nd Lieut. Joined 9th May, 1918. To hospital sick 20th June, 1918. Rejoined Battn. *w.* 1st Aug., 1918.
Marchbank, W. 2nd Lieut. Joined 15th May, 1917. *w.* 31st July, 1917. To U.K. 15th Aug., 1917.
Marshall, A. 2nd Lieut. *w.* 9th April, 1917. Promoted Lieut. 19th Nov., 1917.
Mearns, A. H. Lieut. Joined 14th March, 1916. Transferred to R.F.C. 11th March, 1917.
Menzies, C. E. K. 2nd Lieut. Went to France with Battn. 7th July, 1915.
Menzies, J. N. 2nd Lieut. Joined 2nd Dec., 1917. Left Battn. Aug., 1918.
Millar, J. 2nd Lieut. Went to France with Battn. 7th July, 1915. *k.* 25th Sept., 1915.
Miller, J. D. G. Lieut. Went to France with Battn. 7th July, 1915. *w.* and *d. of w.* 14th Nov., 1915.
Mitchell, W. W. 2nd Lieut. Joined 5th Jan., 1918. To U.K. sick 11th March, 1918.
Morren, J. H. Lieut. Joined 5th Oct., 1918.
Morris, J. W. Lieut. M.O.R.C. United States Army. Joined Battn. as Medical Officer. *w.* 28th March, 1918.
Morrison, A. 2nd Lieut. Joined 8th Oct., 1917.

APPENDIX I

Morrison, L. G. 2nd Lieut. Joined 5th Oct., 1915. Promoted Capt. k. 23rd April, 1917.
Morton, W. T. Capt. C.F. Joined 17th Feb., 1918.
Muir, H. S. 2nd Lieut. Joined 12th June, 1916. w. 9th April, 1917. Awarded M.C. 8th June, 1917. Mentioned in Despatches. Rejoined 8th Oct., 1917.
Murray, H. F. F. Major. Joined 13th Nov., 1916. Assumed command of Battn. 7th May, 1917. k. 23rd Aug., 1917. Buried at Brandhoek Cemetery Aug. 27th, 1917.
Murray, R. J. Lieut. Promoted Capt. 5th Oct., 1917. To U.K. sick 5th Jan., 1918.

Neish, C. F. I. 2nd Lieut. Joined 11th May, 1917. w. 31st July, 1917. To U.K. 19th Aug., 1917.
Norman, N. F. Capt. Sick to hospital 1st Oct., 1916.
Norie-Miller, S. Lieut. Went to France with Battn. 7th July, 1915. Promoted Capt. and Adj. Oct., 1916. Awarded M.C. Mentioned in Despatches 5th Jan., 1917. w. 9th April, 1917. Posted to U.K. for duty 1st Nov., 1917. Rejoined 18th Aug., 1918.

Pattulo, G. L. S. 2nd Lieut. Rejoined from hospital 1st Oct., 1918.
Pitcairn, E. G. Lieut. Joined 1st Oct., 1915.
Porter, R. W. 2nd Lieut. Joined 9th Sept., 1916. Promoted Lieut. 19th Nov., 1917. k. 11th Jan., 1918.
Proudfoot, F. 2nd Lieut. Joined 30th June, 1916. w. 9th April, 1917. Awarded M.C. for gallantry, Battle of Arras, 1917. Rejoined 27th June, 1917. Bar to M.C. 31st July, 1917. Promoted Lieut. from 27th March, 1917. Promoted Capt. To hospital 17th May, 1918. To U.K. 4th June, 1918.
Purvis, R. M. 2nd Lieut. Went to France with Battn. 7th July, 1915.

Raymond, E. N. L. 2nd Lieut. Joined 29th Nov., 1915. w. 5th Feb., 1916. Rejoined from hospital 6th March, 1916.
Read, F. 2nd Lieut. To U.K. sick 17th April, 1918.
Reid, J. M. Capt. Joined 12th Oct., 1916. Seconded 12th Nov., 1917.
Reid, R. W. 2nd Lieut. Joined 5th Oct., 1915. w. 27th April, 1916. d. of w. 15th May, 1916.
Reid, S. M. 2nd Lieut. Joined 31st March, 1916. w. 9th April, 1917.
Reid, T. E. 2nd Lieut. Joined 23rd July, 1916. w. 9th April, 1917.
Reid, W. Capt. Joined 22nd Oct., 1916.
Reid, W. D. G. 2nd Lieut. Gassed 14th Sept., 1918. Rejoined 10th Nov., 1918.
Reynell, H. E. 2nd Lieut. Joined 5th Oct., 1915. Transferred to R.F.C. 20th July, 1916.
Ritchie, C. I. B. 2nd Lieut. Joined 1st May, 1917. w. 25th Aug., 1917.
Ritchie, T. 2nd Lieut. Joined 4th June, 1917. To Instructor XIX Corps School Oct., 1917. Rejoined 30th Dec., 1917.
Robertson, A. L. 2nd Lieut. Joined 27th June, 1918. To U.K. 3rd Sept., 1918.

THE NINTH BATTALION THE BLACK WATCH

Robertson, J. B. 2nd Lieut. Joined 6th Oct., 1915. Promoted Capt. k. 7th Sept., 1916.
Robertson, J. H. 2nd Lieut. Joined 5th Oct., 1915.
Robertson, R. H. 2nd Lieut. Went to France with Battn. 7th July, 1915.
Rusk, G. A. Lieut. Went to France with Battn. 7th July, 1915. Promoted Capt. Gassed 29th April, 1916. w. 8th July, 1916.

Sanderson, K. W. 2nd Lieut. Joined July, 1918.
Scott, A. 2nd Lieut. Joined 8th Oct., 1917. Awarded M.C. 31st Aug., 1918. w. 1st Aug., 1918.
Scott, C. 2nd Lieut. Joined 8th Oct., 1917. To U.K. sick 15th April, 1918.
Scott, R. J. L. 2nd Lieut. Joined 4th Feb., 1916.
Scott-Pearse, G. 2nd Lieut. Went to France with Battn. 7th July, 1915. w. 25th Sept., 1915.
Scoular, J. G. 2nd Lieut. Joined 11th May, 1917. To War Office 7th Sept., 1917.
Sharpe, A. 2nd Lieut. Went to France with Battn. 7th July, 1915. k. 25th Sept, 1915.
Small, J. 2nd Lieut. Joined 6th Oct., 1915. Promoted Lieut. k. 29th April, 1916.
Smythe, P. C. 2nd Lieut. Joined from 6th Battn. 19th Oct., 1917.
Stephen, J. C. 2nd Lieut. Joined 12th July, 1917.
Stevenson, R. 2nd Lieut. Joined 11th May, 1917. k. 23rd Aug., 1917. Buried 27th Aug., 1917.
Stevenson, S. D. Capt. Went to France with Battn. 7th July, 1915. To U.K. Sept., 1915.
Stewart, A. J. Major. Joined 27th Sept., 1918, from 4/5th Black Watch.
Stewart, J. Major (Second-in-Command). Went to France with Battn. 7th July, 1915. Assumed command to Battn. 11th Jan., 1916. To U.K. sick 31st June, 1916. Mentioned in Despatches 1st Jan., 1916, 1st June, 1916.
Stewart-Murray, L. 2nd Lieut. Joined 5th Oct., 1915. To hospital 30th Nov., 1915.
Stirling, J. S. 2nd Lieut. Joined Battn. 13th February, 1916.
Stirling, R. 2nd Lieut. Went to France with Battn. 7th July, 1915. w. 25th Sept., 1915. Rejoined 6th May, 1916. Promoted Capt. w. 8th Sept., 1916.
Story-Wilson, W. S. Lieut. Went to France with Battn. 7th July, 1915. w. 26th June, 1916. Rejoined 30th Sept., 1916. Mentioned in Despatches March, 1917. Italian Silver Medal for Gallantry, 19th March, 1917. w. 9th April, 1917. Rejoined 30th Sept., 1917. Temporary Major, 1917. w. 28th March, 1918. Awarded M.C. July, 1918. Rejoined 5th Oct., 1918. Assumed command of Battn. 11th Oct., 1918.
Strang, J. S. 2nd Lieut. Joined 7th Feb., 1916. w. 18th Aug., 1916. Promoted Lieut. Rejoined Battn. 11th May, 1917. Promoted Capt. from 27th March, 1917. w. 26th Aug., 1917. Awarded M.C. 4th Oct., 1917. Rejoined Battn. 16th Feb., 1918. k. 28th March, 1918.
Stuart, J. 2nd Lieut. Joined 5th Jan., 1918. To hospital sick 19th June, 1918. Rejoined Battn. k. 28th July, 1918.
Studley, R. 2nd Lieut. Joined Battn. 29th April, 1918. To hospital sick 20th June, 1918.

APPENDIX I

Tait, D. G. 2nd Lieut. Joined 9th May, 1918. *w.* 28th July, 1918.
Tatham, A. D. 2nd Lieut. Joined 1st May, 1917. Promoted Lieut. 19th Nov., 1917.
Taylor, I. 2nd Lieut. Joined 11th May, 1917. *k.* 31st July, 1917.
Third, J. B. 2nd Lieut. Joined 14th Oct., 1916. *w.* 23rd April, 1917.
Tovani, W. R. 2nd Lieut. Joined 11th May, 1917. *w.* 31st July, 1917. Awarded M.C. for gallantry 31st July, 1917.
Tuke, C. S. Capt. Went to France with Battn. 7th July, 1915. *k.* 25th Sept., 1915.
Turnbull, T. R. 2nd Lieut. Joined 9th Sept., 1916. *k.* 10th Oct., 1916.
Tweedie, D. O. 2nd Lieut. Shell-shock 24th Aug., 1916. Rejoined Battn. 27th June, 1917. To U.K. 21st Aug., 1917.
Tweedie, T. C. 2nd Lieut. Joined 12th Oct., 1915.

Walcott, E. P. 2nd Lieut. Joined 8th Oct., 1917. Missing 28th March, 1918.
Waldie, J. G. 2nd Lieut. Joined 7th Oct., 1915.
Walker, E. R. C. 2nd Lieut. Joined July, 1918. Gassed 14th Sept., 1918. Rejoined 24th Oct., 1918. To hospital 12th Nov., 1918.
Watson, A. F. 2nd Lieut. Joined 12th June, 1916. *w.* 18th Aug., 1916. Rejoined Battn. 9th Jan., 1917. *k.* 23rd April, 1917.
Watson, W. D. 2nd Lieut. Joined 31st July, 1918.
Webster, C. 2nd Lieut. Joined July, 1918.
Wedderburn, H. F. K. 2nd Lieut.
Whitehead, F. W. F. Lieut. Joined 1st October, 1918.
Wilkie, D. R. R. 2nd Lieut.
Wilkie, J. F. M. L. 2nd Lieut. Joined 22nd Oct., 1916. To U.K. 21st Dec., 1916.
Wilson, D. M. 2nd Lieut. Joined 9th July, 1916. *w.* 13th July, 1916.
Wilson, E. R. Lieut. Went to France with Battn. 7th July, 1915. *w.* 25th Sept., 1915. Awarded M.C. Jan., 1916.
Wilson, E. W. D. 2nd Lieut. Joined 18th Sept., 1917. Promoted Lieut. 7th April, 1918.
Wilson, F. R. 2nd Lieut. *w.* 25th Sept., 1915. Promoted Lieut. Rejoined 10th Sept., 1916. To U.K. sick 22nd March, 1917.
Wilson, J. 2nd Lieut. Joined 22nd Sept., 1916. *k.* 23rd April, 1917.
Wilson, R. O. S. 2nd Lieut. Joined 25th Nov., 1916. Promoted Lieut. 24th April, 1917. Transferred to 8th Battn. 27th Oct., 1918.
Wilson, W. F. Lieut. Joined 28th April, 1918.
Wishart, J. 2nd Lieut. Joined 5th Oct., 1918.
Woodburn, J. C. 2nd Lieut. Joined 21st May, 1917. Shell shock 1st Aug., 1917. To U.K. 30th Aug., 1917 Promoted Lieut. 19th Nov., 1917.

Young, C. K. 2nd Lieut. Joined 16th Aug., 1916. Sick to hospital 1st Oct., 1916. *w.* 23rd April, 1917. Rejoined 27th Aug., 1917. To M.G. Cy. 18th Dec., 1917.
Young, G. E. R. 2nd Lieut. Joined 1st May, 1917. *w.* 23rd Aug., 1917. Relinquished commission on account of ill-health 21st Jan., 1918.
Young, G. F. 2nd Lieut. Joined 4th May, 1917. *w.* 25th Aug., 1917.

APPENDIX II

Summary of Casualties. The Ninth Battalion

OFFICERS, 1914–18

Year.	Killed. D. of Wounds. D. on Service.	Wounded.	Missing.	Total.	Year.
1914	—	—	—	—	1914
1915	14	10	—	24	1915
1916	13	29	1	43	1916
1917	16	44	1	61	1917
1918	3	5	4	12	1918
Totals :	46	88	6	140	

OTHER RANKS, 1914–18

Year.	Killed. D. of Wounds. D. on Service.	Wounded.	Missing.	Total.	Year.
1914	—	—	—	—	1914
1915	303	429	—	732	1915
1916	158	686	50	894	1916
1917	151	788	97	1036	1917
1918	33	126	78	237	1918
Totals :	645	2029	225	2899	

TOTAL:
140 Officers.   2,899 Other Ranks.

APPENDIX III

Casualties—Officers

Abbreviations :—* Killed in action.   † Died of wounds.

The Ninth Battalion

Name.	Rank.	Date.
Anderson, W.	2nd Lieut.	*23.4.17.
Bearn, O. L.	Lieut.	*23.4.17.
Belford, C. R.	2nd Lieut.	*2.9.18.
Bell, J. M.	Captain	*25.9.15.
Bell, T. H.	2nd Lieut.	*9.2.16.
Brown, G. B.	2nd Lieut.	*7.2.16.
Burton, J. L.	2nd Lieut.	*24.4.17.
Cameron, J. H.	Lieut.	*25.9.15.
Clow, G. R.	2nd Lieut.	*17.3.16.
Collins, H. J.	Captain	*9.4.17. R. C. Chaplain, attd.
Crighton, J.	Lieut.	*25.9.15.
Cuthbert, D. W. H.	2nd Lieut.	*9.4.17.
Donaldson, J.	Captain	*23.8.17. From 7th Battalion.
Dow, W.	2nd Lieut.	†2.2.17.
Fraser, J. O.	2nd Lieut.	*9.4.17.
Gilchrist, J.	Captain	†29.8.15.
Graham, A.	Lieut.	*30.12.17. With 44th T.M.B.
Graham, D. H. N.	Captain	*25.9.15.
Harvey, R. E.	Captain and Adjutant	†25.9.15.
Henderson, M. W.	Major	*25.9.15.
Henderson-Hamilton, J. C.	Lieut.	*25.9.15.
Hewat, J. G. A.		
Howard, R. T. P.	2nd Lieut.	*17.3.16.
Ireland, J. B.	Lieut.	*8.9.16.
Johnstone, N. G.	Captain	*30.12.17. With 44th T.M.B.
Leslie, G. C.	2nd Lieut.	†15.8.17. From 5th Battalion.
MacDonald, R. B. A.	2nd Lieut.	*17.8.16.
McKenzie, L.	Lieut.	†2.4.18.
McKenzie, A.	2nd Lieut.	*5.11.15.
MacWilliam, H.	Lieut.	*28.5.16.
McVeigh, J.	2nd Lieut.	*28.3.18. From 3rd Battalion.
Mearns, A. H.	Lieut.	*24.6.17. And R.F.C., 57 Sqd.
Millar, J.	2nd Lieut.	*25.9.15.
Miller, J. D. G.	Lieut.	†15.11.15.
Morrison, L. G.	Captain	*23.4.17.
Murray, H. F. F.	Lieut.-Col.	*23.8.17.

THE NINTH BATTALION THE BLACK WATCH

Name.	Rank.	Date.
Porter, R. W.	Lieut.	*11.1.18. Attd. 4/5th Battalion
Reid, R. W.	2nd Lieut.	†17.5.16.
Reid, T. E.	2nd Lieut.	†18.4.17. From 3rd Battalion.
Robertson, J. B.	Captain	†17.9.16.
Sharpe, A.	2nd Lieut.	*25.9.15.
Small, J.	Lieut.	*29.4.16.
Stevenson, R.	2nd Lieut.	*23.8.17. From 7th Battalion.
Strang, J. S.	Captain (M.C.)	*28.3.18.
Stuart, J.	2nd Lieut.	*28.7.18. From 3rd Battalion.
Taylor, J.	2nd Lieut.	*3.7.17.
Tuke, C. S.	Captain	*25.9.15.
Turnbull, T. R.	2nd Lieut.	*10.10.16. From 11th Batt.
Watson, A. F.	2nd Lieut.	*23.4.17.
Wilson, J.	2nd Lieut.	*23.4.17.

APPENDIX IV

NOMINAL ROLL OF WARRANT OFFICERS, NON-COMMISSIONED OFFICERS AND MEN KILLED IN ACTION OR DIED OF WOUNDS OR DISEASE IN THE GREAT WAR, 1914–18

Abbreviations.—* Killed in action. † Died of wounds. § Died. ¶ Died at sea.

THE NINTH BATTALION

Abercrombie, J. D., Pte., S/7796	* 25.9.15	Beaton, W., A/Cpl., 240391	† 26.10.18
		Beattie, J., Pte., S/7003	* 17.8.16
Addison, J., Pte., S/4238	* 25.9.15	Beattie, W. P., Pte., S/17811	† 30.9.17
Adkins, H., Pte., S/9714	† 25.8.16	Beaty, T., Sgt., S/4796	* 25.9.15
Aiken, J., Pte., S/5354	* 25.9.15	Beeby, H. W., Sgt., S/8772	† 14.4.17
Aitchison, J., Pte., S/5172	* 25.9.15	Bell, F., Pte., 201126	* 22.8.17
Aitken, J. M., Pte., S/4535	* 25.9.15	Bell, W. D., Pte., S/14405	† 11.4.17
Alberti, M., Pte., S/12318	* 26.4.17	Berry, J. I., A/Cpl., S/18428	† 31.3.18
Alker, J., Pte., S/15991	† 28.1.17	Bertie, J., Pte., S/6856	* 25.9.15
Allan, W., Pte., S/6614	* 25.9.15	Bevans, G. P., Pte., S/12225	* 8.9.16
Allison, A., Sgt., S/9863	† 10.10.16	Binnie, W., Pte., S/0707	* 9.4.17
Allison, J., Pte., S/9031	* 26.8.17	Bissett, A. W., Pte., S/16068	* 9.4.17
Anderson, A., Pte., S/12231	* 22.8.17	Black, A., Cpl., S/6563	* 29.4.16
Anderson, D., A/Cpl., S/7637	§ 17.8.19	Black, G., Pte., 240315	* 23.4.17
Anderson, G., Pte., S/5349	† 26.9.15	Black, R., A/Cpl., S/40423	† 11.5.17
Anderson, G., Pte., S/7172	† 10.9.16	Blackall, R., L/Cpl., S/8502	* 25.9.15
Anderson, J. McK., Pte., S/4633	* 25.9.15	Blackwood, J., Pte., S/4659	* 26.1.16
		Blair, J., Pte., S/6799	§ 19.10.18
Anderson, R., Pte., S/12292	† 25.8.17	Blyth, W., Pte., S/43304	* 27.4.17
Anderson, T., Pte., S/4242	* 25.9.15	Bothwell, D. C., Pte., S/24200	* 2.9.18
Anderson, W., Pte., 350912	† 29.9.17	Bowland, T., Pte., S/12355	* 17.8.16
Arbuckle, A., Pte., S/9536	* 18.9.16	Bowman, M., Pte., S/16251	† 26.4.17
Armstrong, T., Pte., S/5339	* 25.9.15	Boyle, H., Pte., S/4905	* 25.9.15
Arnott, J., Pte., 292128	† 17.12.17	Boyle, J., L/Cpl., S/15962	* 23.4.17
Arnott, G. B., Pte., S/4298	† 28.6.16	Boyle, J., Pte., S/16685	* 31.7.17
Aspin, E., L/Cpl., S/12262	* 9.4.17	Bradley, J. F., L/Cpl., S/4911	* 29.8.16
Auchterlonie, G., Pte., S/40332	* 9.4.17	Braithwaite, T., Pte., S/12396	* 10.9.16
		Brannan, M., Pte., S/40810	* 31.7.17
		Brebner, W., Pte., S/12315	* 21.7.16
Bagan, J., Pte., S/7647	* 18.9.16	Bremner, W., Cpl., S/9465	† 22.9.16
Baillie, R., Pte., 2025	* 10.4.17	Brodie, A., L/Cpl., S/15851	* 31.7.17
Bain, A., Pte., S/9435	* 29.4.16	Brough, W., L/Cpl., 202258	* 30.7.17
Baird, P., L/Cpl., S/8233	* 26.4.17	Brown, A., Pte., S/8871	† 1.7.17
Baker, E., Pte., S/12067	* 17.8.16	Brown, A., Pte., S/3334	* 18.7.16
Ballantyne, J., Pte., 9780	* 1.7.17	Brown, A., L/Sgt., S/4295 (M.M.)	* 24.5.16
Barber, J. M., Sgt., S/5164	* 25.9.15		
Barclay, A., Pte., S/12312	† 28.1.17	Brown, A., Sgt., S/9422	* 24.3.18
Barnes, J., Pte., S/19982	† 2.8.17	Brown, A., Pte., S/15951	* 24.5.16
Barnes, T., Pte., S/27568	* 21.10.18	Brown, C. K., Sgt., S/6822	* 25.9.15
Barnett, A., Pte., S/4253	* 11.10.16	Brown, D. R., Pte., S/11990	* 26.4.17
Barnett, R. A., Pte., S/14188	† 23.4.17	Brown, J., Pte., S/11905	* 28.3.18
Barron, T., Pte., S/4871	† 28.9.15	Brown, J. D., Pte., S/6530	* 25.9.15
Barton, H., L/Cpl., S/43406	* 25.8.17	Brown, J., Pte., S/11217	* 29.4.16
Barton, W., Cpl., 4610	* 25.9.15	Brown, M., Pte., S/11106	* 8.9.16
Baxter, J., Pte., S/12350	* 9.4.17	Brown, P., Pte., S/16616	† 24.4.17
Bayne, A. E., Sgt., S/3982 (D.C.M.)	* 29.4.16	Brown, R., Pte., S/4903	* 25.8.17
		Brown, W., Pte., 9584	† 18.3.16

THE NINTH BATTALION THE BLACK WATCH

Bruce, J., Pte., S/9639	*9.4.17		Connell, J., Pte., S/43152	*9.4.17
Buchanan, W., Pte., S/9653	*14.11.15		Cook, H., Pte., 291279	*23.4.17
Buchanan, C. McG., Pte., S/5161			Cookson, P., Pte., S/9141	*17.8.16
	*25.9.15		Cornelius, J., Pte., S/4357	*25.9.16
Buist, W., Pte., S/4915	*25.9.15		Corrigan, P., Pte., 2787	*23.8.17
Burden, T., Pte., S/18145	† 9.4.17		Couldrey, G. R., Pte., S/8788	*29.4.16
Burke, J. F., Pte., S/15940	*9.4.17		Couper, A., L/Cpl., S/4160	†30.4.16
Burnett, J., Pte., 5340	*20.6.16		Couper, J., Pte., S/43290	*18.9.16
Burns, P., Pte., S/7002	*25.9.15		Coutts, J. D., Pte., S/18812	*31.7.17
Burr, W., Pte., S/4315	*25.9.15		Craig, J., L/Cpl., S/6321	*25.9.15
Butterworth, A., A/Sgt., S/12431			Crawford, J., L/Cpl., S/48180	*25.9.15
	† 1.8.17		Crawford, M., Pte., S/4755	*25.9.15
			Creamer, W. B., Pte., 350925	*26.8.17
Cairney, H., Pte., S/11919	*8.9.16		Crerar, J., Cpl., S/4433	*25.9.15
Cairns, J., Pte., S/4427	*25.9.15		Crighton, J., Pte., S/23489	*24.5.18
Caldwell, W., L/Cpl., S/40322			Crilly, M., L/Cpl., S/4605	†23.4.17
	*31.7.17		Crinean, W., L/Cpl., 7930	†17.5.17
Cameron, J., Pte., S/3964	*25.9.15		Crombie, G., Pte., S/27005	*2.9.18
Cameron, J., Pte., S/16850	*22.8.17		Crombie, J., Pte., 290913	*21.10.18
Campbell, J., L/Cpl., 350388	*28.3.18		Cruickshanks, G., Pte., 3/3734	
Campbell, J., Pte., 201488	†30.9.17			*25.9.15
Campbell, J., Pte., S/8893	*29.4.16		Cumming, A., Sgt., 3/3748	*25.9.15
Campbell, J.D., Pte., S/18996	¶27.1.18		Cumming, J. S., Pte., S/7975	†24.5.16
Campbell, M., Pte., S/6609	*25.9.15		Cundall, N., Pte., S/43178	*25.8.17
Campbell, R., Pte., S/7805	*25.9.15		Cunningham, D., A/Cpl., S/9855	
Cane, W., A/Cpl., S/43198	*28.3.18			*13.3.17
Canning, T., Pte., S/3563	*31.7.17		Currie, A., A/Cpl., S/42449	*23.4.17
Carmichael, A., Pte., S/4494	*25.9.15		Cuthbert, C. L. Cpl., 3/3756	*25.9.15
Carmichael, A., Pte., 241204	*26.8.17			
Carmichael, J., Pte., 3/3191	*25.9.15		Dalrymple, J., Pte., S/15836	*25.8.17
Carr, J., Pte., S/15949	*17.8.16		Dand, A., Pte., 2575	*30.5.16
Carr, J. V., Pte., S/15965	†19.9.16		Dargie, J., Sgt., S/6861	† 9.8.17
Carter, J. G., Pte., S/9129	*28.3.18		Davidson, S., Pte., S/9413	†12.3.16
Casciane, J., Pte., S/9964	*29.4.16		Davidson, L. W., L/Cpl., S/4290	
Chalmers, A., Pte., S/27703	†15.11.18			*25.9.15
Chandler, W. L., Pte., S/9332	† 1.5.16		Davis, T., Pte., S/4860	*25.9.15
Chapman, A., Pte., S/6629	*25.9.15		Devine, J., Pte., S/5043	*25.9.15
Christian, F.G., Pte., S/12256	*29.4.16		Devlin, J. A., L/Cpl., S/5319	*25.9.15
Christie, J., Pte., S/4152	*25.9.15		Dick, J., Pte., S/3830	*25.9.15
Clark, J., L/Sgt., S/4240	*25.9.15		Dick, W., Pte., S/4156	*25.9.15
Clark, J., Pte., S/4396	*25.9.15		Dick, W., L/Cpl., S/5351	
Clark, K., Cpl., 268668	*20.3.18		(M.M.)	† 2.11.19
Clark, R., L/Cpl., S/4174	†26.9.15		Dickson, R., Pte., S/4705	*25.9.15
Clark, S. H., Pte., S/4933	*25.9.15		Dickson, R., Pte., 267992	*28.3.18
Clark, T., Pte., S/6617	*25.9.15		Dickson, R.J., Pte., 202557	*12.11.17
Clark, T., Pte., S/9479	*6.11.15		Dickson, W., Pte., S/21330	*28.3.18
Clarkson, M., Pte., S/3988	† 2.10.15		Dickson, W., Pte., 291416	*30.3.18
Clegg, J., Pte., S/9740	*17.3.16		Docherty, E., Pte., S/4882	†28.9.15
Cleghorn, J. K., Pte., S/9552	†20.5.16		Docherty, P., L/Cpl., 3/3317	† 9.9.16
Cockburn, J., Pte., S/9509	* 7.9.16		Doig, G., Pte., S/18101	†11.11.17
Coleman, W., Pte., S/4231	*25.9.15		Doig, J., L/Cpl., S/3765	*17.9.16
Collins, J., Pte., S/13010	*17.8.16		Dolan, M., L/Cpl., S/4663	*9.4.17
Colyin, J., Pte., S/7276	*25.9.15		Donaldson, R., Pte., 291206	*8.2.18
Comrie, J., Pte., S/4506	*25.9.15		Dorward, D., Pte., S/3930	*25.9.15
Connell, E., L/Cpl., S/9398	*22.8.17		Dorward, J., Pte., S/43143	*9.4.17

APPENDIX IV

Douglas, R., C.S.M., 9567 † 6.5.18
Dow, J., Pte., S/4749 *25.9.15
Dow, J., Pte., S/5123 *25.9.15
Dow., J. M., L/Cpl., S/11185 *29.4.16
Dow, T., L/Sgt., S/9848 * 9.4.17
Downey, J., Pte., S/9374 *25.9.15
Downie, J., Pte., S/8775 *31.7.17
Dredge, A. W., Pte., S/16350 † 8.4.17
Drysdale, J. P., L/Cpl., S/11078
§26.2.17
Duff, A., Pte., S/5154 *25.9.15
Duff, M., Pte., 268133 *11.2.18
Duffus, J., A/Sgt., S/8447 * 6.11.15
Duncan, A., Pte., S/17822 *17.5.17
Duncan, A., Pte., S/18558 *26/4/17
Duncan, H. D., Sgt., S/9368 *23.4.17
Duncan, J., Pte., 3/2712 *13.9.16
Duncan, R., Pte., 267918 †14.12.17
Duncan, T., Pte., 235040 *28.3.18
Dunn, R. A., Pte., S/9727 *29.4.16
Dunne, W., L/Cpl., S/4723 *25.8.16
Dunsmuir, D., Pte., S/6649 *26.10.15
Duthie, H. W. S., Pte., 240447
†25.8.17
Duthie, R., Sgt., S/9382 * 6.9.18
Dymock, T., Cpl., S/6865 *29.4.16

Eadie, A., Pte., S/4011 *25.9.15
Easdon, W., Pte., S/40816 *11.2.18
Easson, A., Pte., S/15014 *9.4.17
Easson, W., Pte., S/3771 *25.9.15
Eddie, A. L., A/Cpl., S/43431 *26.4.17
Edmond, R., A/Sgt., 2368 *25.8.17
Edmondson, J., Pte., S/4502 *25.9.15
Edward, J., Pte., S/8371 *17.8.16
Emery, H., Pte., S/10283 *26.4.17
Erskine, T., Pte., S/8385 *29.4.16
Erskine, W., Pte., 3/2807 *25.9.15
Evans, J., Pte., S/4980 *25.9.15
Ewing, J., Pte., S/9371 *29.4.16
Ewing, J., Pte., S/20358 *31.7.17

Fairburn, J., Pte., 3/2764 †10.8.17
Fairley, A., L/Cpl., S/6576 *25.9.15
Fell, L., Pte., S/12160 †16.9.16
Ferguson, A. M. C., L/Cpl., S/4806
*25.9.15
Ferguson, D., Pte., S/4550 *25.9.15
Ferguson, F., Pte., S/16848 *23.4.17
Ferguson, H., Pte., S/9954 * 9.4.17
Ferguson, J., Pte., 11271 * 8.9.16
Ferguson, J., Pte., S/9352 *29.4.16
Ferris, A., Pte., S/5107 *22.5.16
Findlay, A., Pte., S/7311 *25.9.15
Findlay, J., Pte., S/4337 † 3.2.17

Fisher, A., Pte., S/9292 † 1.5.16
Fitzgerald, J., Pte., S/4503 *25.9.15
Flannigan, J., Pte., S/10694 †13.4.17
Fletcher, B., Pte., S/8863 §30.11.15
Foley, T., Pte., S/43135 *23.8.17
Forrester, R. F., Pte., S/5324 *25.9.15
Foster, S., Pte., S/12843 † 6.10.16
Foster, H. S., Pte., S/19579 *22.8.17
Fotheringham, J., Pte., S/43248
†18.9.16
France, T., Pte., 3/2604 *25.9.15
Fraser, H., Pte., S/21394 *28.3.18
Frizzell, Pte., W., S/25282 †21.8.18
Fulton, H., Pte., S/4561 *26.10.15
Fulton, T., Pte., S/6656 †24.4.17
Fulton, W., Pte., 202510 *28.3.18
Fyfe, H. J., Pte., S/16539 *31.7.17
Fyffe, A., Pte., 351301 *25.8.17
Fyffe, T., Pte., S/3680 † 2.10.17

Gabriel, J. J., L/Sgt., 343 *25.9.15
Gallacher, C., Pte., S/6627 *25.9.15
Gallettie, E., Pte., S/12829 *31.7.17
Galloway, T. M., Pte., S/4268 *25.9.15
Gardiner, J., Pte., 3/3082 *25.9.15
Gardyne, C. G., Pte., S/10520 *14.3.17
Garland, J. R., Pte., S/40005 *28.1.17
Geddes, G., Pte., S/6846 *25.9.15
Gemmell, T., Pte., S/4564 †16.10.15
Geyton, W.L., Pte., S/11169 *23.4.17
Gibb, L., Pte., S/9693 *19.1.16
Gibbin, A. E., Pte., S/12181 *27.4.16
Gibson, D., Pte., S/4286 *25.9.15
Gibson, J., Pte., S/4778 *25.9.15
Gibson, R., L/Cpl., S/4742 *25.9.15
Gilchrist, C., Pte., S/8820 *23.8.17
Gillies, D. A., L/Cpl., S/14250
† 6.5.18
Gilman, F., Cpl., S/4345 *16.11.15
Gilroy, W., Pte., S/3962 *25.9.15
Glen, D., L/Cpl., S/4211 *25.9.15
Godfrey, D., Sgt., 3/3761 †26.9.15
Goodall, G., Pte., S/43432 *23.4.17
Goodwin, H., Pte., S/9547 *26.1.16
Goodwin, J., Pte., S/9293 * 8.9.16
Goodwin, J., Pte., S/16005 †24.5.16
Gordon, C. D., Pte., S/43459 * 9.4.17
Gorrie, T., L/Cpl., 350537 *24.10.17
Gouldthorpe, G. F., Sgt., S/4896
*25.9.15
Govenlock, T., Cpl., S/9028 *24.10.16
Graham, A., Pte., S/9234 †30.4.16
Graham, A., Pte., 350632 †27.8.17
Graham, A., Pte., S/24473 * 6.9.18
Graham, G. G., Pte., S/6643 †14.10.15

191

THE NINTH BATTALION THE BLACK WATCH

Graham, H. J., Pte., S/4310	*25.9.15	Hughes, R., Pte., S/4936	* 8.9.16
Grant, A., Pte., S/11952	†29.4.16	Hume, J. H., Pte., S/9610	†22.7.16
Grant, D. S. Pte., 266584	*28.3.18	Hunter, A. W. Pte., 241151	*28.3.18
Grant, J., Pte., S/4246	*13.11.17	Hunter, A., Pte., S/4744	*25.9.15
Gray, C., A/Cpl., 3/3341	*25.8.17	Hunter, D., Pte., S/6805	*25.9.15
Gray, J. T., Pte., S/18687	*26.8.17	Hunter, P., Pte., S/4914	*25.9.15
Gray, N. C., Pte., S/4557	*25.9.15	Hutchison, C., Pte., S/4558	*25.9.15
Gray, P., Pte., S/4683	*25.9.15	Hutton, W., L/Cpl., S/10048	*24.6.16
Gray, P., Pte., S/9158	*17.8.16		
Gray, R., L/Cpl., S/5358	*27.4.16	Imrie, W. S., Pte., S/14149	† 3.8.17
Grelish, E., Pte., 3/2942	† 9.12.15	Ingram, T. B. Pte., S/4521	*25.9.15
Greig, D., C.S.M., 3/3607	*25.9.15	Innes, J., Pte., S/155551	*23.4.17
Grierson, J., Pte., S/2998	† 4.10.15	Irons, H., Pte., S/16689	*31.7.17
Grierson, R., Pte., S/9185	* 9.4.17	Irvine, J., Pte., S/4549	*25.9.15
Grisenthwaite, J., Pte., S/14018		Izatt, P., Sgt., S/3973	*25.9.15
	* 9.4.17		
Guthrie, D., L/Cpl., S/43078	*25.8.17	Jack, J., L/Cpl., S/4830	*17.8.16
Guthrie, J., Pte., S/4861	*25.9.15	Jack, J., A/Cpl., 268184	*28.3.18
Hadley, W. E., Pte., S/11395	*17.8.16	Jack, R., Pte., S/3979	*25.9.15
Haggart, J., Pte., S/4634	*25.9.15	Jack, W. M., A/Cpl., S/5313	*25.9.15
Hall, H., Pte., 201663	†25.3.18	Jaffray, J., Pte., S/7312	*25.9.15
Halley, D. A., Pte., S/9814	*11.10.16	Jamieson, A., Pte., 265920	*31.7.17
Hamilton, C., Pte., S/4259	†26.9.15	Jenkinson, R. W., Pte., S/4309	
Hamilton, C., Pte., S/5328	* 9.4.17		*25.9.15
Hannay, J., Pte., S/6755	*25.9.15	Jess, J., Pte., S/9842	†29.4.16
Hardie, W., L/Sgt., S/4761	*25.9.15	Jessamine, J. W., Pte., 266815	*26.4.17
Harland, H., Cpl., S/4802	† 9.3.16	Johnson, J., Pte., S/12165	§ 8.8.18
Harrison, A., L/Cpl., S/12127	†16.6.17	Johnson, S., Pte., S/15972	* 9.4.17
Harvey, F., Pte., S/12929	*29.3.18	Johnston, H., Pte., S/9112	†31.1.16
Harrison, G. H., Pte., 201454	*23.4.17	Johnston, J., Pte., S/40754	*15.9.18
Hastings, E. M., L/Cpl., S/14145		Johnston, W., Pte., 268106	*22.8.17
	* 9.4.17	Johnstone, J., Pte., S/4667	*31.7.17
Hastie, J., L/Cpl., S/5321	† 9.4.17	Jones, G., Pte., 3/4269	*17.8.16
Hastie, S. P., Pte., S/4421	*25.9.15	Jones, W. E., Pte., 28040	†15.9.18
Havlin, J., Pte., S/11505	§ 7.4.17		
Hay, J., Pte., S/8479	*25.9.15	Kear, P., Pte., S/4184	†20.10.15
Hayburn, R., Pte., S/6777	* 8.9.16	Kelly, J., A/Cpl., S/3946	*31.7.17
Heaney, G., Pte., S/4726	†22.10.15	Kelly, J., Pte., S/7334	*25.9.15
Heaton, J., Pte., S/4608	*25.9.15	Kelly, J., Pte., S/4062	*25.9.15
Heffernan, R., Cpl., S/4540	*29.4.16	Kennedy, A., Cpl., S/4619	*17.8.16
Hegarty, T., Pte., S/3949	*25.9.15	Kennedy, R., Cpl., S/3950	*25.9.15
Henderson, J., Pte., S/3770	*26.9.15	Kenward, J., Pte., S/15942	*31.7.17
Hennerty, J., Pte., S/4725	*25.9.15	Kerr, A., Pte., S/4898	†16.2.16
Herd, W., Pte., 291519	§28.5.18	Kerr. G., Pte., S/15934	† 1.10.17
Herd, W., Pte., 351522	† 3.11.18	Kerr, R., Pte., S/5345	*25.9.15
Herriot, A., A/Cpl., S/4192	*27.9.17	Kerr, T., Pte., S/16592	*28.9.17
Hewitson, R., Pte., S/43291	*18.9.16	Kerry, G. W., Pte., 15932	*24.5.16
Hibbert, F., Pte., S/12122	*17.8.16	Kidd, R. B., Pte., S/15107	*28.3.18
Higgins, J., L/Cpl., 3/2012	†31.7.17	Killin, D., Pte., S/4446	*25.9.15
Hilton, J. B., Pte., S/16679	*28.9.17	Kindred, W., Pte., S/4200	*25.9.15
Hoggan, J., Pte., S/4037	*14.8.16	Kinloch, A., Pte., S/19567	*28.6.17
Horsburgh, W., C.Q.M.S., 7853		Kinnear, R., Pte., S/4158	§ 8.7.16
	*17.3.16	Kinnear, T., Pte., S/16885	*25.8.17
Hossack, G., Pte., S/4251	*25.9.15	Kirkcaldy, C. S., Pte., S/40854	†24.9.17
Howat, E., Pte., S/6841	*21.2.16	Knowles, A. E., Pte., S/8142	*25.9.15

APPENDIX IV

Laing, J. B. B., Pte., S/21374 †16.11.17
Laird, C., Pte., S/11385 * 8.9.16
Law, A., Pte., S/6584 *25.9.15
Law, G. C., L/Cpl., 200459 *31.7.17
Law, W., Pte., S/9078 † 2.4.16
Lawley, W., Pte., S/3936 *25.9.15
Lawrence, D., Pte., S/16801 † 1.5.17
Lawrie, A. W., L/Cpl., S/4768
   *31.7.17
Lawson, A., Pte., S/9211 *17.8.16
Ledingham, J. A., Pte., S/4098
   *25.9.15
Leishman, J., Pte., S/5106 *25.9.15
Leishman, R., Pte., S/40422 *10.10.16
Leitch, J., Pte., S/6722 *25.9.15
Leslie, D., Pte., S/6862 †26.9.15
Leslie, J., L/Cpl., S/4341 *25.9.15
Levin, M., Pte., S/6662 †20.4.17
Lewis, A. G., Pte., S/5055 †25.9.15
Lewthwaite, W., Pte., S/4483 *25.9.15
Lille, D., Pte., S/7335 *25.9.15
Lindsay, J., Pte., S/40025 *18.9.16
Lindsay, J. S., Pte., S/7800 *26.8.17
Lindsay, R. C., L/Sgt., 290801
   *25.4.17
Lindsay, T., Pte., S/43150 *18.9.16
Linn, A., Pte., S/43164 *29.3.17
Lister, A., Pte., S/14606 *26.4.17
Livingstone, A., Pte., S/6529 † 6.2.16
Logan, W. J., Pte., S/4822 *25.9.15
Louden, W., Pte., S/4923 *25.9.15
Louden, W., Pte., S/4399 *27.4.16
Love, R., Pte., S/3912 *25.9.15
Low, A., Pte., 292539 *25.2.18
Low, E., C.S.M., 3/88 *31.7.17
Low, W., Pte., S/16753 * 9.4.17
Lowe, A., Pte., S/9722 *26.8.17
Lowe, C., Pte., S/4126 *25.9.15
Lumsden, J., Pte., 290359, *31.7.17
Lyall, F., Pte., S/4803 *17.8.16
Lyon, R. S., Pte., S/4105 *25.9.15

MacDonald, M., Pte., S/19707
   *24.8.17
MacDougall, A. R., Pte., S/6608
   *25.9.15
Macfarlane, D., Pte., S/8325 *26.4.17
Macfarlane, T., Pte., S/10280 †11.10.16
Mackay, A. C., Pte., 203358 †14.11.18
Mackay, H., Pte., S/17098 * 8.2.18
Mackay, H., Pte., 3/2641 *25.9.15
Mackie, A. S., A/Cpl., 7065 *25.8.17
Mackie, W., Pte., S/40622 † 8.2.18
Mackenzie, W., Pte., S/4033 *25.9.15
Malcolm, J., Pte., S/11220 †13.3.16

Manzie, J., Sgt., S/15953 * 9.4.17
Marsden, A., Pte., 12244 *17.8.16
Marshall, C., Pte., 266442 §13.10.18
Marshall, G., Pte., S/43460 * 9.4.17
Marshall, J., Pte., S/9218 †30.4.16
Martin, A., Pte., 3/3104 *25.9.15
Martin, J., Pte., 3/4148 *25.9.15
Martin, W. H., Sgt., S/6855 *28.3.18
Mason, J., Cpl., S/4501 *29.4.16
Masters, G. T., Pte., S/10529 † 9.9.16
Mathers, J., Pte., 240306 † 2.8.17
Mathers, R., Pte., S/6759 *31.7.17
Matheson, J., L/Cpl., S/4784 *25.9.15
Mathieson, R., Pte., S/43151 *11.4.17
Matthew, A., Pte., S/4095 *25.9.15
Maxwell, J., Pte., S/9226 *26.4.17
McAinsh, J., Pte., S/40230 *26.4.17
McAinsh, J., C.S.M., S/3575 *25.9.15
McAllister, J. D., Pte., S/4902
   *25.9.15
McAvoy, R., Pte., S/3719 *25.9.15
McBride, J., Pte., S/4511 * 5.2.16
McBride, P., Pte., S/4011 †25.9.15
McCabe, A., Pte., S/40858 *31.7.17
McCall, A., Cpl., S/4366 *25.9.15
McCallum, J., Pte., S/4859 *25.9.15
McCann, D., Sgt., S/4480 *25.9.15
McCann, W. J., Piper, S/5335
   *25.9.15
McClusky, N., Pte., S/2812 *20.5.16
McColl, A., L/Cpl., S/9430 *17.8.16
McComb, J., Pte., S/4613 *25.9.15
McCue, H., Pte., S/4146 *25.9.15
McDonald, F. A., Pte., S/16777
   §13.1.17
McDonald, G., Pte., S/10534 *31.7.17
McDonald, H., Pte., S/4078 *25.9.15
McDonald, J., Pte., S/4697 *25.9.15
McDougall, D., Pte., S/8259 *17.8.16
McDougall, J., Pte., 2740 † 2.6.16
McDougall, R., Pte., S/4262 *25.9.15
McDougall, R., Pte., S/43186 *23.8.17
McDougall, W., Pte., S/6684 †26.9.15
McEwan, A H., Pte., S/18122
   †11.4.17
McEwan, J., Pte., S/4714 *25.9.15
McEwan, J., Pte., S/5148 †29.9.15
McEwan, P., Pte., S/40023 * 8.9.16
Mcfarlane, A., Pte., S/4512 †26.9.15
McFeat, T., Pte., 350301 *28.3.18
McGaw, R. S., Sgt., S/4825 *25.9.15
McGee, J., Pte., S/4993 §27.2.17
McGonigill, A., Pte., S/9483 *23.4.17
McGowan, J., L/Cpl. S/40352 *22.8.17
McGregor, G., Pte., S/40856 *31.7.17

THE NINTH BATTALION THE BLACK WATCH

McGregor, H., Pte., S/9287 *29.4.16
McHutchison, J., Pte., S/4767 *25.9.15
McIlhatton, J. St. C., Pte., S/43279 †19.10.16
McIlroy, D. L., Pte., S/4014 *31.7.17
McIntosh, G., Pte., 266476 *28.9.17
McIntosh, N., L/Cpl., 268143 †30.9.17
McIntosh, W., Pte., 202514 *30.9.17
McIntosh, W., Pte., S/9820 *25.8.17
McIntyre, D., Pte., S/40857 †25.3.18
McIntyre, J., Cpl., 7484 *30.4.16
McIntyre, W., Cpl., S/4805 *25.9.15
McIntyre, W. T., Pte., S/4900 *25.9.15
McIsaac, A. N., Sgt., S/40026 †28.4.17
McIvor, T., Sgt., S/8909 *29.4.16
McKay, N., Pte., S/4042 †24.10.15
McKay, R., Pte., S/4402 * 3.9.15
McKay, W., Pte., S/4662 *25.9.15
McKellar, P., Pte., S/9967 *25.9.15
McKendrick, H., L/Sgt., S/4534 *25.9.15
McKenzie, G. R., Pte., S/16557 †10.4.17
McKenzie, J., Pte., S/9132 * 9.4.17
McKenzie, J. C., Pte., S/43434 * 9.4.17
McKenzie, R., L/Cpl., S/2944 *25.9.15
McKenzie, W. J., Pte., S/6524 †27.6.16
McKim, W., Pte., 3/3521 †29.4.16
McKim, J., Pte., 291705 † 1.4.18
McKinnon, A., Pte., S/18269 †30.9.17
McKerrow, G., Pte., S/12232 * 8.9.16
McKissock, G., Pte., S/40828 †31.7.17
McLaggan, G., Pte., 235042 *28.3.18
McLaren, D., Pte., S/4408 *29.4.16
McLaren, G., Pte., S/4823 *25.9.15
McLaren, J., Pte., S/4845 *25.9.15
McLaren, J., Pte., S/40421 *31.7.17
McLaren, W. B., C.S.M., 3/3664 *25.9.15
McLarty, D., Piper, S/5061 *25.9.15
McLauchlan, J., Pte., S/11465 *17.8.16
McLauchlan, R., Pte., S/4437 *25.9.15
McLean, A., Pte., S/15567 †20.9.18
McLean, A., Cpl., 10465 *17.8.16
McLean, C. C., Pte., 265713 *31.7.17
McLean, D., Pte., S/8306 *10.7.16
McLean, J., Pte., S/11624 *17.8.16
McLennan, W., Pte., S/11265 *29.4.16
McLeod, G. McK., Pte., S/4279 *26.8.17
McLeod, J., Pte., S/9111 * 9.4.17
McLinden, J., Cpl., S/4171 *25.9.15
McLure, J., Pte., S/3656 †23.4.17
McManus, H., Pte., S/26697 †20.9.18
McMillan, C., Pte., 241305 *31.7.17
McMillan, J., Pte., S/7631 *31.7.17
McMurtie, W., Pte., S/4498 *25.9.15
McNair, J., Pte., S/6561 *25.9.15
McNeill, J., Sgt., S/3000 *25.9.15
McPherson, J., Sgt., S/4420 *29.4.16
McPherson, W., Cpl., S/4673 *25.9.15
McRosty, W., Pte., 3/3474 *31.7.17
McWhinney, R., Pte., 4122 §11.12.15
McWilliams, G., L/Cpl., S/11806 §11.9.16
Mearns, S., Pte., S/16752 §26.3.17
Meech, W. S., Pte., S/8962 * 6.2.16
Meek, J., Pte., 351250 † 8.9.18
Meek, J., Pte., S/24135 † 4.4.18
Melrose, T., Pte., S/27282 * 6.9.18
Melville, J., Pte., S/5045 *25.9.15
Melville, P., Pte., 292157 †26.8.17
Melville, R. W., Pte., S/24679 †20.9.18
Melvin, J. D., Sgt., S/6557 *31.7.17
Merrylees, J., Pte., S/11401 *17.8.16
Mewha, S., Pte., S/4752 *25.9.15
Millar, D., Pte., S/6622 *25.9.15
Millar, J., Pte., S/13454 §15.10.17
Millar, J., L/Cpl., 3/4200 *25.9.15
Millar, J., Sgt., 1052 *25.9.15
Millar, A., Pte., 266160 *31.7.17
Millar, W., Pte., S/4641 *25.9.15
Miller, F., Pte., S/9480 *11.2.16
Miller, H., Pte., S/8950 *29.10.16
Milne, R., Pte., S/9461 (M.M.) †11.9.16
Milnes, L., Pte., S/9694 *14.8.16
Mitchell, A., Pte., 201624 *29.8.18
Mitchell, F., Pte., S/43034 † 2.8.17
Mitchell, J., Pte., S/11992 †24.6.16
Mitchelson, R., Cpl., S/3242 *11.3.16
Moffat, J., Pte., S43228 †16.3.17
Moffat, W., Sgt., S/4657 *20.5.16
Moir, W., Pte., 268664 *20.3.18
Montgomery, J., Pte., S/8988 *17.8.16
Moore, D., Sgt., S/4769 †26.9.15
Moore, J., Pte., S/8231 †29.4.16
Morgan, J., L/Cpl., S/4255 *25.9.15
Morrison, H., Pte., S/6642 *25.9.15
Morrison, E. R., Pte., S/17739 *28.9.17
Morrison, J. A. McK., L/Cpl., 240986 *22.8.17

APPENDIX IV

Moulton, W., Pte., S/4606 *25.9.15
Muirhead, W., Pte., S/3839 *25.9.15
Mullins, T., Pte., S/9060 *29.4.16
Munns, T. J., Pte., S/11371 *24.7.16
Munro, D., Pte., S/43439 *26.4.17
Munro, R., Sgt., 3/3760 *25.9.15
Munro, W., Pte., S/16845 † 7.4.17
Murdock, D., Pte., S/4904 *25.9.15
Murdock, W., C.S.M., S/3848 *25.9.15
Murray, D., Pte., S/3819 *25.9.15
Murray, R., Pte., S/9380 * 7.12.15
Murray, R. D., Pte., S/6564 *26.10.15
Mutch, J., Pte., S/4563 *25.9.15

Neil, J., L/Cpl., S/4536 *25.9.15
Neillans, J., Pte., S/6559 *25.9.15
Nellies, H., Pte., S/15795 * 9.4.17
Nicholas, W. T., Pte., S/4185 *25.9.15
Normandale, F. L., L/Cpl., S/26705 *29.8.18
Norwood, J. A., Cpl., S/4790 *25.9.15
Nuttall, G., Pte., S/10288 *17.8.16

O'Brien, J., Pte., S/4649 *25.9.15
O'Connor, J., Pte., S/4877 *25.9.15
O'Flacherty, E., Pte., 2805 *25.8.16
Ogilvie, A., Pte., 202012 *31.7.17
Ogilvie, J., Pte., S/4386 *25.9.15
Ogilvie, W., Pte., S/4327 †11.5.18
O'Neill, H., Pte., S/6626 *29.4.16
Orchison, D., Pte., 202745 *26.4.17
Orr, J., Pte., S/25251 § 5.11.18

Page, D. D., L/Cpl., S/16536 *28.3.18
Palethorpe, G. H., Pte., S/12054 * 8.9.16
Park, J. T., Cpl., S/4701 * 6.7.17
Paterson, P., Pte., S/7291 *25.9.15
Paterson, S., Pte., S/4765 †26.9.15
Paterson, W., Pte., S/9052 *29.4.16
Paterson, W., Pte., S/13274 *31.7.17
Paterson, W., Pte., S/9789 *11.10.16
Paton, G., S/9735, Pte. †21.7.16
Paton, M., A/Cpl., S/11487 †25.1.17
Paton, R., Pte., S/27012 * 2.9.18
Patrick, J., Pte., S/9242 * 9.9.16
Patterson, G., L/Cpl., S/4048 *25.9.15
Pearson, T. G., A/Cpl., 3/4231 †27.8.17
Peebles, G., Pte., S/5018 *25.9.15
Pender, J. C., Pte., 266904 *30.9.17
Penman, J., Pte., 9407 †13.11.15
Pert, W., Pte., S/4380 *25.9.15
Pert, W., Pte., 240406 *26.4.17
Philip, G.H., Pte., S/4637 * 9.4.17
Philips, J., Pte., S/15952 *23.8.17

Phillips, A., Pte., 267082 *28.3.18
Phillips, W., Pte., S/43201 *20.1.17
Philp, J., Sgt., S/6714 †26.4.18
Pithkeathly, R., Pte., S/4320 *25.9.15
Player, D. F., Pte., 1358 *25.9.15
Pollock, D., Pte., 292791 * 8.2.18
Pollock, C. H., Pte., S/9912 * 9.4.17
Ponton, R. G., Pte., S/12429 †28.6.16
Potter, A., Cpl., S/9400 * 9.4.17
Pritchard, A., L/Cpl., 265653 *31.7.17
Proctor, L., Pte., S/12448 * 7.7.16

Radcliffe, J., Pte., S/4474 *23.8.17
Ramsay, A., L/Cpl., S/4741 *25.9.15
Ramsay, J., Pte., 453 †26.8.17
Ramsay, R., Pte., S/4587 *25.9.15
Rankine, D. B., Pte., S/4167 *17.8.16
Reddie, J., Pte., S/7823 †26.9.16
Reece, H. E., Pte., S/6081 *25.9.15
Reece, R., Pte., S/10872 *17.8.16
Reid, D., Pte., 291836 †25.8.17
Reid, M., Pte., 3/3187 *25.9.15
Reid, W., L/Cpl., S/4301 † 1.12.15
Reid, W., Pte., S/12234 * 9.4.17
Reid, W., L/Cpl., 265177 (M.M.) *26.4.17
Reilly, H., Pte., S/3947 *25.9.15
Rennie, W. J. G., Pte., S/12514 *27.5.16
Renwick, W. H., L/Cpl., S/6863 *25.9.15
Riddel, A., Pte., S/13324 *31.7.17
Riddle, D., Sgt., 3/3979 *26.9.15
Riley, J., Pte., S11384 *17.8.16
Rintoul, A., Pte., S/40367 * 9.4.17
Risk, A., Sgt., S/9497 * 9.9.16
Ritchie, A., Pte., S/17087 *28.3.18
Ritchie, D., Pte., S/7285 *25.9.15
Ritchie, J., Pte., S/11993 *24.6.16
Robb, J., Pte., S/16891 *28.3.18
Robb, J., Pte., 266694 * 6.9.18
Robbie, D., Pte., S/16222 † 3.5.17
Roberts, E., Pte., S/8223, ,*25.9.15
Roberts, J. S., Pte., S/17810 *31.7.17
Robertson, D., Pte., S/9235 *11.7.16
Robertson, D., Pte., S/40418 *26.4.17
Robertson, G., Pte., 4214 *25.2.16
Robertson, J., Pte., S/13468 *31.7.17
Robertson, J., Sgt., S/4731 *16.11.15
Robertson, J., Pte., S/9072 *25.8.16
Robertson, J., Pte., S/40356 †29.12.16
Robertson, J. B., L/Cpl., 292126 †12.11.17
Robertson, M. B., Cpl., 290160 †18.5.18

THE NINTH BATTALION THE BLACK WATCH

Robertson, R., Pte., 292695	§28.10.18	Smith, G. S., Pte., S/6040	* 8.9.16
Robertson, R., Pte., S/15986	* 9.4.17	Smith, J., Pte., S/6589	*25.9.16
Robertson, R., Sgt., S/3646	*26.8.17	Smith, J., Pte., S/10448	* 8.9.16
Robertson, R., Pte., 3/2859	† 7.4.17	Smith, J. D., L/Cpl., S/6331	*25.9.15
Robertson, T., Pte., S/4688	*25.9.15	Smith, J., Pte., S/40894	† 9.4.17
Robertson, T., Pte., S/4849	*25.9.15	Smith, J., L/Cpl., S/6812	*25.9.15
Robertson, W., Pte., S/4141	*23.4.17	Smith, M., Cpl., S/4777	*25.9.15
Robinson, R., L/Cpl., S/5157	*25.9.15	Smith, R., Pte., S/15678	*25.4.17
Roddick, G., Pte., S/4293	†24.3.16	Smith, R., Pte., S/15722	*23.4.17
Rodgers, A., Cpl., 8248	*13.6.16	Smith, S. G., Pte., 267236	*26.8.17
Rodgor, G., Pte., 266092	*31.7.17	Sneddon, A., L/Cpl., S/4285	*25.9.15
Ronaldson, D., Pte., S/16710	†24.9.17	Sneddon, W., Pte., S/4212	*25.9.15
Ross, D., Pte., 3/3715	† 2.4.17	Somerville, C., Pte., 266644	*23.4.17
Ross, R., Pte., S/9149	*17.9.16	Somerville, W., A/Cpl., 241158	
Rough, J., Pte., S/4063	*27.9.15		*28.3.18
Roxburgh, J., L/Cpl., S/5348	†30.9.15	Souness, J., L/Cpl., 268439	* 2.9.18
Rudd, W., Pte., S/4989	†27.9.15	Soutar, J., Pte., S/9387	†28.1.17
Ruddick, I., Pte., S/11048	§ 1.9.17	Spalding, J., L/Cpl., 240074	§16.6.17
Rust, J., Pte., S/43137	†29.9.16	Spence, S., Pte., S/15998	*17.8.16
Rutherford, T., Sgt., 3/3720	*25.9.15	Stanley, J., Pte., S/4205	†16.3.16
		Steele, S., Pte., S/4542	*25.9.15
Saddler, N., Pte., S/13051	*17.8.16	Stevenson, J., L/Cpl., S/6586	* 1.7.17
Scott, G. H., Pte., S/17466	* 9.4.17	Stewart, A. A. E., Pte., S/16237	
Scott, H., Sgt., 3/2799	†20.9.15		* 9.4.17
Scott, J., Pte., S/9089	†14.7.16	Stewart, C., L/Cpl., S/40379	† 5.9.17
Scott, T., Pte., S/25263	*31.8.18	Stewart, D. S., Pte., S/43147	*26.4.17
Scott, W., Pte., 267892	*31.7.17	Stewart, E. G. B., Pte., S/23891	
Scrimgeour, D., L/Cpl., S/4428			† 3.9.18
	*25.9.15	Stewart, P., Pte., S/27319	* 6.9.18
Seaton, J., Pte., S/16192	*25.12.16	Stewart, W., Pte., S/3032	*25.9.15
Seivwright, J., Pte., 3/3156	*25.9.15	Stobie, G., Pte., S/11957	*26.8.17
Semple, P. R., Sgt., S/7079	* 8.9.16	Stone, A., A/Cpl., S/12320	
Shand, H., Pte., S/2833	*25.1.16	(M.M.)	*30.12.17
Sharp, W., Pte., S/4771	*25.9.15	Storie, G., Pte., S/8922	*17.9.16
Shaw, W., Pte., S/4148	*25.9.15	Stormouth, W., Pte., S/13309	*23.8.17
Shaw, W., Pte., S/43441	†25.8.17	Stothard, J., L/Cpl., S/4429	*25.9.15
Shearer, R., Pte., S/16895	* 8.4.17	Strachan, A., Pte., S/8604	*11.10.16
Sherlock, D. J., Pte., S/28658		Strachan, H. D., C.S.M., 9478	
(M.M.)	* 6.9.18	(D.C.M.)	* 9.4.17
Sim, D., Pte., S/9453	*11.2.16	Strong, W., Pte., S/40628	*28.3.18
Sim, J., Pte., S/11262	*29.4.16	Surgeon, J., Pte., S/21379	*25.2.18
Simmie, A., Pte., S/6635	*11.2.16	Sutherland, E., Pte., 267793	*31.7.17
Simpson, A., Pte., S/16687	*31.7.17	Suttie, J. McD., Pte., S/16516	
Simpson, D., Pte., S/17441	*25.8.17		*26.4.17
Simpson, W., Pte., S/16561	* 6.4.17	Swan, W., Pte., S/4089	*25.9.15
Sinclair, D., Pte., 351491	*21.10.18	Swanwick, W. E. A., Pte., S/12069	
Singleton, E., A/Cpl., S/11252			*17.8.16
	* 8.9.16	Syme, J., Pte., 630	* 8.9.16
Skene, D. N., Pte., S/4465	*25.9.15		
Smedley, J. H., Pte., S/12228	* 7.4.17	Taggart, W., Pte., S/4753	*29.4.16
Smellie, J., Pte., S/17538	† 3.4.18	Tarbet, J., Pte., S/40351	* 6.1.17
Smith, A., Pte., S/43202	†19.9.16	Tawse, P., Pte., 268147	*23.4.17
Smith, A., Pte., S/43462	*26.4.17	Taylor, J., Pte., 351151	*22.8.17
Smith, C., Pte., S/16519	*26.4.17	Taylor, J., Pte., S/11153	†25.1.16
Smith, G. R., Pte., S/43226	* 9.4.17	Taylor, W., Pte., S/43244	†11.2.18

APPENDIX IV

Telfer, R., Pte., 291108	*26.4.17	Webster, G. C., Pte., S/43172	*8.9.16
Tennant, J., Pte., 3/2754	†24.1.17	Webster, J., Pte., S/9342	§22.5.16
Thom., C., Pte., S/15765	†15.4.17	Weir, D. F., Pte., S/5217	*25.9.15
Thomason, C. C., Sgt., S/4197	*26.10.15	Welsh, A., Pte., S/4265	*25.9.15
		Welsh, J., Pte., S/4332	*25.9.15
Thomson, D., Pte., 266238	† 3.8.17	Welsh, J. G., Cpl., S/8228	†21.1.16
Thomson, J., Pte., S/4574	*10.7.16	Wheeler, C., Pte., S/11206	*29.8.16
Thomson, J., Pte., S/27744	* 6.9.18	Whelam, P., Pte., S/9300	* 9.4.17
Thomson, W., Pte., S/4264	*23.4.17	White, A., L/Cpl., S/6325	*25.9.15
Thomson, W. A., Pte., S/10986	* 8.2.18	White, J., Pte., S/9313	*29.4.16
		White, J., Pte., S/6612	*25.9.15
Thornton, P., Pte., S/40836	*31.7.17	White, P., Pte., S/4763	*25.9.15
Todd, J., Sgt., S/6789	*28.3.18	White, W. H., Sgt., S/3808	*25.9.15
Tootell, G., Pte., S/27088	* 6.9.18	Wilkie, W., Sgt., 3/3117	*17.8.16
Tracey, J., Pte., S/40929	†25.1.17	Williams, F., Pte., S/15923	*23.3.18
Trainer, R., Pte., S/17808	*28.9.17	Wilson, F., Pte., S/4469	*25.9.15
Tulloch, D., Pte., 3/3322	†24.3.17	Wilson, J. E., Sgt., 6014	†28.2.18
Turnbull, J. G., Pte., S/15933	*13.7.16	Wilson, J. R., Pte., S/43192	*31.3.18
Turner, W. H. G., Pte., S/12363	† 8.5.16	Wilson, P., Pte., S/4583	* 8.9.16
		Wilson, T., Pte., S/15958	* 6.1.17
		Wilson, W., Pte., S/40863	*28.3.18
Vass, J., Pte., S/9718	*23.8.17	Wilson, W., Cpl., S/5280	*31.7.17
		Wishart, A., Pte., 267906	*31.7.17
Waite, T., Pte., S/11136	* 5.12.15	Wood, J., Pte., S/43211	*26.4.17
Waldie, A., Pte., S/6565	†28.9.15	Wright, D., Pte., S/4215	*25.9.15
Walker, A., Pte., S/11391	†21.2.16	Wright, G., Sgt., S/8435 (M.M.)	*28.3.18
Walker, D., Pte., S/4299	*25.9.15	Wright, J., Pte., S/11724	*26.4.17
Walker, J., Pte., S/4300	*25.9.15	Wylie, J., Pte., S/7791	*25.9.15
Walker, J. P., Pte., S/11022	*13.10.6		
Walker, R. H., Pte., S/27303	*15.9.18		
Wallace, A., Pte., S/12330	* 8.9.16	Yeardly, W., L/Cpl., S/5155	†19.8.16
Wallace, T. I., Pte., S/14574	*23.4.17	Yellowlees, T., Pte., S/10385	*28.9.17
Wallace, W., Pte., S/4785	†16.9.15	Young, A., Pte., S/4140	*25.9.15
Waller, J., Pte., S/16855	*10.12.7	Young, A., Pte., S/7528	§21.5.17
Ward, J., Cpl., S/4554	†15.8.16	Young, A., Pte., S/6615	§25.10.15
Watson, R., Pte., S/4530	*25.9.15	Young, J. A., Pte., S/27256	*16.9.18
Waugh, W., Pte., 351298	* 8.2.18	Young, J. P., Pte., S/12239	*28.9.17
Wear, A., L/Cpl., S/4209	*25.9.15	Young, R., Pte., S/4390	*25.9.15

APPENDIX V

HONOURS AND AWARDS

The Ninth Battalion

C.M.G.
Lieut.-Colonel T. O. Lloyd.

Bar to D.S.O.
Lieut.-Colonel S. A. Innes.

D.S.O.
Capt. F. A. Bearn, R.A.M.C. (attached).
Lieut.-Colonel S. A. Innes.

Bar to M.C.
Capt. W. B. Binnie.
Lieut. S. Graham.
Lieut. M. G. Johnstone.
2nd Lieut. F. Proudfoot.
Capt. J. S. Strang.

M.C.
2nd Lieut. T. J. Addison.
2nd Lieut. B. Allison.
Capt. F. A. Bearn, R.A.M.C. (attached).
Capt. W. B. Binnie.
2nd Lieut. T. Byers.
2nd Lieut. T. Calvert.
Lieut. and Quartermaster W. Clark.
Capt. H. J. Collins, C.F.
2nd Lieut. J. E. Drummond.
Capt. E. Gordon.
2nd Lieut. S. Graham.
Lieut. A. K. Hamilton.
Lieut. A. Marshall.
2nd Lieut. H. S. Muir.
Capt. S. Norie-Miller.
2nd Lieut. F. Proudfoot.
Capt. J. S. Strang.
2nd Lieut. W. R. Tovani.
Lieut. E. W. D. Wilson.
R.S.M. G. D. Bedson.
C.S.M. J. McCall.
C.S.M. J. McKercher.
C.S.M. J. W. Price.

D.C.M.
Sgt. Bayne.
Pte. A. Black.
Pte. W. Cobban.
Corpl. A. Johnstone.
R.Q.M.S. J. Munro.
L/Corpl. J. Sandilands.
L/Corpl. Thomson.

M.S.M.
Sgt. G. Gray.
Pte. W. Scobie.

Bar to M.M.
Pte. T. Beattie.
Pte. A. Jack.
Sgt. T. Mullen.
L/Corpl. R. Ross,

APPENDIX V

M.M.

Pte. T. Beattie.
Pte. J. Beveridge.
Pte. A. Black.
Sgt. T. Booth.
L/Corpl. H. Brown.
Corpl. R. Brown.
Pte. W. Brown.
L/Corpl. T. Callaghan.
Corpl. S. Cashmore.
Corpl. W. Christie.
Corpl. J. Clink.
Sgt. C. Cody.
Sgt. A. Crisp.
L/Corpl. J. H. Davidson.
Pte. W. Dick
Sgt. J. A. Duncan.
Pte. R. Duffy.
Pte. T. Fletcher.
Pte. T. Forrest.
Sgt. J. Gibb.
Sgt. W. Goward.
Pte. A. Gowk.
Pte. J. Grant.
Pte. R. Greig.
Pte. S. Isles.
Pte. J. Johnson.
Pte. J. Keating.
Pte. W. Kennedy.
L/Corpl. W. Lindsay.
Pte. G. W. MacIsaac.
Pte. F. Mackay.
Corpl. J. McCauley.
Corpl. W. McCluchie.
Pte. R. McQueen.
Pte. W. Mechan.
Pte. R. Milne.
Pte. J. Moffat.
L/Corpl. J. Mullen.
Sgt. W. Murphy.
L/Corpl. W. Murray.
Sgt. C. Ogilvie.
Pte. J. Pullar.
Corpl. W. Rankin.
Pte. A. R. Robertson.
Pte. W. Robertson.
L/Corpl. R. Ross.
Pte. T. Ross.
Pte. A. Rowley.
Sgt. J. Saunders.
Corpl. W. Sharples.
Sgt. G. Simpson.
Pte. C. Smith.
L/Corpl. J. Smith.
Pte. J. Somerville.
Pte. A. Stone.
Pte. D. Sullivan.
Pte. H. Thomson.
Pte. D. Wallace.
Pte. T. Ward.
Corpl. W. Wilson.
Corpl. G. Wright.

Mentioned in Despatches

Capt. F. A. Bearn, R.A.M.C. (attached).
Major A. D. Carmichael.
Lieut. and Quartermaster W. Clark (2).
Lieut.-Colonel S. A. Innes (2).
Lieut.-Colonel T. O. Lloyd (2).
2nd Lieut. G. B. Mackie.
2nd Lieut. J. F. N. MacRae.
Capt. S. Norie-Miller.
Major J. Stewart (2).
Capt. C. S. Tuke.
Lieut. E. R. Wilson.
Pte. A. Boak.
L/Corpl. A. Brown.
L/Corpl. J. F. Connely.
Sgt. J. Henderson.
Sgt. A. Jack.
L/Corpl. R. Ledlie.
C.S.M. J. Munro.
C.Q.M.S. A. Naesmith.
Sgt. A. Steele.
W. S. Story-Wilson.

THE NINTH BATTALION THE BLACK WATCH

FOREIGN DECORATIONS

French Medaille Militaire
Corpl. T. Park.

French Croix de Guerre
L/Sgt. J. McKellar.

Belgian Croix de Guerre
Sgt. J. Monkley.

Italian Silver Medal for Military Valour
Capt. W. Story-Wilson.

APPENDIX VI

List of Actions and Operations

The Ninth Battalion

1915. Landed in France. 9th July.
Trench warfare. Maroc, Quality Street. July–September.

BATTLE OF LOOS. Capture of Loos Village and Hill 70. 25th September.
Trench warfare. Loos Salient. October–December.

1916. Trench warfare. Loos Salient, Albert, Contalmaison. January–August.

BATTLE OF DELVILLE WOOD. (Switch Elbow.) 17th August.

BATTLE OF FLERS-COURCELETTE. (Capture of Martinpuich.) 15th–17th September.
Trench warfare. Le Sars Sector. September–December.

1917. Trench warfare. Le Sars Sector, Arras. January–April.

FIRST BATTLE OF THE SCARPE (1917). (Capture of Monchy.) 9th April.

SECOND BATTLE OF THE SCARPE (1917). (Capture of Guémappe.) 23rd April.
Trench warfare. Ypres Area. June–July.

BATTLE OF PILCKEM RIDGE. (Frezenburg.) 31st July–3rd August.

BATTLE OF THE MENIN ROAD. (Gallipoli Farm.) 23rd–25th August.
Trench warfare. Arras Area. September–December.

1918. Trench warfare. Monchy le Preux Sector. January–March.

FIRST BATTLE OF ARRAS (1918.) (Pelves.) 28th March.
Trench warfare. Arras Area. April–May.
Battalion absorbed by 4/5th Battalion at Fampoux. May 15th.

THE TENTH
BATTALION

CHAPTER I

SEPTEMBER, 1914, TO NOVEMBER, 1915

Formation of Battalion

THE formation of the 10th (Service) Battalion was started at Perth, The Black Watch Regimental Depot, in the beginning of September, 1914. The response to the call for recruits was excellent throughout Scotland, and batches of men soon began to arrive from the various recruiting stations. There was little time for training, but the organization of the Battalion was begun, and by the 20th of September some four hundred men were sent to Shrewton in Wiltshire, where the 10th was to form part of the 77th Infantry Brigade, the other Battalions being the 12th Argyll and Sutherland Highlanders, 11th Scottish Rifles and 8th Royal Scots Fusiliers.

On arrival near Codford St. Mary the Brigade pitched camp in a low-lying meadow beside a stream, where nearly eighty thousand troops were encamped in the valley within a radius of half a dozen miles. The country lanes presented a strange appearance in those days; numbers of recruits, still in mufti, and without any sort of badge or uniform to show to what regiment they belonged, roamed round the neighbourhood in search of recreation during their leisure hours.

Throughout the day training in physical drill, musketry, signalling and eventually in company movements was carried out under non-commissioned officers mainly from The Black Watch Depot. Officers arrived daily, some with former military experience gained in either Regular or Territorial battalions, but the majority with none, all, however, full of enthusiasm for the cause and keenness to work.

For some time the weather was fine and October saw a marked improvement in the physique and discipline of all ranks; but the following month the conditions changed, and the mud caused by heavy rain blocked the roads and made the use of training grounds almost impossible. It became increasingly difficult to exercise the men and the health of the troops began to suffer from constant wet days and chilly nights spent in damp tents nearly all without floor boards, where sixteen men lay side by side literally in mud. In the middle of November orders arrived for a move to Bristol, and a few days later the Battalion was comfortably quartered in public buildings in that city; A and C companies occupied Colston Hall, B the Victoria Gallery and D the Coliseum, a large skating rink; the officers being billeted at the Colston Hotel. An ideal training ground was found in Ashton Park, where each company had its own area for practising trench digging.

THE TENTH BATTALION THE BLACK WATCH

Christmas and New Year arrived, and the latter was celebrated by a Brigade inspection and march past on one of the wettest days of the whole winter. Shortly afterwards four days' leave with free passes to Scotland was granted to all ranks, a concession which was greatly appreciated. By this time temporary uniforms, in some cases rather suggestive of comic opera, had been provided for the men; but early in the New Year khaki kilts, red and black hose and leather sporrans were issued and the appearance of the Battalion was much improved.

The citizens of Bristol vied with each other in hospitality to both officers and men, and many entertainments were organized by various clubs and associations. As spring advanced field training became more arduous, the men more fit and the physique and general smartness of the Battalion gave a much more favourable impression. Although the many kindnesses of the townsfolk were keenly appreciated by all ranks yet, as the days lengthened, the longing to go to France grew stronger and stronger, and the monotony of the daily work and the digging of trenches seemed never ending.

In March the Brigade was ordered to move to camp at Sutton Veny, near Warminster in Wiltshire, where huts were being built, and the 10th was soon engaged in field exercises over the wide expanse of downs and hills bordering the southern end of Salisbury Plain. Within a few days of its arrival similar camps extended as far as Longbridge Deverill, and for the first time the whole of the 26th Division was concentrated, making it possible to carry out Divisional exercises. The huts consisted of long, low wooden buildings with raised board floorings, each hut housing half a platoon of about twenty-five men, all of whom slept on their paillasses on the floor. Training was necessarily arduous, and as the programme of work was seldom less than eight hours a day, officers and men had but little leisure except on Sundays. The work consisted chiefly of route marching, field work, drill, musketry practice and shooting on miniature and open ranges. Route marches of twenty miles were frequently carried out, and the high standard of march discipline thus attained proved invaluable later on in France and in the Balkans.

In these days of strenuous training the men had little time for games, and it was not till the Battalion went abroad that the 10th was given a chance of taking a high place in football and other sports. By the end of July the scheme of training had been completed. In August officers and men were sent to their homes on three days' "farewell" leave, and early in September it became clear that the 10th would soon be sent to France. The equipment was completed, and the officers selected who should proceed

MOVE TO FRANCE, SEPTEMBER 17TH, 1915

to France with the Battalion. Unfortunately some most capable subalterns had to be left behind, including Second Lieutenants R. E. Odell, Murdo Mackenzie, Ferguson and David Anderson, all of whom were subsequently killed while serving with other battalions.

The following officers proceeded to France with the Battalion:

Headquarters

Commanding Officer	Lieutenant-Colonel Sir W. Stewart-Dick-Cunyngham, Bart.
Second-in-Command	Major J. N. F. Livingstone.
Adjutant	Captain I. C. Sanderson.
Quartermaster	Lieutenant J. McLachlan.
Transport Officer	Lieutenant J. B. Caldwell.
Major J. Harvey.	2nd Lieut. J. E. Denniston.
Captain M. W. Gloag.	„ P. Stormonth-Darling.
„ J. S. MacLeod.	
„ E. M. Lithgow.	„ R. J. L. Scott.
„ J. P. Sturrock.	„ D. Mathieson.
„ W. Stewart.	„ E. G. M. Phillips.
„ C. A. Nicol.	„ W. Martin.
„ R. C. H. Millar.	„ H. A. F. McLaren.
Lieut. J. M. Scott.	„ W. J. Duffy.
„ M. Macdonald.	„ A. O. Drysdale.
„ R. M. Don.	„ A. W. R. Don.
	„ I. B. Gow.

On the 10th of September mobilization was completed, and on the 17th an advance party consisting of Major Livingstone, Major Harvey, Regimental Quartermaster McLachlan, Lieutenant Caldwell, Second Lieutenant Duffy and 109 other ranks left for France, arriving at Longueau, south-west of Amiens, on the 20th of September. They then marched twenty miles to Bougainville to arrange for the billeting of the Battalion, which had meanwhile arrived at Folkestone on the evening of the 19th, the strength being 24 officers and 858 other ranks. Embarkation was hardly completed when the Commanding Officer received orders that, owing to the presence of floating mines, the Battalion would proceed to Shorncliffe and bivouac for the night. On arrival there arms were piled and at one in the morning the men lay down to sleep with no blankets and only a waterproof sheet to protect them against twelve degrees of frost. Everyone was on the move long before daylight, and officers and men were all grateful for a hot breakfast kindly prepared by the Canadians encamped near Shorncliffe.

THE TENTH BATTALION THE BLACK WATCH

At 6 o'clock that evening the 10th marched back to Folkestone and embarked on s.s. *La Marguerite*, arriving at Boulogne about midnight, where the remainder of the night was spent under canvas at Ostrahove Camp on a hill behind the town. The next morning the Battalion entrained for Sallux near Amiens, and then marched fifteen miles to Bougainville. On the 23rd orders were received to proceed to Salouel, which was reached about midnight after a seven hours' march in torrents of rain. On the following morning the Brigade marched to Villers-Bretonneux, and was inspected on the road by Major-General MacKenzie Kennedy, Commanding 26th Division, and Sir Henry Wilson, Commanding XII Corps, who congratulated the Commanding Officer on the march discipline and fine appearance of the Battalion.

Villers-Bretonneux, destined later to become famous as the turning-point of the enemy's final advance in March, 1918, will long be remembered as one of the most comfortable billets the Battalion ever occupied. During the five days the Battalion remained there, the men were equipped with gas masks and put through a "Gas Chamber," and an issue of khaki Balmoral bonnets replaced the glengarries. A distant rumbling of guns all along the line was subsequently explained. It was the beginning of the Battle of Loos, for which the 10th was held in reserve.

On the 29th of September the 10th, less the service detachments, machine gunners with Second Lieutenants W. J. Duffy, R. J. L. Scott, W. Martin and G. Kirkpatrick and some of the Battalion transport, left for Proyart and arrived there at dusk, A company occupying a large underground cellar without lights of any sort. At daybreak A company under Captain J. S. MacLeod, and D under Captain M. W. Gloag, moved to the front line trenches and were attached to the 2nd Battalion Duke of Cornwall's Light Infantry at Fontaine-les-Cappy for forty-eight hours' instruction. Here these companies had their first experience of digging under fire, and constructed a new line of trenches fifty yards in front of the existing front line. During the day the situation was quiet, though No Man's Land was only about a hundred and fifty yards wide at this point.

Soon after dark on the 2nd of October A and D companies moved back to Proyart in good spirits but tired and wet, as they had found but little sleeping accommodation in the overcrowded trenches. The following day was spent at rest, and many friends were found amongst the Argylls, Royal Scots and Camerons of the 27th Division, and in the "Dandy 9th" Battalion from Edinburgh. B and C companies under Major J. Harvey and Captain J. P. Sturrock followed A and D for instruction, and were attached to the Royal Irish Fusiliers, who had taken over

TRENCH WARFARE, OCTOBER, 1915

from the Duke of Cornwall's Light Infantry. The trenches, originally built by the French, were T-shaped, and much work was required to connect up the crosses of the T. Mining and counter-mining were continuous, as two salients ran out from a wood known as Bois Commun—the total Battalion frontage being nearly 2000 yards—and at one point two craters, one thirty and the other sixty feet deep, separated the two front lines and required permanent bombing posts. Water and rations were brought up through long communication trenches from Battalion Headquarters in the village, and telephonic communication was established. The Battalion was highly praised by Major-General Milne, commanding 27th Division, for its workmanlike conduct during this period of instruction.

On the 4th of October the Battalion reoccupied its former billets at Villers-Bretonneux. These had been vacated the previous day by the service and reserve machine gun detachments, which had moved to Frise for two days' instruction with Princess Patricia's Canadian Light Infantry. These detachments returned on the 6th, having suffered two slight casualties. After a week's training in very bad weather the Battalion proceeded on the 12th of October to Chipilly along the low-lying country by the banks of the Somme, and on the following day to Bray, when the Commanding Officer, Adjutant and Company Commanders and Machine Gun Officer reconnoitred the trenches held by the King's Own Yorkshire Light Infantry, whom it was to relieve two days later.

At dusk on the 14th of October the Battalion started the relief—companies moving off at intervals of ten minutes. The relief was completed without incident, though the communication trenches seemed to have no end and frequently no bottom, and men were often up to their knees in mud. A, C and D companies occupied the front line, with B in reserve, and Battalion Headquarters at Carnoy. The following day Captain J. S. MacLeod and Second Lieutenant J. E. Denniston of A company were wounded while watching a " West " bomb thrower being worked, four of the team being killed owing to the accidental explosion of a bomb. The next morning, during stand-to, two men were killed and three wounded from rifle grenades; luckily most of these grenades landed on the parapet, or the losses would have been far more serious as the bays were all fully manned.

D company also had two men badly wounded by German rifle grenades, but Trench 50 was a sector which those who held it will never forget. It consisted of a number of saps, about three feet deep, pushed out some seventy yards from the front line, each sap ending in a listening post. These saps had been rendered necessary by the explosion of mines in No Man's Land, which at this point was very narrow. The enemy on their side had also pushed out similar saps, with the result that the opposing listening posts were only about ten yards apart and the defenders could plainly hear German voices. Occasionally there was an interchange of bombs between the various posts, but on the whole both sides lay quiet, listening to the perpetual mining and counter-mining going on below them, and wondering at what moment the mines would be "blown." The defence of this trench was exceptionally trying, not only on account of its nearness to the enemy, but also because a platoon's tour of duty lasted twenty-four hours; during the tour each sap head was manned by two sentries who remained there for two hours at a time, isolated from the rest of their company except for visits every hour by the platoon commander or sergeant.

Looking back on this tour it is interesting to note that entries in the Battalion War Diary lay emphasis on two principles: front trenches should not be held in strength unless plenty of dug-outs are available, and the necessity for numerous communication trenches between the front and support lines.

In view of future events it may be mentioned that on the day after the 10th arrived in these trenches England declared war on Bulgaria. The Bulgarian army, acting in conjunction with Von Mackensen's concentration on the Serbian frontier, had entered Serbia four days previously, on the 11th of October. The Austro-Germans occupied Belgrade on the 9th, but for one reason and another the first representatives of the Allied forces did not reach Salonika until the 5th of October.

The 18th to 21st of October was spent in billets at Bray, 200 men being employed nightly and 100 daily on working parties, chiefly digging and deepening trenches in the support and reserve lines. On the 21st the Battalion relieved the 8th Battalion Royal Scots Fusiliers, B and C companies being in the front line with A and D in support. Although a considerable amount of sniping took place, and a bombardment by minenwerfer, only four casualties had been reported by the night of the 24th when the Royal Scots Fusiliers again relieved the 10th.

The Battalion was in billets, two companies at Etinehem and two, with Headquarters, at Chipilly until the 29th, when it reassembled at the latter village on again coming under orders of the 77th Brigade, and the next morning it marched seventeen miles to Cardonette. As only six men fell out it was a creditable performance considering the heavy work done during the five previous days. The next day was spent resting; Second Lieutenant W. F. Bassett reported from the 3rd Battalion and was posted to A company. Rumours of a move to Egypt or Serbia

MOVE TO SALONIKA, NOVEMBER 10TH, 1915

reached the Battalion, and the signallers were ordered to practise visual signalling.

On the 5th of November orders were received for the 10th to organize so as to conform to the Salonika establishment. This entailed an addition of thirty-three personnel to the transport, the return of all heavy and light draught horses, and an increase of mules to the number of 102. About this time a copy of a report made by Major-General C. T. Kavanagh, commanding the 5th Division, to which the 77th Brigade had been attached, was received, reporting on the 10th Battalion as follows:

"Training and efficiency good, work in the trenches very "good. The Battalion on the whole is well above the average, "and there seems to be a good regimental system. Decentraliza-"tion good."

On the 8th the Battalion was warned to expect a sudden move and changes in transport were ordered; the officers' mess cart was also exchanged for a limbered wagon; four limbers replaced the travelling kitchens, and the water and Maltese carts were withdrawn. On the 10th the Battalion paraded at 10.30 a.m. and marched in pouring rain through Amiens to Longueau Station, where it entrained at 1.30 p.m. The transport under Lieutenant J. B. Caldwell remained behind awaiting further orders. Second Lieutenants R. J. L. Scott and I. B. Gow, who were suffering from jaundice and bronchitis, were invalided to hospital. The strength of the Battalion, less transport personnel, was 26 officers and 870 other ranks.

Forty, or even forty-five men, with all their arms and equipment, were allotted to each truck, and the discomfort of the journey to Marseilles will probably remain in the men's memories long after other events have been forgotten. Marseilles was reached soon after midday on the 12th of November, and the Battalion marched straight to the quay. By 5.30 p.m. the embarkation was completed and the 10th was on board H.M.S. *Magnificent*, together with two companies of the 11th Battalion Worcestershire Regiment and two of the 12th Battalion Argyll and Sutherland Highlanders. There is no doubt that, in spite of official protests from the Captain, the ship was overcrowded, so much so indeed that on practising "boat stations" it took at least ten minutes to get all hands on deck. The long voyage now before them was to be a new experience for the 10th, and the rough and icy cold weather in the Gulf of Lyons made the visiting of submarine watches and the many sentry duties unpleasant and arduous. Soon, however, all ranks settled down, and by the morning of the 15th the wind had died down and the sun came out, and from this time on the days passed more pleasantly.

THE TENTH BATTALION THE BLACK WATCH

The Regimental Pipers added much to the pleasure of the voyage, the well-known strains recalling a different scene to the young soldiers of the 10th. The course followed was north of Corsica, passing Elba the same evening, then south through the Straits of Messina, along the coast of Sicily and so to Alexandria, which was reached on the 18th.

CHAPTER II

NOVEMBER, 1915, TO JULY, 1916

Salonika

THE Battalion disembarked at Alexandria during the afternoon of November 18th and proceeded to Maritza Camp, about three miles from the harbour. On the following afternoon it re-embarked in the same ship and sailed that evening for Salonika, which it reached on the 24th. The Battalion disembarked at once and, after a trying march through Salonika, reached Lembert Camp, three miles from the town, about 8.30 p.m.

The camp was pitched on sloping hills gained by a steep ascent from the main road running to Seres through the Derbend Pass. The quarters were crowded, eighteen or twenty men in every tent, but all were thankful to lie down for a night's rest. In the morning half the Battalion was employed in pitching tents for the remainder of the Division, who were due to arrive shortly. The next day it rained heavily and the camp became a sea of mud. It was impossible to drain the ground, as all picks and shovels had been left with the regimental transport at Marseilles and none were procurable locally.

The following week was perhaps the most uncomfortable the 10th experienced throughout the war. During the first night snow fell heavily, followed next morning by hard frost while a "Vardar wind" blew from the north-east off the snow-clad mountains of Serbia. No lamps, fires or stoves were available and, in spite of an issue of fur coats and extra blankets, the men lay shivering in their tents. Sentries, although provided with vests, woollen shirts, cardigans, tunics, fur coats, greatcoats and blankets over everything else, could only stand a tour of duty for twenty minutes. As soon as galvanized iron and wood were procurable a Battalion cook-house and officers' mess were built, and conditions improved.

The military situation up-country was obscure. It was known that the 10th Division had already arrived and, with two French Divisions, was trying to effect a junction with the Serbian army. Hundreds of men suffering from frostbite were seen coming in daily and it was believed that the whole force was retreating before the advancing Bulgarians. But, as the small arms ammunition and transport had not yet arrived, it was hopeless for the Brigade to advance to their relief. It was learned later that the 10th (Irish) Division and two French Divisions had taken up a defensive position astride the Vardar, to the south and west of Strumnitza, but as Bulgaria had attacked Serbia from the east, while Von Mackensen had crossed the Danube and taken

Belgrade, the Serbians were forced to retire westward. In the meantime Greece, in spite of her treaty with Serbia, remained nominally neutral, but the Greek press and the demeanour of the inhabitants towards the Allied troops occupying Salonika was definitely hostile, and an endless stream of Serbian refugees arrived daily barefooted and in rags.

By the end of November regimental stores and warm clothing arrived, also three limbered waggons with ammunition, but there was no trace of the remainder of the transport, and picks and shovels were still unprocurable. The only form of training was route marches across the hills, as any instruction which involved standing was out of the question owing to the weather. Sickness, however, did not increase in spite of the intense cold. A Greek canteen was opened, and although the prices were high they were willingly paid, as no food was procurable beyond the rations of biscuits, jam and bully beef.

Officers and men were allowed into the town on pass, the order being that all Greek officers were to be saluted. This was a most humiliating experience, as few Greek officers returned the salute, and many did not conceal their hostile feelings. The chief rendezvous in Salonika was a restaurant known as Floca's, which at this time was one of the most cosmopolitan spots in the world. Here representatives of nearly every European and several Eastern nations were to be found; British and French soldiers and sailors; Russians and Serbs; Albanians, Greeks and Germans; Indians, Senegalese and Algerians, and Balkan peasants in every conceivable type of costume.

From December 1st one battalion in each brigade was on duty, ready to fall in under arms at a moment's notice, a necessary precaution against surprise, as the Brigade was encamped on the outside of the lines to the north-east. The work of improving the camp was continued; stables for the transport were built and roads laid out, but progress was slow as few tools were yet available. The weather, which had been intensely cold, suddenly changed and twenty-four hours' heavy rain converted the camp into a sea of mud, adding greatly to the difficulties. In spite of the weather, conditions improved daily, and the completion of a road through the camp facilitated the carriage of stores, rations and supplies. The distribution of 300 rounds of ammunition per man gave a more satisfactory feeling of security.

At midnight on December 13th the Battalion received orders to move next morning and march to Aivatli. The distance was only about fourteen kilometres along the Seres road, but the road was very bad, mostly uphill and, in additon to full marching order, each man carried a blanket, fur coat, two days' rations

TRENCH WARFARE

and sufficient firewood to cook one meal. On reaching its destination the Battalion halted in vineyards at the foot of the hills overlooking Langaza Plain; as soon as the lorries arrived camp was quickly pitched, and the whole Brigade settled down soon after dark. The following morning every available man was employed digging trenches on what was to be known as the " Birdcage Defensive Line," the sector allotted to the 10th stretching from Aivatli to Laina.

After eight days of digging news reached the Battalion that its transport had at last arrived at Salonika, but by some error the baggage had been put in a different ship to the personnel, and consequently a large quantity was missing. Fortunately, however, the machine guns and signalling equipment arrived safely. So far there had been no sign of the enemy, which was fortunate for, owing to practically incessant rain, the trenches were waterlogged, the hills behind draining straight into them. Now, however, thorough drainage work was undertaken, long stretches of wire were erected and by Christmas Day the position was fairly secure. The front line lay in cornfields with communicating trenches running back among numerous mud-brick barns dotted about on the plain below the village, which lay on the lower slopes of the hills.

No mail had arrived, so Christmas dinners consisted of what was known as " Balkan stew," made of the contents of bully beef tins emptied into a dixie. A few fortunate platoons managed, in addition, to produce " plum puddings " made from what little flour and currants they obtained in the villages. Three days after Christmas the Battalion moved into billets in the village and surrounding barns, the change from crowded tents being much appreciated. A few days later the first parcel mail arrived and, as large quantities of eggs from the villagers were now obtainable, Hogmanay Night was spent under more cheerful conditions than had existed at Christmas.

Material for trench construction was still difficult to obtain; only a small supply of sandbags was available, demolition of buildings was forbidden and dug-outs could not be completed until timber was available. On January 7th each Brigade was ordered to send its transport to the Base Depot to draw material, and soon the front and support lines were completed, except for shelters and machine gun emplacements. A party of fifty men was provided daily for work on a mule track leading from Artillery Road through Watch Kloof to the village. About the middle of the month an alternative line was sited about 150 yards behind the front line. During these digging operations various interesting relics of bygone days were discovered, including several clay Tanagra statuettes, many beautifully carved heads being found intact, samples of copper gilt ornaments and many sets of "Knuckle-bones," this latter being a common game in ancient times. The most interesting find, however, was a tusk about ten feet long which was discovered about four feet below the surface, and is now preserved in the Sedgwick Museum. The improving of trenches and repairing damage caused by snow, rain and frost continued till the middle of February; two days a week were allowed for battalion and company training, and a rifle range was built near Laina. Practice in manning the trenches by day and night was carried out, also in the transport of wounded over the mule tracks to the field dressing station.

On February 27th a successful sports meeting, in which the Battalion more than held its own, was organized in conjunction with the 12th Battalion Argyll and Sutherland Highlanders. During all this time enemy aeroplanes had done considerable damage to Salonika itself and to the back areas. In February platoons marched in turn across the plain to the old Roman hot spring baths at Langaza, this bathing being very much enjoyed. With the coming of March spring seemed to arrive, and about the middle of the month the Battalion moved out of the village into bivouacs in Watch Kloof on the hill behind, where holes seven feet square were dug, each covered by four bivouac sheets, and in these the 10th spent the next three months—four men to each shelter, the officers having two marquees for a mess. This move was undertaken to avoid sandflies and other insects which appear as soon as warm weather sets in. On a wet day the village streets were converted into rivers, which brought down quantities of refuse and accumulated filth and showed that the move to bivouac was necessary, though until now the health of the Battalion had been excellent.

On March 27th the enemy made an air raid on Salonika; considerable damage was inflicted, but four aeroplanes were brought down on their return journey. A week later a tremendous thunderstorm broke over the camp and huge boulders were washed down the gully. Every bivouac was flooded within a few minutes, and men spent a miserable night sitting on their packs waiting for dawn. Even an extra issue of rum brought little comfort. By the end of April the weather grew very warm. A shower bath, built by Sergeant Weir and the pioneers out of a few sheets of corrugated iron, was in constant use, and slouch hats were issued to officers and men.

On April 12th the Battalion set out for a five days' Brigade tactical exercise, marching across the plain through Langaza village to Balavca, where the Brigade bivouacked for the first night, the Lothian and Border Horse acting as protective cavalry. The route followed was by Kara-Omerli to Visoka, where the

TRENCH WARFARE, APRIL TO JUNE, 1916

Battalion again bivouacked, the march continuing as far as Sarijar. The weather was extremely hot throughout the exercise, but although there was great scarcity of water only one man fell out. The day after the return to Watch Kloof all officers and men were inoculated against cholera for a second time. The remainder of April was spent in training, practice in hill warfare and work on the trenches. Lieutenant and Quartermaster McLachlan reurned to England at the end of the month.

With the beginning of May spring passed into summer; the whole country became a blaze of colour, and storks, pelicans and quail took the place of geese and snipe, which now migrated north. Constant training was carried out and each battalion took its turn in furnishing the many necessary guards and duties, the 10th having to provide four hundred men for these alone during the first week in May. At 1.50 a.m. on the night of May 4th the camp guard reported aircraft passing overhead, and about ten minutes later the Salonika searchlights were seen playing on a Zeppelin, which was brought down by the guns of the Fleet in the Vardar marshes. The remainder of the month was spent in training and included a four-day Brigade scheme near Sarijar.

Hot weather now caused many cases of dysentery and towards the end of the month Captain R. C. H. Millar was invalided, suffering from malaria. Major J. F. Livingstone, who had organized an excellent Battalion canteen, and Captain J. P. Sturrock, commanding C company, sailed for England on receiving orders to report to the War Office. On May 21st the Battalion team defeated the 9th Battalion Gloucester Regiment in the first round of the Army Football competition by six goals.

On May 29th the Greeks surrendered Rupel Pass to the Bulgarians, who immediately swarmed down on the strategic points covering central and eastern Macedonia. The defenders, who had fired blank rounds by way of making a show of resistance, retired on Kavalla, where, early in August, the Greek IV Corps, 10,000 strong, surrendered with many batteries of both mountain and field artillery, large numbers of rifles and ammunition depots. On the other hand, at Demir-Hissar and Seres, the 6th Greek Division, after making a spirited defence, managed with the help of the French Navy to cross to Thasos and later to the mainland. By way of retaliation for this treachery, General Sarrail, commanding the Salonika Allied forces, immediately declared a state of siege in Salonika. Under cover of Allied patrols and machine guns he assumed command over the postal and telegraphic controls, thus closing most of the channels by which news had till now reached the enemy. The Battalion's share in this coup consisted of falling in on the alarm at about 3.20 p.m. on June 3rd and marching over the hills down to Salonika in anticipation of trouble with the Greek inhabitants of the city. No trouble, however, took place, and the 10th took up a position outside the walls of the fort, where it spent the night. A heavy thunderstorm soaked everyone to the skin, but at daybreak news came that Salonika was completely under control and the 10th returned to Watch Kloof Camp.

During the few hours spent in Salonika many fires were seen from blazing dumps, set alight by Greeks in enemy pay. These acts of incendiarism led to the immediate formation in Salonika of the Army of National Defence, and a proclamation was issued calling on the Greek army to join in resisting the Bulgarians. Later when Colonel Lymbrakakis, at the head of the gendarmerie, with an enormous crowd following, marched to General Sarrail's Headquarters and offered himself and his supporters to the Allies, the enthusiasm was tremendous. This was, in fact, the beginning of the entry of Greece into the war, though it was not until early in October that Venizelos arrived in Salonika.

On June 5th a detachment of two hundred men, who had been employed for ten days at Akbunar, was ordered to rejoin immediately as the Brigade was to leave early the following morning to move up-country. As the days were now very hot, the Battalion started at 3.30 a.m., having handed over the camp to the Inniskilling Fusiliers, and at 7.30 a.m. halted for breakfast, arriving at its destination, Ambarkoi, about two hours later.

The camp, selected by the scout officer, Lieutenant Mathieson, was pitched on an open stretch of ground, within three hundred yards of an excellent water supply, but the whole area was infested with flies and mosquitoes. Consequently the following days were spent in cutting down reeds and, as far as possible, draining a large wooded swamp near the camp, using the boughs to roof over shelters for meals, which the medical officer rightly ordered must be eaten well away from the lines. Owing to the excessive heat reveille was now at 3.30 a.m. and breakfast at 4 a.m. Parades were finished by 9.30, as it was too hot after that to work in the sun. In the cool of the evening companies usually marched about two miles to the Galiko River for bathing, dinners being served on their return to camp. Cases of fire breaking out in the dry scrub and grass were of frequent occurrence, and on one occasion the whole Battalion was turned out to extinguish a particularly threatening one with the help of blankets and ration sacks. Pith helmets now replaced the slouch hats, and many were the failures in early attempts at folding the puggarees. In spite of all precautions, such as the chlorination of water and the issue of mosquito netting to fit inside the bivouacs, malaria became very prevalent and admissions to hospital increased daily.

TENTH BATTALION ON THE MARCH TO AMBARKOI, SALONIKA, 1916

TENTH BATTALION: WOUNDED MEN BEING TAKEN TO HOSPITAL ON SALONIKA FRONT, 1918

MOVE TO SARIGOL, JULY 25TH, 1916

The heat in the middle of the day was almost unbearable, the temperature frequently reading 110° in the shade, a striking contrast to the comparative comfort of Aivatli.

The Brigade was now in reserve to the French, and the sound of their ·75 batteries was stimulating after the quiet of Lembert and Aivatli. At the beginning of July the Battalion was inoculated against paratyphoid, and ten grains of quinine were given to every man twice weekly. About this time the Battalion team played the third round of the Army Football Cup against the Scottish Rifles and after a very exciting game defeated their opponents by three goals to nil.

While at Ambarkoi, Captain B. P. Sheldon and Second Lieutenants A. O. Drysdale, A. W. R. Don and E. A. Dobbie were admitted to hospital and Second Lieutenants J. S. Allison and A. Hebden reported from the 3/6th Battalion The Black Watch. On July 19th road making was again started, but after three days this work was cancelled and orders received that the 26th Division would take over part of the line then held by the French along a range of hills averaging 900 feet high, and about thirteen miles long running from the south of Doiran Lake to the Vardar River. All surplus stores were handed to Ordnance and the men classified as unfit were sent to the base.

Starting on the morning of July 25th the Battalion, with the rest of the Brigade, reached Sarigol that night, where it bivouacked after a very dusty march on a bad road. The next evening it proceed to Yenikoi; water was scarce and the road hidden in clouds of sand. Soon after daybreak on the 27th a party of French officers arrived and asked the Commanding Officer to move the bivouacs about two hundred yards and to have them well screened, as their present position was exposed to artillery fire. This was the 10th's first introduction to " camouflage," with which it was soon to become familiar. That same evening the Battalion, moving independently, marched to Rates and bivouacked there, while the Commanding Officer, Adjutant and company commanders proceeded to inspect the position held by the 1st Battalion of the Deuxième Regiment de Marche d'Afrique, 156th (French) Division, a line of defended posts overlooking Lake Doiran, regularly shelled by the enemy. The following evening, July 28th, companies moved off independently about 8 o'clock, but owing to the difficulties experienced in locating the numerous sentry groups pushed out well in front, the relief was not complete till shortly after midnight.

The Battalion held the position as follows: A company, Captain C. A. Nicol, at Les Lunettes and Petit Piton; B, Captain E. M. Lithgow, in reserve with Headquarters; C company, Captain R. C. H. Millar, Piton des Zouaves—which supplied the main Observation Post for the artillery—and D, Captain M. W. Gloag, at Mamelon de Col. The first day was occupied in cleaning up bivouacs and trenches: the latter were in full view of the enemy and untenable by day, as they were only three feet deep and in places even less, owing to much of the ground being solid rock, covered here and there with small oak bushes and prickly scrub. At first the bivouac areas appeared, mainly for sanitary reasons, to be equally uninhabitable, but after a day's work, followed by heavy rain, they were put in better order, although millions of flies remained in spite of all efforts to cope with them. C company lines were the most securely hidden and, the night after taking over, its transport, having wandered all night between the 11th Battalion Scottish Rifles on the right and the Berkshire Regiment on the left, eventually turned up at 5.30 a.m., while a platoon of the 12th Battalion Argyll and Sutherland Highlanders, detailed to strengthen C, having left Yenikoi about 7 p.m., arrived at Headquarters about 10 a.m. next day, the Adjutant of the 10th Battalion The Black Watch having spent a wet and fruitless night searching for them. This was an experience that all ranks were destined to become accustomed to on dark nights, when mule tracks were the sole means of guidance, where one hill looked much the same as the next, and where there were no landmarks to assist the guides.

Except for a few outbursts of shelling, mainly directed against D company, the enemy remained fairly quiet during this tour and gave the Battalion a good opportunity to reconnoitre the Bulgarian position. This was situated in a series of hills gradually rising steeper and steeper, scarred here and there by deep ravines with precipitous banks, up to the main " Pip " Ridge and Grand Couronne (Kala Tepe), 1900 feet high, the latter containing the enemy's main observation post, which commanded the entire country, including Salonika nearly fifty miles away.

This position had been made almost impregnable during the winter, and possessed a road on its northern slope which led to the summit. The " Pip " Ridge, nearly a mile due west, and over 2000 feet high, with spurs running out on either side, lay at right angles to the Battalion line facing north and south, the ridge itself being in places so narrow that only a few men could proceed along it abreast. Immediately south of P. 5 the ridge sloped down through Horseshoe Hill in Serbia to Kidney Hill and to the plain, a stretch of undulating country about a mile wide which formed No Man's Land. On the north, across Lake Doiran, towered the Beles Mountains, nearly 5000 feet high, and to the north-east the Balashitza Range, almost of equal height. This range runs east and west from the Rupel

IN RESERVE NEAR HILL 227, AUGUST 10TH, 1916

Pass to Doiran and forms an almost impregnable barrier between Bulgaria and Greece. On the west of the ridge the enemy line ran along the foothills to the Vardar River just north of Macukovo, the trenches thus being practically along the boundary line.

On August 2nd the 9th Battalion King's Own Lancaster Regiment (22nd Division) relieved the Battalion and the companies marched back to their former bivouacs at Yenikoi, moving next evening to Gavalanci, close to Lake Ardzan, where orders were received that it would remain in Divisional reserve but ready to move at short notice.

Shorts with turned-up flaps buttoning above the knee, which at sunset were turned down inside the hose top as a precaution against mosquitoes, had now been issued. While at Gavalanci, Captain R. C. H. Millar, C company, and Second Lieutenants W. Martin, A. D. Tatham and E. A. Dobbie were admitted to hospital. Captain R. N. Allenby, Seaforth Highlanders, rejoined and took command again of C company. Captain W. Stewart returned to A company from Malta, and Second Lieutenants H. H. Jalland and L. W. Urquhart were posted to D and C companies respectively on arrival from England.

On August 8th instructions were received that the first phase of the coming operations, consisting of the occupation by the French of the line Vladaja to Hill 227, would take place at 5 o'clock the following morning, and that the 12th Battalion Argyll and Sutherland Highlanders and 8th Battalion Royal Scots Fusiliers would move at once to the neighbourhood of Mihalova as Corps reserve, while the 10th Battalion The Black Watch remained in its lines in Division reserve, with the 11th Battalion Scottish Rifles. All that night and next day the Allied artillery bombarded the enemy front from Hill 535 (Pip Ridge) to Lake Doiran, though the main objective, La Tortue, was invisible from the Battalion camp.

On the morning of the 10th news reached the camp that the French had occupied Hill 227 during the night without a shot being fired, but that the bombardment would continue with the intention that the 17th (French) Colonial Division should occupy La Tortue and so link up with the 22nd British Division; consequently, after a heavy bombardment on both sides, the French, after a previous unsuccessful attempt, gained possession of La Tortue and entered Doldzelli, near Horseshoe Hill; the latter was, however, eventually retaken by the enemy.

On the 17th orders were received that the Battalion should hold itself in readiness to move that night, as the battalions of the 79th Brigade were advancing their line to pre-arranged points and were to attack Horseshoe Hill at 8 p.m., and that the 10th Black Watch might be required as reinforcements. These

THE TENTH BATTALION THE BLACK WATCH

operations were preparatory to a further attack by the 17th (French) Colonial Division on Petit Couronne to be made next day. No further orders were received, but on the following morning it was learnt that the 7th Battalion Oxford and Buckinghamshire Light Infantry had taken its objective at 1.30 a.m. at the point of the bayonet, and had beaten off two counter-attacks.

Just as it was getting dark on the 22nd the Battalion received orders to move immediately to Kalinova and report to the General Officer Commanding 79th Brigade. A heavy bombardment was in progress all along the front, and when the 10th arrived it received orders to proceed to Grand Ravine—about one mile south-west of Kalinova—and to remain there in case reinforcements were required. The enemy, having pushed forward strong reconnoitring patrols, had attacked Horseshoe Hill on the north-east side and were massing near Sejdelli, where the Observatoire de Reselli was reported to be surrounded; the French also reported enemy activity on their front in the neighbourhood of La Tortue. After remaining all night in the Ravine orders were received next morning to return to camp as the situation had again become normal.

On the day the 10th returned to Gavlanci it suffered a severe loss; Lieutenant-Colonel Sir W. Stewart-Dick-Cunyngham, who had commanded the Battalion since it was raised, was admitted to the Field Ambulance and was subsequently invalided home suffering from heart trouble. Major John Harvey succeeded to the command. Later on Colonel Sir William Stewart-Dick-Cunyngham served with the British Forces in Italy and, after the war, was appointed Chairman of the British Legion in Scotland. He died in March, 1922, deeply regretted by all who knew him.

The usual training was carried out in the early morning, but the middle of the day was spent in extreme discomfort, due to the great heat and the myriads of flies. Steel helmets had been issued to all ranks, this making the fifth form of headgear now to be carried in each pack, namely, Balmoral bonnet, pith helmet, steel helmet, waterproof cover for Balmoral, and cap comforter. As a slight variation from the ordinary swimming parades, sports were held at Lake Ardzan on the following Sunday, when the Battalion won the Brigade relay race and several other events.

CHAPTER III

JULY, 1916, TO MARCH, 1917

Salonika

ALL this time malaria was raging. Many remedies were tried unavailingly. Between July 3rd and August 26th there were 140 cases in the Field Ambulance including a third of the transport men. The latter was a great loss, as the Division was changing from wheeled to pack transport, and the men who replaced the casualties had little knowledge of their work, and many of the mules were untrained.

On August 28th the Battalion marched to its former camp at Yenikoi. The 26th Division was to take over the line. This was being held by the 22nd, with the 17th (French Colonial) Division on the right, from Doldzeli to Lake Doiran, the 77th Brigade acting as Divisional reserve, in readiness to support the French left if required. On August 29th the Battalion was notified that Headquarters had learned that the enemy had issued definite orders for an attack to be pressed without delay on the whole front. The Brigade was therefore ordered to be in readiness to move at very short notice.

During the next two days parties of officers and guides reconnoitred routes to all parts of the front between Bojuklu and Kilindir, and also the 78th and 79th Brigades' positions, the two battalions on duty being under orders to move at a moment's notice, and the other two at half an hour's notice. Just before midnight on August 31st a telegram was received stating that the French Division reported having observed the enemy massing on the lower slopes of Grand Couronne about dusk, but no action took place. During the next few days, in spite of high winds and heavy storms, reconnaissance parties were out continually; no further news was received from the French front.

Second Lieutenant A. W. R. Don now rejoined from Malta with a draft of a hundred men, and Captain W. Stewart was admitted to hospital and subsequently invalided home; and as mentioned above, Major J. Harvey was appointed to command the Battalion vice Lieutenant-Colonel Sir W. Stewart-Dick-Cunyngham.

In connection with Roumania's entry into the war on July 29th a special order of the day by the General Officer Commanding Salonika Army, General Sir George Milne, G.C.M.G., was published on August 29th, 1916:

" In announcing the entry into the war of our new ally, the
" Army Commander hopes that all ranks will realize that one
" of the most important aims of the military policy adopted in
" this theatre of operations has been effected. He wishes to
" congratulate all ranks on the part they have played in achieving

THE TENTH BATTALION THE BLACK WATCH

" this object, and he takes the opportunity of saying how fully
" he appreciates the splendid work they have done during the
" past ten months, often under very trying conditions."

On September 8th the 77th Infantry Brigade received orders to take over on the next day the line from Ravine de Vladaja (inclusive) to Hill 5, about one mile north-west of Cidemli; the 79th Brigade to hold the line from there to the left. The 10th Black Watch remained in support, with B company at Le Commandant, A at Paillasse, D at La Cantinière, and C, with Battalion Headquarters, at Table Hill—77th Brigade Headquarters being at Gugunci.

On the morning of the 9th Captain R. N. Allenby, commanding C company, and Lieutenant A. W. R. Don, with a number of men reported unfit for the line, were sent to hospital suffering from fever. The plague of flies was responsible for most of the sickness in this camp, while the fever cases came chiefly from the camp at Gavalanci. Captain Allenby was sent to England and, to the great sorrow of all ranks, Lieutenant A. W. R. Don died of malignant malaria within a few hours of his arrival at the 43rd General Hospital, Kalamaria. By his death the Battalion lost one of its best junior officers.

During the evening of the 9th the Battalion moved off by companies and was fortunate in having no casualties although, during the move, the enemy dropped a number of heavy shells close to the cross roads at Gugunci, the relief being carried out in very heavy rain.

On viewing the position by daylight it was found that the front consisted of advanced posts on small hills in the plain, whilst the support line, now occupied by the 10th, was the main line of resistance. A company from Paillasse had to send two platoons forward nightly to Bagatelles and Batignolles. B had two platoons at the north end of Le Commandant and two at the south-west end. D company was in support to B, finding a post by night on Marabout, while C company, in reserve near Battalion Headquarters, was kept busy improving the road to Horseshoe Hill between Gokcelli and La Douane, the only available route for ration parties and evacuating wounded and sick to the field dressing station at the foot of Table Hill.

Enemy artillery was fairly active in this sector, the main target being several batteries close to the camp; none the less the infantry holding the line suffered considerably from this fire. The main observation post on this front was situated on the north end of Le Commandant, and one of the most disagreeable duties of the subalterns was a four hours' watch there at night, with the object of locating flashes from enemy guns by

TRENCH WARFARE, SEPTEMBER, 1916

means of a compass. While in this sector all available men were employed for four nights digging a trench at the foot of Castle Hill, midway between Kidney Hill and Le Commandant, to the Horseshoe Hill road to screen the movement of troops by day.

On September 13th, after three days' artillery preparation, the 12th Battalion Lancashire Fusiliers and 14th Battalion The King's Liverpool Regiment, supported by the 4th Battalion East Lancashire Regiment and the 11th Battalion Royal Welch Fusiliers (22nd Division), captured the trenches held by German troops on Piton des Mitrailleuses. After beating off several counter-attacks the same night they came under heavy enfilade fire from the Guevgheli batteries, and had to withdraw suffering heavy losses. This was in the section next to the Vardar, afterwards known as "M," with which the 10th was to become familiar in 1917.

On September 18th the company commanders, machine gun officer, signalling officer and one guide from each platoon were sent on to the Horseshoe and Kidney Hills as the Battalion had been ordered to relieve the Scottish Rifles in that sector the following night. The relief was completed shortly after midnight, the position being held as follows: B and C companies near the Horseshoe; A company with Battalion Headquarters at Pillar Hill, kept touch with the 8th Battalion Royal Scots Fusiliers in Doldzeli Ravine, while D was in support at Kidney Hill, holding McArthur's post and patrolling down to the 12th Battalion Argyll and Sutherland Highlanders. The Scottish Rifles reported that they had discovered a listening post the previous night, about sixty yards in front of C. 2 with a wire running back to P. 5, which was roughly a hundred and fifty yards in front, and which was held by the enemy at night; Lieutenant R. Don went out with a small covering party, filled up the hole and brought back a Bulgarian greatcoat, cap and some German bombs.

The trenches in this sector were in solid rock, and had been sandbagged breast high. The work of repairing them seemed endless, for whenever the opposing artillery, who were believed to be chiefly Austrian, wanted practice, they selected the Horseshoe trenches and camp as their target.

With the idea of holding the enemy on this front and preventing any further troops being sent to take part in the operations near Monastir, the 8th Battalion Royal Scots Fusiliers on the right of the 10th Battalion The Black Watch was ordered to carry out a raid on the night of September 21st on the Mamelon trenches. Operations of this kind always brought down enemy artillery fire, and as the British batteries engaged in wire cutting were just behind Battalion Headquarters' camp, that camp and the one occupied by the support company were often shelled. Patrols were out each night, the main objectives being an enemy post, P. 5, and the ruins of Doldzeli village, through which Bulgarian patrols passed regularly.

On the night of September 22nd Colonel Harvey sent out a fighting patrol consisting of Lieutenant R. Don and twenty men from B company, Lieutenant W. J. Duffy with a Lewis gun section, and Lieutenant P. Anderson, C company, with ten men to raid P. 5 with the object of obtaining identification. Don's party met with resistance from the post, but, being reinforced by the Lewis gun section, they eventually captured the hill, where they were joined later by Anderson's party of C company. The latter had met about twenty Bulgarians on the Krastali track, at a point south-west of P. 4, and after an exchange of rifle fire at close range they moved east across a gully, only to find that the enemy had retired; they then joined up with the men of B company. The raiders lost Sergeant Rhodes of B company and four other ranks wounded.

Another raid was carried out the following night under Lieutenant W. Duffy and Second Lieutenant L. Urquhart. Several bombs were thrown, bringing down an enemy barrage for half an hour in front of P. 5, but no target was offered to the Lewis gun section which had taken up a position commanding the Doldzeli–Krastali track. The patrol returned an hour before dawn with two men wounded, having located the position of some sangars to which the group on P. 5 were in the habit of retiring. Several patrols were also sent out from A company's line to Doldzeli village and the track north-west of it; but no identification was obtained, although much useful knowledge of the ground was gained. From information given by deserters it seemed that the enemy's patrols usually consisted of parties of about sixty men. Each party was divided into a main body, and three smaller groups which took up positions in front; when one of these groups were attacked the remaining two retired on the main body, which then advanced to the assistance of the group engaged, thus bringing the fire of about fifty rifles on any given point in a very short time.

On the morning of the 25th Battalion Headquarters and A company on Pillar Hill were heavily shelled, enemy aeroplanes directing the fire. Second Lieutenant A. Hebden, B company, Company Sergeant-Major Mackenzie and Company Quartermaster-Sergeant McInnes of A company and 16 other ranks were wounded and twenty-six boxes of ammunition destroyed. Had it not been for the prompt action of the Adjutant, Captain I. Sanderson, most of the Battalion Headquarters' store of ammunition and bombs would also have exploded.

Nightly shelling continued, and directly a wiring party went

RAID ON "THE PILLAR," SEPTEMBER 30TH, 1916

out an enemy barrage was put down, making it more than ever imperative that P. 5 observation post should be captured. On the morning of September 30th a deserter from the 9th Regiment of the II Bulgarian Division gave himself up. That night Lieutenant Macdonald, A company, with twenty men took up a position on the north-east slope of P. 5 to form a flanking party for Lieutenant Duffy, who, with a Lewis gun and twenty men from C company under Lieutenant P. Anderson, was to raid P. 5 from the west, and, if possible, capture the garrison. At "The Pillar" Anderson's party was fired on by about five men, who then retired, and on following them up for about fifty yards they were again fired on by a group of about thirty men, who were driven back to the gully between P. 5 and P. 4. Near the edge of the gully Anderson was met by heavy fire, which compelled him to withdraw. Meanwhile touch had been lost with Duffy's party as the three men who had been left as connecting files had been wounded, but Anderson opened Lewis gun fire on a party of about twenty Bulgarians moving over the skyline to support P. 5, several of whom were either killed or wounded. He was then attacked by about eighty more, who began to outflank him and forced him to retire, during which movement he again caused casualties to the enemy. The Battalion losses during this raid were Privates Thomson and Melville of C company killed, and five wounded. The enemy's loss was undoubtedly heavy.

The next day was comparatively quiet. Just before dark a heavy rain storm came on with a gale of wind, under cover of which the enemy raided the posts held by the 7th Battalion Berkshire Regiment on the right. In the middle of this raid the 8th Battalion Royal Scots Fusiliers arrived to relieve the 10th Battalion The Black Watch. The relief, therefore, was carried out under most trying conditions, and the Battalion only reached its destination, Gugunci, at 4.30 a.m. on October 2nd.

At Gugunci a draft of ninety men joined the Battalion, of whom twenty were ex-yeomanry, the remainder having only had a few months' service and no training in bombing or night work. For the next five days work consisted of improving the road between Table Hill and Asagi Mahala by day, and wiring on the north slopes of Le Commandant by night.

The 10th was now ordered to carry out a raid on P. 5, with the object of obtaining identifications, and Colonel Harvey detailed A and C companies for this purpose.

The raid was carried out from the "Horseshoe," the plan being as follows: Twenty-five men of A company under Lieutenant Phillips, were to proceed to the Doldzeli–Krastali track, at a point behind, and due north of P.5. Lieutenants Macdonald and Allison with another twenty-five of A were to drive the garrison southwards either on the remainder of A company in position near Doldzeli village under Captain Nicol, or else on to a party of C company lined up along the gully between P. 5 and P. 4, the object of Lieutenant Phillips' party on the Doldzeli–Krastali track being to prevent the retirement of the garrison of P. 4 or the arrival of reinforcements.

Everything went well except that the garrison, instead of awaiting the arrival of Macdonald's party, abandoned their sangars and escaped before the raiders were in position, leaving five killed. Macdonald, who had been hit in the hand, was missing when the party reassembled at the starting-point, also Sergeant Halcrow and Private Duncan, A company, and two others were wounded. Captain Nicol and Lieutenant Duffy searched the slopes of P. 5 for these men, but could find no trace of them and were forced to retire, as the enemy was now advancing in strength. The following night Second Lieutenant J. Allison and twenty volunteers marched up from Gugunci to search once more, but found the post strongly held, and after an exchange of bombs and some rifle fire the party withdrew with the loss of one man wounded.

On October 11th the 10th relieved the 12th Battalion Argyll and Sutherland Highlanders in "The Posts," a line in the Plain with Battalion Headquarters in Clinchy Ravine. This was a very quiet sector, but "The Posts" themselves were in the air if attacked, and at that time had little wire in front of them. The only activity in this sector consisted of patrol work towards Krastali village, which was known to be strongly held by the enemy at night. In order to discover how the village was held by day, Colonel Harvey detailed Lieutenant Drysdale to take two men from D company, and, entering the village by night, to lie up there during the day and find out whether any signs of a day garrison were visible. This was a particularly difficult operation to carry out, especially as No Man's Land was covered with thick thorn bush and intersected by gullies, some of which were twenty feet deep; in addition the enemy were known to have numerous defended posts which were held by night, all of which had to be avoided.

Drysdale's small party managed to cross No Man's Land, and arrived safely at the village, but was discovered by the enemy shortly afterwards. Lance-Corporal Harkness, D company, who was leading, was wounded by almost the first shot, and before anything could be done for him, the enemy rushed out; Drysdale, with the remaining survivor, withdrew to a nullah, and eventually regained the Battalion line, both having been wounded several times. Lance-Corporal Harkness, a fine stalker, and one

TRENCH WARFARE, OCTOBER, 1916

of the best of the Battalion snipers, was unfortunately never heard of again.

Many raids were carried out on Krastali; one of the most successful was achieved by D company, under Captain K. S. MacRae. On October 19th B company, under Captain Lithgow, was in support and some of the Scottish Rifles on Whaleback acted as right flankers; D company succeeded in entering the village, having called for the prearranged barrage by sending up a red Very light after their scouts had been fired at. The Bulgarians, however, retreated before them in the ruined village, and in the darkness it was impossible to follow them up. All the time a brisk rifle fire was kept up by the Bulgarians from high ground overlooking the village. The company was then withdrawn and moved back to its line. This raid established beyond any doubt that the Bulgarians used Krastali as an advanced post, but withdrew when attacked.

The general work in this sector consisted of erecting miles of wire, digging new trenches at Post Z and Gully Post and strengthening Worcester Post, which was always flooded after heavy rain. Three Bulgarians who gave themselves up at Gully Post one morning reported having seen a wounded Highlander carried into their lines a few days before, but whether this was Corporal Harkness or not was never ascertained. On returning to the support line at La Table on October 20th work was started on dug-outs for the winter. The plan for these dug-outs, designed by the Royal Engineers, consisted of a large square hole about twenty-seven feet long by eight feet wide dug into the slope of the hill with sandbag walls built on to support a sloping roof of corrugated iron, the entrance being a gap between the front sandbag walls, with a door of waterproof sheeting hanging from the roof. Stoves made of old oil drums and paraffin tins added considerably to the warmth inside. Several deaths were reported from dysentery in hospital, and men of the new drafts fell victims more readily than those who had been on service since 1914.

On October 27th the Battalion returned to the Horseshoe sector which, in spite of many drawbacks, had the advantage of standing high and was therefore comparatively dry. For several days it was misty during this tour, and the Adjutant, with his servant Douglas and Lieutenant Duffy, was able to verify the exact positions of the enemy sangars and extent of their wire. During their reconnaissance they found the sangars unoccupied, but just as they had finished their task the mist lifted and fire was opened on them from behind a low stone wall about two yards away, but without doing any damage. While occupying this sector, T. L. Alexander, one of the original C company sergeants, who had been recommended for a commission, rejoined the Battalion and was posted as Second Lieutenant to A company; Second Lieutenants R. H. Ross and W. A. Carswell were sent to D, and Lieutenant P. B. Hepburn and Second Lieutenant J. Grey, from the Scottish Horse, to B and A respectively.

The 10th next occupied the Clichy sector for ten days, from November 18th to 28th. During this tour patrols visited Scratchbury and Bowls Barrow Hills each night. By day work was concentrated on building winter shelters. Various patrols were also sent out to observe the enemy's action when Krastali was bombarded, and useful information was gained.

During this tour two companies of the Battalion held the line of the Argyll and Sutherland Highlanders while the latter carried out a raid, though this was unsuccessful. About the same time Lieutenant P. W. Anderson and Second Lieutenant J. M. Watson went to Egypt to join the Royal Flying Corps. The Battalion suffered a further loss on the 28th, when Lieutenant Duffy, the Lewis gun officer, was wounded by shell fire as the Battalion moved into the Horseshoe sector.

The first party to go on leave to England started on November 19th; there were six in all, of whom three were officers. The second party went home a month later. The weather during this tour was perhaps the worst experienced by the 10th throughout the war. As the Battalion was holding advanced positions, fires were not allowed. Constant patrols had to be sent out by day and night along the wire, so as to avoid the possibility of a repetition of the disaster which overtook the 10th Division in exactly similar weather the previous winter. Indeed, it would be impossible to exaggerate the discomforts of this tour. Officers and men were soaked through the whole time, and had little chance ever to get dry or warm, owing to the scarcity of charcoal. The weather, however, seemed to have damped the spirits of the Bulgarians, for apart from the usual intermittent shelling which caused several casualties in D company, there was very little enemy activity.

The reserve company, A, at Kidney Hill, spent eight hours daily working on the road between Castle Hill and Battalion Headquarters at Pillar Hill which had become a sea of mud and impassable even for pack mules; luckily, owing to the mist, most of this work could be done by day.

On the night of December 8th the Battalion handed over the sector to the Argyll and Sutherland Highlanders and moved back to the support line with Battalion Headquarters at Table Hill. Fortunately a change in the weather enabled all blankets and clothes to be dried for the first time in eleven days, and three days later the 10th returned to "The Posts" known as F Sector.

TRENCH WARFARE

This tour was uneventful, the usual work on the defences and construction of dug-out accommodation being continued. Christmas Day and New Year were spent in the line, the latter being ushered in by an artillery salvo from the British guns. On January 5th, 1917, Major T. L. Cunningham, D.S.O., 7th Cameron Highlanders, reported his arrival on appointment as Second-in-Command, and two days later Second Lieutenant W. A. Carswell and Sergeant Carrie of D company were wounded by shrapnel.

On the 14th the Royal Scots Fusiliers relieved the Battalion, which then moved back to a new camp between Mektoub and Capitaine. The defences in this area were only half finished and the 10th was now occupied in completing them; also in digging a long communication trench from Capitaine to the south end of Baraka, and in constructing machine gun emplacements on Mektoub. By the end of the month two thousand yards of trench had been dug, over half of it being seven feet deep and the remainder about four feet. For the last eight days of the month the weather was very bad, starting with continual rain followed by snow and very sharp frosts.

The Battalion relieved the Royal Scots Fusiliers in its old sector on February 1st, and two nights later Second Lieutenant J. Grey, A company, with a patrol of six men, visited a house at the south-west corner of Krastali, said to be occupied by the enemy. This proved correct, the house was strongly held and Grey and his party returned to their line. Two nights later Second Lieutenant D. C. Thomson, C company, with a party of eight men, visited the same house. They were fortunate in reaching their goal unseen by the enemy, and, opening fire on the sentry group, they succeeded in hitting the sentry and at least one of his comrades, after which the party withdrew to the Battalion lines.

About this time Lieutenant K. S. MacRae, who had been commanding D company when Major Gloag was acting as Battalion Second-in-Command, went to Egypt on a Staff course; Sergeant H. Kinnear, A company, and A/Sergeant W. Armit, D company, also left the Battalion, having been nominated for commissions. Regimental Sergeant-Major A. F. Ritchie, who had held acting rank since Regimental Sergeant-Major Fairweather left the Battalion at Aivatli, was appointed Second Lieutenant and attached to B company for duty, special application having been made for his retention with the Battalion.

On February 15th the Battalion again relieved the Royal Scots Fusiliers in support and continued the work on the Mektoub and Baraka lines. In addition two hundred men were supplied nightly for work on communications in the front lines.

THE TENTH BATTALION THE BLACK WATCH

A squadron of about twenty enemy aeroplanes were frequently seen passing over to bomb Janes, Railhead and Corps Headquarters.

During the last few days of February a snow blizzard made life most unpleasant, and caused the newly started communication trench to be completely obliterated by snow-drifts. The 10th returned to F Sector on March 3rd. The weather was extremely cold and a " Vardar " wind and sharp frosts accentuated the discomfort caused by the lack of shelters or dug-outs in the recently constructed part of the line.

It was now decided to advance the line across the plain from Whaleback to the north of Bowls Barrow. Two platoons started working by night, making shelter trenches behind these two hills, and after the 8th of March every available man did seven hours' work on the new line. Directly this trench had been completed the enemy artillery registered it with shrapnel, but work was continued for another seven hours and the trenches were deepened throughout and a hundred and fifty yards of new communication trench opened up.

Two men were killed and six wounded before the 18th, when the Battalion was relieved and moved back to camp near Mihalova. Here the Commanding Officer received a letter from the Division Commander expressing his appreciation of the work recently done in F Sector. Colonel Harvey also received a letter from Major-General C. W. Mackenzie-Kennedy, C.B., on relinquishing command of the Division, from which the following is an extract:—

" Please tell all your officers how I regret leaving them. I
" never had a minute's anxiety about the 10th Black Watch, for
" I know they always do well."

The night before the relief the Bulgarian artillery heavily bombarded the front line, using a quantity of gas and high explosive shell. Nothing followed this demonstration, but much damage was done to the newly constructed line.

CHAPTER IV

MARCH TO AUGUST, 1917

Salonika

THE next twelve days were spent quietly at Mihalova carrying out practice attacks and working on a new system of trench digging. The weather was fine and the 10th soon forgot the discomforts of the past months. On March 29th the Battalion was inspected by the Brigade Commander, and the next evening advance parties from each company proceeded to the 79th Brigade front which was to be taken over the following day from the 11th Scottish Rifles, then holding the left sub-sector of the Division line.

The Battalion occupied the new line as follows: One company at Tilbury Camp, one at Rockley Hill, one at Swindon and the fourth with Battalion Headquarters at Minden. The trenches overlooked Lake Doiran on the right. On the immediate front the ground dropped sharply to Jumeaux Ravine; beyond which rose the Petit Couronne, the main feature of the enemy front line, about four hundred yards distant from Rockley Hill. Further behind the Bulgarian line the country rose fold upon fold to the Grand Couronne, which overlooked this position, as it had done Horseshoe and the other sectors. The most striking feature in the Allied line was the "Tortue" on the left of Rockley Hill. In front of the "Tortue," Rockley Hill, Silbury and several smaller ravines, Dorset, Hand and Claw, ran into Jumeaux Ravine, along the top of the far edge of which lay the enemy front line trenches. Such, roughly, was the new sector held by the Battalion. The three days spent there passed pleasantly in glorious weather, the chief work being to strengthen Rockley and Silbury Forts. Enemy field guns registered Jumeaux Ravine regularly every afternoon.

On being relieved by the Royal Scots Fusiliers on April 6th the 10th returned to bivouacs at Yenikoi. On the 9th the Battalion moved to Mamelon in the neighbourhood of Avret Hissar, south-east of Lake Ardzan, where training in open warfare was continued. A party was left behind to repair the road near Kilindir. The next ten days were spent in Battalion and Brigade training in view of the coming operation. Owing to the heat and the strenuous nature of the work there was little inclination for recreation.

The 10th returned to Yenikoi on the 19th, moving from there on the 22nd to a camp south of Switch Hill in readiness for an attack arranged to take place the following day. On the night of the 25th the Battalion moved up from Switch Hill Camp to bivouacs in Deep Cut Ravine.

THE TENTH BATTALION THE BLACK WATCH

The plan of operations was, roughly, as follows: After three days' bombardment the 22nd and 26th Divisions were to make an assault on the whole front from Lake Doiran to the Pip Ridge inclusive; three battalions of the 79th Brigade were to attack from the Lake to Petit Couronne inclusive. The 7th Royal Berkshires and 11th Worcesters of the 78th Brigade were to take the trenches west of Petit Couronne, and the 22nd Division was to attack Hill 380, Mamelon and the Pips, the 77th Brigade being in reserve to the 78th and 79th Brigades.

The 77th Brigade was not actually employed in the fighting. The operation was not a success, and about 2 o'clock in the afternoon a strong Bulgarian counter-attack forced back the few groups of men who had managed to reach the enemy front line at one or two places.

On the night of April 25th the 10th relieved the Duke of Cornwall's Light Infantry in B Sub-sector. Parties were employed all next morning in the Jumeaux and smaller ravines collecting and burying the dead, and in salvage work; the amount of equipment, rifles and bombs saved bore witness to the terrible barrage put down on the ravine. In fairness to the enemy it must be recorded that he showed due respect to the stretcher parties, allowing them to carry out their duties unmolested in the open until they were withdrawn at 2 p.m., when the artillery on both sides again opened fire. As soon as the shelling stopped salvage work was continued, and immense quantities of Lewis gun ammunition, stores, mortar shells and various forms of equipment were brought in.

Next morning it was still raining, and burial parties were fired on by machine guns and had to withdraw, but salvage work continued where the ground was not under enemy observation. That afternoon Second Lieutenant Millar, B company, and 10 men removed all the material which had been left at a dump previous to the operation, making five trips in broad daylight—a fine performance, especially in view of the fact that a patrol had been bombed at this spot only a few hours before. In the evening there was a fierce bombardment round Hill 380 and Mamelon from 6.30 p.m. to 9 p.m., after which, at "stand to," the enemy rushed the latter position held by the 22nd Division. It was, however, recaptured after dark by the battalion holding the Doldzeli sector.

That same night all available men of the 10th dug a communication trench from Rockley Fort down to the Jumeaux Ravine with a view to further operations. As their listening posts had not been able to pass our standing patrols the enemy were unable to locate the working parties, who were thus able to work without loss. On the night of the 28th one of A

ATTACK AT LAKE DOIRAN, MAY 8TH, 1917

company's patrols brought in a wounded man of the Devonshire Regiment who had been lying close to the enemy wire since the 24th.

On the 30th the Royal Scots Fusiliers took over the line, and the Battalion moved back to Piton Rocheux close to the trenches it had held in July, 1916. The next few days were spent in practising attacks on marked out trenches representing the enemy line to be attacked shortly.

The Battalion relieved the Royal Scots Fusiliers at Silbury and Minden on May 7th, A and B companies occupying the former, C and D with Headquarters taking over Minden. All packs and spare kit were sent down to the transport lines, and eight officers and 92 other ranks were left as a reserve to reform the Battalion should heavy losses be incurred. The remainder moved up in battle order and arrived at the trenches about 10 p.m.

The line to be attacked extended from Lake Doiran to Point o6, the 77th Brigade objective being the Bulgarian line between Petit Couronne and the Lake, while the 78th Brigade on the left continued westward. The 77th Brigade attack was carried out by three groups, the 8th Royal Scots Fusiliers being in reserve. Nearest the Lake was the Scottish Rifle group; the Argyll and Sutherland Highlanders group was in the centre and the 10th Black Watch group on the left. This group consisted of the 10th Black Watch, one company 8th Battalion Oxford and Buckinghamshire Light Infantry (Pioneers), one section of 108th Company R.E., two guns 77th Machine Gun Company and two guns 77th Trench Mortar Battery.

The plan of attack was as follows: The 77th Brigade to attack on May 8th at 9.50 p.m. If this attack proved successful the 7th Oxford and Buckinghamshire Light Infantry, 78th Brigade, were then to assault the eastern and higher portion of Petit Couronne, after which the 7th Battalion Berkshire Regiment was to pass through them and take the western portion of the hill. An elaborate artillery programme was arranged to cover the operation.

The bombardment and wire cutting continued throughout the 7th, the latter being assisted by a medium trench mortar on the northern bank of Jumeaux Ravine, but the wire in front of one sector was almost intact at dusk. Profiting by the lesson of the attack on April 24th it had been decided that the assault position should be Sunken Road on the further or northern side of Jumeaux Ravine, as it was possible to get there unobserved. Accordingly at 8.15 p.m. the Adjutant, Captain Sanderson, and Regimental Sergeant-Major Christie, laid a tape 250 yards beyond the British wire, parallel to the objective, and cut three gaps in the wire between Jumeaux Ravine on the left and the Wylye Ravine on the right. Half an hour later companies moved to their positions of assembly: A on the right and B on the left along the tape; one platoon C company to Rocky Knob, the remainder of C company to the covered way leading from Silbury Camp to the Ravine, and D to Silbury in support, all being in position by 9.30 p.m. Each of the two companies in the front line had one platoon in the first wave, another in the second and two in the third.

The attack began punctually at Zero. Touch between companies was lost at the start. The reserve platoons of A company, with which were Captain Nicol and Company Headquarters, lost touch with B company on the left, who then inclined to the left, compelling A to throw its second wave into the first line in an endeavour to keep connection with B. The barrage was good and A company, keeping well up to it, reached the enemy wire, but found it strong. Lieutenant J. Grey, however, with about thirty men and a Lewis gun, got through and into the enemy line. At this moment the enemy barrage fell, and many high explosive shells landed along the line of wire with two belts of shrapnel, one about thirty and the other about eighty yards in front of the wire, while machine gun fire swept the line from the rear of 02 and Petit Couronne, which, according to plan, had not yet been attacked. The enemy meanwhile kept up a steady rifle fire, lying on their parados, thus escaping the British barrage which by this time had lifted on to points behind them. The men of Lieutenant Grey's party were now almost the sole survivors of A company in the trench, and were only able to hold about seventy yards of it just west of Wylye Ravine, while the Argyll and Sutherland Highlanders on the right had in some places penetrated to the enemy's second line. Lieutenant Phillips therefore decided to go back to Sunken Road to report progress to Headquarters and ask for reinforcements. He was then instructed to take up C company about 10.30 p.m.

In the meantime B company had advanced on Z 20, but as a result of not having kept as close to the barrage as A, the third and fourth waves were caught in the enemy's barrage. Don, Hepburn and Hebden, however, with the survivors, had crossed the trench, found no wire and lay in the shell-holes beyond. The garrison of the enemy support line now opened heavy fire on them, and the party was forced to withdraw to the cover of the first line of enemy trenches, from which they were finally ejected by counter-attacks from both flanks. They then retired to Rocky Knob, where they were met by the platoon of C company, under Graham. Don had last been seen on the

LAKE DOIRAN, MAY 8TH, 1917

parapet of the trench encouraging his men, Hebden with a bombing party on his right had not been heard of again, and there was now no officer left in B company. Of A company Captain Nicol with the company sergeant-major and runners were seen in the enemy front line trench in the vicinity of B company, but what subsequently happened to them was never discovered. Alexander was wounded soon after leaving the point of assembly, and must have been hit again later, as no more was heard of him.

Meanwhile, Lieutenant Grey was still holding out at the extreme right of the objective with the remainder of No. 4 platoon when Phillips came up with C company about 10.50 p.m. As the enemy barrage was now on his front line and the counter-attack which had just ousted B company was still in progress, it was impossible for more than a few men to force their way through the uncut wire, and both parties were obliged to withdraw. Grey was able to bring his Lewis gun away intact. McLaren, though badly wounded in two places, carried on magnificently. Two of the other officers, Thomson and Noble, were wounded, Taylor-Lowen alone being unwounded. At this stage the survivors, who had returned to Sunken Road, numbered twenty-five of A company under Phillips and Grey, and about forty of B company who had been reorganized by Graham and had been ordered by McLaren to retire with the remainder of C company, now about half its original strength. When C company was ordered to reinforce A, Major Gloag moved up with D company to Sunken Road, and reorganized A, B and C companies. He received orders from Headquarters to move with them to Rocky Knob and wait there until arrangements were made for artillery support.

The Brigade then ordered a company of Royal Scots Fusiliers at Minden Camp to report to Major Gloag and replace the Pioneer company who were to man the trenches at Silbury Fort; on their arrival Major Gloag reported that he would attack Z 20 at 1.35 a.m. with two waves of The Black Watch in the front line and two of the Royal Scots Fusiliers in support, the total strength being under four hundred men. At 1.35 a.m., however, the enemy barrage was so intense that Major Gloag decided to wait till it should quieten down, and at 2.15 a.m. the Brigade ordered that the attack should be delayed until the 9th Battalion Gloucester Regiment (78th Brigade) had arrived when a general attack would be made. The Gloucester Regiment was given the right of o2, the Argyll and Sutherland Highlanders the left of o2 as their objectives, the 11th Battalion Worcester Regiment taking two hundred yards west of Wylye Valley with The Black Watch and one company Royal Scots Fusiliers on its left.

THE TENTH BATTALION THE BLACK WATCH

Major Gloag at the same time received instructions to get in touch with the Commanding Officer of the Worcester Battalion now coming up to start its attack from Wylye Valley. Major Gloag therefore formed up D company at Rocky Knob as the first wave, the remaining men of A, B and C companies as second wave, half a company of the Fusiliers as the third, and the remaining half company and a carrying party in rear, and arranged with Colonel Barker at Sunken Road to attack simultaneously at 4.30 a.m. He then pushed forward Lewis guns to give covering fire during the advance, and after seeing the Worcester Battalion move into position, his force advanced and found the enemy wire still a formidable obstacle. With difficulty a few men managed to cut and force their way through, but owing to the enemy strength and the increasing daylight Major Gloag realized that his force was too weak and rightly ordered a withdrawal which was carried out in good order, it being broad daylight when the last man returned to camp. Out of the six hundred men who took part in this action five officers were killed, Captain Nicol, Lieutenant Don, Second Lieutenants Alexander, Hebden and Graham, and six were wounded; 63 other ranks were killed and 309 wounded.

For services on this occasion the following awards were made: M.C., Captain Sanderson, Lieutenants McLaren and Duffy and Second Lieutenant Grey; D.C.M., Company Sergeant-Major McArthur; M.M., Sergeant Joss, Corporal Gow, and Privates Macpherson and Stuart.

After the Battalion had been withdrawn from the fighting the Allied attack continued throughout the whole of the 9th and the following night, but with no success, the position being so strongly held as to resist capture. Active operations ceased on the 10th. It is probably true to say that in no case was a Division asked to attack, almost unsupported, so strong a position on so wide a front.

The Battalion was relieved on the night of May 9th by the 2nd King's Own Regiment and returned to Piton Rocheux, moving the following day to Corps reserve at Malovci, where a draft of seventy-six men was received, the majority of whom were old malaria patients. At this camp the time was chiefly spent in instructing new non-commissioned officers and in reorganizing the Battalion. The 10th now moved up to relieve the 2/20th London Regiment in J Sector, and on May 18th the Battalion was 770 strong.

The sector was a quiet one, with Battalion Headquarters close to the ruins of Reselli village. The main position was held by the centre company, and consisted of a low ridge which jutted out conspicuously in the flat surrounding country, and which

TRENCH WARFARE, JUNE, 1917

was shelled by the enemy daily. Except for Piton Boise the posts were weak in the new sector, and the trenches were in a poor state, and two isolated works which formed a salient between Piton Boise and Wagon Hill had no communicating trenches. From most of the isolated posts the field of fire was small, in spite of the ground being almost flat.

Facing the front line the chief enemy works were the Trapeze de Stojakovo on the right, Boyau Hill and The Nose. The last, their main stronghold on this sector, was very heavily wired and contained their chief observation post. In No Man's Land the main features were the Bogorodica track which crossed the Selimli Deresi and passed through the enemy lines to the town, and Bergerie Hill, situated on the further bank of a deep ravine. Down this ravine flowed the Selimli Deresi from the village of Selimli, opposite H Sector, till it emptied itself into Lake Ardzan behind the British lines. The tour was quiet. Concealed wire entanglements were placed in the Selimli Deresi, and a trench was dug to connect Piton Boise to the next isolated post on the left.

On the night of June 3rd the Battalion was relieved and moved into Brigade reserve at The Crag, a camp about a mile and a half behind the front line, close to Brigade Headquarters. Here large working parties were sent out each night to the front line, and parties were also provided for the camp in the neighbourhood of Kalinova, as well as in the Corps reserve area round Gavalanci and Mihalova. A number of wounded men and many former malaria patients now returned from hospital. In spite of all precautions, however, malaria increased each summer. In order to combat this, mosquito-proof huts were built; gloves and head nets were issued for use after sunset, converting an ordinary sentry into something resembling very closely a model bee-keeper. By the end of the summer of 1917 the thirty thousand malaria hospital patients of 1916 had increased to sixty-three thousand, and in 1918 to sixty-seven thousand. In one fortnight in 1916 a cavalry regiment was reduced to forty-five officers and men, and one infantry battalion showed a strength of one officer and 19 other ranks. These figures do not take into account the large number of men who had constant relapses of fever without going to hospital. As the hospital accommodation was inadequate to cope with these numbers some twenty thousand patients were sent to Malta in 1916. This procedure, however, was stopped and more hospitals were afterwards opened in Salonika.

On June 13th the 10th was relieved at The Crag by the 7th Battalion Berkshire Regiment, and moved to a new camp south-east of Kalabak in Corps reserve. Here classes of instruction were started and training continued. Leave to Salonika was granted to those officers who cared to go, but as there was little to do there this concession was of no great value. On the 1st of July the Battalion moved from Kirec Camp to a point on the foothills between Causica and Pyramide, where it bivouacked for a night before relieving the 7th Battalion Wiltshire Regiment, 79th Brigade, in M Sector, on the extreme left of the British line at Glen Smol. Here the Battalion was in Brigade reserve about half a mile behind the front line. Smol Hill rises some 900 feet above sea-level and from the Corps observation post on its summit the Vardar could be traced for about fifteen miles till it lost itself in the Serbian mountains. In line with the Hill, but across the river on its right bank, lay the French second position, around Kara Sinanci and Mayadag.

During this tour the 10th worked on a new support line from the Vardar across the south of Smol to Bald Hill, while B company was attached to the Argyll and Sutherland Highlanders for wiring in L Sector. Nothing of importance occurred throughout the tour. By the middle of the month Lieutenants McLaren, Thomson and Noble and a number of men returned from hospital. There was little shelling in this sector, but on one occasion a high velocity gun at Bogorodica sent two shells into A company's camp, luckily at a moment when it was unoccupied.

On the 17th the Battalion took over from the Scottish Rifles in the line. The same night Lieutenant Jalland and three men from D company were fired on while patrolling just south of Piton des Quatre Arbres, close to the bank of the Vardar. The trenches in M Sector were mostly in solid rock, and though provided with fire-bays had no fire-step, and in places were not more than three feet deep. Work consisted in deepening the trenches and blasting sites for dug-outs, as there were none in the front line. In front of the British line, and nearer to the enemy was the ruined village of Macukovo. Second Lieutenants Thomson and Bushe and eight men of C company spent a whole day there but saw nothing; two evenings later, however, twenty Bulgarians were seen to move down Bangor Ravine towards the village; Second Lieutenants Millar and Forgan with forty men of B company, having made good the junction of Y and Macukovo ravines, crossed to Bangor Ravine and swept back through the village towards the Battalion line, hoping to capture the party. But unfortunately the Bulgarians had already retired to a safer position.

An unfortunate accident occurred during this tour when a Stokes trench mortar exploded, killing Lieutenant Gibbons, Royal Engineers, and two men, and wounding three others—

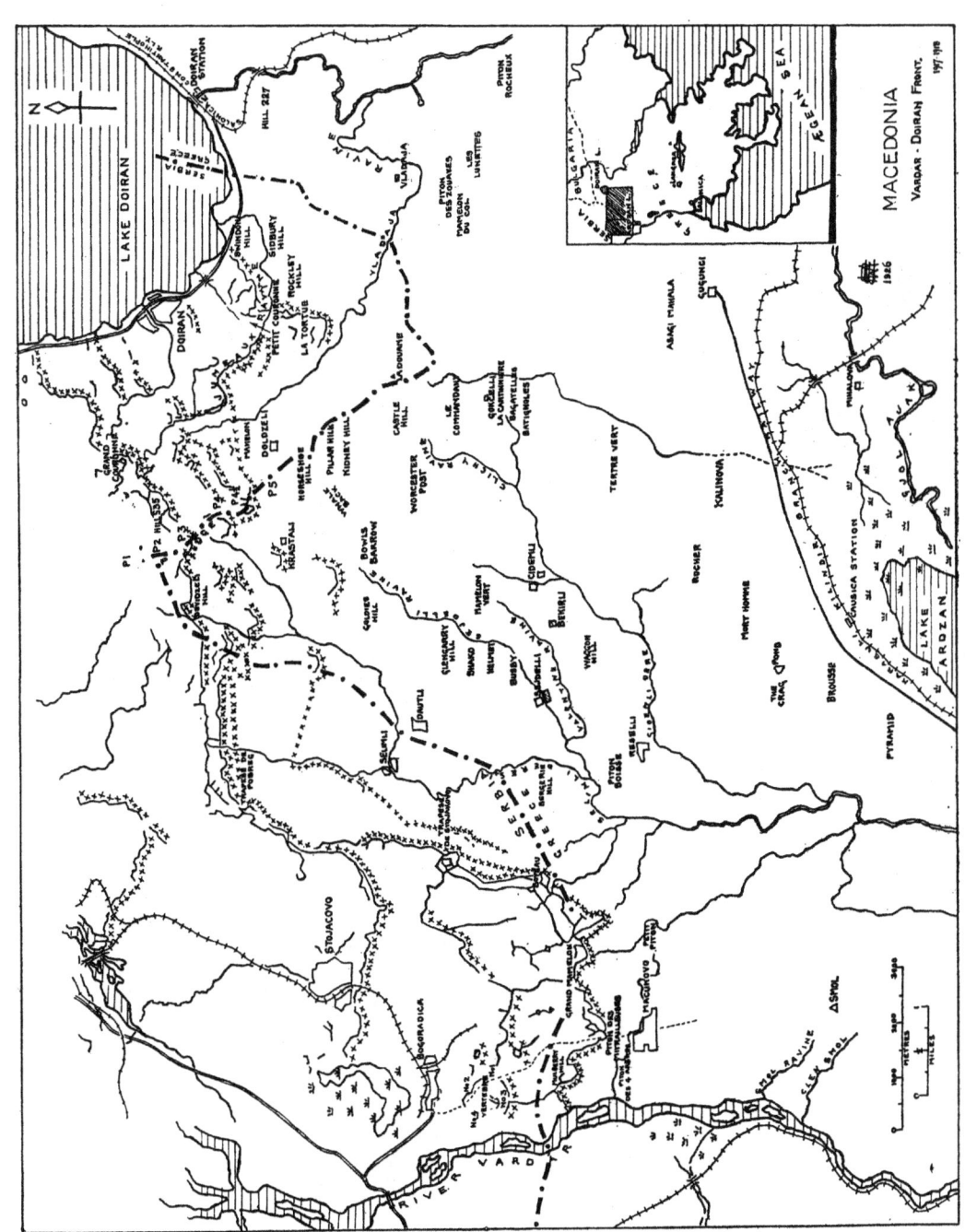

TRENCH WARFARE, KALINOVA, AUGUST, 1917

one of the men killed being Private Campbell, attached to the 77th Trench Mortar Battery. Another night a patrol of fourteen men, under Second Lieutenant Taylor-Lowen, went out at dawn, remaining all day in the ravine north of One Tree Hill, so as to reach Piton des Quatre Arbres before the enemy's garrison should arrive. They were successful in getting there, but found no enemy, and after being fired on from another spot they returned to the line. On the 1st of August the 9th Battalion Gloucester Regiment (78th Brigade) relieved the 10th, which then moved back to Divisional reserve at Gully Ridge south-east of Oreovica, where some tactical schemes were practised. After a fortnight at Gully Ridge the 10th moved to Kalinova in motor lorries, and relieved the 7th Battalion Wiltshire Regiment in I Sector.

This was the quietest part of the front between the Vardar and Lake Doiran, as the enemy's line, after forming a re-entrant, owing to the flatness of the ground in front, ran back to the Trapeze de Pobreg. Battalion Headquarters were at Bekirli. The right company held H. 24 to H. 32 with advanced posts on Shako, Helmet and Busby Hills; the centre company had an advanced post at Round Hill with numerous small isolated bombing posts, and the line of the left company ran to AI. 16. It was not a good position, so it was decided to dig a new line from Busby Hill towards Wagon Hill, thus straightening out a deep re-entrant held by the centre company. During the afternoon of August 18th a fire broke out in Salonika which eventually destroyed nearly a square mile of the town. It started in the Turkish quarter, and there seems little doubt that it was due to enemy action.

The Battalion went back into the line in I Sector on August 19th, and for three days and nights rain fell steadily, causing considerable discomfort and endless work on the trenches. A company at Wagon Hill on the left was shelled, chiefly by 8-inch guns, on two successive days; the range proved so accurate on the second day that the company moved to a narrow ravine on the south-west of the hill. Patrols were sent out across the Selimli Deresi to the enemy's advanced posts in front of the Trapeze de Stojakovo, but found them empty. During the tour a three days' bombardment of the enemy lines was carried out. This drew some fire from the enemy, but the Battalion was fortunate in losing only two men killed and four wounded in the fortnight during which it occupied the lines.

While the Battalion was in the line Major T. Cunningham, D.S.O., Cameron Highlanders, assumed command of the Battalion, replacing Lieutenant-Colonel Harvey, who had been invalided. Second Lieutenant A. E. Boyd also joined and was

THE TENTH BATTALION THE BLACK WATCH

posted to A company. Lieutenant-Colonel John Harvey had served throughout the South African War with the 2nd Battalion The Black Watch. His wide experience, high sense of duty and knowledge of regimental custom made his loss keenly felt both among officers and men of the 10th.

Parties of about twelve malaria patients were now frequently sent for a fortnight to a rest camp at Kara Burun, south of Salonika, and to Janes Convalescent Camp; officers were also sent for a similar period to Stavros. This change had an excellent effect on the health of the Battalion.

On August 27th work was begun on the new line, and the next night Lieutenant R. H. Ross and a small party took up a position in the gully at the north end of Bergerie to observe the wire cutting on Boyau Hill. But at daybreak they found they had to crawl forward 300 yards in the open before they could see the wire near Boyau Hill. At nightfall they were relieved by Second Lieutenant A. S. McKenzie, who was also unable to locate any gaps. The next day the wind was so high that the bombardment was stopped during the morning, and by the time it recommenced in the afternoon the enemy's aeroplanes were busy in great numbers and their howitzers, firing from the direction of Grand Mamelon, sent about sixty shells round a battery on Bastille. The following night the Scottish Rifles relieved the Battalion, which again became Divisional reserve at Dache Camp, some 300 feet above the ruined village of Kalinova.

At the end of August the ration strength of the Battalion was 26 officers and 865 other ranks as against 27 officers and 730 other ranks at the beginning of the month, and the following figures, taken from admissions to Field Hospitals, show how the amount of sickness varied in the summers of 1916 and 1917.

Month.	Admissions.	Average Ration Strength.	Percentage.
June, 1916	47	860	5·5
June, 1917	59	770	7·6
July, 1916	79	800	9·8
July, 1917	101	769	13·1
August, 1916	99	725	13·6
August, 1917	76	815	9·3

The rise in July, 1917, was probably caused by the insanitary state of the camp at Kalabak. The fall in August, 1917, showed a distinct improvement, largely due to sanitation and the general use of mosquito nets.

CHAPTER V

SEPTEMBER, 1917, TO JULY, 1918

Salonika

ON September 5th the Argyll and Sutherland Highlanders in J sector on the left were ordered to make a raid on Boyau Hill, and the 10th was detailed to distract the enemy's attention. Colonel Cunningham therefore prepared a scheme to make a demonstration against one of the works in the enemy outpost line, about 200 yards south-east of the Pyramide. This work adjoined the Trapeze de Stojakovo, and was about half a mile on the far side of the Selimli Deresi. The force detailed was two officers and 40 men, with one officer and 40 other ranks acting as a right flank guard for the main operation on the left. The general idea of the demonstration was to enter and wreck the work if the opposition was not too strong. As there was to be no artillery preparation on the wire, the orders were not to risk heavy casualties, but to make the necessary diversion with rifle grenades.

It was pitch dark on the night of the raid, but the Battalion was in position by Zero hour, which had been fixed for about 10 p.m. There was considerable delay, as the rocket did not go up till after 11 p.m. Meantime, while waiting for the signal, Lieutenant Bushe with three men had crawled forward with Bangalore torpedoes to within fifteen yards of the wire, and was lying waiting to blow the gaps for his men to rush through. Unfortunately the enemy, hearing movements on the right flank, where the 22nd Division were operating against Selimli, sent up two Very lights, which fell amongst his men, and rifle shots were fired in their direction. Lieutenant Bushe thereupon, thinking they had been seen, ordered up the torpedoes, two of which were successfully fired; this caused the enemy posts on his left to start firing. As the barrage had not yet started, Bushe decided not to try and enter the work, so after firing a volley and exploding two Stokes mortar bombs in the wire, he withdrew about two hundred and fifty yards under cover of the rifle grenades. At this moment the rocket went up, and the barrage on Boyau began, whereupon the party again advanced to within sixty yards of the wire and opened fire with rifles and rifle grenades on the garrison. The enemy replied with rifle and machine gun fire from their main line trenches, and put down a heavy barrage in front of the Pyramide, causing The Black Watch party to withdraw to the Selimli Deresi. Four men were wounded, and the party acting as flank guard to the Argyll and Sutherland Highlanders came in about an hour later with one man killed and three wounded. The following night the Battalion moved back to the Crag.

THE TENTH BATTALION THE BLACK WATCH

Training continued at Dache Camp till September 17th, when the Battalion relieved the Scottish Rifles in I Sector. Here, as usual, much work was done in improving the trenches and blasting dug-outs out of the solid rock. The orchards were all heavily wired on the front of this sector, and protective wire was placed from Busby Hill down to I. 14, the wire running immediately behind Sejdelli village, where a night post was established.

As the Scottish Rifles had reported that an enemy patrol of about seventy men had been met along the Selimli Deresi the night before the relief, the 10th sent out patrols every night to reconnoitre the area, but without success. On the 19th Lieutenant D. Tainsh rejoined from hospital and the following officers joined the Battalion: Lieutenants E. G. Pitcairn and J. M. Dewar, and Second Lieutenants R. H. C. Ewart and F. W. Cronne. By the last day of the month the advanced line had been so much improved that the right company moved up to Helmet Hill, the centre company was sent to Little Bekirli, and the reserve company was split up, with two platoons at Battalion Headquarters and two at Mamelon Vert, in support to the right company. The health of the Battalion showed a marked improvement since 1916; the strength was now 887. On October 1st Lieutenant E. R. Wilson, who had been wounded and gained his M.C. at Loos, and Second Lieutenant D. R. McLaren joined the Battalion.

After a very quiet tour the 10th moved back on October 4th to Division reserve at Dache Camp. Here it was employed on road-making, A and B companies moved to a temporary camp at Grand Ravine, and C and D companies went to the Crag for night work on the K. 2 trenches.

About the middle of the month sickness suddenly increased. After the heat of the summer the health of the troops was easily affected by changes in temperature, and many men were unable to do a hard day's work. For example, a three mile march with packs caused about a third of the Battalion to fall out, and the medical officer reported officially that it would be a month before the majority of these men would be fit for duty. In consequence of this, extra transport was sent from the Division to carry packs on all moves.

At this time the 10th suffered a severe loss, as Captain I. C. Sanderson, who had been adjutant since the Battalion left England, went to Egypt to join the Flying Corps. Few battalions have had a more popular and efficient adjutant. He was succeeded by Captain E. G. Phillips, and Captain McLaren took over the command of A company.

The health of the Battalion now slowly improved, but malaria

TRENCH WARFARE, DECEMBER, 1917

was still prevalent, and there were also many cases of "Mediterranean sores," chiefly on the hands and knees, although these were not so serious as in the previous year. Several officers were admitted to hospital about this time, including Captain E. R. Wilson and Lieutenants Dewar, H. Graham, W. Laurence, R. H. Ross and T. Mackenzie; and Second Lieutenant P. V. Lowe left for Egypt on transfer to the Flying Corps. By the middle of the month the weather became colder, and winter clothing was issued, including leather jerkins, though the third blanket per man was not yet drawn on account of the difficulties of transport. The average daily sick parade at this camp was about eighty men. The work during the fortnight in reserve was chiefly roadmaking near Kalinova, and the men were glad to return to the same sector on November 21st.

On the night of December 4th Second Lieutenants R. Ewart and B. Mackinnon, with a party of forty men of A company and flanking parties, raided the same enemy post which C company had attacked a month earlier. The time fixed for the raid was 11 p.m., at which hour the Royal Scots Fusiliers on the left were to raid another post about two hundred yards south-east of Boyau Hill. Mackinnon's party, Sergeant Curran and eight men, successfully worked their way round to the rear of the post, and after cutting two belts of wire by hand they entered the work at the very moment the sentry was starting to light his artillery barrage signal; on the right Ewart found the wire was very strong and the enemy succeeded in escaping back to their main line before the raiders reached the work. The whole party withdrew safely, bringing back one prisoner and having killed four of the garrison before the barrage came down. The success of this small operation brought a telegram of congratulation from the Commander-in-Chief.

The Battalion was relieved and moved to the Crag on the 6th, where it remained for a fortnight working on a new second line of defence, chiefly on the Pyramide and Mort Homme. As this line was overlooked by The Nose, most of the work had to be done at night, and as the weather was bitterly cold, with a freezing Vardar wind, it was not pleasant.

On December 19th the 10th moved to J Sector, relieving the Argyll and Sutherland Highlanders, and having the French "Premier Regiment de Marche" on the left. The line had been altered considerably since the Battalion first took it over in June from the 60th Division. The forward positions of the right company had been abandoned as being too wet to hold in winter; the centre company held Piton Boise, and the left company AK. 2. The company commanders at this time were: A, Captain H. A. F. McLaren, M.C.; B, Captain

THE TENTH BATTALION THE BLACK WATCH

E. R. Wilson, M.C.; C, Captain G. Rusk and D, Captain P. B. Hepburn.

While in this sector the following awards were published: Sergeant J. Curran, A company, was awarded the M.M. for gallantry in the raid of December 4th, and the following were mentioned in General Milne's despatch under date of November 25th, 1917. Colonel John Harvey, Major M. W. Gloag, Captain J. B. Caldwell, Captain P. Stormonth-Darling, Regimental Sergeant-Major Christie, Sergeant A. Weir, Pioneer Sergeant, Sergeant G. Briddick, Transport Sergeant, Private B. Elbra, the Brigade Acting Quartermaster-Sergeant, and Private 7860 A. Jamieson.

Christmas Day passed very quietly in the line, all celebrations for that day and the New Year being postponed until the Battalion should be relieved. The last week of 1917 was uneventful, though much rain necessitated constant work on the trenches. New Year, 1918, was ushered in by a salvo from the artillery, to which the enemy at once replied.

On coming out of the line on the night of January 2nd the Battalion returned to Divisional reserve at the Crag, and Major C. S. Nairne, of the Seaforths, took over command of the 10th, Major T. L. Cunningham, D.S.O., becoming Second-in-Command. The next two days were held as Christmas and New Year holidays, and large parties from the Battalion attended the Brigade and Divisional pantomimes.

About this time Captain K. S. MacRae was appointed adjutant of the New Army Training School at Akbunar, and Captain W. A. Carswell and Lieutenant Grey, M.C., were admitted to hospital. The celebrations in connection with the New Year were somewhat spoilt by a bitterly cold wind and continuous blizzard which lasted for two days and made cooking in the open almost impossible. The work during the tour of " rest " consisted of digging a " Bastion " line, putting men through the gas chamber and washing and disinfecting clothes and blankets.

The Regimental football team defeated the Argyll and Sutherland Highlanders by one goal in the first round of the Corps competition. In the second round the Battalion played three matches against the Royal Scots Fusiliers, each match ending in a draw. In February the match was replayed and the Battalion was defeated.

On taking over from the Argyll and Sutherland Highlanders in the same sector as before, the trench strength was 643 out of a total ration strength, including transport, of 840.

A new convalescent camp was formed about this time at Gramatna, and a more important scheme was also started by which men suffering from chronic malaria and cachexia were sent

TRENCH WARFARE

to England, to be drafted when sufficiently recovered to the Western Front. Under this scheme 30,000 malaria patients were sent home between January and October.

In January the Divisional Commander inspected the transport lines and said that the Battalion transport was the smartest he had seen in the Division. Unfortunately, a day or two later, one man and 11 mules were killed, and several mules wounded by two shells which burst in the lines. About this time Lieutenant-Colonel J. Harvey was awarded the D.S.O., and Captain E. G. Phillips the M.C.

The fortnight in the line, ending in a relief by the Argyll and Sutherland Highlanders on January 31st, was quiet. Four men were wounded when working on the wire, but the work was successfully done. During the month three officers and 40 men were admitted to hospital, and four officers and 91 other ranks rejoined; sickness was now almost entirely confined to malaria.

As usual, when in reserve, after two days' cleaning and resting, work again started under the Royal Engineers; this consisted of six hours' digging by day on fortified bastions, or digging and wiring for four hours by night. On February 10th the Battalion relieved the Argyll and Sutherland Highlanders in J Sector: A company on the left, B on the right and D at Piton Boise; C company having one platoon in support with the other three in reserve at Headquarters. The strength of each company was about 170.

About a week after taking over the sector snow began to fall for the first time since the previous winter. The snow fell for seventy-four hours and all paths and roads were obliterated, making transport work at night extremely difficult. All available men were employed on clearing the trenches and roads and scarcely a shell was fired by either British or enemy artillery for three days. Patrols were out constantly under Lieutenant Noble and Sergeant Carmichael, who wore white smocks, which proved very serviceable in the snow.

When the snow melted on February 24th the trenches were in a terrible state, many of the sand-bag revetments having collapsed and every dug-out being flooded. A company was lucky in losing only one man wounded by shrapnel fire which two minutes earlier would have caught a group of 40 men waiting for dinner to be served. Reinforcements for this month were one officer and 148 other ranks, and 49 men were evacuated sick. After three and a half weeks in the line the 10th was relieved by the Argyll and Sutherland Highlanders and went back to the Crag. The Battalion guard at Division Headquarters was relieved by the 9th Battalion Gloucester Regiment, and the General Officer Commanding wrote saying that he had been much impressed by its smartness and excellent turn-out, which had been a credit to the Battalion and to the Division. On this occasion the tour in reserve lasted for three weeks, Battalion training being carried out every morning. A draft of 33 men arrived, of whom nine had served with the Battalion before; the remainder came from France, Palestine and England. Lieutenant D. C. Thomson, C company, left to take up the appointment of adjutant, Officers' Rest Camp, at Stavros.

On March 20th the Battalion formed a guard of honour at Karasouli for the presentation of medals by the General Officer Commanding. Captains E. G. Phillips and H. A. F. McLaren received the M.C., and Sergeant J. Curran the M.M. About this time Christie, a most capable and popular sergeant-major, received a well-earned commission in the Battalion, and went to England on leave, being succeeded by Company Quartermaster-Sergeant Carstairs.

During the three weeks' training the Battalion practised a trench-to-trench attack on spit-locked trenches near Mihalova, and each company watched a trench mortar and Vickers machine gun overhead barrage demonstration. Platoon football matches and bomb-throwing competitions were also carried out.

In bitterly cold weather the 10th relieved the Royal Scots Fusiliers in I sector on March 30th; B company occupying the right at Helmet Hill, C the centre at Little Bekirli, and D the left at Lang Toon, with A in reserve. After the 11th Battalion Worcester Regiment, 78th Brigade, had relieved the French troops on the left of J Sector earlier in the month, that Brigade held the line right up to the Vardar, and I and J Sectors consequently became the right sub-section of the 26th Division area, while the battalion out of the line at the Crag was now in reserve to the Division instead of to the Corps. Before going into the line a draft of 22 men had arrived, raising the Battalion strength to 19 officers and 691 other ranks, exclusive of the transport and band; 44 men were admitted to hospital during the last week, mostly with malaria.

Since the Battalion had last occupied the line much work had been carried out, and the sector was far more comfortable than it was before. The tour was exceptionally quiet, and the Battalion was relieved on April 17th by the Argyll and Sutherland Highlanders, after which it moved to Grand Ravine in Brigade reserve. During the next fortnight C and D companies were employed in wiring and working on a fresh trench system, the remainder being occupied in sanitation work. By the end of the month summer clothing was issued and the usual steps were taken to guard against flies and mosquitoes, fly-proof mess huts, recreation huts and shelters were built. On April 29th

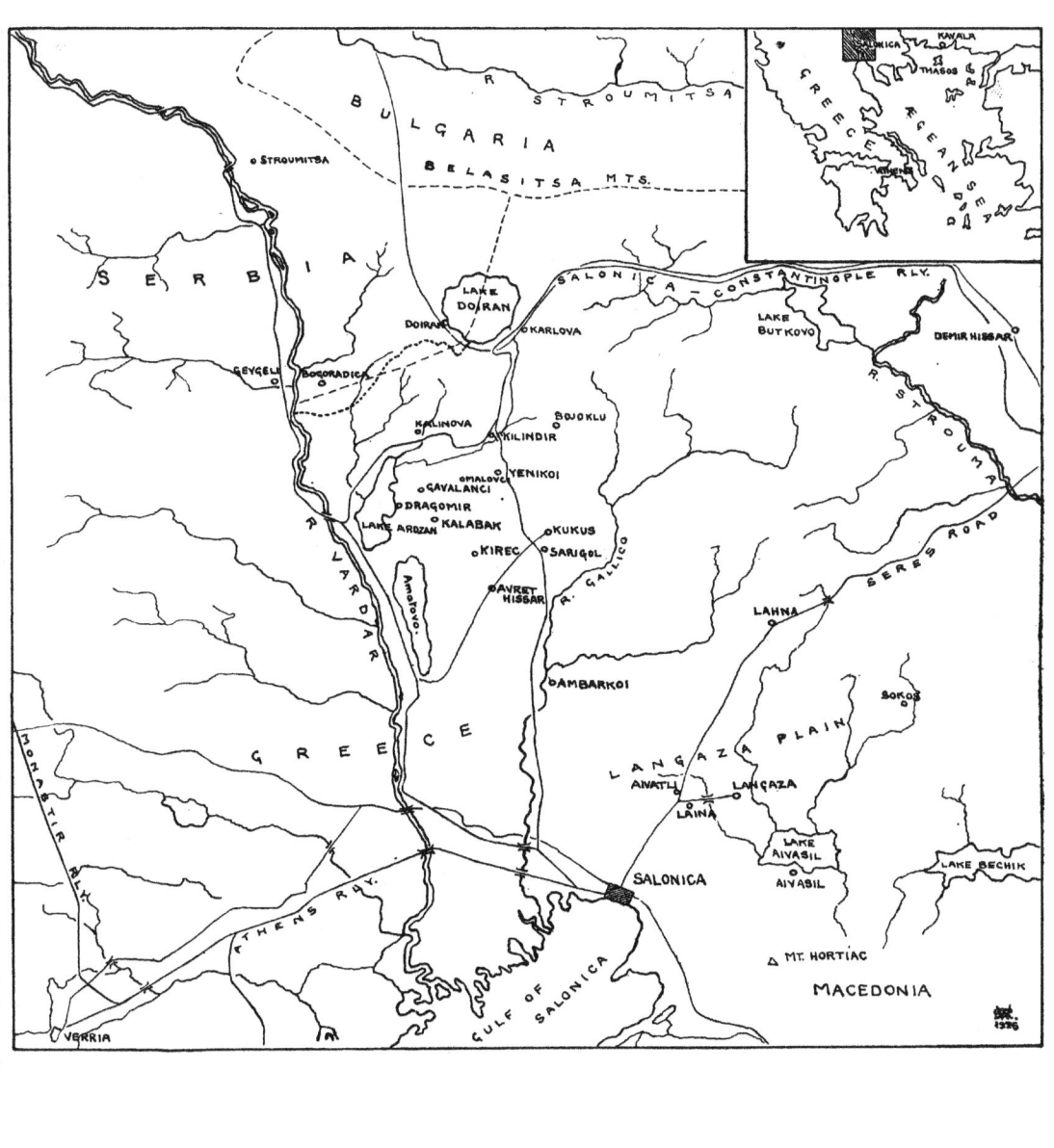

RAID ON BOYAU HILL, MAY 7TH, 1918

Major Cunningham—who had commanded the Battalion from the date of Colonel Harvey's departure till the arrival of Colonel Nairne—left Salonika to attend a senior officers' course in England.

On May 2nd the 10th relieved the Royal Scots Fusiliers in J Sector and one company of the 10th Devons at K. 6. After a few days in the line plans were made for a raid on three enemy outposts in front of Boyau Hill, in conjunction with a similar operation by the Fusiliers near the Trapeze de Stojkovo on May 7th. Owing to the strength of the enemy wire this operation was not successful, and was again attempted ten days later. On the second occasion the wire was successfully blown up, but the enemy heard the raiders approaching and retired on their support line. The 10th lost four men killed, two wounded and one missing in the two raids.

Towards the end of May Captain P. Stormonth-Darling rejoined the Battalion, and took over the duties of Second-in-Command. Second Lieutenant J. Walker also joined during May. On its return to the Crag Camp on May 21st the 10th was again engaged on work in the support line, chiefly in wiring at night. On May 25th the 26th Division opened a three days' horse show, which in spite of the intense heat was extremely well managed. The Battalion won first prize for officers' chargers, the best pair of pack mules and the Lloyd-Lindsay competition.

Early in June a new offensive had begun on the hills northwest of Guevgueli where, by June 3rd, three Greek and two French Divisions with a large number of guns and aeroplanes had gained all their objectives on a six-kilometre front to an average depth of one and a half kilometres, capturing 25 Bulgarian officers and 1500 other ranks, their own casualties being very heavy. They also captured the mountain crest at Skra Di Legen, a supreme achievement as the first action on a large scale of the new Greek army.

When the Battalion relieved the Royal Scots Fusiliers in J and K Sectors on June 2nd, the reserve company moved into K. 2. The chief work there consisted of placing layers of stones and cement on the roofs of bomb-proofs and making doors proof against mosquitoes. The June *Gazette* published the following awards: M.C., Lieutenant B. Mackinnon; D.C.M. to Lieutenant Christie and Scout-Sergeant Carmichael, for splendid work on many occasions in No Man's Land; M.S.M. to Private Souter.

After an uneventful tour in the line the Battalion was relieved on the night of June 12th by the Royal Scots Fusiliers, and after staying a night at Crag Camp moved the following

THE TENTH BATTALION THE BLACK WATCH

evening by motor lorries to Corps reserve at Kirec, where it took over from the 12th Hampshire Regiment. For some time before this it had been rumoured that one battalion from each Infantry Brigade was to be withdrawn and would move to France to fill the gaps caused by the German offensive in March. These rumours proved correct, and on June 14th the 10th Battalion The Black Watch was ordered to hand in all khaki drill clothing and received serge tunics, kilts and greatcoats; the other two battalions chosen being the 7th Battalion Wiltshire Regiment and 9th Battalion Gloucester Regiment.

All spare ammunition and stores were handed in, and on June 24th Major-General Sir A. Gray inspected the Battalion and presented the M.C. to Lieutenant Mackinnon, the D.C.M. to Sergeant Carmichael and the M.M. to Sergeant Roy. A few days later the 10th received orders to proceed to Sarigol. On June 29th Lieutenant Brook, the quartermaster, with an advance party of twenty men, left for Sarigol, followed the next night by the Battalion. After spending two very hot days at Sarigol the Battalion, under Colonel Nairne, moved to Bralo rest camp, travelling thence in forty-three lorries by road to Itea. The country was of extraordinary beauty and interest, and will never be forgotten by those who took part in that journey. The rest camp was pitched on a bare rocky slope, a few miles from Delphi, in a magnificent gorge running almost into the heart of the Parnassus. Only a few hours were spent here; the Battalion embarked on the French transport *Odessa* at midnight, and left at 4 a.m. on the 6th for Italy.

CHAPTER VI

JULY, 1918, TO OCTOBER, 1918

France

ON arrival at Taranto on July 7th the 10th disembarked in lighters and went to the Cimino rest camp, where orders were received to entrain that evening for Serqueux. The day was spent in a hot and dusty camp, but a welcome relief was found in sea-bathing. Second Lieutenants J. H. Fraser, P. Low and R. D. J. Pollexfen joined the Battalion here. Faenza was reached on the evening of the 9th, and after being well entertained at the rest camp that night the Battalion marched through the town before resuming its journey. Another halt was made at Ventimiglia on the French frontier, where one man was drowned when bathing. Travelling by Nice and Marseilles the Battalion eventually reached Abancourt on July 14th, and marched to the rest camp. For the first two days heavy thunderstorms burst at intervals, and as the whole Battalion was under quinine treatment, training was limited to short route marches and special courses of Lewis gun classes, as the establishment of the latter in France was thirty-two guns against sixteen in Salonika. The 10th was now under the administration of the 50th Division, the Battalion strength being 34 officers and 901 other ranks.

As there were still about 350 men who originally went overseas with the Battalion in 1915 who had had no leave to England, parties of four left daily on fourteen days' leave to the United Kingdom. On July 21st the 10th moved to Serqueux, about twelve miles away, where it joined the 197th Infantry Brigade under Brigadier-General L. L. Wheatley; Major-General H. K. Bethell, with the 66th Division Headquarters, was at Gaillefontaine. The other battalions forming the Brigade were the 14th Liverpool Regiment, 5th Connaught Rangers and 6th Royal Dublin Fusiliers. The remaining brigades in the Division were the 198th and 199th. The base Depot was at Calais, and Sergeant Peters, who had been the Battalion orderly room sergeant since Sutton Veny, joined the 3rd echelon at Rouen. The daily routine consisted of three hours' work in the morning and one in the afternoon, with route marches under company arrangements on alternate days, and every man was in some measure trained as a Lewis gunner under the supervision of Lieutenant Laurence. Gas training was also carried out, and all ranks were refitted with box respirators. For the first time since July, 1916, the 10th was able to organize a Battalion officers' mess.

After a week in this camp influenza broke out, and about

fifteen men were sent to hospital daily; many others were only fit for light duty, and by the end of the month the trench strength had diminished to 22 officers and 662 other ranks. August brought no improvement, and owing to bad weather and thunderstorms the camp became a sea of mud, and the transport lines were even worse. Every fourth day the Battalion was battalion on duty, when little training could be done.

On August 5th Lieutenant B. B. Mackinnon, M.C., a most efficient and popular officer, died at No. 2 Red Cross Hospital at Rouen to the deep sorrow of all officers and men. On August 6th Major-General Bethell inspected the Battalion in full marching order. Before the end of the month several new officers had reported their arrival and were posted as follows: Second Lieutenant J. McNeil to A company, Second Lieutenant Gyle to B, Steuart and Keltie to C, and Gilbert to D company; Captain the Reverend J. Rae also joined as chaplain, and Lieutenant Rowan, who had been sent to the Battalion for a short time in Salonika, rejoined; Major Cameron left for Salonika to resume his duties with the Army Service Corps.

Brigade sports were held, in which the Battalion won the cross-country race; unfortunately, Colonel Nairne fractured his collar-bone when running in the Staff relay race; he was sent to hospital, and was never able to rejoin the Battalion. Colonel Nairne had made himself very popular among all ranks of the 10th, and his loss was greatly regretted. Second Lieutenant M. McArthur, D.C.M., who had been wounded in May, when Company Sergeant-Major of B company, rejoined, and seventy-five malaria patients who had left the Battalion in Salonika returned from the Curragh Camp, Dublin.

The 10th, with the rest of the 197th Brigade, moved to Abancourt on September 17th. Three days later Major-General Bethell again visited the Battalion and gave warning that the 10th would probably be disbanded in order to reinforce the 1st, 6th and 14th Battalions of the Regiment; two companies would be sent to the 1st Battalion, one company to the 6th and one to the 14th Battalion The following day the Battalion marched to Haudricourt. All transport and animals were handed over at Abbeville and surplus regimental equipment was sent to the Base, as all men leaving the Battalion were to proceed as ordinary drafts.

On September 29th orders were received that the 10th was to send one complete company next morning to each of the following Battalions of The Black Watch: 1st Battalion, 1st Brigade, 1st Division; 1/6th Battalion, 51st Division; 14th Battalion (late Fife and Forfar Yeomanry), 74th Division. Arrangements for this were immediately made.

DISBANDMENT, SEPTEMBER, 1918

B and C companies were amalgamated and moved to Romescamp in the afternoon. A company, under Captain H. A. F. McLaren, M.C., joined the 6th Battalion, with Lieutenants J. M. Dewar, H. Graham, D. McDowall, J. H. Fraser and Second Lieutenant M. J. McArthur, D.C.M., also Company Sergeant-Major Watson and Company Quartermaster-Sergeant Horn. B and C companies, under Captain G. A. Rusk with Captain E. R. Wilson, M.C., Lieutenants W. Wilson, D.C.M., W. F. Bushe, A. F. Ritchie, Second Lieutenant D. C. Christie, D.C.M., Company Sergeant-Major Gordon and Company Quartermaster-Sergeant Watson joined the 1st Battalion; and D company, under Lieutenant W. T. Laurence with Lieutenants R. H. C. Ewart, A. S. McKenzie, R. H. Ross, G. F. Taylor-Lowen, Second Lieutenant F. R. Gilbert, M.M., Company Sergeant-Major White and Company Quartermaster-Sergeant Malcolm joined the 14th Battalion.

This left Battalion Headquarters with 13 officers and about 170 other ranks, of whom nearly one-third were sick or detained by the medical officer, in addition to five officers and 66 other ranks attached to the 197th Brigade, L.T.M. Battery.

A copy of the following letter from the Commander-in-Chief addressed to Lieutenant-General Sir J. J. Asser, K.C.M.G., C.B., Commanding Lines of Communication area, with reference to the disbandment was received:

" GENERAL HEADQUARTERS,
" BRITISH ARMIES IN FRANCE,
" *20th September*, 1918.

" MY DEAR ASSER,

" 1. The heavy fighting which has taken place since the
" 21st March, and the question of man power generally, had
" rendered it impossible to maintain all the units which were
" in the Field when the operations commenced this Spring.
" It has, therefore, been necessary to disband some battalions
" entirely.

" 2. I fully realize how deeply officers and men will feel the
" disbandment of battalions with which they have been so closely
" connected and which have rendered such valuable services in
" other theatres of war, and I know that since this reorganization
" is unavoidable, all ranks will accept it with a loyalty and devo-
" tion which has been conspicuous during every trial of the war.

" 3. I therefore wish you to convey to the officers, non-
" commissioned officers and men of these battalions my deep
" regret that this step should have been found necessary, and
" my great appreciation of the valuable service these battalions
" have rendered to the Allied Cause.

THE TENTH BATTALION THE BLACK WATCH

" 4. Will you further inform these battalions that they have
" not been selected for reduction or disbandment because they
" have fought any less gallantly than those still existing, but
" solely on account of the impossibility of their maintenance.
  " Yours very truly,
              "(Sgd.)   D. HAIG."

On October 10th the Trench Mortar Battery and Brigade Training School were broken up, the members rejoined their companies, and a mixed company of six officers and 177 other ranks proceeded the following day to the 1st Battalion The Black Watch. The officers were Captain P. B. Hepburn, Lieutenants H. H. Jalland, M. H. Noble, Second Lieutenants J. Walker, L. Urquhart, U. Stewart and E. W. Gyle. After 22 men had been sent to the malarial camp the following officers, Lieutenants A. W. Dickson, L. S. R. Stroyan, Second Lieutenants F. W. Keltie, G. Anderson, T. S. Tait, A. S. Milne, P. Low, G. H. Croucher, together with Sergeant-Major Carstairs and 27 other ranks were sent to the reinforcement camp at Calais on the 13th, leaving only A/Lieutenant-Colonel P. Stormonth-Darling, Captain E. G. Phillips, Adjutant and Quartermaster Lieutenant T. R. Brook and Regimental Quartermaster-Sergeant Stewart with the orderly room staff to carry out the disbanding of the Battalion.

When the first three companies left this camp on October 1st the following were those remaining of the original officers who left Sutton Veny in September, 1915: A/Lieutenant-Colonel P. Stormonth-Darling, Captains J. B. Caldwell, E. G. Phillips and H. A. F. McLaren. Three others had been commissioned since, namely: Quartermaster and Lieutenant R. T. Brook, Lieutenant A. F. Ritchie, and Second Lieutenant D. C. Christie. Of other ranks—Regimental Quartermaster-Sergeant Stewart, Company Sergeant-Major Watson, A company, Company Sergeant-Major Gardner, B company, Company Sergeant-Major Gordon, C company, Company Sergeant-Major White, D company, Company Quartermaster-Sergeant Horn, A company, Company Quartermaster-Sergeant Heron, B company, Company Quartermaster-Sergeant Watson, C company, Company Quartermaster-Sergeant Malcolm, D company—the latter having held his rank the whole time—and 26 sergeants, 22 corporals, 16 lance-corporals and 243 privates.

On October 15th the disbandment of the Battalion was reported to the 197th Infantry Brigade. Colonel P. Stormonth-Darling went the next day to Étaples, Captain E. G. Phillips and the Quartermaster to Calais.

So ends the history of the 10th Battalion almost on the eve

CONCLUSION

of the Armistice. Looking back on it two points will strike the reader: the arduous years spent in Macedonia and the circumstances under which the Battalion was disbanded. Although the fighting was not on the same scale as in other theatres of the war, the conditions there made life very hard. The Salonika front was one of the most unhealthy. Officers and men suffered great hardships. The fierce summer heat, the winter's bitter cold, the myriads of flies and mosquitoes filled the hospitals and led to sickness, fever and death.

The second point was the disbanding of the Battalion. On the very eve of victory, barely a few days before their comrades began the final and successful advance against the Bulgarians, the 10th was transferred to France. Scarcely had the Battalion reached the Western front and settled down, eagerly looking forward to taking part in the last stages of the war, when Fate again stepped in and—for paramount reasons as shown in the Commander-in-Chief's letter to General Sir J. J. Asser—the 10th was one of those battalions selected for disbandment.

If this History contains no record of great battles nor of decisive operations on a scale equal to some on other fronts, none the less it is a tale of long and good service under most trying conditions; and it also shows that the spirit of discipline and determination which has ever been, and ever will be, the character of all Battalions of The Black Watch was ever present and active in the 10th.

APPENDIX I

Record of Officers' Service

Abbreviations :—" K."—Killed.   " D. of W."—Died of Wounds.
" W."—Wounded.   " M."—Missing.

THE TENTH BATTALION

Alexander, T. L. 2nd Lieut. *k.* 8th May, 1917.
Allenby, R. N. Capt. Attached from Seaforth Highlanders. To hospital 9th Sept., 1916. Joined August, 1916.
Allison, J. S. 2nd Lieut. Joined 3rd July, 1916. *d.* 18th Sept., 1917.
Anderson, G. 2nd Lieut. Joined 21st Aug., 1918. To Base details 13th Oct., 1918.
Anderson, P. W. Lieut. Transferred to R.F.C. 20th Nov., 1916.

Bassett, W. F. 2nd Lieut. Joined 31st Oct., 1915. *k.* 27th Oct., 1918. Attached 2nd Royal Scots.
Boyd, A. E. 2nd Lieut. Joined 23rd Oct., 1917. To hospital 10th Aug., 1918.
Brook, T. R. Lieut. and Q.M. Hon. Lieut. 3rd June, 1917.
Bushe, W. F. Lieut. To 1st Battn. 30th Sept., 1918.

Caldwell, J. B. Lieut. Went to France with Battn. Sept., 1915. Mentioned in Despatches 28th Nov., 1917. To 10th A. and S. Highlanders as Transport Officer 8th Oct., 1918.
Cameron, D. C. Major. Attached from general headquarters, Salonika, June, 1918.
Carswell, W. A. 2nd Lieut. Joined 13th Nov., 1916. *w.* 7th Jan., 1917. Promoted Capt. Rejoined Battn. To hospital 18th Oct., 1917. Promoted Major. Rejoined Battn. To Malta 3rd Jan., 1918. *d.* of *w.* March 21st, 1918.
Christie, D. C. A/R.S.M., D.C.M. Appointed 2nd Lieut. 24th March, 1918. To 1st Battn. 30th Sept., 1918.
Christie, G. W. Lieut. R.A.M.C. Went to France with Battn. Sept., 1915. To U.K. 8th June, 1916.
Cronne, F. W. 2nd Lieut. Joined 15th Sept., 1917. To hospital 18th Oct., 1917.
Croucher, G. H. 2nd Lieut. Joined May, 1917. To Base details 13th Oct., 1918. To 6th Battn.
Cruickshank, J. G. Lieut. Transferred to Indian Army 10th Feb., 1918.
Cunningham, T. L. Major. D.S.O. Joined 7th Jan., 1917. Assumed command of Battn. 31st Oct., 1917. Left Battn. for France April, 1918.

Denniston, J. E. 2nd Lieut. Went to France with Battn. Sept., 1915. Accidentally *w.* 15th Oct., 1915. *d.* of *w.* 20th Sept., 1916.
Dewar, J. M. 2nd Lieut. Joined 15th Sept., 1915. To hospital 8th Nov., 1917. Promoted Lieut. To 6th Battn. 30th Sept., 1918.
Dickson, A. W. Lieut. To Base details 13th Oct., 1918.
Dobbie, E. A. 2nd Lieut. Joined 3rd April, 1916.
Don, A. W. R. 2nd Lieut. Went to France with Battn. Sept., 1915. To hospital 19th July, 1916. *d.* of malaria 13th Sept., 1916.

THE TENTH BATTALION THE BLACK WATCH

Don, R. M. Lieut. Went to France with Battn. Sept., 1915. *k*. 8th May, 1917.

Drysdale, A. O. 2nd Lieut. Went to France with Battn. Sept., 1915.

Duffy, W. J. 2nd Lieut. Went to France with Battn. Sept., 1915. *w*. 28th Dec., 1916. Rejoined Battn. Awarded M.C. 4th June, 1917.

Ewart, R. H. C. 2nd Lieut. Joined 15th Sept., 1917. Promoted Lieut. To 14th Battn. 30th Sept., 1918.

Forgan, Lieut.

Fraser, J. H. 2nd Lieut. Joined 11th June, 1918. To 6th Battn. 30th Sept., 1918.

Gilbert, F. R. 2nd Lieut. M.M. Joined 25th Aug., 1918. To 14th Battn. 30th Sept., 1918.

Gloag, M. W. Capt. Went to France with Battn. Sept., 1915. Promoted Major. Mentioned in Despatches 28th Nov., 1917. To 26th Div. Staff 24th Feb., 1918.

Gordon, W. Major. Went to France Sept., 1915.

Gow, I. B. 2nd Lieut. Went to France with Battn. Sept., 1915. To hospital sick 30th Sept., 1915.

Graham, H. Lieut. Joined 4th Jan., 1917. Transferred to 1/7th Battn. 5th Oct., 1918.

Graham, H. B. 2nd Lieut. Joined 1st Aug., 1916. *k*. 9th May, 1917.

Grey, J. 2nd Lieut. Joined 13th Nov., 1916. Awarded M.C. May, 1917. To U.K. 3rd Jan., 1918.

Gyle, E. W. 2nd Lieut. Joined 17th Aug., 1918. To 1st Battn. 12th Oct., 1918.

Harvey, J. Major. Went to France with Battn. Sept., 1915. Mentioned in Despatches 28th Nov., 1917. Promoted Lieut.-Col. Awarded D.S.O. 1st Jan., 1918.

Hay, T. Capt.

Hebden, A. 2nd Lieut. Joined 3rd July, 1916. *w*. 25th Sept., 1916. Rejoined Battn. *m*. 8th May, 1917.

Hepburn, P. B. Lieut. Joined 13th Nov., 1916. Promoted Capt. To 1st Battn. 12th Oct., 1918.

Jalland, H. H. 2nd Lieut. Joined 12th Aug., 1916. To 1st Battn. 12th Oct., 1918. *k*. 18th Oct., 1918.

Keltie, F. W. 2nd Lieut. Joined 25th Aug., 1918. To Base details 13th Oct., 1918.

Kennard, A. Major.

Kirkpatrick, G. P. 2nd Lieut. Went to France with Battn. Sept., 1915.

Lamb, C. C. Major and Adj. No further details available.

Laurence, W. T. 2nd Lieut. Joined 13th June, 1916. To hospital 8th Nov., 1917. Promoted Lieut. To 14th Battn. 30th Sept., 1918.

Lithgow, E. M. Capt. Went to France with Battn. Sept., 1915.

Livingstone, J. N. F. Major. Joined 23rd Sept., 1915. To U.K. to War Office 20th May, 1916.

APPENDIX I

Low, P. 2nd Lieut. Joined 7th July, 1918. To Base details 13th Oct., 1918.
Lowe, P. V. Lieut. Transferred to R.F.C. 10th Nov., 1917.

Mackenzie, T. 2nd Lieut. To hospital 8th Nov., 1917.
Mackinnon, B. B. Lieut. Awarded M.C. 24th June, 1918. To hospital 23rd July, 1918. *d.* in hospital 6th Aug., 1918.
McLachlan, J. M. Lieut. and Q.M. Went to France with Battn. Sept., 1915. To U.K. 22nd April, 1916.
MacLeod, J. S. Capt. Went to France with Battn. Sept., 1915. Accidentally *w.* 15th Oct., 1915.
MacRae, K. S. Lieut. To Egypt 5th Feb., 1917. Promoted Capt.
McArthur, M. J. 2nd Lieut. D.C.M. Rejoined Battn. 15th Sept., 1918.
McCowan, P. K. Lieut. R.A.M.C. Joined Battn. 26th Sept., 1916.
Macdonald, M. 2nd Lieut. Went to France with Battn. Sept., 1915. *k.* 9th Oct., 1916.
McDowall, D. Lieut. Joined 13th Nov., 1917. To 9th Battn. Oct., 1918.
McKenzie, A. S. Lieut. Joined 15th Aug., 1917. To 14th Battn. 30th Sept., 1918.
McLaren, D. R. 2nd Lieut. Joined 1st October, 1917. Transferred to 8th Battn. 30th Sept., 1918.
McLaren, H. A. F. 2nd Lieut. Went to France with Battn. Sept., 1915. Awarded M.C. May, 1917. *w.* 8th May, 1917. Rejoined Battn. 11th July, 1917. Promoted Capt. 28th Jan., 1918. To 6th Battn. 30th Sept., 1918.
McLeod, J. 2nd Lieut. Joined 25th August, 1918.
McNeil, J. 2nd Lieut. To 66th Div. Staff 20th Sept., 1918.
Martin, W. M. 2nd Lieut. Went to France with Battn. Sept., 1915.
Mathieson, D. 2nd Lieut. Went to France with Battn. Sept., 1915. Promoted Lieut. To 74th Div. Staff.
Millar, D. A. 2nd Lieut. To U.K. 31st Aug., 1917.
Millar, R. C. H. Capt. Went to France with Battn. Sept., 1915. To hospital 27th May, 1916.
Milne, A. S. 2nd Lieut. To Base details 13th Oct., 1918.

Nairne, C. S. Major. Assumed command of Battn. 3rd Jan., 1918. Promoted Lieut.-Col. To hospital 15th Sept., 1918.
Nicol, C. A. Lieut. Went to France with Battn. Sept., 1915. To U.K. 21st April, 1916. Promoted Capt. *k.* 8th May, 1917.
Noble, M. H. N. A. 2nd Lieut. *w.* 8th May, 1917. Rejoined 28th June, 1917. To 1st Battn. 12th Oct., 1918.

O'Kelly, J. O. Lieut. R.A.M.C. Joined 13th Sept., 1916.

Phillips, E. G. M. 2nd Lieut. Went to France with Battn. Sept., 1915. Promoted Capt. Appointed Adj. 18th Oct., 1917. Awarded M.C. 1st Jan., 1918.
Pitcairn, E. G. Lieut. Joined 15th Sept., 1917. To 8th Battn. 30th Sept., 1918. *d.* of sickness 4th Oct., 1918.
Pollexfen, R. D. J. Joined from 3rd Battn. 7th July, 1918.

THE TENTH BATTALION THE BLACK WATCH

Rae, J. Capt. C.F. Joined 17th Aug., 1918.
Ritchie, A. F. A/R.S.M. Appointed 2nd Lieut. 15th Feb., 1917. To U.K. 22nd March, 1918. Rejoined Battn. To 1st Battn. 30th Sept., 1918.
Ross, R. H. 2nd Lieut. Joined Oct., 1916. Promoted Lieut. To 14th Battn. 30th Sept., 1918.
Rowan, A. N. Joined from 3rd Battn.
Rusk, G. A. Capt. Joined 12th April, 1917. To 1st Battn. 30th Sept., 1918. Awarded M.C.

Salmond, ———. Lieut. R.A.M.C. Joined Battn. 2nd Sept., 1916. To hospital 13th Sept., 1916.
Sanderson, I. C. Capt. and Adj. Went to France with Battn. Sept., 1915. Awarded M.C. 4th June, 1917. To R.F.C. 18th Oct., 1917. Rejoined Battn. 3rd March, 1918.
Scott, J. M. Lieut. Went to France with Battn. Sept., 1915.
Scott, R. J. L. 2nd Lieut. Went to France with Battn. Sept., 1915. To hospital 10th Oct., 1915.
Sheldon, B. P. Capt. Joined 3rd April, 1916.
Stewart, U. 2nd Lieut. Joined 25th Aug., 1918. Transferred to 1st Battn. 12th Oct., 1918.
Stewart, W. Capt. Went to France with Battn. Sept., 1915.
Stewart-Dick-Cunyngham, Sir W. S. Lieut.-Col. Went to France with Battn. Sept., 1915. Invalided to U.K. 1st Sept., 1916.
Stormonth-Darling, P. 2nd Lieut. Went to France with Battn. Sept., 1915. Promoted Capt. Mentioned in Despatches 28th Nov., 1917. Promoted Major. To 77th Infantry Brigade Headquarters Feb., 1917. Rejoined Battn. 15th May, 1918. To Base 28th Sept., 1918.
Stroyan, L. S. R. Gazetted Lieut. 1st July, 1917. To Base details 13th Oct. 1918.
Sturrock, J. P. Capt. Went to France with Battn. Sept., 1915. To U.K. to War Office 20th May, 1916.

Tainsh, D. Mac H. Lieut. Attached from Queen's Own Cameron Highlanders. Joined Sept., 1917.
Tait, T. S. Joined from 3rd Battn. To Base details 13th Oct., 1918.
Tatham, A. D. Lieut. To hospital sick 27th May, 1916.
Taylor-Lowen, G. F. Lieut. Joined April, 1917. To 14th Battn. 30th Sept., 1918.
Thomson, D. C. 2nd Lieut. w. 8th May, 1917. Rejoined Battn. 11th July, 1917. Left Battn. to take up duties of Adjt., Stavros, 12th March, 1918.

Urquhart, L. W. 2nd Lieut. Joined 12th Aug., 1916.

Walker, J. 2nd Lieut. Joined 15th May, 1918. To 1st Battn. 12th Oct., 1918.
Watson, J. M. 2nd Lieut. Transferred to R.F.C. 20th Nov., 1917.
Wilson, E. R. Lieut. Joined July, 1917. Promoted Capt. To hospital 8th Nov., 1917. To 1st Battn. 30th Sept., 1918.
Wilson, J. D. Lieut. R.A.M.C. Joined 11th June, 1916.
Wilson, W. (Commissioned 2nd Battn. June, 1915.) Joined 10th Battn. March, 1917. Transferred 1st Battn. 30th Sept., 1918.

APPENDIX II

SUMMARY OF CASUALTIES. THE TENTH BATTALION

The discrepancy between these figures and those given by the war diaries is accounted for by the fact that, save in the case of regular battalions, the diaries seldom give a record of casualties other than those suffered in main actions.

OFFICERS, 1914–18

Year.	Killed. D. of wounds. D. on service.	Wounded.	Missing.	Total.	Year.
1914	—	—	—	—	1914
1915	2	2	—	4	1915
1916	1	2	—	3	1916
1917	5	6	—	11	1917
1918	—	—	—	—	1918
Totals:	8	10	—	18	

OTHER RANKS, 1914–18

Year.	Killed. D. of wounds. D. on service.	Wounded.	Missing.	Total.	Year.
1914	—	—	—	—	1914
1915	9	—	—	9	1915
1916	18	2	2	22	1916
1917	80	309	0	389	1917
1918	15	—	—	15	1918
Totals:	122	311	2	435	

TOTAL:

Officers, 18. Other Ranks, 435.

APPENDIX III

CASUALTIES—OFFICERS

* Killed in action.   † Died of wounds.   § Died.

THE TENTH BATTALION

Name.	Rank.	Date.
Alexander, T. L.	2nd Lieut.	*8.5.17.
Allison, J. S.	Lieut.	§18.9.17
Bassett, W. F., M.C.	Lieut.	*27.10.18. Attd. 2nd R. Scots.
Browne, G. B.	2nd Lieut.	*7.2.16. Attd. 9th Battn.
Carswell, W. A., M.C.	Capt.	†21.3.18.
Denniston, J. E.	2nd Lieut.	†20.9.16. Attd. 1st Battn.
Don, A. W. R.	2nd Lieut.	†13.9.16.
Don, R. M.	Lieut.	*9.5.17.
Dow, R. M.	Lieut.	*8.5.17.
Dewar, J. M.	Lieut.	*14th Battn. Oct., 1918.
Ewart, R. H. C.	Lieut.	†16.10.18. Attd. 14th Battn.
Graham, H. B.	2nd Lieut.	*9.5.17. 3rd Battn.
Gyle, E. W.	2nd Lieut.	*1st Battn. Oct., 1918.
Hebden, A.	2nd Lieut.	*8.5.17. 6th Battn.
Jalland, H. H.	Lieut.	*1st Battn. Oct., 1918.
Mackinnon, B. B.	Lieut.	§5.8.18.
Macdonald, M.	Lieut.	*9.10.16.
McGregor, A. W.	2nd Lieut.	*27.2.16. Attd. 9th Battn.
Nicol, C. A.	Capt.	*8.5.17.
Robertson, W. S.	Lieut.	*3.9.16. Attd. 4/5th Battn.

APPENDIX IV

NOMINAL ROLL OF WARRANT OFFICERS, NON-COMMISSIONED OFFICERS AND MEN KILLED IN ACTION OR DIED OF WOUNDS OR DISEASE IN THE GREAT WAR, 1914–18

* Killed in action.   † Died of wounds.   ‡ Died at home.   § Died.

THE TENTH BATTALION

Allan, G., Pte., S/10902	§2.12.17	Hind, J., Pte., S/17460	* 9.5.17
Allan, H., Pte., S/8640	* 9.5.17	Hislop, W., Pte., S/5555	* 8.5.17
Anderson, R., L/Cpl., 3/3951	* 9.5.17	Hopwood, A. E., Cpl., S/14612	§21.10.18
Anderson, J., A/C.Q.M.S., S/5422	* 9.5.17	Howard, W. A., Pte., S/12776	* 9.5.17
Anderson, W. H., Pte., S/15489	* 9.5.17	Hume, H., Pte., S/11428	†21.10.17
		Hutchison, A., Pte., S/15054	†10.5.17
Baxter, A. M., Pte., S/6874	‡27.10.18	Inglis, W., Pte., S/5384	*14.10.15
Bolton, L., Pte., S/5565	*15.3.17	Inkster, T., L/Sgt., S/5630	§6.10.16
Brady, T., Pte., S/5774	‡21.6.15		
Bremner, D., Pte., S/5960	* 9.5.17	Johnstone, J., Pte., S/15099	* 9.5.17
Brunton, G., Pte., S/4967	* 9.5.17	Kennedy, D., Pte., S/13417	* 9.5.17
Campbell, J., Pte., S/...4	*26.7.17	Kennedy, J., Pte., S/6890	*5.11.16
Campbell, R. R., Pte., S/14612	*2.11.17	King, J., Pte., S/6936	* 9.5.17
Cooper, A., Pte., S/17438	* 8.5.17	Kinnear, J., Pte., 4106	‡30.9.18
Cuff, W. G., L/Cpl., S/4238	* 9.5.17	Kinnell, D., A/Cpl., S/6133	* 9.5.17
Culshaw, J., Pte., S/6058	* 9.5.17	Laing, A. M., Pte., S/7988	* 9.5.17
		Lauder, W., Pte., S/17960	* 9.5.17
Dalgetty, J., Pte., S/12880	† 2.7.17	Linklater, D., Pte., S/17933	†18.1.18
Dewar, A., Pte., S/4973	* 9.5.17	Livingston, A., Pte., S/17179	† 7.3.18
Dodds, W., Pte., S/6030	§31.1.18		
Duncan, A., Pte., S/12896	*10.10.16	MacKenzie, A., Pte., S/5521	* 9.5.17
Duthie, A., Pte., S/14542	* 9.5.17	MacKillop, A., L/Cpl., S/5866	§31.8.16
Edwards, P., Pte., 3/2579	* 8.5.17	MacNab, D., Pte., S/13380	* 9.5.17
		Macready, J., Pte., 240605	§20.9.17
Ferguson, D., Pte., S/16327	* 9.5.17	Martin, W., Pte., S/12558	†13.1.17
Fotheringham, D., Pte., S/5999	§13.9.16	McAulay, W., Pte., S/5500	§9.11.18
Fraser, P., Pte., S/17881	†10.5.17	McCorkindale, J., Pte., S/6160	*17.5.18
Fraser, R., Pte., S/14185	*25.4.17	McDougall, A., Pte., S/7871	§11.10.16
Frickleton, D., Pte., S/25465	†25.10.18	McDougall, D., Cpl., S/4789	§28.1.18
		McGill, R. W., Pte., S/5430	* 9.5.17
Garth, D., Pte., S/4985	* 9.5.17	McGregor, J., Pte., S/12868	* 9.5.17
Grant, J., Pte., S/17896	* 9.5.17	McGregor, J., L/Cpl., S/7350	* 9.5.17
Grier, G. C., Pte., S/13310	§6.11.17	McIntyre, H., Pte., S/17969	* 9.5.17
Gunn, R., L/Cpl., S/6104	* 9.5.17	McKay, D., Pte., S/4988	*16.10.15
		McKay, E. G., Pte., S/17629	§7.11.16
Halcrow, J., A/Sgt., S/5391	*10.10.16	McKendrick, G., Pte., S/6078	*24.10.15
Harkness, W., L/Cpl., S/7866	†14.10.16	McKendry, J., Pte., S/5276	*22.1.18
Harris, R., Pte., S/18477	§2.11.16	McKenzie, A., Pte., S/5082	* 9.5.17
Henchilwood, T., C.S.M., S/5619	* 9.5.17	McLaughlin, M., Pte., S/5553	†10.5.17
		McLeod, W., Pte., S/17860	‡ 8.7.17

263

THE TENTH BATTALION THE BLACK WATCH

McNeill, T., Pte., S/5696	*26.10.15	Rollo, W. D., Pte., S/13376	§19.10.16
McQuade, E., Pte., S/6181	†23.10.18	Ross, W., Pte., S/5223	§11.7.18
McWalter, E., Cpl., 2062	†13.5.17	Rowan, N., L/Sgt., S/5888	§13.10.15
Melville, J. M., Pte., S/5721	*1.10.16		
Millar, W., Sgt., S/3863	* 9.5.17	Salmond, J., Pte., S/5279	§23.7.16
Miller, R., Pte., S/17187	* 9.5.17	Simpson, A. M., Pte., S/9232	* 9.5.17
Mitchell, D. L., Pte., S/14039	§15.10.16	Skinner, W., Pte., S/5259	* 9.5.17
Murphy, R., Pte., S/6894	* 9.5.17	Sloan, E., Pte., S/14541	* 9.5.17
		Smith, W., Pte., S/6073	† 9.5.17
Nelson, W., L/Cpl., S/5430	†30.10.17	Spence, J. F., Pte., S/17924	* 9.5.17
Nelson, W., Pte., S/5598	* 9.5.17	Stein, D., Pte., 11419	* 9.5.17
Ness, J., Pte., S/12646	†10.5.17	Stevenson, W., Sgt., S/5554	* 8.5.17
		Stewart, C., Pte., S/5574	* 8.5.17
Ogilvy, J., Pte., S/6008	†18.10.15	Stewart, R., Pte., S/17981	* 9.5.17
Olding, J., Sgt., S/5447	§24.10.18	Strachan, W., Pte., 3/557	† 8.5.17
Owen, F., Pte., S/11768	§5.11.16		
		Thomson, J., Pte., S/5581	*1.10.16
		Turner, T. C., Pte., S/17332	* 9.5.17
Park, H. R., A/Cpl., S/5260	† 9.5.17	Turner, W., Pte., S/5608	* 9.5.17
Paterson, W., Pte., S/15908	* 9.5.17		
Patterson, R., Pte., S/16086	* 9.5.17	Walker, A., Pte., S/5610	* 9.5.17
Peters, J., Pte., S/6142	§ 6.5.17	Webster, W., Pte., S/13392	§27.2.17
Philipson, E., Pte., S/6906	*15.3.17	White, D. J., L/Cpl., S/13320	§20.10.16
Pugsley, A., L/Cpl., S/18479	*27.2.18	Wightman, T., Pte., S/14098	* 9.5.17
		Wood, R., Pte., S/12897	§19.10.16
Rennie, E., Pte., S/17994	* 9.5.17	Wright, R., Pte., S/7910	§18.8.16
Ritchie, J. C., Pte., S/6128	*22.10.15	Wright, W., Pte., S/5547	* 9.5.17
Robertson, D., Pte., S/12887	†16.6.17		
Robertson, D., Pte., S/5575	* 9.5.17	Younger, J. S., Pte., S/13342	* 9.5.17

APPENDIX V

HONOURS AND AWARDS

The Tenth Battalion

C.B.E.
Lieut.-Colonel Sir W. Stewart-Dick-Cunyngham, Bart.

D.S.O.
Lieut.-Colonel J. Harvey.
Major T. L. Cunningham.

M.C.
Lieut. W. J. Duffy.
2nd Lieut. J. Grey.
Lieut. B. B. Mackinnon.
Lieut. H. A. F. McLaren.
Capt. E. G. M. Phillips.
Capt. and Adjutant I. C. Sanderson.

D.C.M.
Sgt. Carmichael.
C.S.M. M. McArthur.
A/R.S.M. D. C. Christie.

M.S.M.
R.Q.M.S. J. T. Brook.
Pte. J. Souter.
R.Q.M.S. J. Stewart.

M.M.
Sgt. J. Curran.
Pte. J. Donelly.
Corpl. A. Gow.
L/Corpl. W. Hanson.
Sgt. E. Joss.
Pte. A. MacGowan.
Pte. W. Macpherson.
Corpl. W. Orr.
Sgt. Roy.
Pte. W. G. Stuart.

Mentioned in Despatches
Major M. W. Gloag.
Capt. J. B. Caldwell.
Sgt. G. Briddick.
Sgt. C. Carmichael.
R.S.M. W. Carstairs.
R.S.M. D. C. Christie.
Corpl. J. Cormack.
Q.M.S. S. B. Elbra.
Sgt. W. Gordon.
Lieut.-Colonel J. Harvey.
Capt. P. Stormonth-Darling.
Pte. G. Gray.
Corpl. J. Heron.
Pte. A. Jamieson.
L/Sgt. R. Morrison.
R.Q.M.S. J. Stewart.
Sgt. A. Weir.

FOREIGN DECORATIONS

Italian Croix de Guerre
Lieut.-Colonel Sir W. Stewart-Dick-Cunyngham, Bart.

Serbian Karageorge
Pte. W. G. Stuart.

APPENDIX VI

LIST OF ACTIONS AND OPERATIONS

THE TENTH BATTALION

1915. Landed in France. 21st September.

    Trench warfare. Proyart, Fontaine les Cappy, Carnoy. September–October.

    Left France. 12th November. Landed at Salonika. 24th November.

    Trench warfare. Aivatli. December.

1916. Trench warfare. Aivatli, Lake Doiran. January–August.

DOIRAN OPERATIONS, 1916. (Vladaja Line.) 9th August.

    Trench warfare. Kalinova, Jenikoi, Horsehoe Hill, Krastali, Clichy Ravine. August–September.

1917. Trench warfare. Clichy Ravine, Jenikoi. January–April.

BATTLE OF DOIRAN. 8th–9th May.

    Trench warfare. Reselli, Macukovo, Bekirli, Reselli. May–December.

1918. Trench warfare. Reselli, Bekirli, Reselli. January–June.

    Left Macedonia. 6th July. Arrived France, 14th July. Battalion disbanded at Haudricourt. 12th October.

THE ELEVENTH
BATTALION

THE ELEVENTH BATTALION

BY October, 1914, the 8th, 9th and 10th Service Battalions The Black Watch had been brought nearly up to strength; the War Office therefore decided to raise another Service unit, the 11th Battalion. During the following winter the resources of the Depot at Perth were so severely drained by the demands made by the British Expeditionary Force for reinforcements from the 3rd Battalion, that it was found impossible to bring the new Battalion up to strength. Indeed, even while its formation was being attempted, the 11th Battalion had to hand over some of its men: on November 13th a draft of 65 other ranks was sent to the 9th Battalion; and on the 25th of December, 279 more were transferred to the 3rd Battalion, leaving only 30 officers and 167 non-commissioned officers and men with the Battalion.

By April, 1915, the Battalion was not yet up to half its war strength; and the decision of the War Office to change it from a Service to a Reserve Battalion became inevitable, and the announcement that it was no longer destined to go overseas as a unit was received with feelings of the keenest disappointment by all ranks. The same fate was shared by the other Service Battalions of the Highland Regiments, with which the Battalion was brigaded.

To train men for the 8th, 9th and 10th Battalions now became the function of the 11th. During the remainder of 1915, drafts of other ranks were supplied to the 8th and 9th Battalions, though the first draft was not sent overseas until August 21st. Officers, on the other hand, were posted to any of the Regular battalions of The Black Watch, and on occasions to other Scottish regiments.

In January, 1916, the system for reinforcements for other ranks became more elastic, and drafts were ordered to be sent to the 1st and 2nd Battalions. At this juncture the Battalion became a receiving as well as a despatching depot for all ranks of the New Army battalions, who arrived continuously from sick leave or hospital, relieving in their turn others as they were ordered to proceed overseas.

On the 1st of September the name of the Battalion was changed to the 38th Training Reserve Battalion. From now onwards it ceased to receive British Expeditionary Force personnel, and was engaged entirely in training young recruits for despatch to any of the Scottish regiments.

In August, 1917, the name of the Battalion was again changed to the 202nd Infantry Reserve Battalion, though its duties remained unaltered. The New Army Infantry Reserve Battalions were now being reduced in number; and on Novem-

THE TENTH BATTALION THE BLACK WATCH

ber 1st those of the Highland regiments were telescoped into two battalions, which, for some arbitrary reason, were called the 51st and 52nd Graduated Battalions Gordon Highlanders. The Battalion from this date bore the name of the 51st (Grad.) Battalion of the Gordon Highlanders.

But throughout all those changes, and until the retirement of Lieutenant-Colonel John MacRae-Gilstrap, in May, 1918, the Battalion retained The Black Watch character, for, though alterations in its personnel were continually occurring, those who formed its permanent establishment belonged to the Regiment and wore its uniform. And it may be here mentioned that no regimental kilt other than that of The Black Watch ever appeared in the Battalion's books, as the men's khaki kilts came into use in the summer of 1916.

Therefore it may justly be claimed that those officers and other ranks of the Battalion sent overseas, were a contribution from the Regiment to the fighting forces. If the thought that they might have to serve under other colours sometimes clouded the men's horizon during their training, it was their consolation to know that whichever units they were to reinforce would be enriched by the traditions of the Regiment under whose auspices they had been trained.

In the autumn of 1914 a station was found for the 11th Battalion in the camp at Nigg, Ross-shire, in lines adjoining those of the 3rd Battalion, and the temporary command was entrusted to Major C. H. Graham-Stirling, of Strowan. The 11th Battalion formed part of the 101st Infantry Brigade (Brigadier-General S. B. Jameson, with headquarters at Saltburn). The other units of the Brigade will be referred to later. Major-General Walter Hunter Blair was in command of the district, with headquarters at Cromarty.

The command of the Battalion was offered to Lieutenant-Colonel John MacRae-Gilstrap, of Eilean Donan, on November 5th. This officer, on the completion of a recruiting campaign which he had undertaken over part of the mainland and islands of the west of Scotland, accompanied by Major A. Carswell (Argyll and Sutherland Highlanders), proceeded to Nigg and assumed command December 2nd. Major Carswell was appointed Adjutant, and the following completed Headquarters' Staff: Hon. Lieutenant and Quartermaster, W. Curtis; Regimental Sergeant-Major, W. B. Laing; Regimental Quartermaster-Sergeant, J. Anderson; Quartermaster-Sergeant (Orderly Room Staff), J. McCheyne.

The formation of the Battalion from October onwards had proceeded very slowly, although twenty-nine junior officers reported before the end of the year; a few had seen

NIGG, 1915

active service before the war; but most of them came from the University Officers' Training Corps, and continued their training for some months after joining the Battalion, mainly under the instruction of non-commissioned officers. Some non-commissioned officers and men, Regular Reservists who had served with the 1st or 2nd Battalions, were received from the 3rd Battalion as a provisional contribution to the Cadre. Most of those wore ribbons of previous campaigns and many were now too old for service overseas; but they were invaluable to a young Battalion, and the influence of the Regular Army was felt through them by all who afterwards joined. A few drafts of recruits had arrived from the Depot, including 200 men on December 2nd. These men came from all the counties of Scotland, which stretch from Ross and Argyll in the north-west to Fife and Forfar in the east; many of them, perhaps most of them, were married men with families; they came from many walks of life, and were very unequal in age and physique; but they had in common a patriotism, a keenness and a soldierly instinct which was not always equalled and certainly never excelled by those who joined the Battalion after them. Out of these rather heterogeneous elements the nucleus of a battalion was formed, consisting at first of only two companies.

Much rain and snow fell at Nigg during this winter, with bitter winds sweeping off the hills. The parade ground was often a sea of mud on which it was difficult to drill; the few roads which led from the camp were little better; and through lack of other accommodation much of the training had to be carried out in the men's sleeping hutments. It speaks highly for the men that these desolate surroundings did not damp their ardour. No case of desertion occurred in the Battalion. But, if the camp itself was unfavourable for winter training, the fields and heather and wooded hills of the promontory afforded excellent ground for practice in skirmishing, entrenching, visual training, and night operations. A pipe band was formed in January, 1915, after the arrival of Pipe-Major M. MacPhee. Thanks to the generosity of the Commanding Officer and of the Clan MacRae Society, very handsome sets of pipes and drums were supplied for the use of the Battalion. Visits by inspecting officers were rare at Nigg in those days; but the Battalion was inspected by Major-General Gaisford on March 1st. It presented a strange spectacle standing in mud, the men dressed in " Kitchener Blue " uniform, and armed with rifles of obsolete patterns.

By the end of April the Battalion's strength did not exceed 500, of whom 45 were officers. On May 15th the Battalion marched from Nigg to Tain, to spend the summer under canvas on the Morrich Mhor, an ideal camping ground

THE ELEVENTH BATTALION THE BLACK WATCH

on seaside turf by the margin of the Dornoch Firth. Brigade Headquarters—now called the 9th Reserve Infantry Brigade—were already at Tain. The Battalion was soon joined by the 10th Battalion Seaforth Highlanders, from Cromarty, and the 8th Battalion Queen's Own Cameron Highlanders, from Invergordon. The 11th Battalion Gordon Highlanders remained at Dornoch, where they had spent the winter. Some weeks later the Brigade was completed by the arrival on the Morrich Mhor of the 13th Battalion Argyll and Sutherland Highlanders, from England.

Major H. G. Wolridge-Gordon reported on May 29th from the 10th Battalion. From this time the Battalion was joined by many officers and a few other ranks, including nine non-commissioned officers employed as Instructors, from the Service Battalions, which were shedding their supernumeraries preparatory to going overseas.

This month a recruiting campaign was conducted by some officers in Edinburgh, Glasgow and Manchester. They were accompanied by a small band of pipes and drums, and raised a considerable number of recruits for the Battalion—one batch cheerfully consented, in the absence of better quarters, to accept the hospitality of the Edinburgh High Street Jail for a night before proceeding to Tain. Two other recruiting expeditions were conducted at later dates.

On the 1st of July the Battalion was formed on a four company basis, a large draft of men having just arrived from the 3rd Battalion.

The system of training companies was now adopted, under which the company commanders handed over their men twice daily on parade to specially selected officers, who were entirely responsible for the men's training in accordance with syllabus issued by Battalion Headquarters. This new departure, in spite of the disadvantages of divided supervision, answered very well. It made it possible to regroup the men of each company for training purposes according to their military age and experience, and thus to expedite the preparation of drafts. The training companies of the 11th Battalion were almost always under the charge of subalterns. At first the Assistant Adjutant exercised immediate supervision; but later, after numbers had increased, this duty was undertaken by the Second-in-Command. In August a detachment under Captain Harnett was posted at Golspie, where the Musketry courses were fired. The results brought much credit to those responsible for the men's instruction.

On August 21st, 60 other ranks left for the 9th Battalion. This was the first draft of other ranks to go overseas. Urgent

LIEUT.-COLONEL. J. MacRAE-GILSTRAP AND THE PIPE BAND OF THE ELEVENTH BATTALION

MOVE TO RICHMOND, OCTOBER, 1915

orders for a second draft were received on September 17th, and 62 other ranks had to be recalled from Golspie, where the railway communication with Tain had just been cut by a landslide. Some fishermen came to the rescue with their boats, and the draft was brought across the Dornoch Firth. It was a final reinforcement to the 9th Battalion before the Battle of Loos, and about half of the men were killed or wounded a week after arrival in France. After the Battle of Loos and before the Battalion moved from Tain, orders for overseas were received for about 70 officers and 145 other ranks. The spirit of those early drafts will always be remembered by those who saw them leave for France.

The training at Tain had continued to run on more or less the same simple lines as at Nigg, but the conditions were brighter and the numbers of men had substantially increased. The highly specialized training of the later years had scarcely begun; even bombing was in its infancy. The summer at Tain was for many reasons the happiest period in the Battalion's history. The dunes and links beside the camp, and the hills and moors with which the district abounds, proved an ideal ground for training and manœuvring. The health of the troops was excellent throughout this summer. It was possible to feed the men better than in the leaner days which followed, and special attention was given to physical training.

In the third week of October the Brigade moved to Richmond, Yorkshire, where the Battalion was accommodated in hutments, first at Hipswell, Catterick, and a few weeks later in the lines of No. 1 Scotton Camp. It was a dismal change from Tain to a muddy scene of endless hutments and much-worn roads; and the town of Richmond offered few attractions to relieve the monotony of camp life.

By the end of the year 155 other ranks had been sent from Richmond to the 8th and 9th Battalions. The Battalion was now receiving from the Service battalions overseas a considerable number of all ranks who reported from hospitals or sick leave; and in January, 1916, a new company (E company) was formed for their reception. At the same time F company was formed for men of Home Service category, whose separation made room in the original companies for the large numbers of recruits which were arriving. The companies were thus increased to six.

On the 27th of January a draft of 20 other ranks left for the 1st Battalion, the first contribution to this or the 2nd Battalion. On the 10th of February, Major C. T. Hunter-Gray, late of the Punjabis, was appointed Second-in-Command, and Second Lieutenant R. D. Duff, Assistant Adjutant. The Battalion was fortunate to secure the services of a Regular officer of much experience, and Major Hunter-Gray's energy and zeal did much to improve the training, which was now assuming rather a complex character. A raw recruit was expected to become a fairly accomplished soldier in three or four months.

The large and ever increasing number of junior officers posted to the battalions of the Brigade had been for over a year a problem calling for special attention. At Tain a class for supernumerary officers had been started under Lieutenant-Colonel G. Staunton. At Richmond an organization was formed on a larger scale called the Young Officers' Training Corps. This was a reserve on which the battalions could draw for their permanent establishment. There were about this time 180 officers on the strength of the 11th Battalion.

From January and before the date of the Battalion's return to Scotland, 253 other ranks had been drafted overseas, including 180 to the 2nd Battalion in Mesopotamia. Even so, the strength on leaving Richmond was nearly 1400.

In April, Lieutenant W. Curtis was compelled to retire, owing to bad health, and Lieutenant J. R. Fullarton, who had acted as Quartermaster-Sergeant at Brigade Headquarters from its formation, was appointed Quartermaster. The Battalion had good cause to appreciate the services of such an experienced soldier during the many changes in its location and dispositions which occurred in the following years. Company Sergeant-Major J. Galloway was appointed Assistant Regimental Sergeant-Major.

In the second week of April, Battalion Headquarters with A C and F companies entrained for Windygates, Fife, where accommodation had been arranged in the distillery. On May 17th this year the right half of the Battalion moved into permanent summer quarters at Lochend Camp from Dunfermline, where it joined the left half battalion which had arrived there on the 10th of May from Richmond, under the Second-in-Command. The Battalion was accommodated with some crowding, half in hutments and half under canvas. Lochend Camp lies high and dry in a secluded fold of the hills above Dunfermline, pleasantly isolated and yet not too remote. Brigade Headquarters were now at Dunfermline, and the Young Officers' Training Corps became No. 1 Company, Y.O.T.C., Kinross.

On the 19th of July, Major Carswell relinquished the Adjutancy prior to joining the 10th Battalion in Macedonia. He had rendered excellent services with the Battalion from the time of its formation. Lieutenant I. D. Brown, who now returned to the 11th after serving with the 1st Battalion, took over the duties of Adjutant, though still suffering from the effects of a wound. On July 29th, Major Hunter-Gray left for the 1st

LOCHEND CAMP, 1916

Battalion; his loss and that of Major Wolridge Gordon, which followed a month later by the reconstruction of the Battalion, added considerably to the strain on the staff. The total strength was now about 1900. It was, however, fortunate that in Major S. D. Stevenson a Second-in-Command arrived who required no introduction to the Battalion or its duties. On August 24th the Brigade was inspected at Dunfermline by Field-Marshal Lord French, Commander-in-Chief of the Home Forces. Twelve drafts were despatched overseas during July and August from Lochend Camp.

On the 1st of September the Battalion became the 38th Training Reserve Battalion. A draft of over 500, consisting of men returned from the British Expeditionary Forces, and men over nineteen years of age who had been recruited under Lord Derby's Scheme, were transferred to the 3rd Battalion. Under the new establishment only two officers were allowed per company, apart from those employed as specialists. The Battalion was now refilled, though not up to full strength, by large drafts of boys; and it should be noted that from this time onwards its recruits all belonged to A 4 category, youths under nineteen.

Mention should here be made of the special arrangements which were instituted at Lochend Camp for training privates to become non-commissioned officers. The system also included advanced training for non-commissioned officers, and was well timed to anticipate the demands of a War Office Order instructing battalion commanders to recommend suitable non-commissioned officers under their command for nomination to the Cadet Corps, with a view to their ultimate promotion to commissioned rank. It may be recorded that out of one company alone twelve non-commissioned officers were nominated for promotion in the course of nine months, all of whom obtained commissions. The subsequent careers of all of these are not known, but at least two obtained captaincies, mentions and decorations in a surprisingly short time.

At the end of September C, D, and E companies were stationed for a month at Milnathort, and afterwards from the 30th of October were quartered in billets in Dunfermline town. These companies, under the Second-in-Command, formed the left half of the Battalion during the winter—Lieutenant R. McKay acted as Assistant Adjutant and Company Sergeant-Major R. Johnston as Assistant Regimental Sergeant-Major—and moved to Cornton Camp, Bridge of Allan, on 20th December. All these moves interrupted the training programme and interior economy was carried out with difficulty in a Battalion so scattered.

In the middle of December, Brigadier-General Jameson relinquished command of the Brigade, to the deep regret of all ranks. On the 6th of February, 1917, Lieutenant-Colonel MacRae-Gilstrap went to France on a tour of duty in the trenches. On his return he received orders to command the 9th Reserve Brigade temporarily. These duties completed, he returned to the Battalion. During his absence, Major Stevenson acted as Commanding Officer.

By the 21st of February 1362 other ranks had been despatched overseas from Lochend Camp. By the end of April the whole Battalion was settled at Cornton Camp, Bridge of Allan, the Brigade, now under the command of Brigadier-General C. P. Higginson, C.M.G., D.S.O., having previously moved to Stirling. On June 12th, Lieutenant W. L. A. W. Urquhart from the 10th Battalion was appointed Adjutant in succession to Captain I. D. Brown, whose energies on behalf of the Battalion had been untiring, and whose devotion to the Regiment had proved a constant stimulus to others. He afterwards returned to France.

On June 26th the Battalion was inspected at Bridge of Allan by Field-Marshal Lord French, Commander-in-Chief of the Home Forces. The total strength on parade was 1500. Lord French congratulated the Commanding Officer on the " splendid physique and ' bearing ' of the young soldiers," and afterwards marked the Battalion as suitable for duty on the Norfolk coast, the invasion of which was considered possible at that time. But before the autumn move most of the soldiers whom Lord French had inspected were transferred to the 41st Training Reserve Battalion, and it was with a different and less trained body of junior recruits that the Battalion arrived in Norfolk.

The general transfer of recruits just mentioned was caused by an inter-battalion grouping of all recruits belonging to the Training Reserve Battalions. They were regrouped into two grades according to age: 18 to $18\frac{1}{2}$ years and $18\frac{1}{2}$ to 19 years, the minimum age for enlistment being 18 years and for overseas service 19 years. In future the 38th Battalion was to train recruits till they were $18\frac{1}{2}$ and then transfer them to the 41st Battalion or elsewhere for final training. This rearrangement added greatly to the work of the headquarters and company staffs, already overtaxed. In order to deal with the emergency a special company (G company) was formed on August 21st, to undertake arrangements for receiving the incoming soldiers as they were transferred to the Battalion from other Training Reserve Battalions, and for handing them over to other companies as these were able to accommodate them. At the conclusion of those disturbing operations, during which the nominal strength of the Battalion reached its maximum of nearly 2300, G company was disbanded. These facts are stated to explain the small number of men (77 other ranks) sent overseas during the year 1917.

MOVE TO NORFOLK, SEPTEMBER, 1917

As the war had advanced, catering had become a more and more difficult problem; and the youth of the recruits did not make matters any easier. Not only had the rations been reduced, but the purchasing power of the allowance for extras was continually falling. Certainly the quantity of food supplied to the kitchens of the Training Battalions during the later stages of the war was insufficient. The officer primarily responsible for the messing of men of the Battalion earned for himself, and justly so, the gratitude of the thousands of soldiers who passed through the Battalion and went overseas. Captain John Birrell was unremitting in his care and trouble over this messing question, and the excellence of his efforts in this direction was perhaps shown by the fact that the men of the Battalion when attached to other Corps, were always glad to get back to the 11th Battalion. An increase in Army pay came very opportunely, enabling the men to buy food in the canteens, even if sometimes at exorbitant prices; and as the Battalion had never prided itself in hoarding the funds of its Regimental Institutes, some assistance was possible from this source.

On the 19th of August, F (Headquarters) company was disbanded, there being now few Home Service men left in the Battalion. On the same day the Battalion became the 202nd Infantry Reserve Battalion, though the change was only in name.

The Battalion Sports were held in the Strathallan Park, and were most successful. A large and well-run Y.M.C.A. hut, and an excellent well-furnished canteen were also much appreciated. At Cornton Camp all the kitchen and mess services were taken over by a very capable contingent of the Women's Army Auxiliary Corps; and ever afterwards those duties were entrusted to members of this Corps, when local conditions permitted.

Late in September the Battalion moved to Kelling Heath, near Holt, in north-east Norfolk, where it was placed under canvas. The accommodation, the cooking and sanitary arrangements, and even the water supply were all inadequate. Discomforts were aggravated by incessant rain and violent winds, which sometimes tore down the tents. Fortunately the Battalion went into permanent winter quarters at Cromer the following month.

On its arrival in Norfolk, the Battalion became part of the 191st Infantry Reserve Brigade and was renamed the 51st Graduated Battalion Gordon Highlanders. Divisional Headquarters (64th Highland Division) were stationed in Norwich. The billets were scattered through the town of Cromer, and it was some weeks before all arrangements for accommodation and food were satisfactorily solved,

During January and February, 1918, 224 other ranks were

THE ELEVENTH BATTALION THE BLACK WATCH

despatched to France. Towards the end of March an urgent message was received that all available men would be required immediately to reinforce the Western Front. This was followed by orders and counter-orders, in consequence of which some hundreds of young soldiers, travelling north on final leave, had to be intercepted at Edinburgh and elsewhere and ordered to return to the Battalion without seeing their homes. No blame rested with the Battalion for this unfortunate occurrence, and it speaks well for its organization that in two days (March 31st and April 1st) 721 other ranks were sent to France. By a strange coincidence several of the first draft were back again at Cromer—this time in a military hospital—within a week. Many were killed soon after their arrival in France. It is fair to say that, although the departure of these drafts was rather hurried, the men were well trained and of excellent fighting material. Out of one company of 193, which landed in France on April 2nd, forty had qualified as marksmen. Before leaving Cromer they were well trained in rapid volley firing and the use of the bayonet. The spirit of these young soldiers was the same spirit which had sustained the army in its earliest struggles, and which finally won the war.

In the early spring, Major R. A. Chrystal (Argyll and Sutherland) succeeded Major Stevenson as Second-in-Command, and Lieutenant A. A. Templeton was appointed Assistant Adjutant, vice Lieutenant P. R. Paul.

On April 15th, the Battalion, very reduced in strength, but comprising about 600 recruits whose training was not yet completed, moved inland to Barnham Cross Camp, Thetford. Here the whole of the Brigade, together with other troops, was placed under canvas at the edge of a moor, whose sandy soil and undulating surface made it a very suitable ground for training. The camp was well equipped.

On the 3rd of May, Lieutenant-Colonel MacRae-Gilstrap gave up the command of the Battalion, which he had held from its formation for a period of three and a half years. He was succeeded by Major (afterwards Lieutenant-Colonel) H. A. Duncan, D.S.O. (Argyll and Sutherland). The high standard of efficiency demanded by the unprecedented character of the war made the duties of Training Battalions difficult and responsible. Year after year the bodies, minds and hearts of men were subjected on the battle fronts to ordeals hitherto unknown, and only a combination of sterling qualities could avail. The recruits of the 11th Battalion had all to be developed and shaped for the special purposes of war. How much the Training Battalions contributed to efficiency in the field can be measured best not by individual reports, but by the

NORFOLK, 1918

successes of the battalions which they reinforced. " By their fruits ye shall know them." The Reserve Battalions of The Black Watch may claim some share in their achievements—those deeds of which the records speak, and those, more numerous and perhaps equally heroic, on which all records are silent. How much the Commanding Officer of the 11th Battalion contributed to such results can be appreciated most fully by those who know in what affectionate esteem he was held by his officers and men, and how much, individually and collectively, they owed to his command.

It is not necessary to enlarge on the remaining history of the Battalion. During May and June the remainder of the Cromer recruits left Thetford for France in drafts which numbered altogether 607 other ranks. These were the last overseas drafts to leave the Battalion. It is estimated that from first to last about 500 officers were furnished for overseas service, and of other ranks 5200. Of this number of other ranks only about two-thirds were fully trained by the Battalion, the remaining third having been transferred to other home units for final training and despatch overseas.

Soon after Lieutenant-Colonel MacRae-Gilstrap's retirement Captain Urquhart resigned the Adjutancy, whose duties he had ably discharged for almost a year. In the meantime, the Battalion had been refilled by young recruits, whose training was not completed before the Armistice. In the course of the summer and autumn the old personnel left the battalion. No attempt has been made to mention those officers and non-commissioned officers who rendered valuable services in the Battalion. Their names are too numerous, and the following remarks must be restricted to a few who rendered long and important services on the Headquarters Staff.

Few quartermasters can have incurred more arduous responsibilities than those which fell to the lot of Lieutenant Fullarton. He studied the best interests of the Battalion unselfishly in the performance of every duty. Regimental Sergeant-Major Laing served in this capacity with the Battalion for over three and a half years. His valuable services were finally rewarded by a commission. From May, 1916, and until the end, Quartermaster-Sergeant (Orderly Room Staff) J. W. Matthews discharged his heavy and responsible duties efficiently. The exact knowledge which he acquired of the Battalion and of administrative detail contributed greatly to the smooth working of all the companies and departments.

The following also deserve to be specially mentioned for valuable services which extended over the whole life of the Battalion: Regimental Quartermaster-Sergeant J. Anderson; Pipe-Major M. MacPhee; Colour-Sergeant J. Hannah, musketry instructor; Colour-Sergeant A. White; Sergeant N. Baxter.

THE ELEVENTH BATTALION THE BLACK WATCH

This account cannot close without some reference to one who was the very true friend of the 11th Battalion through all stages of the war. Mrs. MacRae-Gilstrap not only identified herself with the welfare of all who served under her husband's command, but she followed their subsequent fortunes with keen and sympathetic interest.

The 51st (Grad.) Battalion Gordon Highlanders spent the following winter at Weybourne, on the north coast of Norfolk, where Lieutenant-Colonel J. G. Birch, D.S.O. (K.R.R.C.), succeeded Lieutenant-Colonel Duncan in command. On the 30th of March, 1919, the Battalion travelled to Dunkerque to join the Army of Occupation on the Rhine, where it was finally under the command of Lieutenant-Colonel R. M. Dudgeon, D.S.O., M.C. (Cameron Highlanders). The Battalion returned to England to be demobilized in the spring of 1920.

APPENDIX

Nominal Roll of Non-Commissioned Officers and Men who Died of Disease in the Great War, 1914–18

Abbreviation.—‡ Died at home.

THE ELEVENTH BATTALION

Middlemas, F., L/Cpl., S/3786 ‡29.4.15
Robertson, D. L., Pte., 6663 ‡14.3.16
Robertson, W., Pte., S/10824 ‡6.7.16
Sheldrick, H. D., Pte., S/11524 ‡28.11.15

Sutton, F., A/Sgt., 11701 ‡28.3.16
Varndall, G., C.Q.M.S., 3/3415 ‡14.5.16
Wallace, T., Pte., 6178 ‡9.9.15

THE TWELFTH
(LABOUR)
BATTALION

THE TWELFTH (LABOUR) BATTALION

THE 12th (Labour) Battalion The Black Watch was formed at Blairgowrie in May, 1916. It was the second Scottish Labour Battalion to be formed there, its predecessor being the Labour Battalion of the Royal Scots, which was succeeded by that of the Scottish Rifles.

The command of the Battalion was given to Major H. Jennings-Bramly with the rank of Temporary Lieutenant-Colonel. This officer had joined The Black Watch in 1884, but had retired in 1904. During the past year he had been serving at The Black Watch Depot in Perth. Lieutenant D. C. Campbell, Royal Scots, was appointed Adjutant with the acting rank of captain, and Quartermaster-Sergeant J. Irvine, Argyll and Sutherland Highlanders, Quartermaster with the rank of lieutenant.

The Battalion consisted of four companies, each of 250 all ranks, with two company officers, the senior in each company being given the acting rank of captain. Two of these officers were Second Lieutenants Lace, 3rd Battalion The Black Watch, and Bruce, Gordon Highlanders, who each commanded companies; the other officers, with two exceptions, namely, Second Lieutenants Reid, Cameron Highlanders, and McColl, Royal Scots, came from English regiments. Company Sergeant-Major G. Turner of the 3rd Battalion was appointed Regimental Sergeant-Major. Turner had enlisted in The Black Watch in 1886, and served with the 2nd Battalion throughout the South African war, when he was promoted to the rank of sergeant. Latterly he had served at the Depot in Perth, and before the end of the war he received a well deserved commission as lieutenant.

The personnel of the companies consisted mainly of drafts from the 3rd Battalion The Black Watch, Cameron, Gordon and Seaforth Highlanders, completed by further drafts from the Lowland Scots Regiments.

The men were of the " B " (the vast majority of these " B 2") and " C " classes, and, as a whole, they were elderly and none of them physically very strong. But if they left much to be desired in the latter respect, their hearts at any rate were all in the right place. The following testimony to men of the 12th Battalion deserves to be quoted, as it comes from one who had long experience of the Battalion and whose opinion is worthy of respect:

" The Battalion was composed of men of good character who
" seemed to recognize and appreciate all the efforts put forth by
" the officers to mitigate, as far as possible, the hardships in-
" separable from their work. Their patience and endurance
" under the most difficult circumstances merited the highest

THE TWELFTH BATTALION THE BLACK WATCH

" praise. I often think that were it possible in these days of un-
" rest and dissatisfaction to infuse into the people at home the
" splendid spirit that possesses these men, our troubles would
" soon blow over."

It was a busy time at Blairgowrie, for, in addition to completing the organization of the Battalion, much drill and training had to be carried out, and the value of discipline impressed on all who joined its ranks. Two officers and a number of the non-commissioned officers were of the Regular Army, as also were a sprinkling of old soldiers in the ranks, but the remainder were practically raw. The Battalion was inspected three times by Colonel Mackintosh, Commanding No. 1 District; General Ewart also paid an informal visit, and gave some encouraging criticism. " You will deserve well of your country," he said finally. It was a motley crowd that wet afternoon when the Battalion left Blairgowrie, judged by old, and the best standards; but if the services rendered by the Battalion during the war were not very glorious they were of definite value, and without doubt the Commander-in-Chief in Scotland was justified in his kindly prophecy.

The Battalion embarked at Southampton for Havre on June 27th, 1916, a little over five weeks from the date of its formation. From Havre the Battalion moved to Locre in Belgium on July 1st, 1916, and three days later to La Clyte close by; a bivouac in the first place and a standing camp in the second. The work done here was mainly road repairing—but some entrenching work was also done, and the first casualty was recorded.

On the 17th of July, 1916, the Battalion was moved to the Somme area and encamped first in the Bois de Tailles, and afterwards, for nearly two months, to September 29th, at Carcaillot Farm, below Albert, and close to Méaulte. From that date to November 5th it was camped just below Montauban; at first under canvas but latterly some Nissen huts were run up.

The Battalion at this time was mainly employed on the Méaulte–Fricourt–Mametz and Maricourt roads, and on moving to Montauban on the Carnoy–Montauban–Trones Wood road was frequently working under shell fire. It should be noted that in July, Captain and Quartermaster Irvine was invalided home, his place being filled by Sergeant-Major Turner, who was subsequently appointed lieutenant and quartermaster.

The work was arduous, and, as the maintenance of these roads was all important in that time of crisis, the responsibility was heavy. The supply of repairing material, notwithstanding the most careful organization, frequently ran short; sometimes because the supply of material was deficient, but more often

FRANCE AND BELGIUM, 1916 TO 1917

because the heavy and continuous traffic from and to the front line rendered it impossible to deliver the goods with any attempt at punctuality. For work and traffic went on simultaneously, and it was obviously impossible to keep on working during these dark nights, artificial light being out of the question.

On one evening of pitiless rain—an evening ever to be remembered by all concerned—the road all but " went " for a length of from 50 to 100 yards in Montauban village. Grave would have been the consequences if it had. However, thanks to Providence—and in a measure to the worthy efforts of tired men —the road was just saved; traffic was not held up. And no such catastrophe as then threatened happened again.

On November 5th, 1916, the Battalion was ordered back to Belgium, to the great disappointment of all ranks, for it was on the point of being ordered close up behind the line. The next station was " X " Camp, about two miles out of Poperinghe on the Woosten road—very good quarters at this time, though, as a matter of fact, they were shelled out of existence some six months or so later. Work here was again mostly road making and repairing roads near Poperinghe and Ypres.

On January 19th, 1917, the Battalion was again moved back to France, this time to Lattre St. Quentin, a village on the Frévent–Avesnes–le–Comte–Arras road. The main work here was the construction of a light railway from Noyelle-Vion station to Warlus, a village on the outskirts of Arras. It was an interesting piece of work as the Battalion completed it from " the cutting of the first sod "; in later stages working-parties were usually conveyed to and from work on trains running on the line they themselves had laid, an achievement of which the men were naturally proud.

A strenuous, but generally speaking uneventful, time was spent over the construction of this light railway until on April 12th the Battalion was moved into Arras for employment under the Railway Engineers of the Third Army Headquarters, on the reconstruction of the Arras–Douai railway immediately in the rear of the army advance.

It should be noted that the Battalion had hitherto been under the orders of Chief Engineers of Corps to whose areas it successively moved for work, and under Corps Headquarters Staff for discipline.

During the month the Battalion remained in Arras—until it ceased to exist as a Battalion—the men were comfortably billeted in a school near the railway station.

By the time the railway was restored as far as Fampoux, the advance was arrested, and a series of gun emplacements for heavy artillery were made up the line at intervals. One of the

THE TWELFTH BATTALION THE BLACK WATCH

companies, after a time, was kept at work continuously on the gap where formerly the railway bridge on the Arras–Lens line had crossed the Scarpe.

It may fairly be claimed that the Battalion put in its best work at Arras, very frequently working by day under shell fire which caused a number of casualties, and on most nights in their billets also. But the men stuck to their job cheerfully like good Scotsmen, and in their own line maintained the reputation of their Regiment.

Early in May the Labour Corps came into being, and the Battalion was split up. The Commanding Officer, Adjutant and Quartermaster became " Headquarters, 44th Labour Group," the remainder of the Battalion forming the 5th and 6th Labour Companies under Captain H. Harpham and Captain R. D. Lace respectively.

And so at Arras, on May 11th, 1917, the 12th (Labour) Battalion The Black Watch, ceased to exist. Their services in the war had been useful rather than conspicuous, but all ranks were well justified in feeling that the conduct of the Battalion had been worthy of the Regiment, and their labours had been of good service to the country.

APPENDIX I

Record of Officers' Service

THE TWELFTH BATTALION

Bruce, C. W. 2nd Lieut. Joined 31st May, 1916. Promoted Capt. 22nd June, 1916. Transferred to R.F.C. 16th Nov., 1916.

Campbell, D. C. Capt. and Adjutant. Joined Battn. on formation 27th May, 1916.

Crawford, J. 2nd Lieut. Attached as Technical Supervisor on road construction 2nd Nov., 1916.

Foster, D. 2nd Lieut. Joined 2nd June, 1916.

Gorman, M. E. Capt R.A.M.C. Joined 5th Nov., 1916. Transferred to 17th Div. 12th Jan., 1917.

Hall, P. A. Lieut. R.A.M.C. Joined 12th Jan., 1917.

Harpham, H. D. Capt. Joined 6th June, 1916.

Irvine, J. Hon. Lieut. and Q.M. Joined Battn. on formation 27th May, 1916.

Jennings-Bramly, H. Major. Joined Battn. on formation 27th May, 1916.

Lace, K. R. D. 2nd Lieut. Joined 30th May, 1916. Promoted Capt. 22nd June, 1916.

Lee, W. E. Capt. C.F. Joined 20th Oct., 1916.

McColl, E. E. 2nd Lieut. Joined 19th June, 1916.

McLeod, N. 2nd Lieut. Joined 30th August, 1916.

McVicker, D. Capt. R.A.M.C. Joined Battn on formation 27th May, 1916. Transferred to XIV Corps for duty at dressing station, Bronfay Farm, 16th Aug., 1916.

Moss, W. F. 2nd Lieut. Joined 31st May, 1916.

Reid, A. 2nd Lieut. Joined 31st May, 1916.

Schuller, D. H. Lieut. Joined 30th May, 1916. Promoted Capt. 28th June, 1916.

Tucker, H. S. 2nd Lieut. Attached as Technical Supervisor on Road Construction, 2nd Nov., 1916.

Turner, G. Hon. Lieut. and Q.M. July, 1916

APPENDIX II

Nominal Roll of Non-Commissioned Officers and Men Who Died of Wounds or Disease in the Great War, 1914–18

Abbreviations.—† Died of wounds.   ‡ Died at home.   § Died.

THE TWELFTH BATTALION

Cunningham, P., Pte., S/13570 §17.12.16	Pollock, W., L/Cpl., S/15297 §15.11.16
	Ritchie, A., Pte., S1/3584 §17.8.16
Martin, A., Pte., S/14371 §16.2.17	
McGowan, F. M., Cpl., S/13443 §22.7.16	Thow, A., Pte., S/15449 ‡26.12.16
	Twaddle, J., Cpl., S/13571 †25.4.17
Nicol, W., Pte., S/13557 †1.5.17	Ward, T., Pte., S/14103 24.10.16

THE THIRTEENTH
BATTALION

THE THIRTEENTH BATTALION

THE 13th Battalion was formed from the 1st and 2nd Regiment of Scottish Horse, which had mobilized under the Colonel Commandant, the Marquis of Tullibardine, K.T., in August, 1914.

After serving in Gallipoli, they proceeded to Egypt, being employed on the defence of the Suez Canal and preliminary work in connection with General Allenby's advance to Palestine.

Towards the end of September, 1916, the 1st, 2nd and 3rd Regiments proceeded to Abassia, near Cairo, where, on the 29th of that month, the 1st and 2nd Regiments were formed into an Infantry Battalion, and became the 13th Battalion The Black Watch (Scottish Horse). The 3rd Regiment was formed into a double company, and joined the Lovat's Scouts Battalion of the Cameron Highlanders.

The following is a list of officers with the Regiment when the change was made :—

Lieut.-Colonel A. E. McBarnet, M.V.O., D.S.O. (in Command).
Major R. E. S. Barrington (Second-in-Command).

Company Commanders

| Major R. G. Dawson. | Major A. M. P. Lyle. |
| ,, P. Rattray. | ,, A. J. L. MacGregor. |

Major J. Dewar. Lieut. C. Nicol.
Captain J. D. Couper. ,, H. C. Soundy.
,, G. Hamilton. ,, E. Ferney.
,, J. G. Kennedy. ,, C. Kinloch.
,, A. N. Skelton. ,, R. Gray.
Lieut. R. Inglis. ,, E. Sturrock.
,, A. M. MacLean. ,, C. Schmidt.
,, R. A. Bartram. ,, G. Rutherford.
,, D. W. Rusack. ,, J. Mill.
,, D. G. F. Moore. ,, G. S. Mackay.
,, P. S. Guise.

Captain C. J. Haven. (Q.M.).
,, W. G. Wambeck (M.O.).
,, A. C. McIntyre (Transport Officer).
Lieut. A. Rawson (Adjutant).
,, W. G. Scott (Scout Officer).
,, R. E. Smith (Signalling Officer).

Strength, 35 officers and 922 other ranks.

October 15th was the actual date on which the Battalion was first known as the 13th Black Watch, and the following day it

THE THIRTEENTH BATTALION THE BLACK WATCH

left Abassia for Alexandria, sailing two days later on H.M.T. *Menominee* for Salonika, where it disembarked on the 21st, and camped at Lembet.

On October 28th the Battalion reached the Struma Valley, and joined the 81st Infantry Brigade, 27th Division, XVI Corps, the other battalions in the Brigade being the 1st Royal Scots, 2nd Cameron Highlanders and 1st Argyll and Sutherland Highlanders.

It should be specially noted that when the Scottish Horse became affiliated to The Black Watch, permission was given them to retain their uniform, badges, etc., and throughout their connection with the Regiment—except for correspondence and records—they were always known as the Scottish Horse Battalion.

November was spent in training at Kopaci and Karadzakoj Bala. Nothing of any importance occurred during that month, with the exception of an enemy bombing carried out on the 25th, whereby the Battalion suffered nine casualties.

In addition to training, the 13th was employed on road making, a very necessary work owing to the appalling state of the country roads which, in most cases, were nothing better than tracks, often across marshy ground, and it was some considerable time before these were in a fit state to carry more than pack transport.

December found the Battalion in the line at Hristian Kamila where, on the 1st, it took part in a reconnaisance in force. The month passed in the ordinary routine of trench warfare, three weeks in the line and one in reserve at Bala, Hristian Kamila and Homondos alternately.

The winter passed without incident, neither the Allies nor the enemy showing much initiative, the ground and weather preventing operations on any large scale. It was by no means a pleasant period; the weather was extremely bad, little or no material was available for shelters of any kind; whilst the transport of supplies and engineer stores was ever a problem. The enemy held a particularly fine position on the hills, from which he could see everything that went on for miles behind the Allied lines, and any small movement during the daytime would produce a fairly heavy and accurate artillery fire. In addition, whenever a raid or minor operation was carried out, it meant a long journey from the front line across No Man's Land, which was covered with barbed wire, bush and intersected by several small rivers. In these minor operations the 13th Battalion excelled, their training as scouts standing them in good stead and enabling them to carry out several highly successful operations, among which the following may be mentioned.

On February 21st, 1917, the Battalion successfully raided a

SALONIKA, APRIL, 1917

Turkish post, capturing four and killing two of its garrison, for which Lieutenant Bartram was awarded the M.C., and Sergeant Cowan and Lance-Corporal Cunningham received the M.M.

On March 17th, whilst in the Hristian sector, a party of about 40 Bulgarians attempted to rush one of the forward posts near the Kavakli level crossing. Private A. D. Campbell, who was in charge of the post, defended it gallantly with only himself and one other man of his party unwounded; they were eventually compelled to retire some 200 yards, when, being reinforced, Campbell, with the reinforcements, followed the enemy up some way and obtained valuable information from papers taken from the enemy's dead, of which there were about twenty. For his action on this occasion Private Campbell was later awarded the M.M.

On April 3rd, Lieutenant-Colonel Railston, Rifle Brigade, took over command of the Battalion, vice Lieutenant-Colonel McBarnet, evacuated sick to England.

On the 11th of April, the enemy attacked a party of scouts, and this led to a most gallant episode. When scouting on the Seres railway, Corporal Lewis Finnie, Private McCleod and Private McIntyre were suddenly attacked at close quarters by about 30 Bulgarians. McCleod ran forward to a culvert on the railway embankment through which the enemy were coming and, although shot at from a distance of barely four yards, he killed four of the enemy, thus preventing his two comrades, one of whom had already been wounded, from being further attacked, and enabled them to reach a place of safety. Although the enemy were within only a few yards, and on the embankment above him, he remained alone at his post for nearly an hour until they withdrew.

When the enemy made their first attack on this small party, Corporal Finnie got separated from the other two and was attacked by eight Bulgarians at close quarters. He killed four of them before being slightly wounded in the end by a bomb, which also broke his rifle. The second one wounded him in several places, and he was then attacked by three Bulgarians, one of whom attempted to kill him with the butt of his rifle and the second to stab him, whilst he had the third by his throat. Seeing the situation Finnie was in, Private McIntyre rushed to his assistance, despite the fact that there were about thirty of the enemy on the railway embankment about fifty yards from him. Opening fire on these as he went, and on the party which was attacking Finnie, he wounded one of the enemy, drove the others off, and lifting up Finnie carried him back under heavy fire to a safer place, stopping at intervals to open fire on the enemy on the embankment.

For their conduct on this occasion Corporal Finnie and Private McCleod received the D.C.M., and Private McIntyre the M.M.

The same day another party of scouts was also attacked by a body of some 18 Bulgarians and were forced to retire, but not before they inflicted considerable loss on the enemy. In this operation Private J. Campbell was awarded the M.M.

On the 16th a raid was made on an enemy post, two Bulgarians being killed, and on the 18th another took place, but without result, as the posts were found unoccupied.

May passed without incident, the Battalion taking part in manœuvres behind the line early in the month, and moving back to Osman Kamila on the 21st.

It was now summer and malaria began to develop to an alarming extent. It was, therefore, decided to evacuate the advanced line and hold another which had been prepared on the north bank of the Struma for the summer. Before this could be done, however, it was necessary to dismantle the forward line and move back all stores, etc., to the south of the river. This meant much work and could only be carried out under cover of darkness. The time, therefore, was fully occupied. Only half-battalions now went into the line at one time, each for a tour of ten days, the remainder being employed in constructing a new reserve line in the early morning and evening.

In August malaria and sand-fly fever were very prevalent, in spite of all precautions in the way of providing mosquito nets, ointment, etc., and few escaped one or other of these diseases, which took so heavy a toll of the Battalion.

It is of interest to note that at a Horse Show organized by the Division the 13th Battalion swept the board in the competition for transport mules, winning five firsts and four seconds in the five events, including the championship.

As September drew to a close preparations were made for retaking possession of the old forward line which had been evacuated for the summer. In these measures the Battalion scouts were kept busy night reconnoitring the old line which was then held by the enemy. They gained extremely good information, successfully penetrating the line at several places, and locating machine guns.

On October 12th the 13th moved to Wessex Bridge preparatory to an attack on Homondos in conjunction with the 2nd Battalion Cameron Highlanders. The plan for this operation was that the 13th should work round the right flank of Homondos village and join up with the 2nd Battalion Cameron Highlanders in rear of it, who were to move round the left flank.

The attack took place at 6.30 a.m. on the 14th, and was entirely successful. The Battalion was led through the wire and crossed No Man's Land and behind the enemy line by Lieutenant W. G. Scott, the Scout Officer, and the Battalion scouts, the

MOVE TO FRANCE, JUNE, 1918

leading company being under command of Major A. M. P. Lyle. Half an hour later the village had been taken with a loss of only five other ranks killed.and 11 wounded, the enemy losing over 100 killed, together with 152 prisoners and three machine guns. A counter-attack at 7 a.m. was repulsed, and the village held. Later, Major Lyle and Lieutenant Scott received the M.C., and the Commander-in-Chief complimented the 81st Infantry Brigade on the brilliant manner in which the operation had been carried out.

The winter passed uneventfully; the weather was very bad, with frequent blizzards, floods and snowstorms. Several raids were carried out, one of them by C company on February 7th, 1918, on three enemy posts, 19 of the enemy being killed and wounded. Captain G. Hamilton and Lieutenant Mackay were awarded the M.C. for their services on this occasion.

On April 28th, Major the Hon. R. E. S. Barrington took over command from Lieutenant-Colonel Railston, who proceeded to France, and two days later the 81st Infantry Brigade was relieved by the Greek Army, and went into reserve at Kopaci Ridge. Strength, 35 officers and 934 other ranks.

The Battalion was destined to see no more fighting in Salonika. At the beginning of June, 1918, it was warned to be in readiness to proceed to France, and on the 13th entrained for Bralo, moving from there to Itea on the 16th and embarking the following day on the French transport *Timgard* for Taranto, whence proceeding by rail through Italy and France, it detrained at Forges les Eaux on the 24th, and marched to Serqueux. Strength, 33 officers and 975 other ranks.

The bad effects of malaria and influenza reduced this strength considerably, about a hundred cases on the average attending the medical officer daily.

On July 15th the Battalion moved to Martin Eglise and joined the 149th Infantry Brigade, 50th Division, the other battalions being the 3rd Royal Fusiliers and 2nd Dublin Fusiliers, XVII Corps, Third Army.

The month of August was spent in training, during which the whole Battalion was granted ten days leave to the United Kingdom, the first that had been granted since proceeding overseas just three years before. It was in this month that Her Grace the Duchess of Atholl visited the Battalion.

On September 15th the 13th moved to Le Souich, and on October 1st went into line at Vendhuille. On the 3rd one company was engaged in the attack on Le Catelet and Gouy, where it lost one officer and 13 other ranks killed, and one officer and 24 other ranks wounded.

By this time the " Advance to Victory " had commenced, and on the 6th the Battalion moved forward to the Masnier—

THE THIRTEENTH BATTALION THE BLACK WATCH

Beaurevoir line in front of Gouy, and to Maurois on the 10th where, two days later, Lieutenant-Colonel P. Blair, 9th Royal Scots, assumed command vice Lieutenant-Colonel Barrington, wounded.

The 13th took part in the crossing of the River Selle on October 17th. The 149th Brigade was directed to pass through the 151st when the first objective had been taken, the second being the railway triangle at Le Cateau. The Battalion crossed the river under cover of a thick mist and smoke barrage at 5.45 a.m. Considerable resistance was met with at the railway line, and machine gun fire from the station buildings held up the advance for some hours. At 2 p.m., however, the advance was continued and the first objective was consolidated, the second objective namely, the railway triangle, being taken and occupied during the night, and at 5.20 a.m. the following morning the Battalion attacked and captured the railway triangle, together with 185 prisoners and 30 machine guns, the losses of the 13th being 31 other ranks killed, five officers and 125 other ranks wounded, and one officer wounded and missing.

On the evening of the 19th the Battalion was relieved and moved back to Maritz, where it was visited by General Rawlinson, who said that he had made a special effort to see the Battalion in order to compliment it on its splendid performance at Le Cateau.

In connection with this visit it is interesting to record that General Rawlinson wrote the following letter to the Duke of Atholl, dated October 25th, 1918 :—

"Yesterday I had occasion to visit your splendid Battalion of "Scottish Horse (13th Royal Highlanders) in the 50th Division, "in order to compliment them on their fine attack and capture "of Le Cateau station on 18th inst. They were looking magnifi-"cent, and I was glad to hear that a draft was on its way to join "them so as to replace their losses.

"The attack of the station was a very fine performance, and "less determined troops would hardly have succeeded.

"I went over the ground myself the other day examining the "details of the attack, and so struck was I with the strength of "the hostile position, and the great gallantry displayed by the "Scottish Horse, in the capture of it, that I went personally to the "Battalion to thank them, for they deserved it.

"I cannot often find time to do this, but Scotland has done "so much towards winning this war, that I always do what I can "to show them how much we appreciate their services."

The 13th again moved forward on the 26th, and on November 1st two companies went into the line at Fontaine au Bois, where,

THE ARMISTICE, NOVEMBER 11TH, 1918

on the 3rd, the remaining two companies moved into assembly positions prior to the attack on Haute Cornée, which was to take place the following day.

Zero was 6.15 a.m. and the Battalion objective being Haute Cornée, the early morning mist somewhat hindered the advance, but as soon as it cleared, good progress was made and, with the aid of tanks, the objective was reached and consolidated about noon in spite of a heavy artillery barrage. The Battalion losses were one officer and 23 other ranks killed, and one officer and 99 other ranks wounded. The pursuit of the enemy continued, in spite of machine gun resistance at places.

During this time the Battalion moved as follows :—On the 5th through the Foret de Mormal to Hachette Farm; on the 6th to Chausee Brunehaut and Remy Chausee; on the 8th to St. Aubin, where instructions were received that pressure would be maintained on the retiring enemy and that the Bois de Beugnies would be secured. Semousies was reached at 2 a.m. on the 9th. On the 11th the Commune of Semousies presented the 13th with an address of thanks and a French flag in recognition of their liberation from the Germans, and at 10.15 a.m. news reached the Battalion that hostilities would cease at 11 a.m.

From October 17th until the Armistice the enemy had fought rearguard actions with an ever increasing power of resistance; at times his artillery fire had been intense and accurate, and he was able to get away most of his guns in safety. Only once—at Le Cateau station—was an infantry counter-attack made by the enemy. On all other occasions when the allied troops appeared, those of the enemy rearguard, unable to get away, surrendered freely.

During the last four months of the war the Battalion suffered the following casualties :—six officers killed and 16 wounded; 114 other ranks killed and 333 wounded, whilst its captures included 250 prisoners and 50 machine guns.

The remainder of November was spent by the 13th at Semousies, where it was engaged in salvage work and where, on December 1st, H.M. the King, accompanied by H.R.H. the Prince of Wales, inspected the 149th Brigade on the Maubeuge–Avesnes road.

On December 5th the Battalion moved to Monceau, *en route* to Le Quesnoy. Whilst at Monceau the Duke of Atholl, Commandant Scottish Horse, visited the Battalion, and it should also be mentioned that the Duchess, who was at the time employed with Red Cross work in France, paid the Battalion a visit at Martin Eglise.

The first party to proceed home on demobilization left the Battalion on the 13th, composed of officers and other ranks

THE THIRTEENTH BATTALION THE BLACK WATCH

required for urgent work, and the first party of miners proceeded to Scotland for demobilization three days later.

Le Quesnoy was reached on December 18th, the Battalion moving into barracks there. Here Christmas and New Year was spent, the 13th moving to Villers Pol on January 3rd, 1919, for salvage work.

The following months were occupied on this task and in educational training. During January a colour party had been sent home for the Scottish Horse colours which had been in safe keeping at Blair Castle, and on February 7th a Battalion parade was held for the purpose of receiving them.

By the end of this month the strength of the Battalion was reduced to 39 officers and 300 other ranks, and by March 18th it had been reduced to Cadre, and on that day four officers and 118 other ranks joined the 8th Battalion in the Army of Occupation, the remainder, seven officers and 185 other ranks, being demobilized.

Throughout April and May demobilization proceeded steadily, and on June 3rd the Cadre, strength five officers and 37 other ranks, moved to Le Quesnoy, from which, on the 11th, Second Lieutenant Forster and 18 other ranks proceeded to Scotland with the colours, which were handed over to His Grace the Duke of Atholl, at Blair Castle, for safe custody.

The Battalion, now reduced to two officers and 14 other ranks, remained on at Le Quesnoy until June 29th, when it entrained with regimental transport and equipment for Le Havre. On July 6th the Battalion embarked for Southampton, arriving there the following day, and after handing over stores, proceeded to Scotland for demobilization, and the disbandment of the 13th (Scottish Horse) Battalion The Black Watch, was completed.

Such, in brief, is the history of the 13th (Scottish Horse) Battalion The Black Watch. So short an account cannot do full justice to the fine conduct of the Battalion, far less to the gallantry of many individuals, but enough has been recorded to show how worthily officers and men upheld the traditions of the Regiment, and what good service they were able to give to their King and country.

APPENDIX I

Record of Officers' Service

Abbreviations :—" K."—Killed. " D. of W."—Died of Wounds. " W."—Wounded. " M."—Missing.

THE THIRTEENTH BATTALION

Aitchison, W. Major. *k*. 12th July, 1917.

Ambler, R. Lieut. To hospital 5th July, 1917. Rejoined 11th July, 1917. To Base for Indian Army 18th July, 1917.

Bain, D. 2nd Lieut. Joined 5th July, 1917. To hospital 2nd Sept., 1917.

Barrington, Hon. R. E. S. Major. Joined Battn. when formed. To hospital 27th Sept., 1917. Rejoined. Mentioned in Despatches 25th Oct., 1917. Assumed command of Battn. 29th April, 1918. Promoted Lieut.-Col. 8th May, 1918. Awarded D.S.O. 9th June, 1918. Mentioned in Despatches 4th Aug., 1918. *w*. 6th Oct., 1918.

Bartram, R. A. Lieut. Joined Battn. when formed. To hospital 26th Nov., 1916. Rejoined 18th Dec., 1916. Awarded M.C. for gallantry 21st Feb., 1917.

Bell, D. 2nd Lieut. Joined 21st Sept., 1918. *k*. 6th Oct., 1918.

Bennie, D. 2nd Lieut. Promoted Lieut. 1st July, 1917. *w*. 2nd Feb., 1918. Rejoined Battn. Awarded M.C. 26th Nov., 1918.

Blair, P. J. Temp. Lieut.-Col. 12th Oct., 1918. Commanded Battn. till Cadre demobilized, 1919. Awarded D.S.O. Jan., 1919.

Buy, J. H. 2nd Lieut. Joined 15th July, 1917. Promoted Lieut. 21st Nov., 1917. Appointed Capt. and Adjt. 7th Oct., 1918.

Calder, A. M. 2nd Lieut. Joined 26th Oct., 1918.

Callin, R. W. Capt. C.F. Joined 9th Aug., 1918.

Couper, J. D. Capt. Joined Battn. when formed. To hospital 21st Oct., 1916. Rejoined 10th Jan., 1917.

Cowan, J. 2nd Lieut. *d*. 25th Oct., 1915.

Cunliffe, B. F. G. Lieut. Joined Battn. when formed. To R.F.C. 14th March, 1917.

Dawson, R. G. Major. Joined Battn. when formed. Mentioned in Despatches 4th Aug., 1918. Transferred to 4th Battn. 17th Sept., 1918.

Dewar, J. Capt. Joined Battn. when formed. Attached to 81st Infantry Brigade 10th Jan., 1918. Attached to 27th Div. Staff 23rd Feb., 1918. Rejoined Battn. 24th April, 1918. Awarded M.C. 13th Dec., 1918.

Dewar, J. N. 2nd Lieut. Joined Battn. when formed. To Reinforcement Depot 10th Oct., 1916. Rejoined. To hospital 13th Aug., 1917. Rejoined 25th Aug., 1917. Promoted Lieut. 1st July, 1917. To U.K. 15th Sept., 1918.

Eadie, J.A. Lieut. Joined Battn. 12th June, 1918.

Edwards, Hon. C. Capt. *k*. 20th Nov., 1917.

Ferguson, D. F. 2nd Lieut. *k*. 7th May, 1917.

Ferguson, H. 2nd Lieut. Joined 21st Oct., 1918.

THE THIRTEENTH BATTALION THE BLACK WATCH

Ferney, E. M. 2nd Lieut. Joined Battn. when formed. Promoted Lieut. 1st July, 1917. *w.* 6th Oct., 1918.
Foreman, J. Lieut. M.O.R.C., U.S.A. Joined 13th Oct.
Forster, W. 2nd Lieut. Joined 29th Aug., 1918. *w.* 2nd Oct., 1918.
Forsyth, J. C. 2nd Lieut. Joined 1st Sept., 1918. *k.* 11th Oct., 1918.
Fraser, J. 2nd Lieut. Joined 26th Oct., 1918. Injured 4th Nov., 1918. Awarded M.C. 13th Dec., 1918.

Gibb, J. R. 2nd Lieut. Joined 22nd Oct., 1918. *k.* 4th Nov., 1918.
Gibson, R. 2nd Lieut. Joined 21st Oct., 1918.
Grant-Peterkin, C. G. Capt. Joined Battn. when formed. *d. of w.* 12th Sept., 1917.
Gray, M. W. Lieut. Joined Battn. when formed. Left Battn. for Base 21st June, 1917.
Gray, R. 2nd Lieut. Joined Battn. when formed. Promoted Lieut. 1st July, 1917.
Greening, V. C. 2nd Lieut. Joined 1st Sept., 1918.
Grogan, A. W. Capt. Joined 17th Feb., 1917. To 5th Entrenching Battn. 5th Oct., 1917. Rejoined 9th Jan., 1918.
Guise, P. S. 2nd Lieut. Joined Battn. when formed. To hospital 17th January, 1917. Rejoined 12th Feb., 1917. To A.S.C. 19th July, 1917.

Hamilton, G. Lieut. Joined Battn. when formed. To hospital 1st Jan., 1917. Rejoined 12th Feb., 1917. Promoted Capt. 8th Oct., 1917. Awarded M.C. for gallantry 6th Feb., 1918.
Haven, C. J. Lieut. and Q.M. Joined Battn. when formed. Promoted Capt. March, 1918. Mentioned in Despatches 4th Aug., 1918.
Heard, A. G. Lieut. M.O.R.C., U.S.A. Joined 18th Sept., 1918. To hospital 10th Oct., 1918. Rejoined. *w.* 7th Oct., 1918. Awarded M.C. 5th Dec., 1918.
Hinshelwood, A. W. 2nd Lieut. Joined Battn. when formed. To Reinforcement Depot 13th Oct., 1918.
Hudson, R. C. Lieut. Joined Battn. 5th April, 1917. Appointed A.D.C. to G.O.C. in Command B.S.F. 10th Oct., 1917.
Hunter, G. A. Lieut. *d.* 3rd Aug., 1917.
Hutton, R. Capt. *k.* 22nd Aug., 1917.

Inglis, R. Lieut. Joined Battn. when formed. *w.* 3rd Oct., 1918. *d. of w.* 8th Oct., 1918. Awarded posthumous M.C. 12th Nov., 1918.

Jenkins, A. 2nd Lieut. Joined 26th Oct., 1918.
Jones, I. R. 2nd Lieut. Joined Battn. when formed. To hospital 27th Dec., 1916.
Jones, L. H. 2nd Lieut. Joined Reinforcement Depot 17th Nov., 1916. Rejoined Battn. 7th Sept., 1917. Promoted Lieut. 1st July, 1917. *w.* 3rd Oct., 1918. *d. of w.*

APPENDIX I

Keith, J. A. 2nd Lieut. Joined from 4th Battn. 16th Aug., 1918. *w.* 19th Oct., 1918.

Kennedy, J. G. Capt. Joined Battn. when formed. To 27th Div. Headquarters 2nd June, 1917. To 80th Brigade as Staff Capt. 21st Jan., 1918. Awarded M.C. 26th Nov., 1918.

Kinloch, C. 2nd Lieut. Joined Battn. when formed. Promoted Lieut. 1st July, 1917. *w.* 2nd Oct., 1918.

Lyle, A. M. P. Capt. Joined Battn. when formed. Awarded M.C. 5th Nov., 1917.

Mackay, G. S. 2nd Lieut. Joined Battn. 13th Oct., 1916. Promoted Lieut. 1st July, 1917. Awarded M.C. 6th Feb., 1918. To U.K. 9th May, 1918.

MacLean, A. M. Capt. Joined Battn. when formed. To R.F.C. 1st Feb., 1917.

McBarnet, A. E. Lieut.-Col. M.V.O., D.S.O. Joined Battn. when formed. Relinquished command of Battn. 3rd April, 1917.

McDowall, H. A. 2nd Lieut. Joined 29th Aug., 1918. Gassed 2nd Oct., 1918.

McIntyre, A. C. Lieut. Joined Battn. when formed. Promoted Capt. 1st June, 1916.

MacGregor, A. J. L. Capt. Joined Battn. when formed. Awarded M.C. 9th June, 1917. *w.* 6th Oct., 1918. *d. of w.* 8th Oct., 1918.

MacKinley, R. M. 2nd Lieut. Joined 4th Nov., 1918.

Marshall, P. H. Lieut. Joined Battn. 25th Aug., 1917. Struck off strength 22nd Sept., 1918.

Martin, R. Lieut. *k.* 4th Sept., 1917.

Martin, H. A. S. 2nd Lieut. Joined 22nd Oct., 1918.

Matson, H. A. S. 2nd Lieut. To hospital 1st Nov., 1918.

Mill, J. 2nd Lieut. Joined Battn. when formed. To Army Lewis Gun School as Instructor 13th Sept., 1917. Promoted Lieut. 1st July, 1917. Transferred to U.K. 29th Jan., 1918.

Mitchell, A. T. 2nd Lieut. Joined 29th Aug., 1918. To hospital 10th Nov., 1918.

Mitchell, J. 2nd Lieut. Joined from 4th Battn. 26th Aug., 1918. *w.* and *m.* 19th Aug., 1918. *d. of w.* in enemy hands 23rd Oct., 1918.

Moore, D. G. F. Lieut. Joined Battn. when formed. To hospital 19th Nov., 1917. Rejoined 5th December, 1917. Struck off strength, to U.K. 31st Aug., 1918.

Morgan, L. S. J. 2nd Lieut. Joined 1st Sept., 1918. *w.* 19th Oct., 1918.

Murray, A. Capt. *k.* 14th Aug., 1917.

Myers, J. C. Capt. *k.* 4th May, 1918.

Neilson, F. G. Capt. Joined Reinforcement Depot 17th Nov., 1916. Rejoined Battn. To 27th Division Headquarters as A.D.C. 21st Jan., 1917. Rejoined Battn. 19th March, 1918.

THE THIRTEENTH BATTALION THE BLACK WATCH

Neilson, W. Capt. Joined 12th June, 1918. Transferred to 149th T.M. Batty.

Nicol, C. 2nd Lieut. Joined Battn. when formed. To 245th M.T. Coy. 6th Feb., 1917.

Patrick, J. A. 2nd Lieut. Joined Battn. when formed. To Reinforcement Depot 13th Oct., 1916.

Price, J. 2nd Lieut. Joined 26th Aug., 1918. To hospital 4th Oct., 1918.

Railston, H. G. M. Lieut.-Col. Joined and assumed command of Battn. 4th April, 1917. Promoted Brevet Major for distinguished service in the field 3rd June, 1917. Left Battn to command 4th Battn. Rifle Brigade 28th April, 1918.

Rattray, P. M. Major. D.S.O. Joined Battn. when formed. To U.K. 12th March, 1917.

Rawson, A. Lieut. and Adj. Joined Battn. when formed. Appointed Adj. 28th Nov., 1916. Mentioned in Despatches 29th March, 1917. Promoted Capt. 20th Sept., 1917. k. 6th Oct., 1918.

Reid, G. S. 2nd Lieut. Joined Battn. 15th July, 1917.

Richardson, J. H. Capt. C.F. Joined Battn. when formed.

Riddell, J. E. 2nd Lieut. Joined 1st Sept., 1918. To hospital 2nd Oct., 1918. Rejoined 21st Oct., 1918.

Risk, J. D. 2nd Lieut. Joined 21st Oct., 1918. w. 4th Nov., 1918.

Robertson, A. F. Lieut. Joined Battn. 9th Aug., 1917. Promoted Capt., antedated from 8th May, 1915. To Base 11th Nov., 1917. Rejoined Battn. 10th Aug., 1918. Transferred to 149th Infantry Brigade details 28th Oct., 1918.

Robertson, G. Lieut. Joined Battn. 8th Feb., 1917. w. 19th Oct., 1918. Awarded M.C. 26th Nov., 1918.

Robertson, G. M. 2nd Lieut. Joined 26th Oct., 1918. To hospital 1st Nov., 1918.

Robertson, J. Lieut. Joined Battn. 2nd Feb., 1918. Left Battn. for U.K. 26th Aug., 1918.

Robertson, Ian. Lieut. Joined Battn. 10th April, 1917.

Rowan, R. Lieut. k. 22nd Aug., 1918.

Rundell, W. W. O. Major. Joined 21st June, 1917. To 4th Entrenching Battn. 24th July, 1917.

Rusack, D. W. Lieut. Joined Battn. when formed. w. 11th Nov., 1918.

Rutherford, G. 2nd Lieut. Joined Battn. when formed. To hospital 13th Jan., 1917. Rejoined 28th Jan., 1917. To hospital 16th Oct., 1917. Rejoined 11th Nov., 1917. Promoted Lieut. 6th Nov., 1917. w. 6th Oct., 1918.

Schmidt, C. 2nd Lieut. Joined from Base 6th Oct., 1916. Promoted Lieut. 1st July, 1917. Left Battn. to join Indian Cavalry 21st May, 1918.

Scott, P. W. Capt. R.A.M.C. Rejoined Battn. 30th Aug., 1917. To hospital 18th Sept., 1918.

APPENDIX I

Scott, W. G. 2nd Lieut. Joined Battn. when formed. To 22nd Div. as Instructor 28th June, 1917. Awarded M.C. 5th Nov., 1917. Promoted Lieut. 1st July, 1917. To XVI Corps School 26th Nov., 1917. Mentioned in Despatches 25th Oct., 1917; 4th Aug., 1918. Rejoined Battn. 11th Nov., 1918.

Skelton, A. N. Capt. Joined Battn. when formed. Attached to 27th Div. Headquarters 9th July, 1917. To hospital 16th Oct., 1917. Rejoined 11th Oct., 1918. *w.* 19th Oct., 1918.

Smith, R. E. Lieut. Joined Battn. when formed. To hospital 18th Jan., 1918. Rejoined. Awarded M.C. 13th Dec., 1918.

Soundy, H. C. Lieut. Joined Battn. when formed.

Sturrock, E. W. B. 2nd Lieut. Joined Battn. 13th Oct., 1916. To hospital 21st Dec., 1916.

Tullibardine, Col. the Marquis of. Mobilized the Battn. Aug., 1914.

Wambeck, W. G. L. Capt. R.A.M.C. Joined Battn. when formed.

Watson, R. Lieut. Joined Battn. 24th July, 1917. To Div. School as Instructor 11th Sept., 1917. Promoted Lieut. 21st July, 1917. Rejoined Battn. 9th June, 1918. *w.* 19th Oct., 1918. Awarded M.C. 12th Nov., 1918.

Wilson, W. C. 2nd Lieut. Joined 26th Oct., 1918.

Woods, G. W. M. 2nd Lieut. Joined 26th Oct., 1918.

APPENDIX II

Summary of Casualties

THE THIRTEENTH BATTALION

OFFICERS, 1916–18

Year.	Killed. D. of Wounds. D. on Service.	Wounded.	Missing	Total.	Year.
1916	—	—	—	—	1916
1917	16	—	—	16	1917
1918	13	16	1	30	1918
Totals :	29	16	1	46	

OTHER RANKS, 1916–18

Year.	Killed. D. of Wounds. D. on Service.	Wounded.	Missing.	Total.	Year.
1916	1	9	—	10	1916
1917	16	11	—	27	1917
1918	134	345	—	479	1918
Totals :	151	365	—	516	

TOTAL :

Officers, 46.   Other Ranks, 516.

APPENDIX III

Casualties—Officers

* Killed in action.　† Died of wounds.　§ Died.

THE THIRTEENTH BATTALION

Name.	Rank.	Date.
Aitchison, W.	Major	*12.7.17.
Bell, D.	2nd Lieut.	*6.10.18.
Cowan, J.	2nd Lieut.	§25.10.18.
Edwardes, Hon. C.	Captain	*20.11.17. And Tanks.
Ferguson, D. F.	2nd Lieut.	*7.5.17.
Forsyth, J. C.	2nd Lieut.	*11.10.18.
Gibb, J. R.	2nd Lieut.	*4.11.18.
Grant-Peterkin, C. G.	Captain	†12.9.17.
Hunter, G. A.	Lieut.	§3.8.17. And M.G.C.
Hutton, R.	Captain	*22.8.17.
Inglis, R.	Lieut.	†5.10.18.
MacGregor, A. J. L.	Captain	*6.10.18.
Martin, R.	Lieut.	*4.9.17. And R.F.C.
Mitchell, J.	2nd Lieut.	†23.10.18. In German hands.
Murray, A.	Captain	*14.8.17.
Myers, J. C.	Captain	*4.5.18.
Rawson, A.	Captain	*6.10.18.
Rowan, R.	Lieut.	*22.8.18.

APPENDIX IV

Nominal Roll of Warrant Officers, Non-Commissioned Officers and Men Killed in Action or Died of Wounds or Disease in the Great War, 1914–18

* Killed in action. † Died of wounds. ‡ Died at home. § Died.

THE THIRTEENTH BATTALION

Adair, W. S., Pte., S/17202	* 4.11.18	Farquhar, E. R., Pte., 315845	* 4.11.18
Aird, J. Y., Pte., 316434	* 4.11.18	Ferguson, J., Pte., 315612	* 8.11.18
Allan, J., L/Cpl., 315494	* 4.11.18	Finlay, C., Pte., S/25778	* 4.11.18
Andrews, J. P., Pte., 316437	*17.10.18	Fraser, I. W., Cpl., 316403	* 3.10.18
Armour, A., Pte., 315804	†24.10.18	Frew, J. W., Pte., 315850	*17.10.18
Ashworth, E., Pte., 315566	†30.11.16		
		Galloway, F., Pte., 315861	*17.10.18
Balchin, W., Cpl., 316442	†17.10.18	Gemmell, W. H., Pte., 316349	
Benzie, G., Pte., 316451	*17.10.18		‡19.5.18
Brand, G. E., Pte., S/25808	* 4.11.18	Gentles, A., Pte., 315327	*14.10.17
Brebner, J. P., L/Sgt., 315779	*17.10.18	George, W., L/Cpl., 315799	§ 2.9.17
Brodie, T. S., Pte., 315808	*17.10.18	Gibson, J., Pte., 315865	§25.4.18
Brown, D. W., Pte., 315066	†17.10.18	Gillespie, G. B., Pte., 315618	*17.10.18
Brown, J., Pte., 315812	‡ 4.7.18	Gilmour, W. T., Sgt., 316559	†14.10.18
Bruce, L., Pte., 316463	*17.10.18	Goodfellow, T., Pte., 316561	† 9.10.18
Bryden, J., Pte., 315813	*14.10.17	Graham, D., Pte., 315619	* 3.10.18
Bulloch, J., Pte., 316468	*17.10.18	Grier, J., Pte., 315251	†18.10.18
Calder, H. S., Pte., 315586	*17.10.18	Haig, A., Pte., 315750	* 3.10.18
Cameron, K., Pte., 315072	* 4.11.18	Haigh, P., Pte., 316574	*17.10.18
Campbell, A. B., Sgt., 316475	*17.10.18	Hamilton, W., Pte., S/5296	* 4.11.18
Campbell, A., Pte., 316474	* 4.11.18	Hendry, G., Sgt., 316585	* 4.11.18
Clark, J. W., L/Cpl., 315590	* 4.11.18	Hill, A., Pte., 315129	*17.10.18
Connolly, D., Pte., S/21031	*17.10.18	Horne, D., Pte., S/25644	* 4.11.18
Corson, G. C. W., Pte., 315081		Howatson, W., Pte., 315133	†13.11.18
	†10.11.18	Hunter, D. W. H., Pte., 316353	
Cowieson, R. C., Pte., 316491	*17.10.18		*17.10.18
Craig, C., Pte., 315826	† 4.11.18		
Craig, H. G., Pte., 315084	‡ 5.11.18	Inglis, J. L., Pte., 315633	* 3.10.18
Crawford, D., Pte., 315829	* 8.10.18		
Crerar, A., Pte., 315083	* 4.11.18	Jack, J. W., Pte., 315639	* 4.10.18
Daniels, A., Pte., 316344	§ 5.1.18	Keith, G., Pte., 315641	* 8.10.18
Dawson, T., Pte., 316411	* 8.10.18	Knox, A., L/Cpl., 315495	* 4.11.18
Dickson, J., L/Cpl., 315603	* 3.10.18		
Dobbie, D., L/Cpl., 315744	* 4.11.18	Laidlaw, J. B., Sgt., 315022	* 4.11.18
Donald, D., L/Cpl., 315473	* 8.11.18	Laidlaw, J. T., Pte., 315354	* 8.10.18
Duffus, P., Pte., 315316	*18.10.18	Lathan, L., Pte., 315884	† 4.11.18
Duncan, J., Pte., 316346	* 7.2.18	Liddell, A., Pte., 315648	† 4.11.18
Duncan, W., L/Cpl., 316516	†31.8.17	Low, G. M., Pte., 315647	† 4.10.18
Edgar, M., Pte., 315098	*11.4.17	Mackie, A., Pte., 316638	* 4.11.18
		MacDonald, A., Pte., S/25689	†16.11.18
Falconer, J. H., L/Cpl., 315746		MacDonald, J., Pte., S/25699	* 4.11.18
	*17.10.18	MacDougall, A., Pte., 316688	* 4.11.18
Farmer, F., Pte., S/25634	* 4.11.18	MacKay, C., Pte., 315169	†18.10.18

308

APPENDIX IV

MacKenzie, D., Pte., 315384 *17.10.18
MacNicol, J., Pte., 315752 ‡ 7.11.18
MacPherson, D., Sgt., 315783 * 6.10.18
McAndrew, S., Pte., 316535 *17.10.18
McBean, J., Sgt., 315765 *17.10.18
McCallum, J. A., Pte., 315378 *17.10.18
McCulloch, J., Pte., 315379 *17.10.18
McDade, C., Pte., 315406 † 4.11.18
McDonald, G. D. M., Pte., 315674
 * 3.10.18
McEwan, A., Pte., 315404 †12.11.18
McFarlane, J., Pte., 316009 † 4.11.17
McGregor, W., Pte., S/25702 * 4.11.18
McIntosh, H., Cpl., 315024 § 4.3.18
McIntosh, J. S., C.S.M., 315003
 (M.S.M.) *17.10.18
McKinnon, N., Pte., 315387 * 4.11.18
McLean, R. A., Pte., 315389 †18.10.18
McLennan, J., Pte., 316720 † 3.10.18
McMurdo, A., Pte., 315175 *17.10.18
McQuarrie, A., Pte., 316731 † 1.3.17
McTavish, J., Sgt., 316733 †18.10.18
Matthew, C., Pte., 315149 * 7.10.18
Meadowcroft, J. W., Pte., S/21139
 †10.11.18
Menzies, J., Pte., 316650 †18.10.18
Milligan, J., Pte., 315905 §24.1.18
Milne, G., Pte., 315656 *17.10.18
Milne, R. E., Pte., S/17965 * 4.11.18
Mitchell, W. L., A/Cpl., 315041
 †24.10.18
Muir, W., Pte., S/25995 † 4.11.18
Murchie, W., Pte., 315904 *14.10.17
Murchison, J., Pte., 316671 *17.10.18
Murray, A. E. J., Pte., 315902 *18.10.18

Neil, A., Pte., 315181 †17.10.18
Neil, W., L/Sgt., S/5818 * 8.11.18
Neill, J., Pte., 316740 § 8.10.17
Nelson, O. A., Pte., 316741 * 3.10.18
Nicholson, T., Pte., 316363 †18.10.18

Patterson, D., Pte., 316753 † 6.11.18
Pentland, W., Pte., 315689 † 8.12.18
Pollock, W. Pte. 316758 * 8.10.18

Quaey, J. K., Pte., 316279 * 4.10.18
Quinn, J., Pte., 316760 †28.10.18

Rintoul, W., Pte., 316230 *17.10.18
Robertson, A., Pte., 315962 * 7.10.18
Robertson, J., A/Sgt., 315776 † 5.11.18
Robertson, W. J., Pte., 315431
 * 4.11.18
Ross, H., Pte., 316780 †25.10.18
Russell, G., Pte., 315963 *27.2.17

Samuel, W., Pte., 316789 §14.10.17
Scorgie, G., L/Cpl., 315785 § 9.5.17
Scott, J., Pte., 315704 * 4.10.18
Seaton, R., Pte., 316799 §27.10.17
Simon, G., Pte., 315710 * 8.10.18
Simpson, T. D., Pte., 315709 †19.10.19
Sinclair, R., Pte., 315490 * 4.11.18
Skinner, R., Pte., 315706 * 3.10.18
Smith, D. G., Pte., 315974 *18.10.18
Snodgrass, J. C., Pte., 315219 † 5.11.18
Somerville, D., Pte., 316830 *19.10.18
Stephenson, W., Pte., 316834 * 4.11.18
Stewart, J., L/Cpl., 315755 * 6.11.18
Still, W. S., Pte., 315224 †20.10.18
Strachan, G., C.S.M., 315517
 (M.S.M.) †14.10.17
Sturrock, J., Pte., 315226 * 4.11.18
Sutherland, G. F., Pte., 315714
 §28.7.18

Taylor, J. A. D., Pte., 315980
 ‡11.11.18
Taylor, T. G., Pte., 315717 *17.10.18
Thain, A., L/Cpl., 315718 * 3.10.18
Thomson, W. B., Pte., S/14199
 † 4.11.18
Wallace, A., Pte., 268968 * 3.10.18
Watson, J., Pte., 315462 * 4.11.18
White, J., Pte., 315990 *17.10.18
Whyte, R., Pte., 316870 §16.3.17
Wilson, J., Pte., 316873 †22.10.18
Wilson, N., Pte., 315986 *14.10.17
Wright, J. A., A/Cpl., 315047 * 4.11.18

APPENDIX V

HONOURS AND AWARDS

THE THIRTEENTH BATTALION

D.S.O.
Lieut.-Col. The Hon. R. E. S. Barrington.
Lieut.-Col. P. J. Blair.
Lieut.-Col. H. G. M. Railston.

M.C.
Lieut. R. A. Bartram.
Lieut. D. Bennie.
Capt. The Hon. J. Dewar
Lieut. J. Fraser.
Capt. G. Hamilton.
Lieut. A. G. Heard.
Lieut. R. Inglis.
Capt. J. K. Kennedy.
Major A. M. P. Lyle.
Capt. A. J. L. MacGregor.
Lieut. G. S. Mackay.
Lieut. G. Robertson.
Lieut. W. G. Scott.
Lieut. R. E. Smith.
Lieut. R. Watson.
R.S.M. J. Cowie.

D.C.M.
L/Corpl. P. Farquharson.
Corpl. L. Finnie.
Sgt. C. McFarlane.
Pte. W. McLeod.
Sgt. R. Ross.

M.S.M.
C.M.S. A. Allen.
C.Q.M.S. D. Crichton.
R.Q.M.S. J. Falconer.
C.Q.M.S. R. Greig.
C.Q.M.S. J. McDonald.
Sgt. W. McHardy.
C.S.M. J. S. McIntosh.
L/Corpl. A. Semple.
C.S.M. G. A. Strachan.

BAR TO M.M.
L/Corpl. J. Cameron.
Pte. D. McIntyre.
Sgt. J. Murdoch.

M.M.
C.S.M. A. Allen.
Pte. J. Allen.
Pte. J. Baxter.
Sgt. D. Bruce.
L/Corpl. A. Cameron.
L/Corpl. J. Cameron.
Pte. A. D. Campbell.
Pte. J. Campbell.
Corpl. W. Chalmers.
Sgt. J. Cowan.
L/Corpl. J. Cunningham.
L/Corpl. J. Darroch.
Sgt. A. Fenwick.
Pte. J. Ferguson.
Sgt. G. Gellatly.
Pte. W. Grant.
Pte. A. Halliday.
Pte. J. Hardie.
L/Corpl. C. Hailey.
L/Corpl. M. Jamieson.
Sgt. A. Kirkpatrick.
Pte. A. Knox.
L/Corpl. A. Lees.
Pte. C. Low.
Pte. A. Malcolm.
Pte. J. Matthewson.

APPENDIX V

M.M. (*continued*)

C.S.M. J. Munro.
Sgt. J. Murdoch.
Pte. T. McAuley.
L/Corpl. J. McDonald.
Corpl. G. McGibbon.
Pte. D. McIntyre.
L/Corpl. K. McLean.
Sgt. A. McNaughton.
Pte. K. McRae.
L/Corpl. D. Pirie.
Pte. Z. Pollard.
L/Corpl. J. Reid.
Sgt. D. Roy.
Pte. J. B. Shand.
Pte. T. Smellie.
Pte. P. L. Smith.
Corpl. J. Spark.
Sgt. G. Templeton.
Pte. R. Thomson.
Sgt. J. Walker.

Mentioned in Despatches

Capt. Hon. R. E. S. Barrington (2)
Capt. T. Buy.
Capt. E. W. Callin, C.F.
Capt. J. D. Couper.
Major R. G. Dawson.
Lieut. R. Gibson.
Capt. & Q.M. C. J. Haven (3)

Major A. M. Lyle.
Capt. A. C. McIntyre.
Lieut. Col. H. G. M. Railston.
Capt. A. Rawson (2).
Lieut. W. G. Scott.
Capt. A. N. Skelton.

C.S.M. A. Allen.
Corpl. A. Donald.
R.Q.M.S. J. Falconer.
Sgt. J. Farquhar (2).
R.Q.M.S. J. Hay.
A/Sgt. D. Jamieson.
Sgt. J. Japp.
Sgt. J. Miller.
C.S.M. J. Munro.

C.Q.M.S. J. McDonald.
Sgt. J. McHardy (2).
C.S.M. J. McIntosh (2).
Sgt. A. McNaughton.
L/Sgt. D. McPherson.
Corpl. W. Simpson.
C.Q.M.S. J. Turner.
L/Corpl. A. Wrench.

APPENDIX VI

LIST OF ACTIONS AND OPERATIONS

THE THIRTEENTH BATTALION

1916. Became 13th Black Watch in Egypt. 29th September. Landed in Macedonia. 21st October.

    Trench warfare. Karadzakoj, Hristian Kamila, Kavakli. November–December.

1917. Trench warfare. Bala-Homondos Sector, Hristian Sector, Osman Kamila, River Line, Homondos. January–December.

1918. Trench warfare. Homondos Sector. January–June.

    Left Macedonia. 17th June. Arrived France. 24th June.

    Trench warfare. Vendhuille Sector.

    BATTLE OF THE RIVER SELLE. (Le Cateau.) 17th–18th October.

    BATTLE OF THE SAMBRE. (Haute Cornée.) 4th November.

    ADVANCE TO VICTORY. 11th November.

THE FOURTEENTH BATTALION

PREFACE TO THE FOURTEENTH BATTALION

THE Fife and Forfar Yeomanry was raised in 1794 when, in response to Pitt's famous appeal, regiments of Yeomanry were formed throughout the country to repel any invasion that might be attempted by the armies of Napoleon. It was not, however, until the Boer War that the Regiment first saw active service.

In August, 1914, the fear of invasion was no less acute than it had been in the last years of the eighteenth century, and the Regiment was at once despatched to the east coast of England, for defence duty, remaining there some time.

In 1916 the main armies were still engaged in position warfare, and it was evident that the need for infantry was greater than for regiments of Cavalry or Yeomanry. It was therefore decided that a number of mounted regiments should be converted into infantry battalions, and in November, 1916, the Fife and Forfar Yeomanry received orders that the regiment was to be converted into the 14th Battalion, The Black Watch, and that the men were at once to learn infantry drill.

Until the Fife and Forfar Yeomanry became an infantry battalion its deeds and story have no part in the history of The Black Watch. But the Regiment played an equally honourable part in the earlier, as in the later years, of the Great War. It served with marked distinction at Gallipoli, losing many officers and men and enduring the appalling conditions which prevailed during that unfortunate campaign. On the evacuation of the Peninsula, the Regiment proceeded to Egypt, where it did good service with the South-Western Mounted Brigade, and later, in April, 1916, became part of the Kharga Oasis Detachment in which it spent a quiet, but hot, summer.

New Year's Day, 1917, found the Regiment at Moascar on the Suez Canal, and it was here that it became the 14th (Fife and Forfar Yeomanry) Battalion, The Black Watch. Much as every officer, non-commissioned officer and man regretted the change and the temporary closing of the records of a regiment which had such a career as had the Fife and Forfar Yeomanry, it was realized that it was necessary. No other regiment in His Majesty's service appealed to all ranks as did that of its own Territorial and Yeomany regiments, and if change there were to be, all ranks were proud to learn that The Black Watch had been selected as the regiment into which they were now to be incorporated.

New Year's Day, 1917.

THE FOURTEENTH BATTALION THE BLACK WATCH

OPERATIONS IN PALESTINE, 1917-18

CHAPTER I

JANUARY, 1917—APRIL, 1918

Palestine

ON January 2nd the 14th moved to El Fedran, where for two months it carried out infantry training and brigade exercises, during which period reinforcements, amounting to 12 officers and 393 other ranks arrived, and by the end of February the Battalion was reorganized.

On March 4th it moved to Kantara, entrained for El Arish, and arrived there the following day. Here it formed part of the 229th Infantry Brigade—Brigadier-General R. Hoare—the other battalions being the 12th Royal Scots (late Ayr and Lanark Yeomanry), the 12th Somerset L.I. (late West Somerset Yeomanry), and the 16th Devonshire Regiment (late N. Devon Yeomanry), 74th Division, under Major-General E. S. Girdwood, C. B., C.M.G.

At Kantara further drafts were received, the following officers commanding —

> Lieut.-Colonel J. Gilmour (Commanding Officer).
> Major J. Younger (Second-in-Command).
> Lieut. A. C. Smith (Adjutant).
> Captain G. E. B. Osborne (A company).
> Captain R. W. Stewart (B company).
> Captain I. C. Nairn (C company).
> Captain H. S. Sharp (D company).

Moving up from El Arish on March 22nd, the Battalion took part in the first battle of Gaza, forming part of the Reserve of the XX Corps and occupying a position at Rafa. The following ten to twelve weeks were spent in front of Gaza digging trenches and holding the line, rendered especially unpleasant owing to the dry and fiercely hot wind from the desert and the scarcity of water.

In July General Allenby took over command of the Mediterranean Expeditionary Force, and a general reorganization took place, the 74th Division being withdrawn from the line for training purposes. The training was severe, and after a fortnight the Battalion was sent to dig trenches in the hills facing Gaza, an extremely difficult work.

At the end of August the 14th moved to Wadi Selke, where it took part in Divisional training, for an attack on Beersheba, designed to take place about the end of October, and spent the whole of September and most of October so employed.

On October 25th the Battalion moved to Abu Sitta, the concentrating point of the attacking force.

Beersheba itself occupied a commanding position, well

defended with wire. The main attack was to be pushed home south of the Wadi Saba by the 60th and 74th Divisions, while the enemy's extreme left, that is, the desert flank, was to be turned by cavalry, who, making a wide detour through difficult and waterless country, were to attack Beersheba from the east with a view of cutting off the retreat of the Turkish garrison. The arrangements for troop movements worked well, and before dawn on the 30th both the 60th and 74th Divisions were in position.

The attack was a complete success, the enemy's advanced positions being carried by 8.45 a.m., and the 74th Division crossed the Wadi Saba and cleared the enemy trenches northwards as far as the barrier on the Fara–Beersheba road. Beersheba itself was occupied that night, few of the Turkish garrison escaping.

On October 30th the cavalry had passed through the front line, and the 229th Brigade moved up to Dundee Wadi, the 231st then passing through and taking up a more forward position. On November 2nd the 14th took over the outpost line from the 2/10th Middlesex Regiment (53rd Division), and on the 4th advanced its line some way with little opposition.

At 7 p.m. on the 5th, orders were received for an attack on the Turkish position the following morning by the 229th Brigade. The 14th was, therefore, relieved at 9 p.m. by a battalion from the 230th Brigade, and at 11 p.m. moved off to the point of deployment.

The objective was the Sheria defences, part of the Kuwauka system. The 229th was the spear-head of the attack, the 14th Black Watch and the 12th Battalion Somerset L.I. being in the front line, while echeloned on the right and left respectively were the 230th Brigade, 74th Division and a brigade of the 60th Division.

The attack was launched at 5 a.m. on the 6th, and by 2.30 p.m. all objectives had been captured and the position consolidated.

The 10th Division then took over the line from the 60th, on the left, and attacked the wells and railway station at Tel El Sheria. By this time it was getting dark and direction was lost. The enemy resisted stubbornly, and it was not until the following morning that both these objectives had been gained, although it was apparent by the brilliant light from fires behind the Turkish lines that they intended to retreat, and were burning all surplus material.

The advance began at 5 a.m., and although badly enfiladed from the right and held up for a short time, the Turkish positions were carried by 6.15 a.m. The first objective was taken at 5.55 a.m., together with four guns, limbered up and trying to

CAPTURE OF SHERIA POSITION

get away. The next position, the ridge behind the first objective, was taken twenty minutes later, and the Battalion continued its advance, and by midday had penetrated 10,000 yards.

At noon another advance was made, this time under fairly heavy fire, but the Battalion Lewis guns were exceedingly well handled and succeeded in knocking out the crew and teams of two field guns in position beyond the railway, and the 14th was able to advance just east of this.

The Battalion casualties during this fighting were Major G. E. B. Osborne, Lieutenants J. D. Kinniburgh and E. A. Thomson, and 47 other ranks killed,[1] and five officers and 182 other ranks wounded, of whom 13 subsequently died in hospital. Amongst the wounded was Lieutenant-Colonel J. Gilmour, who was hit at the very end of the day, and to whom was due no small part of the credit for the victory. The élan and dash of the 14th on this occasion gained for it the highest praise from all quarters. During the operations the Battalion captured 99 Turks, six field guns and a large quantity of S.A.A.

For services rendered at the battle of Sheria, the following honours were awarded to members of the Battalion: one D.S.O., four M.C.'s, five D.C.M.'s, and one M.M.

Major J. Younger, who had been acting as liaison officer between the 60th and 74th Divisions, assumed command from Lieutenant-Colonel Gilmour.

Two days were spent in clearing the battle-field, after which, on the 9th, the Battalion moved to Goz El Gelieb, where it remained a fortnight, moving to Wadi Ghuzzeh, in the Gaza area, being employed there on salvage work.

The advance, which ended in the capture of Jerusalem, was resumed on the 24th, the Battalion moving to Ali El Muntar, Mejd El, Wadi Sukharieh and Ludd, which was reached on the 27th. From Ludd the 14th moved into the Judæan Hills via Latron and Beit Sirra, reaching Likia on November 30th.

The country the 14th was now in was a series of rocky hills, many steep, all covered with huge boulders, and each separated from its neighbour by dry wadis (water courses). To find the way in such a country was exceedingly difficult, and more so in Palestine, where the maps were obsolete and not contoured. Consequently, when told to make good, say, Hill 1750, the difficulty was first to find the hill on the map and, having located it, to take it, since the hills were generally occupied by the Turks in force, and before any particular hill could be taken it was usually found necessary to capture others which either flanked or overlooked the original objective.

The first operation in this—to them—new country the 14th

[1] The dead were buried in the "Cactus Garden."

THE FOURTEENTH BATTALION THE BLACK WATCH

had to undertake was the capture of "Hill 1750," and as explained, the Battalion could not turn the enemy off it without the assistance of the 16th Battalion Devonshire Regiment, who had been detailed to carry out a similar operation on the Hill of Foka, which appeared to command "Hill 1750."

This combined operation took place on December 1st near Likia, and the 14th rushed the hill successfully, taking many prisoners, but it proved impossible to hold the position. It was exposed to fire from three sides, with no cover available, and digging—owing to the nature of the rocky ground—was impossible. There was nothing for it, therefore, but to retire.

On the 4th the Battalion was relieved in the line, and, after a couple of days' rest, orders were received to the effect that the Division would take part in a sweeping movement by which it was intended to capture Jerusalem. The operation started the following day, and four days later the city fell into the hands of the Allies with no resistance.

Throughout this successful operation, the 14th was in reserve, but it played no small part in the victorious advance and had to undergo, like all others, an exceedingly arduous time, climbing up and down mountains varying from 2500 feet to 600 feet at top speed, carrying full packs, in pouring rain and a hurricane of wind; in addition it was difficult and sometimes impossible to obtain rations; consequently the news of the fall of Jerusalem was hardly received by the Battalion with the joyfulness the occasion demanded.

On December 11th the Battalion moved to Beit Iksa, where it was employed for ten days on road construction. During this time orders were received and arrangements made for a turning movement along the Zeitun Ridge, the object being to place Jerusalem out of reach of the Turkish guns. The 60th Division was detailed to make an advance by the Nablus road, while the 10th, to which the 229th Infantry Brigade was attached, was to advance on Bireh and Ram Allah from the west, the 14th Battalion being the right, or inside wheel, made by brigades in echelon from the right.

Christmas Day was spent under rather trying conditions. The rapidity with which the operations had been carried out so successfully in a country whose nature made things unpleasant, and in addition the appalling weather, continuous rain and wind adding to the general discomfort, it may be well understood that the Battalion did not spend a Merry Christmas in Palestine in 1917.

The attack on the ridge was timed for 8 a.m. on the 28th, the 12th Royal Scots and 12th Somerset Light Infantry being detailed to lead with the 14th Black Watch in support, and the 16th

CAPTURE OF HILL OF SHAFA

Battalion Devonshire Regiment in reserve. By 9 a.m. the ridge Sheikh Abu El Zeitun was taken with slight loss, and a number of prisoners were captured. The ground leading up to the objective was so steep that the enemy had no chance to fire at the advancing line, and the attack itself was carried out so rapidly that they had little time to resist the swift and well planned assault.

Having completed its task of taking the ridge, the 229th Brigade was given another objective, namely, the Hill of Shafa, a mile and a half away, but before this could be carried out it received instructions to wait until the 10th Division, on the left, had got up level. The 10th, however, was delayed until evening, and the 14th Black Watch remained on the sheltered side of the ridge all day, watching a stubborn contest going on on the left between the 10th Division and the enemy, where a hill—" Hill 2450 "—was taken and lost more than once.

At night the Battalion was ordered to attack the hill of Shafa. It was a moonlight night and no difficulty was experienced until half-way up the hill when resistance was encountered. " A " wild fight took place and still wilder firing with great expendi-" ture of ammunition, but about midnight the Turks retreated."

In the morning the Battalion found itself far in advance of those on its right and left and enfiladed from the Turkish position on the left, but it held on to its gains without difficulty. It was, however, impossible to relieve the Battalion, and the 14th, therefore, had to lead the next advance on Beit Ania with the 12th Somerset Light Infantry on the left, the 12th Royal Scots Fusiliers and the 16th Battalion Devonshire Regiment being in support. This attack was carried out at 2 p.m. on the 28th, and was entirely successful.

" Here again the rapidity of our advance proved our salva-" tion, as we were over the crest, and down into the wadi, and " shelter, before the Turkish machine guns got properly going. " Here we reorganized the main attack in our own time and, after " being held up by fire from our right, we got through to the " village and consolidated the position."

The captures by the 14th on this occasion were 150 prisoners, including a battalion commander and nine machine guns, in addition to which about 100 enemy dead were counted. The Battalion lost in this fight three officers killed and three wounded, 11 other ranks killed and 38 wounded. The last two days of 1917 were spent in clearing the battlefield and in reorganizing.

It should be mentioned that one officer and 50 other ranks were sent to furnish guards for Jerusalem, so to the 14th Black Watch fell the honour of supplying the first Christian guard over the holy places in Jerusalem, after a Moslem occupation of over seven centuries.

From Beit Ania the 14th moved, on New Year's Day, 1918, to Tahta, thence to Beit Serra, and finally reached the Rest Camp at Yalo on the 3rd.

So far the advance had been rapid, and the success of the operations astonishing. It was now found necessary to pause before proceeding further north. The greatest difficulty was experienced in bringing supplies up to the front line over the roadless and mountainous country which had just been wrested from the Turk. There were only two metalled roads, namely, one running north from Jerusalem to Nablus, and the other running west from Jerusalem to Jaffa; the remainder were mere tracks over cultivated ground in the valleys, winding up and down the Judæan Hills, impassable to motors and often so to camels and mules. It was therefore necessary to make roads strong enough and wide enough to bear continuous mechanical traffic, and to enable heavy guns to be brought up in support of a further advance.

The 14th was employed on road making from January 4th to the middle of March, 1918, firstly near Yalo, and then, gradually moving northwards, bivouacking as it went at the end of the road it was making. Fortunately this was an easy task, any amount of stone suitable for the work being close at hand. The road was 16 feet broad and the Battalion on some occasions were able to construct as much as $1\frac{1}{2}$ yards per man per day.

On March 14th the Battalion went once more into the front line at Wadi Kolah, taking over about $2\frac{1}{2}$ miles of line previously held by nine companies of the 53rd Division. It was a difficult sector to occupy as it contained three mountains with steep wadis in between. Each of these was occupied by one company, the fourth being in support. Touch between companies was difficult to maintain at night, and quite impossible with neighbouring units. So sketchy was the line that Turkish deserters were sometimes found at daybreak behind the Battalion front line looking vainly for someone to whom to surrender.

The only operation of note which took place during this period was a half-hearted enemy raid on April 7th, which was easily driven off with loss to the enemy. The weather, however, was bad and made outpost work extremely uncomfortable.

This finished the work of the Battalion in Palestine. On April 9th it was ordered to Kantara, where it arrived on the 16th.

" When we arrived (at Kantara) we were a dishevelled
" crowd, out at toe and elbow, but we were completely refitted,
" and presented a very smart appearance once more when we
" embarked on H.M.T. *Indarra* at Alexandria on the 29th."

CHAPTER II

APRIL, 1918, TO MAY, 1919

France

LEAVING Egypt on April 31st, 1918, the Battalion reached Marseilles seven days later, proceeding to Noyelles and marching to billets in St. Firman, where for ten days it was busy training in gas warfare, etc.

The next ten weeks the 14th spent in various places training, during which period leave to England was granted, some of the men never having been home since the Fife and Forfar Yeomen left England in 1915.

In July the 74th Division went into the line in the Lys area, but it was not until the 31st that the Battalion took over the front line in the Robecq sector, XI Corps, Fifth Army. After six days in the line an officers' patrol reported that the enemy were evacuating their front line. Captain R. A. Andrew immediately ordered his company (D) to advance, and to them fell the distinction of beginning the " Advance to Victory " on the XI Corps front.

The advance was continued the following day, and on the 11th the Battalion was relieved and moved to Robecq, and thence, on the 16th August, to La Micquelerie, where, for the first time, it was completely equipped with the kilt, there having been some difficulty in obtaining the proper sizes until this time.

While in this place the 14th was inspected and complimented by both the Army and Corps Commanders, General Sir W. Birdwood and Lieutenant-General R. Haking.

After a short tour in the line, the 14th was withdrawn on August 31st, and moved to Maricourt, where it embussed for the Somme, together with the remainder of the 229th Brigade. The following day, September 1st, the Battalion went into the line again at Moislains, III Corps, Fourth Army, and spent the day reconnoitring the ground east of Bouchavesnes, from which the Germans had been pushed that morning, in preparation for an attack on the enemy trenches (Opera–Monastir trenches) on the far side of the Canal du Nord the following day. The second objective was a strong system of trenches some way behind the first, and the final one the crest of the ridge south of Nurlu village, about four miles further east.

The Battalion was to advance across the Tortille river, keeping Moislains on its left, then cross the canal swinging north-east and push on to the high ground. The 12th Battalion Somerset L.I. was to lead the attack of the 229th Brigade, with the 14th Black Watch behind, and once the two battalions were clear of the village the 14th were to come up on the left of the Somerset L.I. and take the first objective. This meant squeezing through

THE FOURTEENTH BATTALION THE BLACK WATCH

the narrow neck between the villages of Moislains and Allaines, after which the Battalion was to change direction and extend its front on the left of the Somerset L.I., a somewhat complicated manœuvre.

By 3 a.m. on September 2nd, the Battalion had relieved the 2/4th London Regiment, and was in position in assembly trenches.

Zero was 5.30 a.m., at which time it was barely light and rather misty. At the appointed hour the advance commenced under an artillery barrage, which fell some way in front of the advancing troops, and left untouched a party of the enemy holding a trench immediately in front of the Battalion. This caused a momentary delay, but it was unimportant as the Somerset Light Infantry met with some resistance from the direction of Allaines, and enabled the 14th to get up level with, and indeed a little in front of, them. The advance was again momentarily held up on the canal by the heavy machine gun fire, but pushing on in most gallant style the leading companies of the 14th got across and up the slope, driving the enemy out of some wooden huts at the point of the bayonet, killing a number of them.

So far the advance had gone exceedingly well. The first objective had been taken, and an advance commenced towards the second, when the Battalion came under heavy machine gun fire on the left, from Moislains and left rear. The village itself had never been cleared, and the enemy machine gunners holding it moved quickly to the south of the village after the 14th had passed and opened fire on them from behind. They were also successful in holding up a battalion of another brigade, on the left of the 14th, forcing it to withdraw.

In addition to this machine gun fire the 14th was now subjected to heavy artillery fire on the left flank, the enemy gun teams being actually within sight on the crest of the ridge. To advance under such conditions was out of the question, and as casualties were by now very heavy there was nothing left to do but to withdraw to the west side of the canal and reorganize. It was found afterwards that the enemy had rushed up his best troops to meet the 74th Division attack, and certainly they did their work well.

In this fighting the Battalion casualties were heavy; Lieutenant-Colonel Gilmour was wounded, Captains R. W. Stewart and I. C. Nairn were killed, and the remaining two company commanders, Captain J. McNab and Lieutenant C. G. Duncan, wounded; in addition Lieutenant Darney was killed, the total losses being three officers and 38 other ranks killed; 14 officers and 157 other ranks wounded.

Although the operation, from the 14th's point of view, was not entirely unsuccessful, it had advanced further than higher

FRANCE—TRENCH WARFARE, SEPTEMBER, 1918

authority had expected, and it also had the gratification of seeing the 230th Brigade pass through and make good an advance of about six miles.

The Battalion was commended for this gallant performance on the 2nd, and there is no doubt that it very materially assisted in the victorious advance of the 230th Brigade.

The following day the Battalion advanced to the trenches south of Moislains and to the slag heap on the canal bank where, at dusk on the evening of the 4th, it was relieved by the 19th Battalion London Regiment and moved back to Aizecourt to rest and reorganize, moving to Longavesnes on the 7th, and into the line once more at St. Emilie the same day.

While at Aizecourt the Battalion learned that the transport officer, Lieutenant J. C. Drysdale, had been killed by a shell which had landed at the mouth of his bivouac at least six miles behind the line. The news was received with great regret by all ranks, for in him the Battalion lost a most efficient and hard-working transport officer.

At St. Emilie the 14th relieved the 25th Battalion Welch Regiment in the left sector of the Divisional front, and held a horse-shoe line of trenches round St. Emilie, A company of the Somerset L.I. being attached as the line was long. The 16th Battalion Devonshire Regiment was on the right, and a battalion of the 58th Division on the left, but considerably to the rear.

The length of the Battalion line was about one and a half miles, and consisted of partially dug trenches which had to be held with less than 400 men, all told. The trenches themselves were badly sited, not continuous and with no field of fire and were completely dominated by the German guns at Epehy, and also by snipers. The latter, by crawling through the broken country on the left of the Battalion could, and did, effectively enfilade a great part of the line, and until the enemy were pushed out of Epehy, the salient held by the 74th Division was an exceptionally dangerous one.

On the evening of September 8th, D company, under Lieutenant T. B. Brown, was ordered to establish itself, if possible, on the Ronssoy-Bassé Boulogne Ridge beyond the valley in front of the Battalion. D company advanced about threequarters of the way across the valley when patrols reported at least two companies of the enemy going into the trenches it had been ordered to occupy, with strong enemy parties working forward on either side. To push on was impossible, and the company returned to the trenches it had left.

Late that night orders reached the Battalion to push forward at dawn and occupy the ridge. These were not received until 2 a.m., and although company commanders were summoned to

THE FOURTEENTH BATTALION THE BLACK WATCH

Battalion Headquarters at once, A company (Sergeant W. Collier) only received them at dawn.

The Battalion plan of attack was as follows —

C company (Lieutenant J. W. Cruickshank) was on the right, with B company (Lieutenant J. McLean) on the left, and D company (Lieutenant T. B. Brown) was in reserve. A company (Sergeant Collier) was detailed to keep in touch with a battalion of the London Regiment (58th Division) on the left, and to advance in conjunction with it. On the right of C there was a company of the 12th Somerset L.I.

The time for the opening of the barrage was postponed, but the wire from Brigade announcing this never reached the Battalion, and it advanced without any preliminary bombardment. C company, with that of the Somerset L.I., almost reached their objective unobserved, when they were met and held up by heavy machine gun and rifle fire. B on the left was unable to get on, thus leaving C's left flank exposed. Into this gap the Germans quickly pushed fresh troops, and attacked in force, with the result that both companies were overwhelmed by numbers and very nearly surrounded. They were ordered to retire, but not more than a quarter got back. The Battalion was, therefore, forced to hold its original position as a defensive line and gain touch with the 58th Division, who had also found the enemy in great strength and was unable to hold what it had gained. It was afterwards found that three battalions of the enemy were holding the line between Ronssoy and Templeux le Guerard with orders to fight to the last. It is therefore not astonishing that no progress was made.

By this time the 14th was exhausted. The trenches were knee-deep in water owing to torrential rain, and a great number of Lewis guns and rifles were out of action, due to mud and water. Major Ogilvie and Lieutenant T. B. Brown were the only officers left in the line, telephonic communication was almost impossible owing to broken wires, and it was, therefore, with feelings of relief that news reached the Battalion that it would be relieved by the 10th Battalion East Kent Regiment (230th Brigade) that night, and move back to Longavesnes for reorganization.

During this fighting the Battalion lost three officers wounded, 13 other ranks killed, 25 wounded and 17 missing.

After two days at Longavesnes, the Battalion moved to Templeux la Fosse on the 12th where Lieutenant-Colonel J. M. McKenzie, the Royal Scots, took over command, vice Lieutenant-Colonel Younger, wounded on the 2nd.

Six days were spent here, after which, on the 17th, the Battalion moved to Faustine Quarry in reserve for an attack by the Division on Templeux le Guerard the following day.

The attack on the 18th was designed to secure a position

CAPTURE OF TEMPLEUX LE GUERARD

affording good observation on the Hindenburg line. The 1st Australian Division were on the right, and the 16th on the left. The 38th (German) Division held the line opposite from Templeux le Guerard to Ronssoy.

The Division attack was carried out by the 230th Brigade, with the 12th Somerset L.I. and A company 14th Black Watch on the right, the 231st, with the 16th Battalion Devonshire Regiment on the left, leaving the 14th Black Watch, less A company, in Divisional reserve.

Aided by a haze and a very effective barrage, the attack was a complete success, the first objective being taken by 7.45 a.m., together with many prisoners, and at a trifling loss. On advancing over the ridge towards the second objective, A company came under heavy machine gun fire from Rifleman Post, but this was soon silenced by artillery fire and the position occupied by one o'clock—an advance of 4500 yards. The position was consolidated, and here A remained until relieved by a battalion of the Sussex Regiment. A company's losses were one officer wounded, four other ranks killed and 24 wounded. The Division captured that day 18 officers and 873 other ranks, 13 guns, five trench mortars and 90 machine guns.

The 20th of September was spent in salvage work on the battlefield, and at 10 p.m. that night the 14th moved forward, relieving a battalion of the Suffolk Regiment at Toine and Pimple Posts. On the 22nd it relieved the 25th Royal Welch Fusiliers in the front line, and held from Carbine Trench to Benjamin Post, with A company in support at Artaxerxes Post. The enemy shelled this position heavily, both with high explosives and gas shells, the Battalion losing one officer (Second Lieutenant McL. Innes) wounded, who died of wounds a fortnight later, 50 other ranks and 15 wounded.

On the 25th the 74th Division was relieved by the Americans, the 14th by two companies of the 106th American Battalion, after which it moved back to Tincourt, where it entrained for Villers Bretonneux, detrained there and marched to Corbie, 15 miles east of Amiens.

Whilst here the following letter from General Rawlinson, commanding the Fourth Army, was received on the 28th :—

" The 74th Division has taken a prominent part in the suc-
" cessful advance of the Fourth Army during the past month
" and, much to my regret, has been ordered to another part of the
" British front.
" The work of this Division during a period of severe and
" continuous fighting is worthy of the best traditions of the yeo-
" man stock of Great Britain.

THE FOURTEENTH BATTALION THE BLACK WATCH

" Brought to this country from a hot climate, where they took
" part in a very different method of warfare, the 74th Division
" has quickly adapted itself to the altered conditions, and has
" fought with determination and courage which is beyond praise.

" In the capture of Aizecourt, Driencourt, Templeux la
" Fosse, Longavesnes, Villers Faucon, and Templeux le Guerard,
" the Division has made a name for itself which ranks with the
" best Division fighting in the British Army, and I desire to offer
" to all ranks my warmest thanks for their gallantry and self-
" sacrifice.

" In addition to the considerable area of ground gained the
" Division has captured over 1700 prisoners.

" I greatly regret that the Division is leaving the Fourth Army,
" and in wishing all ranks every good fortune I trust I may at
" some future time find the 74th Division once more under my
" command."

Early in the morning of the 28th the Battalion left Corbie for Méricourt, where it entrained for Berguette, reaching Bourecq and entering the Second Army the following day. On October 2nd it moved to Locon, and on the 4th to Herlies. Here ten days were spent, after which the Battalion moved into the front line at Ligny, relieving the 12th Battalion Somerset L.I.

On October 15th a slight advance was made east of Ligny, and the following day the Battalion patrols had pushed forward to the outskirts of Haubourdin (a suburb of Lille). On October 17th the crossings of Haute Deule canal were secured, and the 74th Division again advanced, the 14th Battalion moving to Petit Ronchin, and the following day to Ascq (on the Lille–Tournai road), eventually reaching Marquain on the 21st.

The Division at this time was advancing on a one-battalion front, and, on the 22nd, the 14th Battalion took over the outpost line in front of Orcq from the 12th Somerset L.I. By this time the enemy resistance was stiffening, their trenches being well wired and strongly manned.

On the 23rd B company made an attack on the enemy position, but was held up within a hundred yards of the trenches by intense trench mortar and machine gun fire, and the two leading platoons were compelled to withdraw after a loss of one officer killed, two wounded, 18 other ranks killed and 27 wounded.

On the 24th the Battalion was relieved by the 10th Buffs, and moved back to billets in Baisieux, where it remained for ten days. Here a most unfortunate occurrence took place. On the evening of November 1st the enemy slightly shelled the village, and whilst assisting in getting the men under cover, Captain and Adjutant R. H. Colthart was mortally wounded. His death was a great loss

AFTER THE ARMISTICE

to the Battalion. As a sergeant he had gone out with the Regiment to Gallipoli, was appointed Quartermaster and then Adjutant, and had been with the Regiment or Battalion in very engagement in which it had taken part. He was succeeded as Adjutant by Lieutenant J. W. Ormiston.

Tournai was evacuated by the Germans on November 9th, when the 231st Brigade passed through it and formed a bridgehead east of the town, with the 55th Division on its right, and the 57th on its left, the 230th Brigade occupying the town, whilst the 229th moved forward to Lamian.

Next day the 14th Battalion, with the remainder of the 229th Brigade, marched through Tournai, where it had a tremendous reception, the skirl of the pipes and the sight of the kilted soldiers moving the population to great enthusiasm. That night the Battalion reached Beclers, five miles east of Tournai.

The advance eastward was continued on the 11th, and the 14th had reached the main road just west of Frasnes, when, at twenty minutes to eleven in the morning, the Brigade Major brought the news that an armistice had been signed and would come into force at 11 a.m. That night the Battalion reached Pironche. Moving to Izitres on November 12th, and to Moustier on the 17th, it was there transferred back to the Fifth Army, and two days later, with the remainder of the 74th Division was again transferred to the Second Army.

The rest of its stay in Belgium was uneventful. On December 16th it moved to Grammont, where demobilization commenced and went on smoothly throughout the winter of 1918 and the following spring. In March a hundred men were sent to the 8th Battalion, and half a dozen officers to the 6th, then in the Army on the Rhine.

By the beginning of May the Battalion had been reduced to Cadre strength, and on June 18th the Cadre, consisting of two officers and 22 men, left for Scotland, travelling via Boulogne, there meeting the Cadre of the 1st Battalion. Kirkcaldy was reached on the 25th, where the Cadre was entertained by the Provost on behalf of the Corporation, and later that day proceeded to Kinross where the men were demobilized the same evening.

Of the original regiment of the Fife and Forfar Yeomanry who proceeded overseas in 1915 only four remained at this time, namely, Lieutenant-Colonel Ogilvie, Captain Andrew, Regimental Quartermaster-Sergeant Galbraith and Company Sergeant-Major Nisbet.

So ends the history of the 14th (Fife and Forfar Yeomanry) Battalion The Black Watch. One word more remains to be said; on September 6th, 1915, as he embarked for the East, Lord Lovat received the following telegram from Windsor Castle:—

THE FOURTEENTH BATTALION THE BLACK WATCH

" I send you and your Brigade my best wishes on your depar-
" ture for Active Service. I feel sure that the great and traditional
" fighting reputation of Scotsmen will be more than safe with
" you, and that your Brigade will spare no effort in the interests
" of the Empire's cause, to bring this war to a victorious conclu-
" sion.

" GEORGE R.I."

This short account of the actions and fighting of the 14th shows how bravely both officers and men endeavoured to carry out His Majesty's command during the period the Battalion formed a unit of The Black Watch.

APPENDIX I

Record of Officers' Services

Abbreviations :—" K."—Killed.   " D. of W."—Died of Wounds.
" W."—Wounded.   " M."—Missing.

THE FOURTEENTH BATTALION

Adamson, H. 2nd Lieut. Joined 2nd March, 1918. To hospital 26th June, 1918. Rejoined 11th July, 1918. Mentioned in Despatches.
Anderson, G. 2nd Lieut. Joined 25th Oct., 1918.
Andrew, R. A. Capt. Awarded M.C. (date unknown). Mentioned in Despatches.
Armstrong, W. W. 2nd Lieut. Joined 17th Dec., 1917. *k.* 27th Dec., 1917.
Arnott, J. W. Lieut. Joined 1st Feb., 1917.

Baldie, T. B. Joined 5th Feb., 1917. Promoted Lieut. 1st July, 1917. Transferred to R.F.C. 11th Nov., 1917. *k. in a.* whilst with Royal Air Force 6th Nov., 1918.
Beard, G. D. M. 2nd Lieut. Joined 25th July, 1918.
Beard, S. A. Joined 1st Feb., 1917. To hospital 26th Nov., 1917. Rejoined 7th Jan., 1918. Transferred to R.F.C. 19th July, 1918.
Bevan, C. M. Joined 15th Jan., 1917. To U.K. 26th June, 1918.
Bremner, C. D. 2nd Lieut. To hospital 20th Dec., 1916. Rejoined 8th Jan., 1917. Seconded to R.F.C. 25th Oct., 1917.
Brown, E. P. Joined 11th Sept., 1918.
Brown, T. B. 2nd Lieut. Joined 2nd July, 1918.
Brown, W. D. 2nd Lieut. Joined 1st Feb., 1917. Promoted Capt. and Adjt. *d. of w.* 27th Dec., 1917.

Campbell, Sir W. A. A. Lieut. Promoted Capt. *w.* 6th Nov., 1917. Awarded M.C. (date unknown). Rejoined 30th Dec., 1917. Mentioned in Despatches.
Clydesdale, R. A. 2nd Lieut. Joined 22nd Dec., 1917. *w.* 2nd Sept., 1918.
Colthart, R. H. 2nd Lieut. Promoted, on probation, from ranks. Fife and Forfar Yeomanry 24th May, 1916. Promoted Q.M. and Hon. Lieut. 9th July, 1916. Promoted Lieut. 24th Nov., 1917. Promoted Capt. and Adjt. 1st Feb., 1918. *d. of w.* 2nd Nov., 1918.
Colville, Lieut. Mentioned in Despatches.
Craigen, J. W. W. 2nd Lieut. Joined 5th Jan., 1918. *w.* 2nd Sept., 1918.
Crawford, W. S. 2nd Lieut. Joined 1st Feb., 1917. *w.* 29th Aug., 1917. Rejoined 20th Oct., 1917. To hospital 3rd Nov., 1917. Rejoined 22nd Dec., 1917.
Cruickshank, J. W. 2nd Lieut. *w.* 2nd Sept., 1918.
Cumming, D. 2nd Lieut. Joined 11th Nov., 1917. *w.* 28th Dec., 1917.
Cumming, F. K. 2nd Lieut. Joined 11th Sept., 1918. *k.* 23rd Oct., 1918.
Cummins, W. W. Capt. *w.* 6th Nov., 1917. Rejoined 3rd Dec., 1917.

Dane, P. W. 2nd Lieut. Joined 5th Feb., 1918.
Daniel, R. D. M. 2nd Lieut. Joined 7th Feb., 1918. Transferred to 231st Infantry Brigade Headquarters 16th July, 1918.

THE FOURTEENTH BATTALION THE BLACK WATCH

Darney, C. E. Joined 5th Jan., 1918. *k.* 2nd Sept., 1918.
Davidson, J. D. 2nd Lieut. Joined 11th Sept., 1918.
Dawes, J. W. 2nd Lieut. Joined 30th Dec., 1917. *w.* 2nd Sept., 1918.
De Pree. Major. Mentioned in Despatches.
Dickie, J. A. 2nd Lieut. Joined 28th Dec., 1917. *w.* 2nd Sept., 1918.
Dickson, R. W. Lieut. Joined 27th Oct., 1918. To T.M. Battery 9th Nov., 1918.
Down, N. C. S. Capt. Joined 28th Dec., 1917. *w.* 6th April, 1918. Rejoined 25th Oct., 1918.
Doyle, R. B. Capt. C.F. Joined 19th April, 1918. To hospital 14th Aug., 1918.
Drummond, P. McF. 2nd Lieut. Joined 11th Sept., 1918.
Drysdale, J. C. 2nd Lieut. Joined Fife and Forfar Yeomanry Sept., 1915. *k.* 2nd Sept., 1918.
Duncan, C. G. 2nd Lieut. Joined Fife and Forfar Yeomanry Feb., 1916. *w.* 2nd Sept., 1918.
Duncan, P. F. Capt. Joined 29th Sept., 1917. *w.* 28th Dec., 1917.

Ewart, R. H. Lieut. Joined 7th Oct., 1918. *w.* 16th Oct., 1918. *d. of w.* 18th Oct., 1918.

Fell, F. J. 2nd Lieut. Joined 1st Aug., 1918. *w.* 24th Sept., 1918.
Forrest, B. T. A. 2nd Lieut. Joined 1st Feb., 1917. To hospital 12th April, 1917. *k.* 27th Dec., 1917.
Forth, C. O. 2nd Lieut. Joined 15th Dec., 1916. To India to join Indian Army 15th July, 1917.
Fraser, H. L. 2nd Lieut. Joined 25th June, 1918. *w.* 3rd Aug., 1918.
Fyfe, A. J. 2nd Lieut. Joined 24th March, 1918. Transferred to R.F.C. 13th July, 1918.

Gilbert, F. 2nd Lieut. M.M. Joined 7th Oct., 1918.
Gilchrist, W. O. 2nd Lieut. Joined 30th Aug., 1918.
Gillan, J. R. W. Capt. Joined 12th Jan., 1918. Transferred to Egyptian Army 18th Jan., 1918.
Gilmour, J. Lieut.-Col. Served in Gallipoli and Egypt with Fife and Forfar Yeomanry. *w.* Egypt 6th Nov., 1917. Awarded D.S.O. and Bar.
Grant, J. N. 2nd Lieut. Joined 25th June, 1918. *w.* 2nd Sept., 1918.
Gray, W. 2nd Lieut. Joined 1/1st Fife and Forfar Yeomanry 4th March, 1915. Promoted Lieut. 1st June, 1916. Served with Remount Depot Sept. to Dec., 1917. Rejoined Battn. 1918.
Greenless, G. D. 2nd Lieut. Joined 20th Nov., 1917. *k.* 1st Dec., 1917.

Haggart, J. 2nd Lieut. Joined 17th Dec., 1917. *w.* 28th Dec., 1917. *d. of w.* 3rd Jan., 1918.
Houston, J. C. 2nd Lieut. Joined 15th Dec., 1916. To R.F.C. 31st Dec., 1917. Awarded M.C. 20th Jan., 1918.

Innes, D. Mc.L. 2nd Lieut. Joined 11th Sept., 1918. *w.* 22nd Sept., 1918. *d. of w.* 7th Oct., 1918.

APPENDIX I

Johnston, W. 2nd Lieut. Joined 14th March, 1917.
Johnstone, W. J. Lieut. Joined 3/1st Fife and Forfar Yeomanry Dec., 1915. Awarded M.C. (date unknown). *k.* 28th Dec., 1917.

Kinniburgh, J. D. 2nd Lieut. Joined 19th Feb., 1917. *k.* 6th Nov., 1917.

Laing, J. E. 2nd Lieut. *w.* 2nd Sept., 1918.
Laird, J. S. 2nd Lieut. Joined 1st Feb., 1917. To hospital 2nd April, 1917. Rejoined 3rd May, 1917. Transferred to R.F.C. 13th July, 1918.
Laurence, W. T. Lieut. Joined 9th Oct., 1918.
Lindsay. Capt. Mentioned in Despatches.
Little, D. A. D. 2nd Lieut. Joined 1st Feb., 1917.
Loutet, J. C. 2nd Lieut. Joined 20th Feb., 1918.
Lowen, C. F. T. Lieut. Joined 7th Oct., 1918.
Lumsden, R. D. Lieut. Joined Fife and Forfar Yeomanry, Cairo, 25th Jan., 1916. To hospital 2nd Aug., 1917. Rejoined 19th Aug., 1917. To hospital 17th Jan., 1918.

MacKenzie, A. S. Lieut. Joined 7th Oct., 1918.
McBain, J. 2nd Lieut. Joined 28th March, 1917. To R.F.C. 25th July, 1917.
McCarrick, F. 2nd Lieut. Joined 19th Feb., 1917. To hospital 14th June, 1917. Rejoined 11th Aug., 1917. *w.* 6th Nov., 1917. Rejoined 20th Nov., 1917. To hospital 25th Dec., 1917.
McDougal, A. R. 2nd Lieut. Served in Gallipoli and Egypt with Fife and Forfar Yeomanry, and in France. Promoted Capt. 9th April, 1918.
McIlhatton, G. A. 2nd Lieut. Joined 11th Sept., 1918.
McKenzie, J. M. Lieut.-Col. D.S.O. Joined 17th Sept., 1918.
McKenzie, V. W. 2nd Lieut. Joined 1st Feb., 1917. Accidentally *w.* 21st May, 1917.
McLaren, D. 2nd Lieut. Joined 25th July, 1918.
McLean, J. 2nd Lieut. Joined 28th Oct., 1917. *w.* 5th Nov., 1917. Rejoined 18th April, 1918. *w.* 2nd Sept., 1918.
McNab, J. B. Capt. Joined 11th Nov., 1917. *w.* 2nd Sept., 1918.
Mair, H. 2nd Lieut. Joined 27th Aug., 1918.
Martin, T. M. 2nd Lieut. Joined 25th July, 1917. *w.* 6th Nov., 1917.
Masson, S. E. 2nd Lieut. Transferred to Egyptian Army 18th Jan., 1918.
Mathewson, J. S. 2nd Lieut. Joined 11th Sept., 1918.
Milligen, D. F. V. 2nd Lieut. Joined 2nd July, 1918. *w.* 2nd Sept., 1918.
Mills, A. S. Lieut. Joined 15th Jan., 1917.
Mitchell, S. Major. Served with Fife and Forfar Yeomanry in Gallipoli and Egypt 1915–17. Attached Australian Corps Headquarters May, 1917, to Feb., 1919.

Nairn, I. C. Capt. Joined 10th March, 1917. Awarded M.C. (date unknown). *k.* 2nd Sept., 1918.

Ogilvie, D. D. Capt. Joined 23rd Jan., 1918. Mentioned in Despatches.
Ormiston, J. W. 2nd Lieut. Joined 7th Feb., 1918.
Osborne, G. E. B. Major. Served in Gallipoli and Egypt with Fife and Forfar Yeomanry. To France with Battn. *k.* 6th Nov., 1917.

THE FOURTEENTH BATTALION THE BLACK WATCH

Paisley, G. D. 2nd Lieut. Joined 10th Dec., 1917. *k.* 27th Dec., 1917.
Peebles, D. A. 2nd Lieut. Joined 1st Feb., 1917. To U.K. 29th June, 1918.
Prentice, J. R. Lieut. Joined 24th Sept., 1918.

Robertson, W. G. 2nd Lieut. Joined 12th Jan., 1918.
Robertson, R. 2nd Lieut. Joined 11th Sept., 1918. *w.* 23rd Oct., 1918.
Robson, P. L. 2nd Lieut. Joined 10th Dec., 1917. *w.* 28th Dec., 1917.
Ross, J. 2nd Lieut. Joined 11th Sept., 1918.
Ross, R. H. Lieut. Joined 7th Oct., 1918.
Russell, W. S. M. 2nd Lieut. Joined 20th Feb., 1918.

Scott, W. 2nd Lieut. Joined 22nd Dec., 1917.
Seaton, J. 2nd Lieut. Joined 7th Feb., 1918.
Sharp, H. S. Capt. To 24th Divisional Headquarters 16th July, 1918.
Smith, A. C. Lieut. and Adjutant. Served with Fife and Forfar Yeomanry in Gallipoli and Egypt and with Battn. in France. To U.K. 22nd Oct., 1918. Awarded M.C. (date unknown). Mentioned in Despatches.
Steel, W. J. O. Lieut. Joined 11th Sept., 1918.
Stevenson, E. J. 2nd Lieut. Joined 27th Aug., 1918. *w.* 15th Oct., 1918.
Stewart, R. W. Capt. Served in Gallipoli and Egypt with Fife and Forfar Yeomanry 1915-17 and with Battn. in France. *k.* 2nd Sept., 1918.
Stroyan, L. S. R. Joined 27th Oct., 1918.
Stuart, N. C. 2nd Lieut. Joined 11th Sept., 1918. *w.* 18th Sept., 1918.

Thom, J. F. Capt. *d.* of *w.* 27th Sept., 1918.
Thomson, A. G. 2nd Lieut. Joined 5th Jan., 1918. Transferred to R.F.C. 12th April, 1918.
Thomson, E. A. 2nd Lieut. Joined 28th Oct., 1917. *k.* 6th Nov., 1917.
Tuke. Capt. Awarded M.C. (date unknown).

Watherston, J. H. 2nd Lieut. Joined 7th Feb., 1918.
Williams, T. L. Capt. C.F. Joined 14th Aug., 1918.
Wood, A. R. 2nd Lieut. D.C.M., M.M. Joined 25th June, 1918. *w.* 16th Oct., 1918. Awarded M.C. (date unknown).

Younger, J. Lieut.-Col. To hospital 7th Jan., 1918. Rejoined. *w.* 2nd Sept., 1918. Awarded D.S.O. 27th Nov., 1918. Mentioned in Despatches.

APPENDIX II

Summary of Casualties

The Fourteenth Battalion

OFFICERS, 1917-18

Year.	Killed. Died of Wounds. Died on Service.	Wounded.	Missing.	Total.	Year.
1917	10	15	—	25	1917
1918	12	18	—	30	1918
Totals:	22	33	—	55	

OTHER RANKS, 1917-18

Year.	Killed. Died of Wounds. Died on Service.	Wounded.	Missing.	Total.	Year.
1917	113	226	—	339	1917
1918	118	248	17	383	1918
Totals:	231	474	17	722	

TOTAL:

Officers, 55.   Other Ranks, 722.

APPENDIX III

Casualties—Officers

* Killed in action. † Died of wounds.

THE FOURTEENTH BATTALION

Name.	Rank.	Date.
Armstrong, W. W.	2nd Lieut.	*27.12.17.
Baldie, J. B.	Lieut.	*6.11.18. And R.A.F.
Brown, W. D.	Capt.	*27.12.17.
Colthart, R. H.	Capt.	†2.11.18.
Cumming, F. K.	2nd Lieut.	*23.10.18.
Darney, C. E.	2nd Lieut.	*2.9.18.
Darsie, G.	Lieut.	†31.7.18.
Drysdale, J. C.	2nd Lieut.	*2.9.18
Ewart, R. H.	Lieut.	†16.10.18. Attd. from 10th Battn.
Ewart, W. G.	Lieut.	*18.10.18.
Forrest, P. T. A.	2nd Lieut.	*27.12.17.
Greenlees, G. D.	2nd Lieut.	*1.12.17.
Haggart, J.	2nd Lieut.	†3.1.18. Attd. from 4th Battn.
Innes, D. McL.	2nd Lieut.	†7.10.18. Attd. from 10th Battn.
Johnstone, W. J.	Lieut.	*28.12.17.
Kinniburgh, J. D.	2nd Lieut.	*6.11.17.
Nairn, I. C.	Capt.	*2.9.18. M.C.
Osborne, G. E. B.	Major.	*6.11.17.
Paisley, G. W.	2nd Lieut.	*28.12.17.
Robertson, J. R.	Lieut.	*12.5.17. And R.F.C.
Stewart, R. W.	Major.	*2.9.18.
Thom, J. F.	Capt.	†27.9.18. And M.G.C.
Thomson, E. A.	2nd Lieut.	*6.11.17.

APPENDIX IV

Nominal Roll of Warrant Officers, Non-Commissioned Officers and Men Killed in Action or Died of Wounds or Disease in the Great War, 1914–18

* Killed in action. † Died of wounds. ‡ Died at home. § Died. ¶ Died at sea.

THE FOURTEENTH BATTALION

Adamson, H., L/Cpl., 345627	*6.11.17
Aitken, A., C.S.M., 345001	† 2.9.18
Aitken, J., Pte., 268173	* 8.8.18
Anderson, D., Pte., S/14539	†26.10.16
Anderson, D. B., Pte., S/21840	*27.12.17
Anderson, J., Pte., S/20382	* 8.11.17
Anderson, R., Pte., 345553	* 2.9.18
Armstrong, W., Pte., 345576	†29.1.18
Aston, T. W., Pte., 3/2819	*6.11.17
Bane, J. W., Cpl., 293009	¶30.12.17
Bannigan, P., L/Sgt., 345945	*25.5.17
Barber, J., Pte., S/25462	*23.10.18
Bartie, T., Pte., S/9729	*23.10.18
Baxter, R., L/Cpl., 345953	*6.11.17
Bayne, A., Sgt., 345055	†22.10.18
Bell, A., Pte., 203525	*30.12.17
Benson, H., Pte., 345638	* 2.9.18
Bissett, A., Pte., 345577	* 2.9.18
Blair, D., Pte., S/22250	* 2.9.18
Bonar, G., Pte., 200328	*18.9.18
Boyd, W. G., L/Cpl., 345105	* 2.9.18
Braid, D., Pte., 345332	*6.11.17
Braid, T., Pte., 345425	†29.12.17
Brand, J., Pte., S/9388	*27.12.17
Brebner, C., Pte., 310082	†10.9.18
Brookland, F. J., Pte., 345698	*27.12.17
Brown, W. J., Pte., S/20373	¶ 4.5.17
Bryne, T., Pte., 345751	*28.12.17
Calder, J., Pte., 345561	* 2.9.18
Chalmers, G. C., Cpl., 345251	†8.11.17
Campbell, J., Pte., S/15814	*23.10.18
Cant, A., Pte., S/18725	*21.9.18
Chisholm, A., Pte., S/20880	¶ 4.5.17
Clunie, R. S., Pte., 268867	†28.12.17
Cockburn, T., Pte., S/12506	*23.10.18
Combe, W. N., Pte., 540004	*6.11.17
Cooper, W., Pte., 22141	* 2.9.18
Coupar, D. L., L/Cpl., 345092	*10.9.18
Coutts, A. J., Pte., S/22207	*24.9.18
Crighton, C., Pte., 345815	*28.12.17
Cubbon, E., Pte., S/22151	*21.9.18
Dalgleish, W., Pte., S/16294	*6.11.17
Davidson, A., Pte., S/14709	†30.12.17
Davidson, J., L/Cpl., S/15546	*10.9.18
Dawson, J., Pte., 345959	*10.9.18
Denham, J., Pte., S/20386	¶ 4.5.17
Dickie, H. A., L/Cpl., 345094 (D.C.M.)	† 4.9.18
Dickson, D., Pte., 345353	*1.12.17
Dickson, W., L/Cpl., 345270	*28.12.17
Donaldson, T., Pte., 308	*10.9.18
Douglas, S. R., A/Cpl., 18847	† 5.9.18
Dow, J., Cpl., 345633	*6.11.17
Downie, H., A/L/Cpl., 345545	*6.11.17
Drinnan, G., L/Cpl., S/12701	¶15.4.17
Duffin, J., Pte., 345707	†23.11.17
Duncan, T., Pte., S/16513	* 2.9.18
Dunipace, W., Pte., 202972	† 6.9.18
Easson, W. W., Pte., 340025	*21.9.18
Edwards, D., Pte., S/20381	†8.11.17
Elder, G., Pte., 203208	* 2.9.18
Ewing, A., Pte., 345499	§4.12.17
Ferguson, J., Pte., 201336	* 2.9.18
Ferguson, R., Pte. 345445	*26.3.18
Findlater, J. P., Pte., S/18724	¶15.4.17
Findlay, W., Pte., S/18192	§25.7.18
Forbes, J. A., Pte., 346049	*21.9.18
Ford, J., Pte., 340017	*10.9.18
Flynn, W., L/Cpl., 345174	†6.11.17
Fraser, D., Pte., S/15200	* 8.8.18
Freel, S., Pte., S/7194	† 2.1.18
Frizzell, R., Pte., 6153	*10.8.18
Fyfe, T. M., Pte., 345605	*6.11.17
Galt, J., Pte., S/21841	*6.11.17
Geddes, C., Pte., 345962	*6.11.17
Geekie, J. A. P., Pte., 345253	*10.9.18
Gibson, A. S., Pte., 291851	¶30.12.17
Goodfellow, T., Pte., S/21826	*27.12.17
Greig, W. T., L/Cpl., 345342	‡6.12.18
Grieve, J., A/L/Cpl., 345331	¶30.12.17
Gunn, D., Pte., S/22331	* 2.9.18
Guyan, D., Pte., 345713	†11.11.17

THE FOURTEENTH BATTALION THE BLACK WATCH

Haggart, J., Pte., S/19537 *21.10.18
Halliday, D., Pte., S/20365 *10.9.18
Hamilton, R., Pte., 345760 * 2.9.18
Harley, R., A/L/Copl., 345461 *1.11.17
Heddleston, J., Pte., S/22177 * 2.9.18
Hedley, W., L/Sgt., 345950 * 2.9.18
Hendrie, J., Pte., S/20370 *6.11.17
Hickman, C., Pte., 345842 * 2.9.18
Hoban, P., Pte., S/8913 *6.11.17
Houston, W., Pte., S/20380 ¶ 4.5.17
Howie, G., Pte., 345301 *6.11 17
Husband, W., A/L/Cpl., 345355
    * 2.9.18
Hynd, H., Pte., S/8224 *6.11.17

Inglis, J., Pte., S/22027 *24.9.18
Irwin, J., Pte., 203207 * 2.9.18
Izatt, R., A/L/Cpl., S/26870 *23.10.18

Jack, A., Pte., 345964 *27.12.17
Johnston, J. R., Pte., 345247 *6.11.17
Jones, W. L., Pte., S/20393 ¶ 4.5.17

Keith, J., Pte., S/20121 * 2.9.18
Keith, W., A/Cpl., 345390 * 2.9.18
Kemp, W., Pte., 345609 *6.11.17
King, B., Pte., 345763 † 6.1.18
King, L., Pte., 345717 *6.11.17
Kilpatrick, W., L/Cpl., 345404
    †29.12.17
Lambie, H., Pte., 201992 * 2.9.18
Lawrence, A. H., L/Cpl., 345358
    *6.11.17
Legg, A., Pte., S/20884 ‡15.9.18
Lessels, W., Pte., 345220 *22.9.18
Lawson, D. S., Pte., S/18799 †11.9.18
Lyall, T., Pte., 3/3752 †7.11.17

Macdonald, A., Pte., 345266 *18.9.18
Macilwain, A., Pte., S/13703 * 3.9.18
Mackenzie, W., Sgt., 345028 * 2.9.18
Maloney, J., Pte., 345184 †29.9.18
Mann, G., Pte., 345968 * 2.9.18
Martin, W., Pte., 345659 *10.9.18
McConnachie, W., Pte., S/41665
    *10.9.18
McDonald, D., Pte., 3/9916 *6.11.17
McDonald, F., Pte., 345269 †13.11.17
McDonald, G., L/Cpl., S/13133
    *6.11.17
McDonald, J. R., Pte., 203189
    †25.9.18
McEwan, T., Pte., 345354 †7.11.17
McIntyre, W., Pte., 345586 †11.4.18
McKendrick, A., Pte., 345662 *16.10.18

McKinnon, A., Pte., 241316 *28.12.17
McLagan, J., Pte., 345587 * 2.9.18
McLaren, P. L., Sgt., S/3796 † 3.9.18
McLean, J., Pte., S/18460 *18.9.18
McLean, T., Pte., 345726 * 2.9.18
McMillan, D., Pte., 340018 *6.11.17
McMillan, J., Pte., 345680 †6.11.17
Melville, G., Pte., 345881 § 4.1.18
Melville, J., Pte., 345411 §12.11.17
Melville, L. W., Pte., 345149 * 2.9.18
Mercer, H., Pte., S/20394 † 8.11.17
Millar, R., Pte., 345526 * 2.9.18
Milne, J., Pte., 345679 *6.11.17
Milne, J. W., Pte., 340016 *16.11.17
Milne, J. R., Pte., 345871 *6.11.17
Mitchell, D. J., Pte., 345660 ‡14.12.18
Moonie, J. W., Pte., 345260 * 2.9.18
Morrison, D. L., Pte., S/25324
    *21.9.18
Morrison, G. B., Pte., 345305 §14.4.18
Mudie, F. T., Pte., S/16758 *6.11.17
Muir, J. K., Pte., 345350 *6.11.17
Munro, W., Pte., 203406 *10.9.18
Murray, W. J., Pte., S/9344 * 2.9.18
Mutch, C., Pte., S/20362 *6.11.17

Nairn, J., Pte., S/43045 *10.9.18
Nicol, J., Pte., 345115 *6.11.17
Niven, R., Pte., 345119 † 6.9.18
Notman, J. S., Pte., 345769 *6.11.17

Okey, J., Pte., 34007 *10.9.18
Oliver, R., A/L/Sgt., 345009 *28.12.17
Ovenstone, P. M., Cpl., 345161
    *6.11.17

Pake, J., Pte., 345394 *6.11.17
Paterson, J. C., Pte., 346009 *27.12.17
Peattie, D., Pte., S/16204 *6.11.17
Perston, W., Pte., S/21830 *10.9.18
Petrie, J., Pte., 266109 ¶30.12.17
Philip, A., Pte., S/25317 †23.9.18
Prain, G., L/Cpl., 345289 *6.11.17

Ramsay, J. W. B., Pte., 345313
    *10.9.18
Rattray, J. M., Cpl., 345264 *6.11.17
Rattray, W., Cpl., 266108 ¶30.12.17
Reid, J., Pte., 345311 *28.12.17
Reid, J., Pte., 203204 * 2.9.18
Reid, J, Pte., 345774 §20.3.17
Reid, R., Pte., S/20875 * 2.9.18
Rennie, H., Pte., 345978 *10.9.18
Ritchie, J., Pte., 345598 *6.11.17
Ritchie, J. W., Cpl., 345125 *10.9.18

APPENDIX IV

Robertson, W., Pte., 345392 †12.11.17
Rodger, J., Pte., 345733 * 2.9.18
Rodger, W., Pte., 345239 *6.11.17
Roper, J. J., Pte., S/20390 †12.9.18
Ross, D. T., Pte., S/21819 *6.11.17
Ross, D., Pte., S/18698 *28.12.17
Ross, T., Pte., 345979 *16.10.18

Saunders, A. M., Sgt., 345334 †18.11.17
Scott, R., Pte., 345735 *6.11.17
Shanks, A., Pte., S/20371 * 2.9.18
Sharp, J., Sgt., 345951 *6.11.17
Shenken, P., Pte., S/20366 ¶ 4.5.17
Shepherd, J., Pte., 345736 §14.4.17
Slater, A. M., Pte., 346033 *10.9.18
Small, R., Pte., 266648 ¶30.12.17
Smart, J., Pte., 345807 †4.10.18
Smart, J., Pte., S/25217 *23.9.18
Smith, J., Pte., S/18102 † 2.9.18
Smith, J., Pte., S/20890 ¶ 4.5.17
Smith, R., Pte., S/22831 * 2.9.18
Smith, R., Pte., S/20361 *10.9.18
Snaddon, P., Pte., S/22180 * 2.9.18
Sowerby, E., Pte., S/6158 *23.10.18
Spence, A., A/Sgt., 345172 *6.11.17
Spence, J., Sgt., 345886 † 7.9.18
Staff, J. W., Pte., S/20889 *6.11.17
Stenhouse, T., L/Cpl., 202466
 ¶30.12.17
Stewart, A., Pte., 345861 *6.11.17
Stewart, C., Pte., S/20893 ¶ 4.5.17
Strachan, J., L/Cpl., S/20879 * 8.8.18

Swift, J., Pte., S/43388 †24.10.18
Syme, W., Sgt., 345200
 (D.C.M.) *28.12.17
Symon, A. H., Pte., 345622 *6.11.17

Taylor, D., Sgt., 345164 †11.11.17
Taylor, J., Pte., S/21837 † 5.8.18
Taylor, T., Pte., S/21820 †29.12.17
Thomson, C., Pte., 350163 ‡30.9.18
Thomson, J., Pte., S/3875 * 2.9.18
Thomson, J., Pte., S/20867 ¶ 4.5.17

Walker, D., Pte., S/11944 * 7.8.18
Walker, H., Pte., 265831 § 1.2.18
Waller, T., Pte., S/25347 *23.10.18
Walton, F., L/Sgt., 345988 * 2.9.18
Wann, R., Pte., S/18703 ¶15.4.17
Watson, N., Pte., 345444 *6.11.17
Webb, A., Pte., S/25378 *23.10.18
Wilkie, A., Pte., 345866 * 2.9.18
Williams, A., Pte., S/18697 ¶15.4.17
Wilson, A., Pte., S/22157 * 8.8.18
Wilson, D., Pte., 345325 *6.11.17
Wilson, G., Pte., S/16403 * 9.8.18
Williams, J. P., Pte., S/21715 †28.12.17
Wood, E., Pte., 292849 ¶30.12.17
Woodward, J., Pte., S/19663 *6.11.17
Woodward, R. A., Pte., S/20376
 †27.9.18

Young, P., Pte., 345524 *27.12.17
Younger, C., L/Cpl., S/15545 *10.9.18

APPENDIX V

HONOURS AND AWARDS

The Fourteenth Battalion

D.S.O.

Lieut.-Col. J. Gilmour.
Lieut.-Col. J. Younger.

M.C.

Lieut. R. A. Andrew.
2nd Lieut. T. B. Brown.
C.S.M. J. Cameron.
Capt. Sir Wm. A. A. Campbell, Bart.
2nd Lieut. J. C. Houston.
2nd Lieut. W. J. Johnstone.
Capt. Ian Couper Nairn.
2nd Lieut. A. C. Smith.
Capt. A. L. S. Tuke, R.A.M.C. (T.).
2nd Lieut. A. R. Wood, D.C.M., M.M.

D.C.M.

Pte. J. Birrell.
Sgt. W. R. Chalmers.
Sgt. W. Collier.
Pte. H. A. Dickie.
C.S.M. W. Henderson.
S.S.M. A. Ogilvie.
Pte. W. Roger.
Pte. T. Spence.
Sgt. W. Syme.
L/Sgt. J. Valentine.

M.S.M.

C.Q.M.S. W. Blyth.
R.Q.M.S. W. J. Galbraith.
R.S.M. G. Gall.
C.S.M. J. S. Lumsden.
C.Q.M.S. J. McNiven.

M.M.

Pte. J. Armour.
Pte. A. Black, D.C.M.
Corpl. J. Black.
Pte. W. Blair.
Pte. A. Campbell.
Sgt. A. P. Gordon.
Sgt. W. Herd.
Pte. R. Izatt.
Sgt. J. Johnston.
L/Corpl. J. J. Leitch.
L/Corpl. E. Lippiatt.
Pte. D. Rodger.
Corpl. J. Ross, R.A.M.C.
L/Corpl. A. Sinclair.
Pte. W. T. Smith.
L/Corpl. D. M. Telfer.

Mentioned in Despatches

Lieut. H. Adamson.
Lieut. R. A. Andrew.
Capt. Sir W. A. A. Campbell, Bart.
Lieut. (A/Capt.) R. H. Colthart.
Lieut. D. Colville.
Lieut. Col. J. Gilmour.
2nd Lieut. A. S. Lindsay.
Capt. M. E. Lindsay.
Capt. D. D. Ogilvie.
2nd Lieut. (A/Capt.) J. W. Ormiston.
Major C. G. de Pree.
2nd Lieut. A. C. Smith.
Major J. Younger.

APPENDIX V

Mentioned in Despatches (*contd.*)

L/Sgt. J. R. Barron.
Pte. T. Blease.
L/Corpl. J. Brown.
Sgt. D. Campbell.
L/Corpl. J. Clark.
Pte. W. Dunn.
S.Q.M.S. J. Edmund.
L/Sgt. R. M. Hogg.
Sgt. B. Low.

Sgt. N. Mack.
Corpl. W. A. Milne.
S.S.M. A. Ogilvie.
Pte. F. Paterson.
Corpl. A. J. Ross, R.A.M.C.
Sgt. W. Scott.
Sgt. A. Sievewright.
L/Corpl. A. Wilson.

FOREIGN DECORATIONS

Serbian Gold Medal

S.S. D. H. Pringle.

Italian Bronze Medal

L/Corpl. Alexander Wilson.

Roumanian Medaille Barbatie si Credinta, 1st Class

Sgt. R. Ballantyne.

APPENDIX VI

LIST OF ACTIONS AND OPERATIONS

THE FOURTEENTH BATTALION

1917. Became 14th Battalion The Black Watch in Egypt on 1st January, 1917.

    Arrived in Palestine. 5th March.

    FIRST BATTLE OF GAZA. 25th–27th March.

    SECOND BATTLE OF GAZA. 17th–19th April.

    Trench warfare. El Mandur, Sheikh Abbas Line, " Regents Park." May–October.

    THIRD BATTLE OF GAZA. (Beersheba and Capture of the Sheria Position.) 27th October–7th November.

    Trench warfare and salvage work. Wadi Ghuzzeh, Wadi Selman. November.

    CAPTURE OF JERUSALEM. (Kubeibe.) 7th–9th December.

    DEFENCE OF JERUSALEM. (Sheikh Abu, El Zeitun, Hill of Shafa and Beit Ania.) 26th–30th December.

1918. Trench warfare and road making. Beit Ania, Ram Allah, Wadi Kolah. January–April.

    Left Palestine. 15th April. Arrived France. 7th May.

    Trench warfare and in reserve. Ham en Artois, Lys Sector, La Micquelerie, Calonne, Moislains. May–September.

    BATTLE OF EPEHY. (Templeux le Guerard.) 18th September. Crossing of Haute Deule Canal. 17th October.

    ADVANCE TO VICTORY. October–11th November.

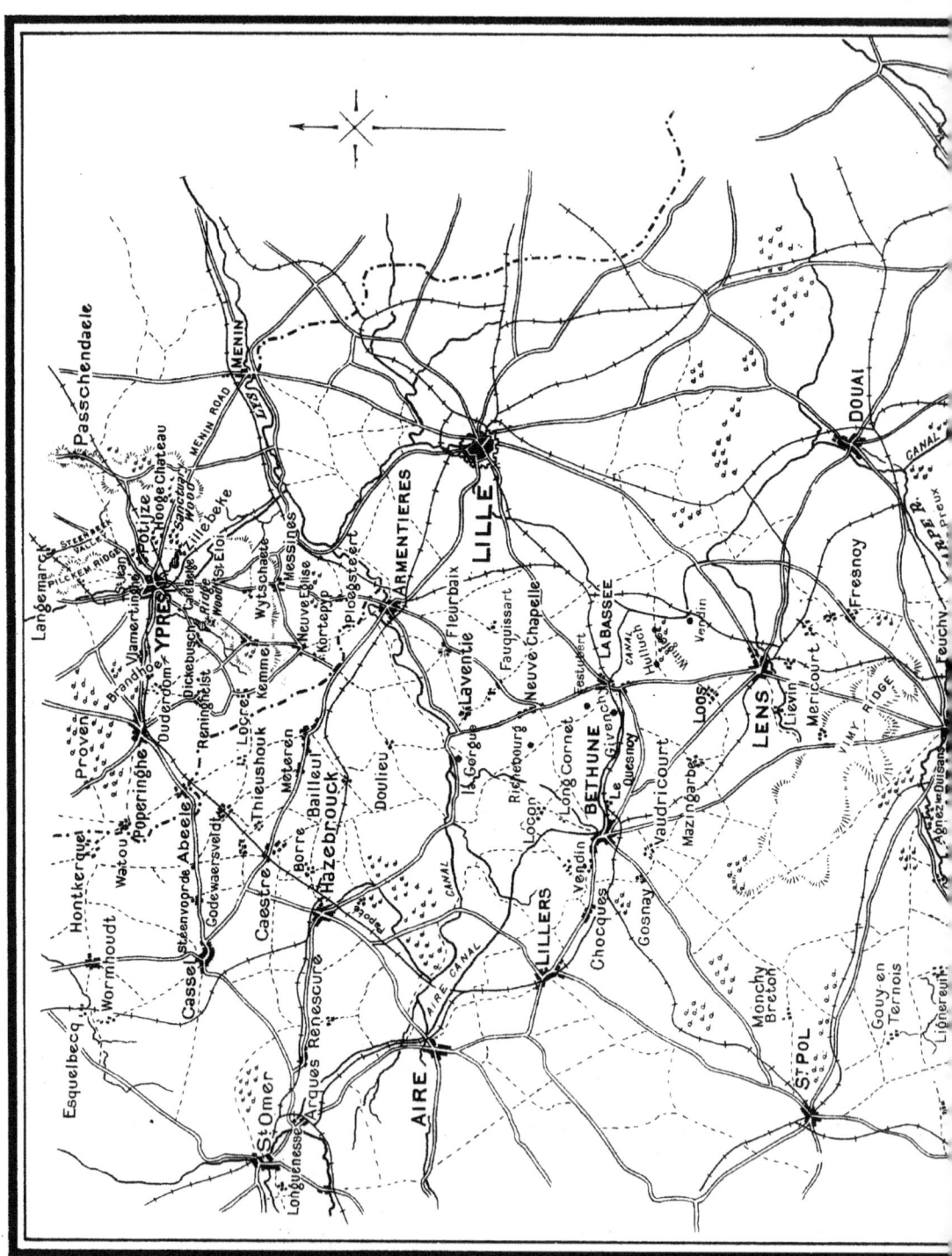

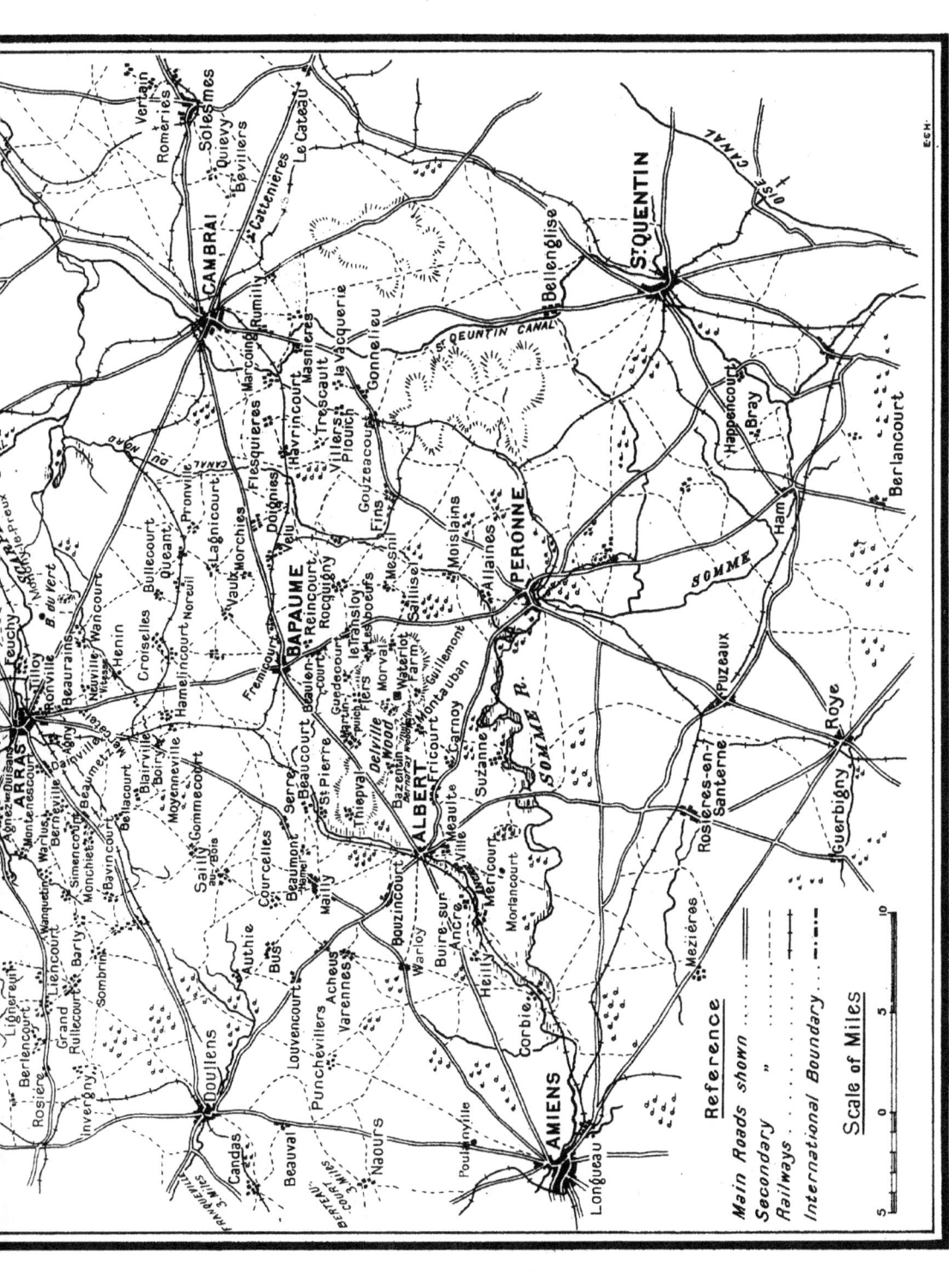

INDEX

The Roman numerals (VIII), (IX), (X), (XI), (XII), (XIII), (XIV), after the entry, indicate the Battalion to which the entry refers

Abercromby, Captain Sir George, 3, 19, 21, Major, 25, Lieut.-Colonel, 27, 28, 34, 35, 38, 39, 41 (VIII)
Actions and Operations, List of
  8th Bn., 103
  9th Bn., 201
  10th Bn., 266
  13th Bn., 312
  14th Bn., 342
Addison, 2nd Lieut. J., 166 (IX)
Advance, The, to Victory, 64 *sqq.*, 103 (VIII), 297, 312 (XIII), 333 (XIV)
Albert, King of the Belgians, 70
Alexander, Company Sergt.-Major T. L., 229, 2nd Lieut., 229–30, 237, 238 (X)
Alexander, 2nd Lieut. P. J. A., 31, 37, 45 (VIII)
Alexandria, 213 (X)
Allan, 2nd Lieut. J., 136 (IX)
Allenby, Capt. R. N., 221, 224, (X)
Allenby, General Sir E. H. H., 17, 141, 144, 147, 160, 293, 317
Allison, 2nd Lieut. T. B., 150, 154 (IX)
Alport, 2nd Lieut. C. M., 22, 25 (VIII)
American Bn., 106th, 327
Anderson, Sergt. C., 13 (VIII)
Anderson, Lieut. D. S., 5, 16, Captain, 20 (VIII)
Anderson, 2nd Lieut. David, 207 (X)
Anderson, 2nd Lieut. G., 254 (X)
Anderson, Regtl. Q.M.-Sergt. J., 270, 279 (XI)
Anderson, 2nd Lieut. J. A., 26, 29, 30 (VIII)
Anderson, Lieut. P. W., 226, 227, 230, (X)
Andrew, Captain R. A., 323, 329 (XIV)
Anstruther, Major R. E., 34, 35, 36, 41, Lieut.-Colonel 72, 73 (VIII)

Argyll and Sutherland Highlanders, 208, 270, 287
  1st Bn., 294
  10th Bn., 23, 24, 28, 32, 33, 36, 37, 38, 39, 40, 41, 44
  Reserve Bn., 26
  12th Bn., 205, 211, 216, 220, 221, 225, 228, 230, 236, 237, 240, 243, 245, 246, 247, 248
  13th Bn., 272
Armstice, the, 6, 9, 70, 299
Armit, A/Sergt. W., 231 (X)
Army
  American, 173, 174
  Austro-German, 210, 213–14
  Belgian, 64
  British
    First, 3 *sqq.*, 107, 121, 174
    Second, 16, 22, 55, 64, 107 *sqq.*, 328
    Third, 144, 160, 165, 287, 297, 329
    Fourth, 141, 144, 323, 327
    Fifth, 163, 323, 329
    Infantry Reserve Bns., 269
    of Occupation on the Rhine, 70 *sqq.*, 280, 329
    Salonika, 223
  Bulgarian, 210
  French 10th, 121
  Greek, 217
  of National Defence, 218, 249, 297
  Serbian, 213
Army Football Cup Matches 71, (VIII), 217, 219 (X)
Army Service Corps, Draft from, 38–9 (VIII)
Arras Area, French warfare in, 145 *sqq.*, 201 (IX)
Arras, Battles of, 145 *sqq.*, 165 *sqq.*, 201 (IX)
  First, 31 *sqq.*, 103 (VIII)
Arras-Douai Railway, Reconstruction, 287, 288 (XII)
Artillery Barrages, 152, 159, 236, 299, 326, 327

343

INDEX

Ashfield, 2nd Lieut. R. C., 26, 30 (VIII)
Asser, Lieut.-General Sir J. J., 253, 255
Athies, Attack on, 36, 38
Atholl, Duchess of, 297, 299
Atholl, Duke of, 298, 299, 300
Austin, 2nd Lieut. W., 22, Lieut., 26, 37, Captain, 50, 52, 53, 65 (VIII)
Australian Infantry, 47th Bn., 55
Austro-German Forces in Belgrade, 210, 213–14
Ayr and Lanark Yeomanry, 317

"Balkan Stew," 215 (X)
Balkwill, 2nd Lieut. A. T. J., 28, 30 (VIII)
Bapaume, First Battle of, 50, 103 (VIII)
Barker, Lieut.-Colonel, 238
Barlow, Comp. Sergt.-Major W., 5, Regtl. Sergt.-Major, 21, 26 (VIII)
Barr, 2nd Lieut. J. W., 54 (VIII), 146 (IX)
Barrington, Major the Hon. R. E. S., 293, 297, 298 (XIII)
Bartman, 2nd Lieut. N., 136 (IX)
Bartram, Lieut. R. A., 293, 295 (XIII)
Bassett, 2nd Lieut. W. F., 210 (X)
Bavarian Regt., 18th, 148 n.
Baxter, Sergt. N., 279 (XI)
Bayne, Sergt., 135 (IX)
Bazentin Ridge, Battle of, 24, 103 (VIII)
Bearn, Lieut. F. A., R.A.M.C., 110, Captain, 127, 132, 139–40, 143 (att. as M.O.IX)
Bearne, Lieut., O. L., 132, 149 (IX)
Bedfordshire Regt., 6
Bedson, Regtl. Sergt.-Major G. D., 108, 143 (IX)
Beit Ania, Attack on, 321 (XIV)
Belgian Battalion, 64, 65, 66
Belgian Regt., 9th, 67, 68
Belgians, King and Queen of, 70
Belgrade, 210, 214
Bell, 2nd Lieut. H., 40 (VIII)

Bell, Captain J. M., 111, 123, 124, 127, 131 (IX)
Bellamy, 2nd Lieut. C. W., 31 (VIII)
Bennett, 2nd Lieut. R. B., 22, 25 (VIII)
Berthonval Sector Raid, successful, 27 (VIII and 5th Camerons)
Bethell, Major-General, H. K., 251, 252
Beveridge, Pte. T., 166 (IX)
Binnie, Lieut. W. B., 134, Captain, 139, 140, Major, A/Lieut.-Colonel 162, 165, 166, 168, 170, 171 (IX)
Birch, Lieut.-Colonel J. G., 280 (XI)
Birdwood, General Sir W., 323
Birrell, Captain John, 277 (XI)
Bissett, Company Sergt.-Major, 5 (VIII)
Black, Pte. A., 153, 156 (IX)
Black, Regtl. Sergt.-Major W. H., 5, 14 (VIII)
Black Watch, The
  Battalions
    1st, 72, 107, 118, 129, 138, 139, 252, 253, 254, 269, 270, 271, 273, 274, 329
    2nd, 109, 110, 118, 242, 246, 269, 271, 273, 274
    3rd, 210, 269, 271, 285
    4/5th, 107, 173, 201
    6th, 72, 252, 253, 329
    7th, 38, 51
    8th (Service), 3, 4 *sqq.*, *passim*
      Demobilization, 71–3
      Educational Classes during, 71–2
      Pioneer Platoon, 52
      Sports, 72
      Strength of, on departure for France, 5
    9th, 26, 107 *sqq.*, 208, 269, 272, 273
      Lewis Gun Team, cup won by, 167
    10th, 205 *sqq.*, 272
      Disbandment, 252, 253–5

INDEX

Black Watch (*contd.*)
  Battalions (*contd.*)
    Equipment for Salonika Campaign, 213, 214–15, 245
    Malaria and other Diseases, 217, 218, 224, 239, 244, 246–7
    Pipers, 212
    Sports Meeting, 216
    Strength on leaving for France, 207
    on Returning thither, 251
    3rd Echelon, 251
    Transport, 213, 214, 215
    11th Reserve, 26, 132, 141, 269 *sqq.*, 280
    B.W. Kilt worn, 270
    38th Training Reserve Bn., 269, 275, 276
    41st Training Reserve Bn., 276
    51st and 52nd (Grad.) Bns. Gordon Highlanders, 270, 279, 280
    Pipe Band of, 271
    Recruiting Campaigns for, 270, 272
    Reservists in, 271
    with Rhine Army of Occupation, 280
    Sports, 277
    202nd Inf. Res. Bn., 269, 277
    12th (Labour), 285 *sqq.*
    13th (Scottish Horse), 293 *sqq.*, 299–300
    Strengths, 293, 297
    14th, 252, 253
    (Fife and Forfar Yeomanry), 315 *sqq.*
    Reserve, 279
Black Watch Farm, Mazingarbe, 123 & *n.*
Black Watch Tartan, issue of, 111 (IX)
Blair, Lieut.-Colonel P., 298 (XIII)
Bombs and Bombing, 14, 19, 20, 26, 29, 32, 33, 34 (VIII)
Bonsargent, Sergt. André, Interpreter, 116 (IX)

Border Regt., 16
Bowes-Lyon, Captain the Hon. F., 5, 14 (VIII)
Boyd, 2nd Lieut. A. E., 241 (X)
Bradley, 2nd Lieut. F. H., 39 (VIII)
Briddick, Trans. Sergt. G., 246 (X)
Brigades
  British
    Cavalry, 9th, 70
    Infantry
      6th (London Infantry), 117
      9th (Reserve) 272, 275, 276
      11th, 41
      16th, 6
      18th, 6
      21st, 6, 29
      26th (Highland), 3, 4, 9, 10, 12, 14, 19, 22, 23, 27, 28, 31, 32, 33, 35, 36, 38, 39, 41, 44, 51, 55, 56, 58, 62, 68
      Games held at Dainville Wood, 42
      Horse Show, 22
      27th (Lowland), 17, 19, 32, 38, 39, 40, 41, 43, 53, 56, 58, 59, 62, 65, 66, 68
      28th, 57, 65
      44th (Highland), 109, 110, 113, 116, 117, 118, 119, 121, 122, 125, 126, 127, 128, 132, 135, 136, 138, 139, 140, 141, 142, 144, 146, 148, 149, 150, 156, 157, 158, 159, 160, 163, 167, 170
      M.G. Company, 156
      Trench Mortar Battery, 156
      45th, 109, 118, 121, 127, 128, 132, 138, 139, 140, 149, 158, 159, 160, 170, 139, 140, 149, 158, 159, 160, 170
      46th, 109, 118, 121, 125, 126, 132, 135, 138, 139, 146, 147, 148, 149, 155, 156, 158, 160, 161, 167, 173
      47th, 159, 174

INDEX

Brigades (*contd.*)
  British (*contd.*)
    Infantry (*contd.*)
      62nd, 126, 128
      77th, 205, 210, 211, 213, 214, 215, 216, 218, 219, 222, 223, 224, 233, 234, 235, 237
        Trench Mortar Battery, 241
      78th, 223, 234, 235, 237, 241, 248
      79th, 221, 223, 224, 233, 234, 238
      81st, 294, 297
      92nd, 58
      94th, 63
      101st, 270
      103rd, 140
      124th, 47
      149th, 297, 298, 299
      187th, 71
      191st (Reserve), 277
      197th, 251, 252, 254
        L.T.M. Battery, 253, 254
        Sports, 252
        Training School, 254
      198th, 251
      199th, 251
      229th, 317, 323, 329
      230th, 325, 326, 329
  Canadian, 10th, 173
  New Zealand Rifles, 3rd, 44, 45
  South African, 29, 36, 38, 39, 43, 57
  S.W. Mounted, 315
Brook, Lieut. and Q.M. T. R., 250, 254 (x)
Brown, L/Corpl. H., 164 (ix)
Brown, Lieut. I. D., Adjt., 274, Captain, 276 (xi)
Brown, Major H. R., 17 (viii)
Brown, Pte. W., 164 (ix)
Brown, 2nd Lieut. J. M., 163 (ix)
Brown, 2nd Lieut. R. L., 61 (viii)
Brown, Lieut. T. B., 325 (xiv)
Brownlie, 2nd Lieut. A. A. S., 61 (viii)
Bruce, Captain R. F., 137 (ix)
Bruce, 2nd Lieut. C. W., A/Captain, 285 (xii)

Bryson, 2nd Lieut. H. L., 31, 37, A/Captain, 61 (viii)
Buchan, Lieut. J. I. 163 (ix)
Buchanan, 2nd Lieut. J. C. R., 25 (viii)
Buffs, the, 10th Bn., 328
Bulgaria, War declared with, 210
Bulgarian Army, 210, 213–14
  Rupel Pass surrendered to, 217
Bulloch, Lieut.-Colonel R. A., 172, 173 (ix)
Burnett, Captain G. H. M., 34 (viii)
Burnett-Stuart, Lieut.-Colonel J. (later Major-General Sir John), 124, 129
Burt, 2nd Lieut. J., 61 (viii)
Burton, 2nd Lieut. J. L., 20 (viii), 144, 145, 149, 150 (ix)
Bushe, 2nd Lieut. W. F., 240, Lieut., 243, 253 (x)
Butte de Warlencourt, Attack on, 28 (viii)
Butter, Lieut. H., 5, Captain 20, 23, 25 (viii)
Byers, 2nd Lieut. T., 144, 154 (ix)

Calder, Lieut. H. F., 64 (viii)
Caldwell, Lieut. J. B., 207, 211, Captain, 246, 254 (x)
Callaghan, L/Corpl. T., 173 (ix)
Callan, 2nd Lieut. J., 146 (ix)
Calvert, 2nd Lieut. T., 166 (ix)
Cameron, Lieut. J. H., 111, 124, 127 (ix)
Cameron Highlanders, Qn's Own, 3, 171, 208, 280, 285
  1st Bn., 71
  2nd Bn., 294, 296
  5th Bn., 3, 4, 6, 9, 10, 12, 13, 16, 21, 23, 27, 28, 29, 34, 35, 36, 38, 39, 40, 41, 44, 50, 51, 52, 53, 55, 56, 65, 66, 68, 71
  6th Bn., 113, 167
  7th Bn., 109, 122, 123, 126-7, 132, 139, 140, 147, 148, 149, 150, 161, 231
  8th Bn., 272
  Lovat's Scouts Bn., 293

INDEX

Cameron of Lochiel, Lieut.-Colonel, 13
Cameron, Major D. C., 252 (x)
Campbell, Lieut. and Adjt. D. C., A/Captain, 285 (xii)
Cameron, 2nd Lieut. W. McA., 22, 25 (viii)
Campbell, Major-General Sir Pitcairn, 112
Campbell, Pte. J., 241 (77th T.M.B.)
Campbell, Pte. A. D., 295 (xiii)
Campbell, Pte. J., 296 (xiii)
Campbell, 2nd Lieut. J., 110, 127 (ix)
Campsie, 2nd Lieut. A., 26, 29, 30 (viii)
Canal du Nord, Crossing of, 323 (xiv)
Carmichael, Captain A. D., 111, 123, 131, Major, 141, 143 (ix)
Carmichael, Scout-Sergt. C., 247, 249, 250 (x)
Carrie, Sergt. 231 (x)
Carstairs, Company Q.M.-Sergt., 248, Regtl. Sergt.-Major, 254 (x)
Carswell, Captain J. D., 20, 25 (viii)
Carswell, 2nd Lieut. R., 132 (ix)
Carswell, 2nd Lieut. W. A., 230, 231, Captain 246 (x)
Carswell, Major A., Adjt., 270, 274 (xi)
Casualties, All Ranks, Lists of
  8th Bn., 84 *sqq*.
  9th Bn., 186 *sqq*.
  10th Bn., 261 *sqq*.
  12th Bn., 290
  13th Bn., 306 *sqq*.
  14th Bn., 335 *sqq*.
Chambers, 2nd Lieut. T. E., 35 (viii)
Cheshire Regt.
  6th Bn., 49
  8th Bn., 112
Christie, Regtl. Sergt.-Major D. C., 235, 246, 2nd Lieut., 248, 249, 253, 254 (x)

Chrystal, Major R. A., 278 (xi)
Clan MacRae Society, 271
Clark, Lieut. and Q.M. W., 107, 110, 142, 143, 165 (ix)
Clement, 2nd Lieut. H. A., 25, 39, 40 (viii)
Clink, L/Corpl. J., 173 (ix)
Clow, 2nd Lieut. G. R., 135 (ix)
Coast Defence Sector, 47 (viii)
Cody, Sergt. C., 164 (xi)
Coldstream Guards
  1st Bn., 167
  2nd Bn., 48
Collier, Sergt. W., 326 (xiv)
Collins, Captain H. J., R.C. Chaplain, 147 (att. ix)
Collins, Major J. G., 3, 4, 7, 12, 14, 15 (viii)
Colquhoun, Lieut. P. H. L. C., 34 (viii)
Colthart, Captain and Adjt. R. H., 328–9 (xiv)
Commissions Conferred on Other Ranks during the War
  9th Bn., 154
  10th Bn., 229–30, 231, 248, 252, 254
  12th Bn., 285
  14th Bn., 328
Connaught Rangers, 5th Bn., 251
Connely, Corpl. J., 125, 126 (ix)
Cook, 2nd Lieut. K. R., 25 (viii)
Corps
  British
    Chief Engineers of, 287
    H.Q. Staffs of, 287
    Labour, 288
  I., 121, 174
  II., 64, 70
  III., 138, 323
  IV., 26, 42, 116, 117, 132, 134
    Artillery of, 121
  V., 17, 43
  VI., 144, 145
  XI., 323
  XII., 208
  XIII., 155, 172
  XV., 58
    Reserve, 58
    Signal Company, 58, 59

347

INDEX

Corps (*contd.*)
  British (*contd.*)
    XVI., 294
    XVII., 27, 34, 165, 171, 172, 173, 297
    XVIII., 153
    XIX., 153, 155
  French, XXI, 118
  Greek, IV., 217
"Corps de Liaison," 116
Couper, Captain J. D., 293 (XIII)
Courtrai, Battle of, 67–8, 103 (VIII)
Cousins, 2nd Lieut. J. K., 22 (VIII)
Cowan, Sergt. J., 295 (XIII)
Cox, Lieut. P. A., 5, 16 (VIII)
Craven, 2nd Lieut. A., 26, 29, 30 (VIII)
Crichton, 2nd Lieut. J. F., 25 (VIII)
Crighton, Lieut. J., 110, 127, 131 (IX)
Crisp, Sergt. A., 154 (IX)
Cronne, 2nd Lieut. F. W., 244 (X)
Croucher, 2nd Lieut. G. H., 254 (X)
Cruickshank, Lieut. J. W., 326 (XIV)
Cunningham, L/Corpl., J. (XIII)
Cunningham, Maj. T. L., A/Lieut.-Colonel, 231, 232, 241, 243, 246, 248–9 (X)
Curran, Sergt. J., 245, 246, 248 (X)
Curtis, Hon. Lieut. and Q.M. W., 270, 274 (XI)
Cuthbert, 2nd Lieut. D. W. H., 137, 146, 147 (IX)

Dale, 2nd Lieut. E. E., 144 (IX)
Dandy 9th Bn. (Royal Scots), 208
Darney, Lieut. C. E., 324 (XIV)
Davidson, Corpl. J. H., 164 (IX)
Dawson, Major R. G., 293 (XIII)
Daylight Raid, 33 (VIII)
Deasy, 2nd Lieut. J. C., 153 (IX)
Deaths from Disease, 11th Bn., 281
Delville Wood, Attacks on, 23, 24 (VIII)
  Battle of, 139 201 (IX)
Denniston, 2nd Lieut. J. E., 207, 209 (X)
Dennistoun, 2nd Lieut. A. O., 110, 127 (IX)

Dent, Brig.-General B. C., 174
Derby Scheme, 275
Deuxième Regiment de Marche d'Afrique, 1st Bn., 219
Devonshire Regt., 235
  10th Bn., 249
  16th Bn., 317, 320–1, 325, 327
Dewar, 2nd Lieut. J. M., 132, 136 (IX)
Dewar, Lieut. J. M., 244, 245, 253 (X)
Dewar, Major J., 293
Dick, Pte. W., 154 (IX)
Dickson, Lieut. A. W., 254 (X)
Dickson, 2nd Lieut. H. B., 25, 31, Lieut., 46 (VIII)
Dinwiddie, 2nd Lieut. R. M., Transport Officer, 147 (IX)
Divisions
  American 78th, 59
  Australian
    1st, 327
    2nd, 143
    16th, 327
  British
    1st, 121, 122, 252
    2nd, 9
    3rd, 43
    4th, 38, 39, 171
    5th, 211
    7th, 6, 9
    8th, 158, 159
    Guards, 167
    Lowland, 72
    New Army, 9th to 14th, 107
    9th (Scottish), 3, 6, 9, 14, 18, 19, 21, 23, 26, 27, 28, 29, 31, 38, 45, 55, 69, 70, 71
      Gas Bombardment by, 62
      M.G. Corps, 70
      (Reserve) 6, 39
    10th (Irish), 213, 230, 321
    12th, 34, 136
    14th (Reserve) 64
    15th (Scottish) 107, 109, 110, 112, 113, 114, 116, 121 *sqq.*, 125, 126, 129, 132, 134, 135, 141, 142, 143, 144, 145, 150, 153, 155, 158, 160, 162–3, 165, 166, 167, 171, 172, 173

INDEX

Divisions (*contd.*)
  British (*contd.*)
    Artillery, 114
    Horse Show and Football Match, 153
    Massed Pipes and Drums of, playing together, 153
    16th (Irish), 159, 174, 175
    19th, 56
    21st, 127
    22nd, 221, 225, 234, 243
    23rd, 141
    24th, 13, 17
    25th, 19
    26th, 206, 208, 213, 221, 223, 232, 233, 242, 244, 246, 249
    Horse Show, 249
    27th, 208, 209, 294
    Horse Show, 296 (XIII)
    29th, 68, 148
    30th, 29
    31st, 69
    35th, 31, 55
    36th, 43, 62
    37th, 145
    39th, 49, 173
    41st, 21, 27
    44th, 155
    47th, (London) 26, 52, 121, 122, 124, 126, 134
    50th, 148, 251, 297
    51st, 145, 252
    53rd, 322
    55th, 155, 329
    56th, 150
    58th (London), 42, 325, 326
    60th, 245
    61st, 158, 160
    62nd, 71
    64th (Highland), 277
    66th, 251
    74th, 252, 317, 323, 324, 325, 327–8, 329
    87th, 148
  Bulgarian, II., 227
  French, 213, 249
    17th (Colonial), 213, 221, 222, 223
    58th, 118
    156th, 213, 219

Divisions (*contd.*)
  German
    3rd, 148 *n.*
    38th, 327
  Greek, 249
    6th, 217
Dobbie, 2nd Lieut. E. A., 219, 221 (X)
Don, Lieut. R. M., 207, 225, 226, 236, 238 (X)
Don, 2nd Lieut. A. W. R., 207, 219, 223, 224 (X)
Don, 2nd Lieut. T. D., 61 (VIII)
Donaldson, Capt. J., 153, 162 (IX)
Donaldson, Pte. V., 71 (VIII)
Doiran, Battle of, 235 *sqq.*, 266 (X)
Doiran Operations, 234 *sqq.*, 266(X)
"Double Crassier," the, 117, 121, 125, 126, 127 (IX)
Douglas, Pte., 229 (X)
Dow, Lieut. W., 138 (IX)
Drumlanrig, Lieut. Viscount F. A. K. D., 163 (IX)
Drummond, Captain A., 31, 32, 33 (VIII)
Drummond, 2nd Lieut. E. M., 153 160 (IX)
Drummond, Lieut. H. M., 5 (VIII)
Drummond, 2nd Lieut. H. M., 5, 135, 136, 140 (IX)
Drummond, 2nd Lieut. J. E., 153, 160, 164 (IX)
Drysdale, Lieut. J. C., 325 (XIV)
Drysdale, 2nd Lieut. A. O., 207, 219, 228 (X)
Dublin Fusiliers, 2nd Bn., 297
Dudgeon, Lieut.-Colonel R. M., 171, 172, 280 (IX)
Duff, Major G. B. (Camerons), 17 (C.O. VIII), Lieut.-Colonel, 19, 21
Duff, 2nd Lieut. R. D., Asst. Adjt., 273 (XI)
Duffy, Pte. R., 166 (IX)
Duffy, 2nd Lieut. W. J., 207, 208, 226, 227, 228, 229, 230, 238 (X)
Duggan, 2nd Lieut. M., 144 (IX)
Duke, Lieut. R. N., M.G.O., 5, Capt., 16, 21, 25, 28, 32 (VIII)

349

INDEX

Duke of Cornwall's Light Infantry, 209, 234
  2nd Bn., 208
  13th Bn., 142
"Dump, the," 16, 17, 19 (VIII), 122 (IX)
Dunbar, 2nd Lieut. W. P., 22 (VIII)
Duncan, Lieut. C. G., 324 (XIV)
Duncan, Major, later Lieut.-Colonel, H. A., 278, 280 (XI)
Duncan, Pte. A., 228 (X)
Dupont, M., 116
Durham Light Infantry
  2nd Bn., 6
  15th Bn., 56
  19th Bn., 24

East Kent Regt., 10th Bn., 326
East Lancashire Regt., 4th Bn., 225
East Yorks Regt.
  1st Bn., 56
  11th Bn., 58, 69
Edwards, 2nd Lieut. T., 144, 156 (IX)
Eglington, Lieut. D. C., 139 (IX)
Egyptian Campaigns, 108
Elbra, Pte. S. B., 246 (X)
Elder, Lieut. W., 67 (VIII)
Equipment, 4 (VIII)
Ewart, 2nd Lieut. R. H. C., 111, 132 (IX), 244, 245, Lieut., 253 (X)
Ewart, General, C.-in-C., Scotland, 286
Ewing, Captain J. L. S., Adjt., 3, 4, 14, 16, 17, 19, 21, 29 (VIII)

Fairley, 2nd Lieut. J. R., 40 (VIII)
Fairweather, Regtl. Sergt.-Major, 231 (X)
Fanshaw, Lieut.-General Sir E. A., 43
Farmer, Lieut. G. A., 69 (VIII)
Fergusson, Lieut.-General Sir Charles, 3, 172
Ferguson, 2nd Lieut., 207 (X)
Ferguson, 2nd Lieut. W., 142 (IX)
Fergusson, 2nd Lieut. J. G., 23, 25 (VIII)
Ferney, Lieut. E., 293 (XIII)

Fife and Forfar Yeomanry (14th Bn. Black Watch), 252
  Earlier War Service of, 315
Finnie, Corpl. L., 295 (XIII)
"First Hundred Thousand," the, 3
Flers-Courcelette, Battle of, 138 sqq., 201 (IX)
Football (see also Army Cup), 246 (X)
Football Cup, Divisional, won by 9th Bn. Black Watch, 153
Forbes, Lieut. W. R. J., 5, 39 (VIII)
Forgan, 2nd Lieut., 240 (X)
Forrest, 2nd Lieut. W. A., 171 (IX)
Forrester, 2nd Lieut. P. H., 5, 13, 14 (VIII)
Forsyth, Captain H., 26 (VIII)
Forsyth, Lieut. G., 141 (IX)
Fortune, Lieut.-Colonel V. M., 72 (VIII)
Fortune, 2nd Lieut. H. R., 26 (VIII)
Fraser, 2nd Lieut. D. C., 142 (IX)
Fraser, Company Sergt.-Major F., 5, 7 (VIII)
Fraser, 2nd Lieut. J. H., 153, 160 (IX), 251, Lieut., 253 (X)
Fraser, 2nd Lieut. J. O., 146 (IX)
Fraser, 2nd Lieut. P. G., 40 (VIII)
Frezenburg, Attack on, 158, 201 (IX)
French, Captain W., 44, Major, 60 (VIII)
French, General Sir John, C.-in-C., 116, 121, F.M. Lord., C.-in-C. Home Forces, 275, 276
French Infantry Regts.
  3rd, 1st Bn., 47
  160th, 58
Fricourt, German dug-out at, 138
Fullarton, Lieut. and Q.M. J. R., 274, 279 (XI)
Fusiliers, 146

Gaisford, Major General, 271
Galbraith, Regtl. Q.M.-Sergt., 329 (XIV)
Gallipoli, 293, 315
Gallipoli Farm, Attack on, 160, 162, 201 (IX)

350

INDEX

Galloway, Asst. Regtl. Sergt.-Major J., 274 (XI)
Gardner, Company Sergt.-Major, 254 (X)
Gas Attacks
  British, 9–10, 12, 62 (VIII), 120, 121, 122, 123 (IX)
  Bulgarian, 232
  German, 24, 32-3, 43, 49, 50, 67, 68, 161
Gas Helmets, Issue of, 135, 136 (IX)
Gauldie, Lieut., 25, 26 (VIII)
Gawne, 2nd Lieut. W. Z., 37 (VIII)
Gaza, Battles of
  First, 317, 342 (XIV)
  Second, 342 (XIV)
  Third, 342 (XIV)
George V, His Majesty, 4, 109, 113, 114, 141, 299, 329–30
German Divisions, *see under* Divisions
  Offensive, March–May, 1918, 50 *sqq.*
Germany, British Army of Occupation in, 70 *sqq.* (VIII), 280 (XI), 329 (XIV)
Gibb, Sergt. J., 149, 154 (IX)
Gibbons, Lieut., R.E., 240
Gilbert, 2nd Lieut. F. R., 252, 253 (X)
Gilchrist, Captain J., 111, 119 (IX)
Gilmour, Lieut.-Colonel J., 317, 324 (XIV)
Gilroy, Lieut. G. B., 5, 13, 16, Captain, 19, 20, 23, 25 (VIII)
Girdwood, Major-Gen. E. S., 317
Glen, 2nd Lieut. A., Signalling Officer, 28 (VIII), Lieut., 38
Glenny, 2nd Lieut. D. J., 110, 127 (IX)
Gloag, Captain M. W., 207, 208, 220, Major, 231, 237, 238, 246 (X)
Gloucester Regt.
  9th Bn., 217, 237, 241, 247, 250
" Glory Hole," the, 7 (VIII)
Gordon, Company Sergt.-Major., 253, 254 (X)

Gordon Highlanders
  2nd Bn., 24
  3rd Bn., 31
  8th Bn., 4, 7, 9, 12, 18, 119, 127, 132
  9th Bn., 109, 122, 134, 161
  10th Bn., 109, 122, 125, 134, 135
  8/10th Bn., 146, 148, 150, 153, 154, 158, 161
  11th Bn., 272
  51st and 52nd Graduated Bns., 270, 277, 280
Gordon, 2nd Lieut. G. H., 140, 163 (IX)
Gordon, Lieut.-Colonel C. W. E., 21, 24, 25, 27 (VIII)
Goudy, Lieut. and Q.M. P., 5, 13, 16, 30, Captain, 35 (VIII)
Gough, General Sir H., 163, 166
Govan, 2nd Lieut. H. F. C., 45, 52, Lieut., 55 (VIII)
Gow, Corpl. A., 238
Gow, 2nd Lieut. I. B., 207, 211 (X)
Gowk, Pte. A., 164 (IX)
Gowan, 2nd Lieut. G. E., 171 (IX)
Graham, 2nd Lieut. A., 22 (VIII)
Graham, Captain D. H. N., 110, 123, 124, 127, 131 (IX)
Graham, Lieut. H. B., 236, 237, 238, (X)
Graham, 2nd Lieut. A., 153 (IX)
Graham, 2nd Lieut. H., 245, 253, (X)
Graham, 2nd Lieut. S., 162, 166 (IX)
Graham-Stirling, Major C. H., A/Lieut.-Colonel, 270 (X)
Grant, Captain G. R. B., R.A.M.C., 47 (VIII)
Grant, Captain N. A., 158, 160, 174 (IX)
Grant, Pte. J., 164 (IX)
Grant-Wilkinson, Brig.-General M., 109, 110, 111, 113, 114, 118, 126–7, 136
Gray, Lieut. R., 293 (XIII)
Gray, Major-General Sir A., 250
Greece, Attitude of (end of 1915), 214
Greek Army, Treachery of, 217
  New, of National Defence, 218, 249

351

INDEX

Greenland Hill (Battle of Arras), Assault on, 39 *sqq.* (VIII)
Grenades, *see* Bombs
Grey, 2nd Lieut., 37 (VIII)
Grey, 2nd Lieut. J., 230, 231, 236, 237, 238, 246 (X)
Grogan, Brig.-General E. G., 4
Guémappe, Capture of, 148 *sqq.*, 201 (IX)
Guise, Lieut. P. S., 293 (XIII)
Gyle, 2nd Lieut. E. W., 252, 254 (X)

Hadow, Captain R., 38, Major, 41 (VIII)
Haig, Sir Douglas, F.M. and C.-in-C., 72, 121, 129, 141, 142, 144, 163, 253, 254, 255
"Hairpin, The" (trench), 133, 134 (IX)
Haking, Lieut.-General R., 323
Halcrow, A/Sergt. J., 228 (X)
Haldane, Lieut.-General, 144, 145, 147, 152, 160
Hall, Major, M.G.C., 126 (attd. IX)
Hamilton, Captain G., 293, 297 (XIII)
Hamilton, Company Q.M.-Sergt. E., 5 (VIII)
Hamilton, Lieut. A. L. G., 27 (VIII)
Hamilton, Lieut. A. K., 173 (IX)
Hampshire Regt.
  12th Bn., 250
  15th Bn., 21
Hampton, Regtl. Q.M.-Sergt. J., 108 (IX)
Hannah, Colour-Sergt. J., 279 (XI)
Harkness, L/Corpl. W., 228, 229 (X)
Harley, 2nd Lieut. W. C., 39–40 (VIII)
Harnett, Captain 272 (XI)
Harnett, Captain E. St. C., 41 (VIII)
Harper, 2nd Lieut. A. S., 26, 27, 46 (VIII)
Harpham, Captain H. D., 288 (XII, 5th Labour Coy.)
Harrison, 2nd Lieut. D. R. 36, 40 (VIII)

Harvey, Lieut. R. E., 110, Captain & Adjt., 127, 130, 166 (IX)
Harvey, Major J., 207, 208, Lieut.-Colonel, 222, 223, 227, 228, 241, 242, 246, 247, 249 (X)
Hastings, 2nd Lieut. J. E., 22, 25 (VIII)
Hastings, 2nd Lieut. R. A. M., 141, 143, 149 (IX)
Haute Cornée captured, 299 (XIII)
Haute Deule Canal, Crossings, 328 (XIV)
Haven, Captain and Q.M. C. J., 293 (XIII)
Hay, Lieut. W. G., 25, 26 (VIII)
Hebden, 2nd Lieut. A., 219, 226, 236, 237, 238 (X)
Henderson, Company Q.M.-Sergt. W., 5, Regtl. Sergt.-Major, 25–6 (VIII)
Henderson, Major N. G. B., 3, 4, 12 (VIII)
Henderson, Major M. W. H., 110, 123, 124, 127, 131 (IX)
Henderson-Hamilton, Lieut. J. C., 110, 124, 127, 131 (IX)
Hennequet, M., and Mlle. Henriette, 123 *n.*
Hepburn, Lieut. P. B., 230, 236, Captain, 246, 254 (X)
Herd, 2nd Lieut. G. G., 61 (VIII)
Heron, Company Q.M.-Sergt., 254 (X)
Higginson, Brig.-General C. P., 276
Highland Games, etc., 113, 167,
Highland Light Infantry
  10th Bn., 7
  10/11th Bn., 155, 156
  12th Bn., 156
High Wood, bivouac near, 28, 29, 30 (VIII)
Hill, Company Sergt.-Major A. G., 5 (VIII)
Hill 70, 122, 125, 126, 127, 128, 129, 201 (IX)
Hindenburg Line, the, 327 (XIV)
Hoare, Brig.-General R., 317
Hodge, 2nd Lieut. D. G., 141 (IX)

INDEX

Hohenzollern Redoubt, 9, Attack on, 10, 103 (VIII), 132 *sqq.*, 141 (IX)
Homondos, Attack on, 296–7, 312 (XIII)
Hondeghem Area, Operations in, 58 *sqq.* (VIII)
Honours and Awards, Lists of
    8th Bn., 102
    9th Bn., 198 *sqq.*
    10th Bn., 265
    13th Bn., 310–11
    14th Bn., 340–1
Horn, Company Q.M.-Sergt., 253, 254 (X)
Horne, General Sir H. S., 174
Howard, 2nd Lieut. A. J., 132, (IX)
Howard, 2nd Lieut. R. T. P., 135 (IX)
Houston-Boswell, Captain W. E., 5 (VIII)
Howitzer *v.* Minenwerfer, 17
Hulluch Sector, 133 *sqq.* (IX)
Humble, 2nd Lieut. J. N., 140, 149 (IX)
Hunter, L/Sergt. 119 (IX)
Hunter, General Sir A., 111
Hunter, 2nd Lieut. T. W., 146 (IX)
Hunter, 2nd Lieut. W. A. D., 31, 33 (VIII)
Hunter-Blair, Major-General, 270
Hunter-Gray, Major C. T., 273, 274
Hussars, 15th, 70
Hutchison, 2nd Lieut. A. D., 26, 28, 30 (VIII)
Hutton, 2nd Lieut. W. F., 22, 25 (VIII)
Hyslop, Lieut. W. D., 54 (VIII)

Indarra, H.M.T., 322 (XIV)
Infantry Reserve Bn., 202nd, 277 (XI)
Ingles, Lieut. J., 27, 30, Captain, 50, 52 (VIII)
Inglis, Lieut. R., 293 (XIII)
Innes, Lieut.-Colonel S. A., 26, 136, 140, 143, 153, 154, 159, 160, 161–2, 163, 165, 166, 168 (IX)
Innes, 2nd Lt. D. Mc.L., 327 (XIV)

Inniskilling Fusiliers, 218
Invicta, ss., 114
Ireland, Lieut. J. B., 140 (IX)
Irvine, Captain and Q.M. J., 286 (XII)
Isles, Pte. S., 154 (IX)

Jacob, Lieut.-General Sir Claud, 67, 70, 71
Jack, Pte. A., 164 (IX)
Jalland, 2nd Lieut. H. H., 221, 240, Lieut. 254 (X)
Jameson, Brig.-General S. B., 270, 275
Jamieson, Pte. A., 246 (X)
Jennings-Bramly, Major H., A/Lieut.-Colonel, 285, 288 (XII)
Jerusalem, Capture of, 320 (XIV)
    Defence of, 320–1 (XIV)
    Guards at, for Holy Places, the first, 321 (XIV)
"Jew's Nose," Lens, 124, 128 (IX)
Johnson, Pte. J., 164 (IX)
Johnston, Asst. Regtl. Sergt.-Major, R. 275 (XI)
Johnston, 2nd Lieut. D. K., 68 (VIII)
Johnstone, Corpl. A., 164 (IX)
Johnstone, 2nd Lieut. H. B., 140 (IX)
Johnstone, 2nd Lieut. N. G., 153, 166 (IX)
Joss, Sergt. E., 238

Kavalla, Greek IV Corps' surrender at, 217
Kavanagh, Major-General C. T., 211
Keating, Pte. J., 156 (IX)
Keltie, 2nd Lieut. F. W., 252, 254 (X)
Kemmel Ridge, Battles of
    First, 56–7, 103 (VIII)
    Second, 59, 103, (VIII)
Kennedy, Captain J. G., 293 (XIII)
Kennedy, Lieut.-Colonel J., 32, 33
Kennedy, Pte. W., 166 (IX)
Kerr, 2nd Lieut. G. R. M., 153, 161, 162 (IX)

INDEX

Kerr, 2nd Lieut. P. E., 163 (IX)
Khaki, Uniform and Bonnets, Issue of, 112, 118 (IX), 206, 208 (X)
Kharga Oasis Detachment, 315
Kilts of Black Watch Tartan, Issue of, 111 (IX), 323 (XIV)
King's Liverpool Regt.
  14th Bn., 225, 251
King's Own Lancaster Regt.
  9th Bn., 221
King's Own Regt.
  2nd Bn., 238
King's Own Scottish Borderers
  1st Bn., 147-8
  6th Bn., 27, 58, 59
  7/8th Bn., 156, 167, 168 170
King's Own Yorkshire Light Infantry, 209
King's Royal Rifle Corps
  22nd Bn., 117
Kinloch, Lieut. C., 293 (XIII)
Kinnear, Sergt. H., 231 (X)
Kirkpatrick, 2nd Lieut. G. P., 208 (X)
Kit and Kat Pillboxes, 64 (VIII)
Kitchener of Khartoum, F.M., and "the New Army," 3, 4, 7, 107, 108, 109, 111, 113
Knox, Lieut.-Colonel H. H. S., 152

Labour Companies
  5th, 288
  6th, 288
Labour Corps, the, 288
Labour Group
  44th, H.Q., 288
Lace, 2nd Lieut. K. D., A/Captain, 285, Captain, 288 (XII)
"Ladies from Hell," the, at Tournai, 329
Laing, Regtl. Sergt.-Major W. B., 270, 279 (XI)
Laing, 2nd Lieut. B. M., 64 (VIII)
La Marguerite, ss., 208
Lancashire Fusiliers
  12th Bn., 225
  17th Bn., 32
Landon, Major-General, 6
Langaza Hot Springs, 216 (X)

Laurence, Lieut. W. T., 245, 251, 253 (X)
Le Cateau, Battle of (1918), 298, 299, 312 (XIII)
Le Catelet and Gouy, Attack on, 297 (XIII)
Leicestershire Regt., 14th Bn., 174
Leitham, 2nd Lieut. H. W., 68 (VIII)
Leslie, 2nd Lieut. G. C., 149 (IX)
Leslie, 2nd Lieut. W. J., 127 (IX)
Lindsay, L/Corpl. W., 154 (IX)
Lindsay, Orderly Room Q.M.-Sergt. J., 108 (IX)
Linked Battalions., 20
Lithgow, Captain E. M., 207, 219 (X)
Little Willie Trench, Assault on, 10 (VIII)
Livingstone, Major J. N. F., 207, 217 (X)
Lloyd, Major T. O., A/Lieut.-Colonel, 107, 108, 110, 118, 119, 122, 124, 126, 127, 128, 129, 130, 133-4, 166 (IX)
Logan, 2nd Lieut. G. C., 31 (VIII)
London Regt. (T.)
  2/4th Bn., 324
  2/10th Bn., 42
  2/20th Bn., 238
  18th Bn., 134
  19th Bn., 122, 125, 126, 325
  21st Bn., 117
  22nd Bn., 117
  23rd Bn., 117
  24th Bn., 117
Longueval, Assault and Capture of, 23-4, 103 (VIII)
Loos, Battle of, 9 *sqq.*, 103 (VIII), 121 *sqq.*, 150-1, 201 (IX), 208 (X, in Reserve), 273 (IX)
Loos Village, Capture of, 122, 125, 127, 201 (IX)
Lothian and Border Horse, 216
Lovat, Lord, 329-30
Lovat's Scouts, 3
Low, 2nd Lieut. P., 251, 254 (X)
Lowe, 2nd Lieut. P. V., 245 (X)
Lowen, 2nd Lieut. A. T., 26, 27, 30 (VIII)

354

INDEX

Lowland Scots Regiments, 285
Loxton, 2nd Lieut. A. S. G., 171 (IX)
Loyal North Lancashire Regt., 7
Lumsden, Brig.-General A. F., 167, 173
Lyle, Major A. M. P., 293 297 (XIII)
Lymbrakakis, Colonel, 218

McArthur, Company Sergt.-Major M., 40 (VIII), 238, 2nd Lieut., 252, 253 (X)
McBarnet, Lieut.-Colonel A. E., 293, 295 (XIII)
McCall, Company Sergt.-Major J., 164 (IX)
McCann, Sergt., 119 (IX)
McCash, 2nd Lieut. W. M., 52 (VIII)
McCheyne, Q.M.- (O.R.S.) Sergt. J., 270 (XI)
McClure, Lieut. G. B., 5, 12 (VIII)
McColl, 2nd Lieut. E. E., A/Captain, 285 (XII)
McCracken, Major-General F. W. N., 112, 113, 114, 115, 118, 119, 120, 121, 129, 130, 132, 135, 141, 143, 146, 147, 149, 152, 155, 160
McDiarmid, 2nd Lieut. A. D., 142, 150 (IX)
Macdonald, Lieut. M., 207, 227, 228 (X)
Macdonald, Lieut. R. B. A., 135, 139 (IX)
McDonald, 2nd Lieut. J. M., 60 (VIII)
McDouall, 2nd Lieut. C. G., 141 (IX)
McDowall, Lieut. D., 253 (X)
MacGregor, Major A. J. L., 293 (XIII)
MacGregor, Major T. W., Lieut.-Colonel, 134 (IX)
McGregor, 2nd Lieut. A. W., 132 (IX)
McGregor, 2nd Lieut. T., 158, 160 (IX)
McGregor, 2nd Lieut. W. K., 153, 156, (IX)
McHardy, Sergt. (M.G.S.), 7 (VIII)
Mackie, 2nd Lieut. C. B., 143 (IX)
McInnes, Company Q.M.-Sergt., 226 (X)
MacIntosh, Lieut., G. E., 5, 12 (VIII)
MacIntosh, Lieut. C. O. C., 14 (VIII)
Macintyre, 2nd Lieut. T., 136 (IX)
Mackay, Lieut. G. S., 293, 297 (XIII)
McKay, Lieut. R., Asst. Adjt., 275 (XI)
McKellar, L/Sergt. J., 130, 134 (IX)
Mackenzie, Company Sergt.-Major, 226 (X)
Mackenzie, Lieut., 39 (VIII)
Mackenzie, Lieut. L., 5, 6, 25, 39 (VIII)
Mackenzie, Lieut. L., 163, 171 (IX)
Mackenzie, Lieut. T., 245 (X)
Mackenzie, Major-General Colin J., 110, 112
Mackenzie, 2nd Lieut. Murdo, 207 (X)
Mackenzie-Kennedy, Major-General C. W., 208, 232
McKenzie, Lieut.-Colonel J. M., 326 (XIV)
McKenzie, 2nd Lieut. A., 132, 133 (IX)
McKenzie, 2nd Lieut. A. J., 61 (VIII)
McKenzie, 2nd Lieut. A. S., 242, Lieut., 253 (X)
McKercher, Colour Sergt.-Major J., 154 (IX)
Mackinnon, 2nd Lieut. B. B., 245, Lieut., 249, 250, 252 (X)
Mackintosh, Colonel, 286
McIntyre, Captain A. C., Transport Officer, 293 (XIII)
McIntyre, Pte. D., 295 (XIII)
MacIsaac, Pte. G. W., 166 (IX)
McLachlan, Lieut. and Q.M. J., 207, 217 (X)

355

INDEX

Maclaren, Lieut. T. D. S., Bombing Officer, 19, 26, 27, 37, 50, 52, 55 (VIII)
McLaren, 2nd Lieut. D. R., 244 (X)
McLaren, 2nd Lieut. H. A. F., 207, 237, 240, Captain, 244, 245, 248, 253, 254 (X)
MacLean, Lieut. A. M., 293 (XIII)
McLean, Lieut. A. L., R.A.M.C., 5, 16 (VIII)
McLean, Lieut. J., 326 (XIV)
MacLeod, Captain J. S., 207, 208, 209 (X)
McLeod, Captain A. K., Adjt., 107, 110, 123, 124, 127 (IX)
McLeod, 2nd Lieut. A. W., 153 (IX)
McLeod, Pte. W., 295 (XIII)
McMillan, Lieut. H. D., 39, A/Captain, 61 (VIII)
McMurray, 2nd Lieut. R. J., 139, 153 (IX)
McNab, Captain J. B., 324 (XIV)
McNeal, 2nd Lieut. T. D. F., 40 (VIII)
McNeil, 2nd Lieut. J., 252 (X)
MacPhee, Pipe-Major M., 271, 279 (XI)
McPhee, 2nd Lieut. I. D. A., 132 (IX)
Macpherson, Pte. W., 238 (X)
MacRae, Captain K. S., 229, Lieut., 231, Captain, 246 (X)
McRae, 2nd Lieut. J. A., 22, 25 (VIII)
MacRae, 2nd Lieut. J. L. N., 139, 143 (IX)
MacRae-Gilstrap, Lieut.-Colonel John, 270, 271, 276, 278, 279, 280 (XI)
  Mrs., 280
McRoberts, 2nd Lieut. R., 141, 145, 146 (IX)
McTavish, Captain F. H. C., 5 (VIII)
McVeigh, 2nd Lieut. J., 171 (IX)
Magnificent, H.M.S., 211 (X)
Malaria, 218, 224, 239, 244, 246–7 (X), 296, 297 (XIII)

Malcolm, Company Q.M.-Sergt., 253, 254 (X)
Malcolm, Sergt., 7 (VIII)
Malta, Malaria patients at, 239 (X)
Manchester Regt., 5th Bn., 43
Mann, 2nd Lieut. A. J., 26, 37 (VIII)
Marchbank, 2nd Lieut. W., 158, 160 (IX)
Marshall, Brig.-General F. J., 136, 146, 149, 158, 161, 166
Marshall, 2nd Lieut. A., 146, Lieut., 173 (IX)
Martin, 2nd Lieut. W. M., 207, 208, 221 (X)
Martinpuich, Capture of, 138, 142, 144, 201 (IX)
Mary, H.M. the Queen, 109
Matthews, Q.M.- (O.R.S.) Sergt. J. W., 279 (XI)
Mathieson, 2nd Lieut. D., 207, Lieut., 218 (X)
Maxwell, Colonel the Hon. H. E., 109–10 (IX)
Mechan, Pte. W., 154 (IX)
Mediterranean Expeditionary Force, 317
Melville, Pte. J. M., 227 (X)
Menin Road, Battle of the, 160, 162, 201 (IX)
Menominee, H.M.T., 294 (XIII)
Messines, Battle of, 56 *sqq.*, 103 (VIII)
Meteren, Capture of, 59, 60, 103 (VIII)
Middlesex Regt.
  4th Bn., 26
  11th Bn., 136
Miles, Captain L. G., 23, 25 (VIII)
Mill, Lieut. J., 293 (XIII)
Millar, Captain R. C. H., 207, 217, 219, 221 (X)
Millar, 2nd Lieut. D. A., 234, 240 (X)
Millar, 2nd Lieut. J., 124, 127, 131 (IX)
Miller, 2nd Lieut. A. W. R., 50 (VIII)
Miller, 2nd Lieut. J. D. G., 111, 123, 133 (IX)
Millerand, M., 4, 111

INDEX

Milligan, Captain the Rev. O. B., C.F., 5, 69 (VIII)
Milne, General Sir George, 209, 223–4, 246
Milne, 2nd Lieut. A. S., 254 (X)
Milroy, 2nd Lieut. A. L., 45, Captain, 72 (VIII)
Mitchell, Company Sergt.-Major D., 5, Regtl. Sergt.-Major, 21, 52 (VIII)
Moffatt, Pte. J., 164 (IX)
Monchy-le-Preux, Capture of, 145 sqq., 201 (IX)
Monday, 2nd Lieut. J. C., 36, 39 (VIII)
Montgomerie, 2nd Lieut. W. D., 25 (VIII)
Montaubon, Operations around, 22 sqq. (VIII)
Moore, Lieut. D., 293 (XIII)
Morris, Lieut. J. W., 171 (IX, ex. U.S. Army Med. Service)
Morrison, 2nd Lieut. L. G., 132, Captain, 148, 149 (IX)
Mount Temple, ss., 114
Mowbray, Captain J. S. S., 5, 7, 12 (VIII)
Muir, 2nd Lieut. H. S., 136, 147, 154 (IX)
Mullen, Sergt. J., 166 (IX)
Munro, Regtl. Sergt.-Major (IX), later Lieut. and Q.M. 8/10th Gordon Highlanders, 154
Murphy, Sergt. W., 166, (IX)
Murray, Captain E. M., 5, 7, 32 (VIII)
Murray, Major H. F. F., 142, A/Lieut.-Colonel, 153, 159, 161–2 (IX)
Murray, 2nd Lieut. E. D., 25 (VIII)
Murray, 2nd Lieut. R. N. M., 5, 26, Captain, 27, 39 (VIII)
Musgrove, 2nd Lieut. J. W., 61 (VIII)
Musketry, v. Bayonet and Bomb, 41

Nairn, Captain I. C., 317, 324 (XIV)
Nairne, Major C. S., Lieut.-Colonel, 246, 249, 250, 252 (X)
Navy, French, 217

Neish, 2nd Lieut. C. F., 153, 160 (IX)
"New Army," the, 3
New Army Training School, Akbunar, 246
New Zealand Regt., 12th Bn., 55
Nicol, Captain C. A., 207, 219, 228, 236, 237, 238 (X)
Nicol, Lieut. C., 293 (XIII)
Nisbet, Company Sergt.-Major, 329 (XIV)
Nisbet, Sergt., 119 (IX)
Noble, 2nd Lieut. M. H. N. A., 237, 240, 247, Lieut., 254 (X)
Norfolk Regt., 12th Bn., 63
Norie-Miller, Lieut. S., 110, 123, Adjt., 130, Captain, 143, 147, 160, 165, 166 (IX)
North Devon Yeomanry, 317
Northumberland Fusiliers 27th Bn., 140

O'Connor, Captain, 116
Odell, 2nd Lieut. R. E., 26, 27, 32 (VIII), 207 (X)
Odessa, ss., 250
Officers, Lists of
  8th Bn., 3, 4–5, 75 sqq.
  9th Bn., 107 sqq., 110–11, 132, 177 sqq.
  10th Bn., 207, 257 sqq.
  11th Bn., 270
  12th Bn., 285, 289
  13th Bn., 293, 301 sqq.
  14th Bn., 317, 331 sqq.
Ogilvie, Major D. D., 326, Lieut.-Colonel, 329 (XIV)
Ogilvie, 2nd Lieut. A. M. L., 33 (VIII)
Ogilvie, Sergt. C., 164 (IX)
Ormiston, Lieut. J. W., 329 (XIV)
Osborne, Captain G. E. B., 317 (XIV)
Oxford and Buckinghamshire Light Infantry
  7th Bn., 222, 235
  8th Bn., 235

Palestine Campaign, 317 sqq., 342 (XIV)

INDEX

Park, Corpl., T. 154 (IX)
Passchendaele Ridge, Battle of, 64 sqq., 103 (VIII)
Paul, Lieut. J. R., 65, 66 (VIII)
Paul, Lieut. P. R., Asst. Adjt., 278 (XI)
Peace Day in German Occupied Territory, 72 (VIII)
Peace Treaty (Treaty of Versailles) Signed, 72
Peebles, 2nd Lieut. P., 61 (VIII)
Pelham-Burn, Lieut. M. E., 5, 34, 37 (VIII)
Peters, O.R. Sergt., 251 (X)
Phillips, 2nd Lieut. E. G. M., 207, 227, 228, 236, 237, Captain, 244, 247, 248, 254 (X)
Piggeries, the, Ploegsteert Wood, 19 sqq. (VIII)
Pilckem Ridge, Battle of, 158, 201 (IX)
Pitcairn, Lieut., 132 (IX)
Pitcairn, Lieut. E. G., 244 (X)
Pith Helmets, Issue of, 218, 222 (X)
Ploegsteert Wood, 19-20 (VIII)
Plumer, General Sir H., 16, 22
Pollexfen, 2nd Lieut. R. D. J., 251 (X)
Potter, Lieut. R., 59, 67 (VIII)
Premier Régiment de Marche, French, 245
Price, Compy. Sergt.-Major J. W., 154 (IX)
Princess Patricia's Canadian Light Infantry, 209
Proudfoot, 2nd Lieut. A., 31, 33, 37, 39, 40 (VIII)
Proudfoot, 2nd Lieut. F., 137, 146, 153, 164 (IX)
Pulteney, General W. P., 128, 142

Queen's, 6th (12th Division) 34

Rae, Captain the Rev. J., 252 (X)
Railston, Lieut.-Colonel, H. G. M., 295, 297 (XIII)
Railway Engineers, Third Army H.Q., 287 (XII)
Rankin, Corpl. W., 166 (IX)
Rattray, Major P. M., 293 (XIII)

Rawlinson, General Sir H., 116, 129, 141, 144, 298, 327-8
Rawson, Lieut., A/Adjt., 293 (XIII)
Ray, 2nd Lieut. P. O., M.G.O., 28 (VIII)
Raymond, 2nd Lieut. E. N. L., 111, 134 (IX)
Recruiting Campaigns, 270, 272 (X)
Red Hackle, the, Permission to Wear accorded to 9th Bn., 118-19
Reed, Major-General H. L., 165, 166, 167, 168, 172
Reid, Captain (Seaforths), 45
Reid, 2nd Lieut. A., A/Captain, 285 (XII)
Reid, 2nd Lieut. R. W., 110, 132, 136 (IX)
Reid, 2nd Lieut. S. M., 146 (IX)
Reid, 2nd Lieut. T. E., 137, 146 (IX)
Reynell, Lieut. H. E., 132 (IX)
Rhine, On the, 70 (VIII). 329 (XIV)
Rhodes, Sergt., 226 (X)
Richardson, Captain J. H. S., 111 (IX)
Ritchie, Major-General A. B., 6, 16, 32, 174
Ritchie, Regtl. Sergt.-Major A. F., 2nd Lieut., 231, 253, 254 (X)
Ritchie, 2nd Lieut. A. S., 25, 26, Captain, 66 (VIII)
Ritchie, 2nd Lieut. C. J. B., 153, 162 (IX)
Robertson, 2nd Lieut., J. K. F., 39, 52 (VIII)
Robertson, Lieut. J. H., 25 (V.III)
Robertson, Pte. A. R., 173 (IX)
Robertson, 2nd Lieut. J. B., 132, Captain 140 (IX)
Robertson, 2nd Lieut. R. H., 110 (IX)
Robson, 2nd Lieut. J., 41, 46 (VIII)
Ronsoy - Bassé - Boulogne Ridge, Occupation of, 325-6 (XIV)
Ross, L/Corpl. R., 164, 166 (IX)
Ross, Pte. T., 166 (IX)
Ross, 2nd Lieut. G. D., 37 (VIII)

INDEX

Ross, 2nd Lieut. R. H., 230, Lieut., 242, 245, 253 (x)
Roumania, Entry of, into the War, 223
Rowan, Lieut. A. N., 252 (x)
Rowley, Pte. A., 173 (IX)
Roy, Sergt., 250 (x)
Royal Artillery, Working Parties for, 35 (VIII)
Royal Berkshire Regt., 220
  7th Bn., 227, 234, 235, 239
Royal Dublin Fusiliers
  6th Bn., 251
Royal Engineers, 68, 70, 229, 240
  Companies
    73rd Field, 122
    108th, 235
    187th, 123
    289th, 47
  Sections, 121
  Working Parties for, 49, 58, 62 (VIII), 120 (IX)
Royal Flying Corps, 230, 244, 245
Royal Fusiliers
  3rd Bn., 297
Royal Irish Fusiliers, 208
  9th Bn., 43
Royal Scots, 285
  1st Bn., 294
  Labour Bn., 285
  12th Bn., 317, 320, 321
  13th Bn., 145
Royal Scots Fusiliers, 119, 208
  2nd Bn., 58, 59, 67
  6th Bn., 7, 8, 17
  7th Bn., 146
  8th Bn., 205, 210, 221, 225, 227, 231, 233, 235, 237, 245, 246, 248, 249
  11th Bn., 7, 20, 21, 22, 58
  12th Bn., 7, 17, 29, 35, 45, 55, 60, 66
Royal Welch Fusiliers, 54
  11th Bn., 225
Royal West Surrey Regt.
  10th Bn., 47
Rupel Pass, 217
Rusk, Lieut. G. A., 110, 123, Captain, 136 (IX), 246 (x)
Rusack, Lieut. D. W., 293 (XIII)

Rutherford, Lieut. G., 293 (XIII)
Salonika Allied Forces, 217
Salonika Campaign, 210 *sqq.*, 266 (x), 294 *sqq.* (XIII)
  Archæological Finds, 215–16 (x)
  Malaria and other Diseases during, 217, 218, 224, 239, 244, 246–7 (x)
Salonika, City of, 213, 216, 217, 218
  Fire at, 241
Sambre, Battle of the, 299, 312 (XIII)
Sanderson, Captain I. C., Adjt., 207, 209, 219, 226, 229, 235, 238, 244 (x)
Sanderson, Lieut. H. S., 5, 12 (VIII)
Sandilands, L/Corpl. J., 154 (IX)
Sandilands, Lieut.-Colonel J., 122
Sarrail, General, 217, 218, 245
Scarpe, Battles of the
  First, 36, 103 (VIII), 201 (IX)
  Second, 201 (IX)
  Third, 39, 103 (VIII)
Schmidt, Lieut. C., 293 (XIII)
Scots Guards, 1st Bn., 167
Scott, Captain J. M., 43 (VIII)
Scott, Lieut. J. M., 207 (x)
Scott, Lieut. R. J. L., 135 (IX), 207, 208, 211 (x)
Scott, Lieut. W. G., Scout Officer, 293, 296, 297 (XIII)
Scott, 2nd Lieut. W. H., 5, 25 (VIII)
Scottish Horse, 230
  1st and 2nd Bns., 293
Scottish Rifles
  9th Bn., 35, 57, 58, 62, 72
  10th Bn., 118, 135, 161, 167, 170
  11th Bn., 205, 219, 220, 221, 225, 229, 233, 235, 240, 244
  Labour Bn., 285
Scott-Pearse, 2nd Lieut. G., 110, 127 (IX)
Scoular, 2nd Lieut. J. G., 153 (IX)
Seaforth Highlanders, 221, 246, 285
  7th Bn., 4, 6, 7, 9, 12, 16, 23, 28, 32, 34, 35, 36, 37, 39, 40, 42, 44, 45, 47, 48, 51, 52, 57, 58, 59, 60, 61, 62, 64, 65, 66, 68, 71

INDEX

8th Bn., 109, 111, 114, 119, 120, 122, 125, 132, 135, 139, 140, 148, 149, 159, 161, 165
9th Bn., 53
10th Bn., 272
Other Bns., 44
Selle Battle of the, 298, 312 (XIII)
Sempill, Lieut.-Colonel Lord, 3, 4, 10–12, 15, 107 (VIII)
Serbia, Bulgarian Invasion of, 210, 213
Serbian Army, 213, 214
Seres Road, the, 214
Shafa, Hill of, captured, 321 (XIV)
Sharp, Captain H. S., 317 (XIV)
Sharpe, Lieut. A., treacherously killed, 125, 127 (IX)
Sharples, Corpl. W., 164 (IX)
Shaw, Lieut. P. H., 5, 12 (VIII)
Sheldon, Captain B. P., 219 (X)
Shell-scarcity, 27 (VIII)
Shepherd, Captain I. W. W., 31, 32, 37, 45, Major, 58, 70 (VIII)
Shirran, Company Q.M.-Sergt. G., 5 (VIII)
Sickness Statistics, 10th Bn., 242
Sim, 2nd Lieut. W. G., 67 (VIII)
Simpson, Sergt. G., 5 (VIII)
Skelton, Captain A. N., 293 (XIII)
Slag Heap, the, 325 (XIV)
Small, 2nd Lieut. J., 132, 136 (IX)
Smith, Corpl. W., 12 (VIII)
Smith, L/Corpl. J., 166 (IX)
Smith, Lieut. A. C., Adjt., 317 (XIV)
Smith, Lieut. R. E., Signalling Officer, 293 (XIII)
Snag Trench, Attack on, 28–9 (VIII)
Snipers, German, 325
Socket, 2nd Lieut. A., 22, 23 (VIII)
Solingen, Demobilization at, 71 (VIII)
Somerset Light Infantry
12th Bn., 317, 320, 321, 323, 324, 325, 326, 327, 328
Somerville, Pte. J., 166 (IX)
Somme, Battle of the, 22 *sqq.* (VIII), 137, 138 *sqq.*, 150–1 (IX)

Soudan Campaign, 1886, 3
Soundy, Lieut. H. C., 293 (XIII)
Soutar, 2nd Lieut. D. A., 30, Captain, 35, 39, 40, 70 (VIII)
Souter, Pte. J., 249 (X)
South African Battalions
Composite, 62
1st, 43, 46, 47
South African Regt.
2nd Bn., 27
4th Bn., 26
South African Trench Mortar, Company, 24
South African War, 3, 109, 242
South Staffordshire Regt., 16
Speed, 2nd Lieut. T. D., 39, 40 (VIII)
Sprake, 2nd Lieut. G. H., 25 (VIII)
Staunton, Lieut.-Colonel G., 274 (XI)
Steel Helmets, Issue and Adoption of, 19 (VIII), 119 (IX), 222 (X)
Steuart, Captain B. C. A., 21, 25 (VIII)
Stevenson, Captain S. D., 110 (IX), Major, 270, A/Lieut.-Colonel, 276, 278 (XI)
Stevenson, 2nd Lieut. R., 153, 162 (IX)
Steward, Major O. H. D'A., 3, 4, 5, 12 (VIII)
Stewart, Captain J., 107, Major, 107 (IX)
Stewart, Captain R. W., 317 (XIV)
Stewart, Captain W., 207, 221, 223 (X)
Stewart, Company Q.M.-Sergt., 52 (VIII)
Stewart, Lieut.-Colonel C. E., 129
Stewart-Murray, Lieut. L., 132 (IX)
Stewart, Major J., 110, 112, 114, 116, 117, 120, 129, Lieut.-Colonel, 134, 136 (IX)
Stewart, Regtl. Q.M. Sergt.-Major, 254 (X)
Stewart, 2nd Lieut. U., 254 (X)

INDEX

Stewart-Dick-Cunyngham, Lieut.-Colonel Sir W., 207, 209, 219, 222, 223 (x)
Stewart-Richardson, Captain J. H., 21 (viii)
Stirling, Lieut. J. S., 135 (ix)
Stirling, 2nd Lieut. R., 110, 127, Captain, 140 (ix)
Stone, Pte. A., 164 (ix)
Stormonth-Darling, 2nd Lieut. P., 207, Captain, 246, 249, A/Lieut.-Colonel 254 (x)
Story-Wilson, 2nd Lieut. W. S., 111, Transport Officer, 112, 114, Captain, 141, 145, 146, 165, A/Lieut.-Colonel, 171 (ix)
Strang, Lieut. J. S., 139, 153, 162, Captain, 166, 171 (ix)
Strange, Lieut. H. St. J. B., 5 (viii)
Stroyan, Lieut. L. S. R., 254 (x)
Stuart, Pte. W. G., 238 (x)
Stuart, 2nd Lieut. M. S., 59 (viii)
Sturrock, Captain J. P., 207, 208, 217 (x)
Sturrock, Lieut. E., 293 (xiii)
Suez Canal Defence (Scottish Horse), 293
Suffolk Regt., 327
Sussex Regt., 327
  2nd Bn., 117

Tainsh, Lieut. D. MacH., 244 (x)
Tait, Pte., 29 (viii)
Tait, 2nd Lieut. T. S., 254 (x)
Taping, 44
Tatham, 2nd Lieut. A. D., 153 (ix), 221 (x)
Taylor, Captain N. R., 25, 27, 28, 29, 32, 39, 40 (viii)
Taylor, 2nd Lieut. J., 153, Lieut., 160 (ix)
Taylor, 2nd Lieut. J. McK., 26, 30 (viii)
Taylor-Lowen, 2nd Lieut. G. F., 237, 241, Lieut., 253 (x)
Templeton, Lieut. A. A., Asst. Adjt., 278 (xi)

Templeux le Guerard, Attack on, 326–7 (xiv)
Thesiger, Major-General, 9, 14
Third, 2nd Lieut. J. B., 149 (ix)
Thomson, L/Corpl., 135 (ix)
Thomson, Lieut.-Colonel, 122
Thomson, Pte. J., 227 (x)
Thomson, 2nd Lieut. D. C., 231, 237, 240, 248 (x)
Thuillier, Brig.-General H. F., 128, 155, 156, 158, 160, 165
Tillie, 2nd Lieut. J. A., 61 (viii)
Timgard, French transport, 297 (xiii)
Tindal, 2nd Lieut. D., 22, 25 (viii)
Tinley, Regtl. Q.M.-Sergt. T., 5 (viii)
Tovani, 2nd Lieut. W. R., 153, 160, 164 (ix)
Training Reserve Battalions, 275, 276, 277, 278–9
  38th, 269, 275, 276
  41st, 276
Trench 50, 209–10 (x)
Tuke, Lieut. C. S., 111, Captain, Brigade M.G. Officer, 127 (ix)
Tullibardine, Colonel the Marquis of, 293
Turnbull, 2nd Lieut. T. R., 142 (ix)
Turner, Regtl. Sergt.-Major G., later Lieut. and Q.M., 285, 286, 287 (xii)
Tweedie, 2nd Lieut. T. C., 132, 140 (ix)
Tyser, 2nd Lieut. H. E., 37 (viii)

Uniforms Issued to 9th Bn., 109
University Officers' Training Corps, 3, 271
Urquhart, 2nd Lieut. L. W. A. W., 221, 226, 254 (x), Lieut., 276, Captain, 276 (xi)

Venizelos, M., 218
Victory, The Advance to, 64 *sqq.*, 103 (viii), 297, 312 (xii), 329, 342 (xiv)
Vimy Ridge, Attack on, 145 (ix)

INDEX

Von Mackensen, General, 210, 213

Walcott, 2nd Lieut. E. P. M., 41 (VIII)
Walcott, 2nd Lieut. E., 171 (IX)
Waldie, 2nd Lieut. J. G., 132, 135 (IX)
Wales, H.R.H. the Prince of, 299
Walker, 2nd Lieut. H. J., 40 (VIII)
Walker, 2nd Lieut. J., 249, 254 (X)
Wallace, Lieut.-Colonel, 122, 127
Wallace, Major-General A., 109, 110
Wallace, 2nd Lieut. A. M. D., 21, Captain, 39, 50, 52 (VIII)
Wambeck, Captain W. G., M.O., 293 (XIII)
Watson, Company Q.M.-Sergt., 253, 254 (X)
Watson, Company Sergt.-Major, 253, 254 (X)
Watson, 2nd Lieut. A. F., 136, 139, 149 (IX)
Watson, 2nd Lieut. J. M., 230 (X)
Watt, 2nd Lieut. G. H., 31, 61 (VIII)
Webster, 2nd Lieut. B., 22, 25, 67 (VIII)
Welch Regt.
  18th Bn., 174, 175
  25th Bn., 325
West Riding Regt., 2nd Bn., 57
West Somerset Yeomanry, 317
West Yorkshire Regt., 6th Bn., 57
Wheatley, Brig.-General L. L., 251
White, Col.-Sergt. A., 279 (XI)
White, Company Sergt.-Major, 253, 254 (X)
Whitecross, 2nd Lieut. J. M., 26, 33, 40 (VIII)
Whitwright, 2nd Lieut. J. A., 26, 33 (VIII)
Weir, Sergt. A., 216, 246 (X)
Wilson, Col.-Sergt. A., O.R.S., 5 (VIII)
Wilson, Corpl. W., 154 (IX)
Wilson, General Sir Henry, 208
Wilson, Lieut. W., 253 (X)
Wilson, 2nd Lieut., 40 (VIII)
Wilson, 2nd Lieut. E. R., 111, 127 (IX), 244, Captain, 245-6, 253 (X)
Wilson, 2nd Lieut. E. W. D., 166, 173 (IX)
Wilson, 2nd Lieut. J., 141, 149 (IX)
Wiltshire Regt.
  7th Bn., 240, 241, 250
Woodburn, 2nd Lieut. J. C., 160 (IX)
Worcestershire Regt.
  11th Bn., 211, 234, 237, 238, 248
Wolridge-Gordon, Major H. G., 272, 275 (XI)
Women's Army Auxiliary Corps, 277
Wright, Corpl. G., 164 (IX)

Yalo, Road making at, and beyond, 322 (XIV)
Yeoman, 2nd Lieut. W. G., 68 (VIII)
York and Lancaster Regt.
  13th Bn., 58, 64
Young, Captain G. F., 162 (IX)
Young Officers' Training Corps, 274
  No. 1 Company, 274
Young, 2nd Lieut. C. K., 149, 163 (IX)
Young, 2nd Lieut. G. E. R., 153, A/Adjt., 162 (IX)
Young, 2nd Lieut. J. L., 26, 35, Lieut., 61 (VIII)
Younger, Major J., 317, Lieut.-Colonel, 326 (XIV)
Ypres Area, 6, 43 (VIII)
Ypres, Third Battle of, 64 *sqq.*, 103 (VIII), 158 *sqq.* (IX)
Ypres Salient, 155 *sqq.* (IX)
  Trench Warfare in, 16 *sqq.*, 103 (VIII)
Yule, 2nd Lieut. G. L., 46 (VIII)

Zeitun Ridge, Capture of, 320-1 (XIV)

NOTES

NOTES

NOTES

NOTES

NOTES

www.ingramcontent.com/pod-product-compliance
Lightning Source LLC
Chambersburg PA
CBHW070805300426
44111CB00014B/2430